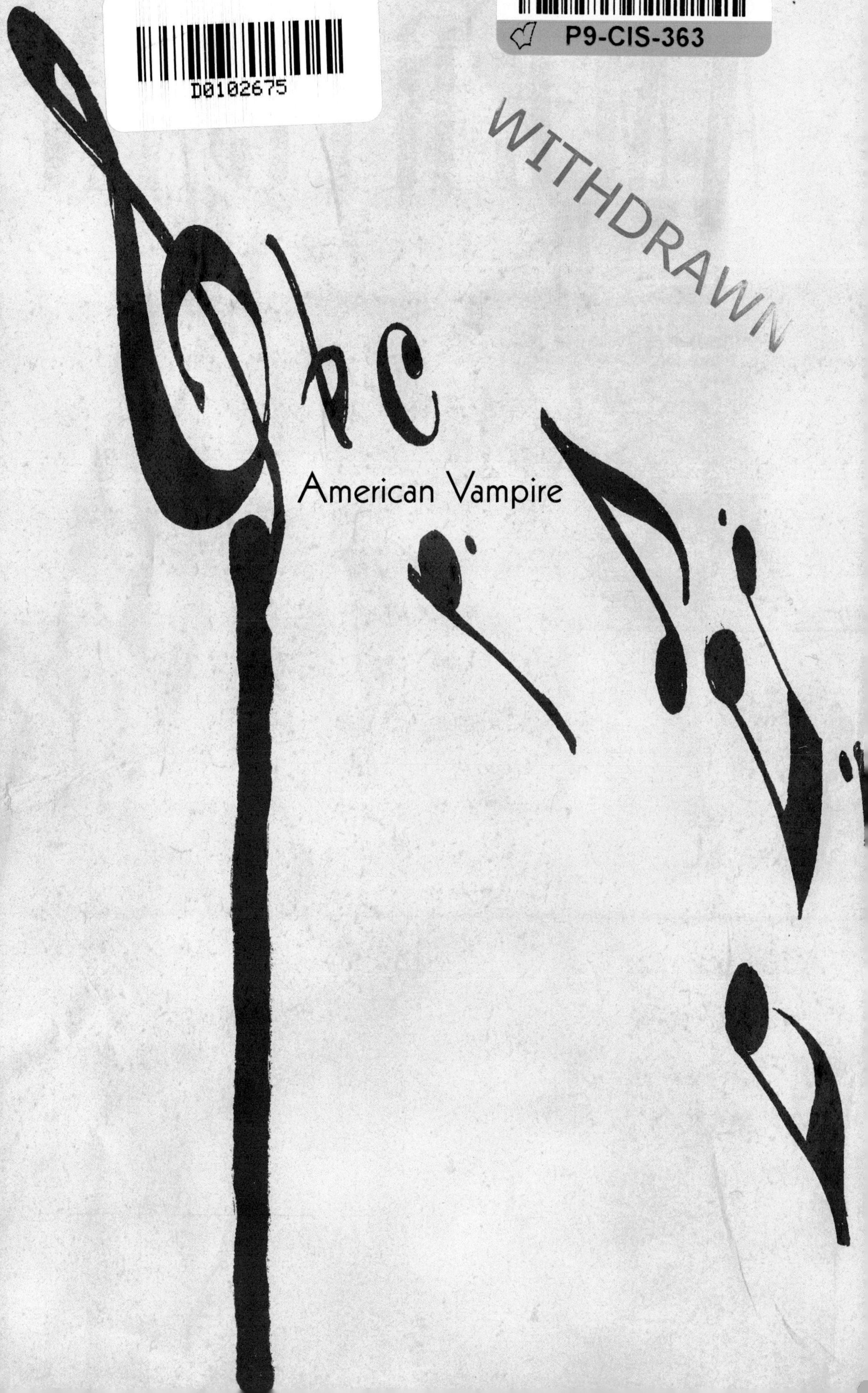
The
American Vampire

AMERICAN

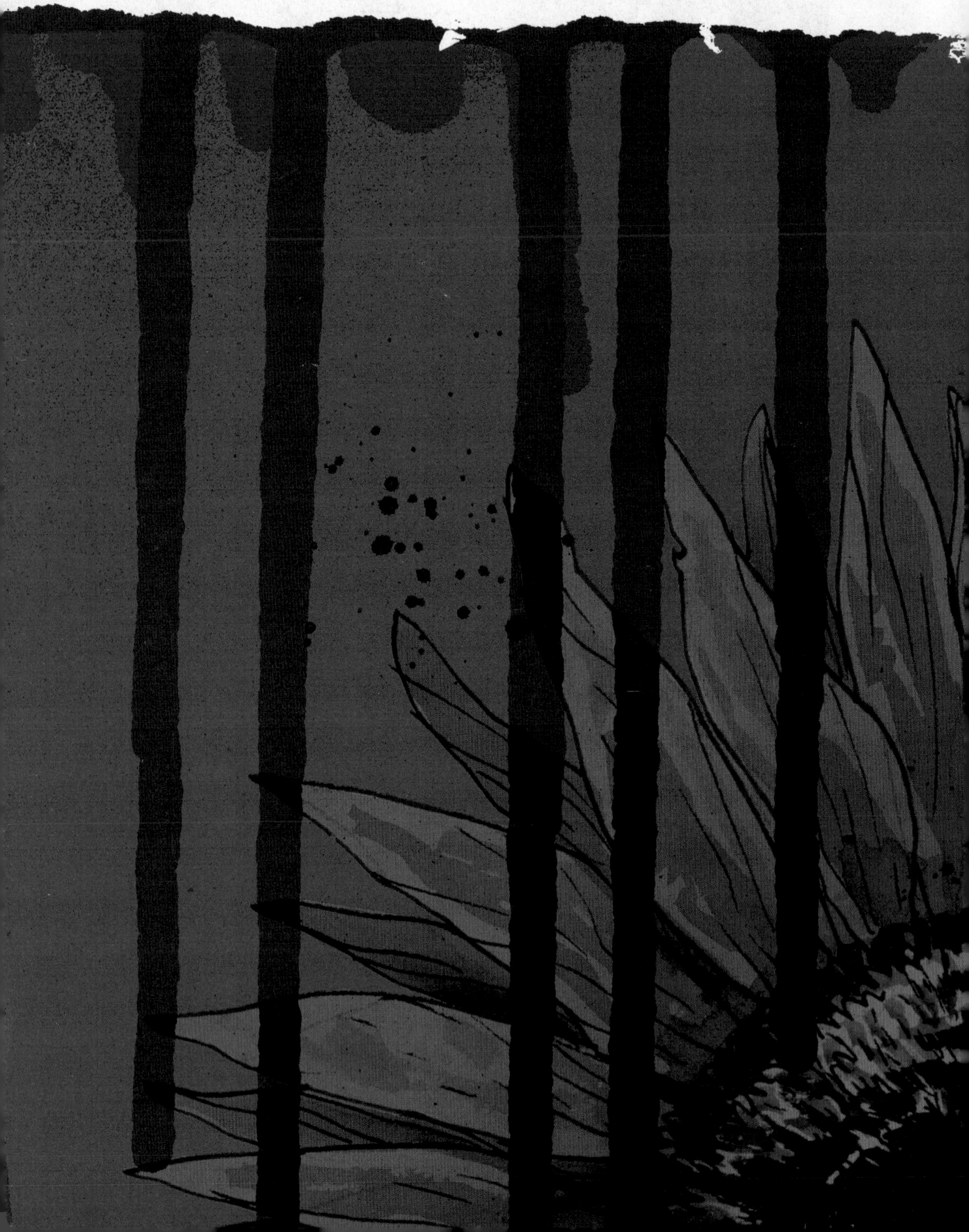

VAMPIRE

VOLUME FIVE

Scott Snyder Writer

Rafael Albuquerque Dustin Nguyen Artists

Dave McCaig John Kalisz Colorists

Jared K. Fletcher Steve Wands Letterers

Rafael Albuquerque Cover Artist

American Vampire created by Scott Snyder and Rafael Albuquerque

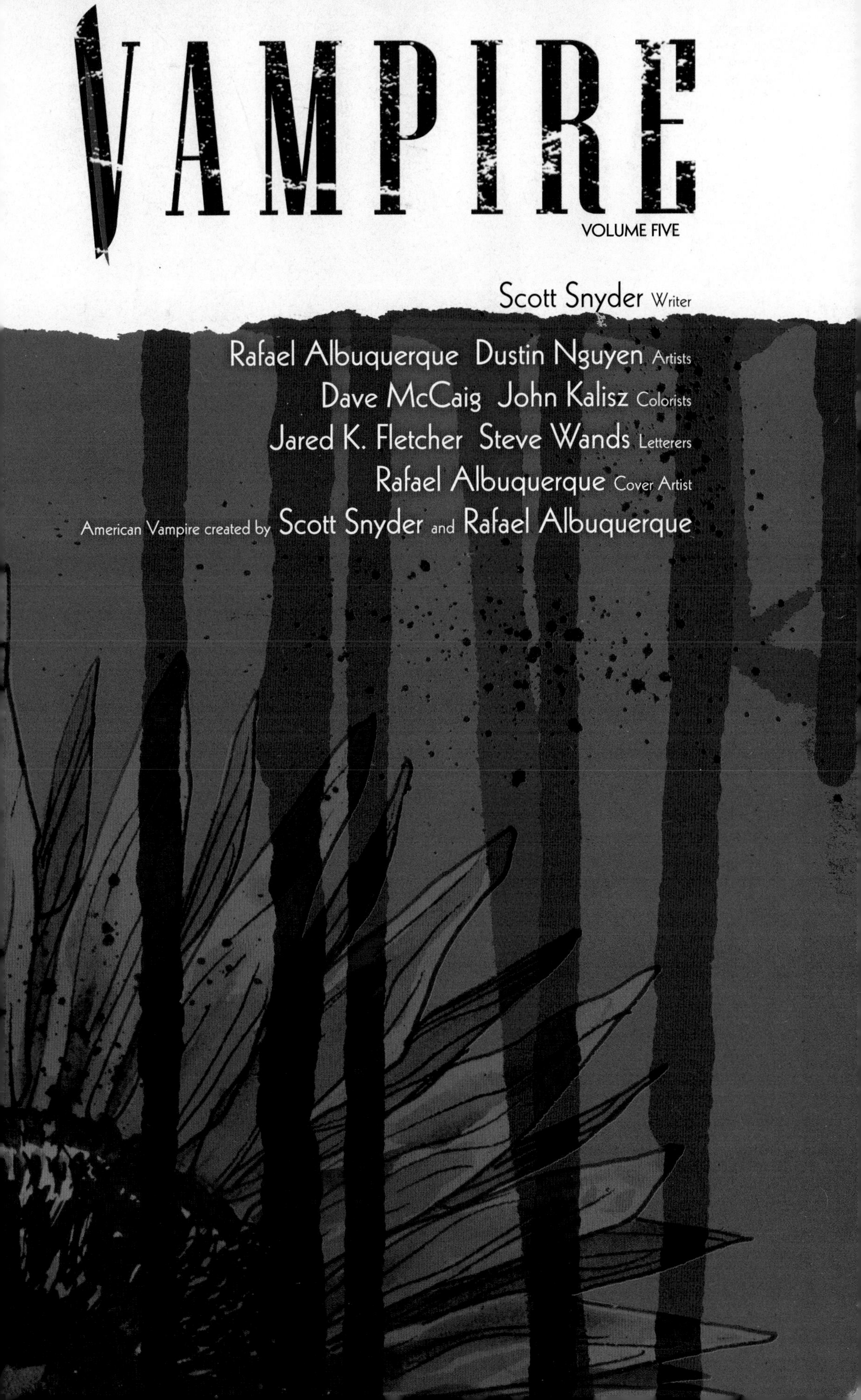

Mark Doyle Editor – Original Series
Gregory Lockard Assistant Editor – Original Series
Peter Hamboussi Editor
Robbin Brosterman Design Director – Books
Louis Prandi Publication Design

Shelly Bond Executive Editor – Vertigo
Hank Kanalz Senior VP – Vertigo and Integrated Publishing

Diane Nelson President
Dan DiDio and Jim Lee Co-Publishers
Geoff Johns Chief Creative Officer
John Rood Executive VP – Sales, Marketing and Business Development
Amy Genkins Senior VP – Business and Legal Affairs
Nairi Gardiner Senior VP – Finance
Jeff Boison VP – Publishing Planning
Mark Chiarello VP – Art Direction and Design
John Cunningham VP – Marketing
Terri Cunningham VP – Editorial Administration
Alison Gill Senior VP – Manufacturing and Operations
Jay Kogan VP – Business and Legal Affairs, Publishing
Jack Mahan VP – Business Affairs, Talent
Nick Napolitano VP – Manufacturing Administration
Sue Pohja VP – Book Sales
Courtney Simmons Senior VP – Publicity
Bob Wayne Senior VP – Sales

AMERICAN VAMPIRE Volume Five

DC Comics, 1700 Broadway, New York, NY 10019
A Warner Bros. Entertainment Company.
Printed in the USA. First Printing.
ISBN: 978-1-4012-3771-4

Library of Congress Cataloging-in-Publication Data

Snyder, Scott.
American Vampire volume 5 / Scott Snyder, Rafael Albuquerque, Dustin Nguyen.
pages cm
"Originally published in single magazine form in American Vampire 28-34, American Vampire: Lord of Nightmares 1-5."
ISBN 978-1-4012-3770-7
1. Vampires--Comic books, strips, etc. 2. Graphic novels. I. Albuquerque, Rafael, 1981- illustrator. II. Nguyen, Dustin, illustrator. III. Title.
PN6727.S555A47 2012
741.5'973--dc23

2012047803

SUSTAINABLE FORESTRY INITIATIVE
Certified Chain of Custody
At Least 20% Certified Forest Content
www.sfiprogram.org
SFI-01042
APPLIES TO TEXT STOCK ONLY

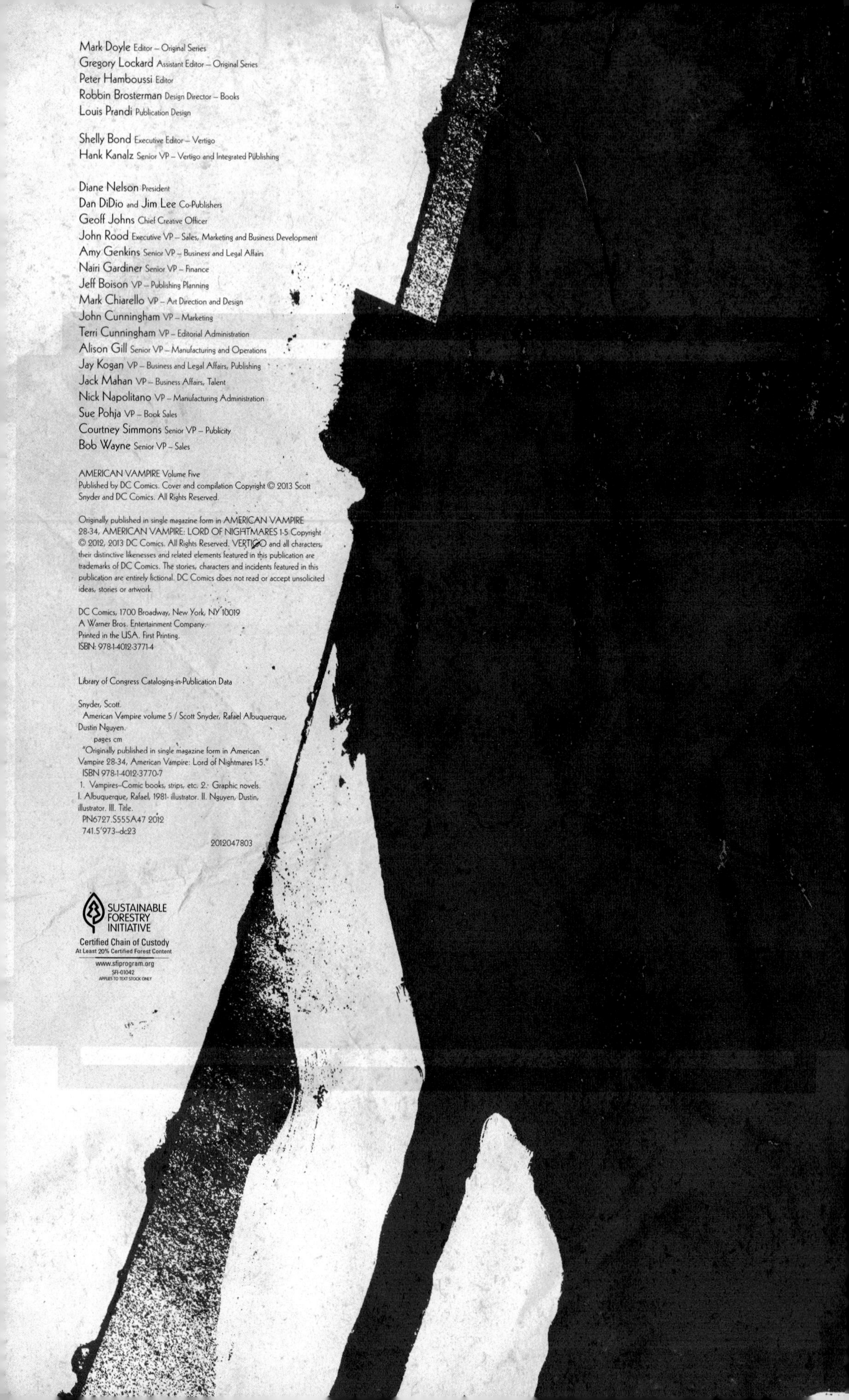

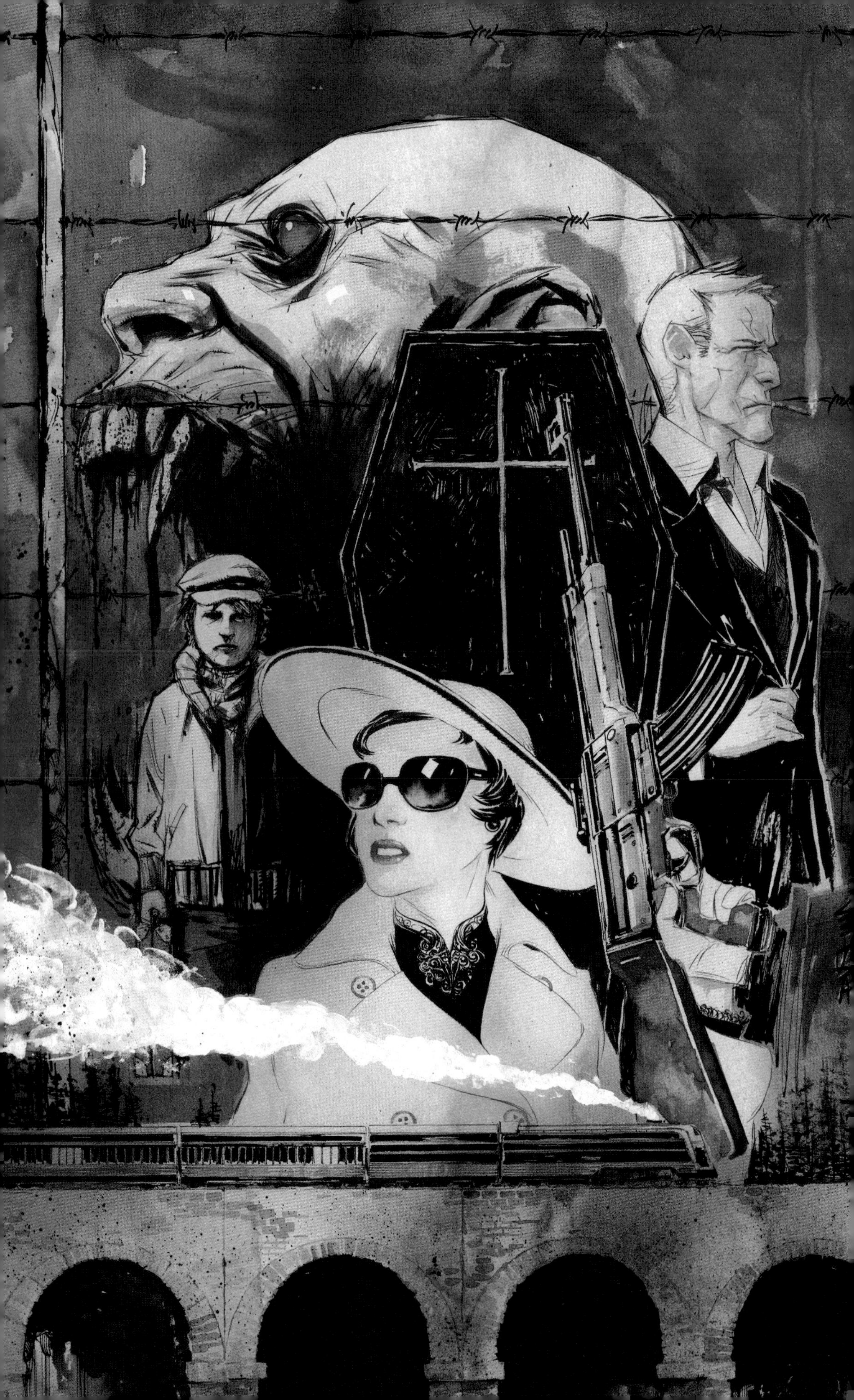

Lord of Nightmares

Scott Snyder
Writer

Dustin Nguyen
Artist and covers

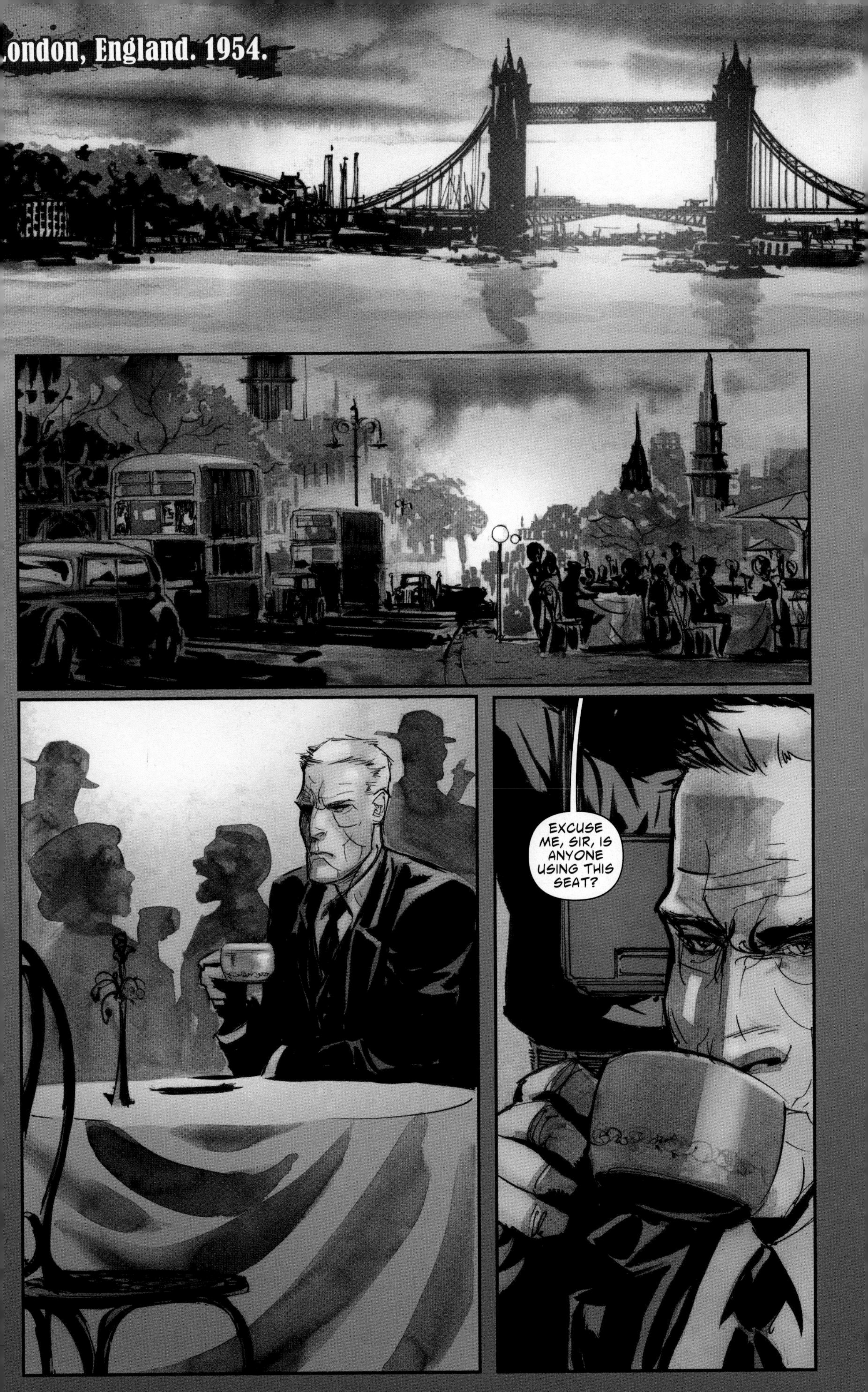
London, England. 1954.
EXCUSE ME, SIR, IS ANYONE USING THIS SEAT?

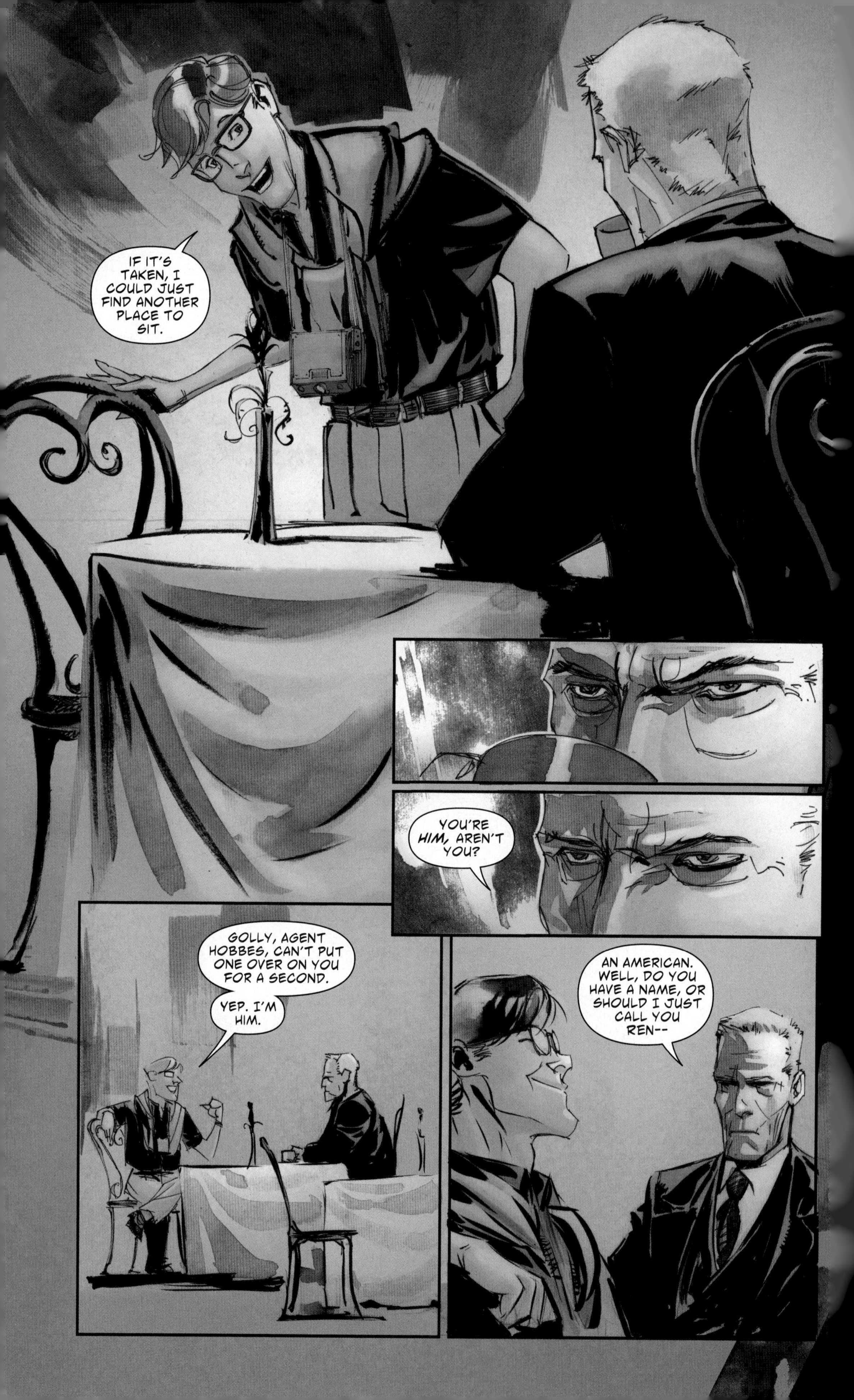
IF IT'S TAKEN, I COULD JUST FIND ANOTHER PLACE TO SIT.
YOU'RE *HIM*, AREN'T YOU?
GOLLY, AGENT HOBBES, CAN'T PUT ONE OVER ON YOU FOR A SECOND.
YEP. I'M HIM.
AN AMERICAN. WELL, DO YOU HAVE A NAME, OR SHOULD I JUST CALL YOU REN--

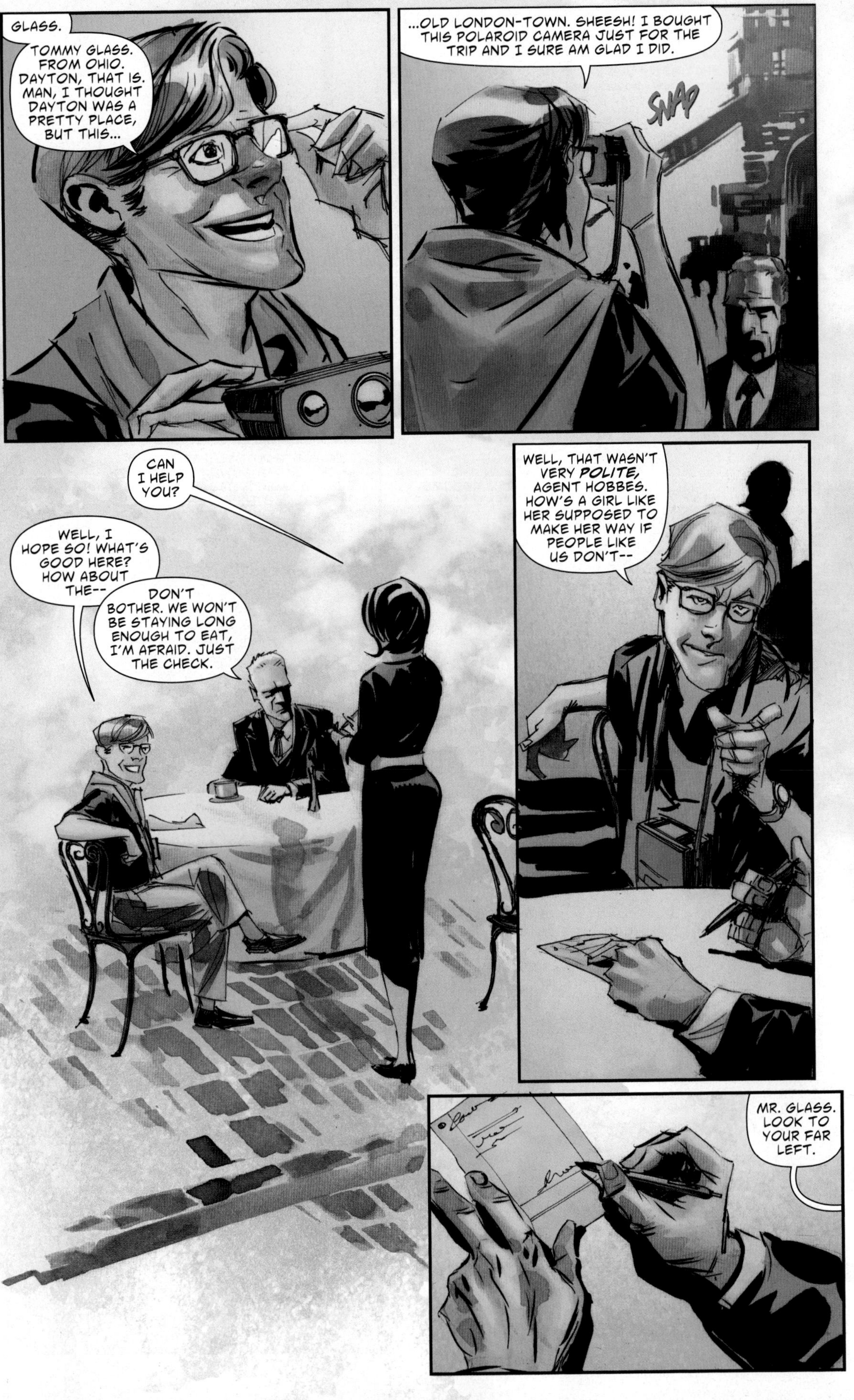
GLASS.
TOMMY GLASS. FROM OHIO. DAYTON, THAT IS. MAN, I THOUGHT DAYTON WAS A PRETTY PLACE, BUT THIS...
...OLD LONDON-TOWN. SHEESH! I BOUGHT THIS POLAROID CAMERA JUST FOR THE TRIP AND I SURE AM GLAD I DID.
SNAP
CAN I HELP YOU?
WELL, I HOPE SO! WHAT'S GOOD HERE? HOW ABOUT THE--
DON'T BOTHER. WE WON'T BE STAYING LONG ENOUGH TO EAT, I'M AFRAID. JUST THE CHECK.
WELL, THAT WASN'T VERY POLITE, AGENT HOBBES. HOW'S A GIRL LIKE HER SUPPOSED TO MAKE HER WAY IF PEOPLE LIKE US DON'T--
MR. GLASS. LOOK TO YOUR FAR LEFT.

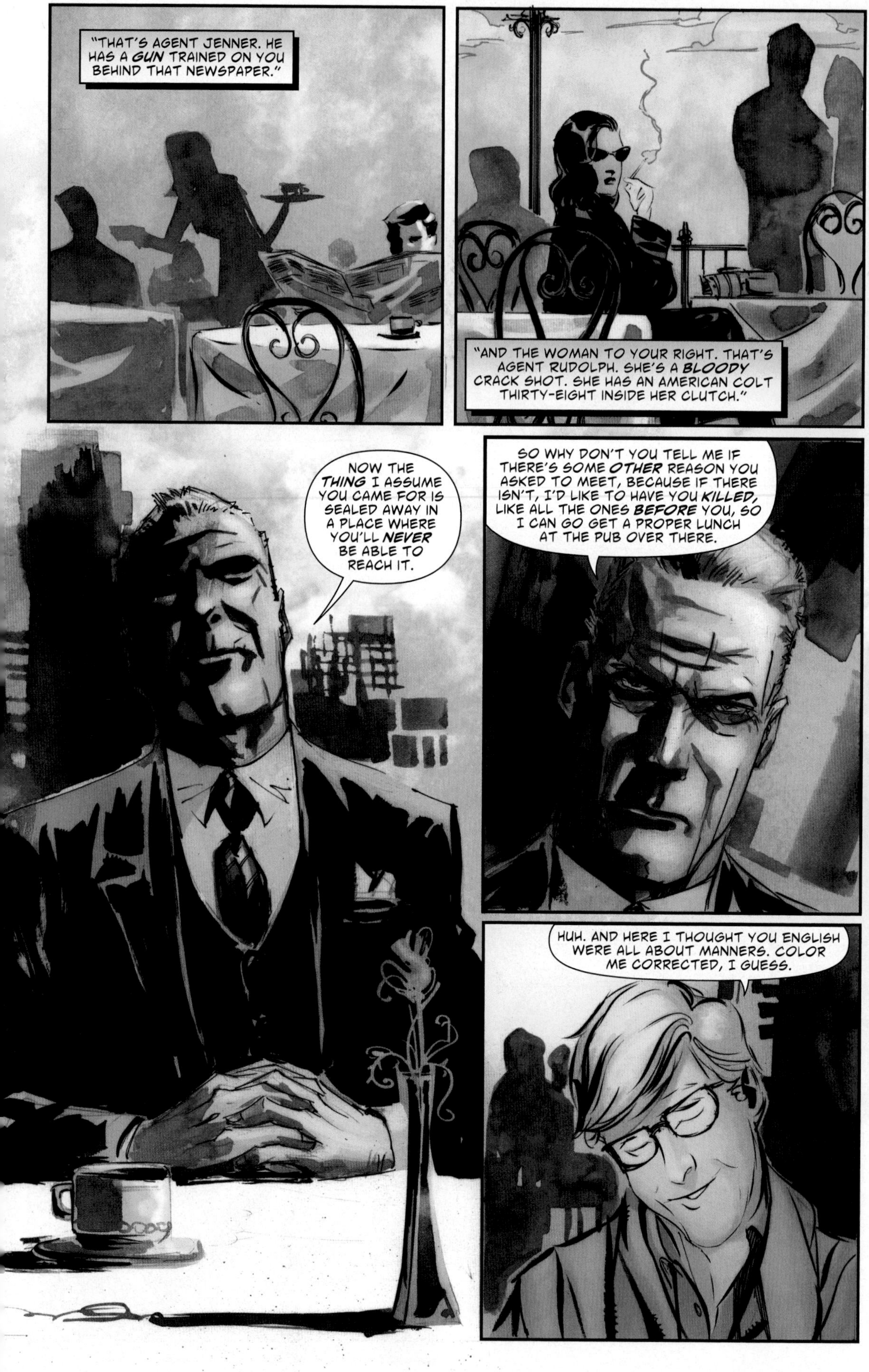
"THAT'S AGENT JENNER. HE HAS A GUN TRAINED ON YOU BEHIND THAT NEWSPAPER."
"AND THE WOMAN TO YOUR RIGHT. THAT'S AGENT RUDOLPH. SHE'S A BLOODY CRACK SHOT. SHE HAS AN AMERICAN COLT THIRTY-EIGHT INSIDE HER CLUTCH."
NOW THE THING I ASSUME YOU CAME FOR IS SEALED AWAY IN A PLACE WHERE YOU'LL NEVER BE ABLE TO REACH IT.
SO WHY DON'T YOU TELL ME IF THERE'S SOME OTHER REASON YOU ASKED TO MEET, BECAUSE IF THERE ISN'T, I'D LIKE TO HAVE YOU KILLED, LIKE ALL THE ONES BEFORE YOU, SO I CAN GO GET A PROPER LUNCH AT THE PUB OVER THERE.
HUH. AND HERE I THOUGHT YOU ENGLISH WERE ALL ABOUT MANNERS. COLOR ME CORRECTED, I GUESS.

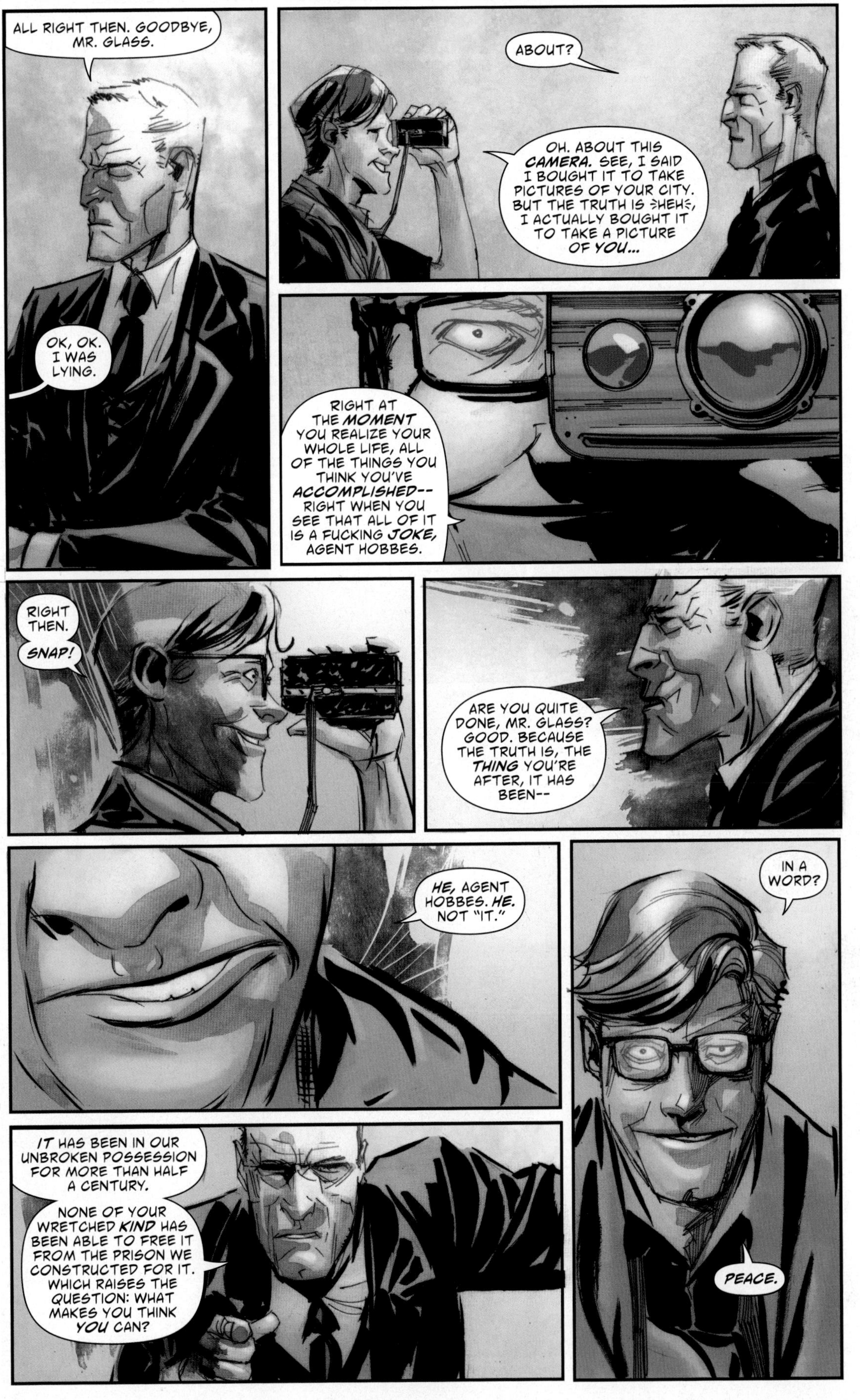

ALL RIGHT THEN. GOODBYE, MR. GLASS.
OK, OK. I WAS LYING.
ABOUT?
OH. ABOUT THIS CAMERA. SEE, I SAID I BOUGHT IT TO TAKE PICTURES OF YOUR CITY. BUT THE TRUTH IS ~HEH~, I ACTUALLY BOUGHT IT TO TAKE A PICTURE OF YOU...
RIGHT AT THE MOMENT YOU REALIZE YOUR WHOLE LIFE, ALL OF THE THINGS YOU THINK YOU'VE ACCOMPLISHED-- RIGHT WHEN YOU SEE THAT ALL OF IT IS A FUCKING JOKE, AGENT HOBBES.
RIGHT THEN. SNAP!
ARE YOU QUITE DONE, MR. GLASS? GOOD. BECAUSE THE TRUTH IS, THE THING YOU'RE AFTER, IT HAS BEEN--
HE, AGENT HOBBES. HE. NOT "IT."
IN A WORD?
IT HAS BEEN IN OUR UNBROKEN POSSESSION FOR MORE THAN HALF A CENTURY.
NONE OF YOUR WRETCHED KIND HAS BEEN ABLE TO FREE IT FROM THE PRISON WE CONSTRUCTED FOR IT. WHICH RAISES THE QUESTION: WHAT MAKES YOU THINK YOU CAN?
PEACE.

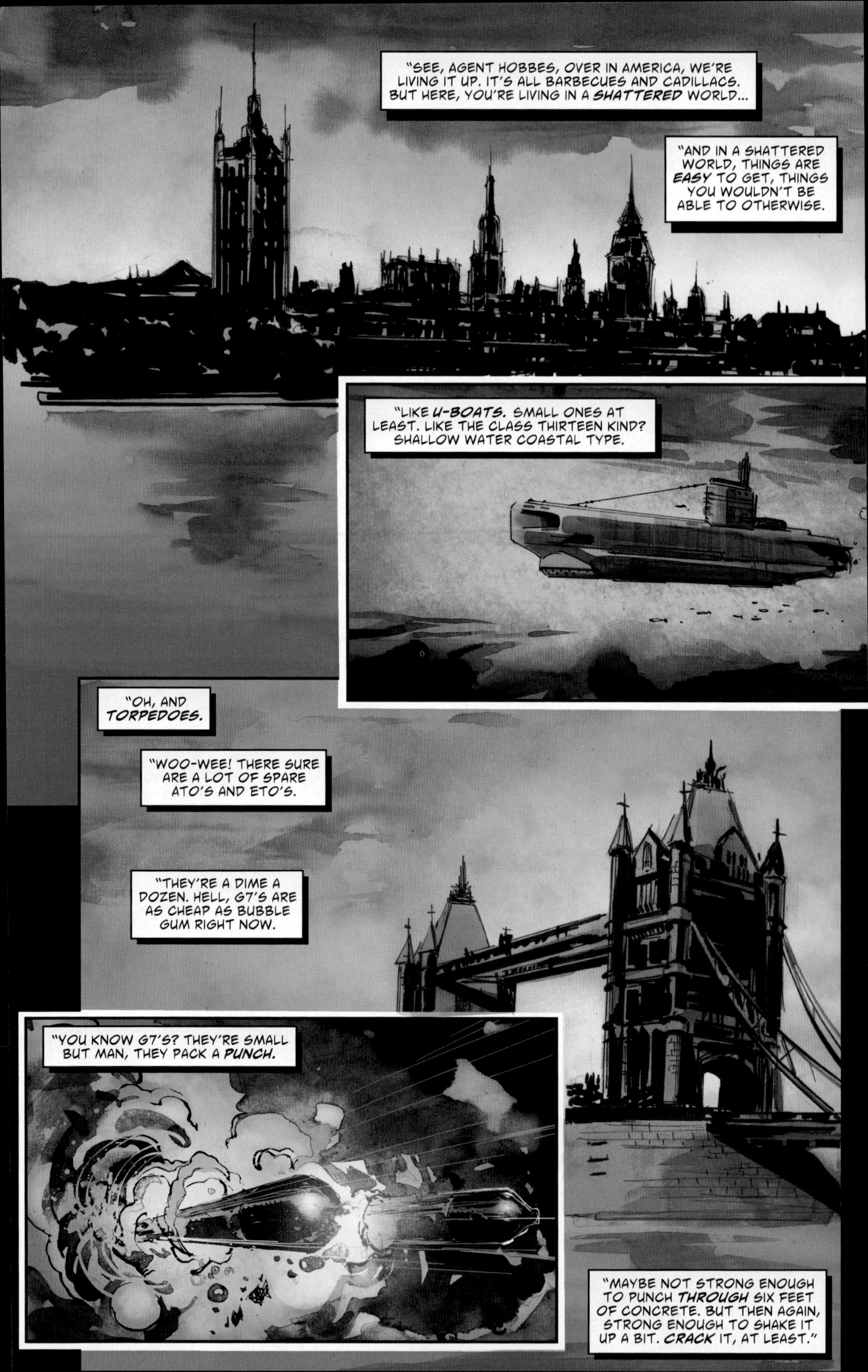
"SEE, AGENT HOBBES, OVER IN AMERICA, WE'RE LIVING IT UP. IT'S ALL BARBECUES AND CADILLACS. BUT HERE, YOU'RE LIVING IN A *SHATTERED* WORLD...
"AND IN A SHATTERED WORLD, THINGS ARE *EASY* TO GET, THINGS YOU WOULDN'T BE ABLE TO OTHERWISE.
"LIKE *U-BOATS.* SMALL ONES AT LEAST. LIKE THE CLASS THIRTEEN KIND? SHALLOW WATER COASTAL TYPE.
"OH, AND *TORPEDOES.*
"WOO-WEE! THERE SURE ARE A LOT OF SPARE ATO'S AND ETO'S.
"THEY'RE A DIME A DOZEN. HELL, G7'S ARE AS CHEAP AS BUBBLE GUM RIGHT NOW.
"YOU KNOW G7'S? THEY'RE SMALL BUT MAN, THEY PACK A *PUNCH.*
"MAYBE NOT STRONG ENOUGH TO PUNCH *THROUGH* SIX FEET OF CONCRETE. BUT THEN AGAIN, STRONG ENOUGH TO SHAKE IT UP A BIT. *CRACK* IT, AT LEAST."

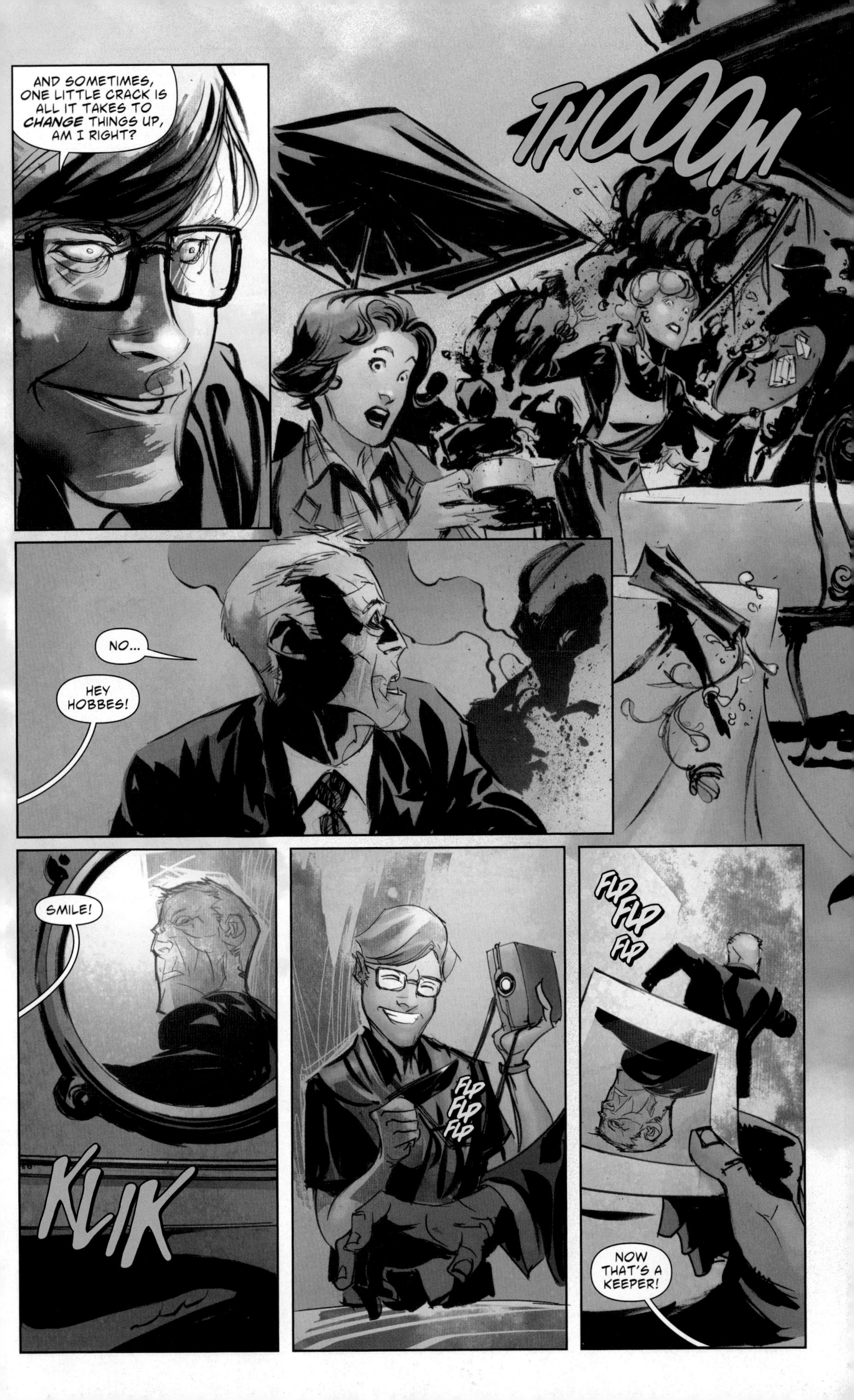
AND SOMETIMES, ONE LITTLE CRACK IS ALL IT TAKES TO CHANGE THINGS UP, AM I RIGHT?
THOOOM
NO...
HEY HOBBES!
SMILE!
KLIK
FLP FLP FLP
FLP FLP FLP
NOW THAT'S A KEEPER!

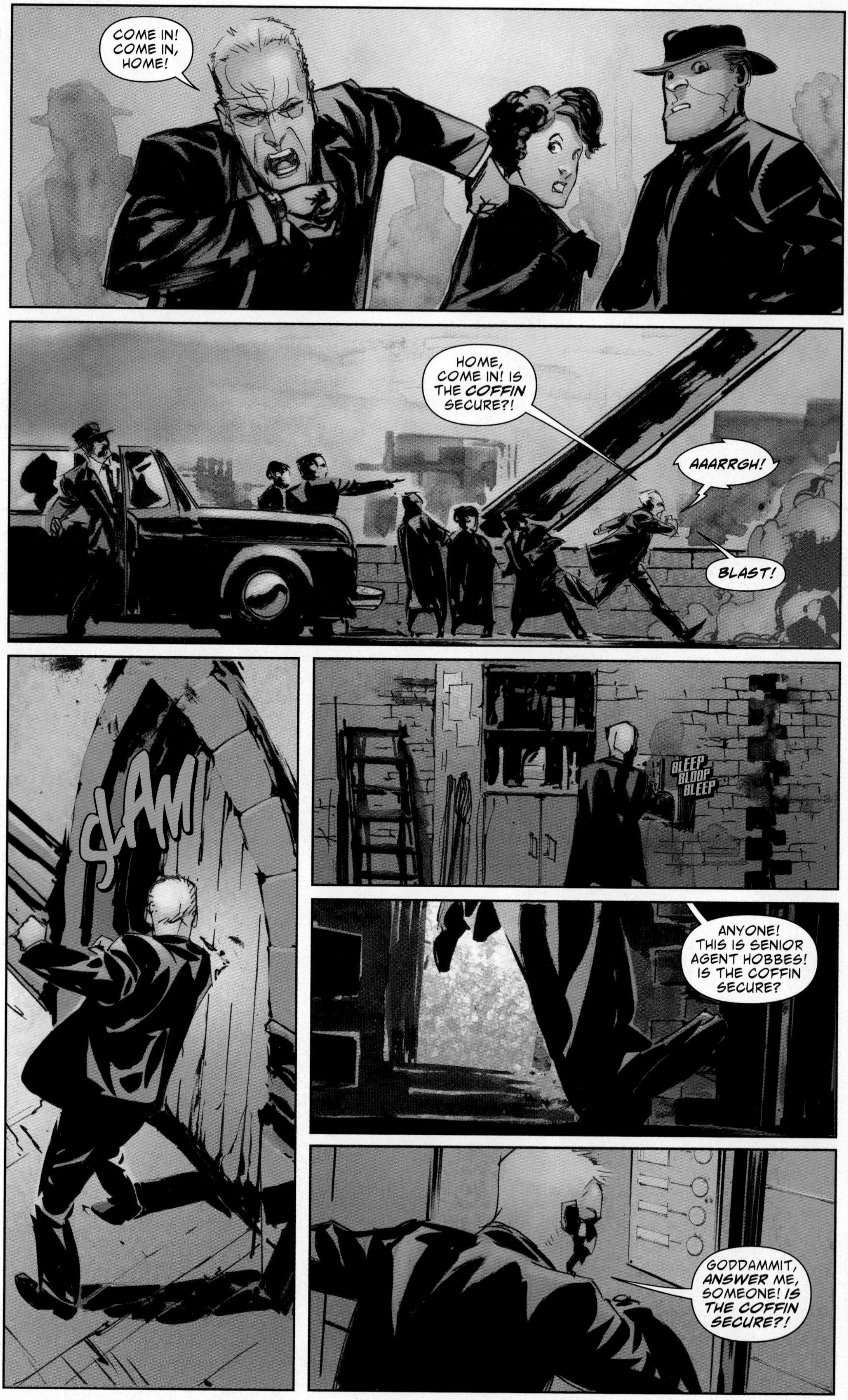
COME IN! COME IN, HOME!
HOME, COME IN! IS THE COFFIN SECURE?!
AAARRGH!
BLAST!
SLAM
BLEEP BLOOP BLEEP
ANYONE! THIS IS SENIOR AGENT HOBBES! IS THE COFFIN SECURE?
GODDAMMIT, ANSWER ME, SOMEONE! IS THE COFFIN SECURE?!

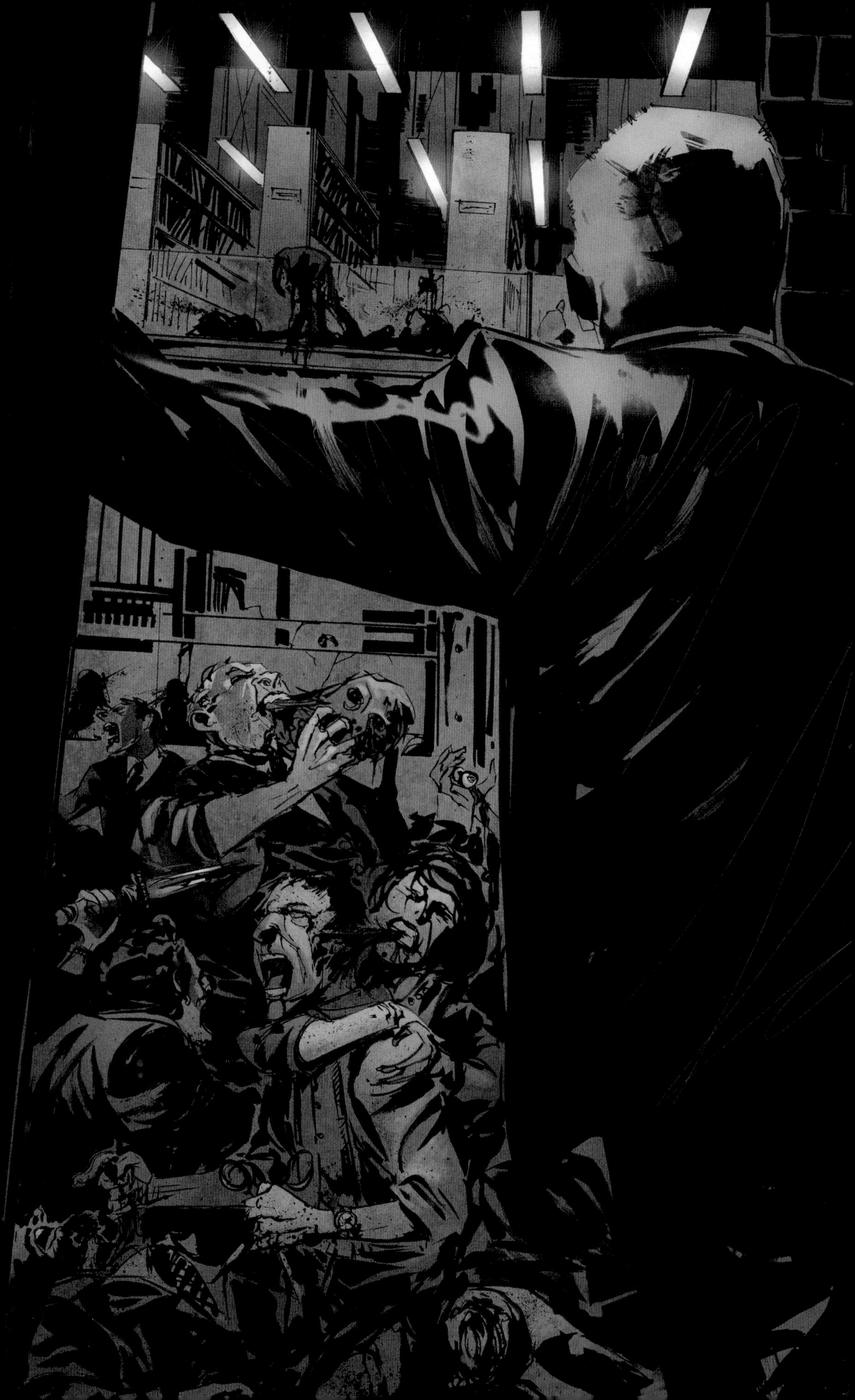

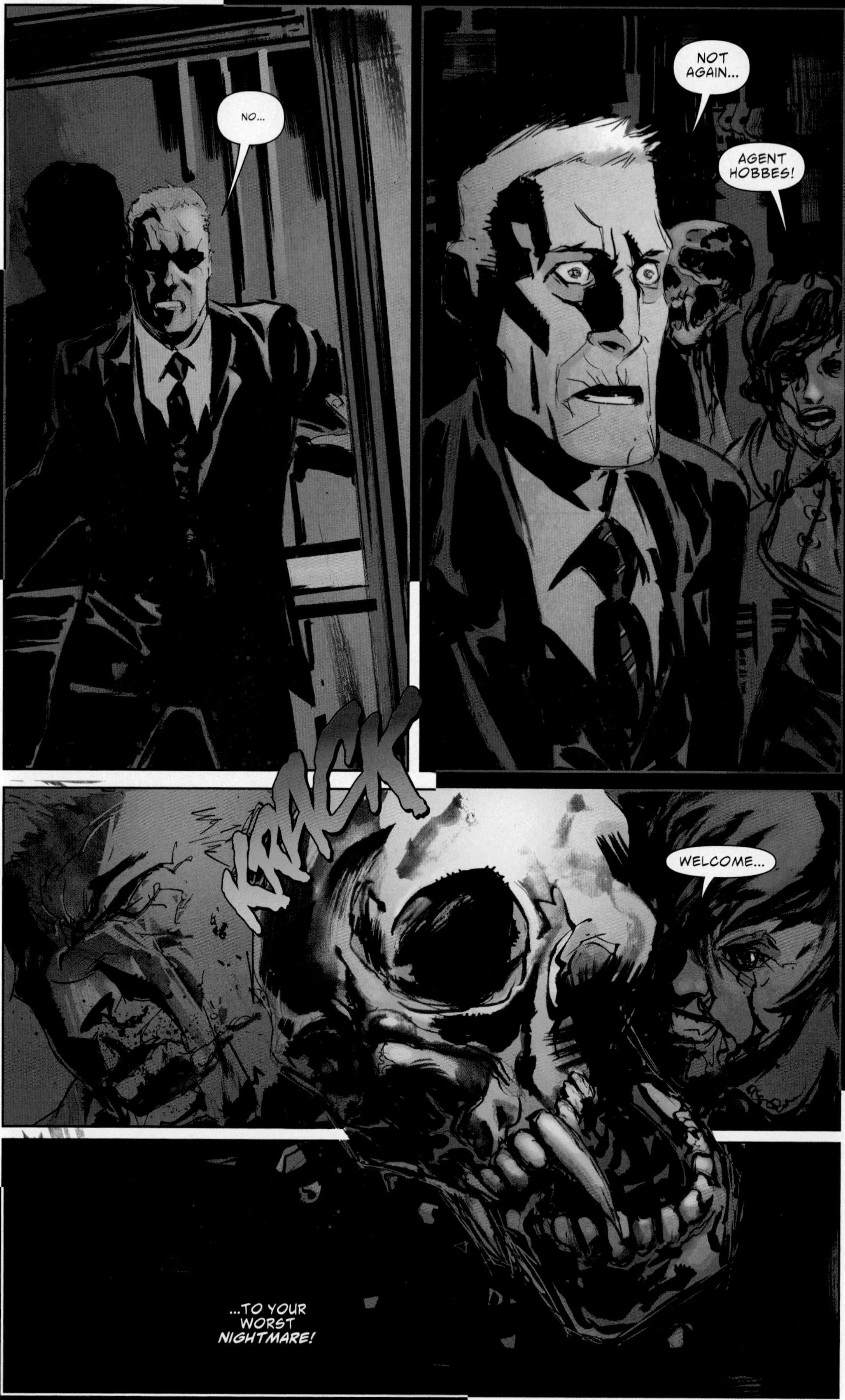
NO...
NOT AGAIN...
AGENT HOBBES!
KRACK
WELCOME...
...TO YOUR WORST NIGHTMARE!

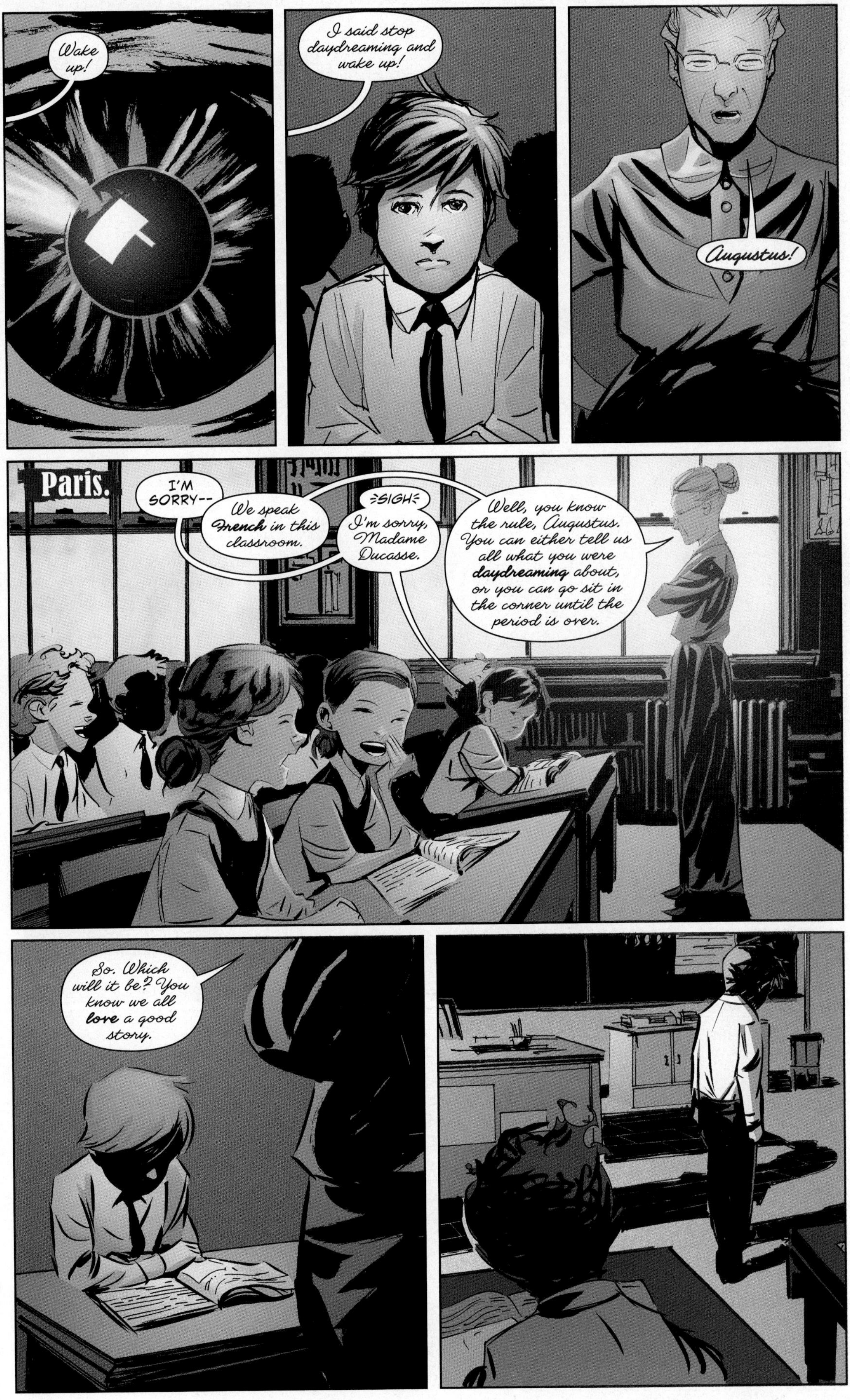
Wake up!
I said stop daydreaming and wake up!
Augustus!
Paris.
I'M SORRY--
We speak French in this classroom.
SIGH
I'm sorry, Madame Ducasse.
Well, you know the rule, Augustus. You can either tell us all what you were daydreaming about, or you can go sit in the corner until the period is over.
So. Which will it be? You know we all love a good story.

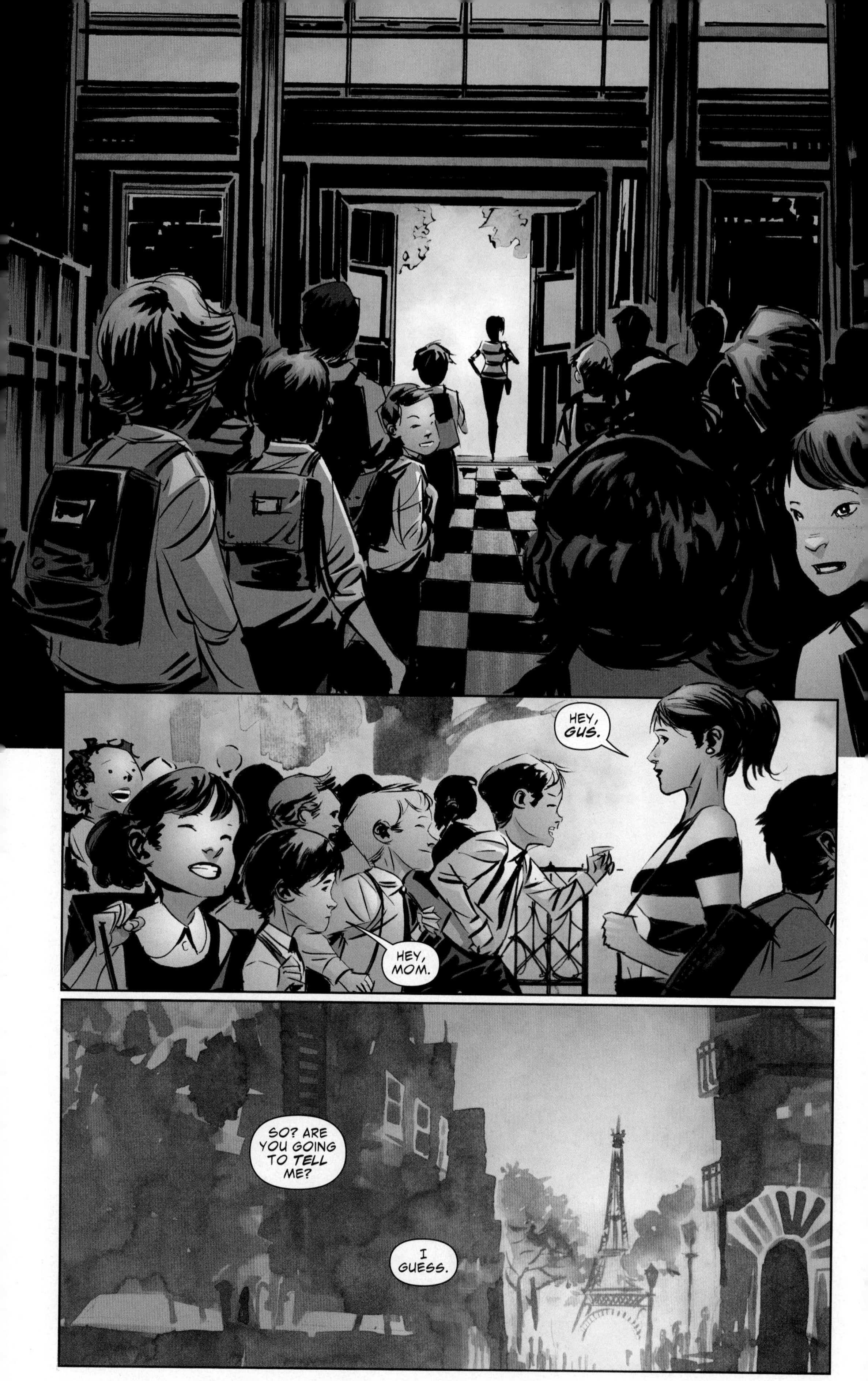
HEY, GUS.
HEY, MOM.
SO? ARE YOU GOING TO TELL ME?
I GUESS.

C-? BUT WE **STUDIED** THIS. WAS IT THE SINE AND COSINE PROBLEMS?

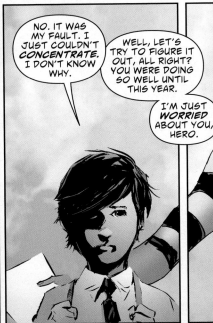

NO. IT WAS MY FAULT. I JUST COULDN'T **CONCENTRATE.** I DON'T KNOW WHY.

WELL, LET'S TRY TO FIGURE IT OUT, ALL RIGHT? YOU WERE DOING SO WELL UNTIL THIS YEAR.

I'M JUST **WORRIED** ABOUT YOU, HERO.

I KNOW.

MOM, WAS **DAD** GOOD AT MATH?

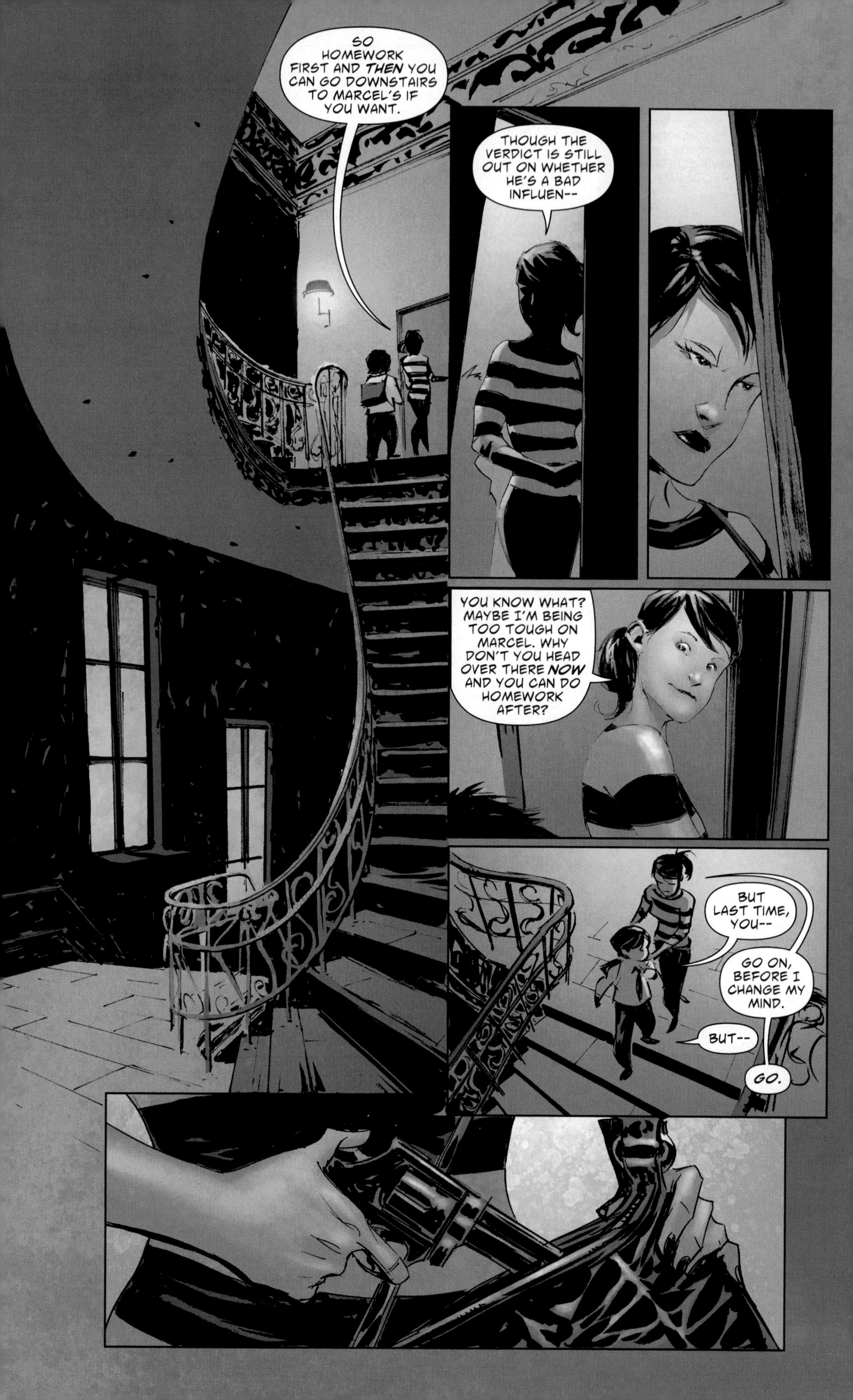

SO HOMEWORK FIRST AND THEN YOU CAN GO DOWNSTAIRS TO MARCEL'S IF YOU WANT.
THOUGH THE VERDICT IS STILL OUT ON WHETHER HE'S A BAD INFLUEN--
YOU KNOW WHAT? MAYBE I'M BEING TOO TOUGH ON MARCEL. WHY DON'T YOU HEAD OVER THERE NOW AND YOU CAN DO HOMEWORK AFTER?
BUT LAST TIME, YOU--
GO ON, BEFORE I CHANGE MY MIND.
BUT--
GO.

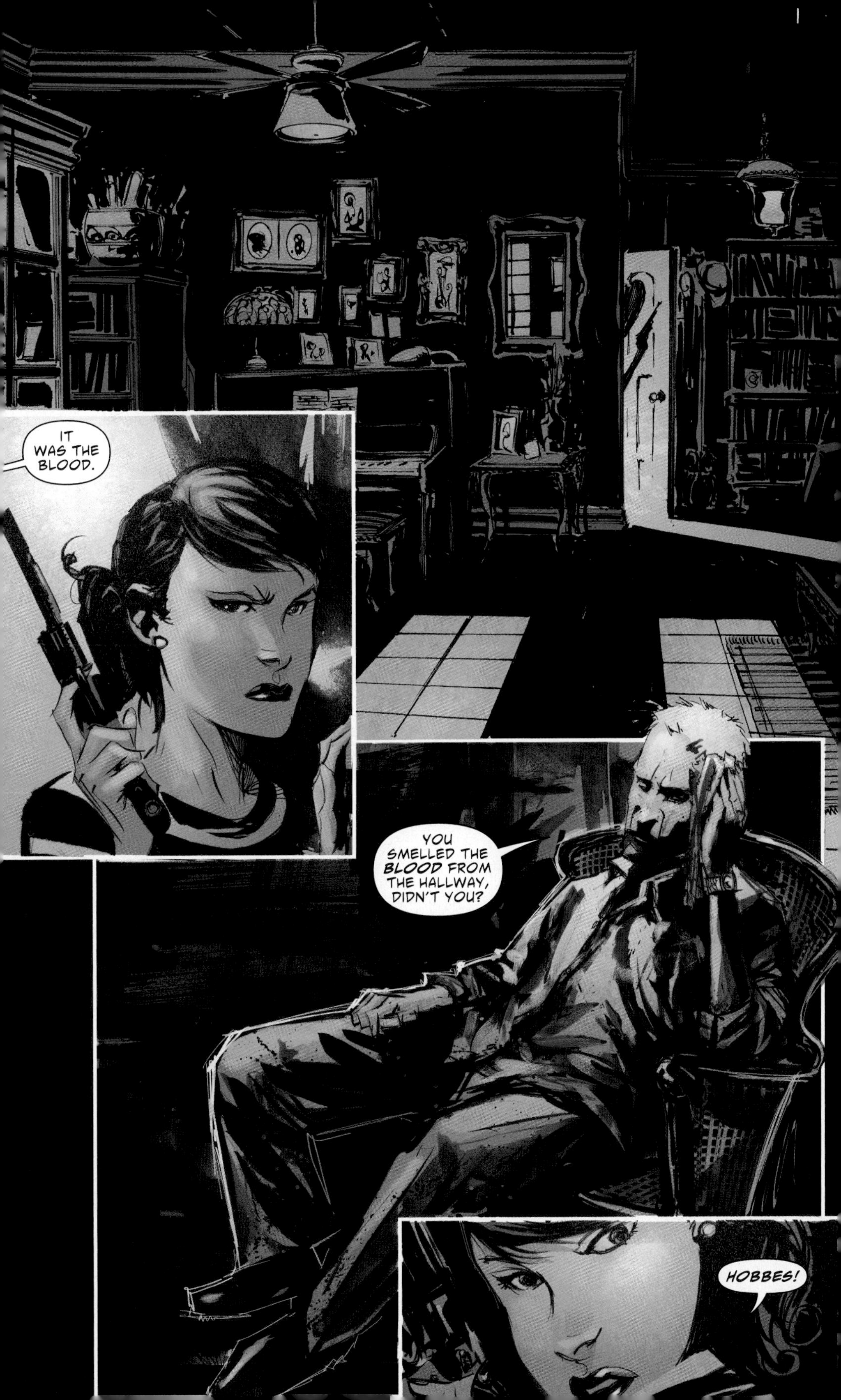
IT WAS THE BLOOD.
YOU SMELLED THE BLOOD FROM THE HALLWAY, DIDN'T YOU?
HOBBES!

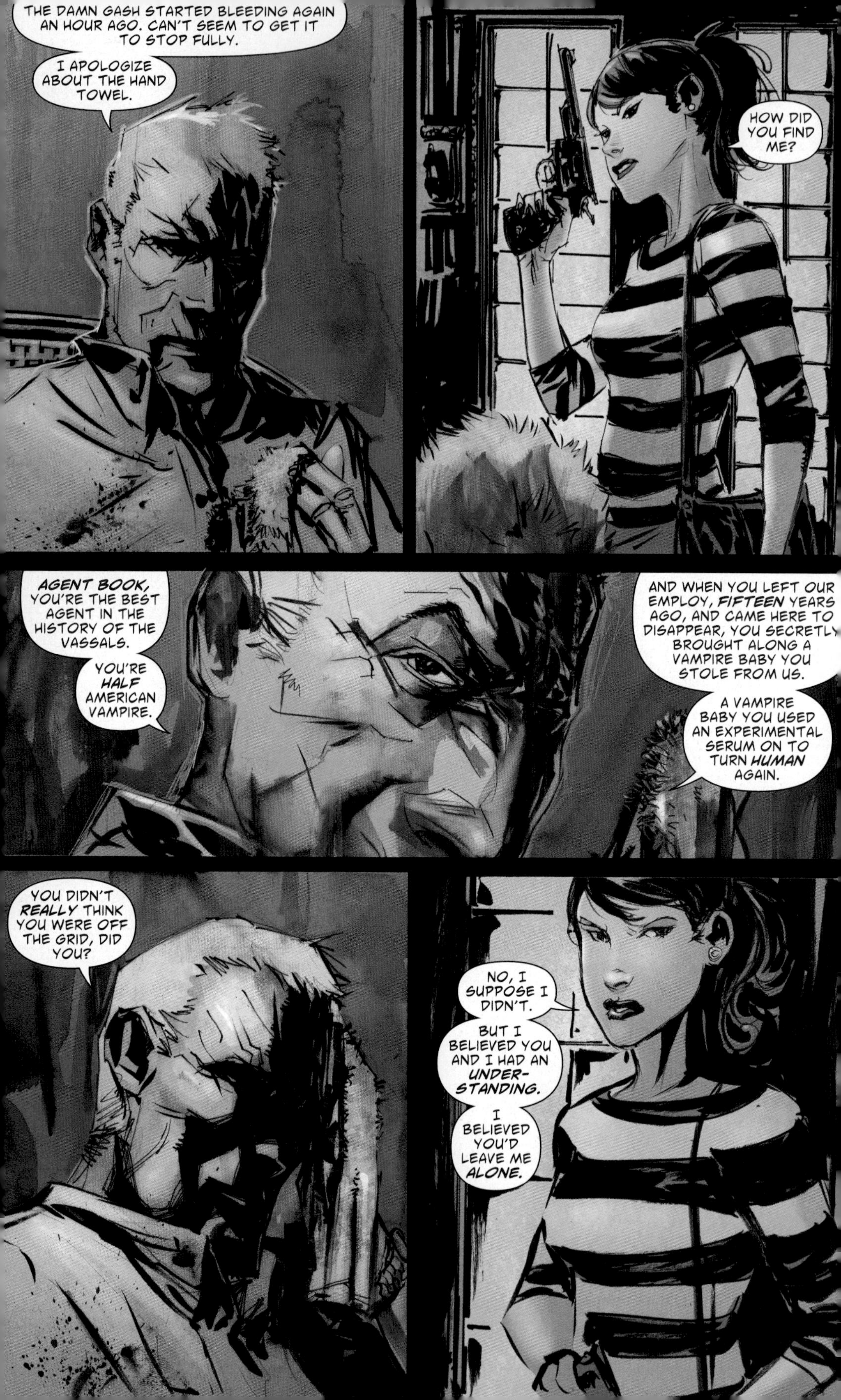
THE DAMN GASH STARTED BLEEDING AGAIN AN HOUR AGO. CAN'T SEEM TO GET IT TO STOP FULLY.
I APOLOGIZE ABOUT THE HAND TOWEL.
HOW DID YOU FIND ME?
AGENT BOOK, YOU'RE THE BEST AGENT IN THE HISTORY OF THE VASSALS.
YOU'RE HALF AMERICAN VAMPIRE.
AND WHEN YOU LEFT OUR EMPLOY, FIFTEEN YEARS AGO, AND CAME HERE TO DISAPPEAR, YOU SECRETLY BROUGHT ALONG A VAMPIRE BABY YOU STOLE FROM US.
A VAMPIRE BABY YOU USED AN EXPERIMENTAL SERUM ON TO TURN HUMAN AGAIN.
YOU DIDN'T REALLY THINK YOU WERE OFF THE GRID, DID YOU?
NO, I SUPPOSE I DIDN'T.
BUT I BELIEVED YOU AND I HAD AN UNDER-STANDING.
I BELIEVED YOU'D LEAVE ME ALONE.

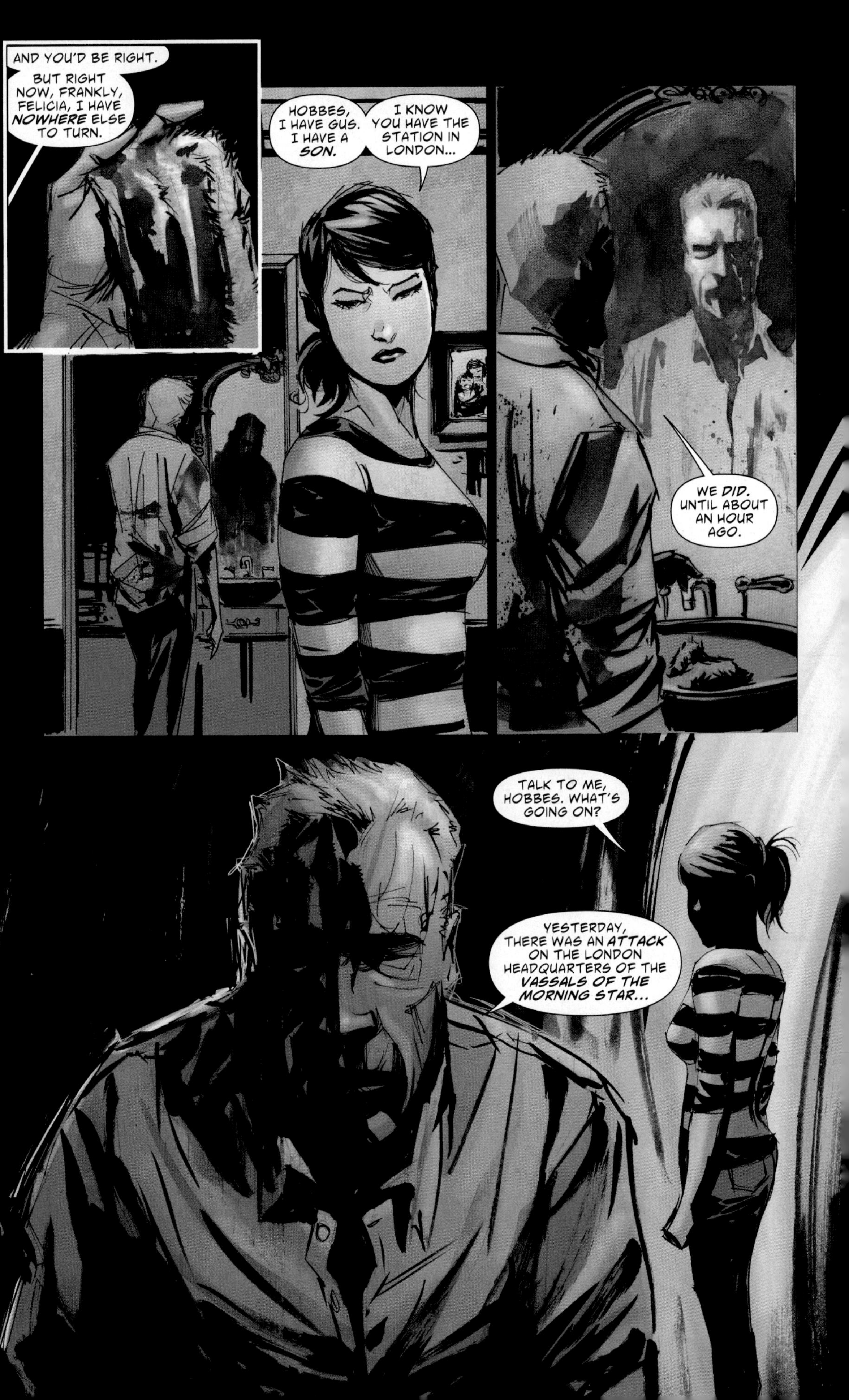
AND YOU'D BE RIGHT.
BUT RIGHT NOW, FRANKLY, FELICIA, I HAVE NOWHERE ELSE TO TURN.
HOBBES, I HAVE GUS. I HAVE A SON.
I KNOW YOU HAVE THE STATION IN LONDON...
WE DID. UNTIL ABOUT AN HOUR AGO.
TALK TO ME, HOBBES. WHAT'S GOING ON?
YESTERDAY, THERE WAS AN ATTACK ON THE LONDON HEADQUARTERS OF THE VASSALS OF THE MORNING STAR...

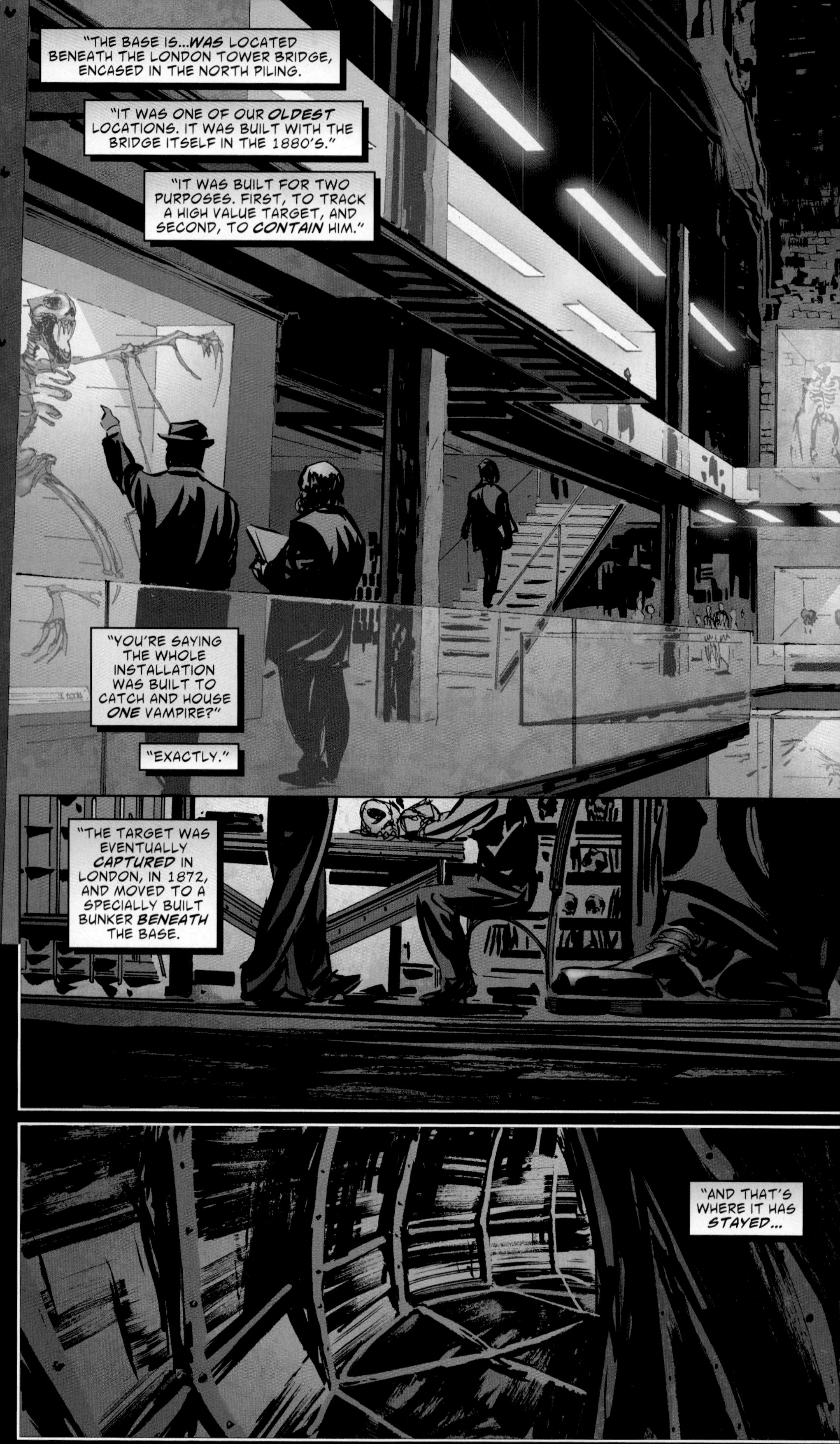
"THE BASE IS...WAS LOCATED BENEATH THE LONDON TOWER BRIDGE, ENCASED IN THE NORTH PILING.
"IT WAS ONE OF OUR OLDEST LOCATIONS. IT WAS BUILT WITH THE BRIDGE ITSELF IN THE 1880'S."
"IT WAS BUILT FOR TWO PURPOSES. FIRST, TO TRACK A HIGH VALUE TARGET, AND SECOND, TO CONTAIN HIM."
"YOU'RE SAYING THE WHOLE INSTALLATION WAS BUILT TO CATCH AND HOUSE ONE VAMPIRE?"
"EXACTLY."
"THE TARGET WAS EVENTUALLY CAPTURED IN LONDON, IN 1872, AND MOVED TO A SPECIALLY BUILT BUNKER BENEATH THE BASE.
"AND THAT'S WHERE IT HAS STAYED...

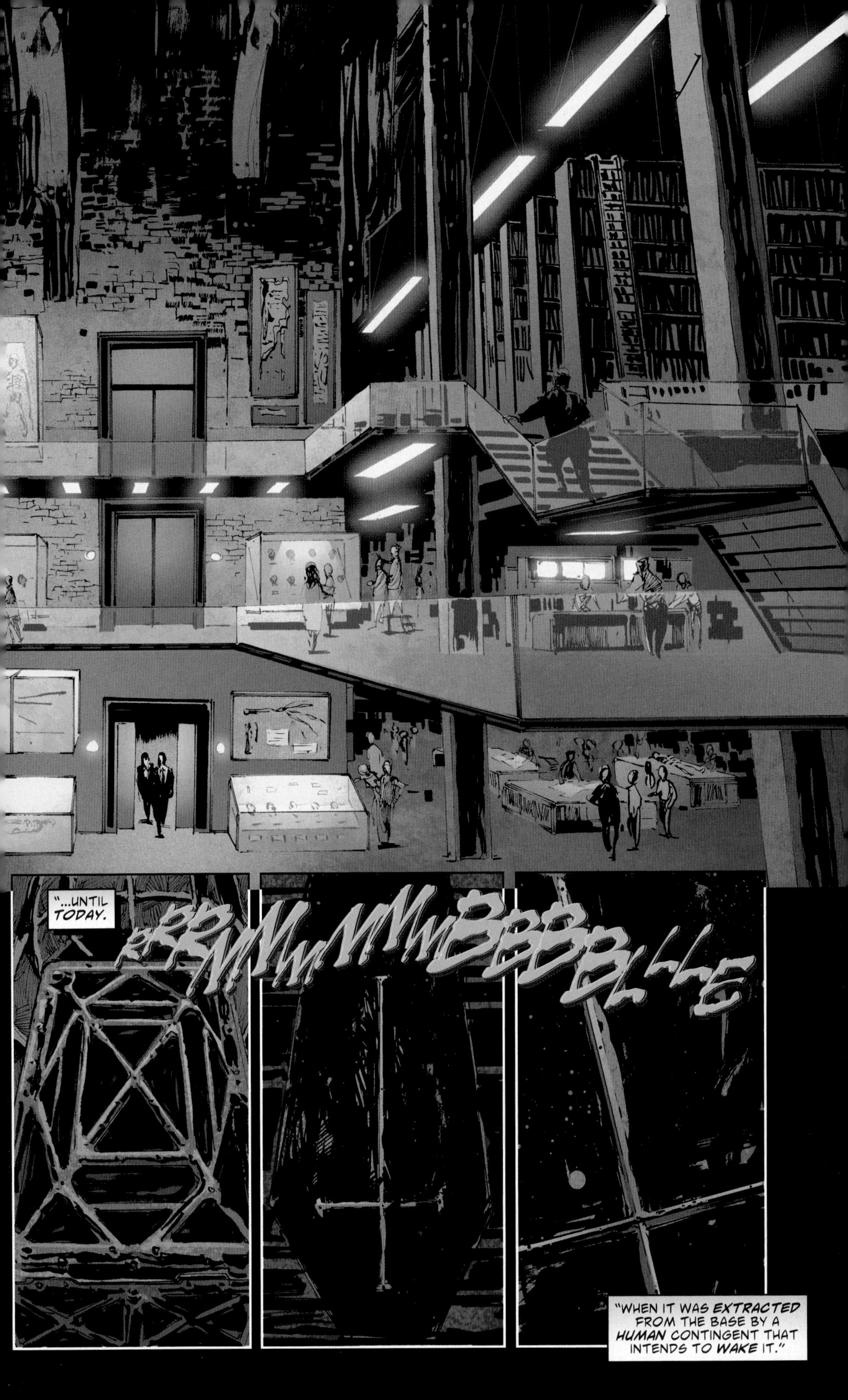

"...UNTIL TODAY.
RRRMMMMMMMBBBBLLLE
"WHEN IT WAS EXTRACTED FROM THE BASE BY A HUMAN CONTINGENT THAT INTENDS TO WAKE IT."

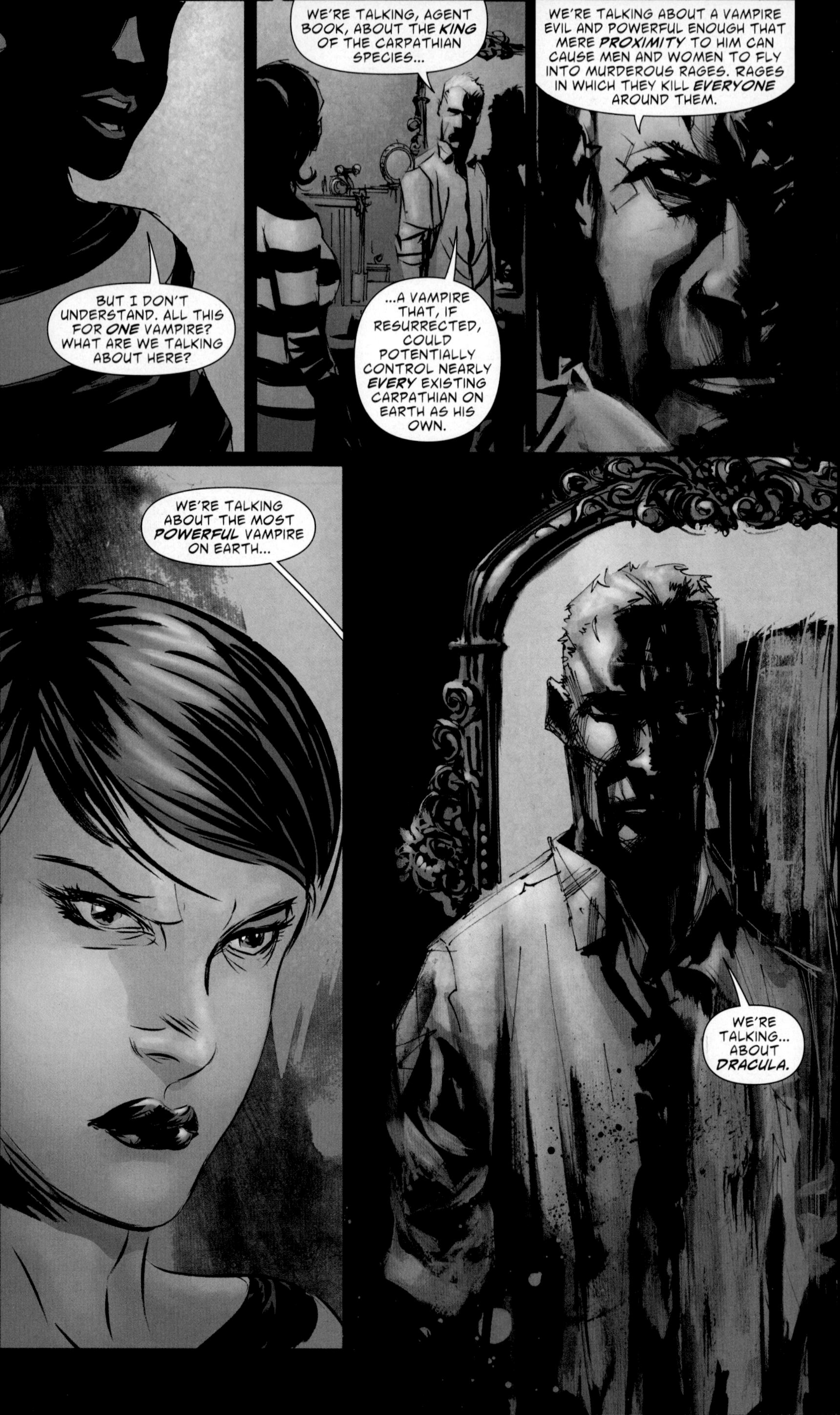
BUT I DON'T UNDERSTAND. ALL THIS FOR ONE VAMPIRE? WHAT ARE WE TALKING ABOUT HERE?
WE'RE TALKING, AGENT BOOK, ABOUT THE KING OF THE CARPATHIAN SPECIES...
...A VAMPIRE THAT, IF RESURRECTED, COULD POTENTIALLY CONTROL NEARLY EVERY EXISTING CARPATHIAN ON EARTH AS HIS OWN.
WE'RE TALKING ABOUT A VAMPIRE EVIL AND POWERFUL ENOUGH THAT MERE PROXIMITY TO HIM CAN CAUSE MEN AND WOMEN TO FLY INTO MURDEROUS RAGES. RAGES IN WHICH THEY KILL EVERYONE AROUND THEM.
WE'RE TALKING ABOUT THE MOST POWERFUL VAMPIRE ON EARTH...
WE'RE TALKING... ABOUT DRACULA.

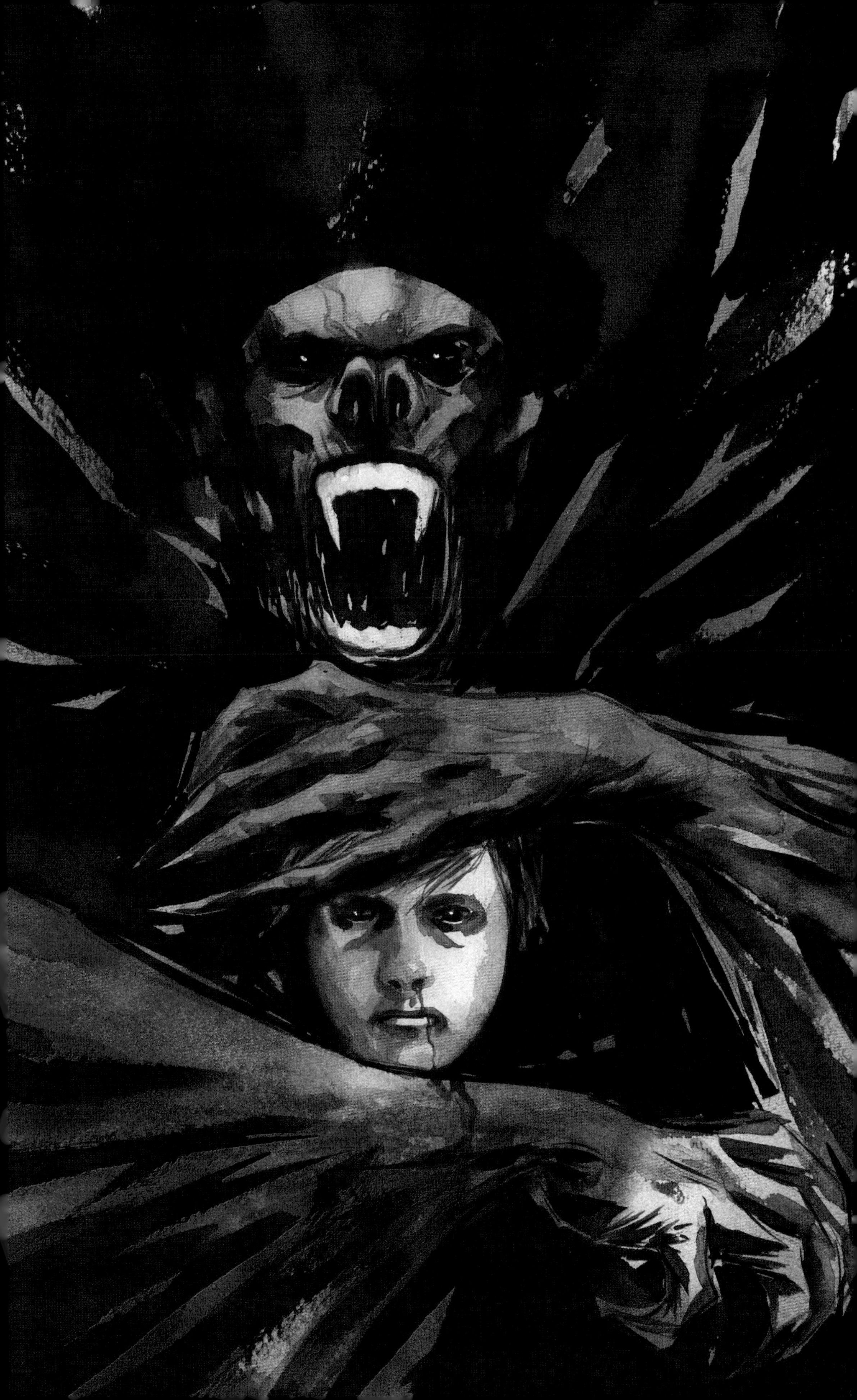

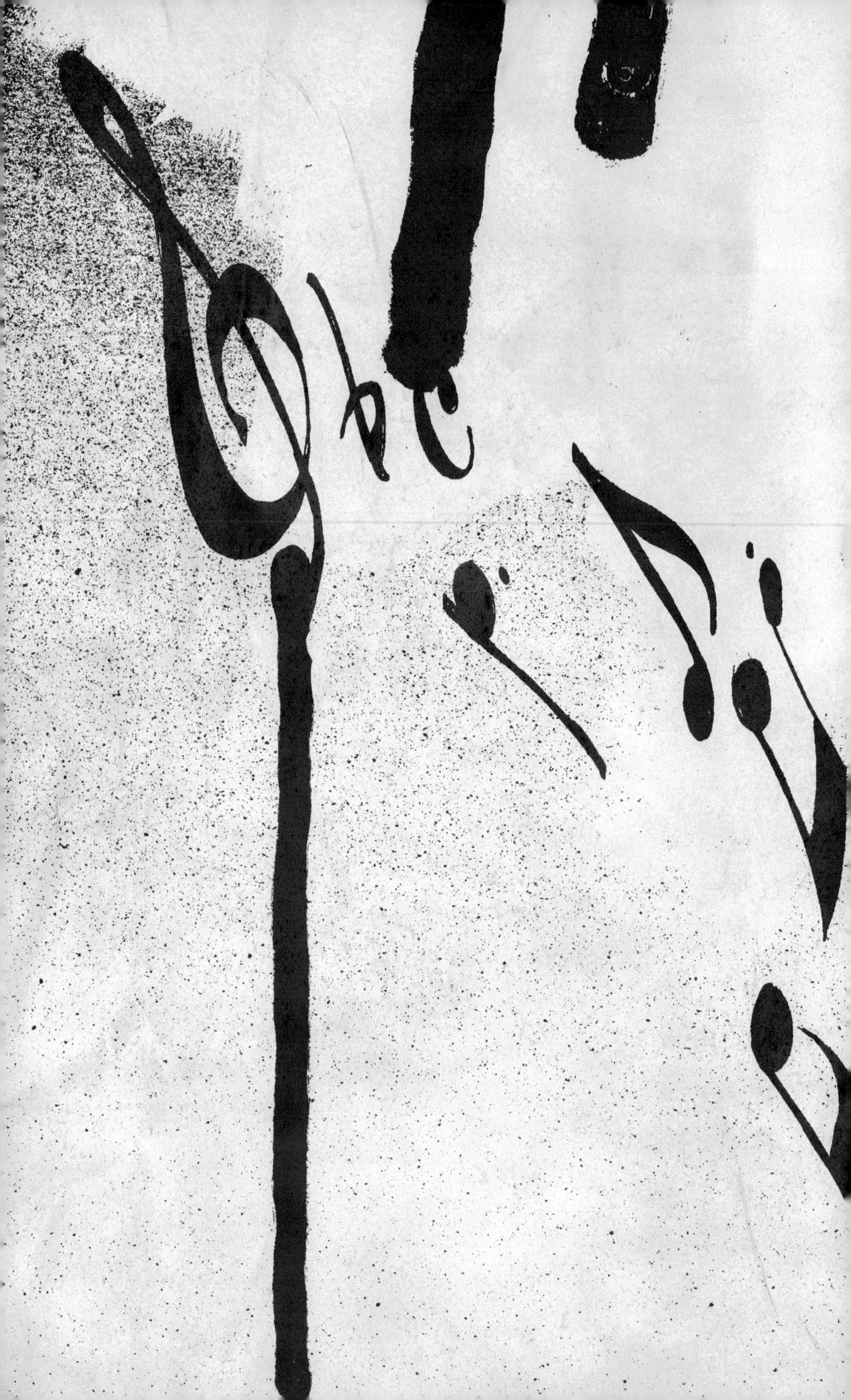

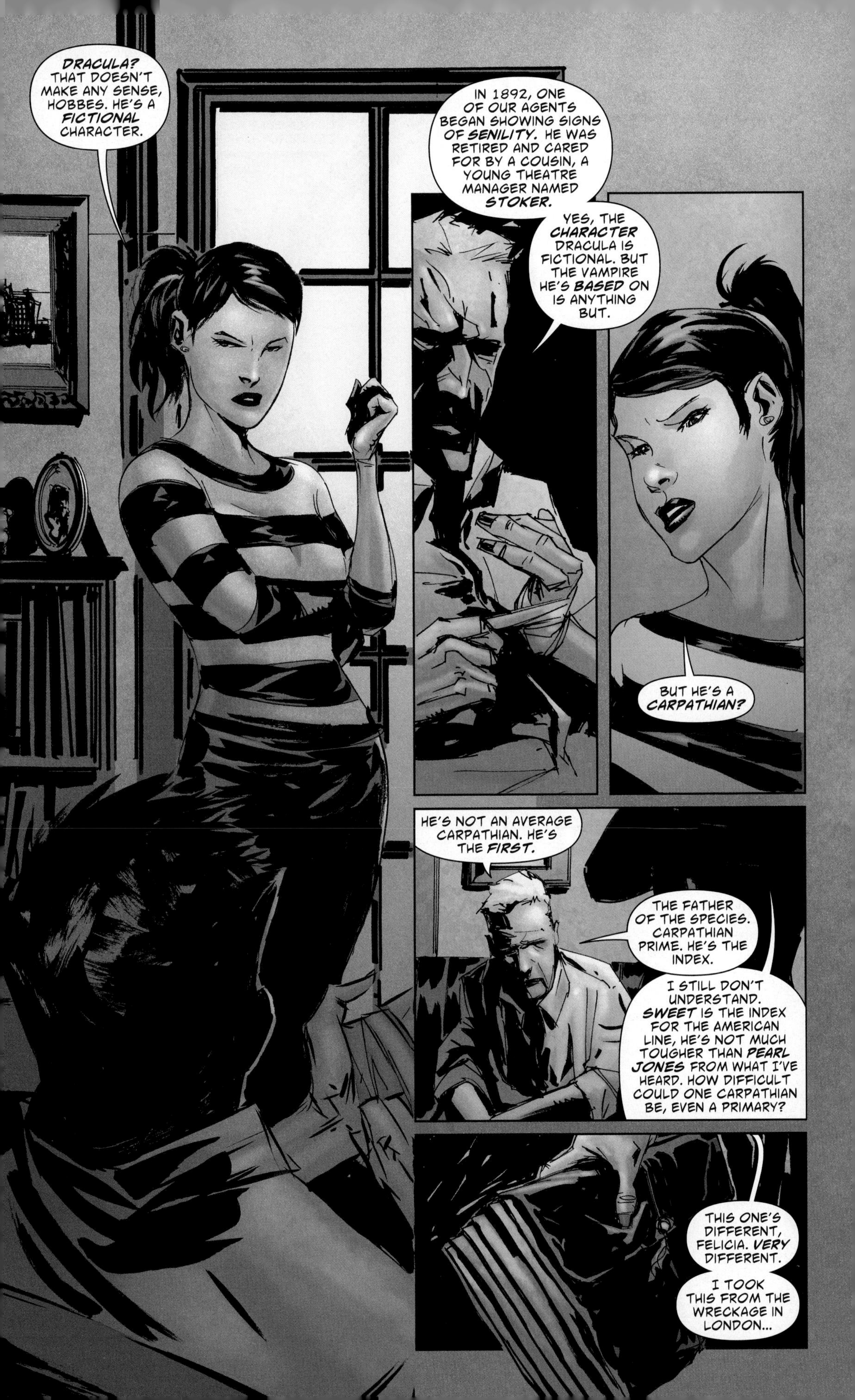
DRACULA? THAT DOESN'T MAKE ANY SENSE, HOBBES. HE'S A FICTIONAL CHARACTER.
IN 1892, ONE OF OUR AGENTS BEGAN SHOWING SIGNS OF SENILITY. HE WAS RETIRED AND CARED FOR BY A COUSIN, A YOUNG THEATRE MANAGER NAMED STOKER.
YES, THE CHARACTER DRACULA IS FICTIONAL. BUT THE VAMPIRE HE'S BASED ON IS ANYTHING BUT.
BUT HE'S A CARPATHIAN?
HE'S NOT AN AVERAGE CARPATHIAN. HE'S THE FIRST.
THE FATHER OF THE SPECIES. CARPATHIAN PRIME. HE'S THE INDEX.
I STILL DON'T UNDERSTAND. SWEET IS THE INDEX FOR THE AMERICAN LINE, HE'S NOT MUCH TOUGHER THAN PEARL JONES FROM WHAT I'VE HEARD. HOW DIFFICULT COULD ONE CARPATHIAN BE, EVEN A PRIMARY?
THIS ONE'S DIFFERENT, FELICIA. VERY DIFFERENT.
I TOOK THIS FROM THE WRECKAGE IN LONDON...

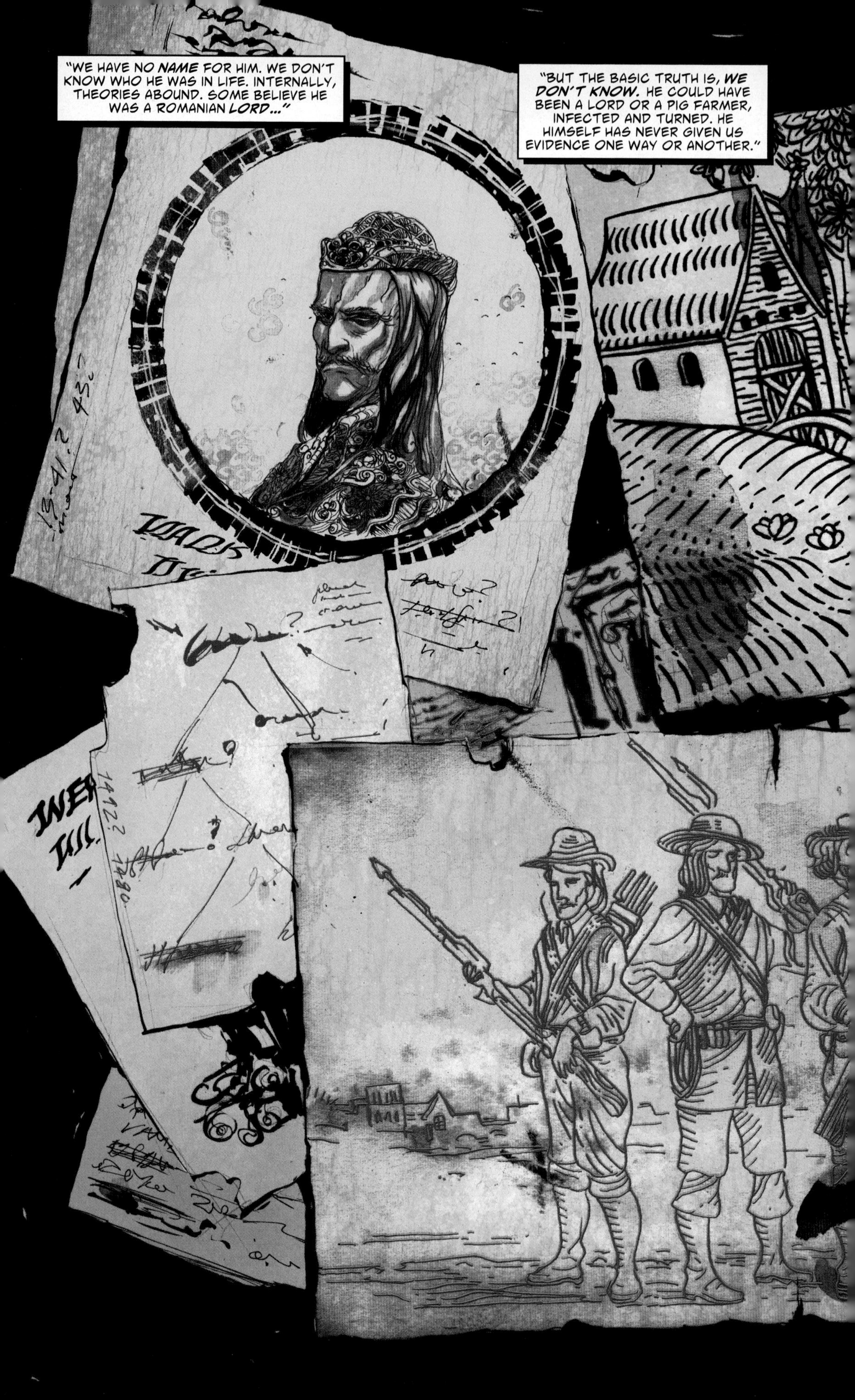
"WE HAVE NO NAME FOR HIM. WE DON'T KNOW WHO HE WAS IN LIFE. INTERNALLY, THEORIES ABOUND. SOME BELIEVE HE WAS A ROMANIAN LORD..."
"BUT THE BASIC TRUTH IS, WE DON'T KNOW. HE COULD HAVE BEEN A LORD OR A PIG FARMER, INFECTED AND TURNED. HE HIMSELF HAS NEVER GIVEN US EVIDENCE ONE WAY OR ANOTHER."

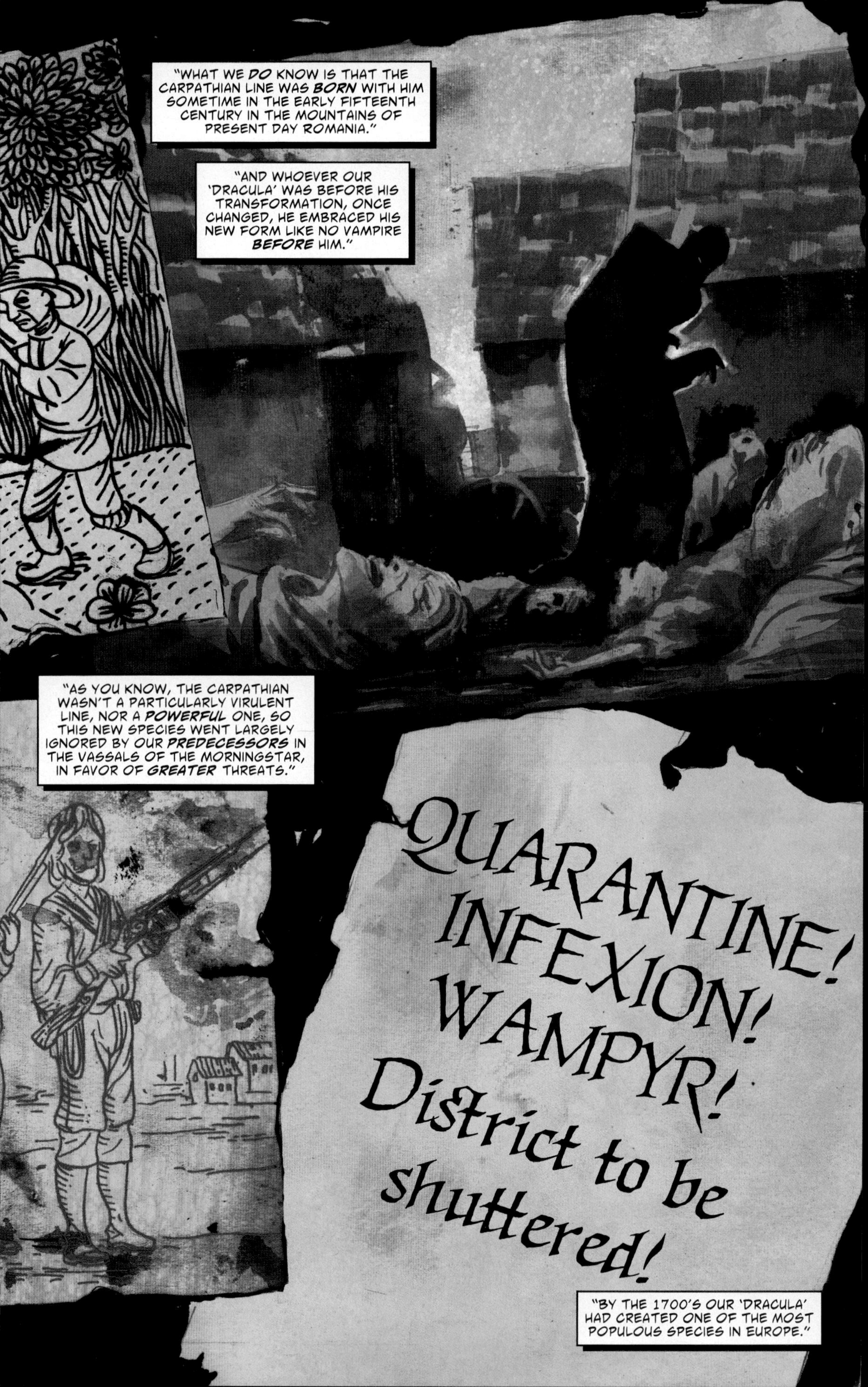
"WHAT WE DO KNOW IS THAT THE CARPATHIAN LINE WAS BORN WITH HIM SOMETIME IN THE EARLY FIFTEENTH CENTURY IN THE MOUNTAINS OF PRESENT DAY ROMANIA."
"AND WHOEVER OUR 'DRACULA' WAS BEFORE HIS TRANSFORMATION, ONCE CHANGED, HE EMBRACED HIS NEW FORM LIKE NO VAMPIRE BEFORE HIM."
"AS YOU KNOW, THE CARPATHIAN WASN'T A PARTICULARLY VIRULENT LINE, NOR A POWERFUL ONE, SO THIS NEW SPECIES WENT LARGELY IGNORED BY OUR PREDECESSORS IN THE VASSALS OF THE MORNINGSTAR, IN FAVOR OF GREATER THREATS."
QUARANTINE! INFEXION! WAMPYR! District to be shuttered!
"BY THE 1700'S OUR 'DRACULA' HAD CREATED ONE OF THE MOST POPULOUS SPECIES IN EUROPE."

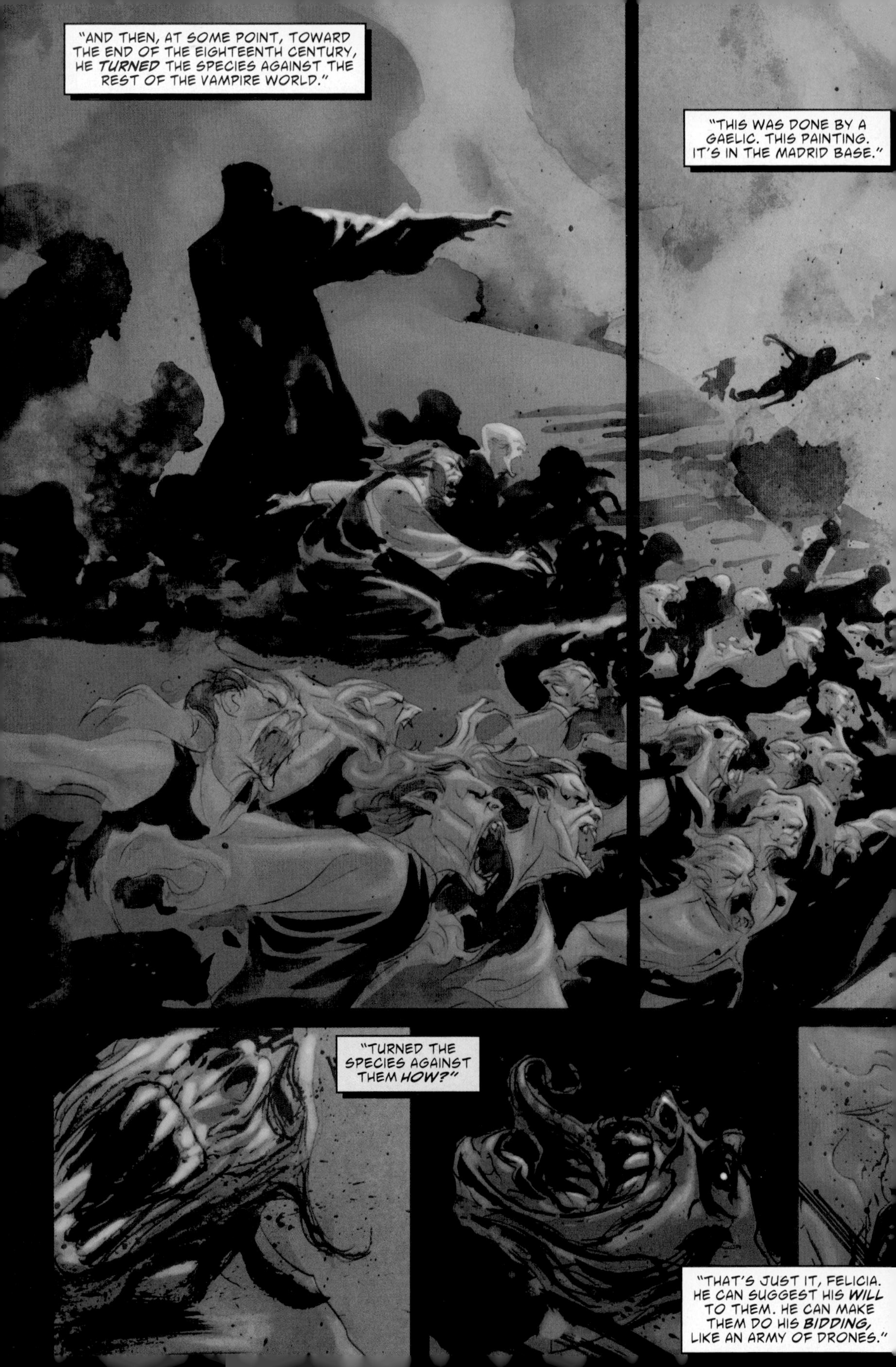
"AND THEN, AT SOME POINT, TOWARD THE END OF THE EIGHTEENTH CENTURY, HE *TURNED* THE SPECIES AGAINST THE REST OF THE VAMPIRE WORLD."
"THIS WAS DONE BY A GAELIC. THIS PAINTING. IT'S IN THE MADRID BASE."
"TURNED THE SPECIES AGAINST THEM *HOW?*"
"THAT'S JUST IT, FELICIA. HE CAN SUGGEST HIS *WILL* TO THEM. HE CAN MAKE THEM DO HIS *BIDDING*, LIKE AN ARMY OF DRONES."

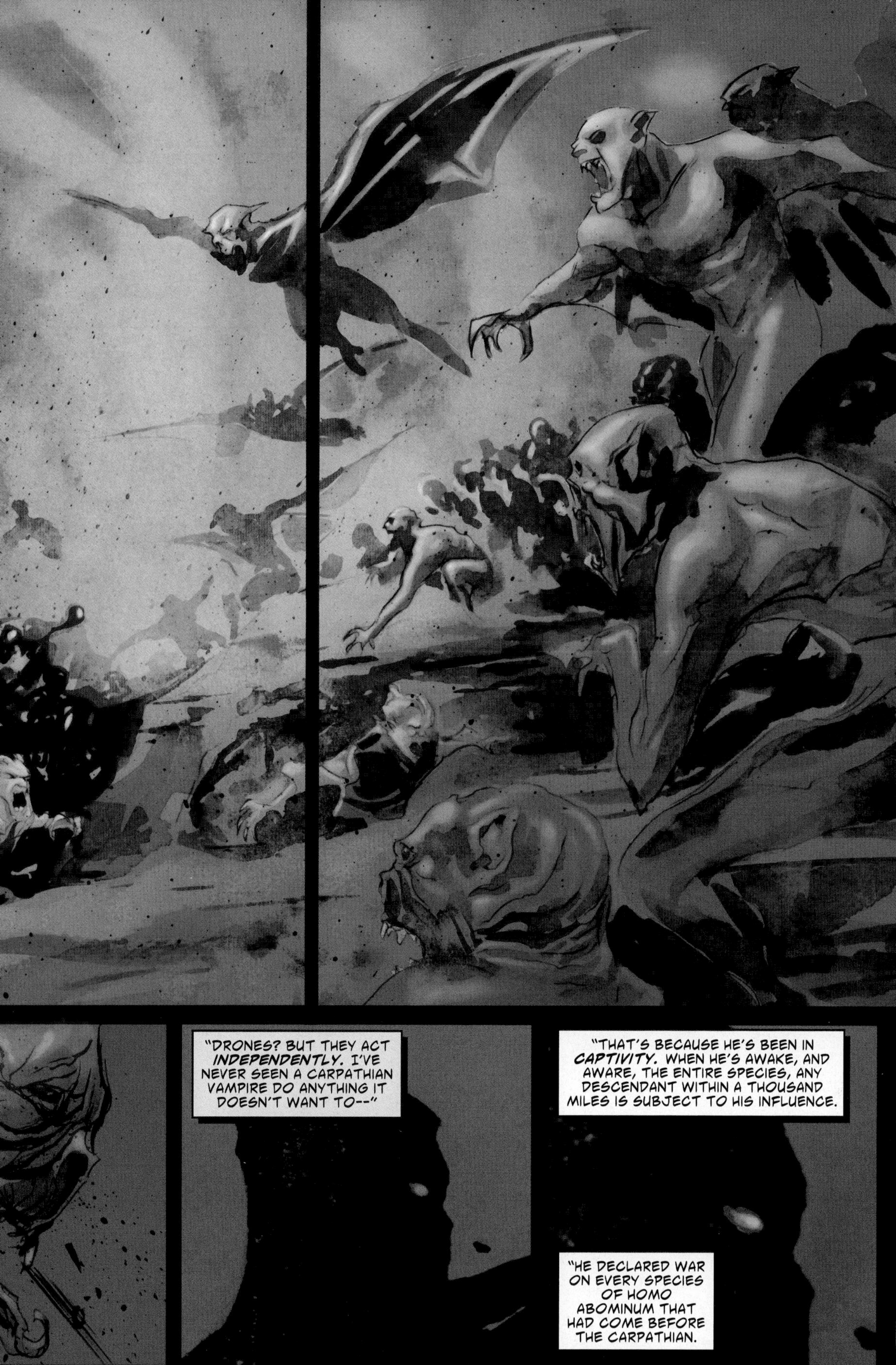
"DRONES? BUT THEY ACT *INDEPENDENTLY.* I'VE NEVER SEEN A CARPATHIAN VAMPIRE DO ANYTHING IT DOESN'T WANT TO--"
"THAT'S BECAUSE HE'S BEEN IN *CAPTIVITY.* WHEN HE'S AWAKE, AND AWARE, THE ENTIRE SPECIES, ANY DESCENDANT WITHIN A THOUSAND MILES IS SUBJECT TO HIS INFLUENCE.
"HE DECLARED WAR ON EVERY SPECIES OF HOMO ABOMINUM THAT HAD COME BEFORE THE CARPATHIAN.

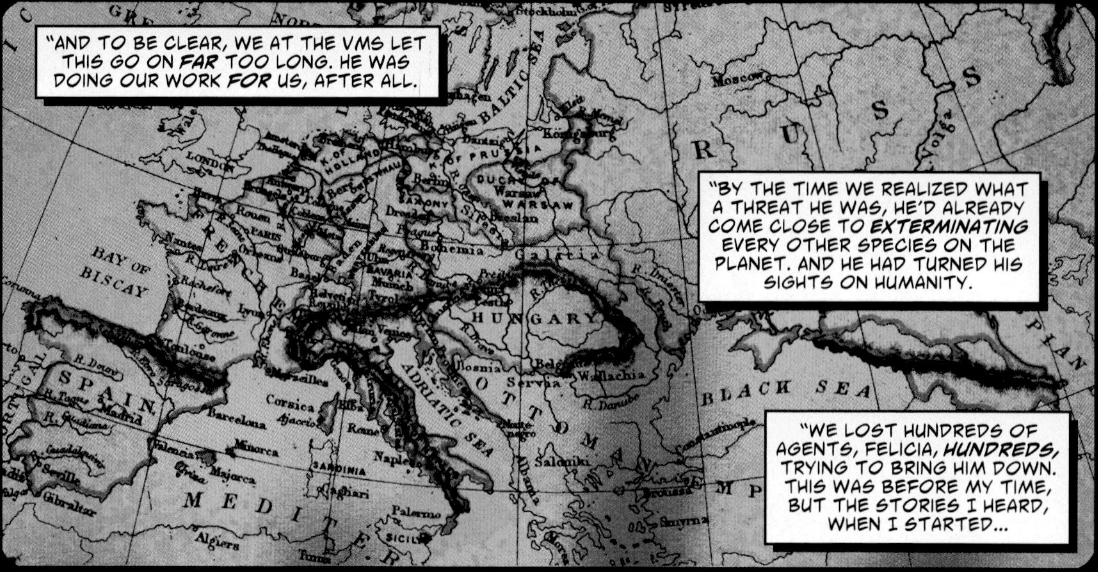
"AND TO BE CLEAR, WE AT THE VMS LET THIS GO ON **FAR** TOO LONG. HE WAS DOING OUR WORK **FOR** US, AFTER ALL.
"BY THE TIME WE REALIZED WHAT A THREAT HE WAS, HE'D ALREADY COME CLOSE TO **EXTERMINATING** EVERY OTHER SPECIES ON THE PLANET. AND HE HAD TURNED HIS SIGHTS ON HUMANITY.
"WE LOST HUNDREDS OF AGENTS, FELICIA, **HUNDREDS,** TRYING TO BRING HIM DOWN. THIS WAS BEFORE MY TIME, BUT THE STORIES I HEARD, WHEN I STARTED...
BALTIC SEA
Moscow
LONDON
PARIS
BAY OF BISCAY
SPAIN
Madrid
HUNGARY
Bohemia
Wallachia
BLACK SEA
ADRIATIC SEA
Corsica
Barcelona
Minorca
Majorca
SARDINIA
Naples
Palermo
Algiers

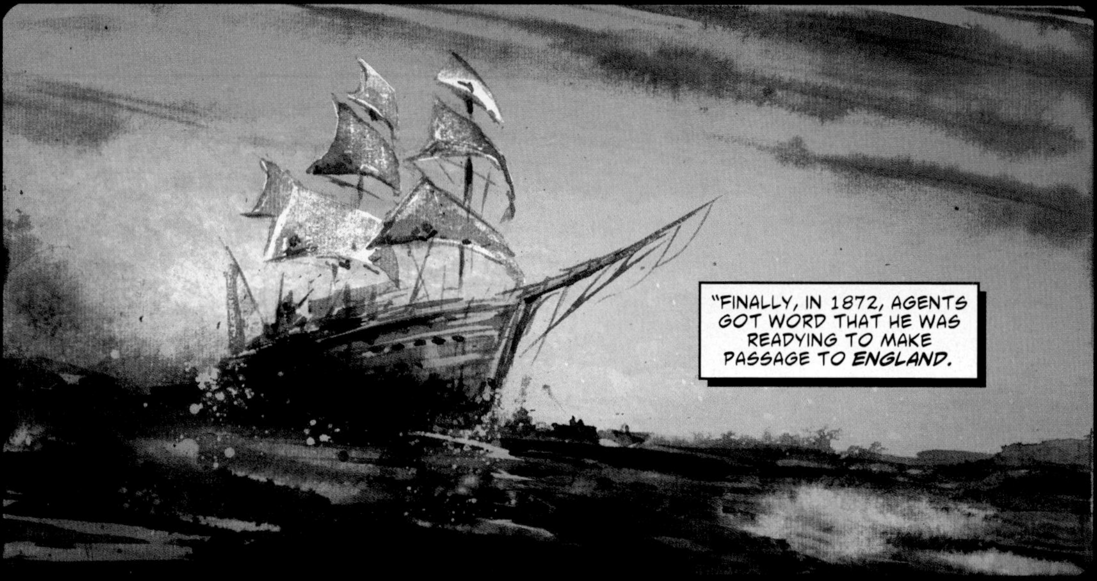
"FINALLY, IN 1872, AGENTS GOT WORD THAT HE WAS READYING TO MAKE PASSAGE TO **ENGLAND.**

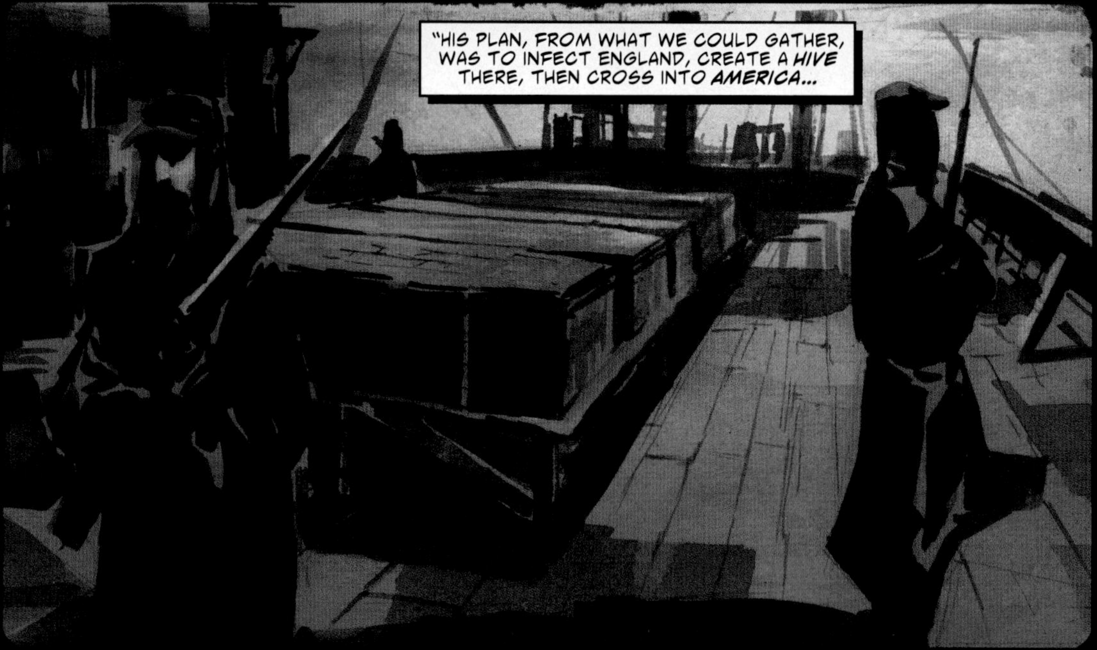
"HIS PLAN, FROM WHAT WE COULD GATHER, WAS TO INFECT ENGLAND, CREATE A **HIVE** THERE, THEN CROSS INTO **AMERICA...**

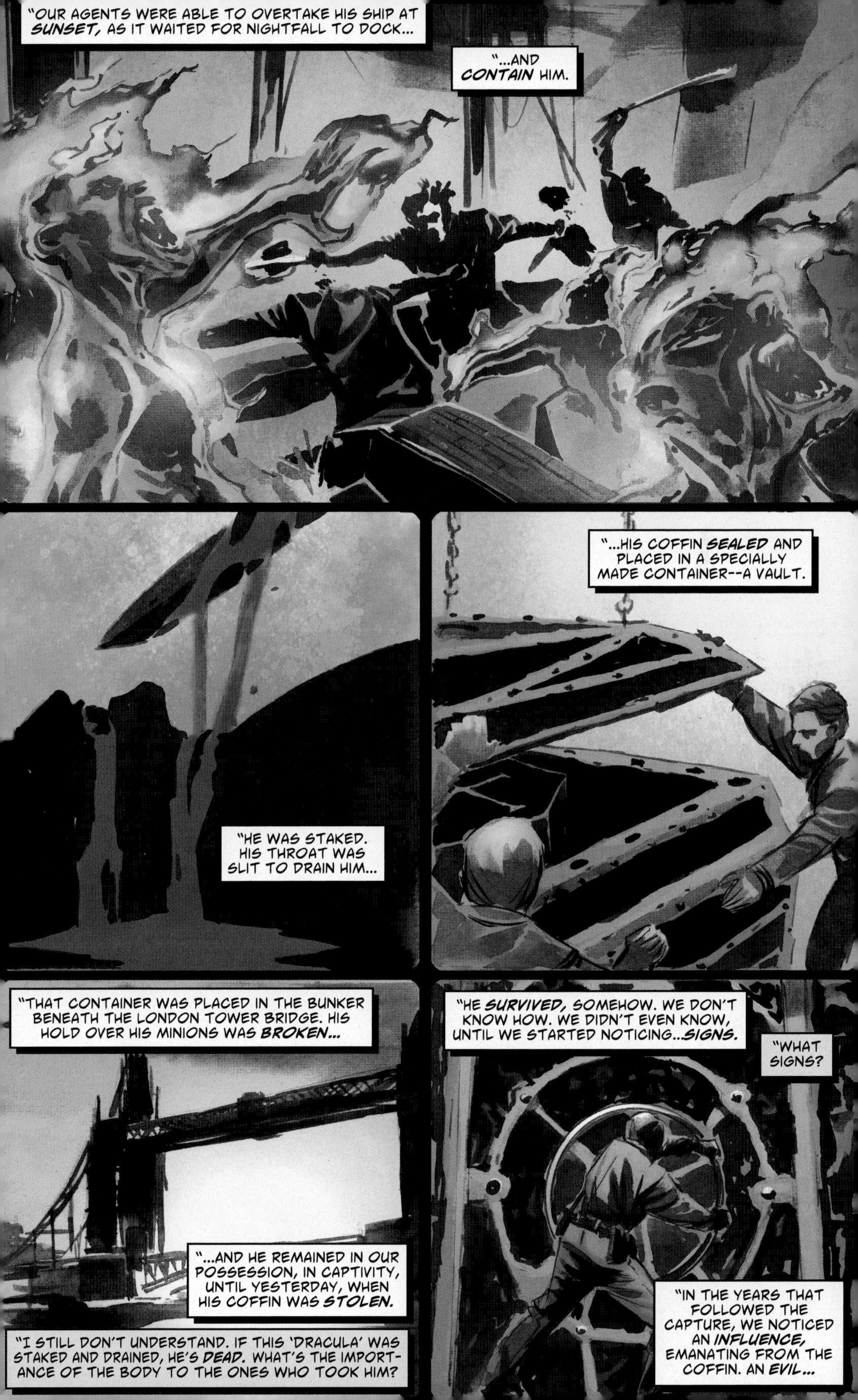
"OUR AGENTS WERE ABLE TO OVERTAKE HIS SHIP AT SUNSET, AS IT WAITED FOR NIGHTFALL TO DOCK...
"...AND CONTAIN HIM.
"HE WAS STAKED. HIS THROAT WAS SLIT TO DRAIN HIM...
"...HIS COFFIN SEALED AND PLACED IN A SPECIALLY MADE CONTAINER--A VAULT.
"THAT CONTAINER WAS PLACED IN THE BUNKER BENEATH THE LONDON TOWER BRIDGE. HIS HOLD OVER HIS MINIONS WAS BROKEN...
"...AND HE REMAINED IN OUR POSSESSION, IN CAPTIVITY, UNTIL YESTERDAY, WHEN HIS COFFIN WAS STOLEN.
"I STILL DON'T UNDERSTAND. IF THIS 'DRACULA' WAS STAKED AND DRAINED, HE'S DEAD. WHAT'S THE IMPORTANCE OF THE BODY TO THE ONES WHO TOOK HIM?
"HE SURVIVED, SOMEHOW. WE DON'T KNOW HOW. WE DIDN'T EVEN KNOW, UNTIL WE STARTED NOTICING...SIGNS.
"WHAT SIGNS?
"IN THE YEARS THAT FOLLOWED THE CAPTURE, WE NOTICED AN INFLUENCE, EMANATING FROM THE COFFIN. AN EVIL...

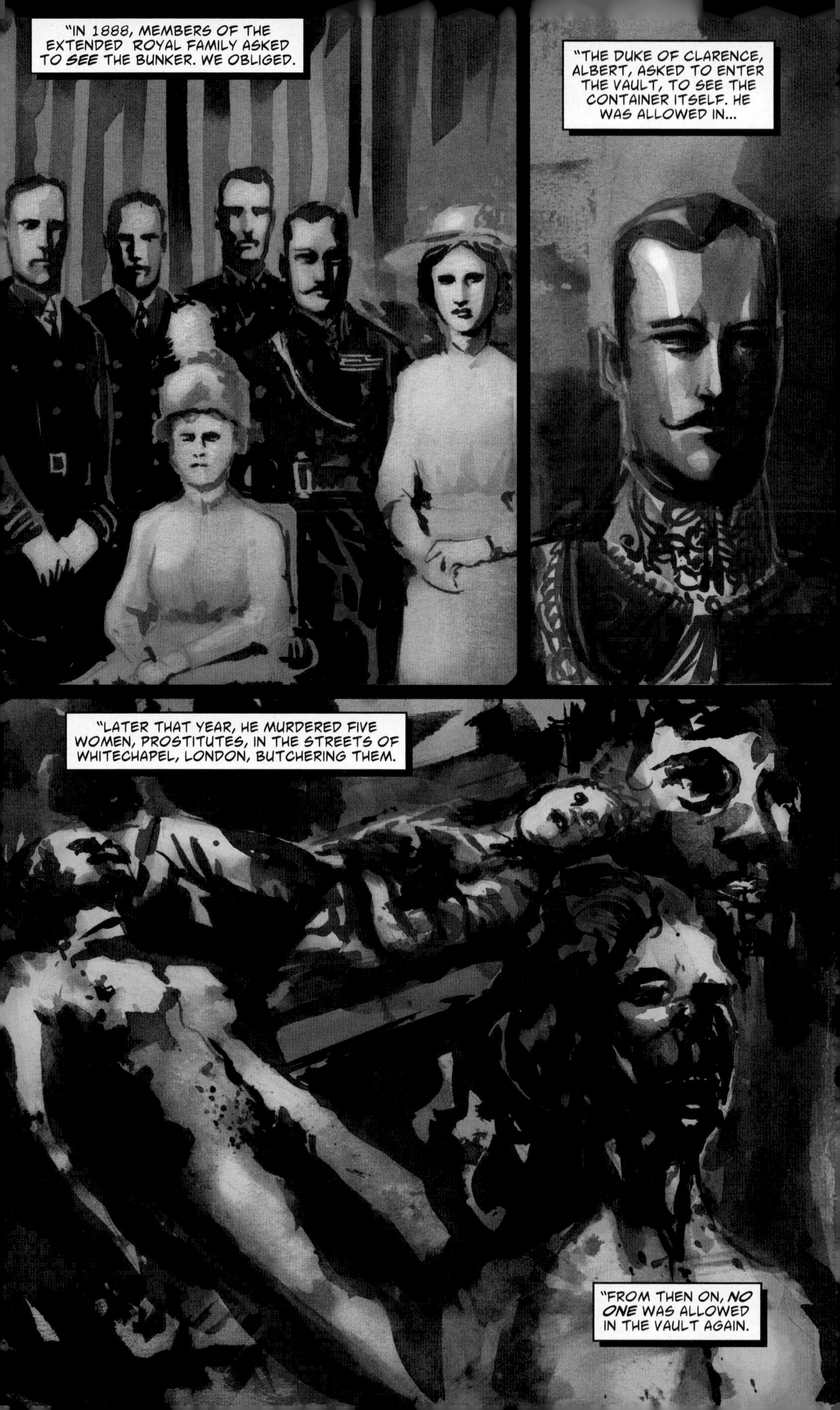
"IN 1888, MEMBERS OF THE EXTENDED ROYAL FAMILY ASKED TO *SEE* THE BUNKER. WE OBLIGED.
"THE DUKE OF CLARENCE, ALBERT, ASKED TO ENTER THE VAULT, TO SEE THE CONTAINER ITSELF. HE WAS ALLOWED IN...
"LATER THAT YEAR, HE MURDERED FIVE WOMEN, PROSTITUTES, IN THE STREETS OF WHITECHAPEL, LONDON, BUTCHERING THEM.
"FROM THEN ON, *NO ONE* WAS ALLOWED IN THE VAULT AGAIN.

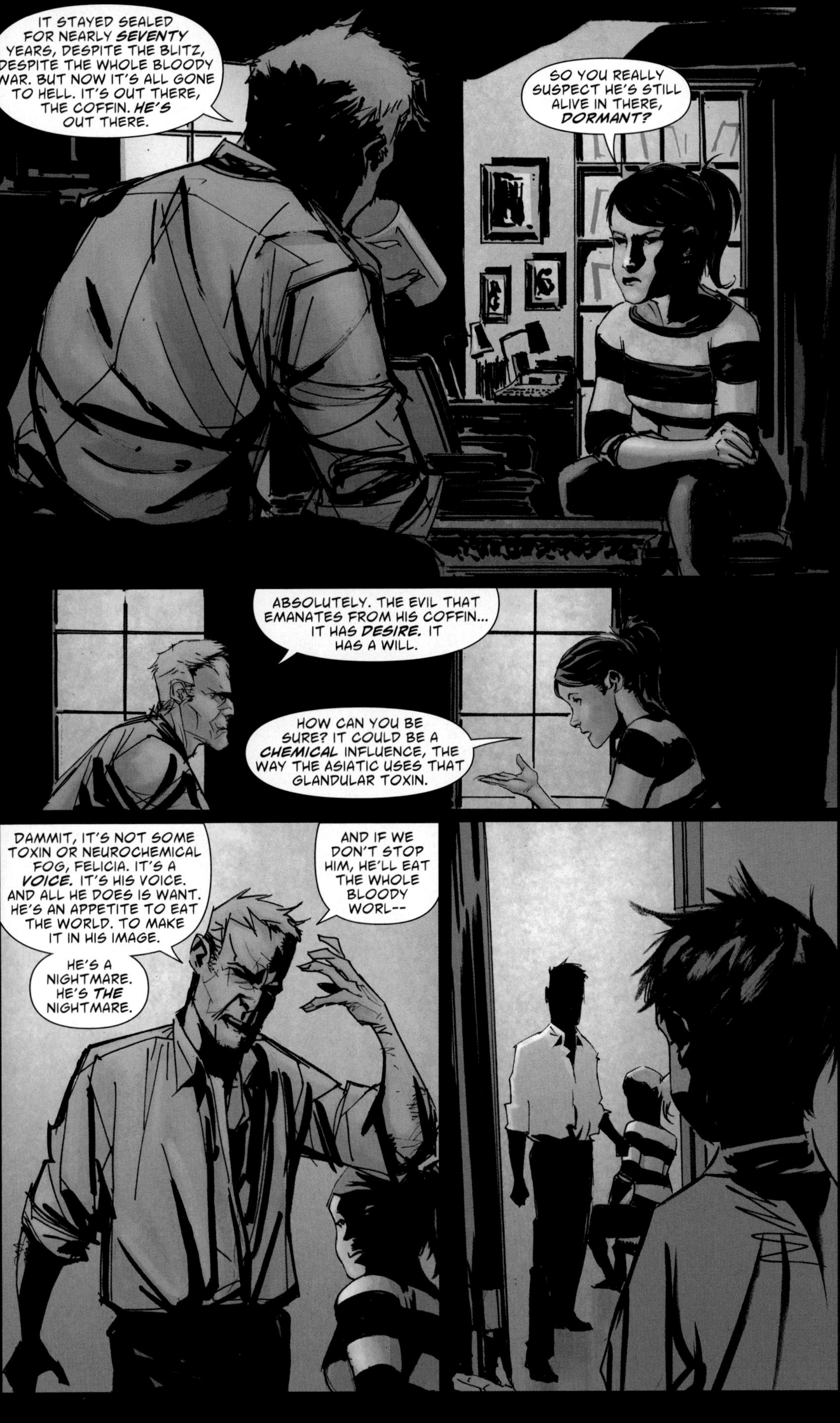
IT STAYED SEALED FOR NEARLY SEVENTY YEARS, DESPITE THE BLITZ, DESPITE THE WHOLE BLOODY WAR. BUT NOW IT'S ALL GONE TO HELL. IT'S OUT THERE, THE COFFIN. HE'S OUT THERE.
SO YOU REALLY SUSPECT HE'S STILL ALIVE IN THERE, DORMANT?
ABSOLUTELY. THE EVIL THAT EMANATES FROM HIS COFFIN... IT HAS DESIRE. IT HAS A WILL.
HOW CAN YOU BE SURE? IT COULD BE A CHEMICAL INFLUENCE, THE WAY THE ASIATIC USES THAT GLANDULAR TOXIN.
DAMMIT, IT'S NOT SOME TOXIN OR NEUROCHEMICAL FOG, FELICIA. IT'S A VOICE. IT'S HIS VOICE. AND ALL HE DOES IS WANT. HE'S AN APPETITE TO EAT THE WORLD. TO MAKE IT IN HIS IMAGE.
HE'S A NIGHTMARE. HE'S THE NIGHTMARE.
AND IF WE DON'T STOP HIM, HE'LL EAT THE WHOLE BLOODY WORL--

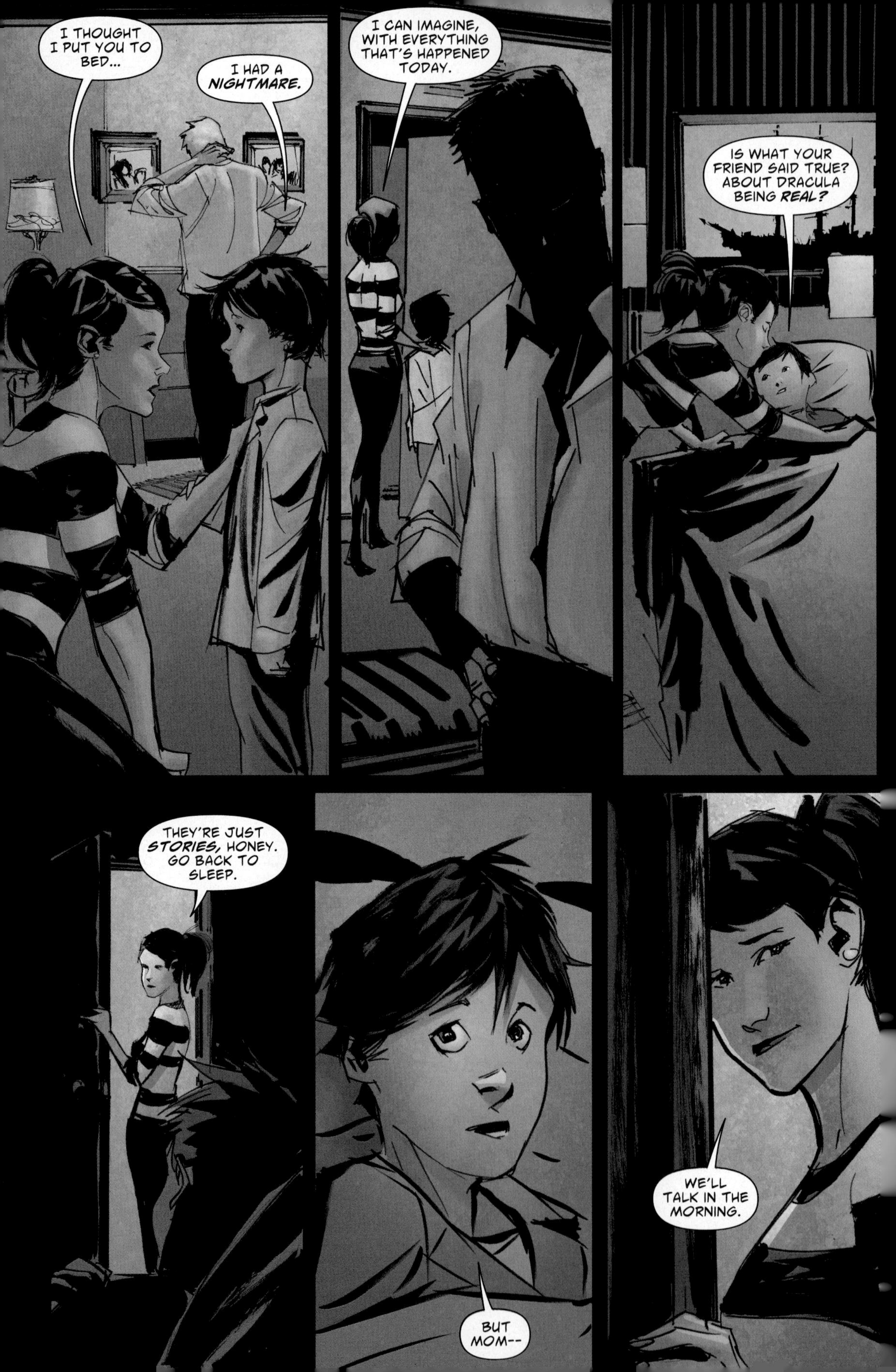
I THOUGHT I PUT YOU TO BED...
I HAD A *NIGHTMARE.*
I CAN IMAGINE, WITH EVERYTHING THAT'S HAPPENED TODAY.
IS WHAT YOUR FRIEND SAID TRUE? ABOUT DRACULA BEING *REAL?*
THEY'RE JUST *STORIES,* HONEY. GO BACK TO SLEEP.
BUT MOM--
WE'LL TALK IN THE MORNING.

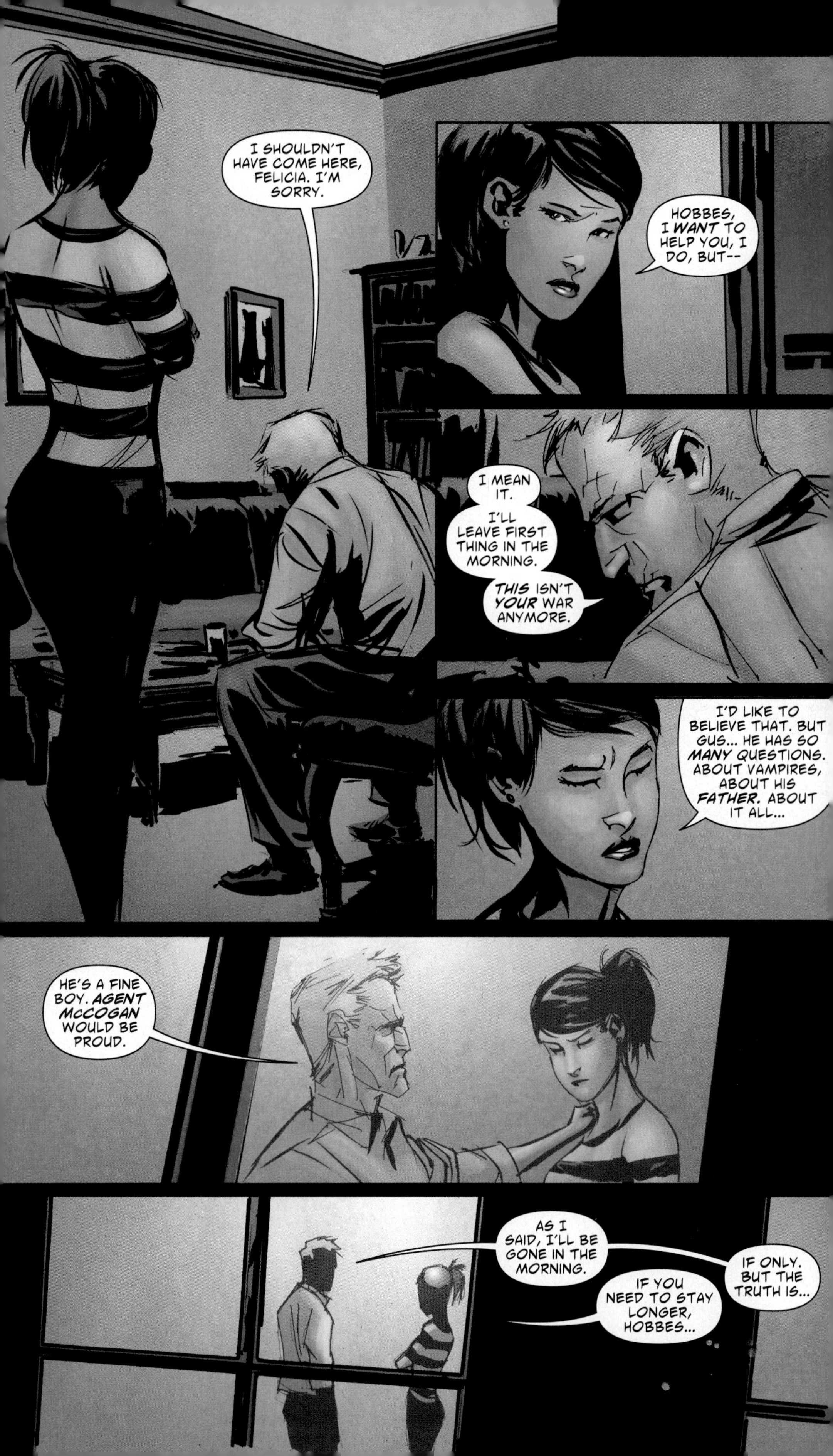
I SHOULDN'T HAVE COME HERE, FELICIA. I'M SORRY.
HOBBES, I WANT TO HELP YOU, I DO, BUT--
I MEAN IT.
I'LL LEAVE FIRST THING IN THE MORNING.
THIS ISN'T YOUR WAR ANYMORE.
I'D LIKE TO BELIEVE THAT. BUT GUS... HE HAS SO MANY QUESTIONS. ABOUT VAMPIRES, ABOUT HIS FATHER. ABOUT IT ALL...
HE'S A FINE BOY. AGENT McCOGAN WOULD BE PROUD.
AS I SAID, I'LL BE GONE IN THE MORNING.
IF YOU NEED TO STAY LONGER, HOBBES...
IF ONLY. BUT THE TRUTH IS...

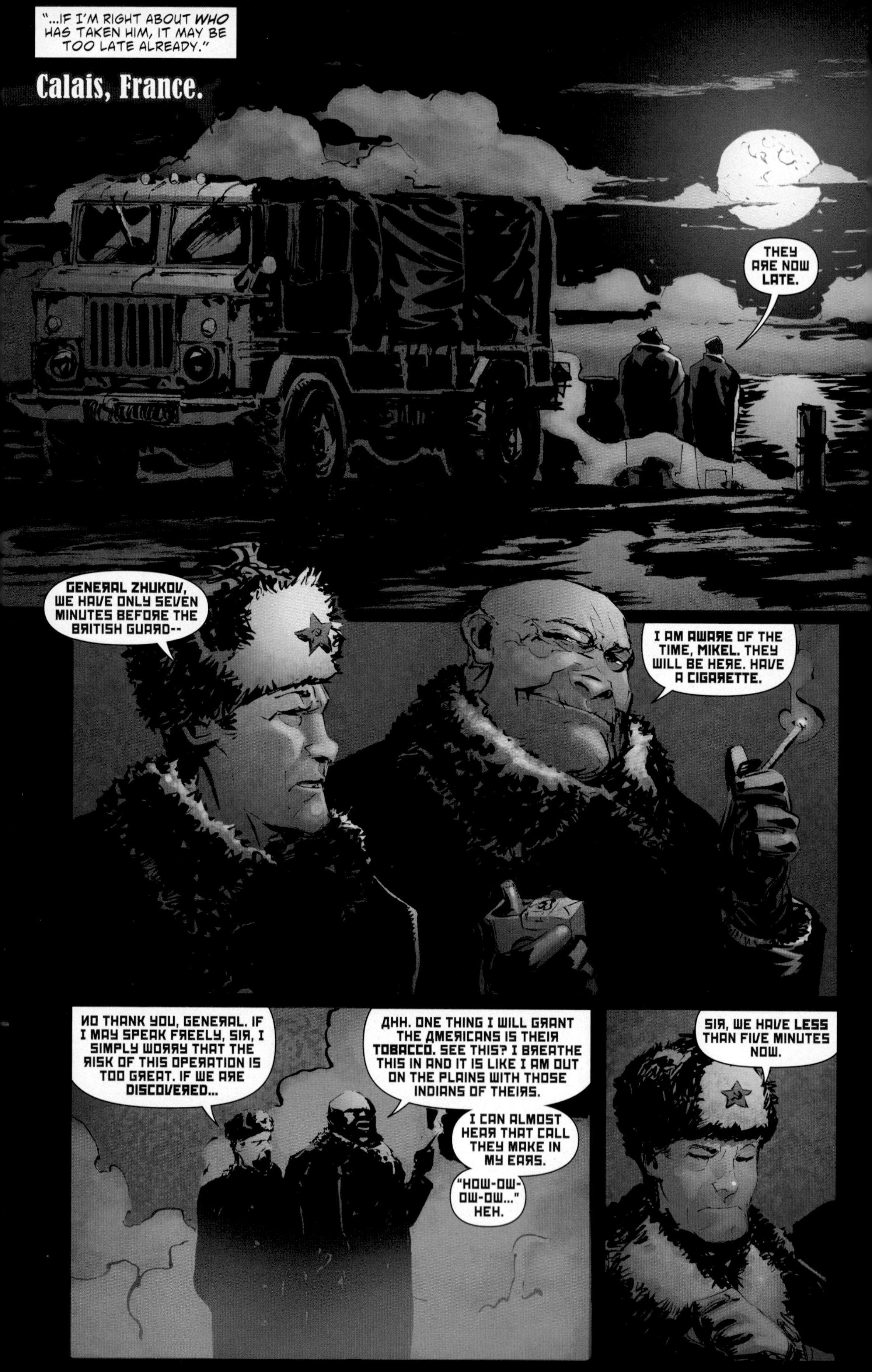

"...IF I'M RIGHT ABOUT WHO HAS TAKEN HIM, IT MAY BE TOO LATE ALREADY."
Calais, France.
THEY ARE NOW LATE.
GENERAL ZHUKOV, WE HAVE ONLY SEVEN MINUTES BEFORE THE BRITISH GUARD--
I AM AWARE OF THE TIME, MIKEL. THEY WILL BE HERE. HAVE A CIGARETTE.
NO THANK YOU, GENERAL. IF I MAY SPEAK FREELY, SIR, I SIMPLY WORRY THAT THE RISK OF THIS OPERATION IS TOO GREAT. IF WE ARE DISCOVERED...
AHH. ONE THING I WILL GRANT THE AMERICANS IS THEIR TOBACCO. SEE THIS? I BREATHE THIS IN AND IT IS LIKE I AM OUT ON THE PLAINS WITH THOSE INDIANS OF THEIRS.
I CAN ALMOST HEAR THAT CALL THEY MAKE IN MY EARS.
"HOW-OW-OW-OW..." HEH.
SIR, WE HAVE LESS THAN FIVE MINUTES NOW.

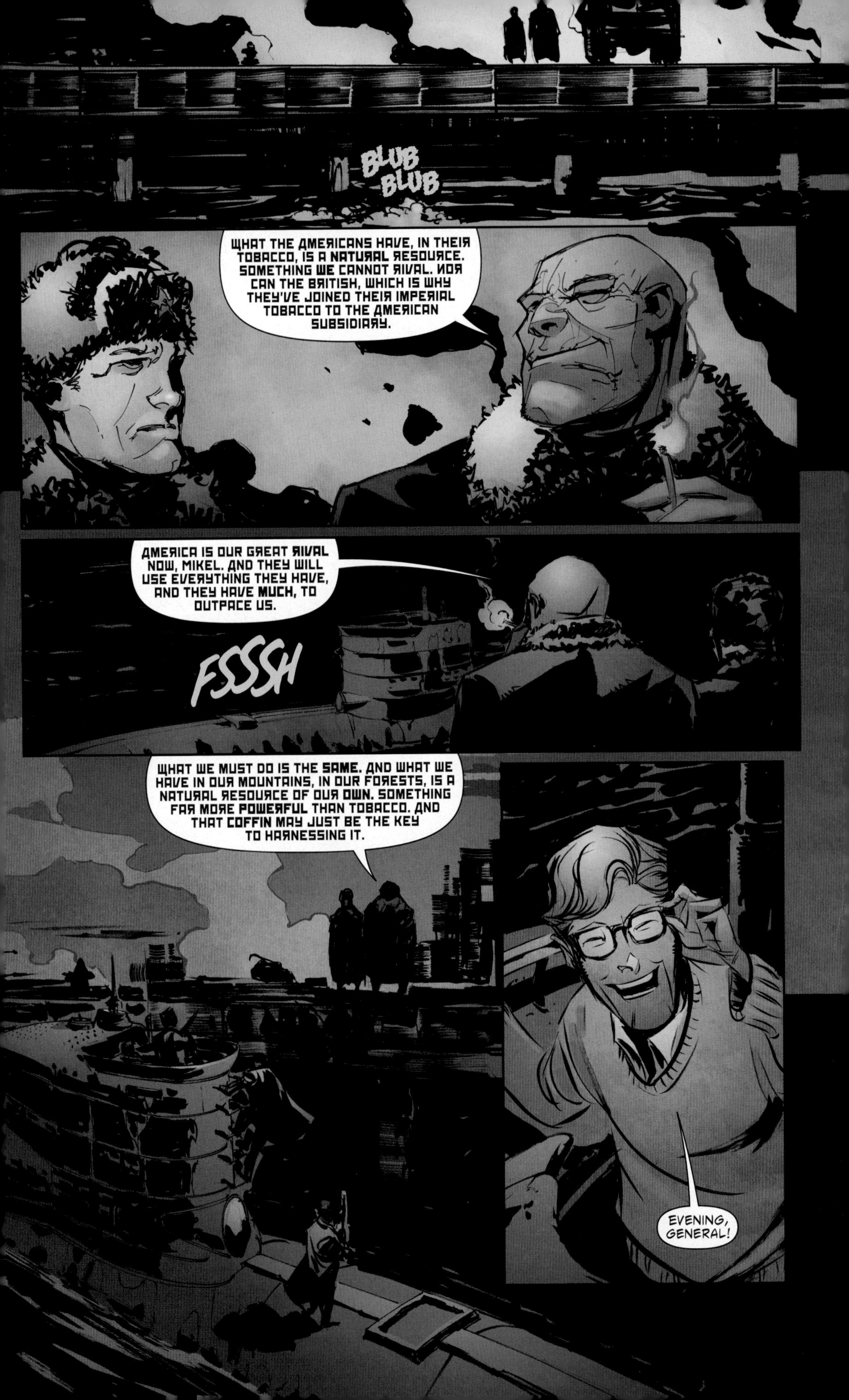
BLUB BLUB
WHAT THE AMERICANS HAVE, IN THEIR TOBACCO, IS A NATURAL RESOURCE. SOMETHING WE CANNOT RIVAL. NOR CAN THE BRITISH, WHICH IS WHY THEY'VE JOINED THEIR IMPERIAL TOBACCO TO THE AMERICAN SUBSIDIARY.
AMERICA IS OUR GREAT RIVAL NOW, MIKEL. AND THEY WILL USE EVERYTHING THEY HAVE, AND THEY HAVE MUCH, TO OUTPACE US.
FSSSH
WHAT WE MUST DO IS THE SAME. AND WHAT WE HAVE IN OUR MOUNTAINS, IN OUR FORESTS, IS A NATURAL RESOURCE OF OUR OWN. SOMETHING FAR MORE POWERFUL THAN TOBACCO. AND THAT COFFIN MAY JUST BE THE KEY TO HARNESSING IT.
EVENING, GENERAL!

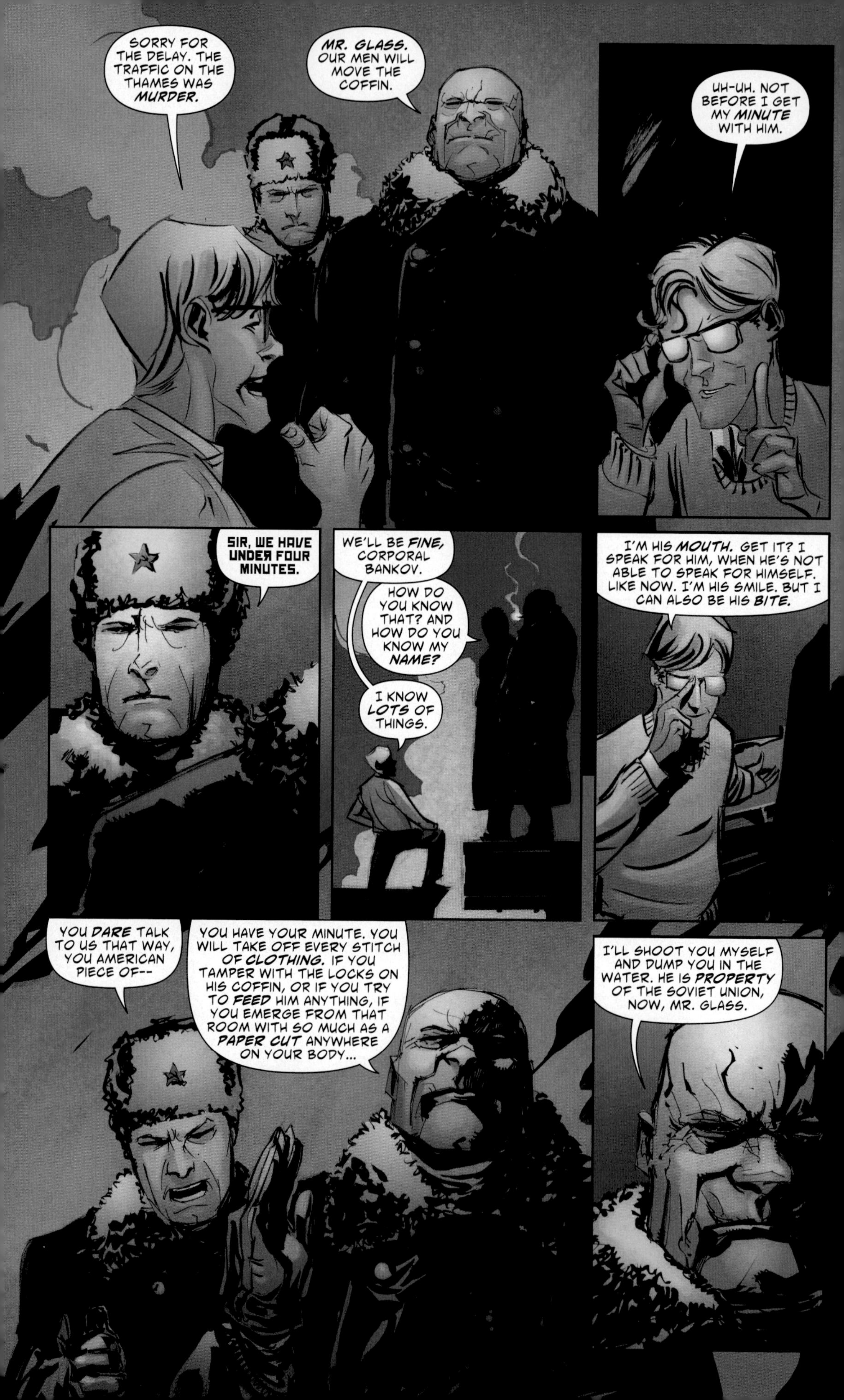
SORRY FOR THE DELAY. THE TRAFFIC ON THE THAMES WAS *MURDER.*
MR. GLASS. OUR MEN WILL MOVE THE COFFIN.
UH-UH. NOT BEFORE I GET MY *MINUTE* WITH HIM.
SIR, WE HAVE UNDER FOUR MINUTES.
WE'LL BE *FINE,* CORPORAL BANKOV.
HOW DO YOU KNOW THAT? AND HOW DO YOU KNOW MY *NAME?*
I KNOW *LOTS* OF THINGS.
I'M HIS *MOUTH.* GET IT? I SPEAK FOR HIM, WHEN HE'S NOT ABLE TO SPEAK FOR HIMSELF. LIKE NOW. I'M HIS SMILE. BUT I CAN ALSO BE HIS *BITE.*
YOU *DARE* TALK TO US THAT WAY, YOU AMERICAN PIECE OF--
YOU HAVE YOUR MINUTE. YOU WILL TAKE OFF EVERY STITCH OF *CLOTHING.* IF YOU TAMPER WITH THE LOCKS ON HIS COFFIN, OR IF YOU TRY TO *FEED* HIM ANYTHING, IF YOU EMERGE FROM THAT ROOM WITH SO MUCH AS A *PAPER CUT* ANYWHERE ON YOUR BODY...
I'LL SHOOT YOU MYSELF AND DUMP YOU IN THE WATER. HE IS *PROPERTY* OF THE SOVIET UNION, NOW, MR. GLASS.

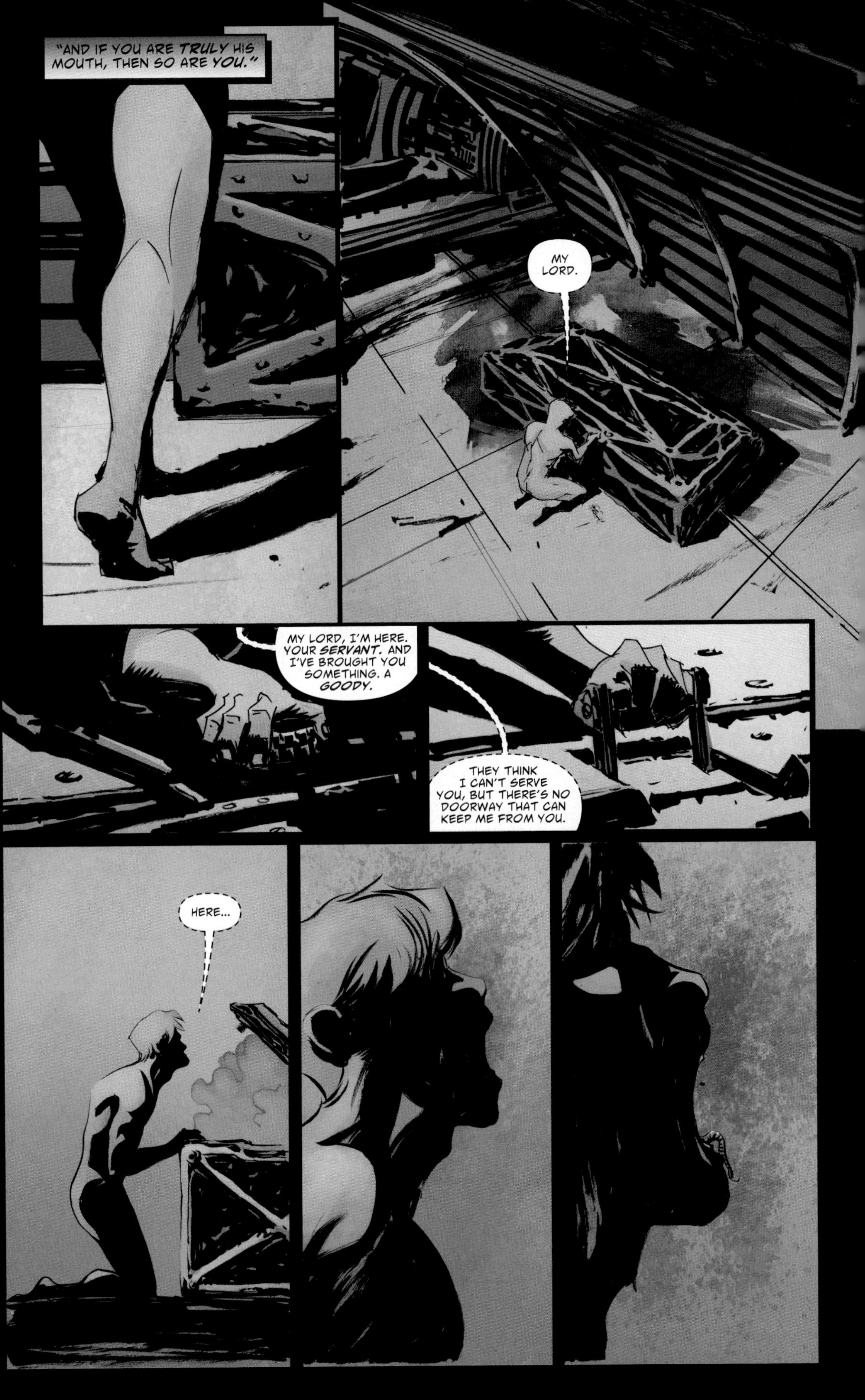
"AND IF YOU ARE TRULY HIS MOUTH, THEN SO ARE YOU."
MY LORD.
MY LORD, I'M HERE. YOUR SERVANT. AND I'VE BROUGHT YOU SOMETHING. A GOODY.
THEY THINK I CAN'T SERVE YOU, BUT THERE'S NO DOORWAY THAT CAN KEEP ME FROM YOU.
HERE...

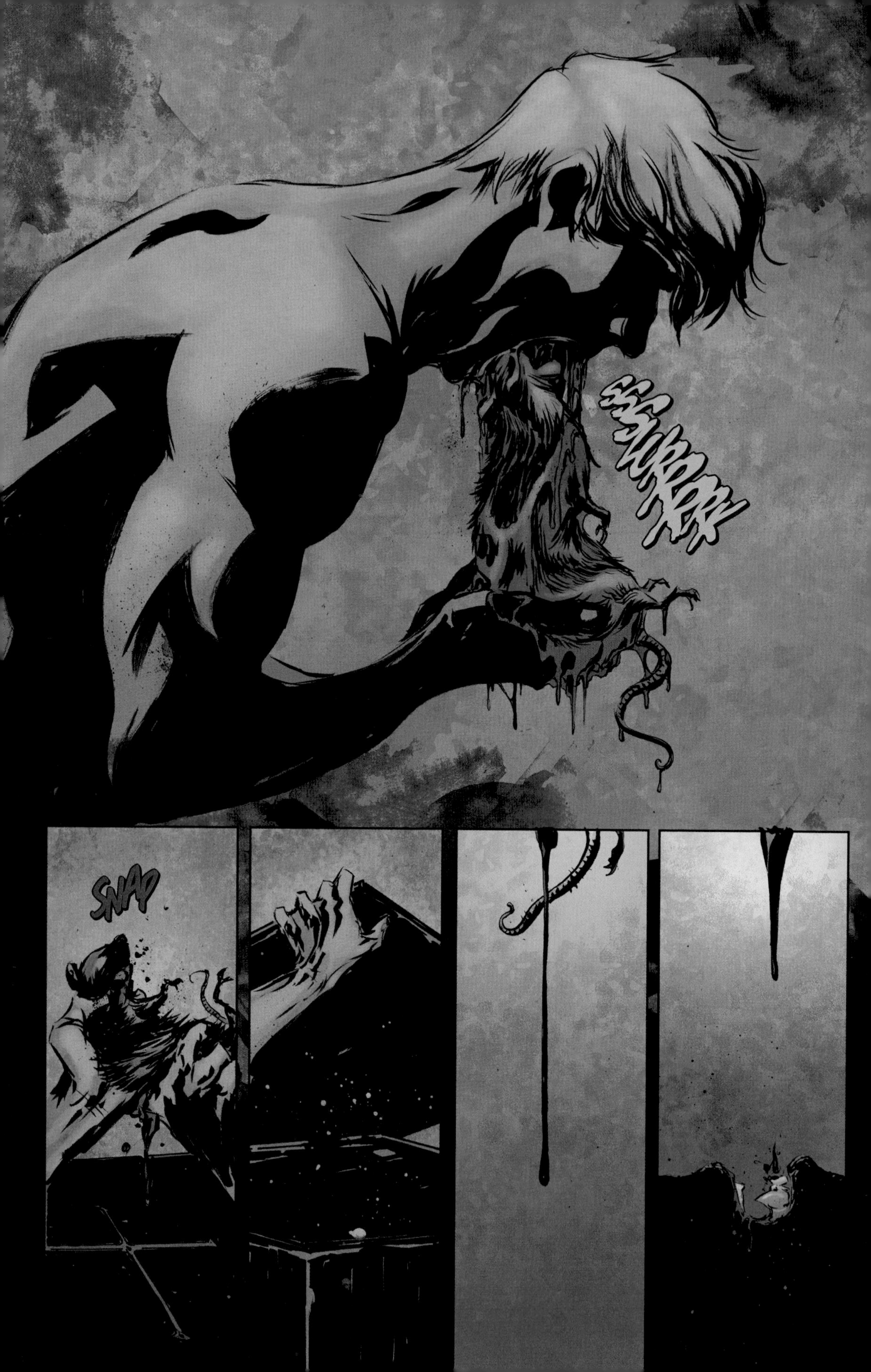
SSSLURRRK
SNAP

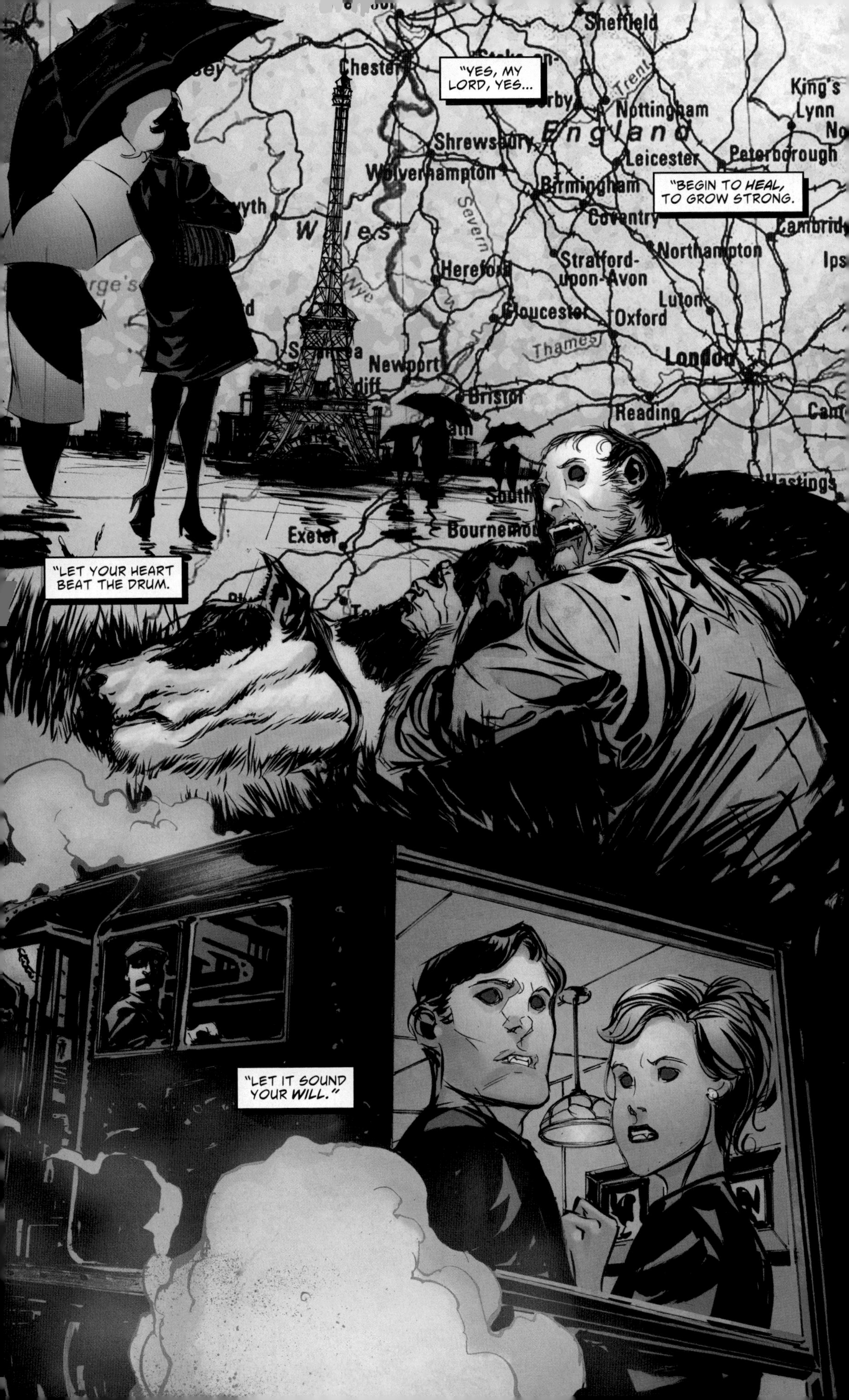
"YES, MY LORD, YES...
"BEGIN TO HEAL, TO GROW STRONG.
"LET YOUR HEART BEAT THE DRUM.
"LET IT SOUND YOUR WILL."

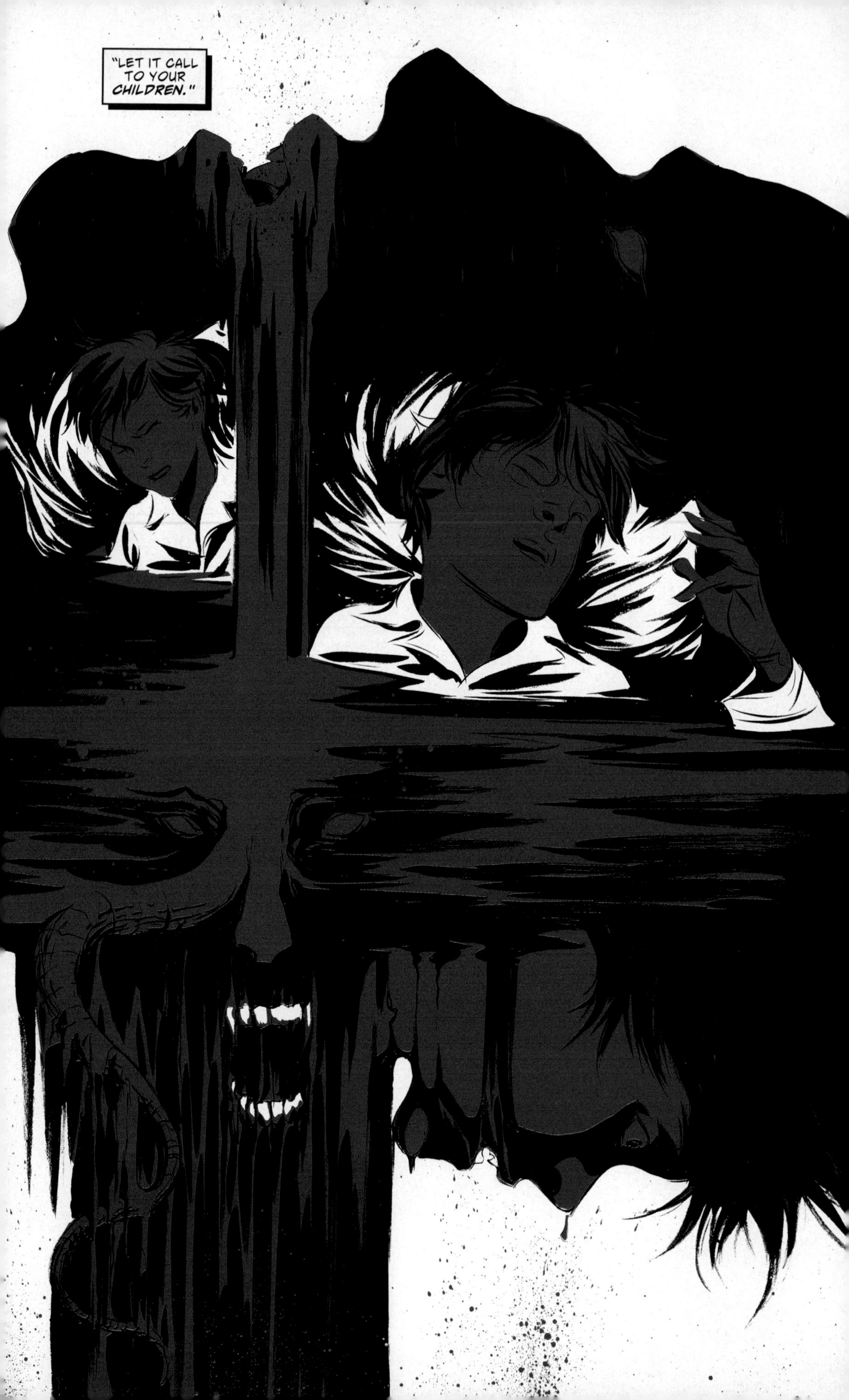
"LET IT CALL TO YOUR CHILDREN."

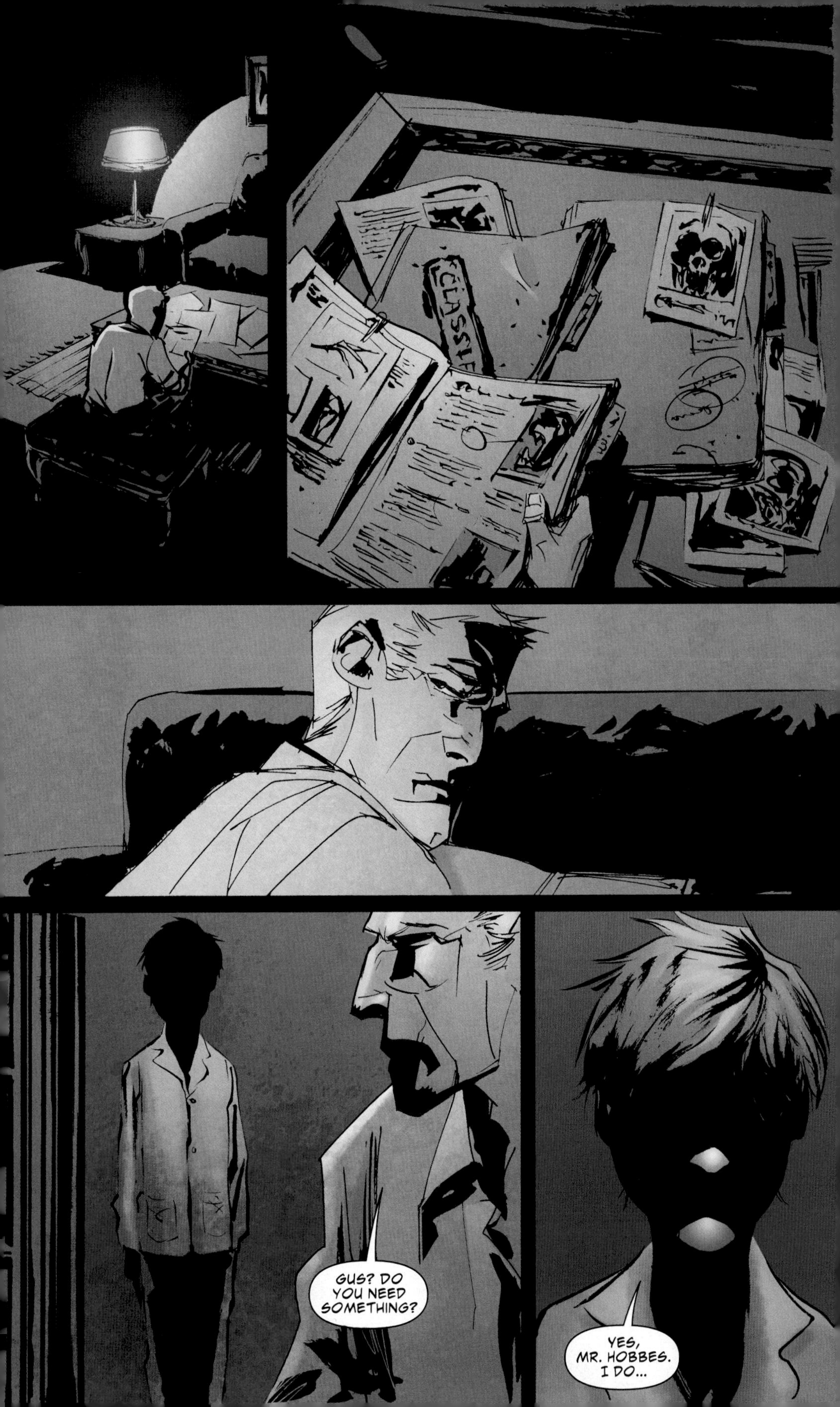

CLASSIF
GUS? DO YOU NEED SOMETHING?
YES, MR. HOBBES. I DO...

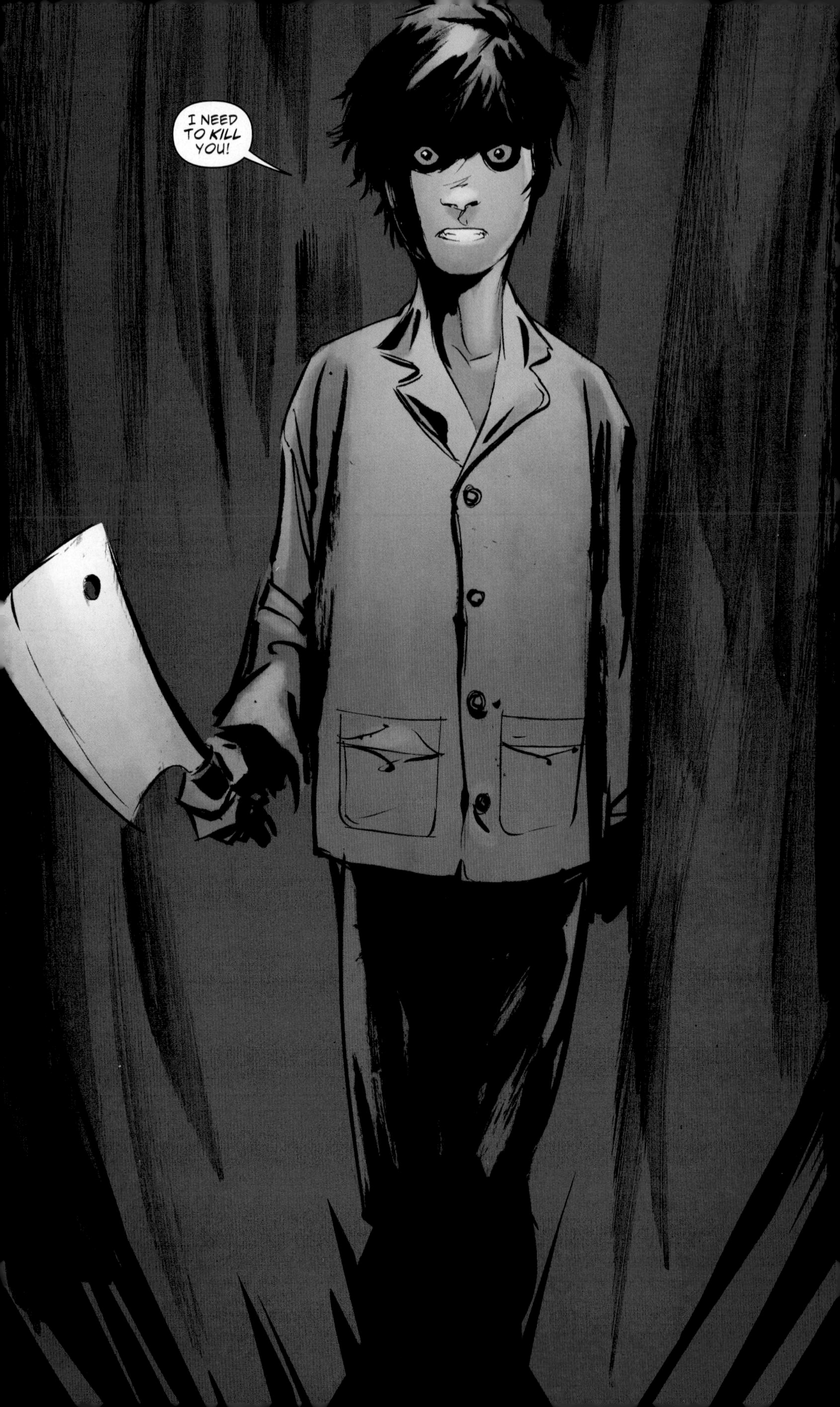
I NEED TO KILL YOU!

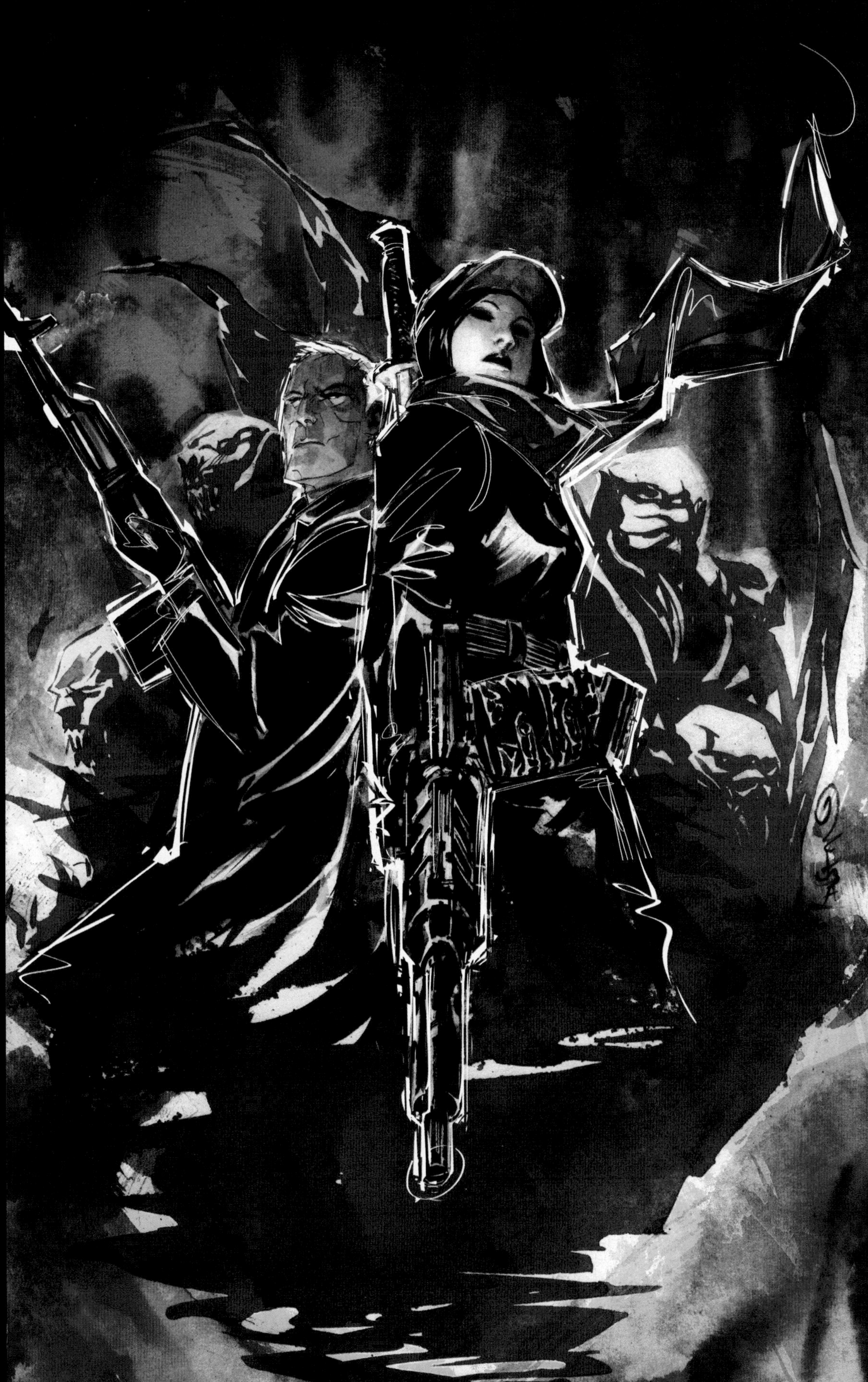

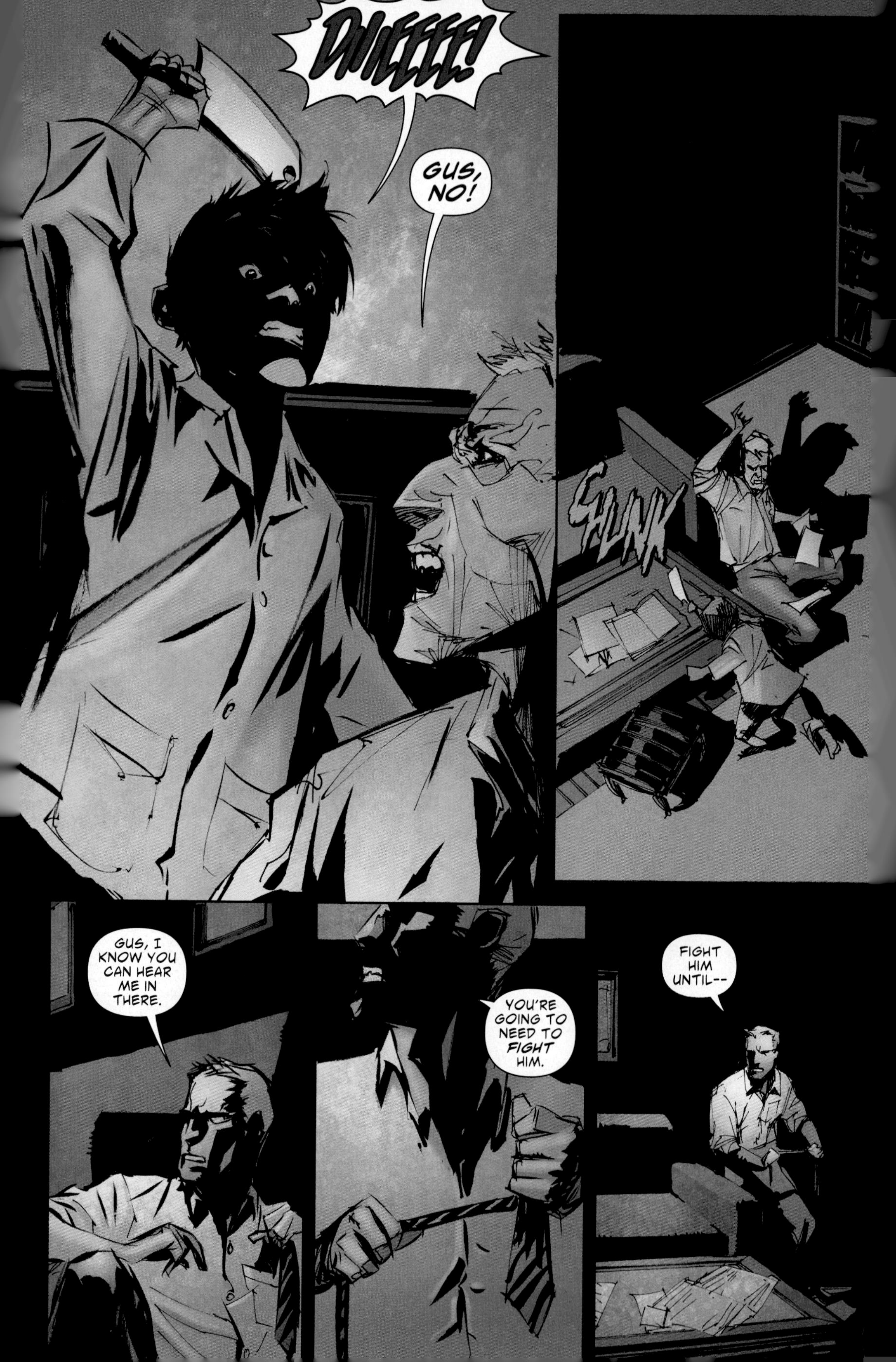
DIIEEEE!
GUS, NO!
SHUNK
GUS, I KNOW YOU CAN HEAR ME IN THERE.
YOU'RE GOING TO NEED TO *FIGHT* HIM.
FIGHT HIM UNTIL--

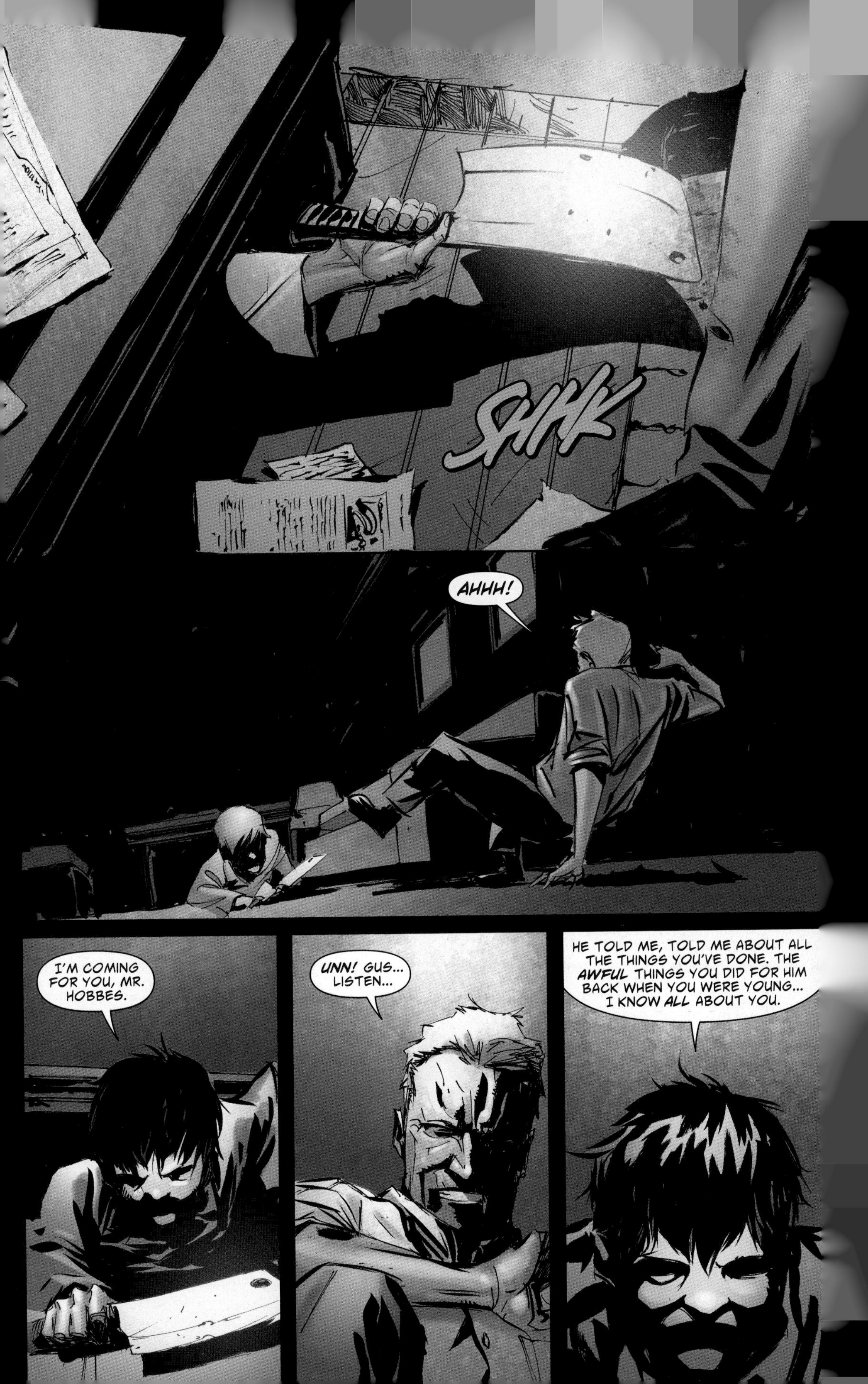
SHHK
AHHH!
I'M COMING FOR YOU, MR. HOBBES.
UNN! GUS... LISTEN...
HE TOLD ME, TOLD ME ABOUT ALL THE THINGS YOU'VE DONE. THE AWFUL THINGS YOU DID FOR HIM BACK WHEN YOU WERE YOUNG... I KNOW ALL ABOUT YOU.

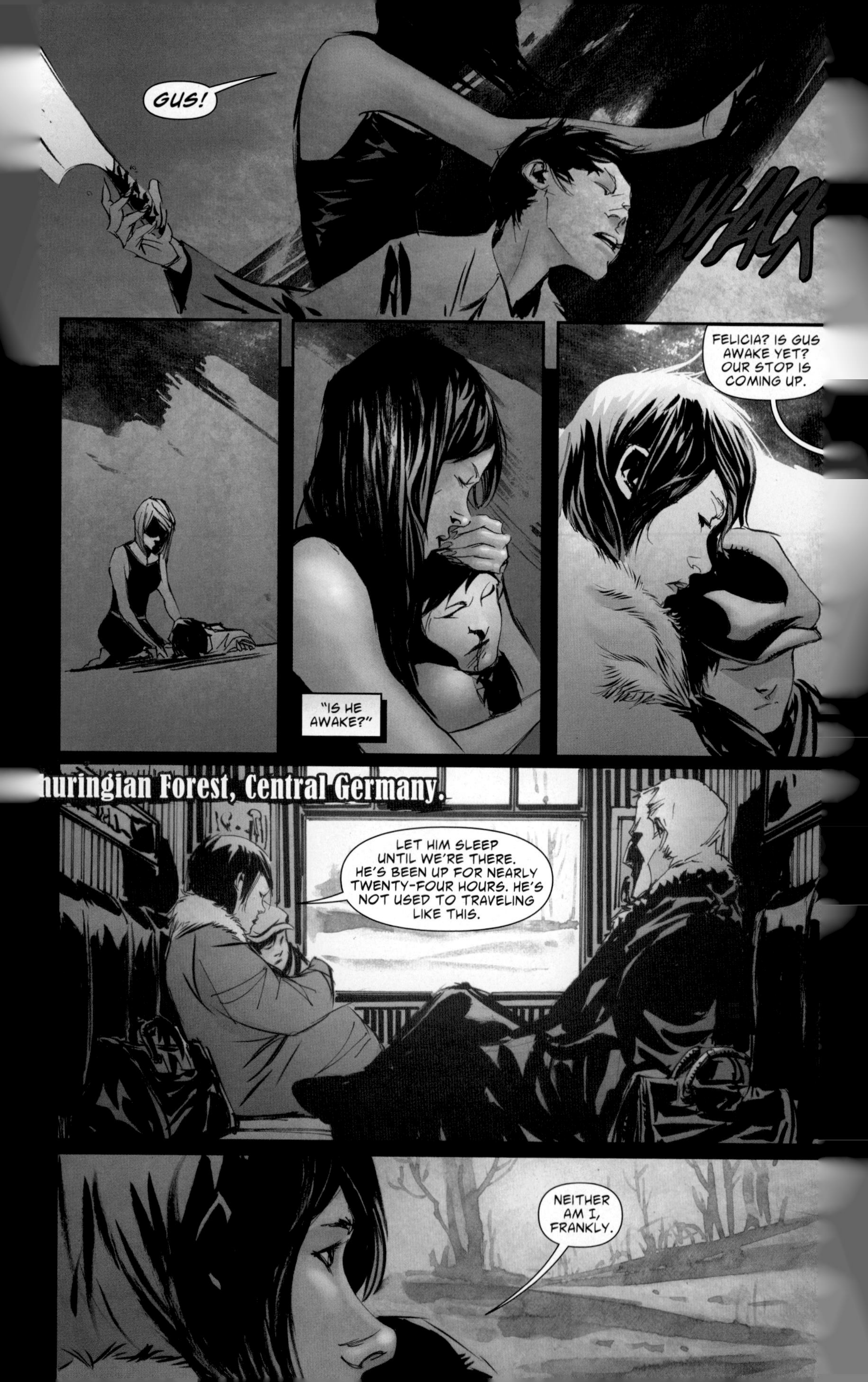
GUS!
WHACK
FELICIA? IS GUS AWAKE YET? OUR STOP IS COMING UP.
"IS HE AWAKE?"
huringian Forest, Central Germany.
LET HIM SLEEP UNTIL WE'RE THERE. HE'S BEEN UP FOR NEARLY TWENTY-FOUR HOURS. HE'S NOT USED TO TRAVELING LIKE THIS.
NEITHER AM I, FRANKLY.

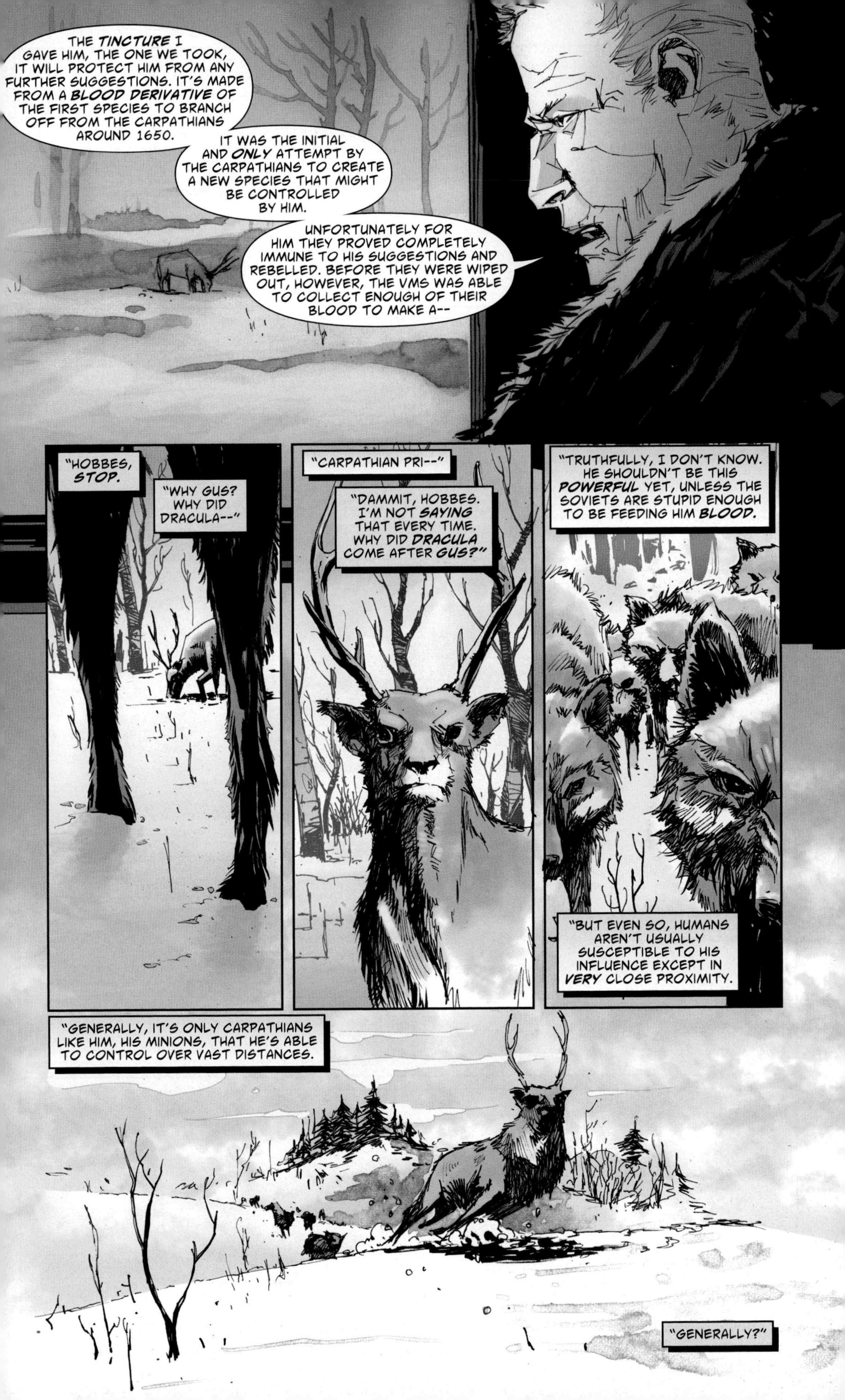
THE *TINCTURE* I GAVE HIM, THE ONE WE TOOK, IT WILL PROTECT HIM FROM ANY FURTHER SUGGESTIONS. IT'S MADE FROM A *BLOOD DERIVATIVE* OF THE FIRST SPECIES TO BRANCH OFF FROM THE CARPATHIANS AROUND 1650.
IT WAS THE INITIAL AND *ONLY* ATTEMPT BY THE CARPATHIANS TO CREATE A NEW SPECIES THAT MIGHT BE CONTROLLED BY HIM.
UNFORTUNATELY FOR HIM THEY PROVED COMPLETELY IMMUNE TO HIS SUGGESTIONS AND REBELLED. BEFORE THEY WERE WIPED OUT, HOWEVER, THE VMS WAS ABLE TO COLLECT ENOUGH OF THEIR BLOOD TO MAKE A--
"HOBBES, *STOP.*
"WHY GUS? WHY DID DRACULA--"
"CARPATHIAN PRI--"
"DAMMIT, HOBBES. I'M NOT *SAYING* THAT EVERY TIME. WHY DID *DRACULA* COME AFTER *GUS?*"
"TRUTHFULLY, I DON'T KNOW. HE SHOULDN'T BE THIS *POWERFUL* YET, UNLESS THE SOVIETS ARE STUPID ENOUGH TO BE FEEDING HIM *BLOOD.*
"BUT EVEN SO, HUMANS AREN'T USUALLY SUSCEPTIBLE TO HIS INFLUENCE EXCEPT IN *VERY* CLOSE PROXIMITY.
"GENERALLY, IT'S ONLY CARPATHIANS LIKE HIM, HIS MINIONS, THAT HE'S ABLE TO CONTROL OVER VAST DISTANCES.
"GENERALLY?"

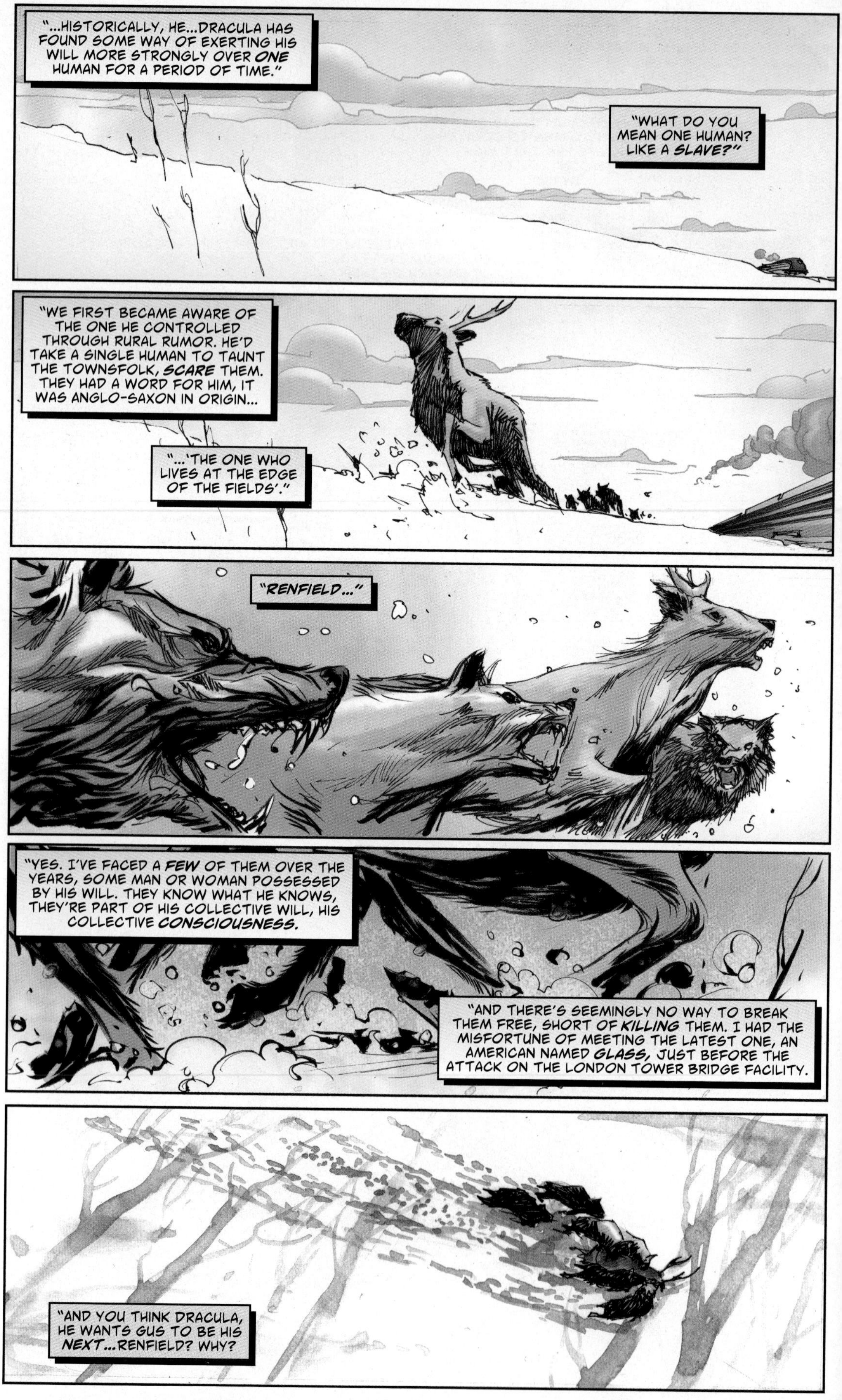

"...HISTORICALLY, HE...DRACULA HAS FOUND SOME WAY OF EXERTING HIS WILL MORE STRONGLY OVER ONE HUMAN FOR A PERIOD OF TIME."
"WHAT DO YOU MEAN ONE HUMAN? LIKE A SLAVE?"
"WE FIRST BECAME AWARE OF THE ONE HE CONTROLLED THROUGH RURAL RUMOR. HE'D TAKE A SINGLE HUMAN TO TAUNT THE TOWNSFOLK, SCARE THEM. THEY HAD A WORD FOR HIM, IT WAS ANGLO-SAXON IN ORIGIN...
"...'THE ONE WHO LIVES AT THE EDGE OF THE FIELDS'."
"RENFIELD..."
"YES. I'VE FACED A FEW OF THEM OVER THE YEARS, SOME MAN OR WOMAN POSSESSED BY HIS WILL. THEY KNOW WHAT HE KNOWS, THEY'RE PART OF HIS COLLECTIVE WILL, HIS COLLECTIVE CONSCIOUSNESS.
"AND THERE'S SEEMINGLY NO WAY TO BREAK THEM FREE, SHORT OF KILLING THEM. I HAD THE MISFORTUNE OF MEETING THE LATEST ONE, AN AMERICAN NAMED GLASS, JUST BEFORE THE ATTACK ON THE LONDON TOWER BRIDGE FACILITY.
"AND YOU THINK DRACULA, HE WANTS GUS TO BE HIS NEXT...RENFIELD? WHY?

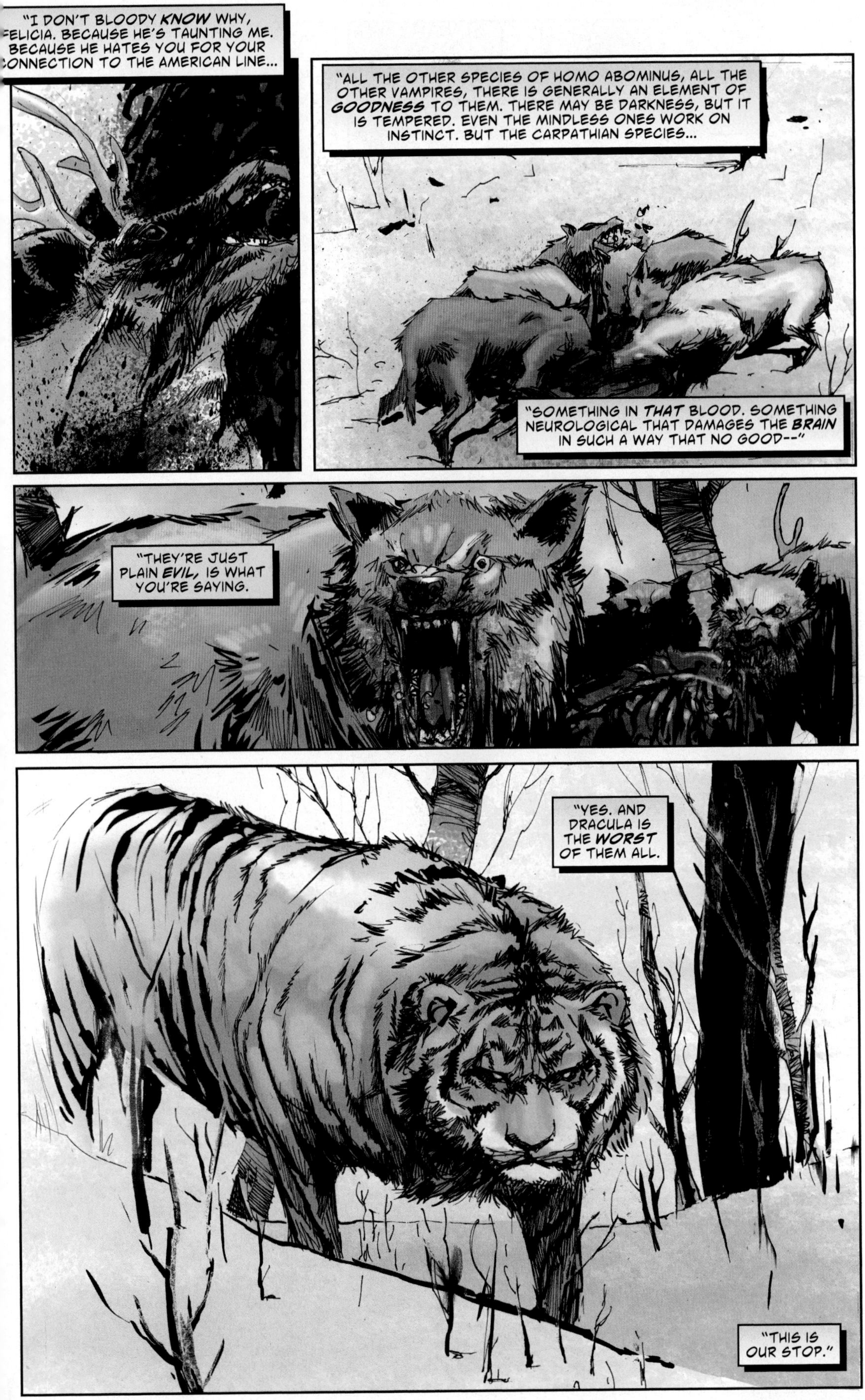
"I DON'T BLOODY KNOW WHY, FELICIA. BECAUSE HE'S TAUNTING ME. BECAUSE HE HATES YOU FOR YOUR CONNECTION TO THE AMERICAN LINE...
"ALL THE OTHER SPECIES OF HOMO ABOMINUS, ALL THE OTHER VAMPIRES, THERE IS GENERALLY AN ELEMENT OF GOODNESS TO THEM. THERE MAY BE DARKNESS, BUT IT IS TEMPERED. EVEN THE MINDLESS ONES WORK ON INSTINCT. BUT THE CARPATHIAN SPECIES...
"SOMETHING IN THAT BLOOD. SOMETHING NEUROLOGICAL THAT DAMAGES THE BRAIN IN SUCH A WAY THAT NO GOOD--"
"THEY'RE JUST PLAIN EVIL, IS WHAT YOU'RE SAYING.
"YES. AND DRACULA IS THE WORST OF THEM ALL.
"THIS IS OUR STOP."

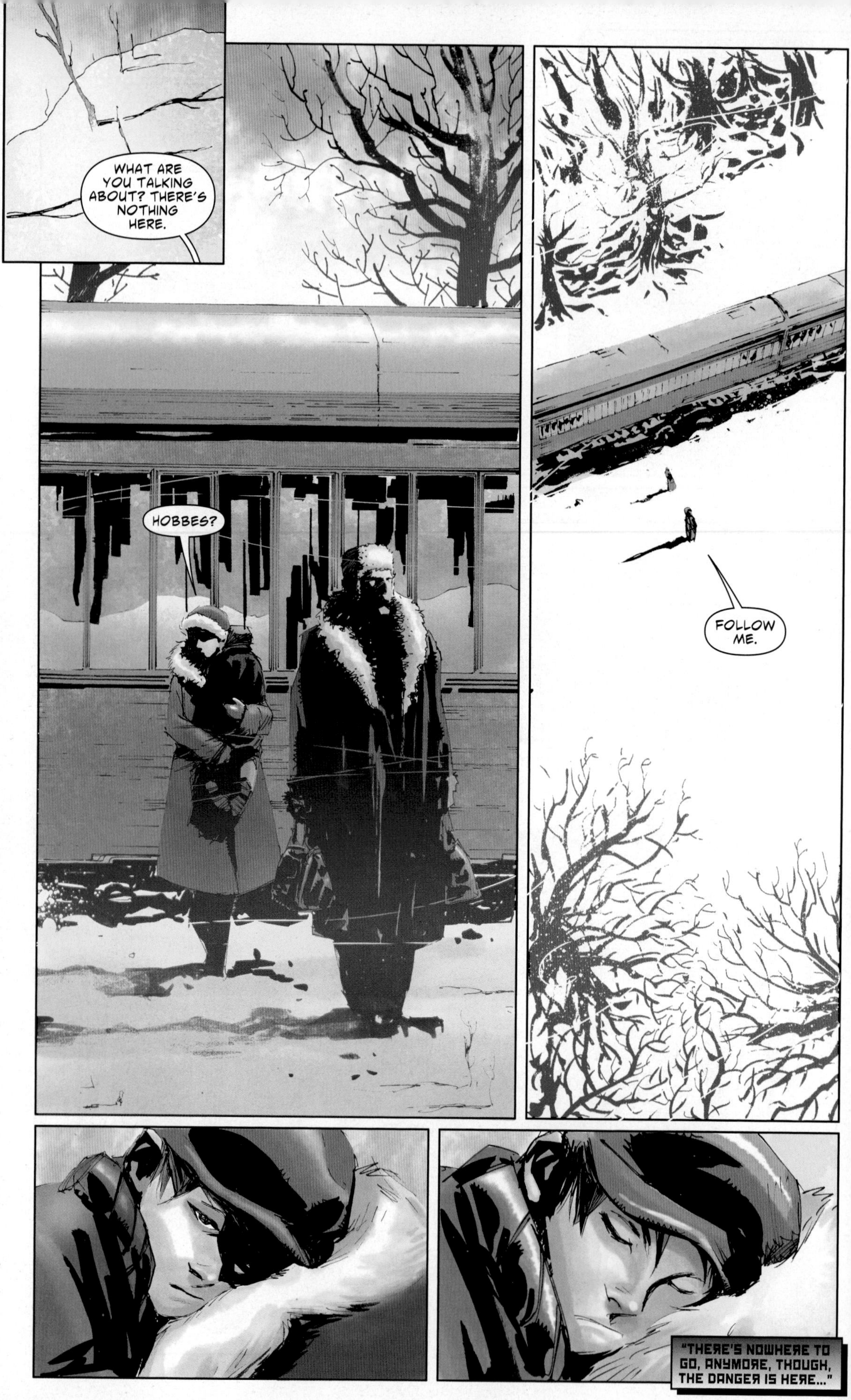
WHAT ARE YOU TALKING ABOUT? THERE'S NOTHING HERE.
HOBBES?
FOLLOW ME.
"THERE'S NOWHERE TO GO, ANYMORE, THOUGH, THE DANGER IS HERE..."

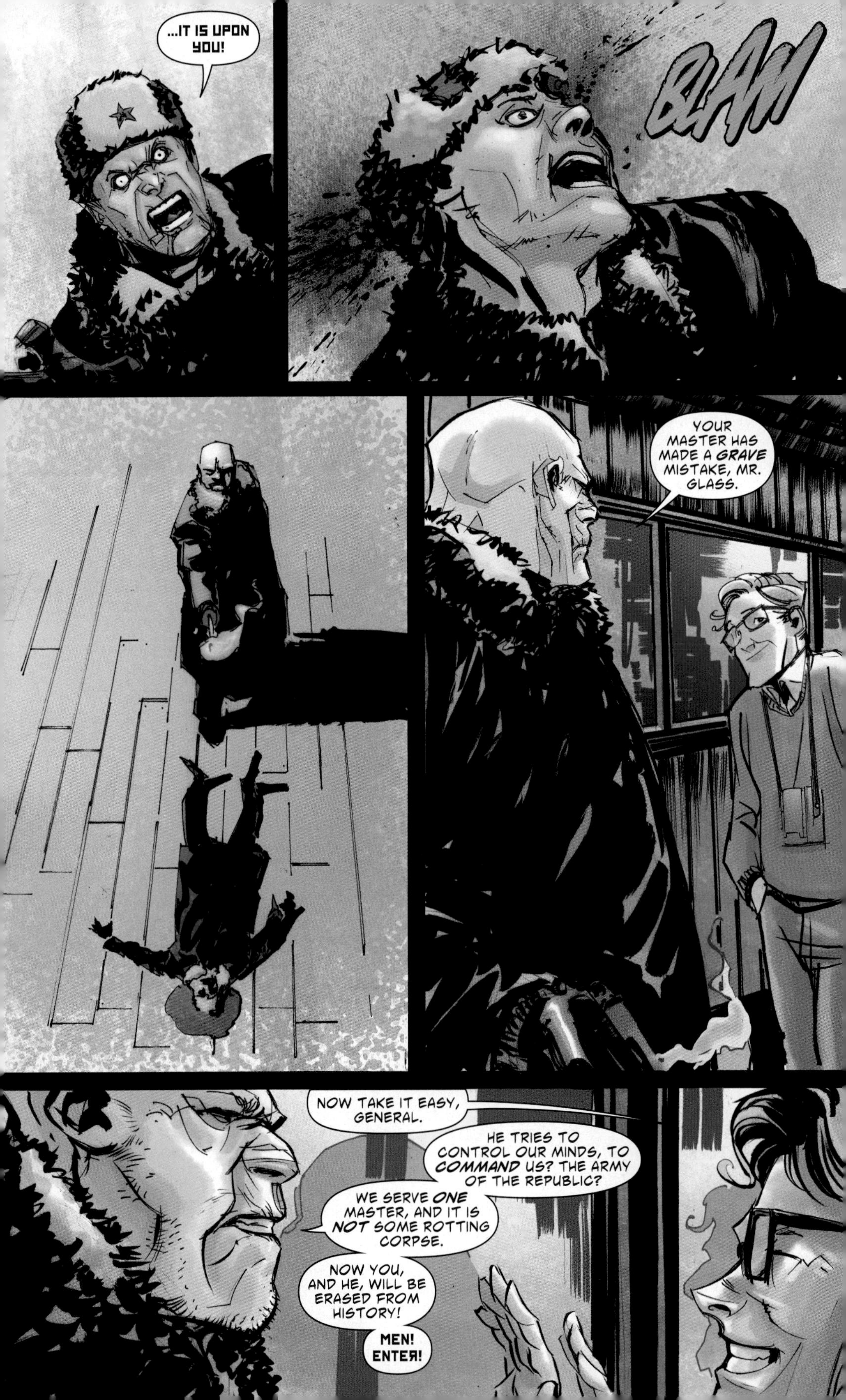
...IT IS UPON YOU!
BLAM
YOUR MASTER HAS MADE A *GRAVE* MISTAKE, MR. GLASS.
NOW TAKE IT EASY, GENERAL.
HE TRIES TO CONTROL OUR MINDS, TO *COMMAND* US? THE ARMY OF THE REPUBLIC?
WE SERVE *ONE* MASTER, AND IT IS *NOT* SOME ROTTING CORPSE.
NOW YOU, AND HE, WILL BE ERASED FROM HISTORY!
MEN! ENTEЯ!

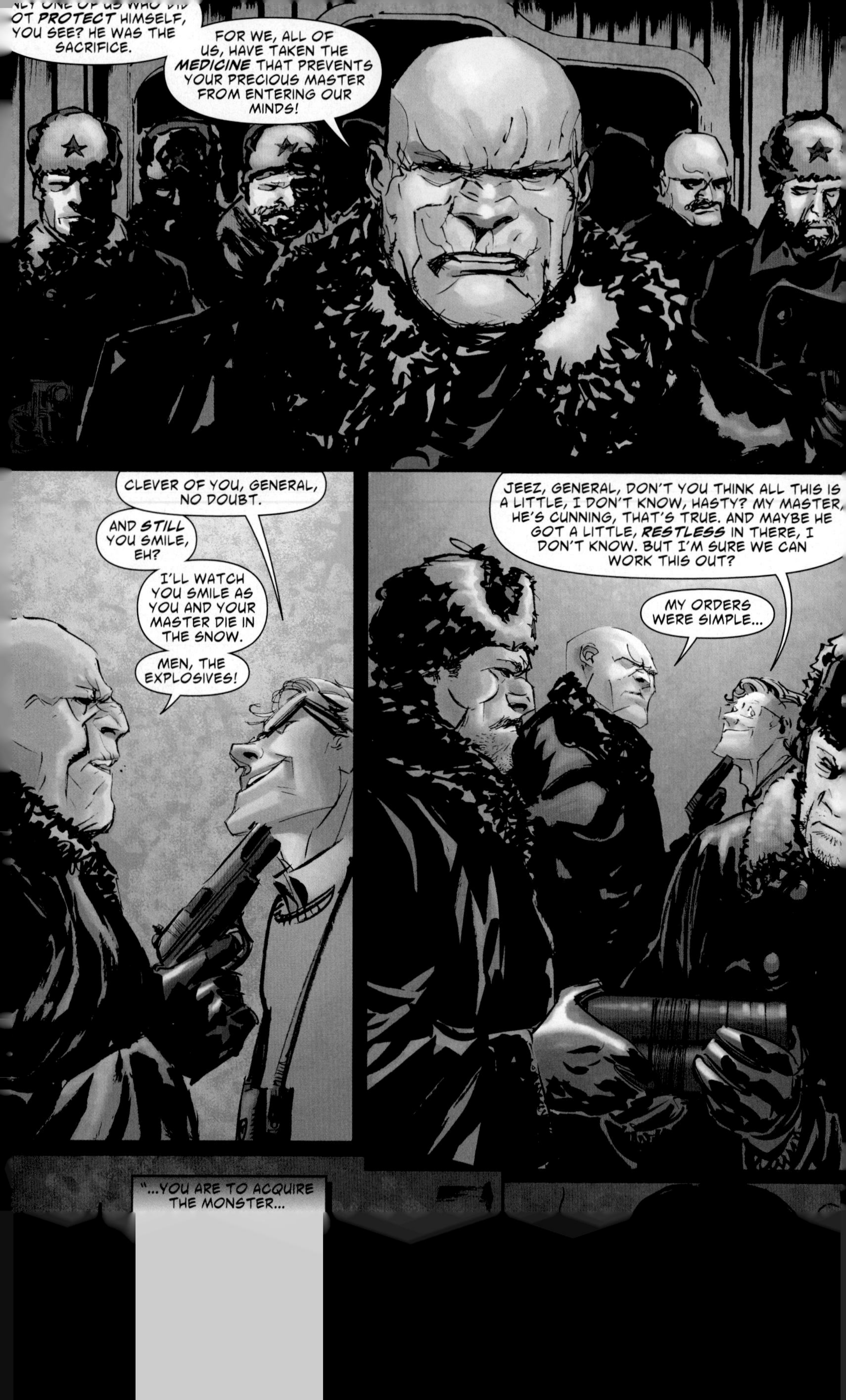
OT PROTECT HIMSELF, YOU SEE? HE WAS THE SACRIFICE.
FOR WE, ALL OF US, HAVE TAKEN THE MEDICINE THAT PREVENTS YOUR PRECIOUS MASTER FROM ENTERING OUR MINDS!
CLEVER OF YOU, GENERAL, NO DOUBT.
AND STILL YOU SMILE, EH?
I'LL WATCH YOU SMILE AS YOU AND YOUR MASTER DIE IN THE SNOW.
MEN, THE EXPLOSIVES!
JEEZ, GENERAL, DON'T YOU THINK ALL THIS IS A LITTLE, I DON'T KNOW, HASTY? MY MASTER, HE'S CUNNING, THAT'S TRUE. AND MAYBE HE GOT A LITTLE, RESTLESS IN THERE, I DON'T KNOW. BUT I'M SURE WE CAN WORK THIS OUT?
MY ORDERS WERE SIMPLE...
"...YOU ARE TO ACQUIRE THE MONSTER...

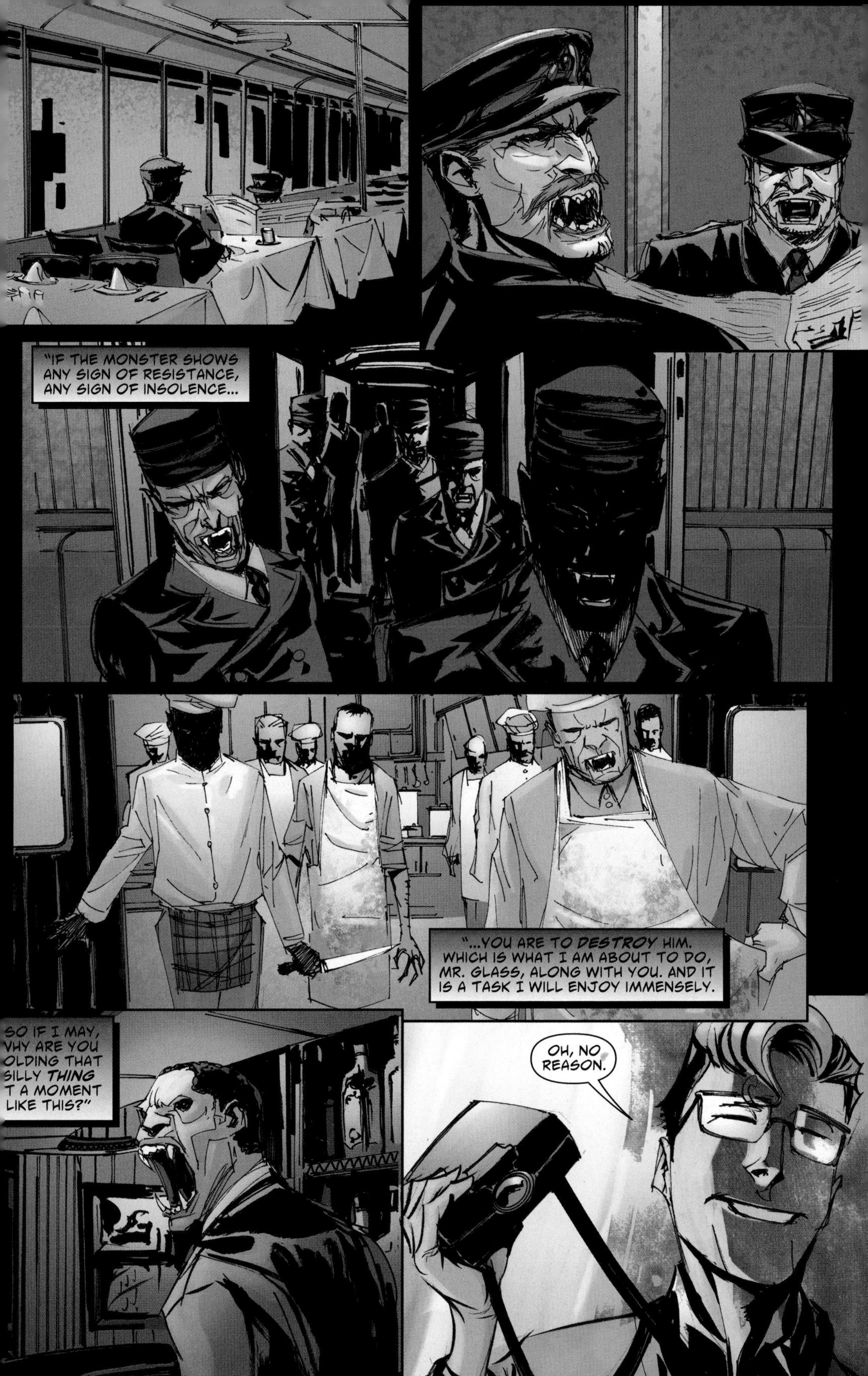
"IF THE MONSTER SHOWS ANY SIGN OF RESISTANCE, ANY SIGN OF INSOLENCE...
"...YOU ARE TO *DESTROY* HIM. WHICH IS WHAT I AM ABOUT TO DO, MR. GLASS, ALONG WITH YOU. AND IT IS A TASK I WILL ENJOY IMMENSELY.
SO IF I MAY, WHY ARE YOU OLDING THAT SILLY *THING* T A MOMENT LIKE THIS?"
OH, NO REASON.

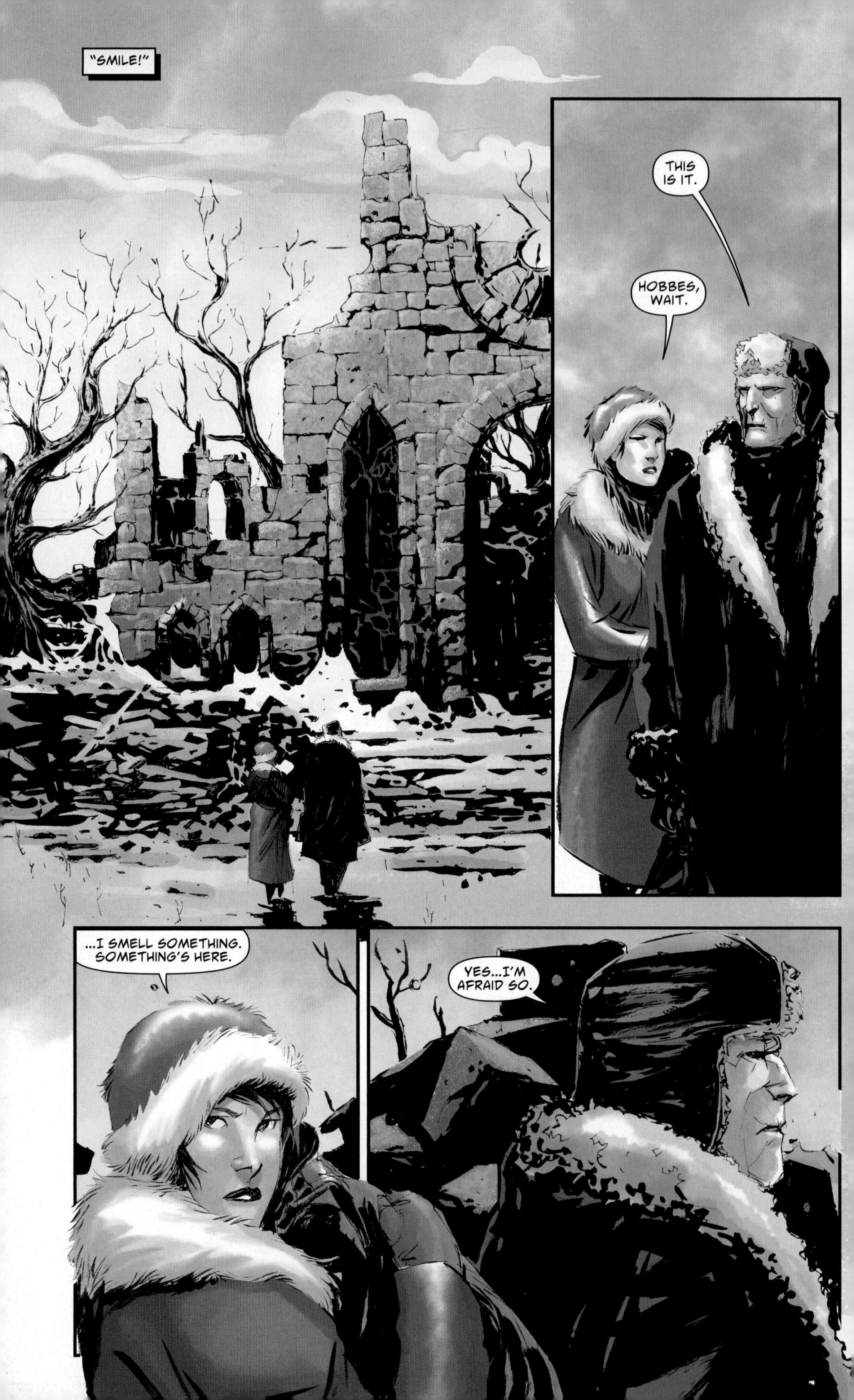
"SMILE!"
THIS IS IT.
HOBBES, WAIT.
...I SMELL SOMETHING. SOMETHING'S HERE.
YES...I'M AFRAID SO.

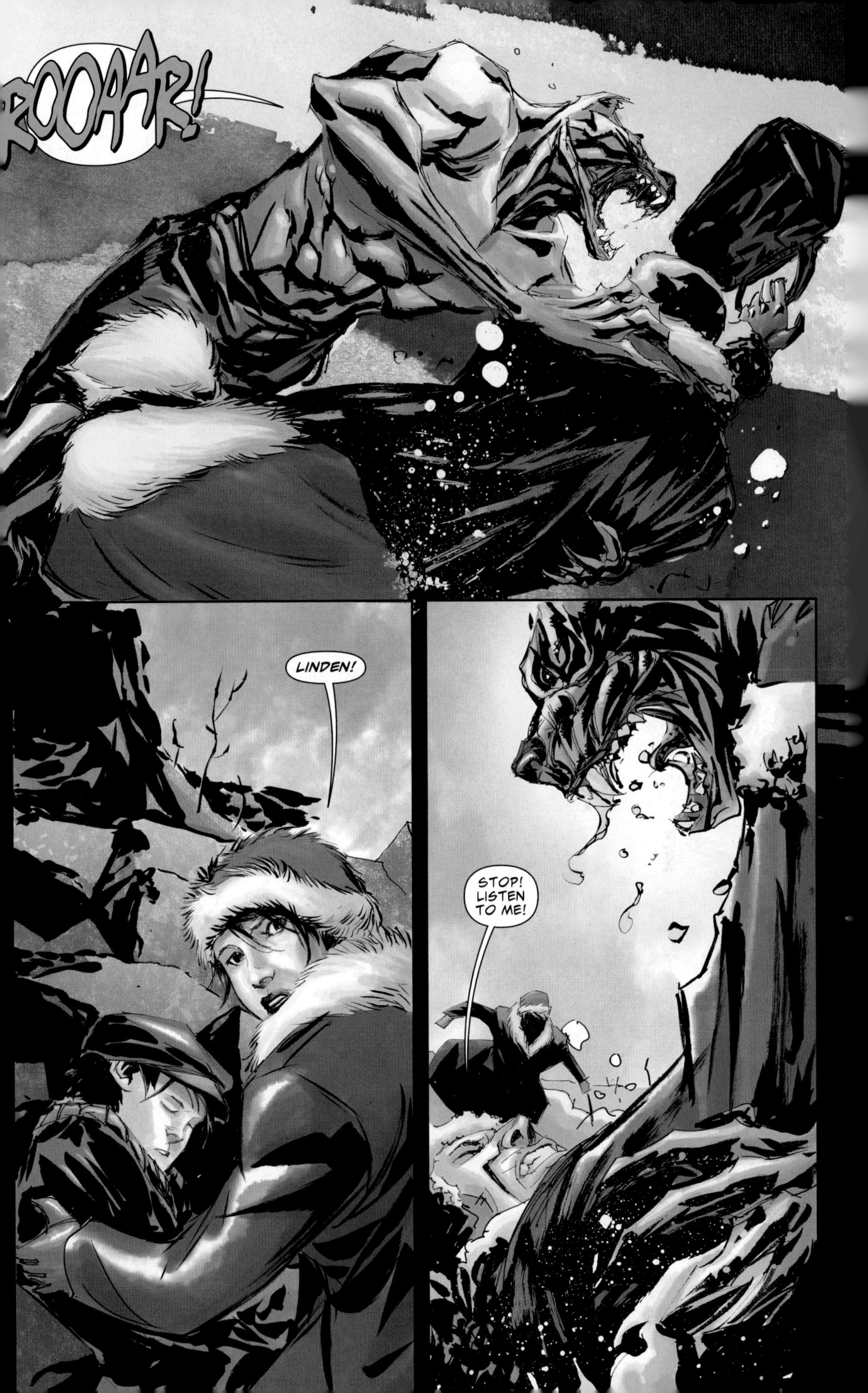
ROOAAR!
LINDEN!
STOP! LISTEN TO ME!

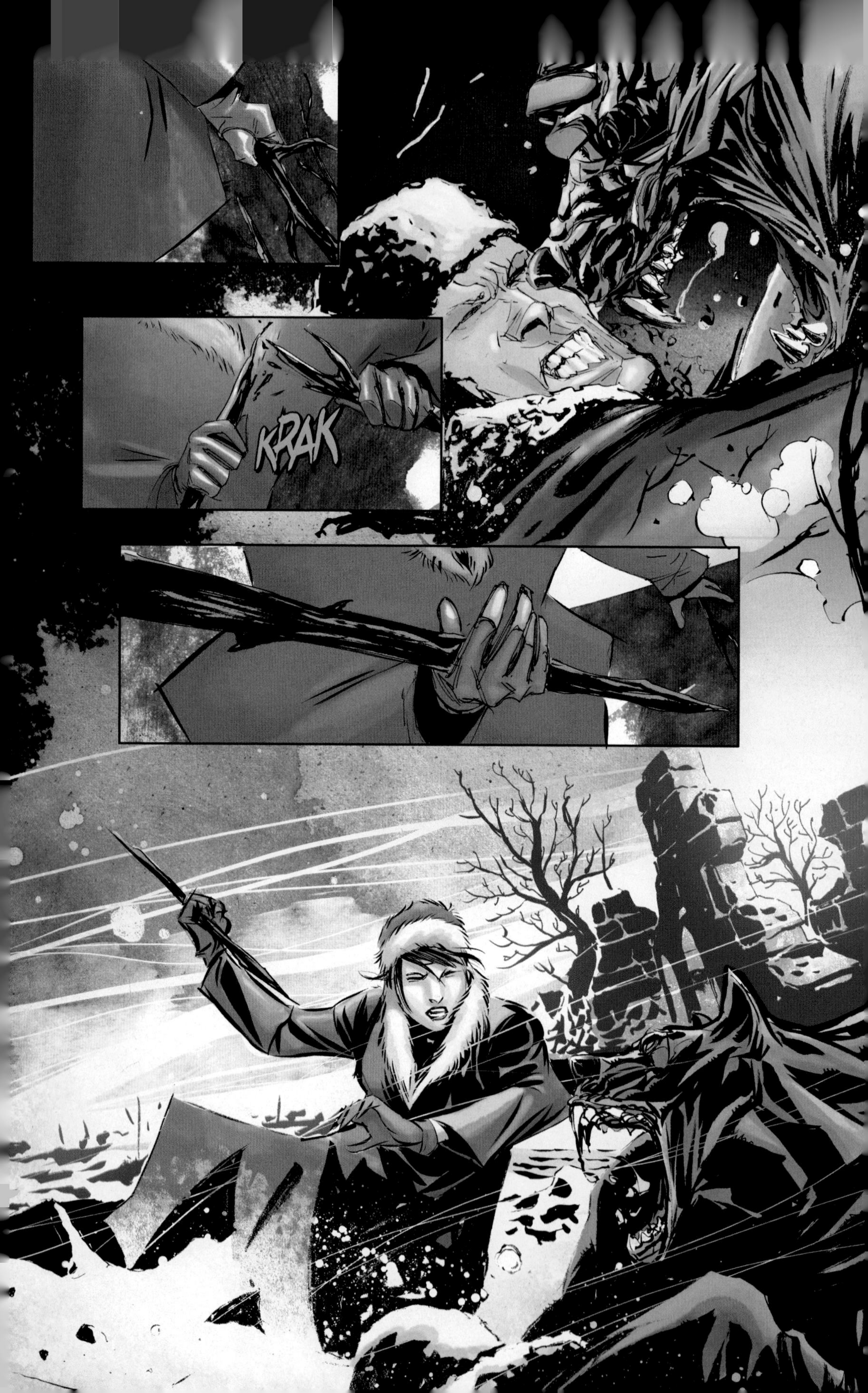
KRAK

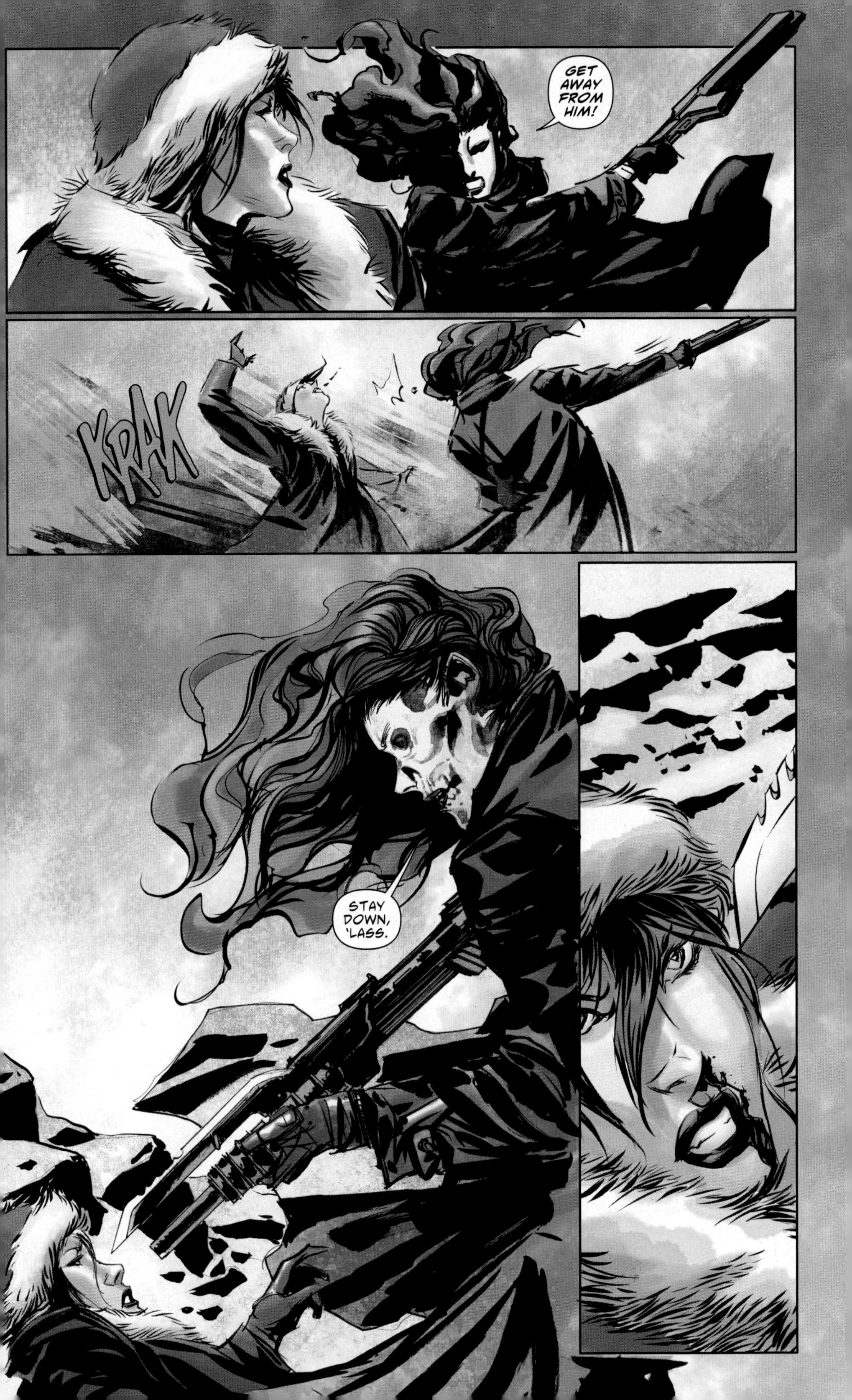
GET AWAY FROM HIM!
KRAK
STAY DOWN, 'LASS.

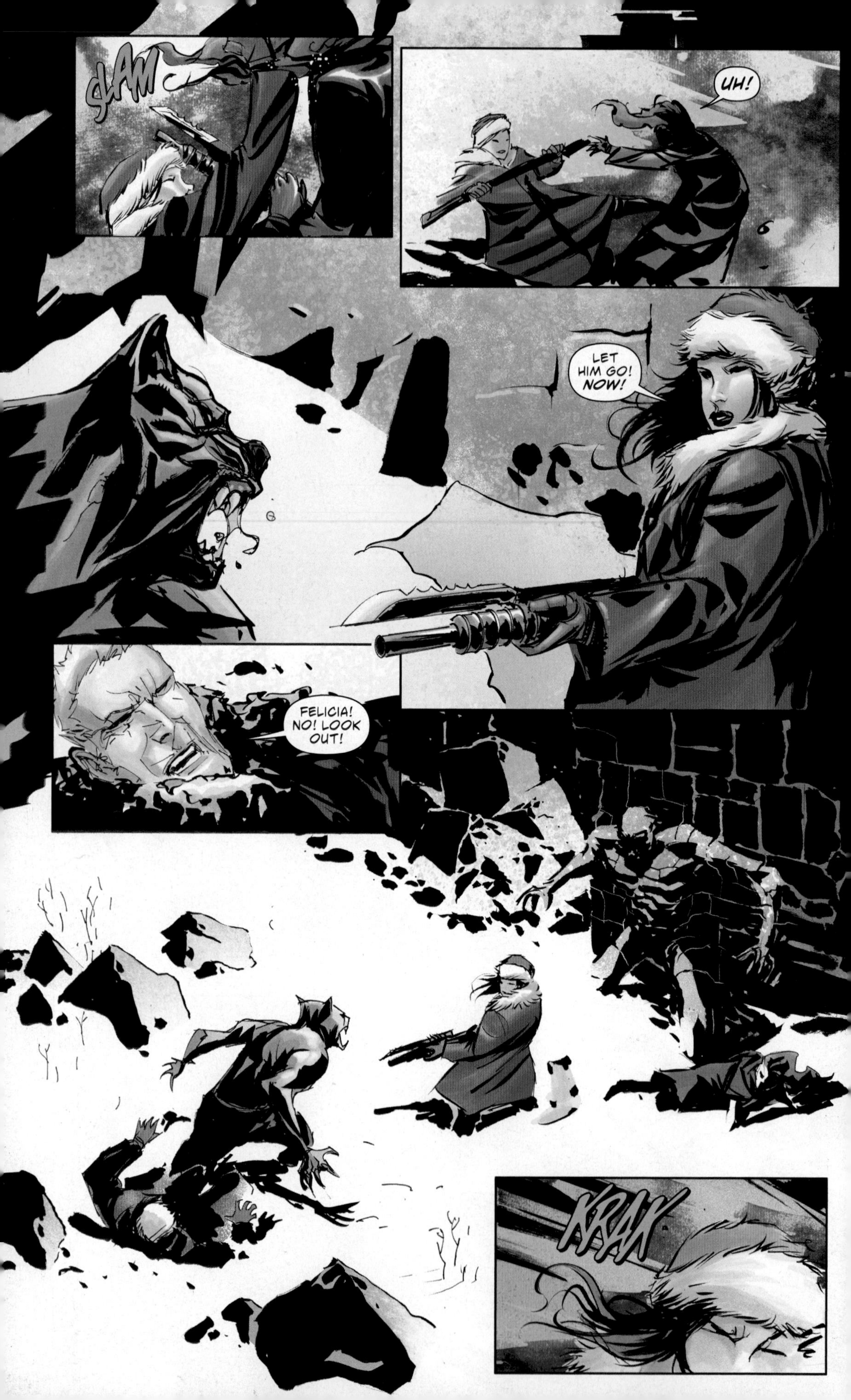
SLAM
UH!
LET HIM GO! NOW!
FELICIA! NO! LOOK OUT!
KRAK

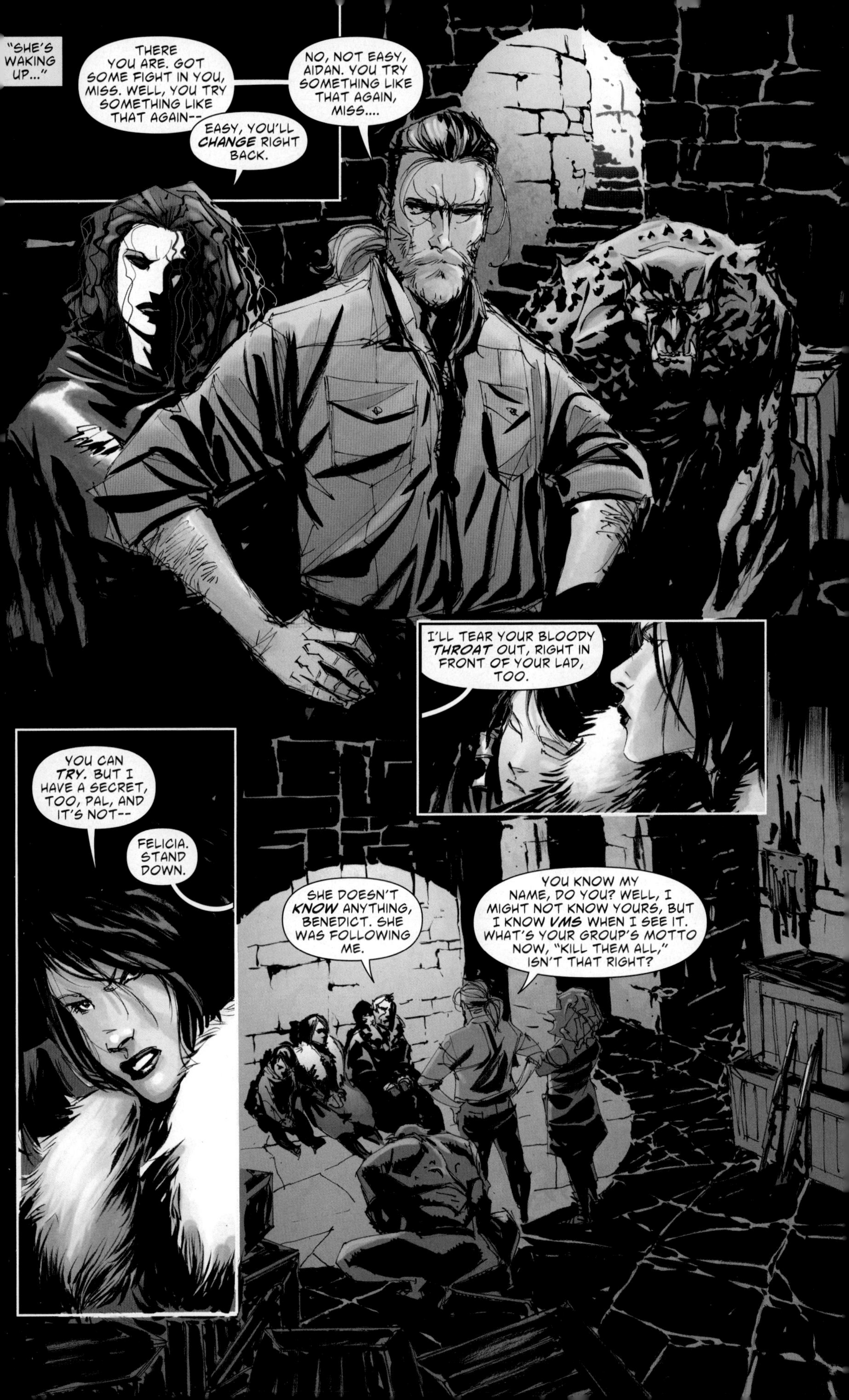
"SHE'S WAKING UP..."
THERE YOU ARE. GOT SOME FIGHT IN YOU, MISS. WELL, YOU TRY SOMETHING LIKE THAT AGAIN--
EASY, YOU'LL CHANGE RIGHT BACK.
NO, NOT EASY, AIDAN. YOU TRY SOMETHING LIKE THAT AGAIN, MISS....
I'LL TEAR YOUR BLOODY THROAT OUT, RIGHT IN FRONT OF YOUR LAD, TOO.
YOU CAN TRY. BUT I HAVE A SECRET, TOO, PAL, AND IT'S NOT--
FELICIA. STAND DOWN.
SHE DOESN'T KNOW ANYTHING, BENEDICT. SHE WAS FOLLOWING ME.
YOU KNOW MY NAME, DO YOU? WELL, I MIGHT NOT KNOW YOURS, BUT I KNOW VMS WHEN I SEE IT. WHAT'S YOUR GROUP'S MOTTO NOW, "KILL THEM ALL," ISN'T THAT RIGHT?

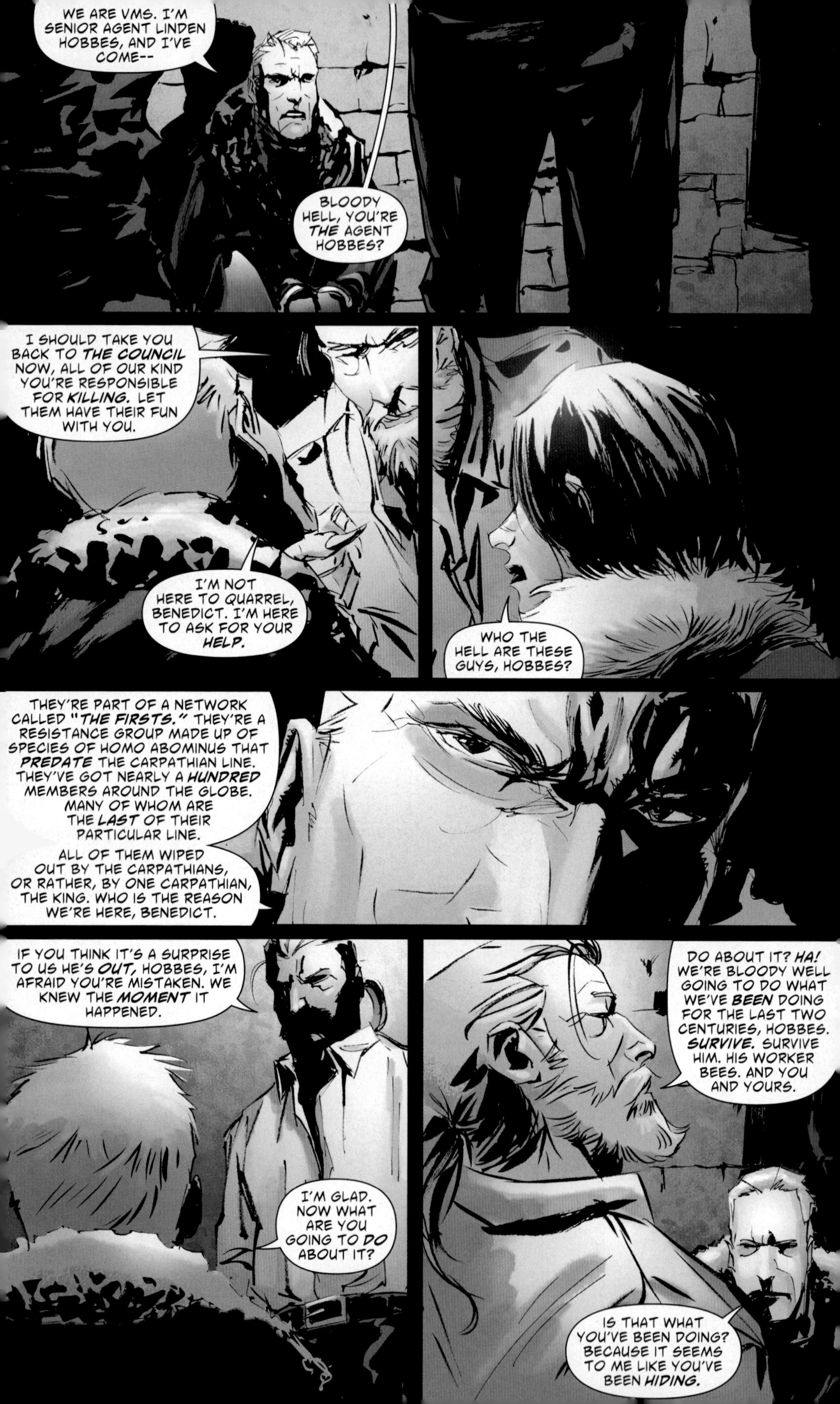
WE ARE VMS. I'M SENIOR AGENT LINDEN HOBBES, AND I'VE COME--
BLOODY HELL, YOU'RE *THE* AGENT HOBBES?
I SHOULD TAKE YOU BACK TO *THE COUNCIL* NOW, ALL OF OUR KIND YOU'RE RESPONSIBLE FOR *KILLING.* LET THEM HAVE THEIR FUN WITH YOU.
I'M NOT HERE TO QUARREL, BENEDICT. I'M HERE TO ASK FOR YOUR *HELP.*
WHO THE HELL ARE THESE GUYS, HOBBES?
THEY'RE PART OF A NETWORK CALLED *"THE FIRSTS."* THEY'RE A RESISTANCE GROUP MADE UP OF SPECIES OF HOMO ABOMINUS THAT *PREDATE* THE CARPATHIAN LINE. THEY'VE GOT NEARLY A *HUNDRED* MEMBERS AROUND THE GLOBE. MANY OF WHOM ARE THE *LAST* OF THEIR PARTICULAR LINE.
ALL OF THEM WIPED OUT BY THE CARPATHIANS, OR RATHER, BY ONE CARPATHIAN, THE KING. WHO IS THE REASON WE'RE HERE, BENEDICT.
IF YOU THINK IT'S A SURPRISE TO US HE'S *OUT,* HOBBES, I'M AFRAID YOU'RE MISTAKEN. WE KNEW THE *MOMENT* IT HAPPENED.
I'M GLAD. NOW WHAT ARE YOU GOING TO *DO* ABOUT IT?
DO ABOUT IT? *HA!* WE'RE BLOODY WELL GOING TO DO WHAT WE'VE *BEEN* DOING FOR THE LAST TWO CENTURIES, HOBBES. *SURVIVE.* SURVIVE HIM. HIS WORKER BEES. AND YOU AND YOURS.
IS THAT WHAT YOU'VE BEEN DOING? BECAUSE IT SEEMS TO ME LIKE YOU'VE BEEN *HIDING.*

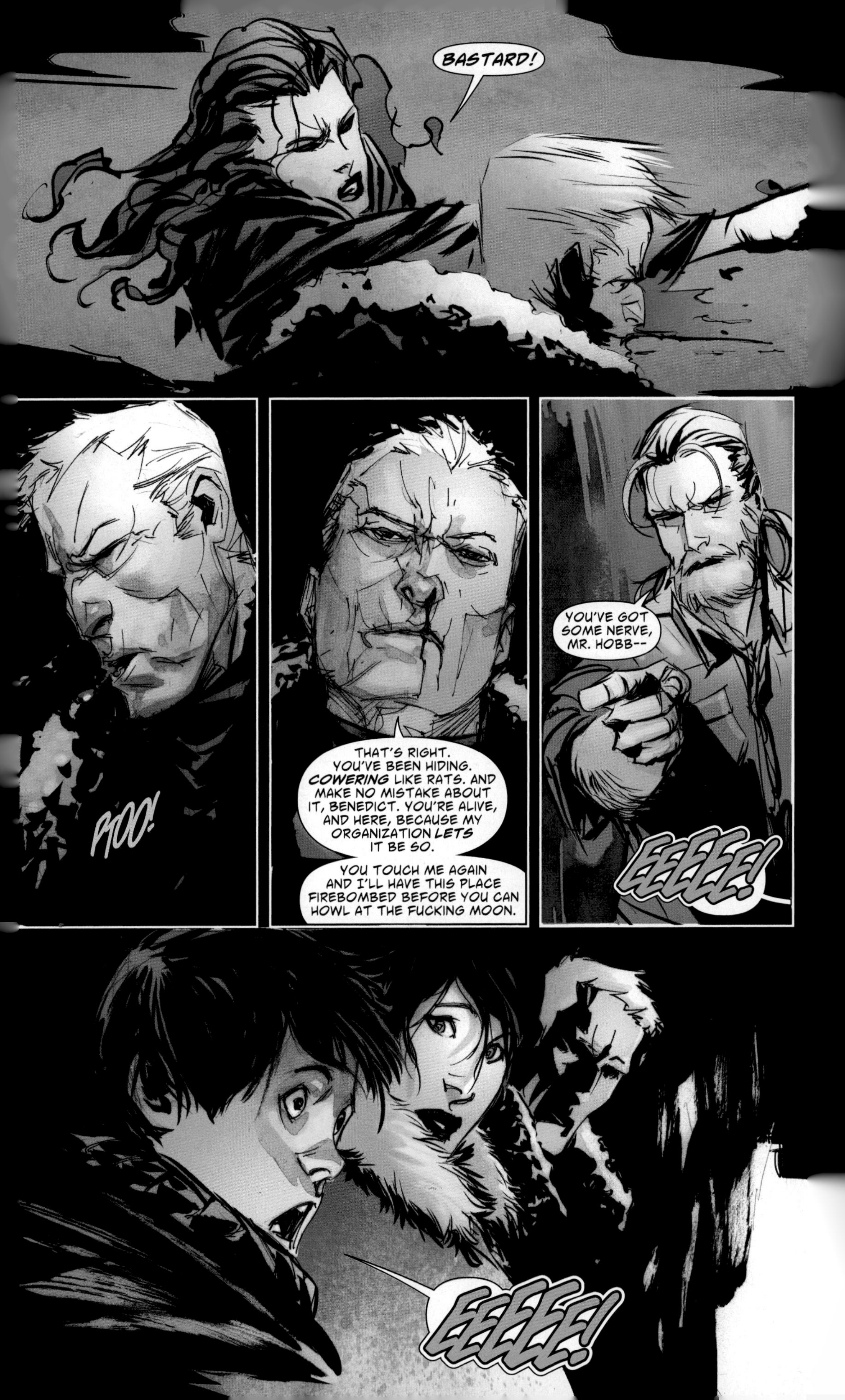
BASTARD!
PTOO!
THAT'S RIGHT. YOU'VE BEEN HIDING. COWERING LIKE RATS. AND MAKE NO MISTAKE ABOUT IT, BENEDICT. YOU'RE ALIVE, AND HERE, BECAUSE MY ORGANIZATION LETS IT BE SO.
YOU TOUCH ME AGAIN AND I'LL HAVE THIS PLACE FIREBOMBED BEFORE YOU CAN HOWL AT THE FUCKING MOON.
YOU'VE GOT SOME NERVE, MR. HOBB--
EEEEEE!
EEEEE!

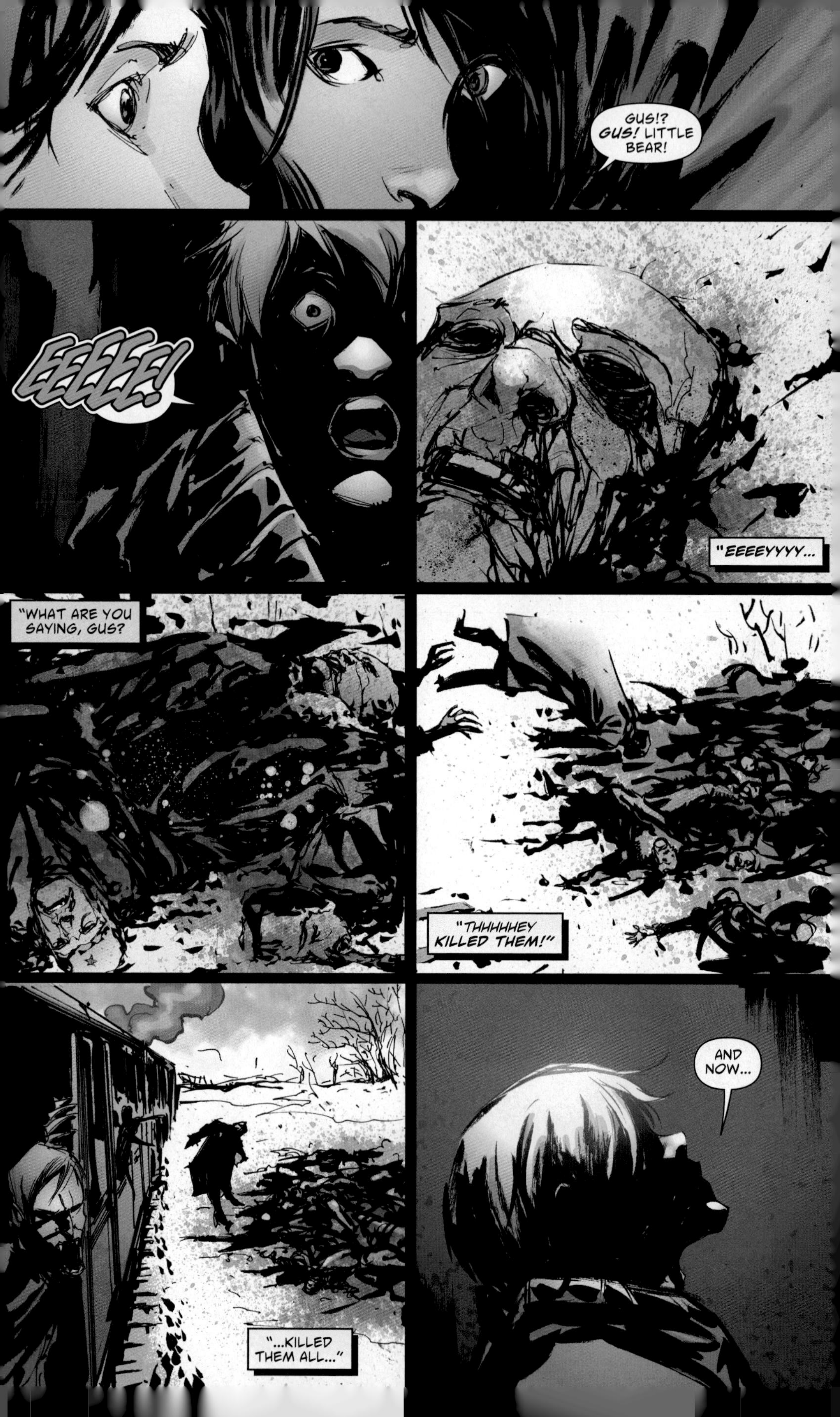
GUS!? GUS! LITTLE BEAR!
EEEEE!
"EEEEYYYY...
"WHAT ARE YOU SAYING, GUS?
"THHHHHEY KILLED THEM!"
"...KILLED THEM ALL..."
AND NOW...

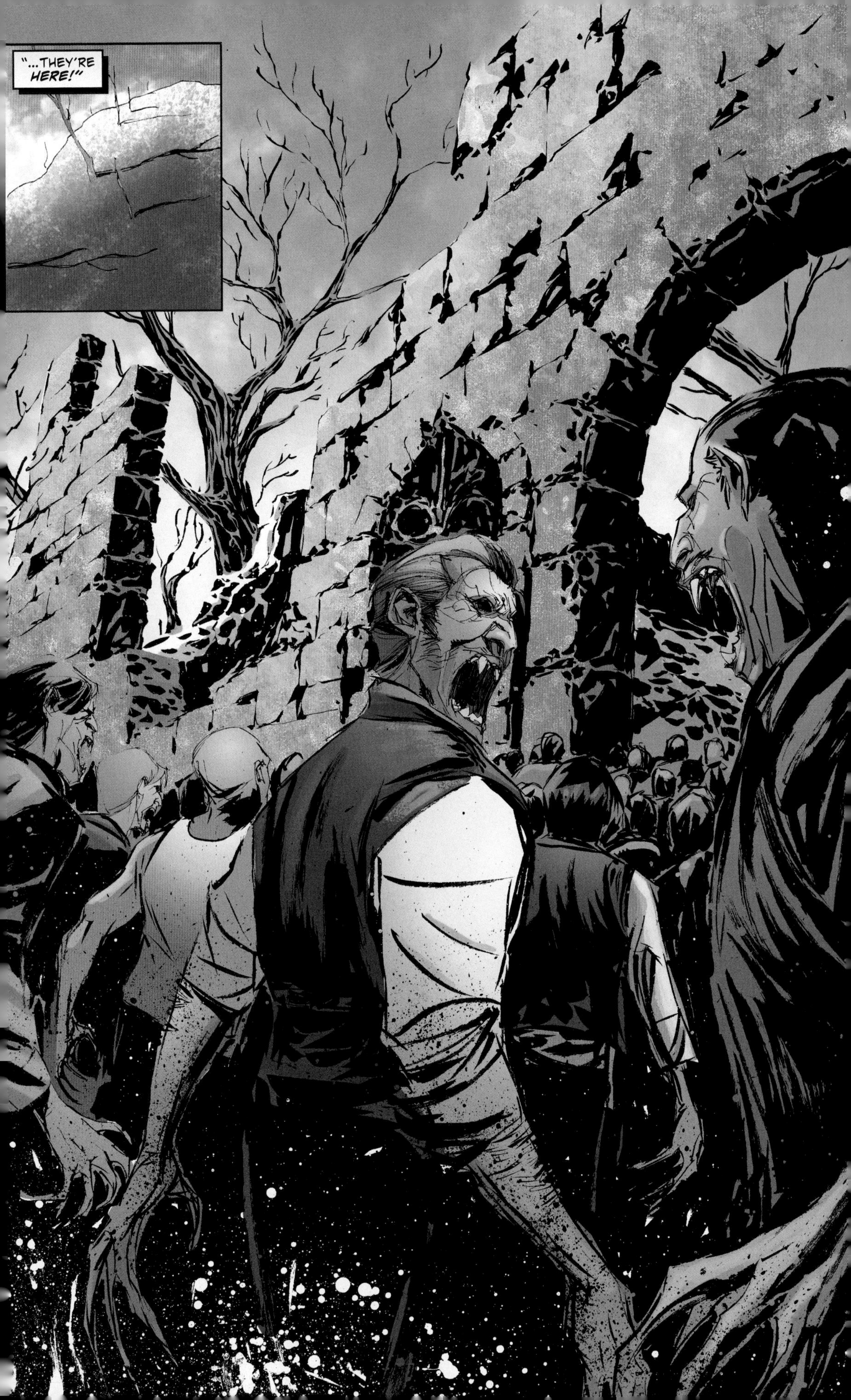
"...THEY'RE HERE!"

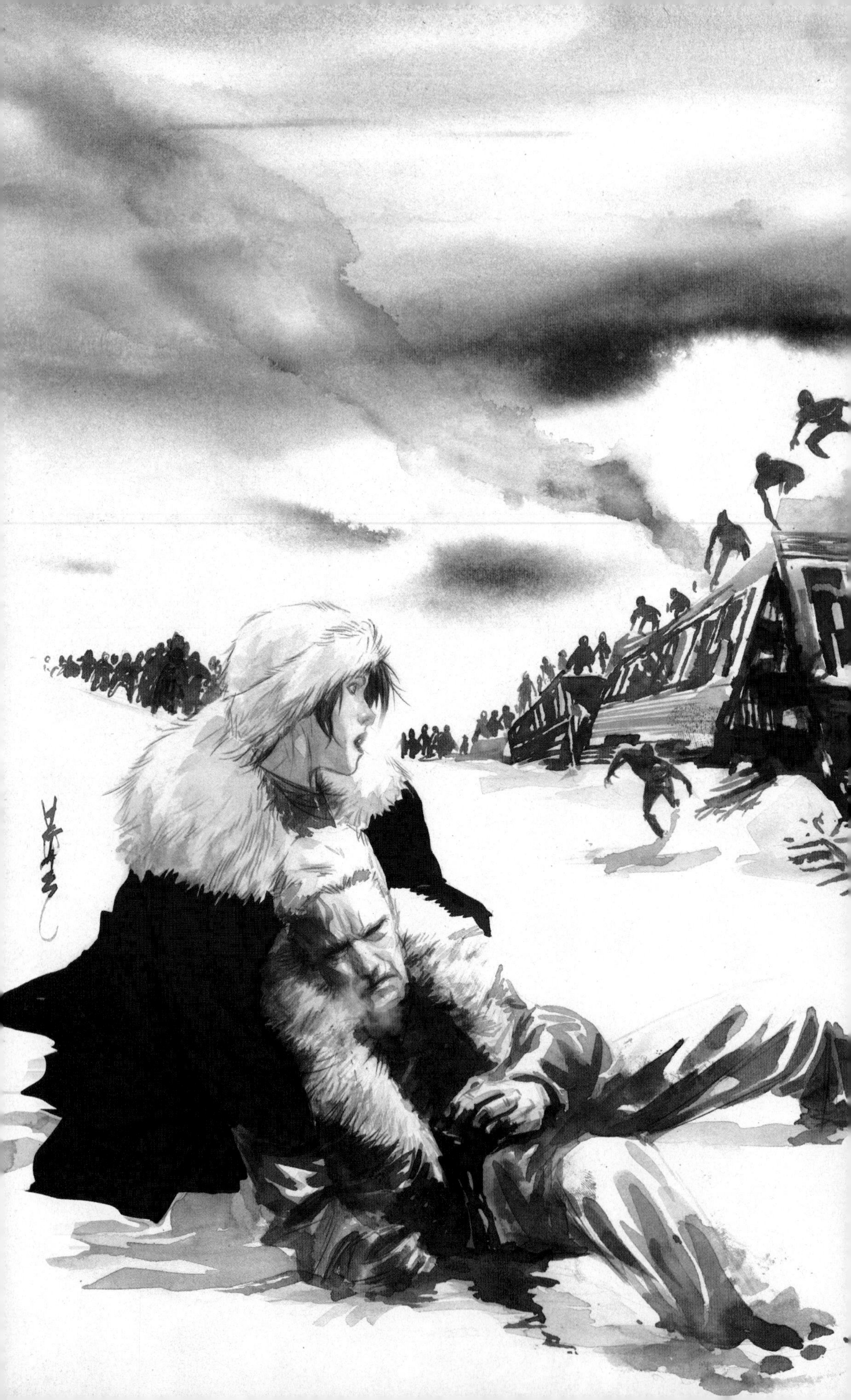

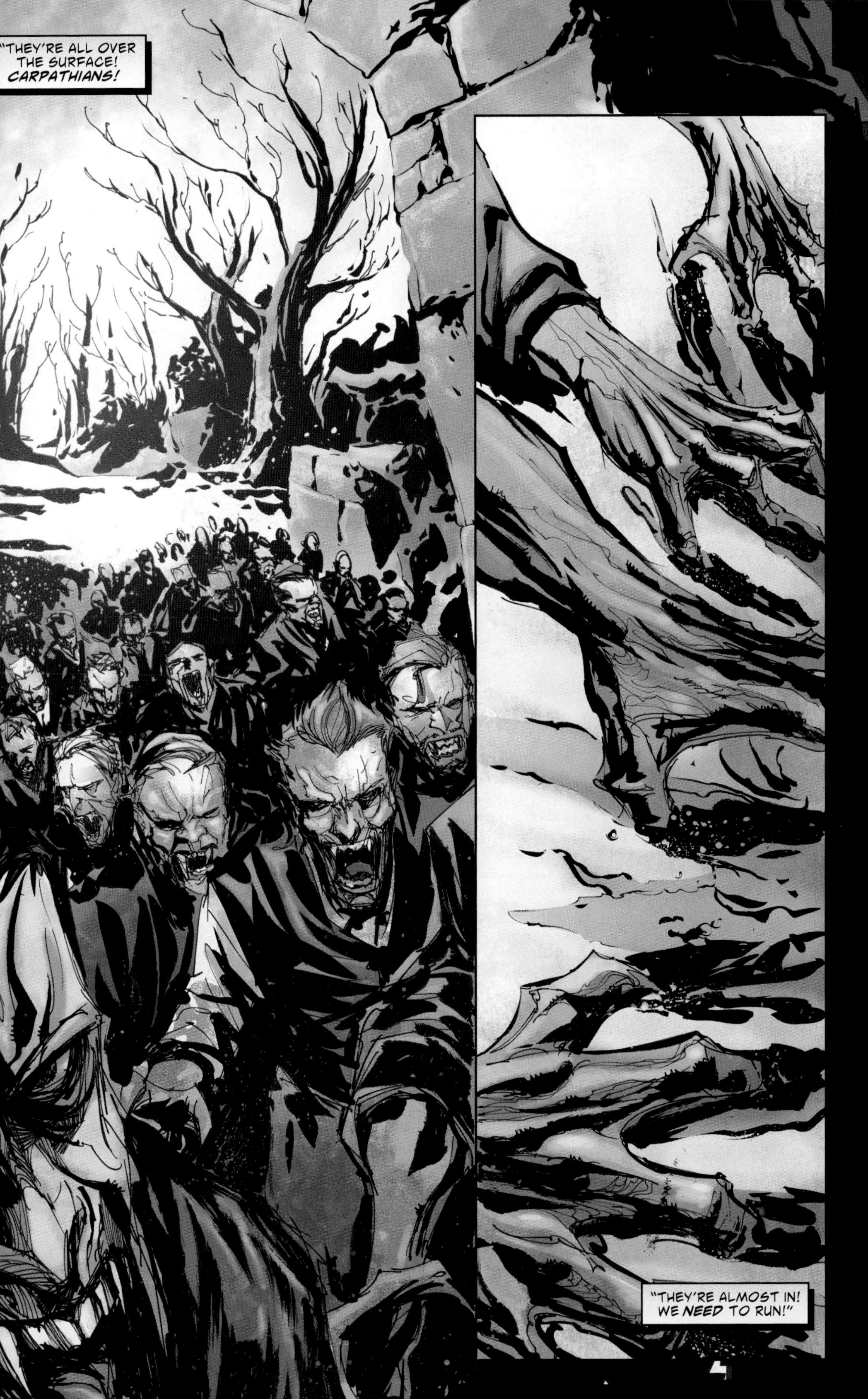
"THEY'RE ALL OVER THE SURFACE! CARPATHIANS!
"THEY'RE ALMOST IN! WE NEED TO RUN!"

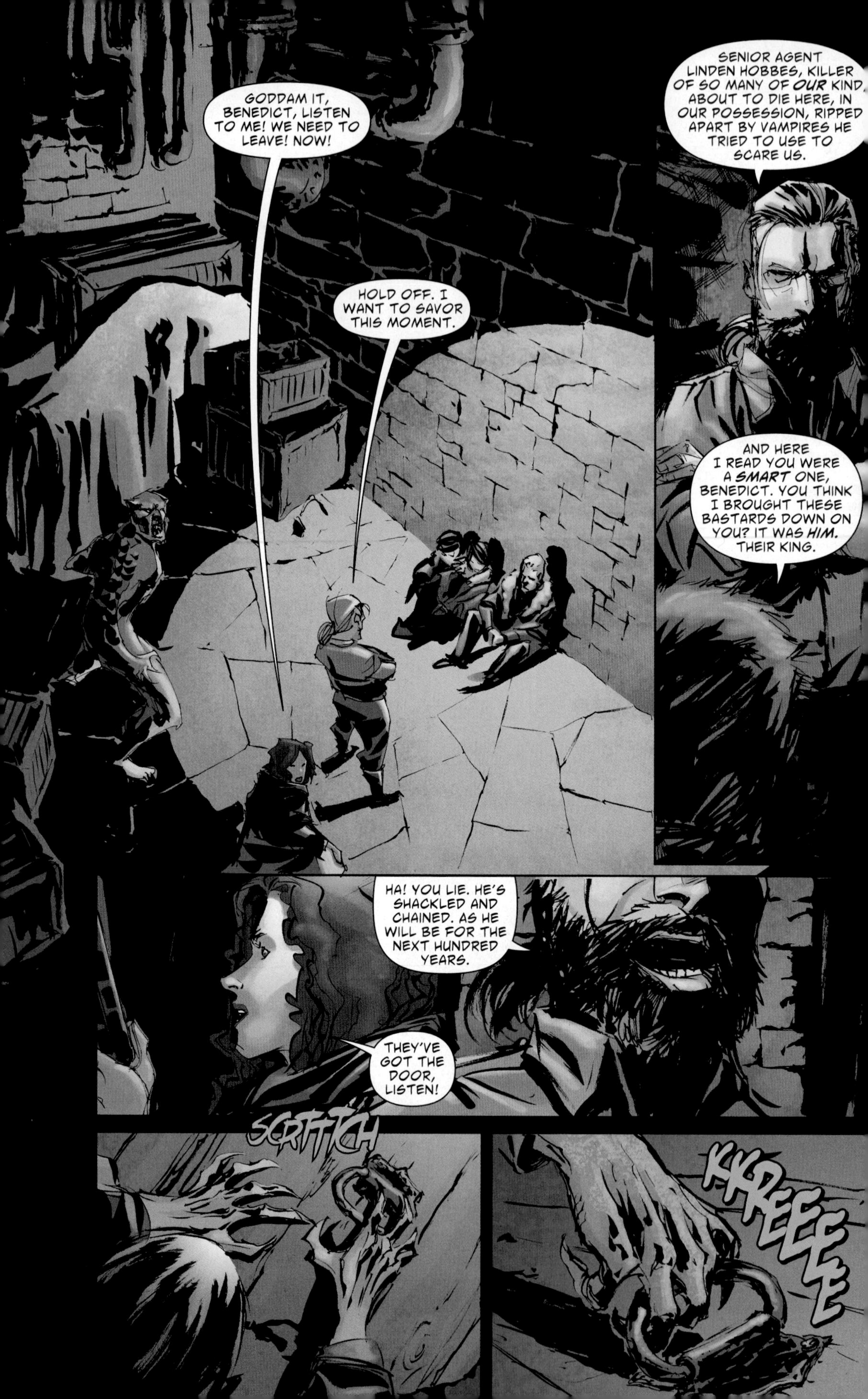
GODDAM IT, BENEDICT, LISTEN TO ME! WE NEED TO LEAVE! NOW!
HOLD OFF. I WANT TO SAVOR THIS MOMENT.
SENIOR AGENT LINDEN HOBBES, KILLER OF SO MANY OF OUR KIND ABOUT TO DIE HERE, IN OUR POSSESSION, RIPPED APART BY VAMPIRES HE TRIED TO USE TO SCARE US.
AND HERE I READ YOU WERE A SMART ONE, BENEDICT. YOU THINK I BROUGHT THESE BASTARDS DOWN ON YOU? IT WAS HIM. THEIR KING.
HA! YOU LIE. HE'S SHACKLED AND CHAINED. AS HE WILL BE FOR THE NEXT HUNDRED YEARS.
THEY'VE GOT THE DOOR, LISTEN!
SCRITTCH
KKREEEEE

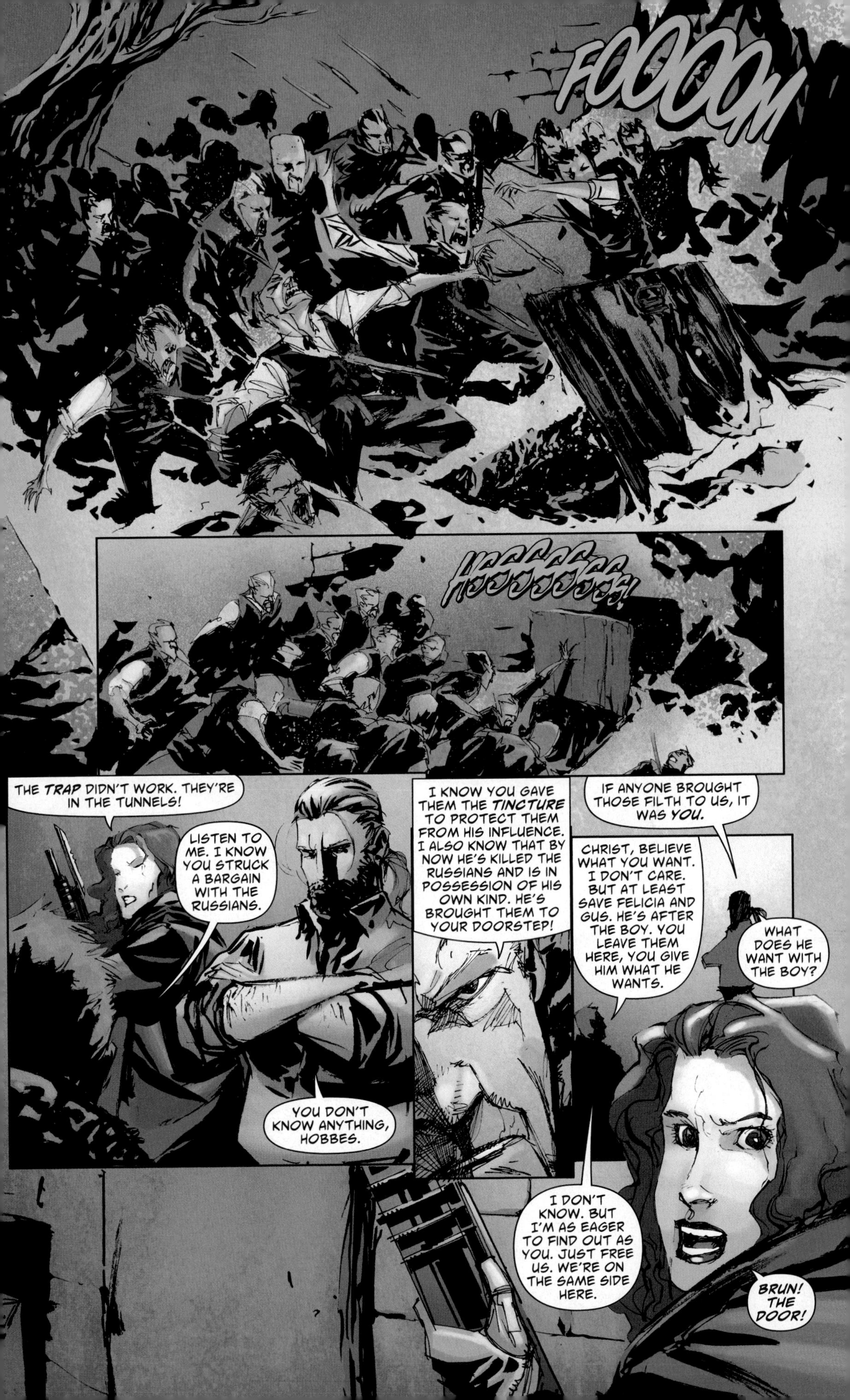
FOOOOM
HSSSSSSS!
THE *TRAP* DIDN'T WORK. THEY'RE IN THE TUNNELS!
LISTEN TO ME. I KNOW YOU STRUCK A BARGAIN WITH THE RUSSIANS.
YOU DON'T KNOW ANYTHING, HOBBES.
I KNOW YOU GAVE THEM THE *TINCTURE* TO PROTECT THEM FROM HIS INFLUENCE. I ALSO KNOW THAT BY NOW HE'S KILLED THE RUSSIANS AND IS IN POSSESSION OF HIS OWN KIND. HE'S BROUGHT THEM TO YOUR DOORSTEP!
IF ANYONE BROUGHT THOSE FILTH TO US, IT WAS *YOU.*
CHRIST, BELIEVE WHAT YOU WANT. I DON'T CARE. BUT AT LEAST SAVE FELICIA AND GUS. HE'S AFTER THE BOY. YOU LEAVE THEM HERE, YOU GIVE HIM WHAT HE WANTS.
WHAT DOES HE WANT WITH THE BOY?
I DON'T KNOW. BUT I'M AS EAGER TO FIND OUT AS YOU. JUST FREE US. WE'RE ON THE SAME SIDE HERE.
BRUN! THE DOOR!

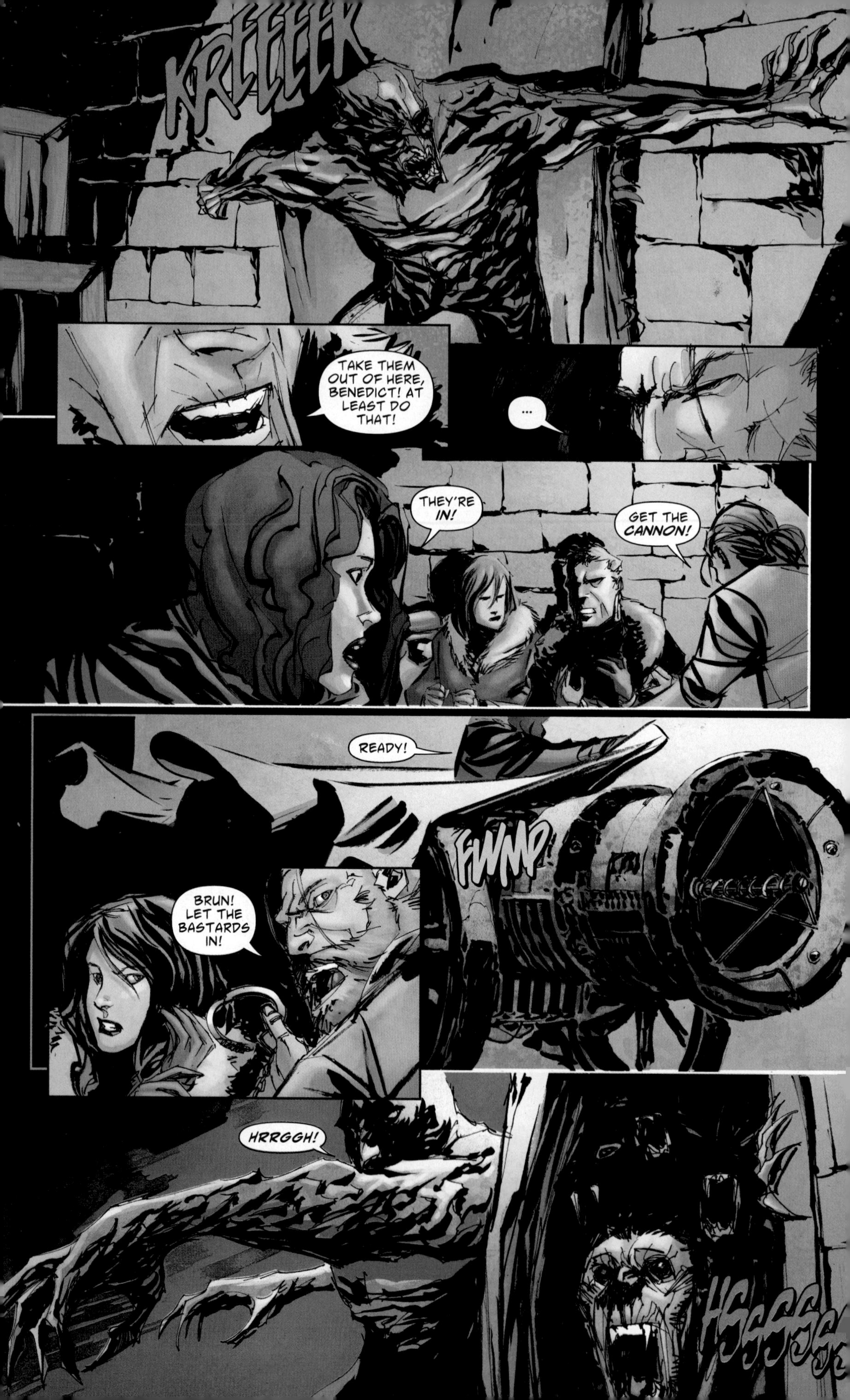
KREEEEK
TAKE THEM OUT OF HERE, BENEDICT! AT LEAST DO THAT!
...
THEY'RE IN!
GET THE CANNON!
READY!
FWMP
BRUN! LET THE BASTARDS IN!
HRRGGH!
HSSSSK

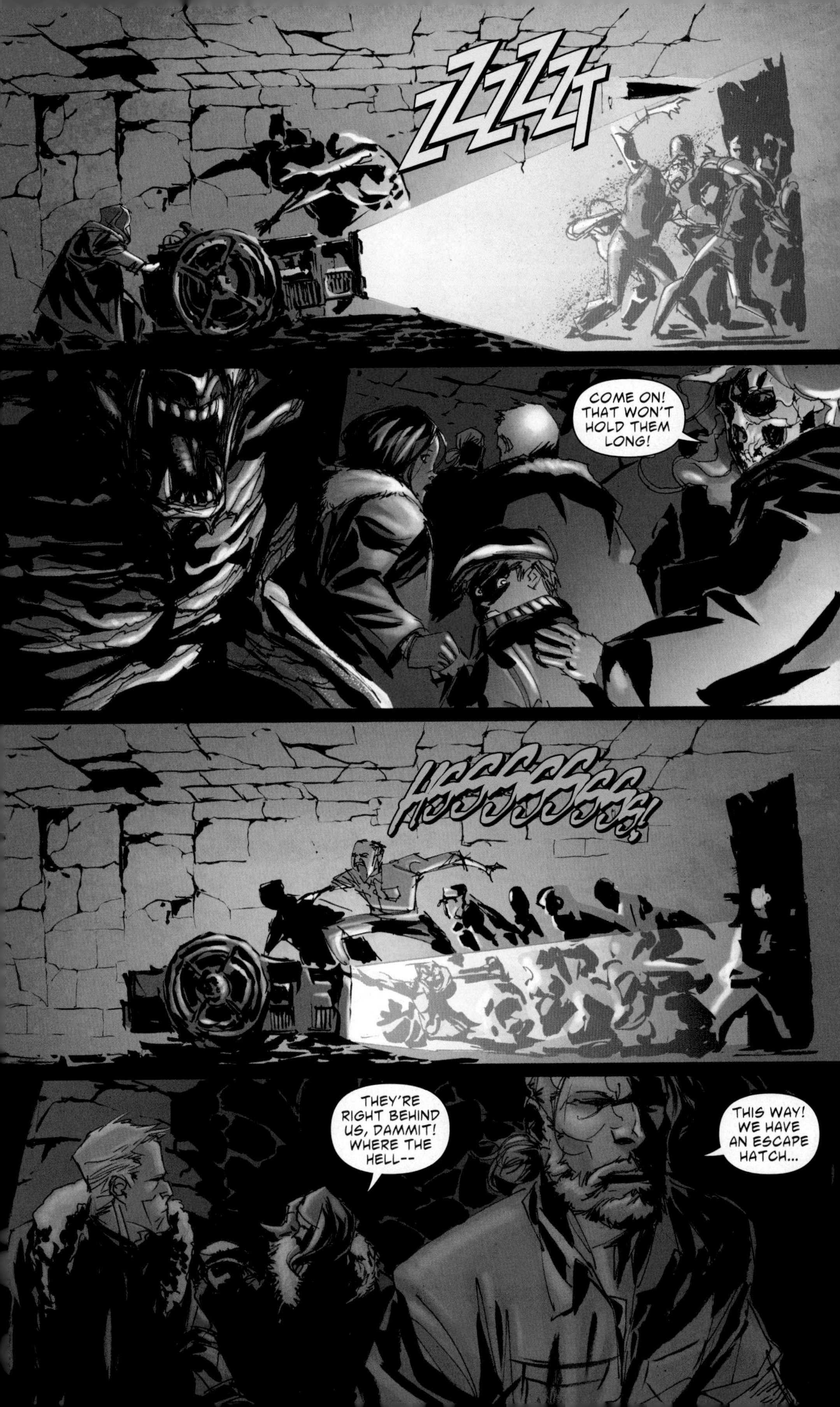
ZZZZZT
COME ON! THAT WON'T HOLD THEM LONG!
HSSSSSSS!
THEY'RE RIGHT BEHIND US, DAMMIT! WHERE THE HELL--
THIS WAY! WE HAVE AN ESCAPE HATCH...

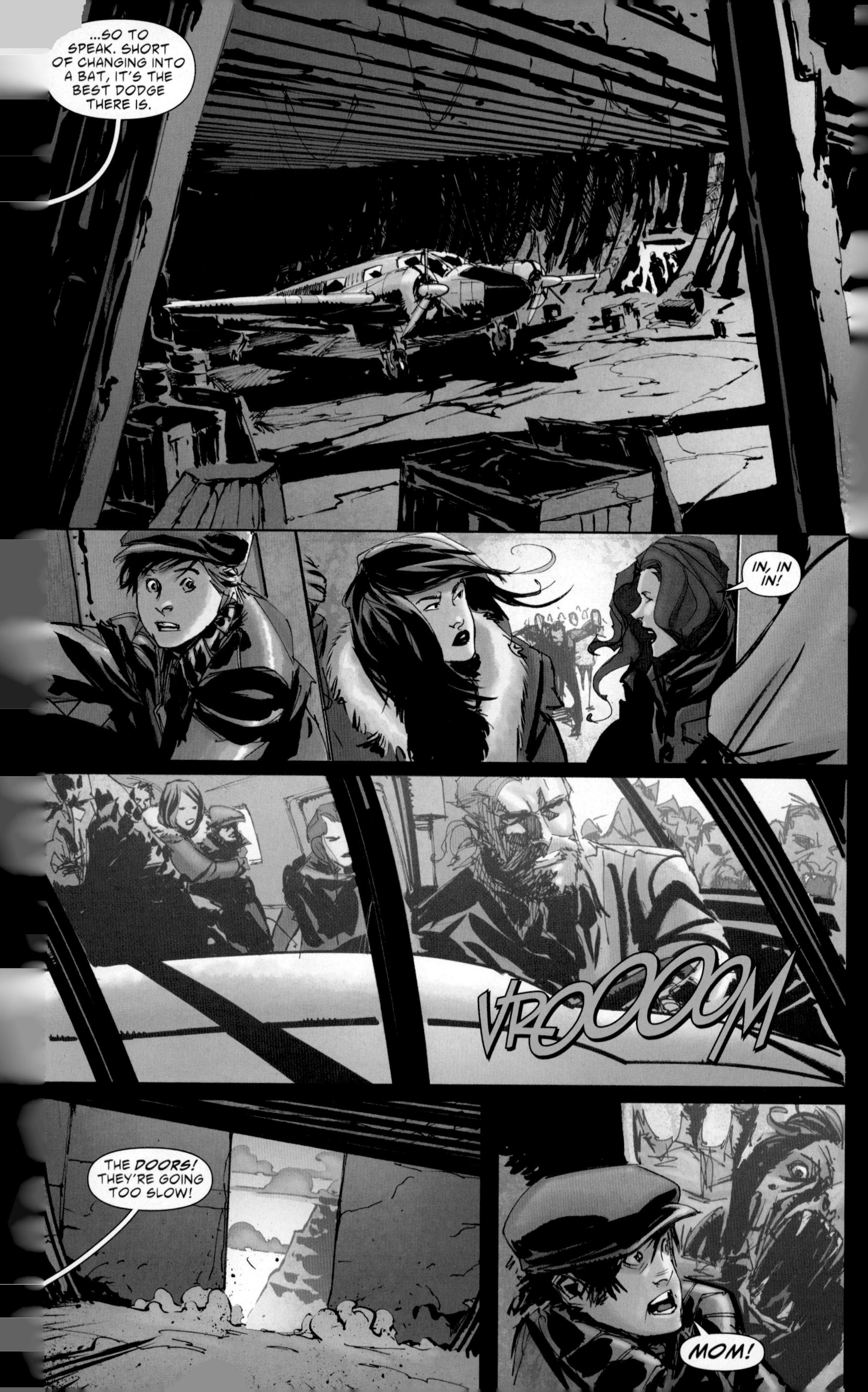
...SO TO SPEAK. SHORT OF CHANGING INTO A BAT, IT'S THE BEST DODGE THERE IS.
IN, IN IN!
VROOOOOM
THE DOORS! THEY'RE GOING TOO SLOW!
MOM!

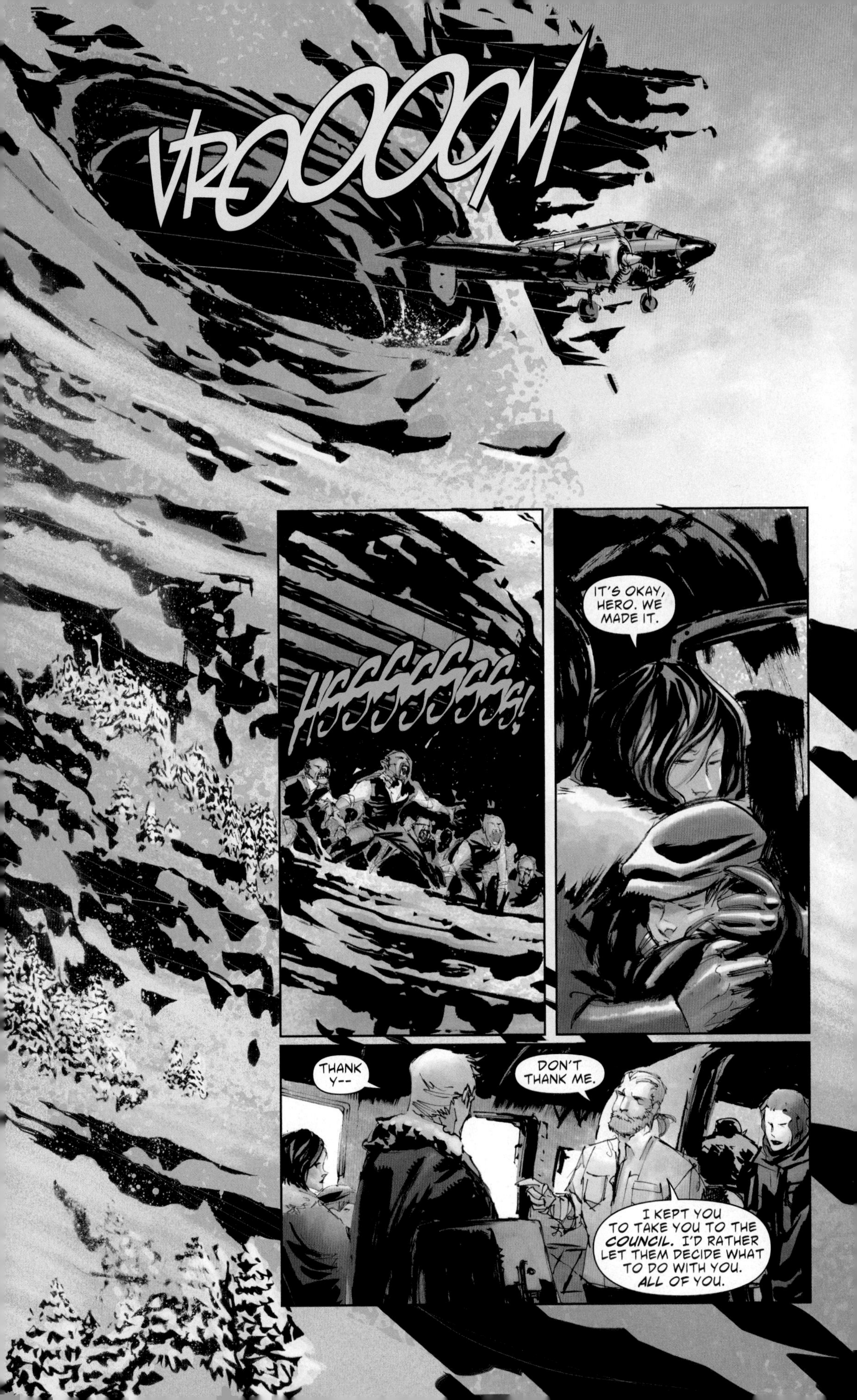
VROOOOM
HSSSSSSSS!
IT'S OKAY, HERO. WE MADE IT.
THANK Y--
DON'T THANK ME.
I KEPT YOU TO TAKE YOU TO THE COUNCIL. I'D RATHER LET THEM DECIDE WHAT TO DO WITH YOU. ALL OF YOU.

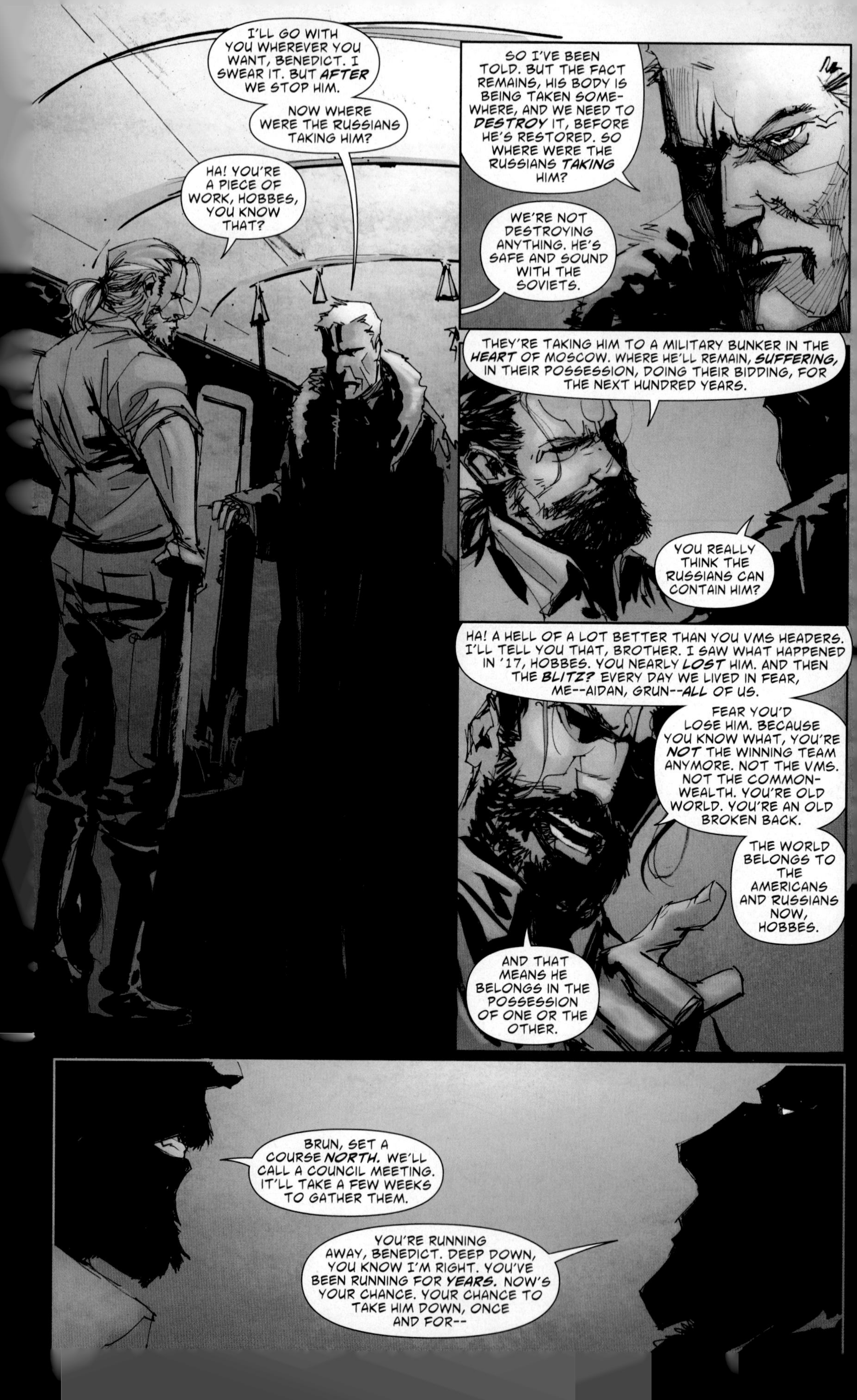
I'LL GO WITH YOU WHEREVER YOU WANT, BENEDICT. I SWEAR IT. BUT AFTER WE STOP HIM.
NOW WHERE WERE THE RUSSIANS TAKING HIM?
HA! YOU'RE A PIECE OF WORK, HOBBES, YOU KNOW THAT?
SO I'VE BEEN TOLD. BUT THE FACT REMAINS, HIS BODY IS BEING TAKEN SOMEWHERE, AND WE NEED TO DESTROY IT, BEFORE HE'S RESTORED. SO WHERE WERE THE RUSSIANS TAKING HIM?
WE'RE NOT DESTROYING ANYTHING. HE'S SAFE AND SOUND WITH THE SOVIETS.
THEY'RE TAKING HIM TO A MILITARY BUNKER IN THE HEART OF MOSCOW. WHERE HE'LL REMAIN, SUFFERING, IN THEIR POSSESSION, DOING THEIR BIDDING, FOR THE NEXT HUNDRED YEARS.
YOU REALLY THINK THE RUSSIANS CAN CONTAIN HIM?
HA! A HELL OF A LOT BETTER THAN YOU VMS HEADERS. I'LL TELL YOU THAT, BROTHER. I SAW WHAT HAPPENED IN '17, HOBBES. YOU NEARLY LOST HIM. AND THEN THE BLITZ? EVERY DAY WE LIVED IN FEAR, ME--AIDAN, GRUN--ALL OF US.
FEAR YOU'D LOSE HIM. BECAUSE YOU KNOW WHAT, YOU'RE NOT THE WINNING TEAM ANYMORE. NOT THE VMS. NOT THE COMMONWEALTH. YOU'RE OLD WORLD. YOU'RE AN OLD BROKEN BACK.
THE WORLD BELONGS TO THE AMERICANS AND RUSSIANS NOW, HOBBES.
AND THAT MEANS HE BELONGS IN THE POSSESSION OF ONE OR THE OTHER.
BRUN, SET A COURSE NORTH. WE'LL CALL A COUNCIL MEETING. IT'LL TAKE A FEW WEEKS TO GATHER THEM.
YOU'RE RUNNING AWAY, BENEDICT. DEEP DOWN, YOU KNOW I'M RIGHT. YOU'VE BEEN RUNNING FOR YEARS. NOW'S YOUR CHANCE. YOUR CHANCE TO TAKE HIM DOWN, ONCE AND FOR--

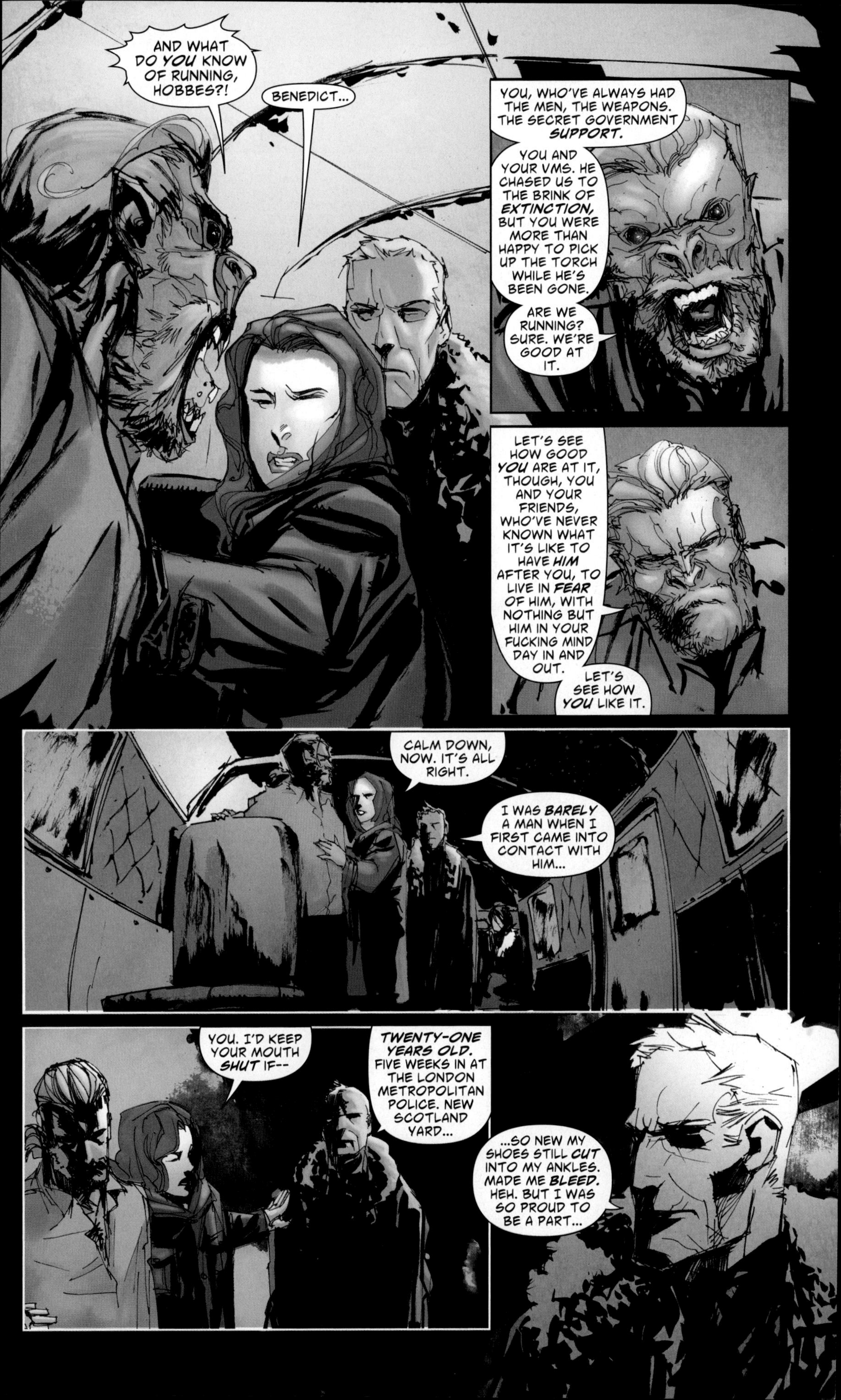

AND WHAT DO *YOU* KNOW OF RUNNING, HOBBES?!
BENEDICT...
YOU, WHO'VE ALWAYS HAD THE MEN, THE WEAPONS. THE SECRET GOVERNMENT *SUPPORT.*
YOU AND YOUR VMS. HE CHASED US TO THE BRINK OF *EXTINCTION,* BUT YOU WERE MORE THAN HAPPY TO PICK UP THE TORCH WHILE HE'S BEEN GONE.
ARE WE RUNNING? SURE. WE'RE GOOD AT IT.
LET'S SEE HOW GOOD *YOU* ARE AT IT, THOUGH, YOU AND YOUR FRIENDS, WHO'VE NEVER KNOWN WHAT IT'S LIKE TO HAVE *HIM* AFTER YOU, TO LIVE IN *FEAR* OF HIM, WITH NOTHING BUT HIM IN YOUR FUCKING MIND DAY IN AND OUT.
LET'S SEE HOW *YOU* LIKE IT.
CALM DOWN, NOW. IT'S ALL RIGHT.
I WAS *BARELY* A MAN WHEN I FIRST CAME INTO CONTACT WITH HIM...
YOU. I'D KEEP YOUR MOUTH *SHUT* IF--
TWENTY-ONE YEARS OLD. FIVE WEEKS IN AT THE LONDON METROPOLITAN POLICE. NEW SCOTLAND YARD...
...SO NEW MY SHOES STILL *CUT* INTO MY ANKLES. MADE ME *BLEED.* HEH. BUT I WAS SO PROUD TO BE A PART...

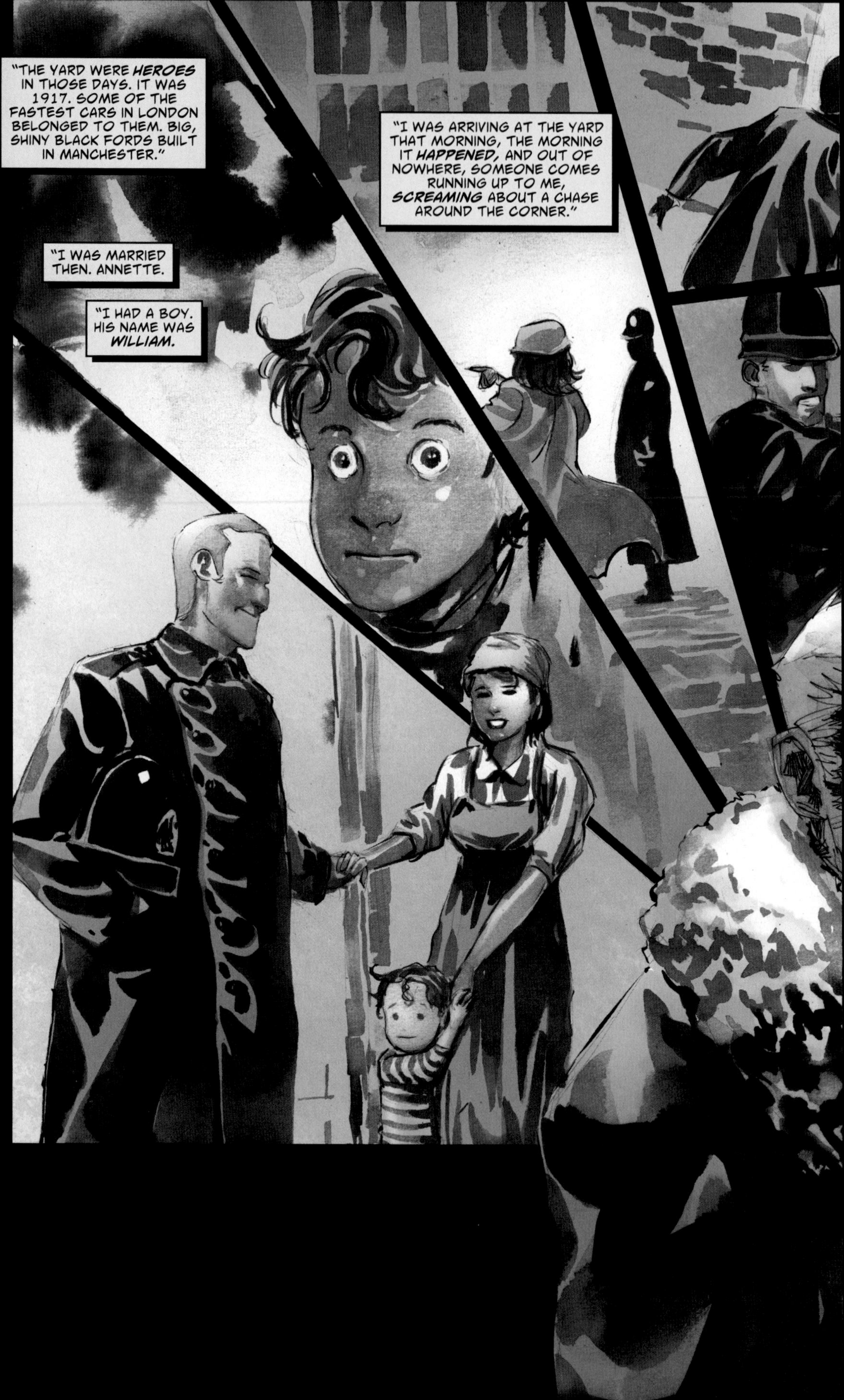
"THE YARD WERE HEROES IN THOSE DAYS. IT WAS 1917. SOME OF THE FASTEST CARS IN LONDON BELONGED TO THEM. BIG, SHINY BLACK FORDS BUILT IN MANCHESTER."
"I WAS ARRIVING AT THE YARD THAT MORNING, THE MORNING IT HAPPENED, AND OUT OF NOWHERE, SOMEONE COMES RUNNING UP TO ME, SCREAMING ABOUT A CHASE AROUND THE CORNER."
"I WAS MARRIED THEN. ANNETTE.
"I HAD A BOY. HIS NAME WAS WILLIAM.

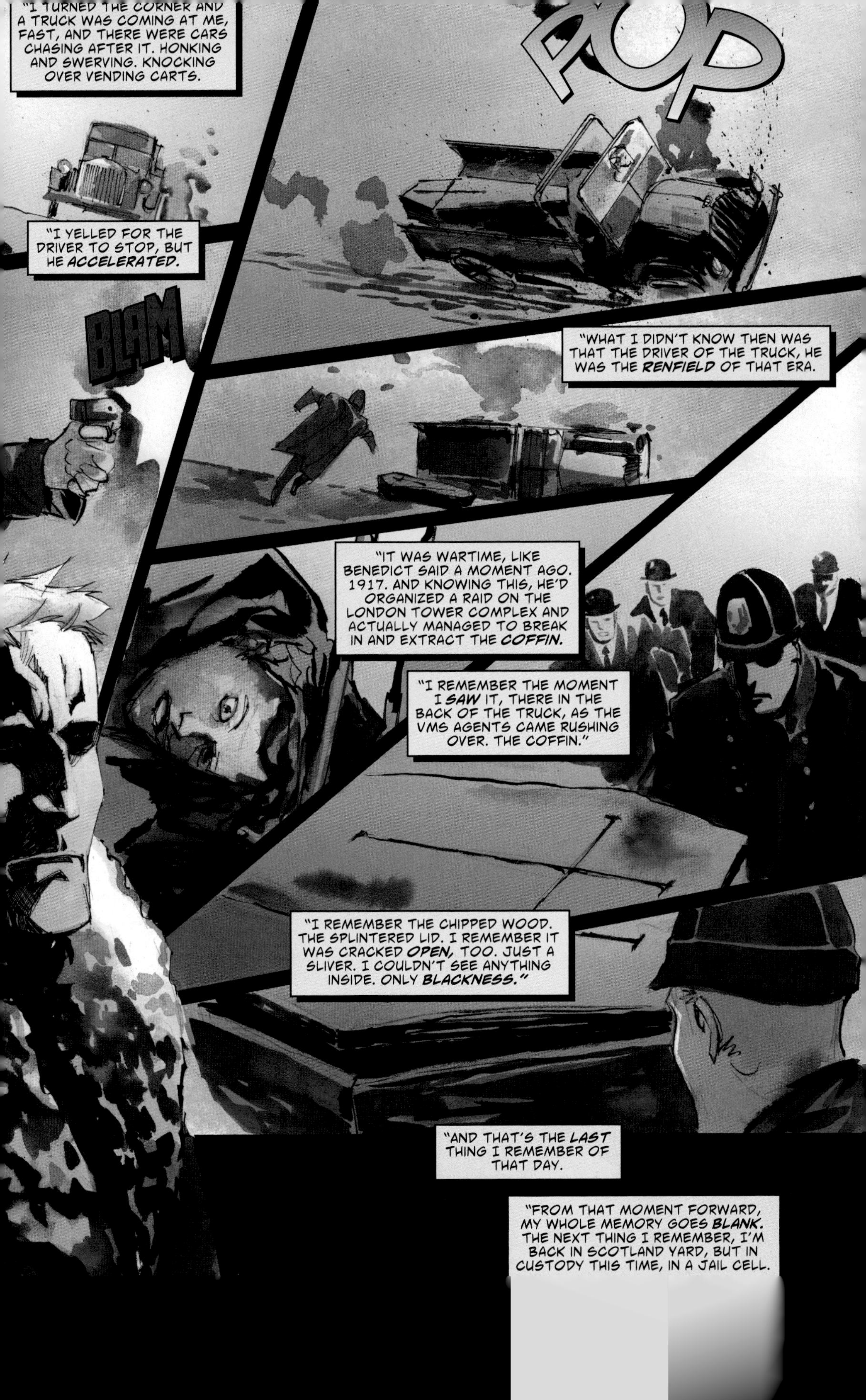
"I TURNED THE CORNER AND A TRUCK WAS COMING AT ME, FAST, AND THERE WERE CARS CHASING AFTER IT. HONKING AND SWERVING. KNOCKING OVER VENDING CARTS.
POP
"I YELLED FOR THE DRIVER TO STOP, BUT HE ACCELERATED.
BLAM
"WHAT I DIDN'T KNOW THEN WAS THAT THE DRIVER OF THE TRUCK, HE WAS THE RENFIELD OF THAT ERA.
"IT WAS WARTIME, LIKE BENEDICT SAID A MOMENT AGO. 1917. AND KNOWING THIS, HE'D ORGANIZED A RAID ON THE LONDON TOWER COMPLEX AND ACTUALLY MANAGED TO BREAK IN AND EXTRACT THE COFFIN.
"I REMEMBER THE MOMENT I SAW IT, THERE IN THE BACK OF THE TRUCK, AS THE VMS AGENTS CAME RUSHING OVER. THE COFFIN."
"I REMEMBER THE CHIPPED WOOD. THE SPLINTERED LID. I REMEMBER IT WAS CRACKED OPEN, TOO. JUST A SLIVER. I COULDN'T SEE ANYTHING INSIDE. ONLY BLACKNESS."
"AND THAT'S THE LAST THING I REMEMBER OF THAT DAY.
"FROM THAT MOMENT FORWARD, MY WHOLE MEMORY GOES BLANK. THE NEXT THING I REMEMBER, I'M BACK IN SCOTLAND YARD, BUT IN CUSTODY THIS TIME, IN A JAIL CELL.

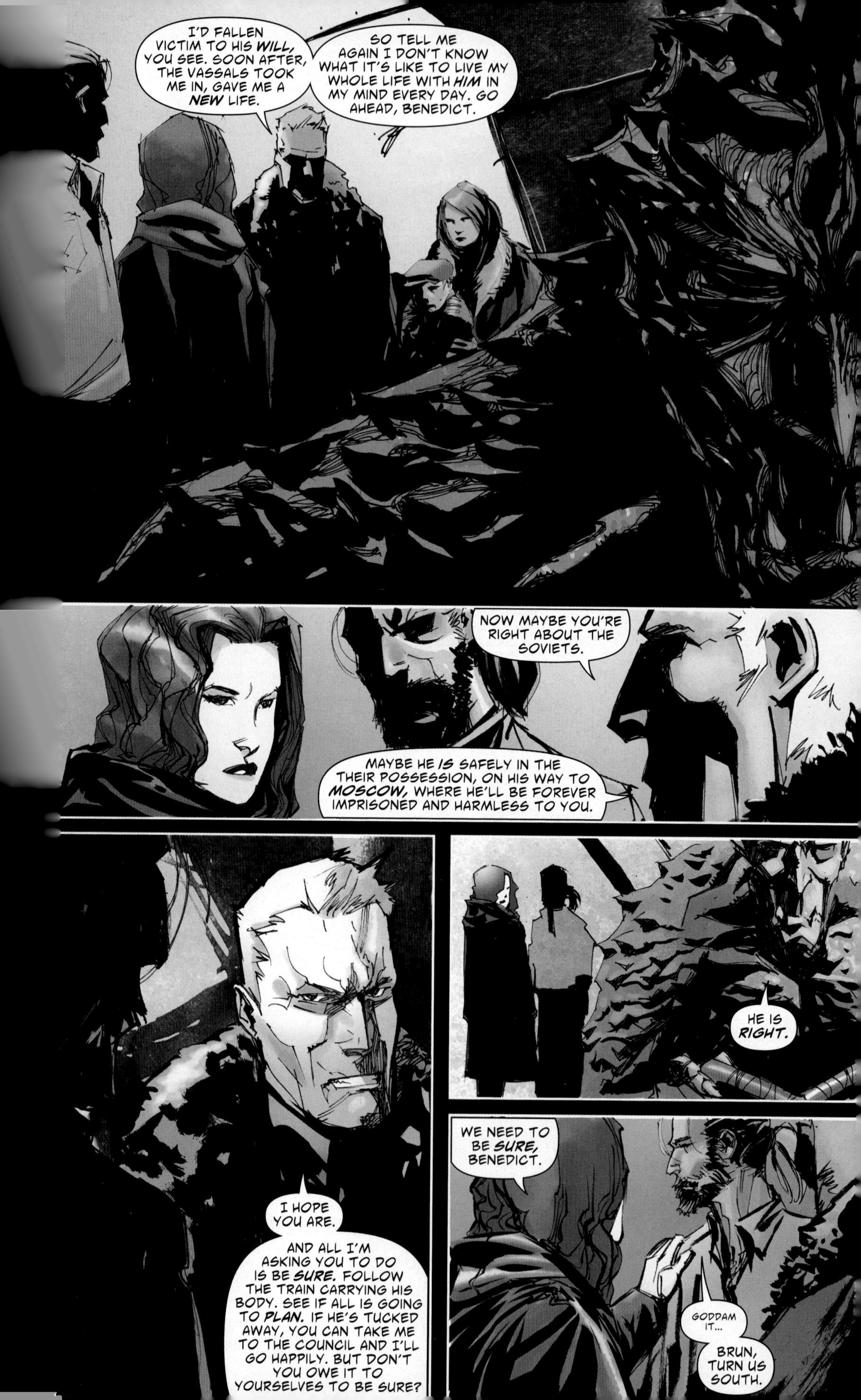
I'D FALLEN VICTIM TO HIS WILL, YOU SEE. SOON AFTER, THE VASSALS TOOK ME IN, GAVE ME A NEW LIFE.
SO TELL ME AGAIN I DON'T KNOW WHAT IT'S LIKE TO LIVE MY WHOLE LIFE WITH HIM IN MY MIND EVERY DAY. GO AHEAD, BENEDICT.
NOW MAYBE YOU'RE RIGHT ABOUT THE SOVIETS.
MAYBE HE IS SAFELY IN THE THEIR POSSESSION, ON HIS WAY TO MOSCOW, WHERE HE'LL BE FOREVER IMPRISONED AND HARMLESS TO YOU.
I HOPE YOU ARE.
AND ALL I'M ASKING YOU TO DO IS BE SURE. FOLLOW THE TRAIN CARRYING HIS BODY. SEE IF ALL IS GOING TO PLAN. IF HE'S TUCKED AWAY, YOU CAN TAKE ME TO THE COUNCIL AND I'LL GO HAPPILY. BUT DON'T YOU OWE IT TO YOURSELVES TO BE SURE?
HE IS RIGHT.
WE NEED TO BE SURE, BENEDICT.
GODDAM IT...
BRUN, TURN US SOUTH.

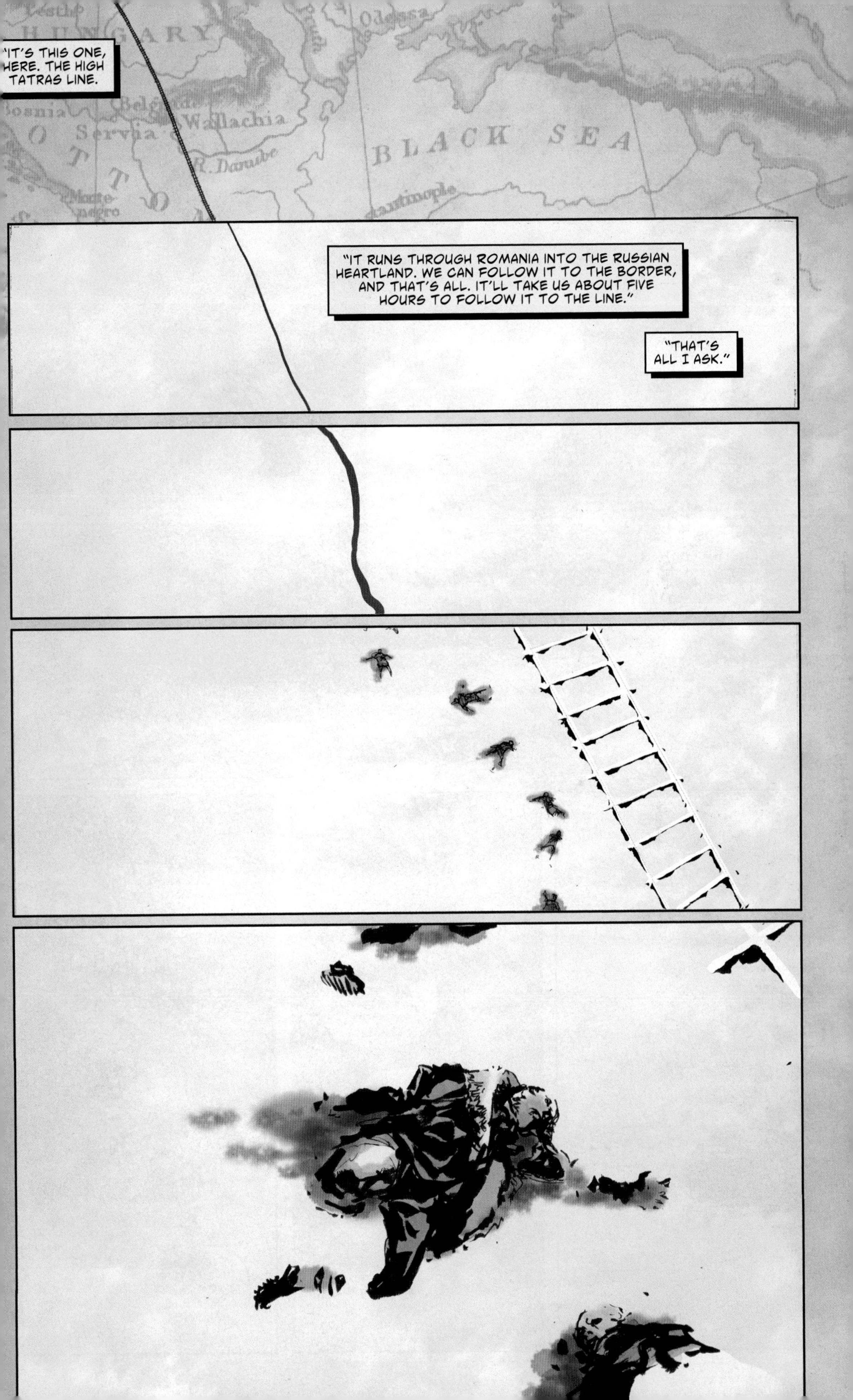

"IT'S THIS ONE, HERE. THE HIGH TATRAS LINE.
HUNGARY
Odessa
Belgrade
Wallachia
Servia
BLACK SEA
R. Danube
Monte-negro
"IT RUNS THROUGH ROMANIA INTO THE RUSSIAN HEARTLAND. WE CAN FOLLOW IT TO THE BORDER, AND THAT'S ALL. IT'LL TAKE US ABOUT FIVE HOURS TO FOLLOW IT TO THE LINE."
"THAT'S ALL I ASK."

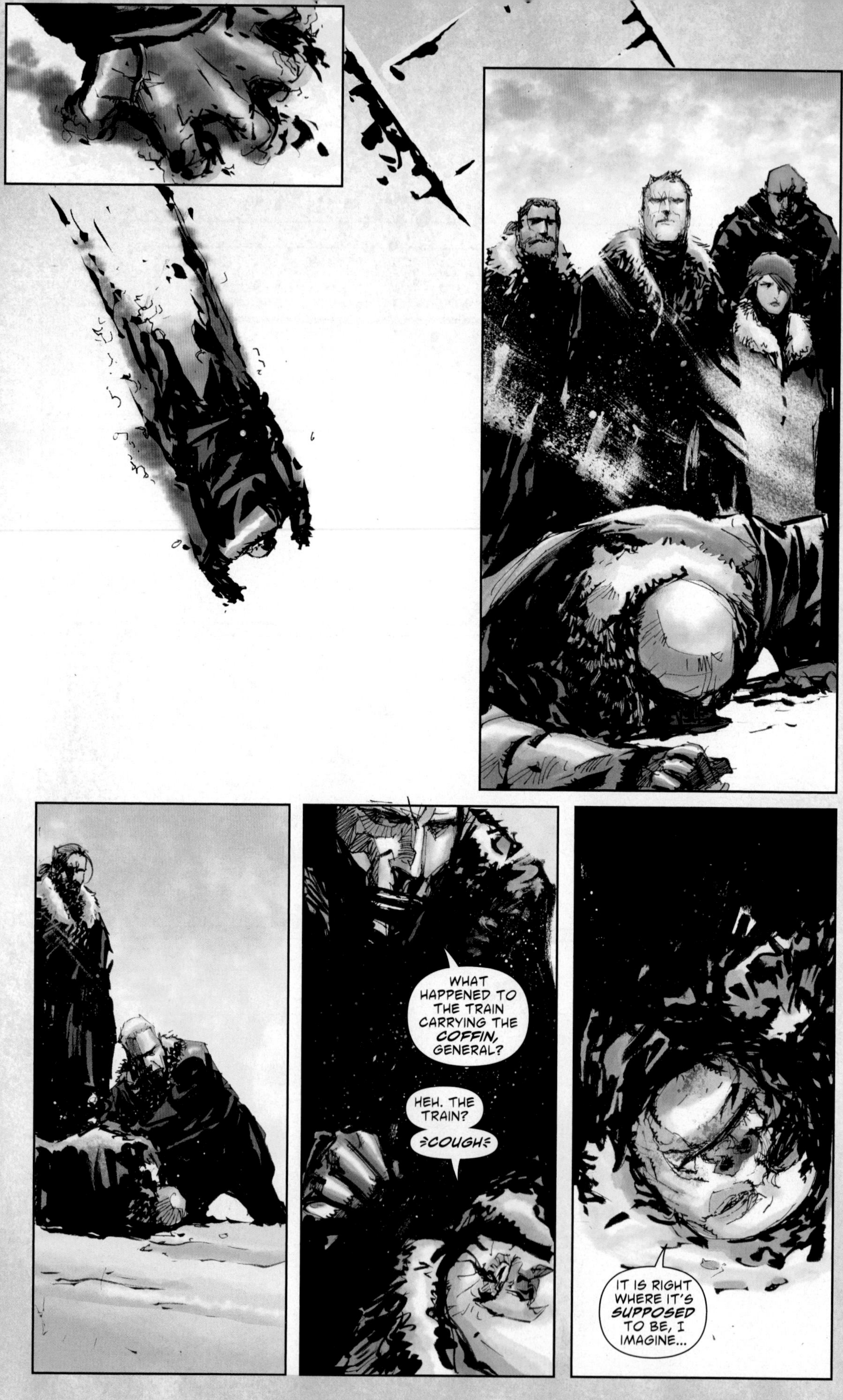
WHAT HAPPENED TO THE TRAIN CARRYING THE COFFIN, GENERAL?
HEH. THE TRAIN?
COUGH
IT IS RIGHT WHERE IT'S SUPPOSED TO BE, I IMAGINE...

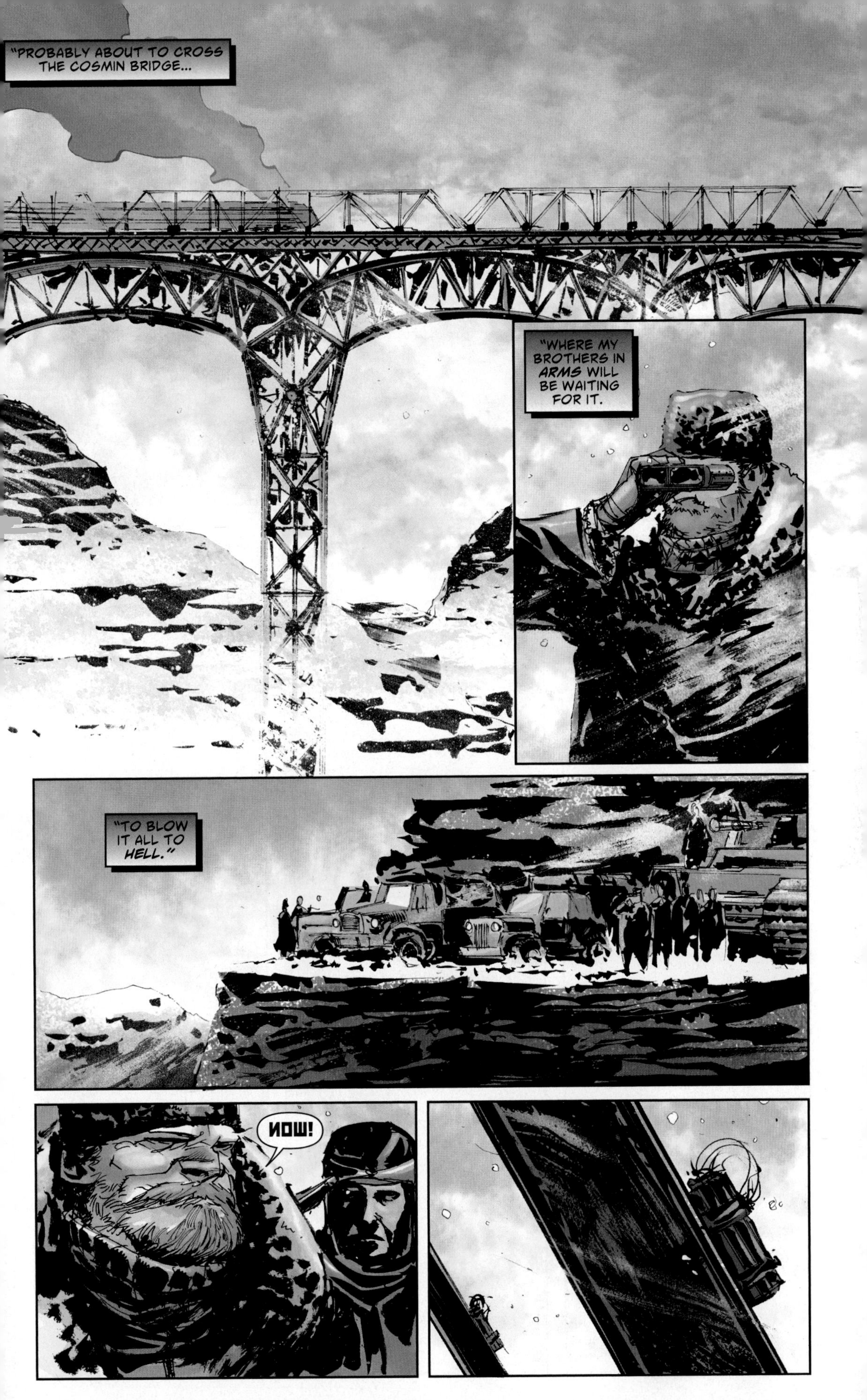
"PROBABLY ABOUT TO CROSS THE COSMIN BRIDGE...
"WHERE MY BROTHERS IN ARMS WILL BE WAITING FOR IT.
"TO BLOW IT ALL TO HELL."
NOW!

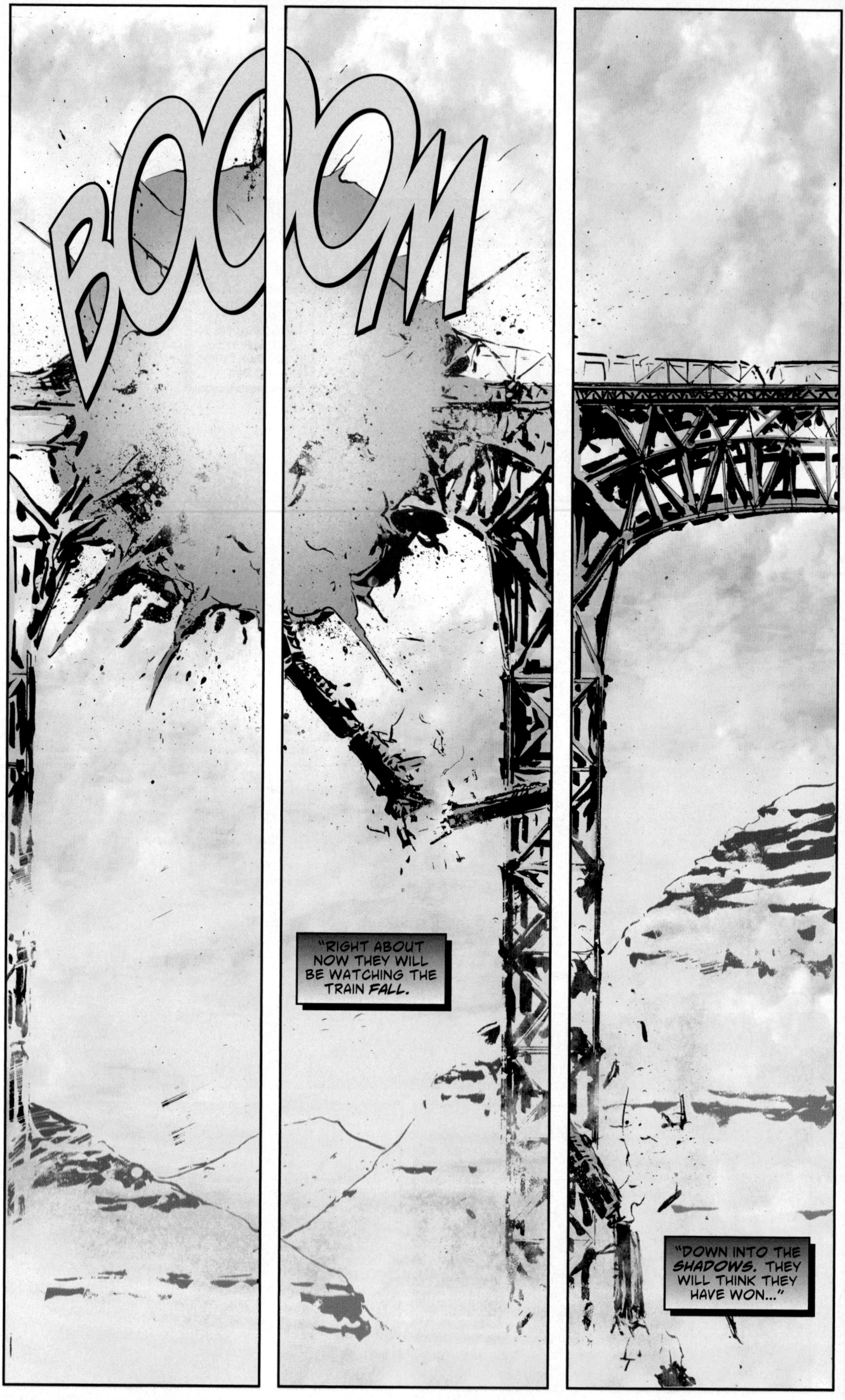
BOOOM
"RIGHT ABOUT NOW THEY WILL BE WATCHING THE TRAIN FALL.
"DOWN INTO THE SHADOWS. THEY WILL THINK THEY HAVE WON..."

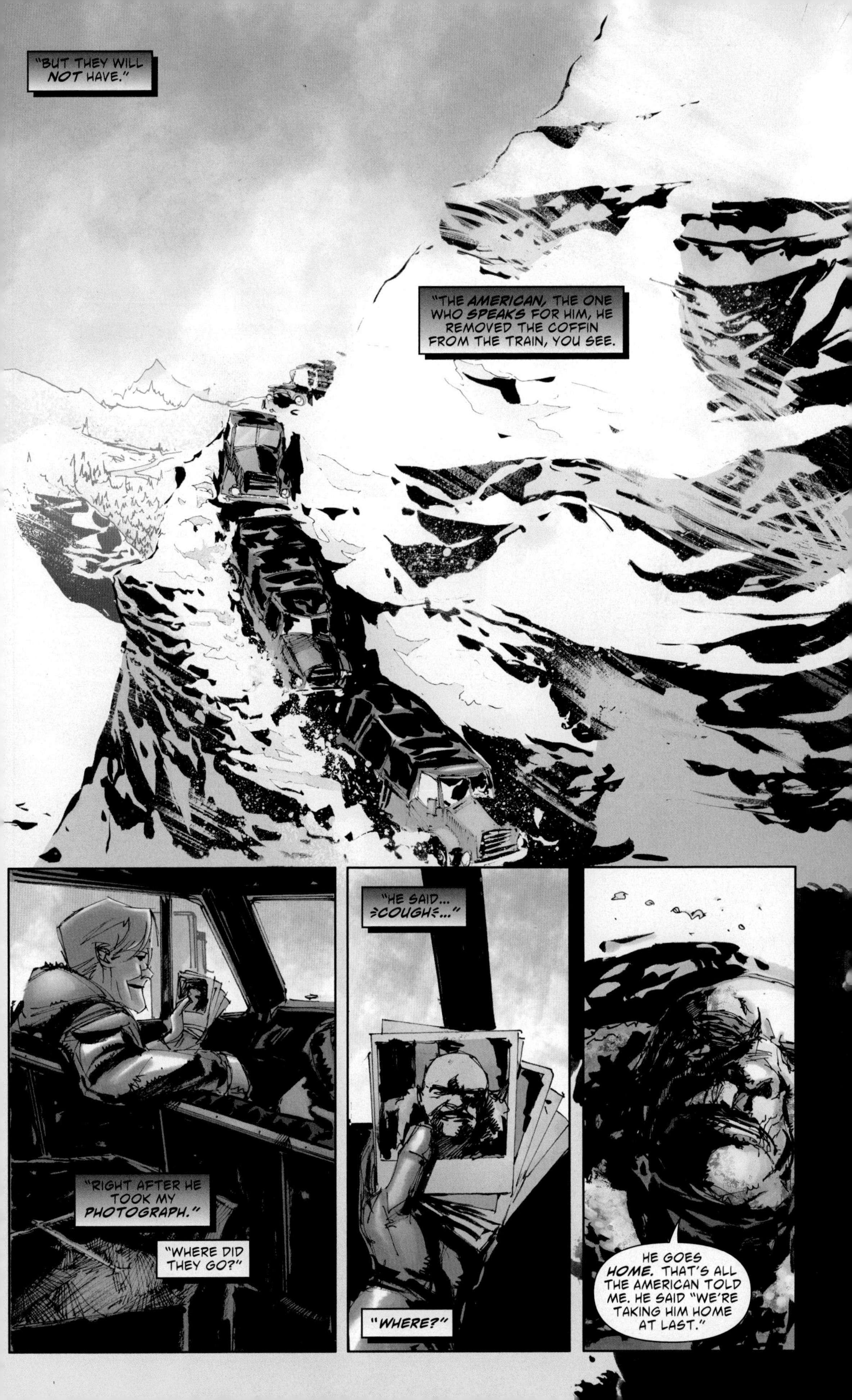
"BUT THEY WILL NOT HAVE."
"THE AMERICAN, THE ONE WHO SPEAKS FOR HIM, HE REMOVED THE COFFIN FROM THE TRAIN, YOU SEE.
"RIGHT AFTER HE TOOK MY PHOTOGRAPH."
"WHERE DID THEY GO?"
"HE SAID... <COUGH>..."
"WHERE?"
HE GOES HOME. THAT'S ALL THE AMERICAN TOLD ME. HE SAID "WE'RE TAKING HIM HOME AT LAST."

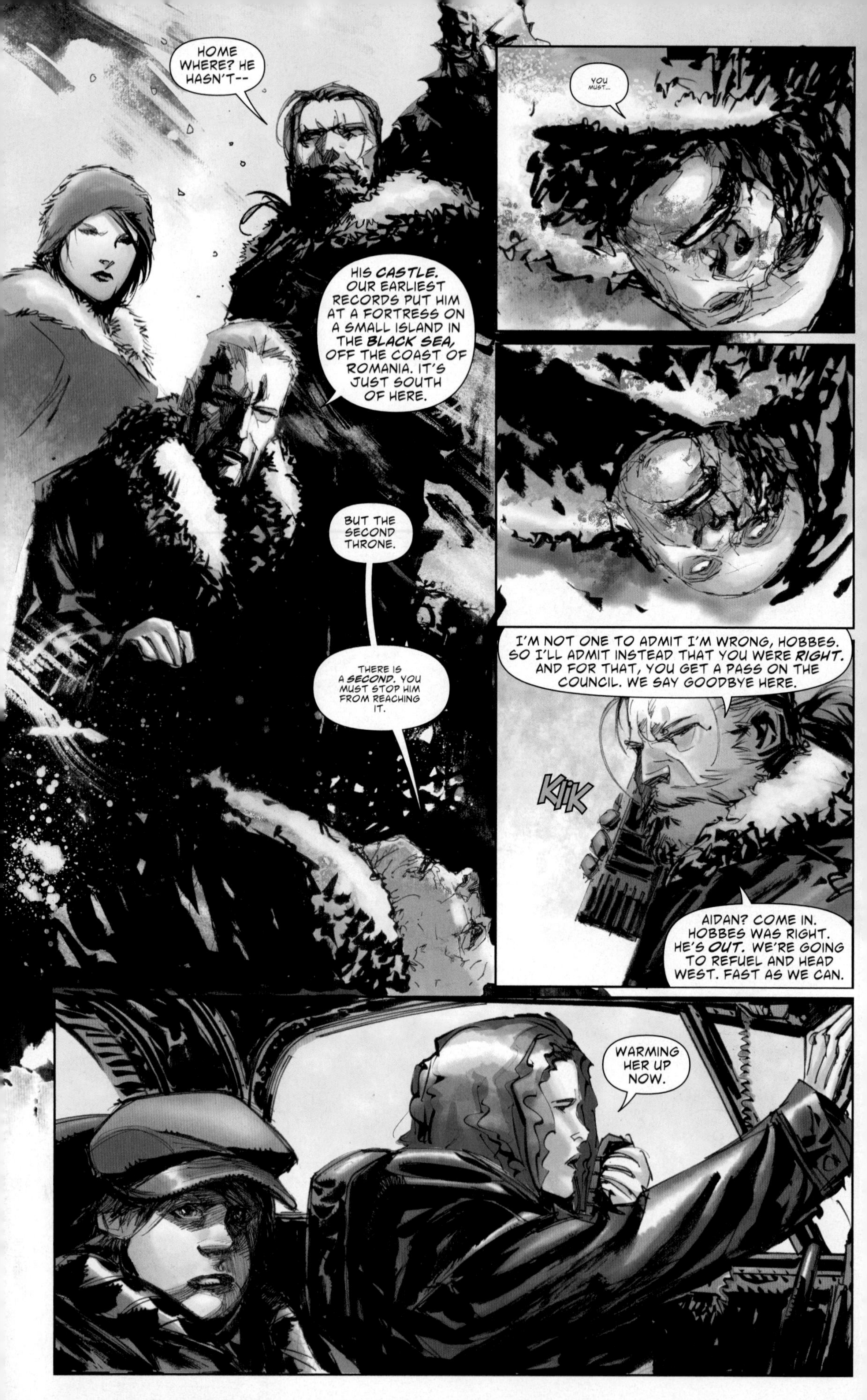

HOME WHERE? HE HASN'T--
HIS CASTLE. OUR EARLIEST RECORDS PUT HIM AT A FORTRESS ON A SMALL ISLAND IN THE BLACK SEA, OFF THE COAST OF ROMANIA. IT'S JUST SOUTH OF HERE.
BUT THE SECOND THRONE.
THERE IS A SECOND. YOU MUST STOP HIM FROM REACHING IT.
YOU MUST...
I'M NOT ONE TO ADMIT I'M WRONG, HOBBES. SO I'LL ADMIT INSTEAD THAT YOU WERE RIGHT. AND FOR THAT, YOU GET A PASS ON THE COUNCIL. WE SAY GOODBYE HERE.
KLIK
AIDAN? COME IN. HOBBES WAS RIGHT. HE'S OUT. WE'RE GOING TO REFUEL AND HEAD WEST. FAST AS WE CAN.
WARMING HER UP NOW.

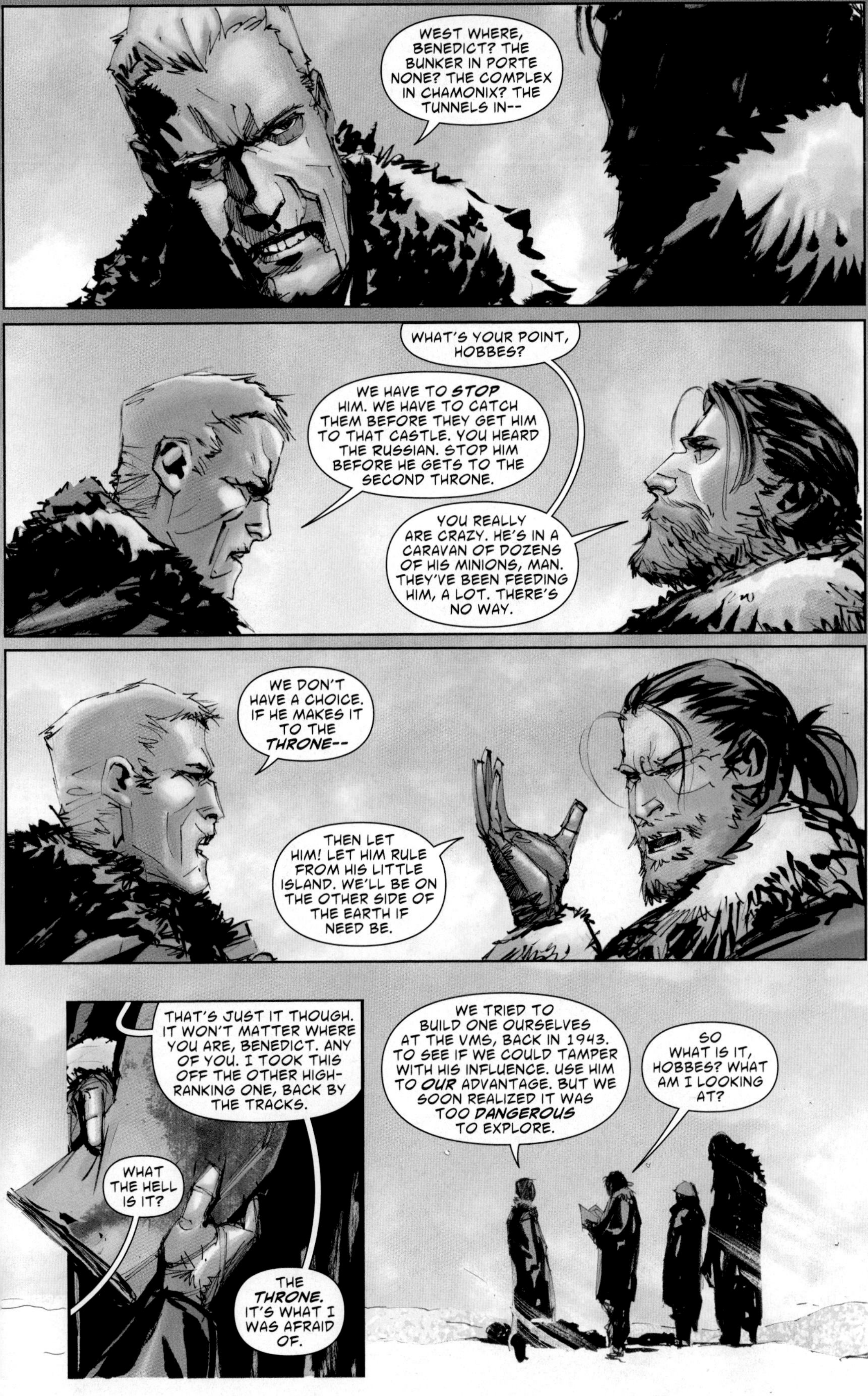
WEST WHERE, BENEDICT? THE BUNKER IN PORTE NONE? THE COMPLEX IN CHAMONIX? THE TUNNELS IN--
WHAT'S YOUR POINT, HOBBES?
WE HAVE TO STOP HIM. WE HAVE TO CATCH THEM BEFORE THEY GET HIM TO THAT CASTLE. YOU HEARD THE RUSSIAN. STOP HIM BEFORE HE GETS TO THE SECOND THRONE.
YOU REALLY ARE CRAZY. HE'S IN A CARAVAN OF DOZENS OF HIS MINIONS, MAN. THEY'VE BEEN FEEDING HIM, A LOT. THERE'S NO WAY.
WE DON'T HAVE A CHOICE. IF HE MAKES IT TO THE THRONE--
THEN LET HIM! LET HIM RULE FROM HIS LITTLE ISLAND. WE'LL BE ON THE OTHER SIDE OF THE EARTH IF NEED BE.
THAT'S JUST IT THOUGH. IT WON'T MATTER WHERE YOU ARE, BENEDICT. ANY OF YOU. I TOOK THIS OFF THE OTHER HIGH-RANKING ONE, BACK BY THE TRACKS.
WHAT THE HELL IS IT?
THE THRONE. IT'S WHAT I WAS AFRAID OF.
WE TRIED TO BUILD ONE OURSELVES AT THE VMS, BACK IN 1943. TO SEE IF WE COULD TAMPER WITH HIS INFLUENCE. USE HIM TO OUR ADVANTAGE. BUT WE SOON REALIZED IT WAS TOO DANGEROUS TO EXPLORE.
SO WHAT IS IT, HOBBES? WHAT AM I LOOKING AT?

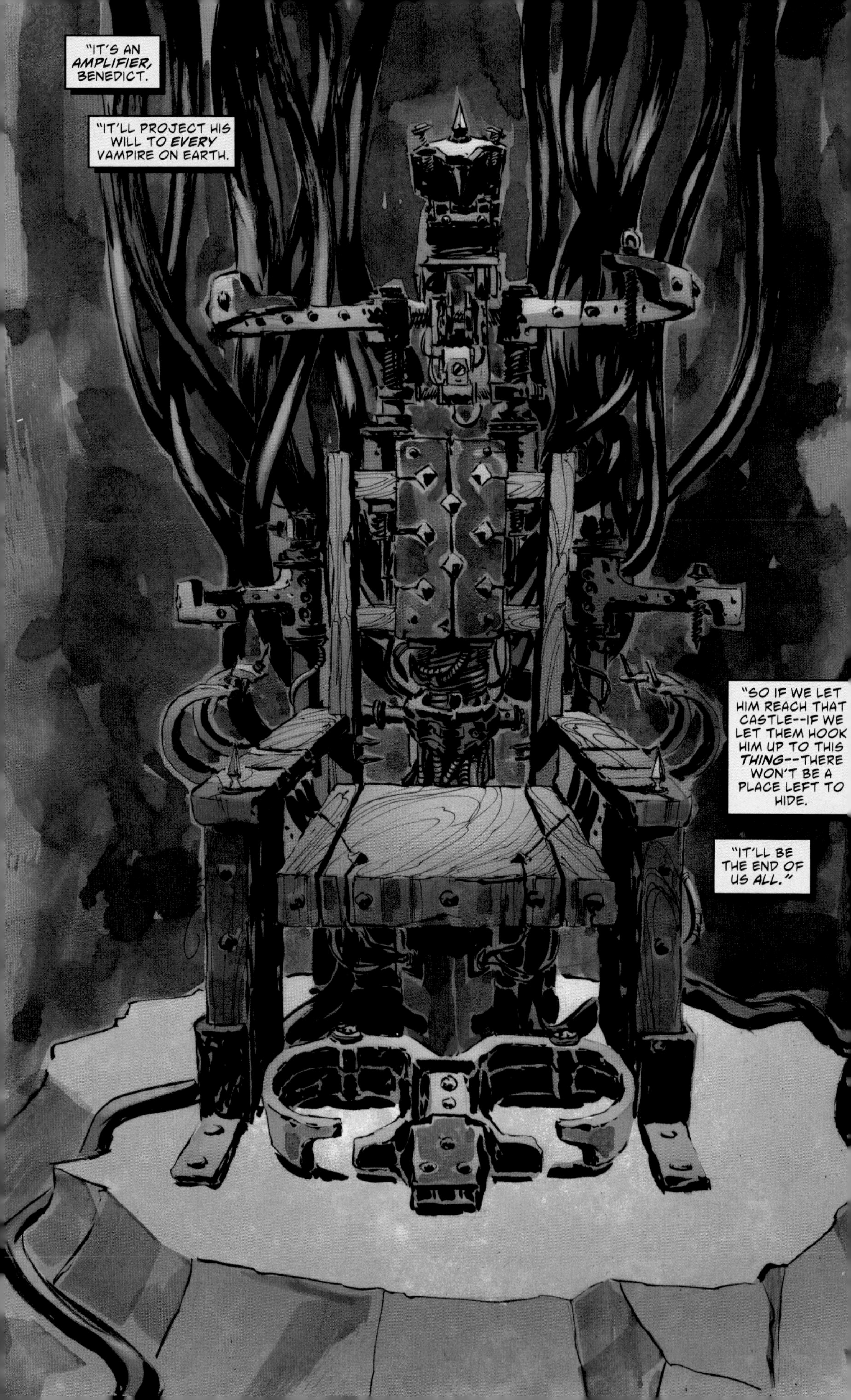
"IT'S AN *AMPLIFIER,* BENEDICT.
"IT'LL PROJECT HIS WILL TO *EVERY* VAMPIRE ON EARTH.
"SO IF WE LET HIM REACH THAT CASTLE--IF WE LET THEM HOOK HIM UP TO THIS *THING*--THERE WON'T BE A PLACE LEFT TO HIDE.
"IT'LL BE THE END OF US *ALL*."

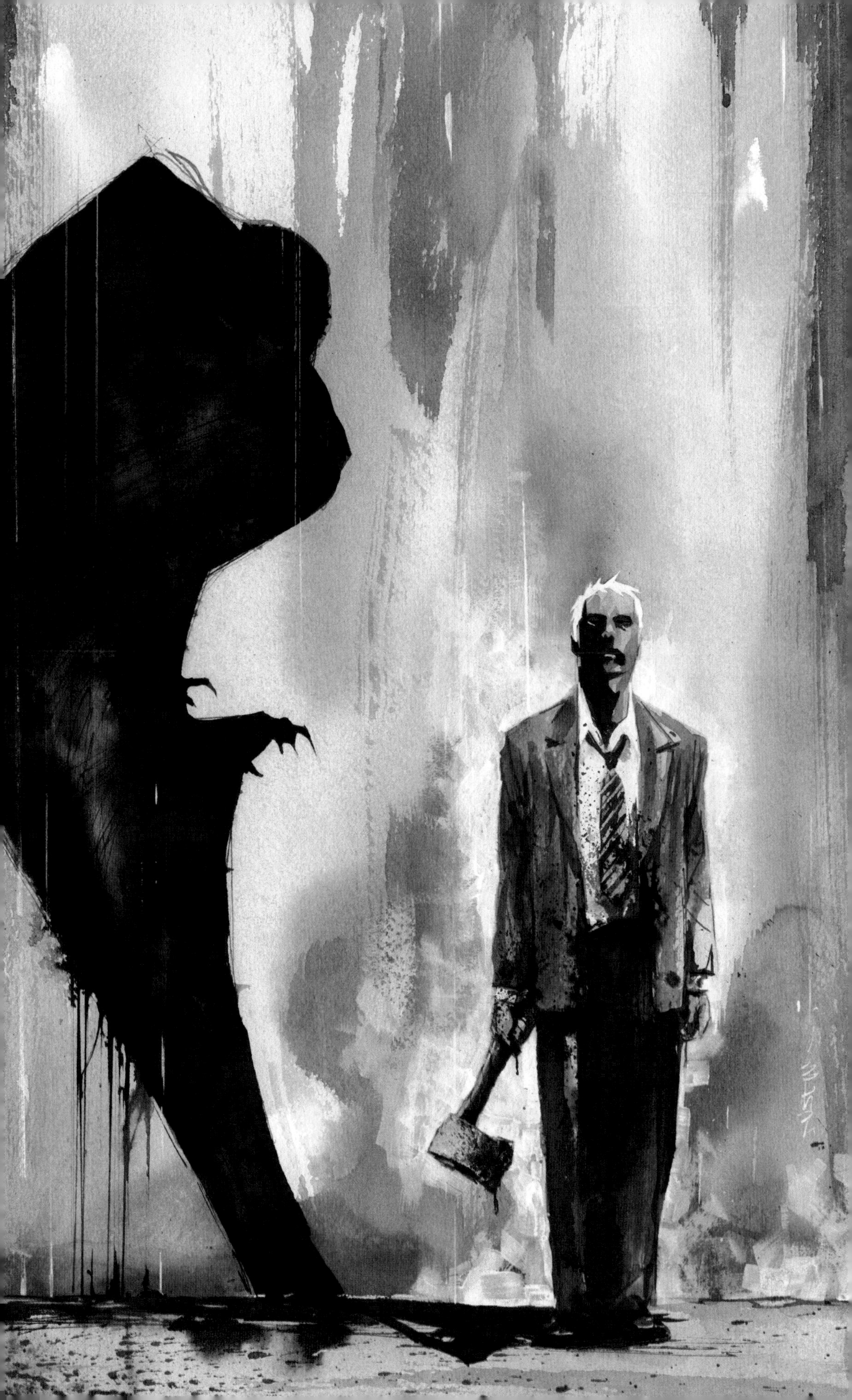

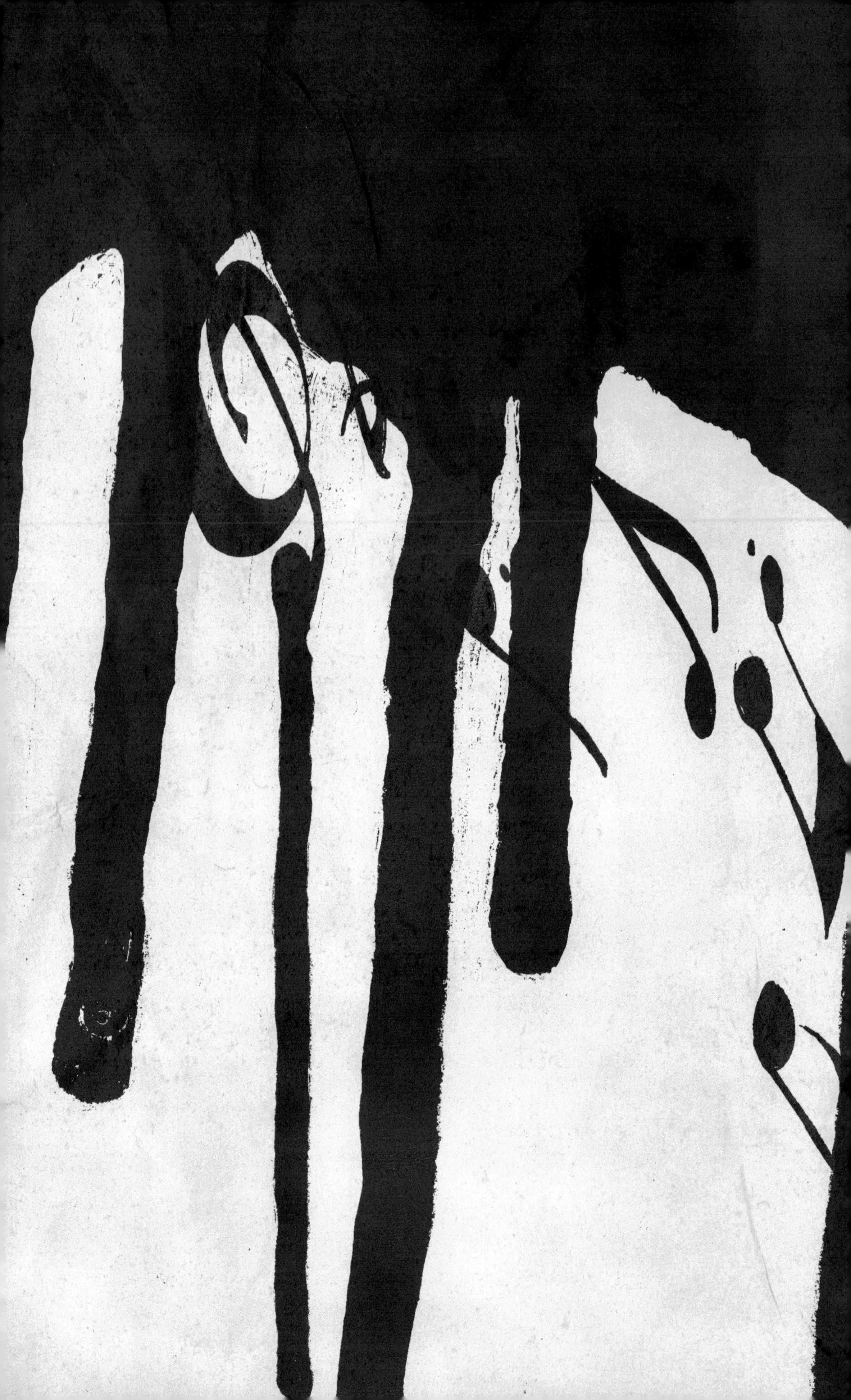

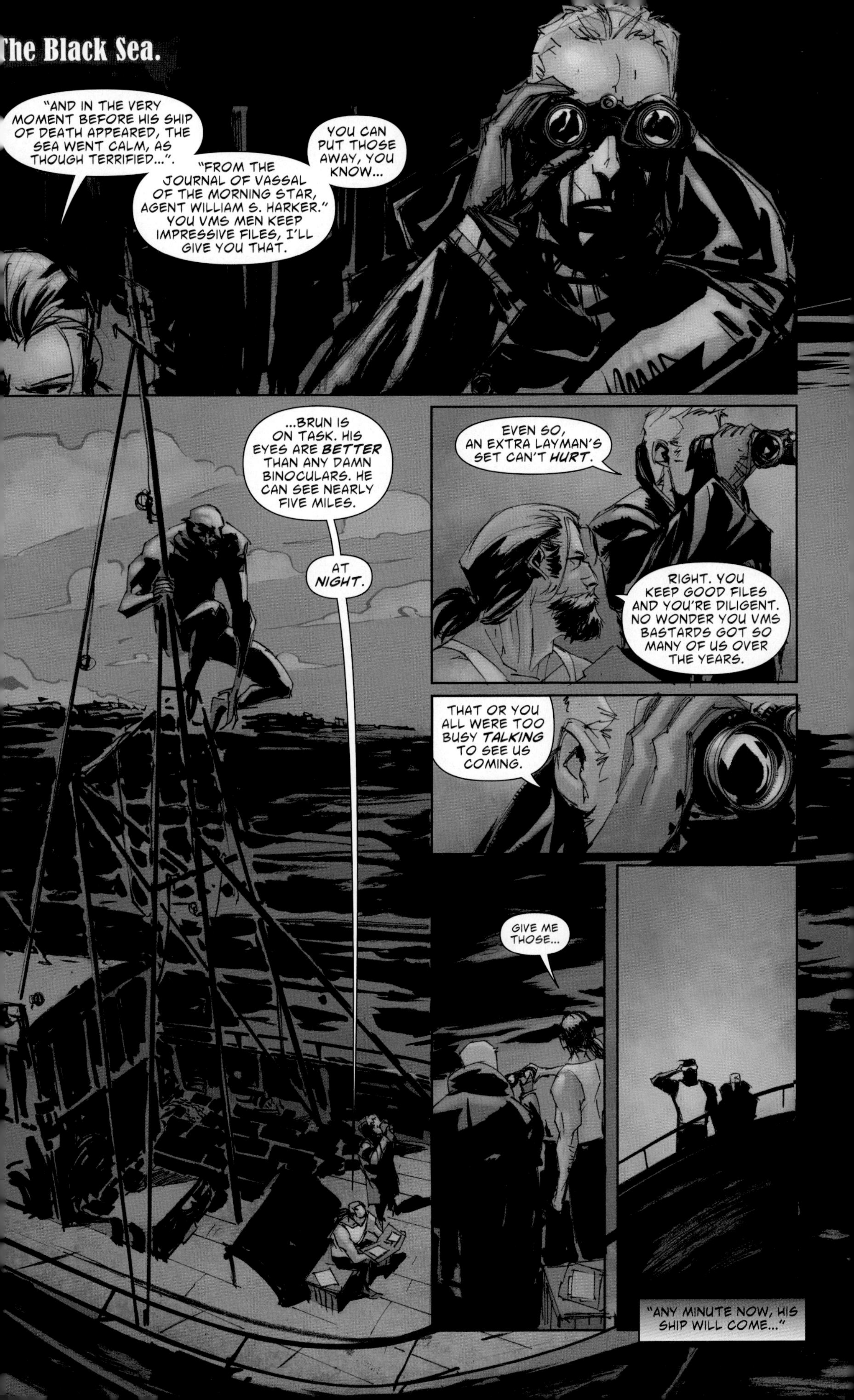
The Black Sea.
"AND IN THE VERY MOMENT BEFORE HIS SHIP OF DEATH APPEARED, THE SEA WENT CALM, AS THOUGH TERRIFIED...".
"FROM THE JOURNAL OF VASSAL OF THE MORNING STAR, AGENT WILLIAM S. HARKER." YOU VMS MEN KEEP IMPRESSIVE FILES, I'LL GIVE YOU THAT.
YOU CAN PUT THOSE AWAY, YOU KNOW...
...BRUN IS ON TASK. HIS EYES ARE BETTER THAN ANY DAMN BINOCULARS. HE CAN SEE NEARLY FIVE MILES.
AT NIGHT.
EVEN SO, AN EXTRA LAYMAN'S SET CAN'T HURT.
RIGHT. YOU KEEP GOOD FILES AND YOU'RE DILIGENT. NO WONDER YOU VMS BASTARDS GOT SO MANY OF US OVER THE YEARS.
THAT OR YOU ALL WERE TOO BUSY TALKING TO SEE US COMING.
GIVE ME THOSE...
"ANY MINUTE NOW, HIS SHIP WILL COME..."

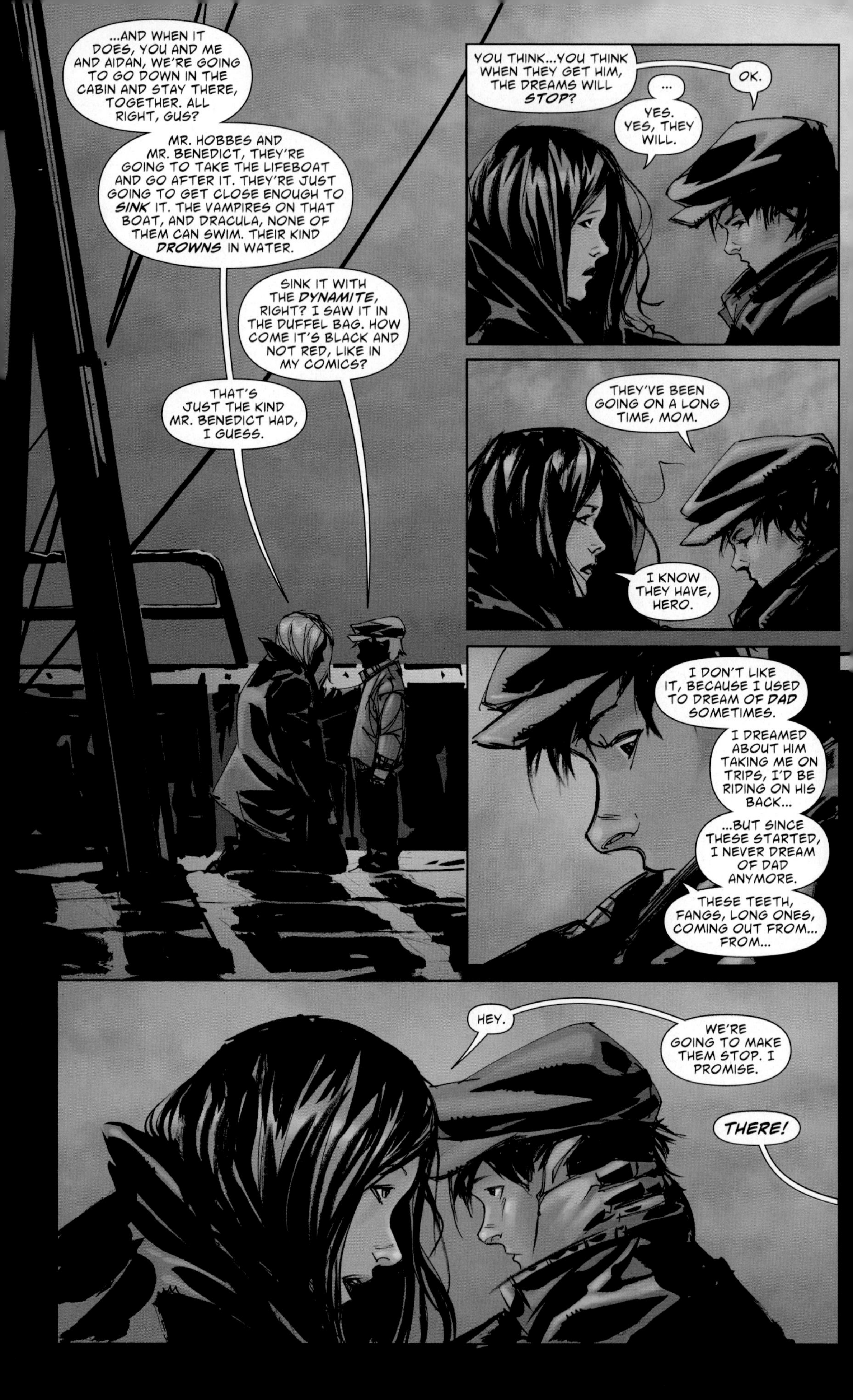
...AND WHEN IT DOES, YOU AND ME AND AIDAN, WE'RE GOING TO GO DOWN IN THE CABIN AND STAY THERE, TOGETHER. ALL RIGHT, GUS?
MR. HOBBES AND MR. BENEDICT, THEY'RE GOING TO TAKE THE LIFEBOAT AND GO AFTER IT. THEY'RE JUST GOING TO GET CLOSE ENOUGH TO *SINK* IT. THE VAMPIRES ON THAT BOAT, AND DRACULA, NONE OF THEM CAN SWIM. THEIR KIND *DROWNS* IN WATER.
SINK IT WITH THE *DYNAMITE*, RIGHT? I SAW IT IN THE DUFFEL BAG. HOW COME IT'S BLACK AND NOT RED, LIKE IN MY COMICS?
THAT'S JUST THE KIND MR. BENEDICT HAD, I GUESS.
YOU THINK...YOU THINK WHEN THEY GET HIM, THE DREAMS WILL *STOP*?
...
YES. YES, THEY WILL.
OK.
THEY'VE BEEN GOING ON A LONG TIME, MOM.
I KNOW THEY HAVE, HERO.
I DON'T LIKE IT, BECAUSE I USED TO DREAM OF *DAD* SOMETIMES.
I DREAMED ABOUT HIM TAKING ME ON TRIPS, I'D BE RIDING ON HIS BACK...
...BUT SINCE THESE STARTED, I NEVER DREAM OF DAD ANYMORE.
THESE TEETH, FANGS, LONG ONES, COMING OUT FROM... FROM...
HEY.
WE'RE GOING TO MAKE THEM STOP. I PROMISE.
THERE!

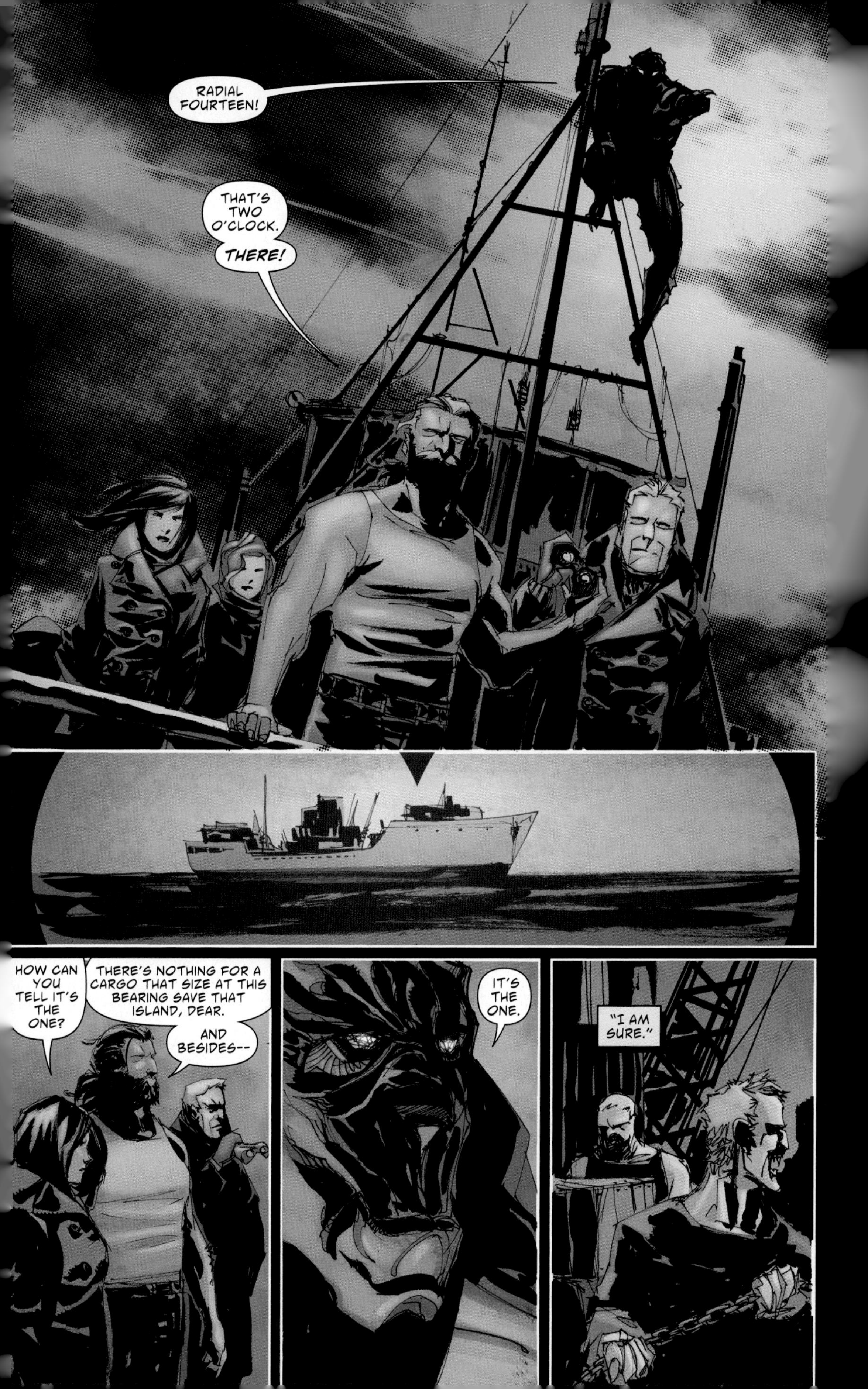
RADIAL FOURTEEN!
THAT'S TWO O'CLOCK. THERE!
HOW CAN YOU TELL IT'S THE ONE?
THERE'S NOTHING FOR A CARGO THAT SIZE AT THIS BEARING SAVE THAT ISLAND, DEAR.
AND BESIDES--
IT'S THE ONE.
"I AM SURE."

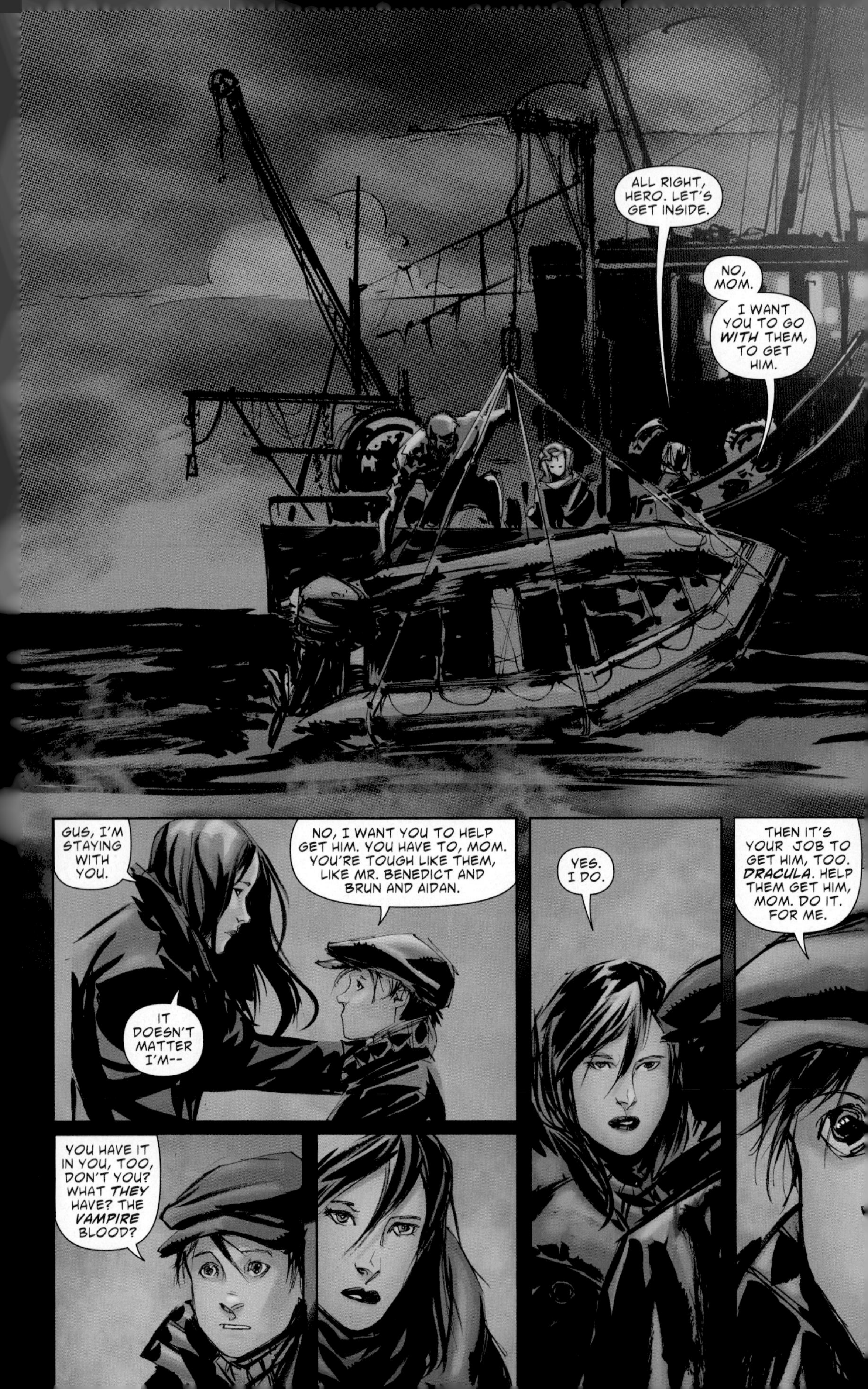
ALL RIGHT, HERO. LET'S GET INSIDE.
NO, MOM.
I WANT YOU TO GO WITH THEM, TO GET HIM.
GUS, I'M STAYING WITH YOU.
NO, I WANT YOU TO HELP GET HIM. YOU HAVE TO, MOM. YOU'RE TOUGH LIKE THEM, LIKE MR. BENEDICT AND BRUN AND AIDAN.
IT DOESN'T MATTER I'M--
YOU HAVE IT IN YOU, TOO, DON'T YOU? WHAT THEY HAVE? THE VAMPIRE BLOOD?
YES. I DO.
THEN IT'S YOUR JOB TO GET HIM, TOO. DRACULA. HELP THEM GET HIM, MOM. DO IT. FOR ME.

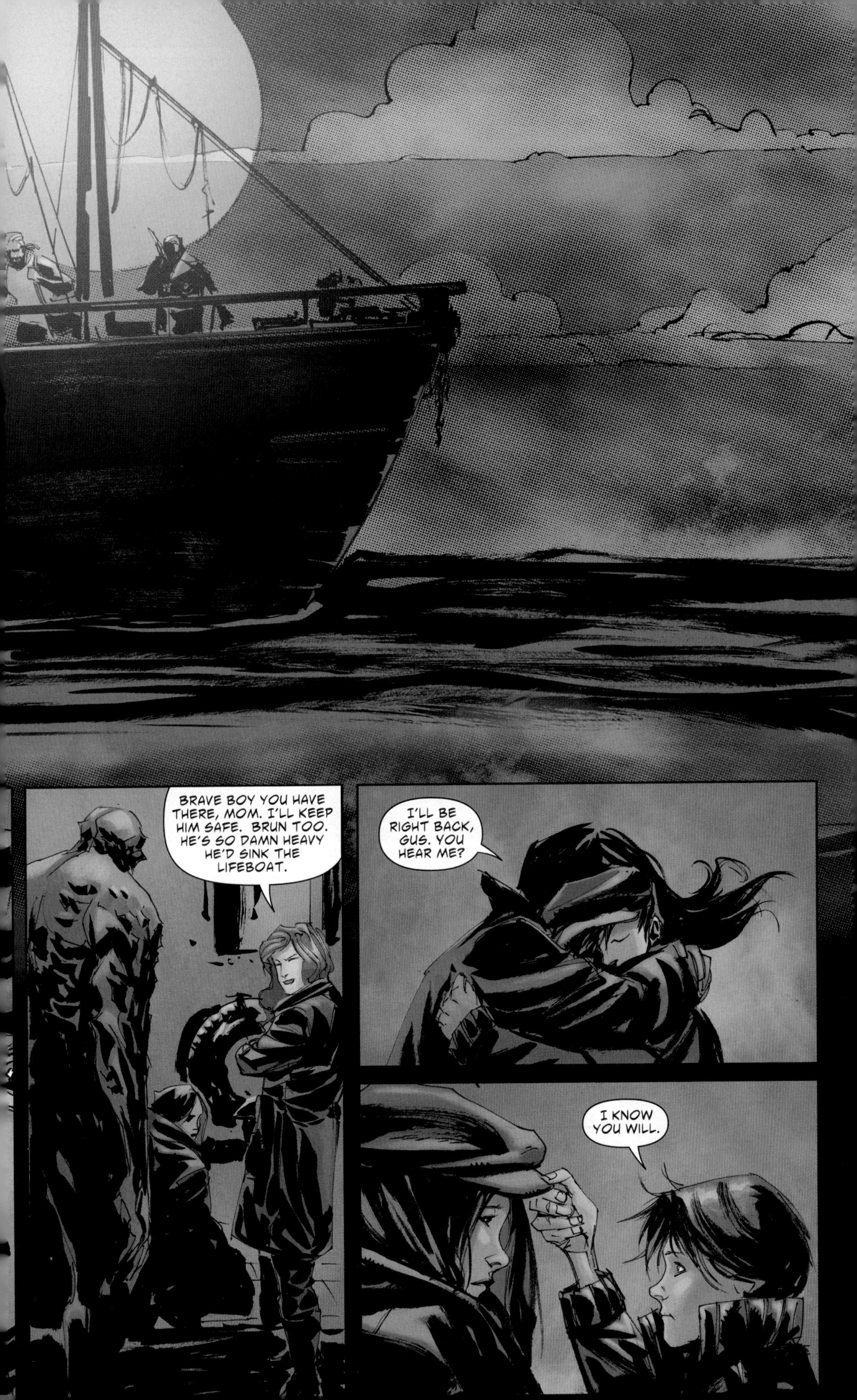
BRAVE BOY YOU HAVE THERE, MOM. I'LL KEEP HIM SAFE. BRUN TOO. HE'S SO DAMN HEAVY HE'D SINK THE LIFEBOAT.
I'LL BE RIGHT BACK, GUS. YOU HEAR ME?
I KNOW YOU WILL.

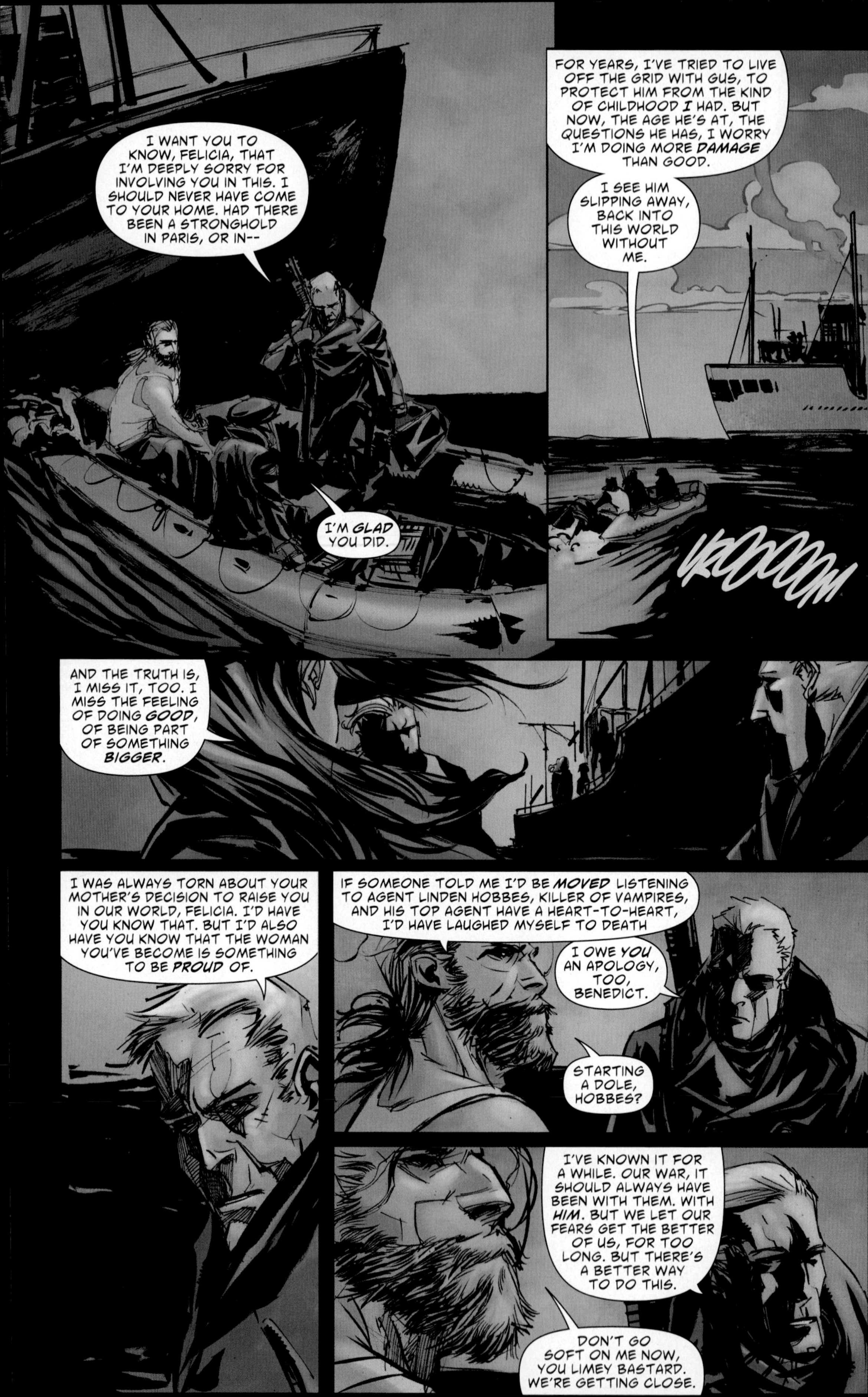
I WANT YOU TO KNOW, FELICIA, THAT I'M DEEPLY SORRY FOR INVOLVING YOU IN THIS. I SHOULD NEVER HAVE COME TO YOUR HOME. HAD THERE BEEN A STRONGHOLD IN PARIS, OR IN--
I'M GLAD YOU DID.
FOR YEARS, I'VE TRIED TO LIVE OFF THE GRID WITH GUS, TO PROTECT HIM FROM THE KIND OF CHILDHOOD I HAD. BUT NOW, THE AGE HE'S AT, THE QUESTIONS HE HAS, I WORRY I'M DOING MORE DAMAGE THAN GOOD.
I SEE HIM SLIPPING AWAY, BACK INTO THIS WORLD WITHOUT ME.
VROOOOM
AND THE TRUTH IS, I MISS IT, TOO. I MISS THE FEELING OF DOING GOOD, OF BEING PART OF SOMETHING BIGGER.
I WAS ALWAYS TORN ABOUT YOUR MOTHER'S DECISION TO RAISE YOU IN OUR WORLD, FELICIA. I'D HAVE YOU KNOW THAT. BUT I'D ALSO HAVE YOU KNOW THAT THE WOMAN YOU'VE BECOME IS SOMETHING TO BE PROUD OF.
IF SOMEONE TOLD ME I'D BE MOVED LISTENING TO AGENT LINDEN HOBBES, KILLER OF VAMPIRES, AND HIS TOP AGENT HAVE A HEART-TO-HEART, I'D HAVE LAUGHED MYSELF TO DEATH
I OWE YOU AN APOLOGY, TOO, BENEDICT.
STARTING A DOLE, HOBBES?
I'VE KNOWN IT FOR A WHILE. OUR WAR, IT SHOULD ALWAYS HAVE BEEN WITH THEM. WITH HIM. BUT WE LET OUR FEARS GET THE BETTER OF US, FOR TOO LONG. BUT THERE'S A BETTER WAY TO DO THIS.
DON'T GO SOFT ON ME NOW, YOU LIMEY BASTARD. WE'RE GETTING CLOSE.

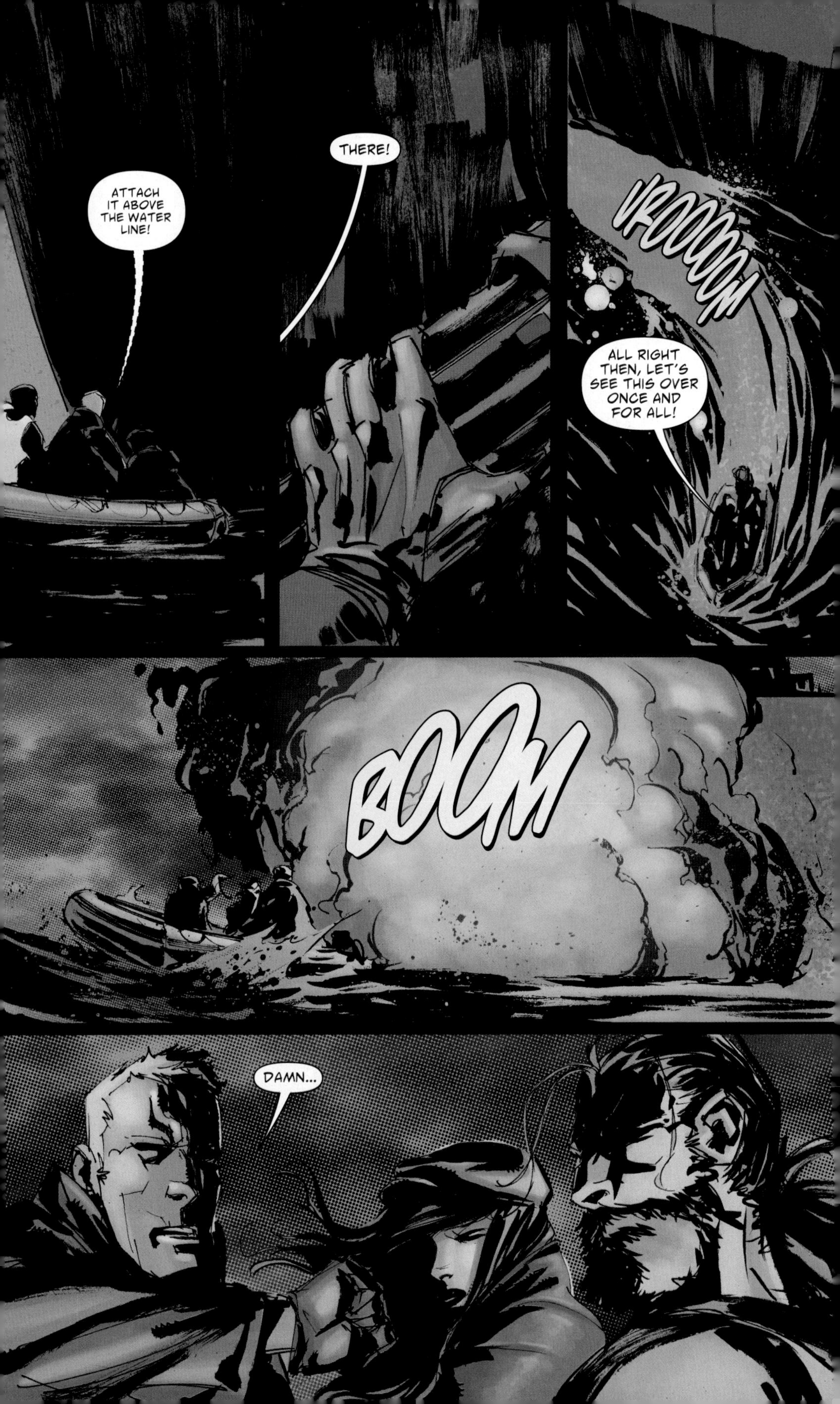
ATTACH IT ABOVE THE WATER LINE!
THERE!
VROOOOOM
ALL RIGHT THEN, LET'S SEE THIS OVER ONCE AND FOR ALL!
BOOM
DAMN...

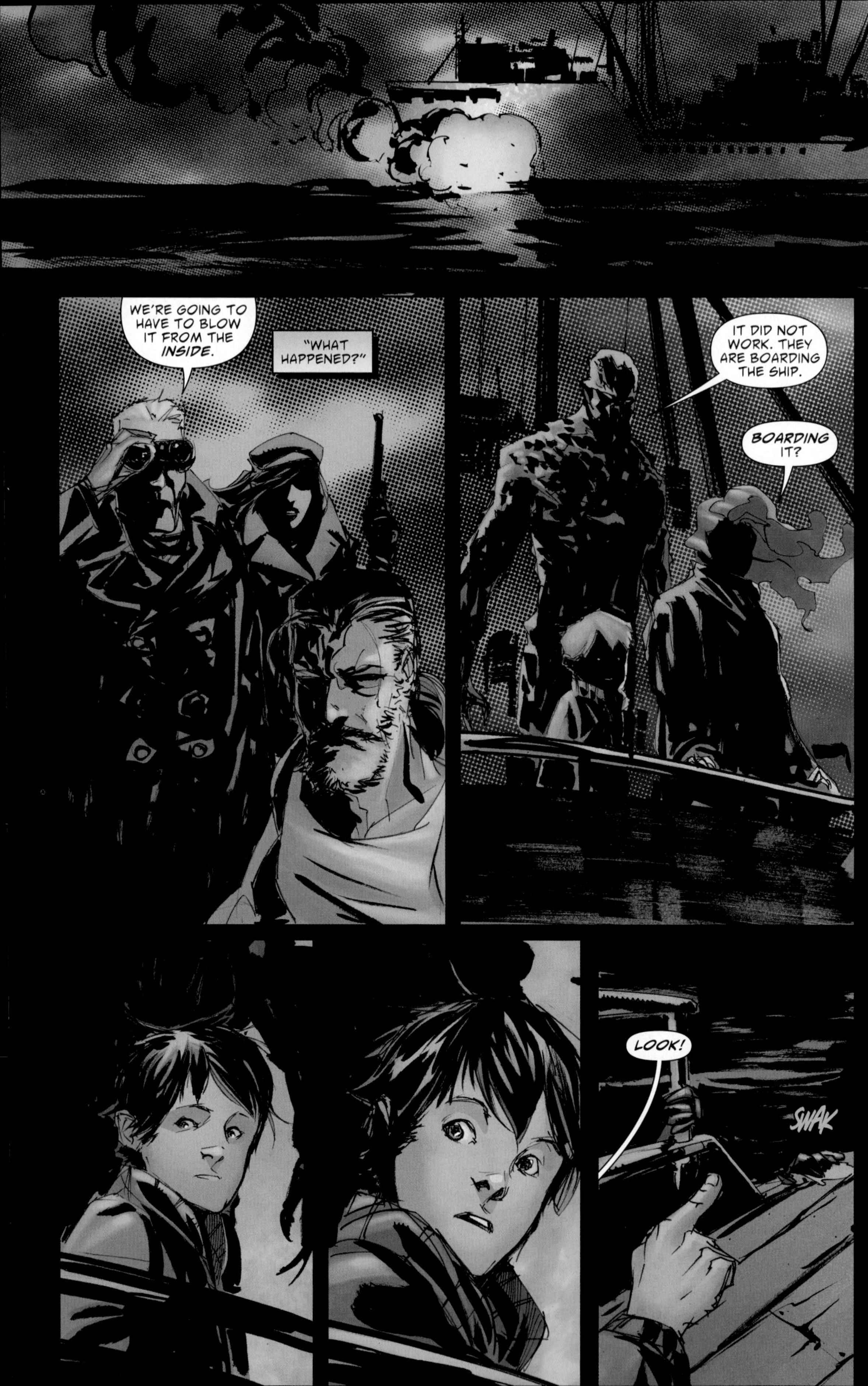
WE'RE GOING TO HAVE TO BLOW IT FROM THE INSIDE.
"WHAT HAPPENED?"
IT DID NOT WORK. THEY ARE BOARDING THE SHIP.
BOARDING IT?
LOOK!
SWAK

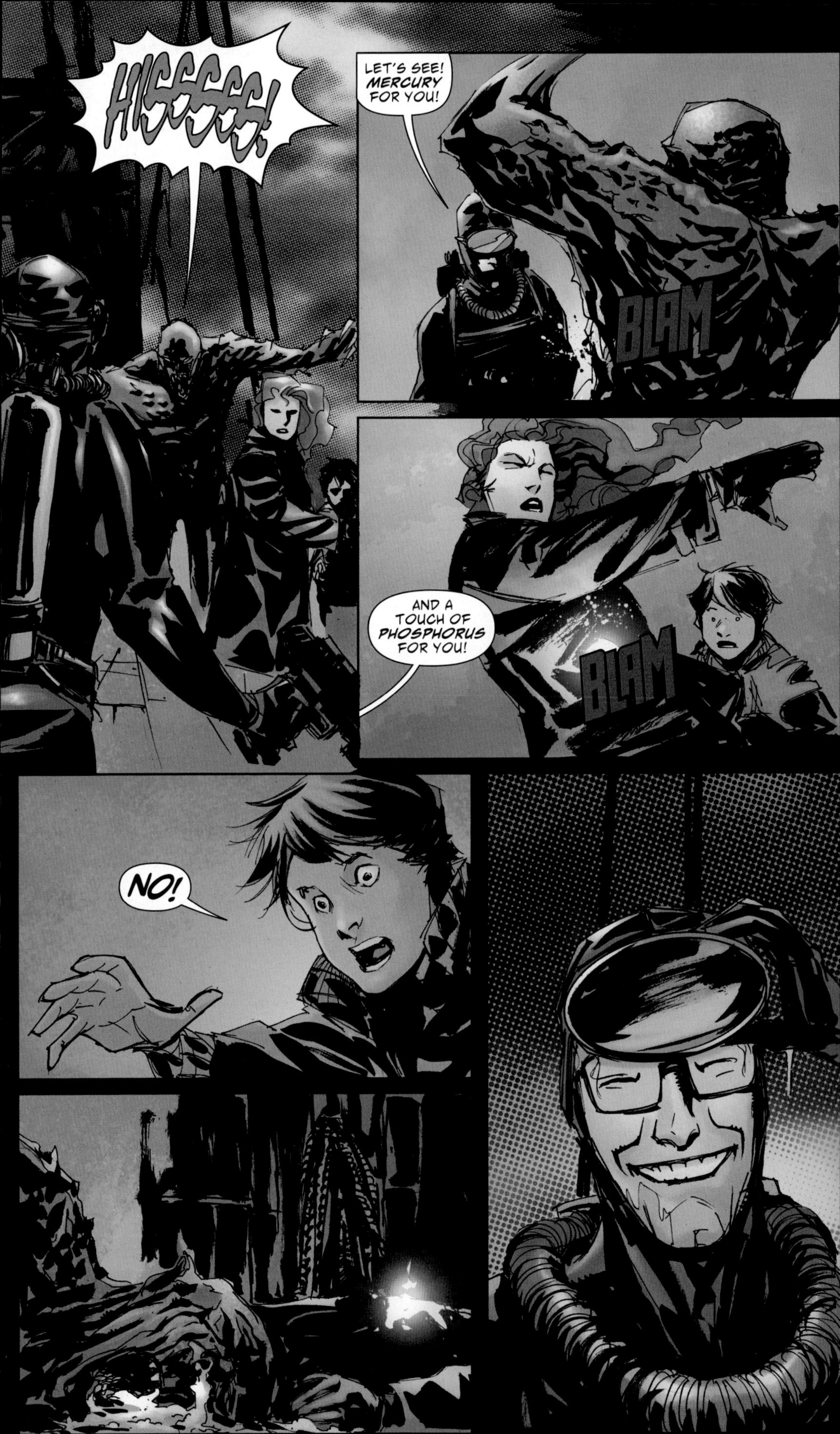
HISSSSSS!
LET'S SEE! MERCURY FOR YOU!
BLAM
AND A TOUCH OF PHOSPHORUS FOR YOU!
BLAM
NO!

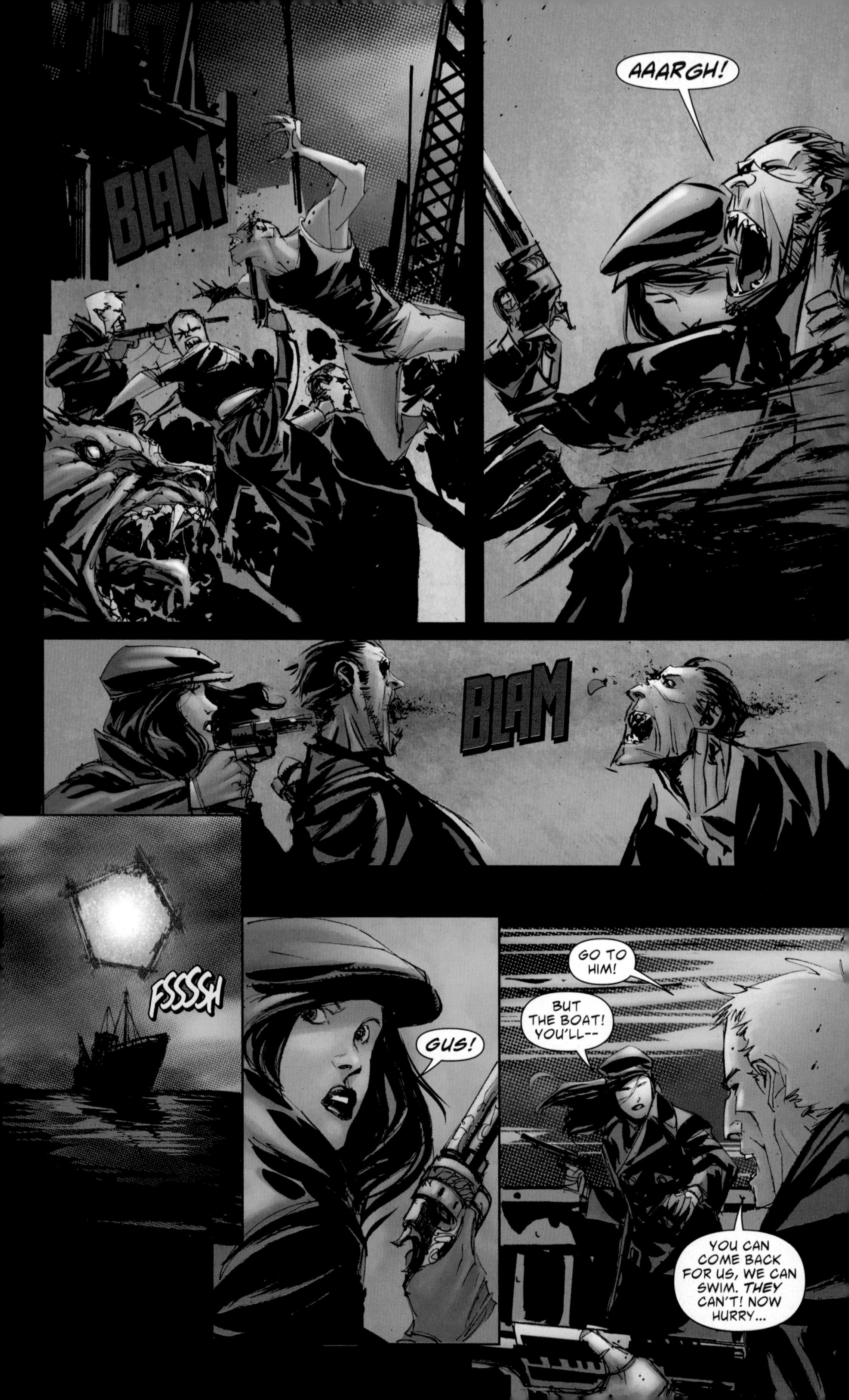
BLAM
AAARGH!
BLAM
FSSSSH
GUS!
GO TO HIM!
BUT THE BOAT! YOU'LL--
YOU CAN COME BACK FOR US, WE CAN SWIM. THEY CAN'T! NOW HURRY...

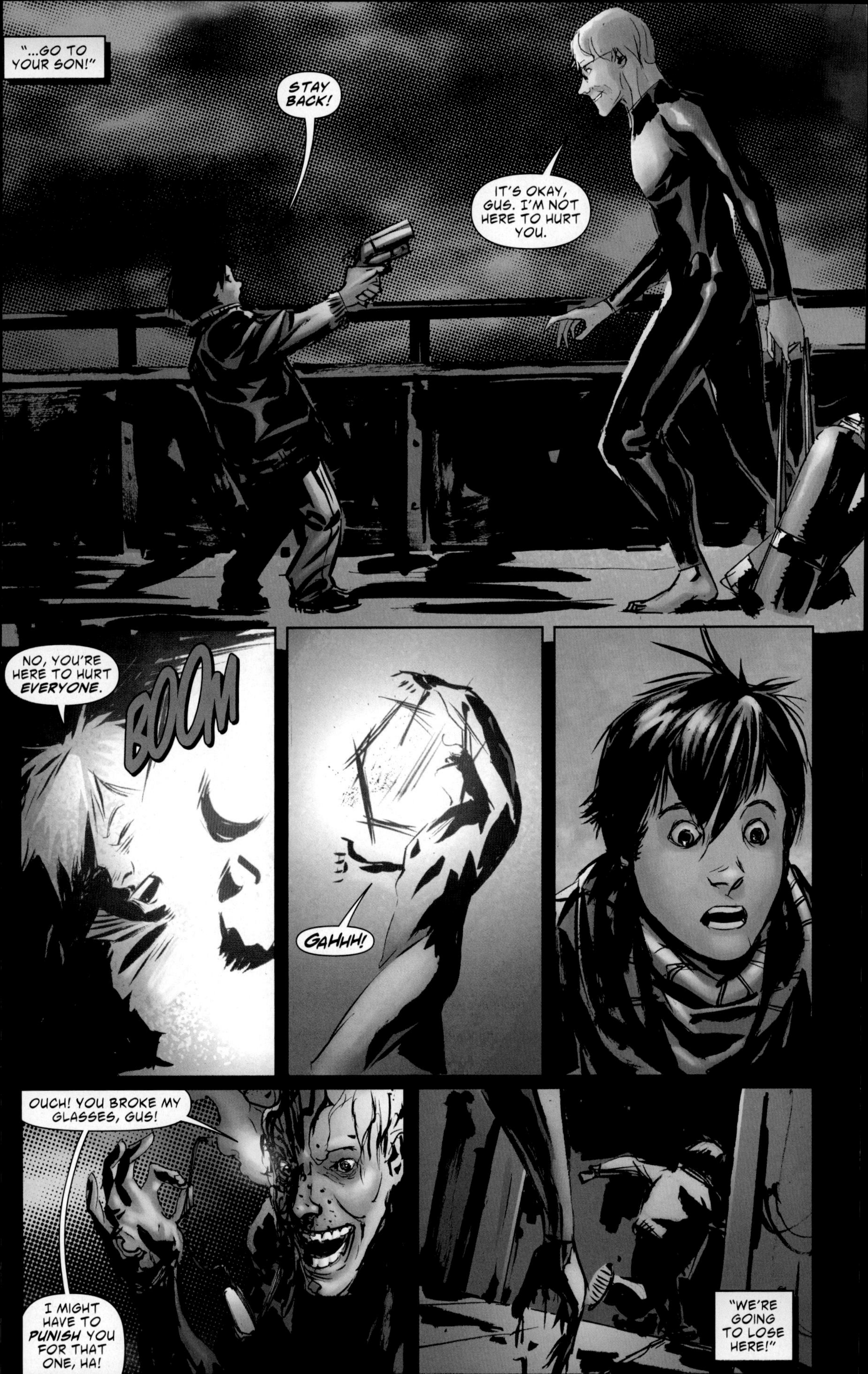
"...GO TO YOUR SON!"
STAY BACK!
IT'S OKAY, GUS. I'M NOT HERE TO HURT YOU.
NO, YOU'RE HERE TO HURT *EVERYONE*.
BOOM
GAHHH!
OUCH! YOU BROKE MY GLASSES, GUS!
I MIGHT HAVE TO *PUNISH* YOU FOR THAT ONE, HA!
"WE'RE GOING TO LOSE HERE!"

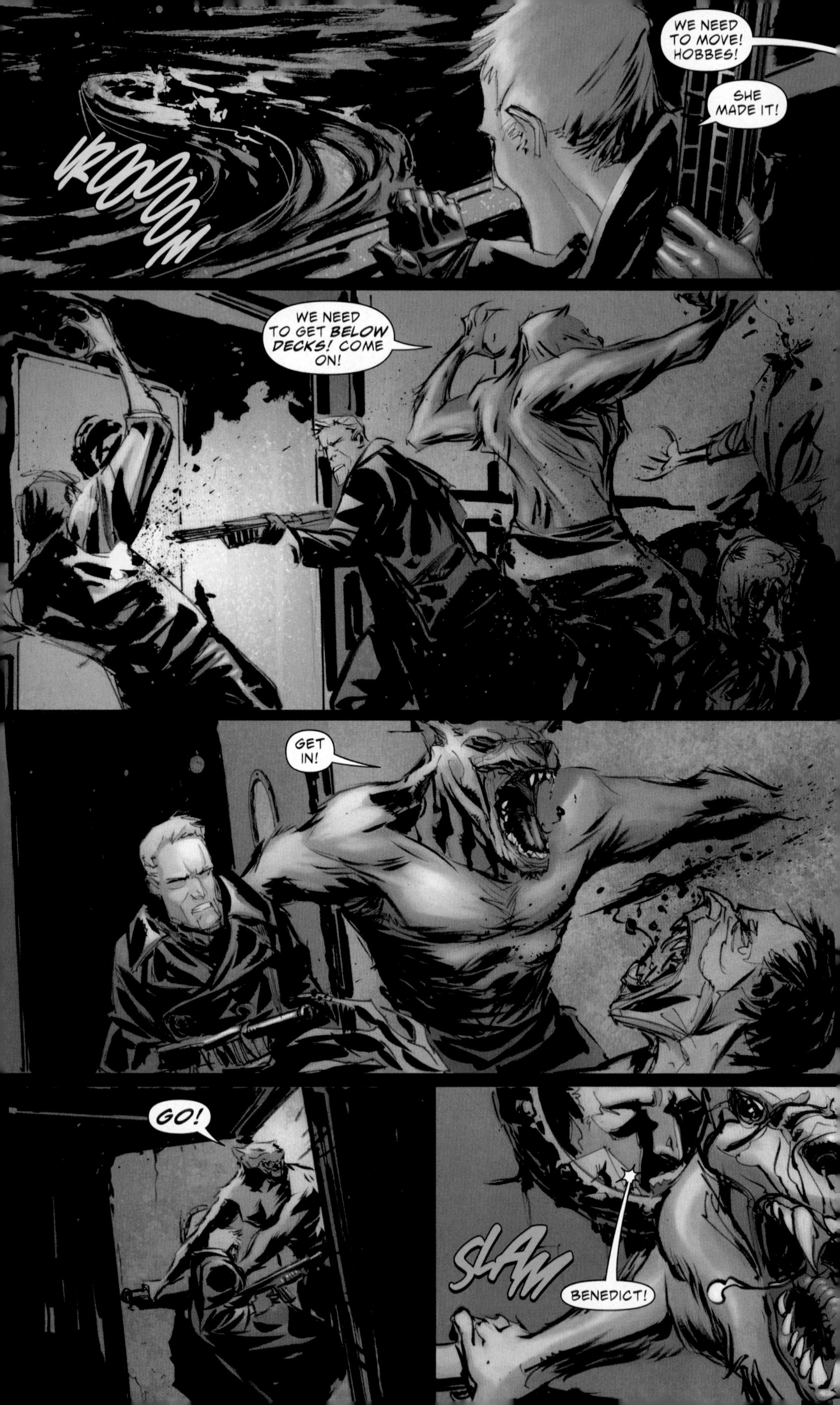
VROOOOOM
WE NEED TO MOVE! HOBBES!
SHE MADE IT!
WE NEED TO GET BELOW DECKS! COME ON!
GET IN!
GO!
SLAM
BENEDICT!

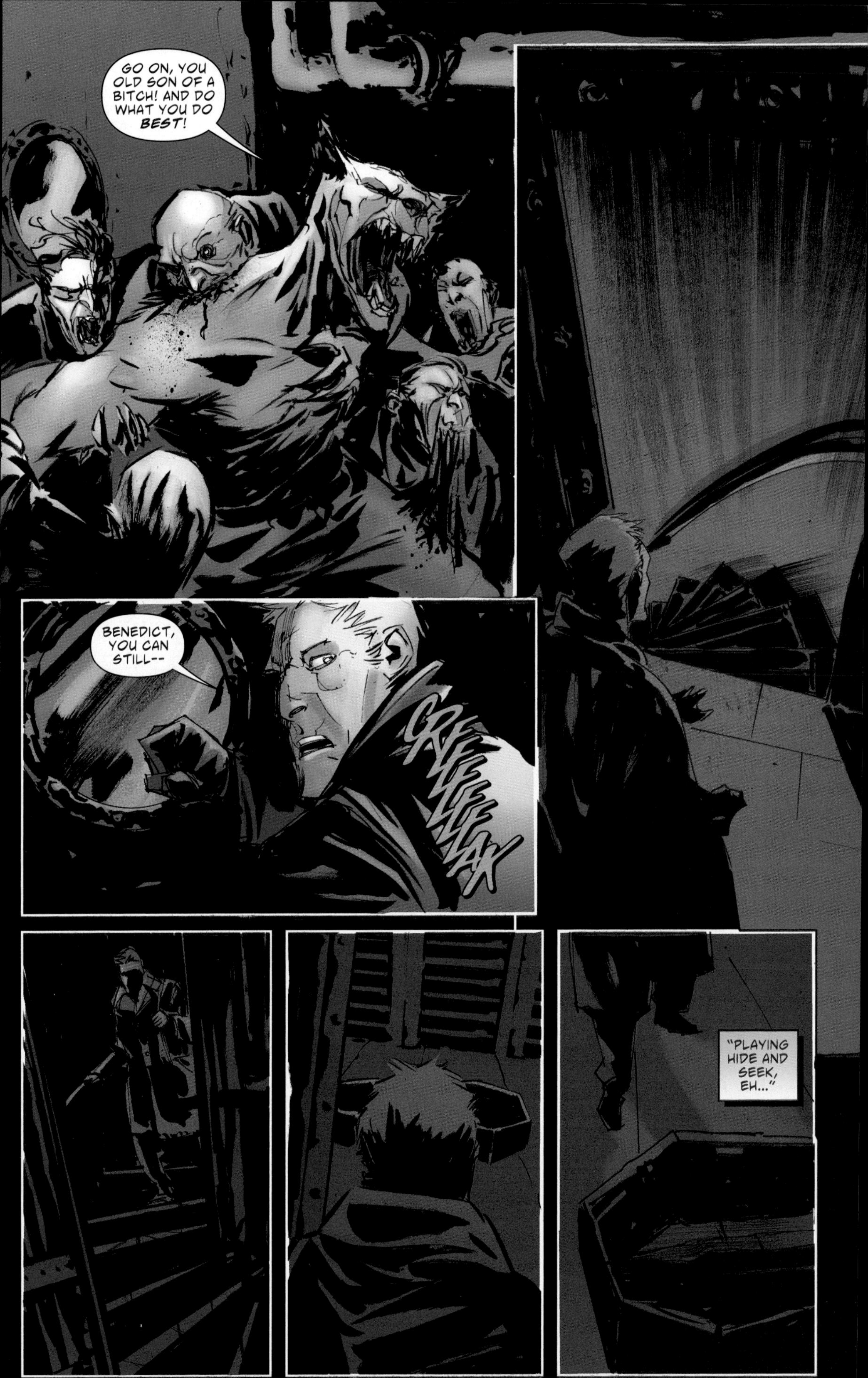
GO ON, YOU OLD SON OF A BITCH! AND DO WHAT YOU DO BEST!
BENEDICT, YOU CAN STILL--
CREEEEAK
"PLAYING HIDE AND SEEK, EH..."

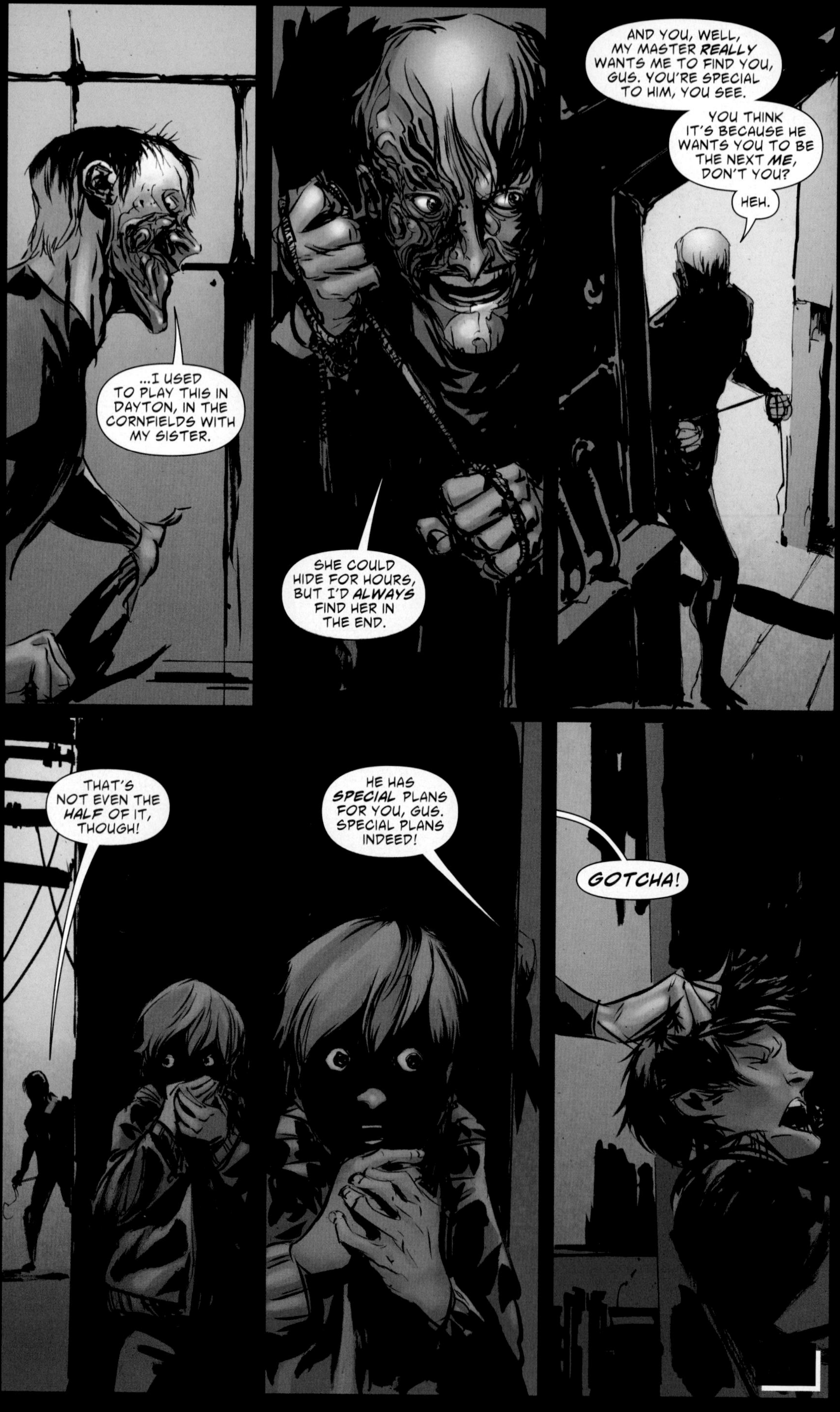
...I USED TO PLAY THIS IN DAYTON, IN THE CORNFIELDS WITH MY SISTER.
SHE COULD HIDE FOR HOURS, BUT I'D ALWAYS FIND HER IN THE END.
AND YOU, WELL, MY MASTER REALLY WANTS ME TO FIND YOU, GUS. YOU'RE SPECIAL TO HIM, YOU SEE.
YOU THINK IT'S BECAUSE HE WANTS YOU TO BE THE NEXT ME, DON'T YOU?
HEH.
THAT'S NOT EVEN THE HALF OF IT, THOUGH!
HE HAS SPECIAL PLANS FOR YOU, GUS. SPECIAL PLANS INDEED!
GOTCHA!

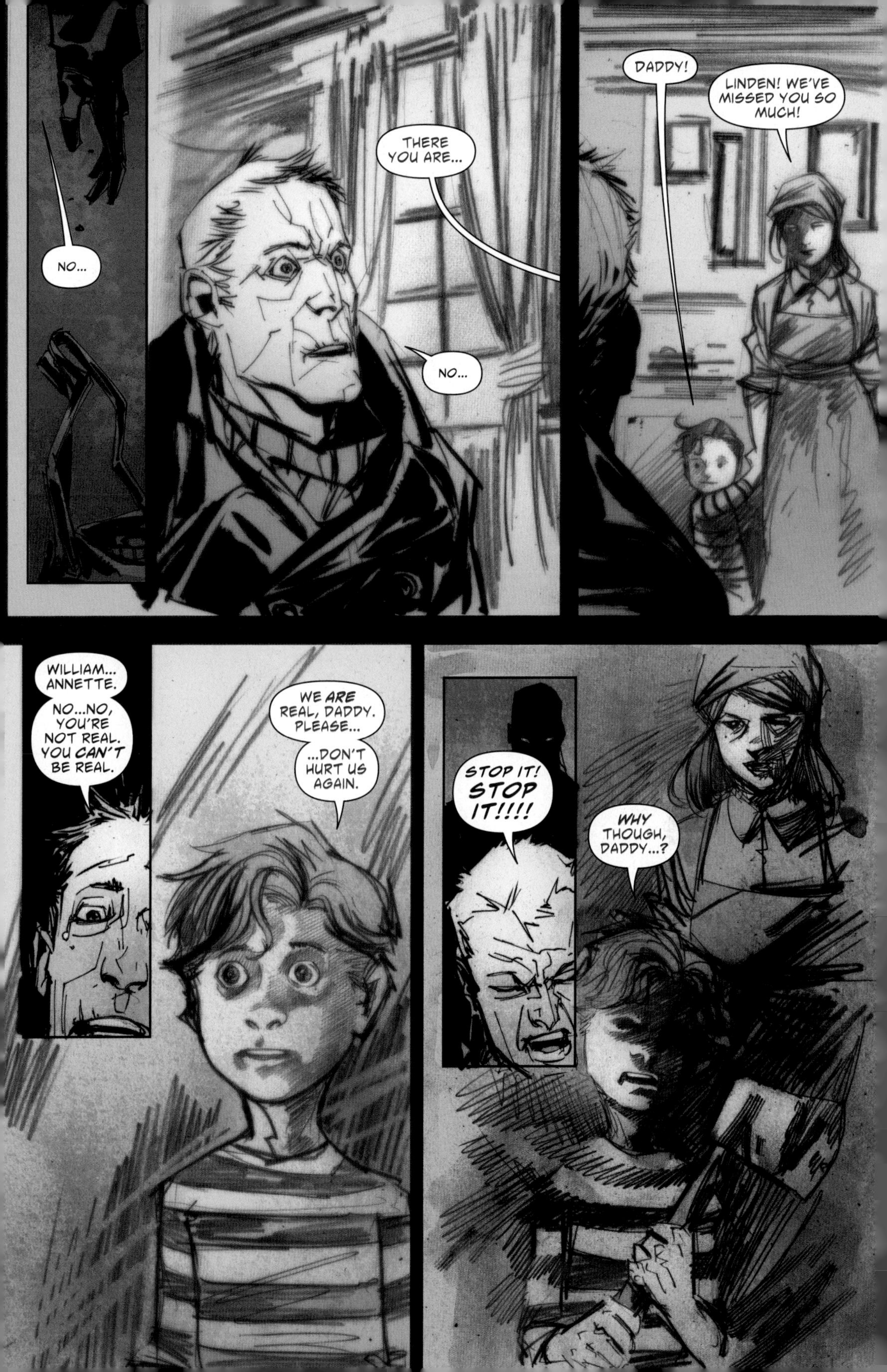
NO...
THERE YOU ARE...
NO...
DADDY!
LINDEN! WE'VE MISSED YOU SO MUCH!
WILLIAM... ANNETTE.
NO...NO, YOU'RE NOT REAL. YOU CAN'T BE REAL.
WE ARE REAL, DADDY. PLEASE...
...DON'T HURT US AGAIN.
STOP IT! STOP IT!!!!
WHY THOUGH, DADDY...?

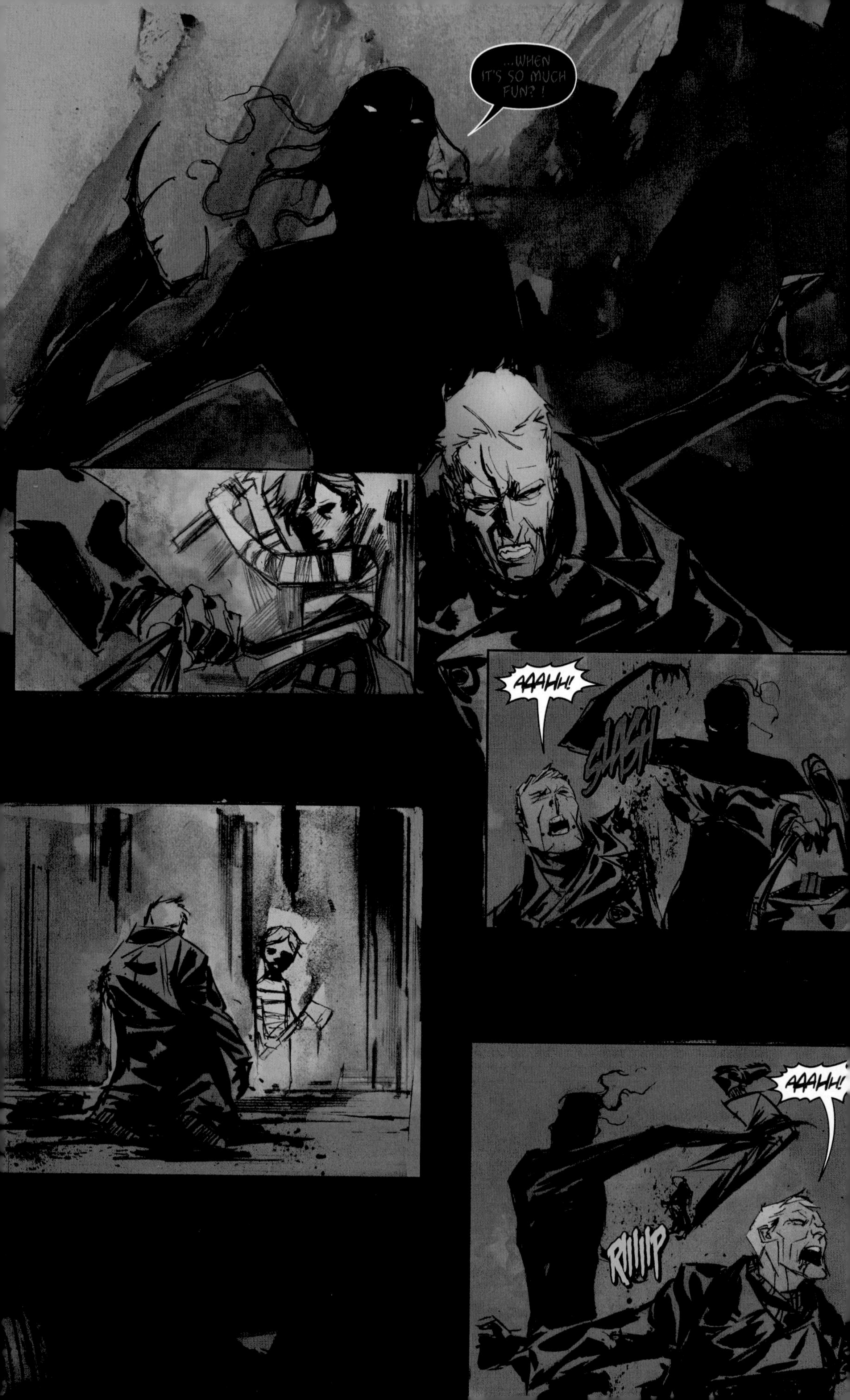
...WHEN IT'S SO MUCH FUN? !
AAAHH!
SLASH
AAAHH!
RIIIIP

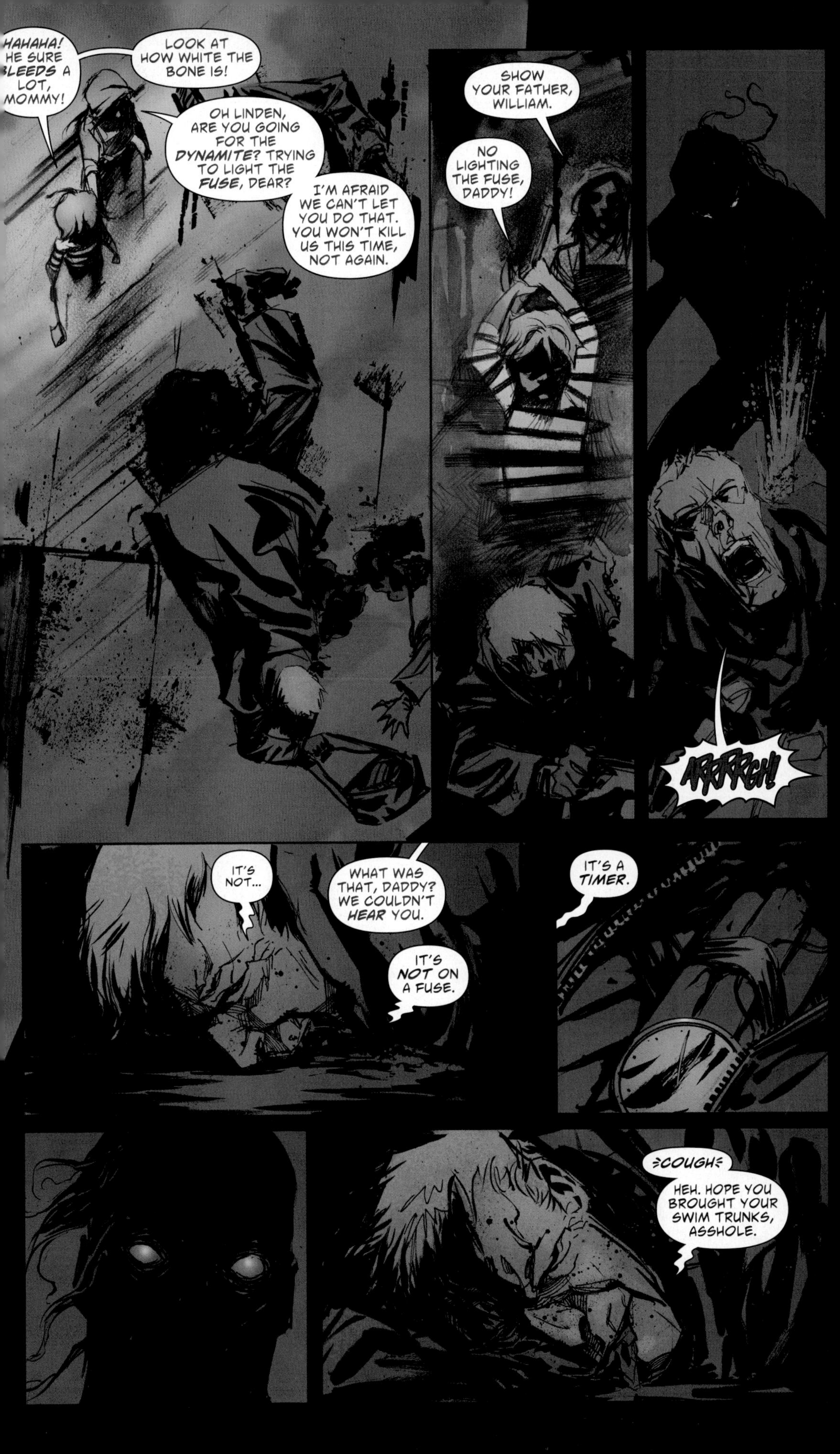
HAHAHA! HE SURE BLEEDS A LOT, MOMMY!
LOOK AT HOW WHITE THE BONE IS!
OH LINDEN, ARE YOU GOING FOR THE DYNAMITE? TRYING TO LIGHT THE FUSE, DEAR?
I'M AFRAID WE CAN'T LET YOU DO THAT. YOU WON'T KILL US THIS TIME, NOT AGAIN.
SHOW YOUR FATHER, WILLIAM.
NO LIGHTING THE FUSE, DADDY!
ARRRRGH!
IT'S NOT...
WHAT WAS THAT, DADDY? WE COULDN'T HEAR YOU.
IT'S NOT ON A FUSE.
IT'S A TIMER.
COUGH
HEH. HOPE YOU BROUGHT YOUR SWIM TRUNKS, ASSHOLE.

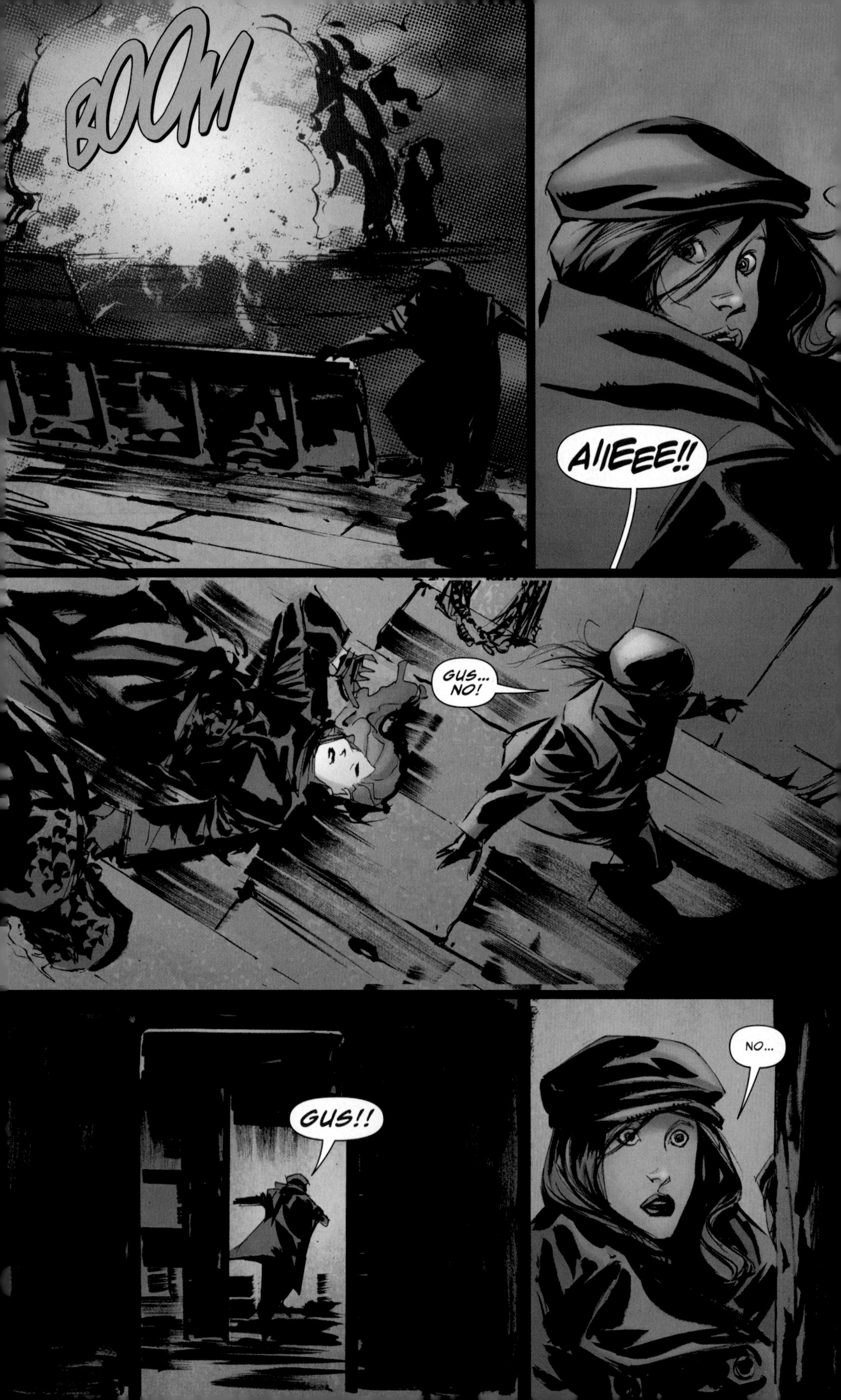

BOOM
AIIEEE!!
GUS... NO!
GUS!!
NO...

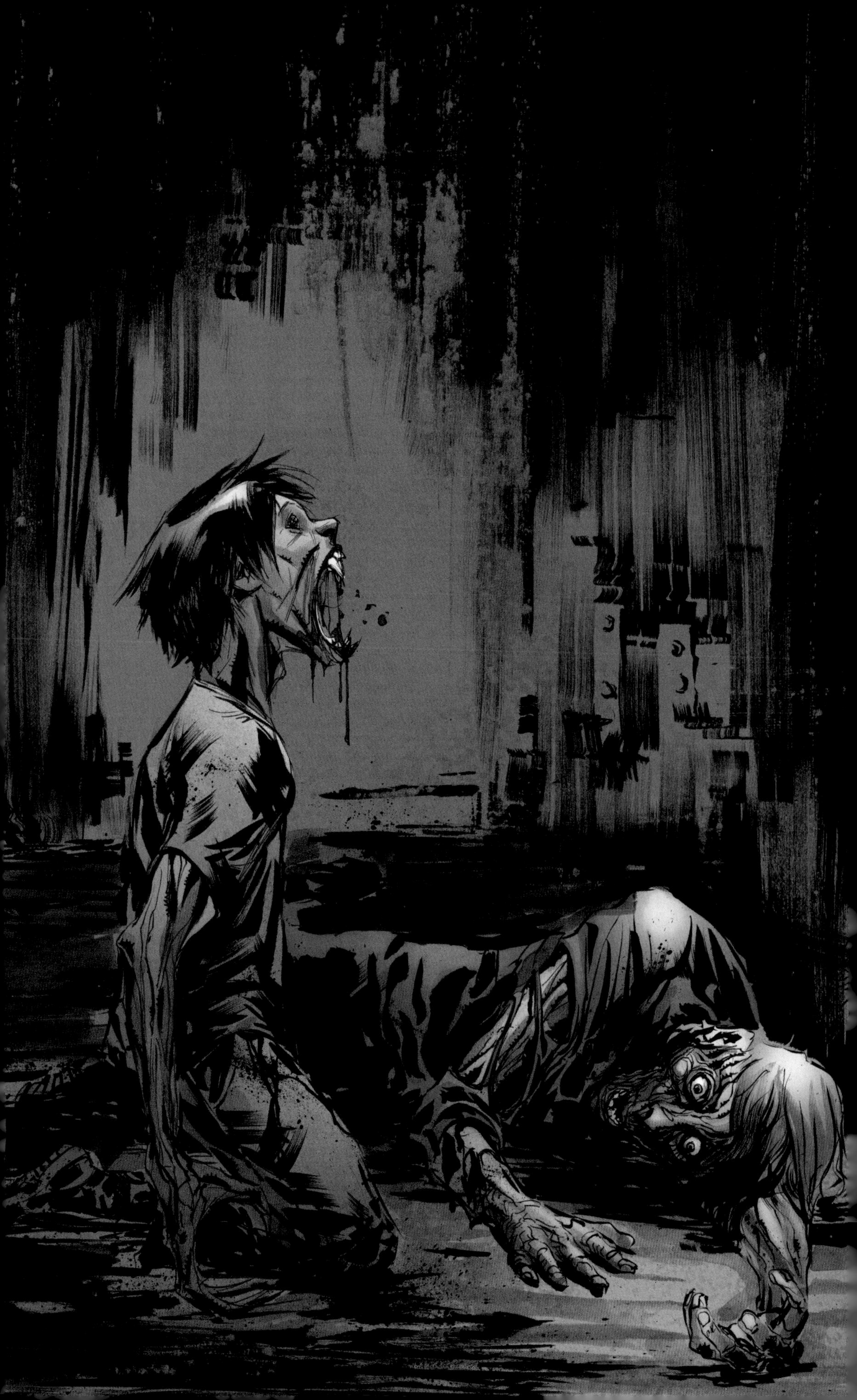

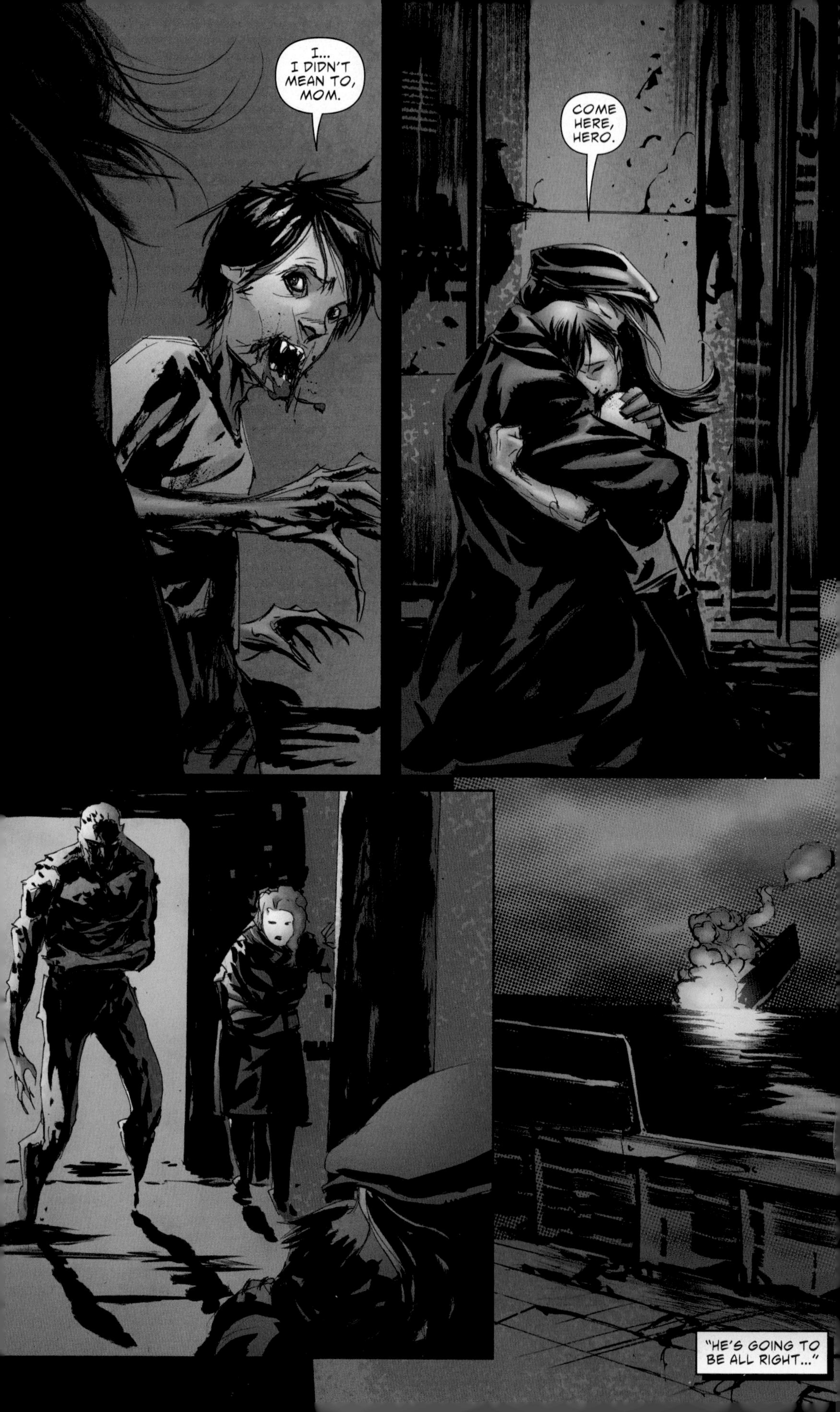
I... I DIDN'T MEAN TO, MOM.
COME HERE, HERO.
"HE'S GOING TO BE ALL RIGHT..."

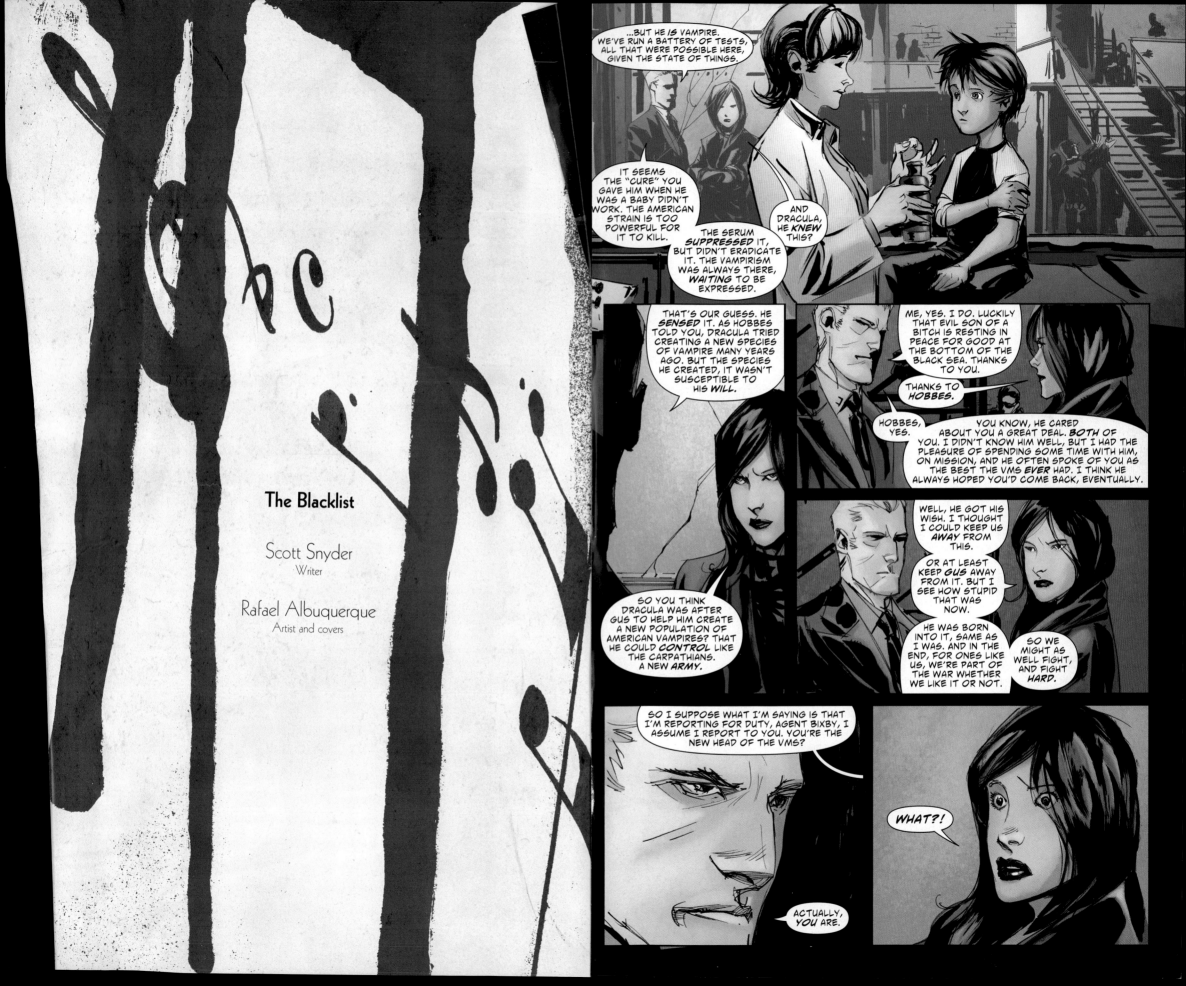

The Blacklist

Scott Snyder
Writer

Rafael Albuquerque
Artist and covers

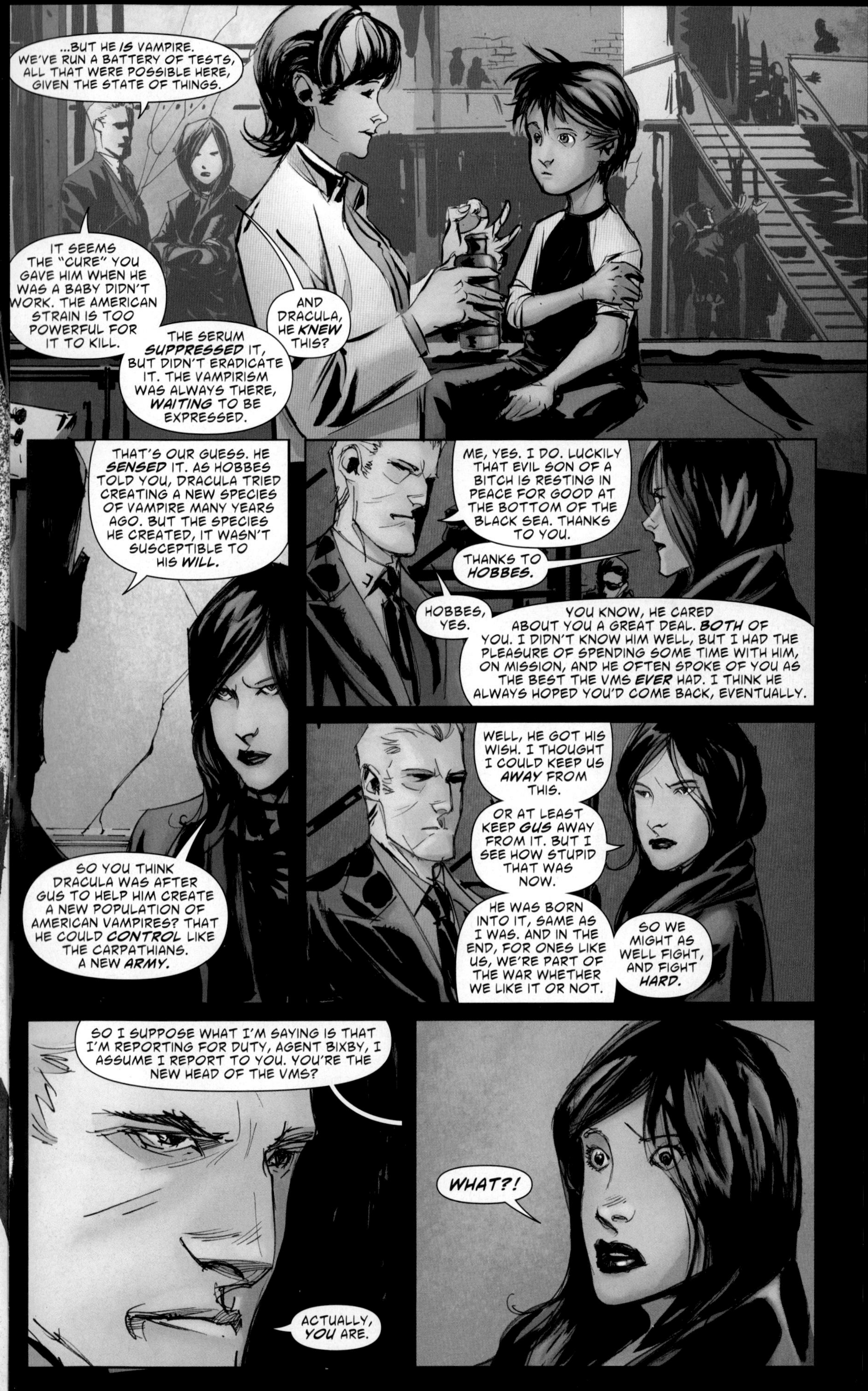
...BUT HE *IS* VAMPIRE. WE'VE RUN A BATTERY OF TESTS, ALL THAT WERE POSSIBLE HERE, GIVEN THE STATE OF THINGS.
IT SEEMS THE "CURE" YOU GAVE HIM WHEN HE WAS A BABY DIDN'T WORK. THE AMERICAN STRAIN IS TOO POWERFUL FOR IT TO KILL.
THE SERUM *SUPPRESSED* IT, BUT DIDN'T ERADICATE IT. THE VAMPIRISM WAS ALWAYS THERE, *WAITING* TO BE EXPRESSED.
AND DRACULA, HE *KNEW* THIS?
THAT'S OUR GUESS. HE *SENSED* IT. AS HOBBES TOLD YOU, DRACULA TRIED CREATING A NEW SPECIES OF VAMPIRE MANY YEARS AGO. BUT THE SPECIES HE CREATED, IT WASN'T SUSCEPTIBLE TO HIS *WILL.*
SO YOU THINK DRACULA WAS AFTER GUS TO HELP HIM CREATE A NEW POPULATION OF AMERICAN VAMPIRES? THAT HE COULD *CONTROL* LIKE THE CARPATHIANS. A NEW *ARMY.*
ME, YES. I DO. LUCKILY THAT EVIL SON OF A BITCH IS RESTING IN PEACE FOR GOOD AT THE BOTTOM OF THE BLACK SEA. THANKS TO YOU.
THANKS TO *HOBBES.*
HOBBES, YES.
YOU KNOW, HE CARED ABOUT YOU A GREAT DEAL. *BOTH* OF YOU. I DIDN'T KNOW HIM WELL, BUT I HAD THE PLEASURE OF SPENDING SOME TIME WITH HIM, ON MISSION, AND HE OFTEN SPOKE OF YOU AS THE BEST THE VMS *EVER* HAD. I THINK HE ALWAYS HOPED YOU'D COME BACK, EVENTUALLY.
WELL, HE GOT HIS WISH. I THOUGHT I COULD KEEP US *AWAY* FROM THIS.
OR AT LEAST KEEP *GUS* AWAY FROM IT. BUT I SEE HOW STUPID THAT WAS NOW.
HE WAS BORN INTO IT, SAME AS I WAS. AND IN THE END, FOR ONES LIKE US, WE'RE PART OF THE WAR WHETHER WE LIKE IT OR NOT.
SO WE MIGHT AS WELL FIGHT, AND FIGHT *HARD.*
SO I SUPPOSE WHAT I'M SAYING IS THAT I'M REPORTING FOR DUTY, AGENT BIXBY, I ASSUME I REPORT TO YOU. YOU'RE THE NEW HEAD OF THE VMS?
ACTUALLY, *YOU* ARE.
WHAT?!

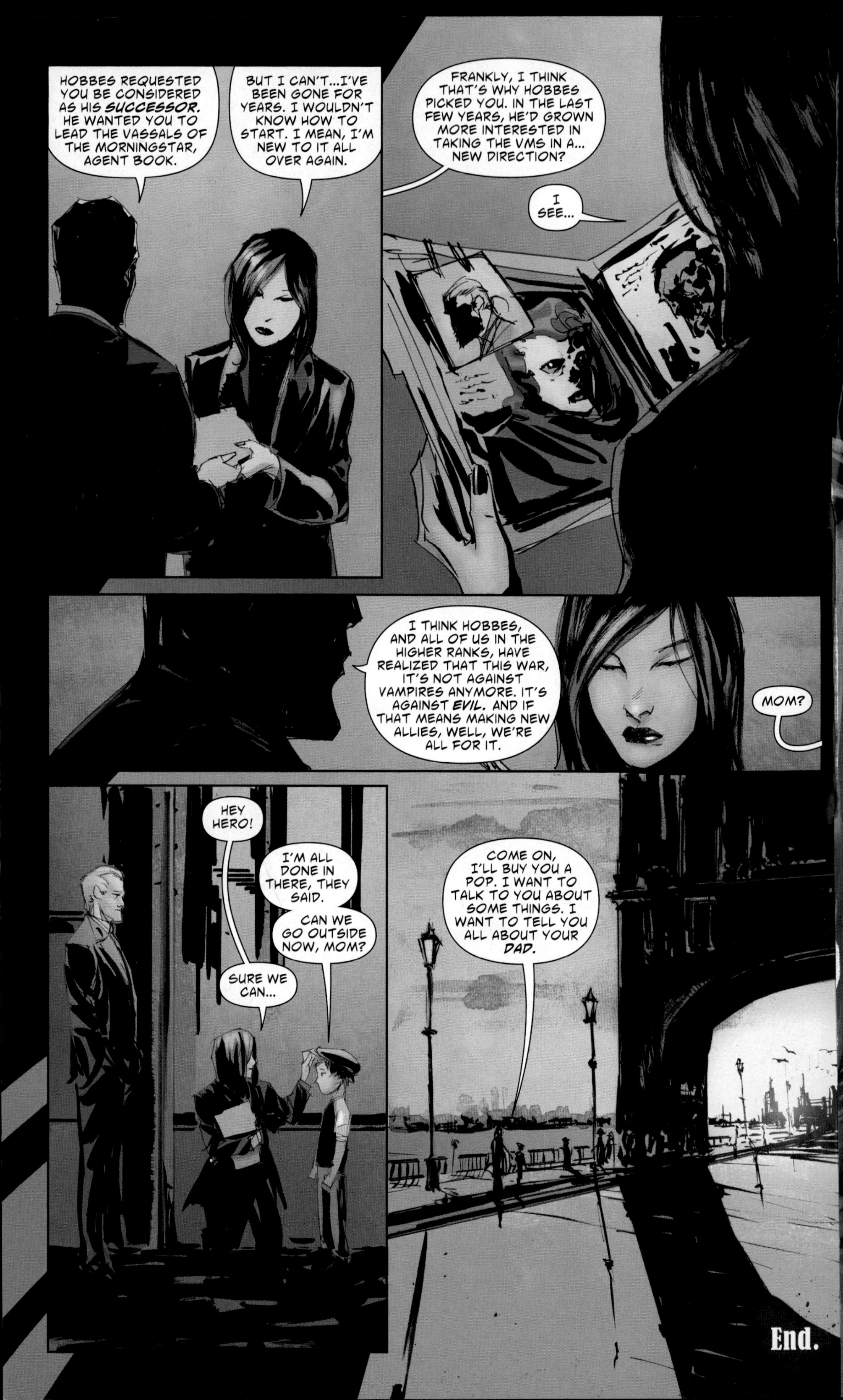
HOBBES REQUESTED YOU BE CONSIDERED AS HIS **SUCCESSOR.** HE WANTED YOU TO LEAD THE VASSALS OF THE MORNINGSTAR, AGENT BOOK.
BUT I CAN'T...I'VE BEEN GONE FOR YEARS. I WOULDN'T KNOW HOW TO START. I MEAN, I'M NEW TO IT ALL OVER AGAIN.
FRANKLY, I THINK THAT'S WHY HOBBES PICKED YOU. IN THE LAST FEW YEARS, HE'D GROWN MORE INTERESTED IN TAKING THE VMS IN A... NEW DIRECTION?
I SEE...
I THINK HOBBES, AND ALL OF US IN THE HIGHER RANKS, HAVE REALIZED THAT THIS WAR, IT'S NOT AGAINST VAMPIRES ANYMORE. IT'S AGAINST **EVIL.** AND IF THAT MEANS MAKING NEW ALLIES, WELL, WE'RE ALL FOR IT.
MOM?
HEY HERO!
I'M ALL DONE IN THERE, THEY SAID.
CAN WE GO OUTSIDE NOW, MOM?
SURE WE CAN...
COME ON, I'LL BUY YOU A POP. I WANT TO TALK TO YOU ABOUT SOME THINGS. I WANT TO TELL YOU ALL ABOUT YOUR ***DAD.***
End.

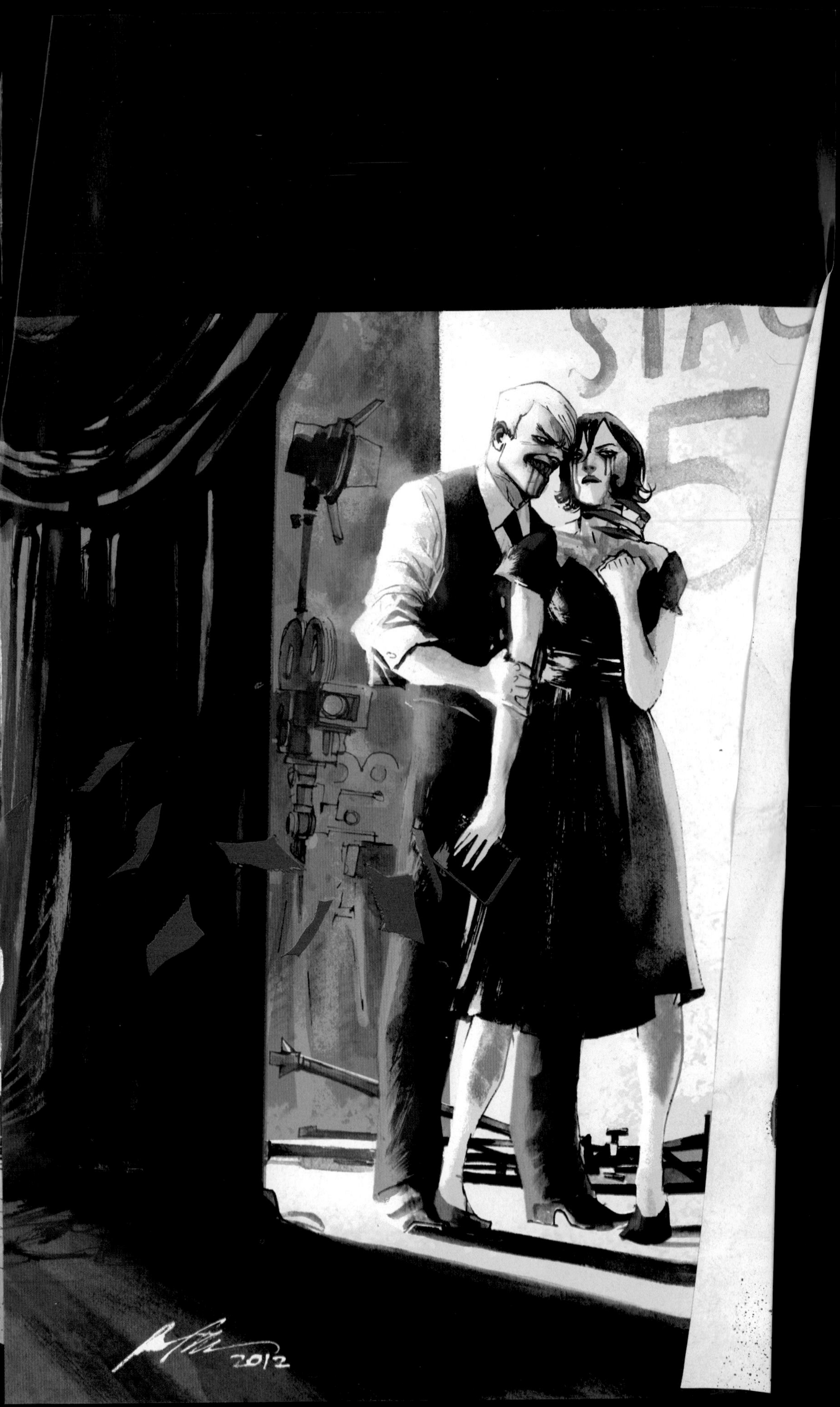
2012

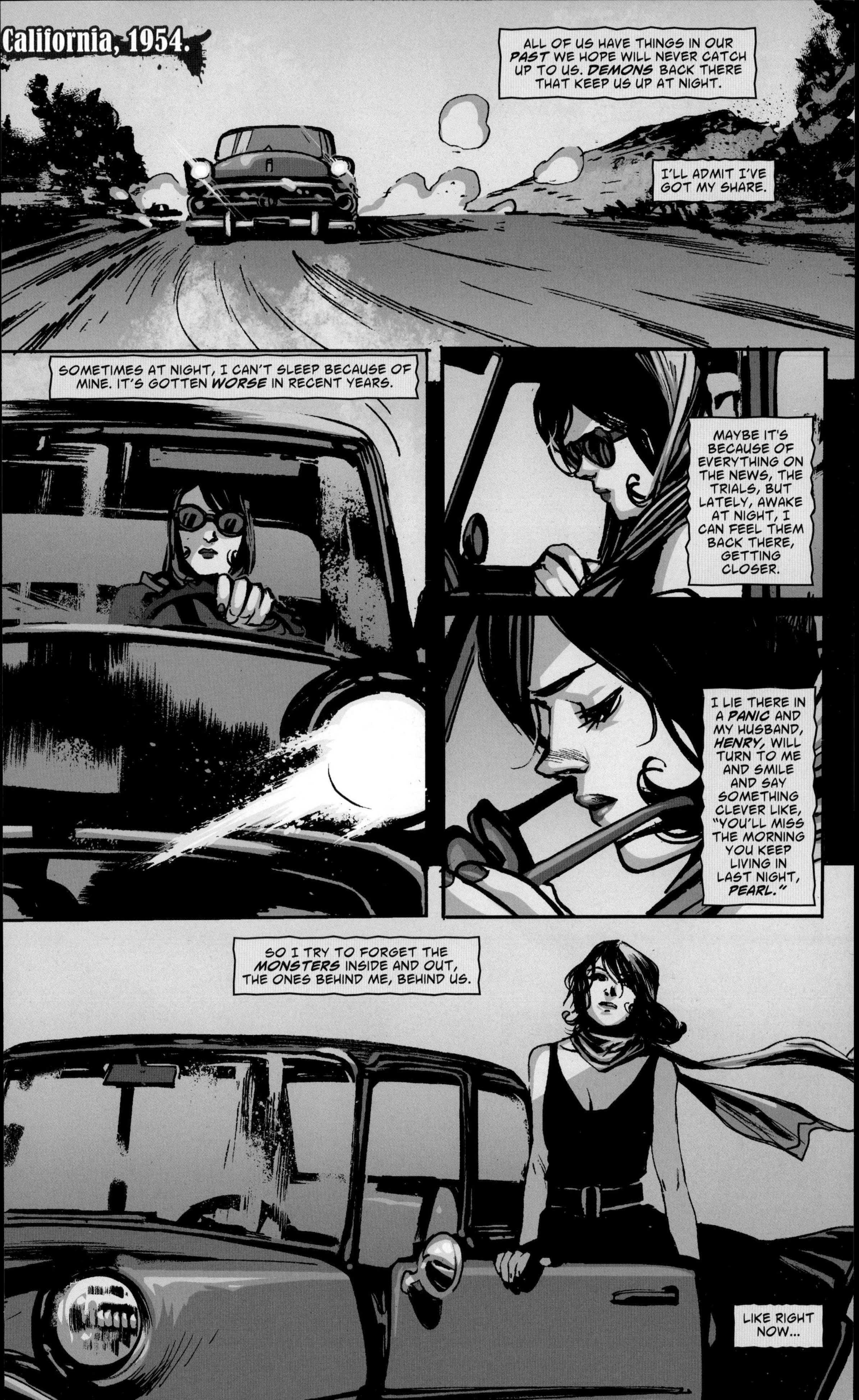
California, 1954.
ALL OF US HAVE THINGS IN OUR PAST WE HOPE WILL NEVER CATCH UP TO US. DEMONS BACK THERE THAT KEEP US UP AT NIGHT.
I'LL ADMIT I'VE GOT MY SHARE.
SOMETIMES AT NIGHT, I CAN'T SLEEP BECAUSE OF MINE. IT'S GOTTEN WORSE IN RECENT YEARS.
MAYBE IT'S BECAUSE OF EVERYTHING ON THE NEWS, THE TRIALS, BUT LATELY, AWAKE AT NIGHT, I CAN FEEL THEM BACK THERE, GETTING CLOSER.
I LIE THERE IN A PANIC AND MY HUSBAND, HENRY, WILL TURN TO ME AND SMILE AND SAY SOMETHING CLEVER LIKE, "YOU'LL MISS THE MORNING YOU KEEP LIVING IN LAST NIGHT, PEARL."
SO I TRY TO FORGET THE MONSTERS INSIDE AND OUT, THE ONES BEHIND ME, BEHIND US.
LIKE RIGHT NOW...

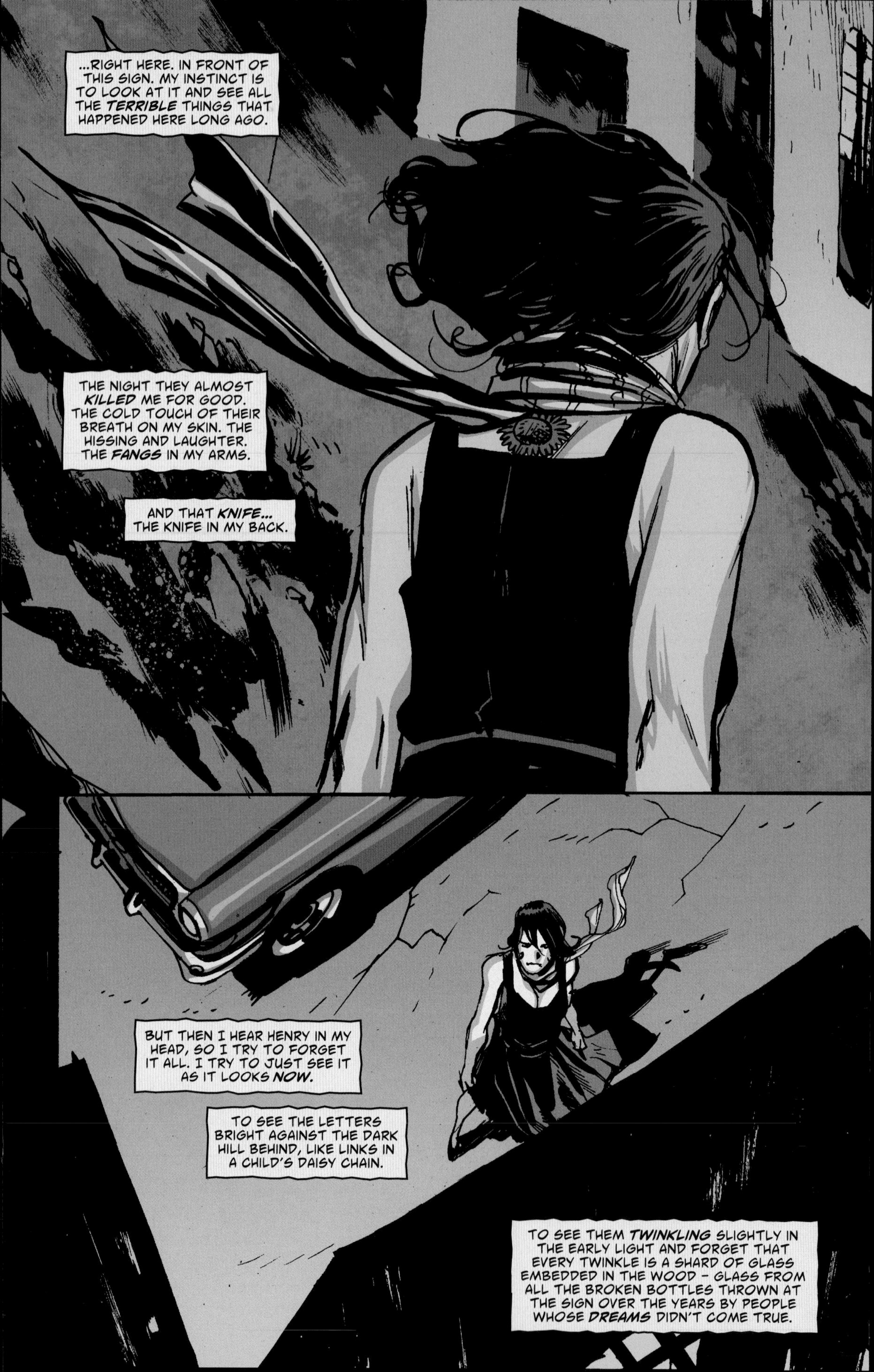

...RIGHT HERE. IN FRONT OF THIS SIGN. MY INSTINCT IS TO LOOK AT IT AND SEE ALL THE *TERRIBLE* THINGS THAT HAPPENED HERE LONG AGO.
THE NIGHT THEY ALMOST *KILLED* ME FOR GOOD. THE COLD TOUCH OF THEIR BREATH ON MY SKIN. THE HISSING AND LAUGHTER. THE *FANGS* IN MY ARMS.
AND THAT *KNIFE*... THE KNIFE IN MY BACK.
BUT THEN I HEAR HENRY IN MY HEAD, SO I TRY TO FORGET IT ALL. I TRY TO JUST SEE IT AS IT LOOKS *NOW*.
TO SEE THE LETTERS BRIGHT AGAINST THE DARK HILL BEHIND, LIKE LINKS IN A CHILD'S DAISY CHAIN.
TO SEE THEM *TWINKLING* SLIGHTLY IN THE EARLY LIGHT AND FORGET THAT EVERY TWINKLE IS A SHARD OF GLASS EMBEDDED IN THE WOOD – GLASS FROM ALL THE BROKEN BOTTLES THROWN AT THE SIGN OVER THE YEARS BY PEOPLE WHOSE *DREAMS* DIDN'T COME TRUE.

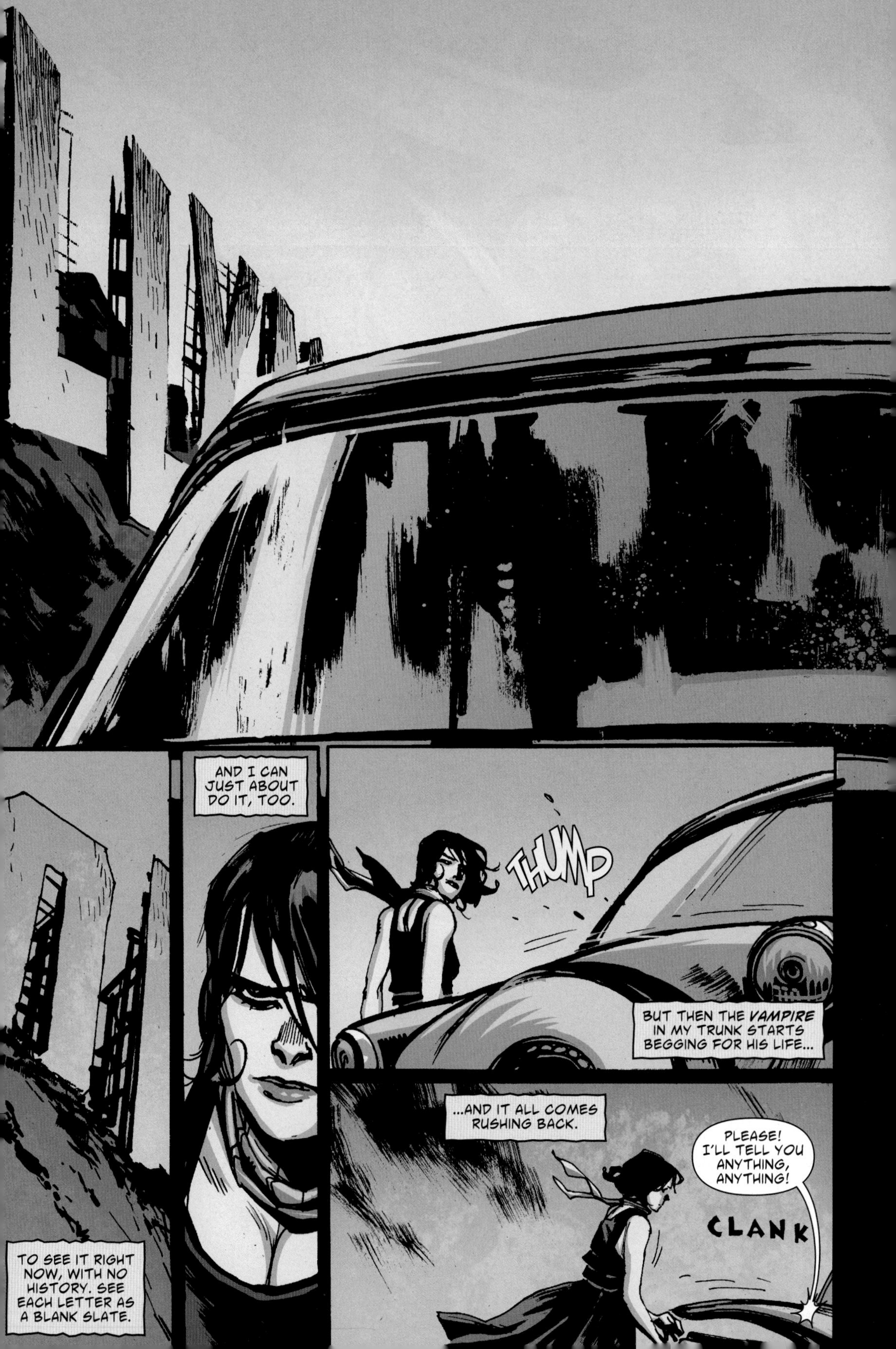
TO SEE IT RIGHT NOW, WITH NO HISTORY. SEE EACH LETTER AS A BLANK SLATE.
AND I CAN JUST ABOUT DO IT, TOO.
THUMP
BUT THEN THE VAMPIRE IN MY TRUNK STARTS BEGGING FOR HIS LIFE...
...AND IT ALL COMES RUSHING BACK.
PLEASE! I'LL TELL YOU ANYTHING, ANYTHING!
CLANK

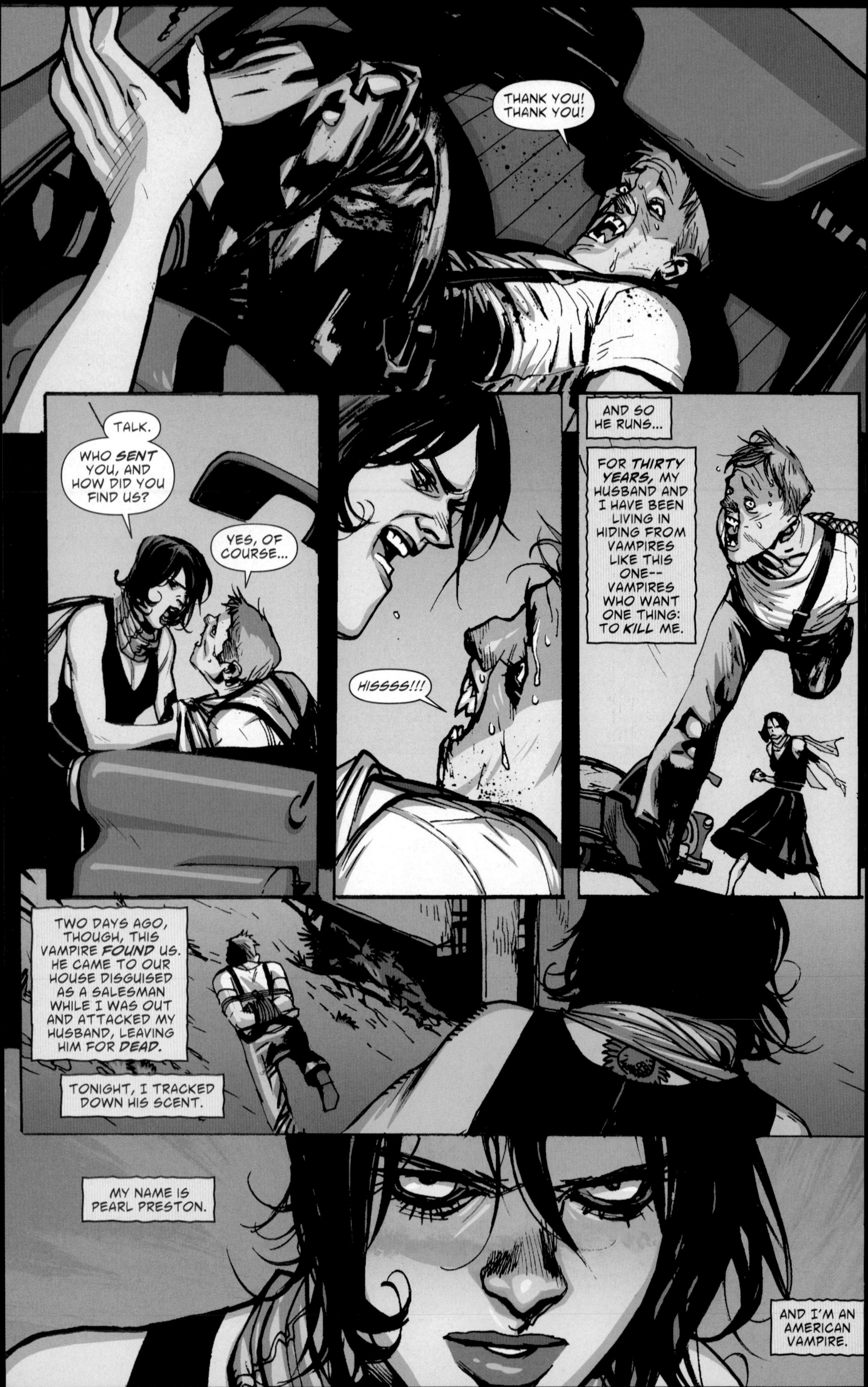
THANK YOU! THANK YOU!
TALK.
WHO SENT YOU, AND HOW DID YOU FIND US?
YES, OF COURSE...
HISSSS!!!
AND SO HE RUNS...
FOR THIRTY YEARS, MY HUSBAND AND I HAVE BEEN LIVING IN HIDING FROM VAMPIRES LIKE THIS ONE--VAMPIRES WHO WANT ONE THING: TO KILL ME.
TWO DAYS AGO, THOUGH, THIS VAMPIRE FOUND US. HE CAME TO OUR HOUSE DISGUISED AS A SALESMAN WHILE I WAS OUT AND ATTACKED MY HUSBAND, LEAVING HIM FOR DEAD.
TONIGHT, I TRACKED DOWN HIS SCENT.
MY NAME IS PEARL PRESTON.
AND I'M AN AMERICAN VAMPIRE.

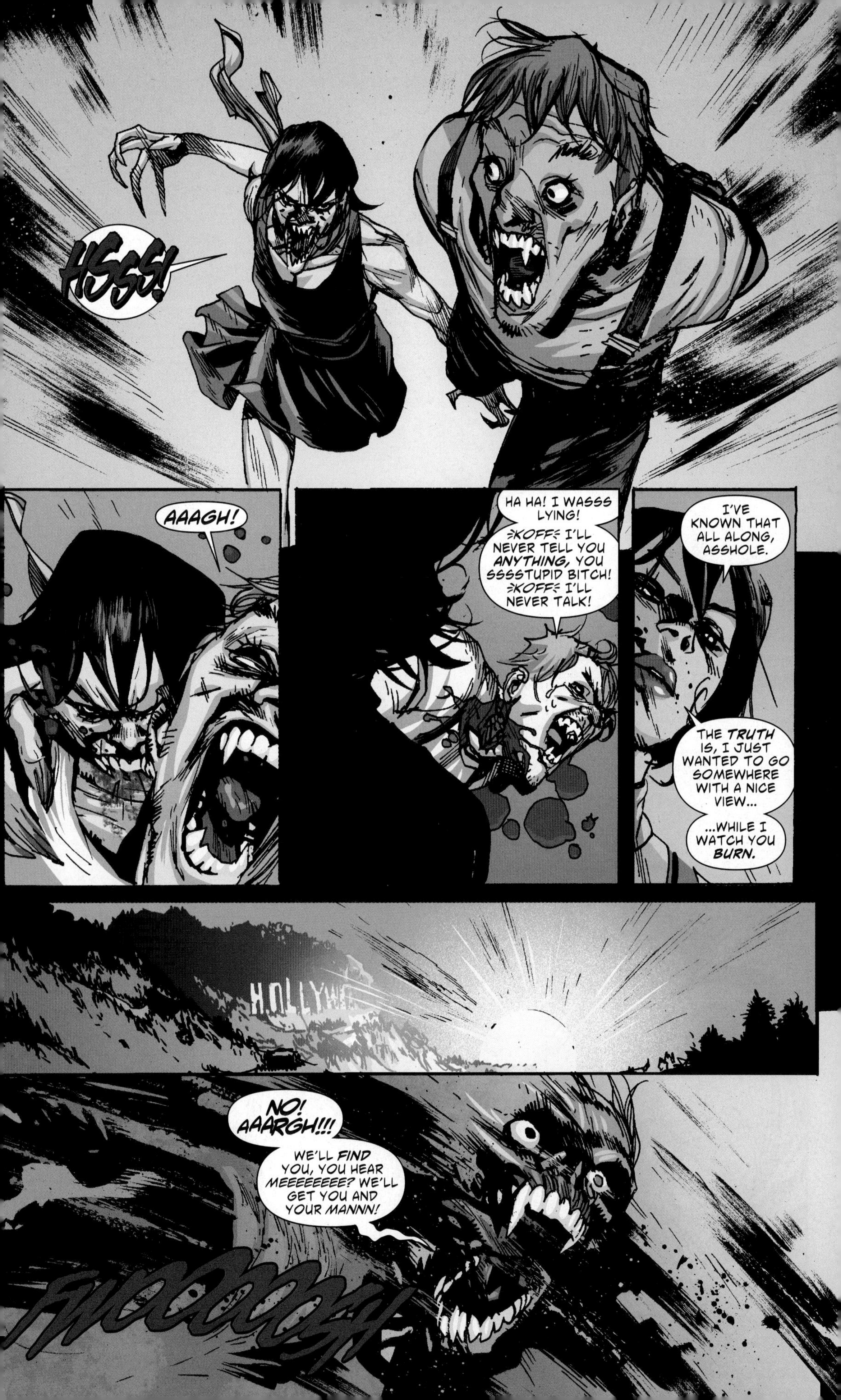
HSSS!
AAAGH!
HA HA! I WASSS LYING!
KOFF I'LL NEVER TELL YOU *ANYTHING,* YOU SSSSTUPID BITCH! *KOFF* I'LL NEVER TALK!
I'VE KNOWN THAT ALL ALONG, ASSHOLE.
THE *TRUTH* IS, I JUST WANTED TO GO SOMEWHERE WITH A NICE VIEW...
...WHILE I WATCH YOU *BURN.*
HOLLYW
NO! AAARGH!!!
WE'LL *FIND* YOU, YOU HEAR *MEEEEEEEE?* WE'LL GET YOU AND YOUR *MANNN!*
FWOOOOSH

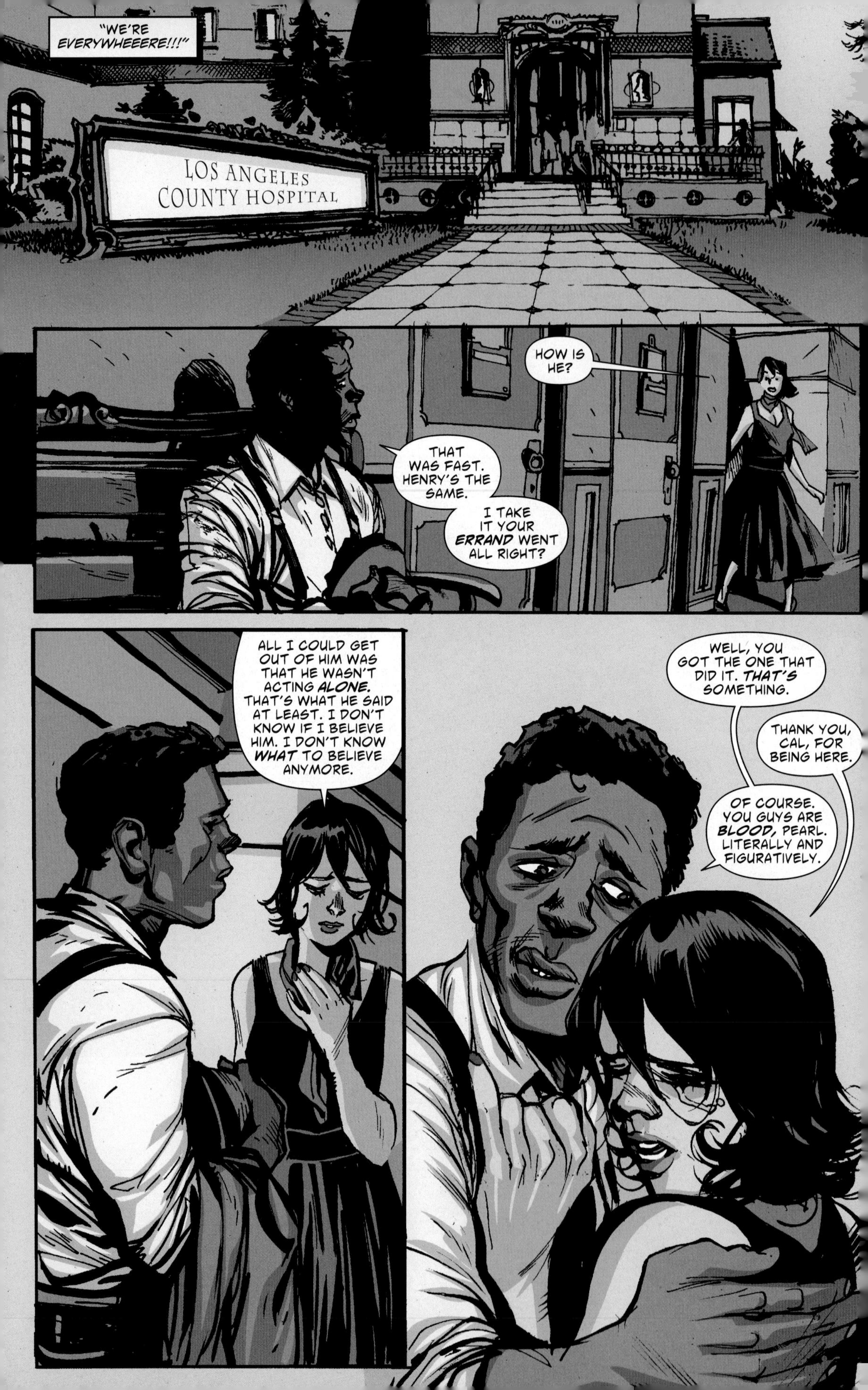
"WE'RE EVERYWHEEERE!!!"
LOS ANGELES COUNTY HOSPITAL
HOW IS HE?
THAT WAS FAST. HENRY'S THE SAME.
I TAKE IT YOUR ERRAND WENT ALL RIGHT?
ALL I COULD GET OUT OF HIM WAS THAT HE WASN'T ACTING ALONE. THAT'S WHAT HE SAID AT LEAST. I DON'T KNOW IF I BELIEVE HIM. I DON'T KNOW WHAT TO BELIEVE ANYMORE.
WELL, YOU GOT THE ONE THAT DID IT. THAT'S SOMETHING.
THANK YOU, CAL, FOR BEING HERE.
OF COURSE. YOU GUYS ARE BLOOD, PEARL. LITERALLY AND FIGURATIVELY.

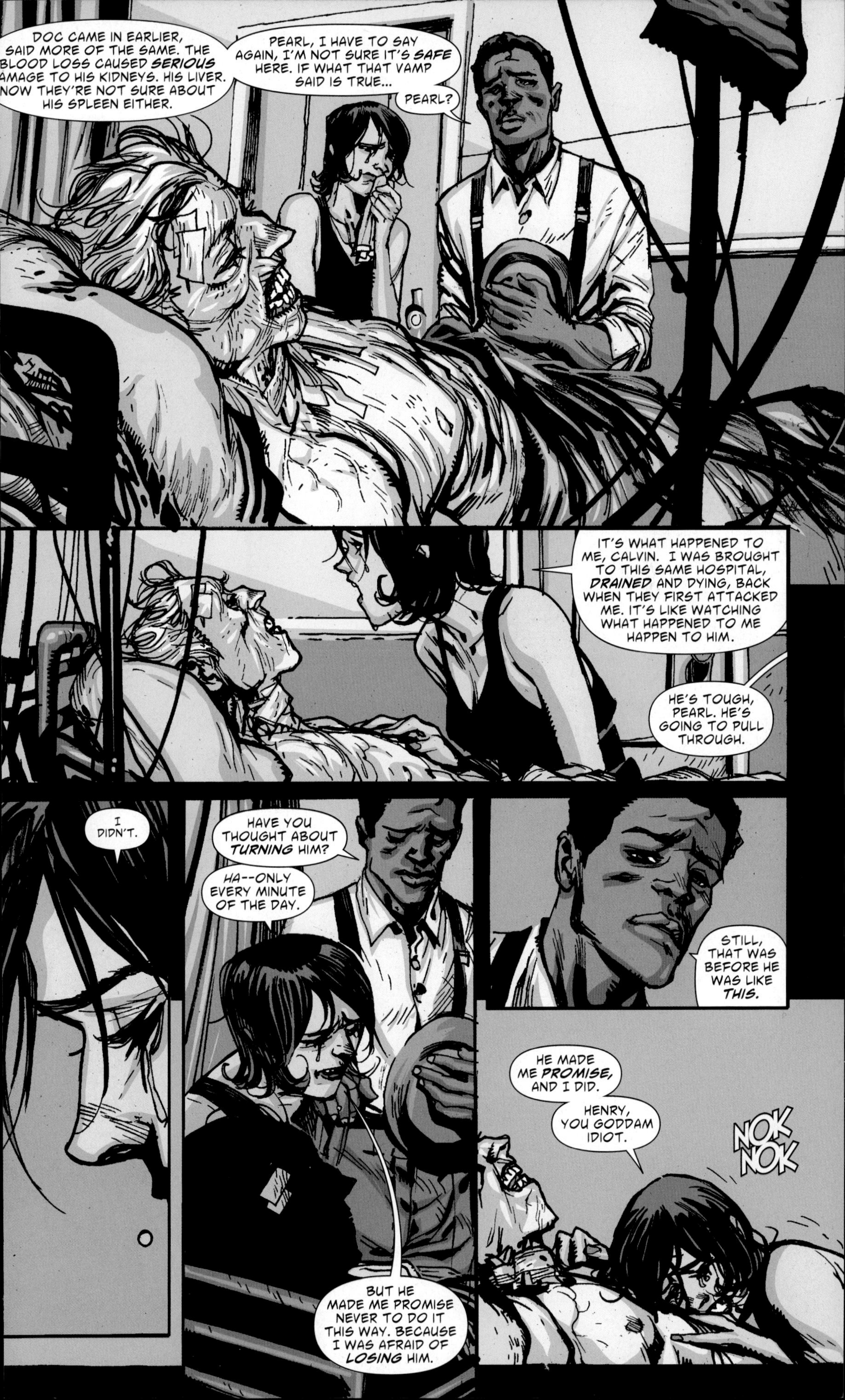
DOC CAME IN EARLIER, SAID MORE OF THE SAME. THE BLOOD LOSS CAUSED SERIOUS AMAGE TO HIS KIDNEYS. HIS LIVER. NOW THEY'RE NOT SURE ABOUT HIS SPLEEN EITHER.
PEARL, I HAVE TO SAY AGAIN, I'M NOT SURE IT'S SAFE HERE. IF WHAT THAT VAMP SAID IS TRUE...
PEARL?
IT'S WHAT HAPPENED TO ME, CALVIN. I WAS BROUGHT TO THIS SAME HOSPITAL, DRAINED AND DYING, BACK WHEN THEY FIRST ATTACKED ME. IT'S LIKE WATCHING WHAT HAPPENED TO ME HAPPEN TO HIM.
HE'S TOUGH, PEARL. HE'S GOING TO PULL THROUGH.
I DIDN'T.
HAVE YOU THOUGHT ABOUT TURNING HIM?
HA--ONLY EVERY MINUTE OF THE DAY.
BUT HE MADE ME PROMISE NEVER TO DO IT THIS WAY. BECAUSE I WAS AFRAID OF LOSING HIM.
STILL, THAT WAS BEFORE HE WAS LIKE THIS.
HE MADE ME PROMISE, AND I DID.
HENRY, YOU GODDAM IDIOT.
NOK NOK

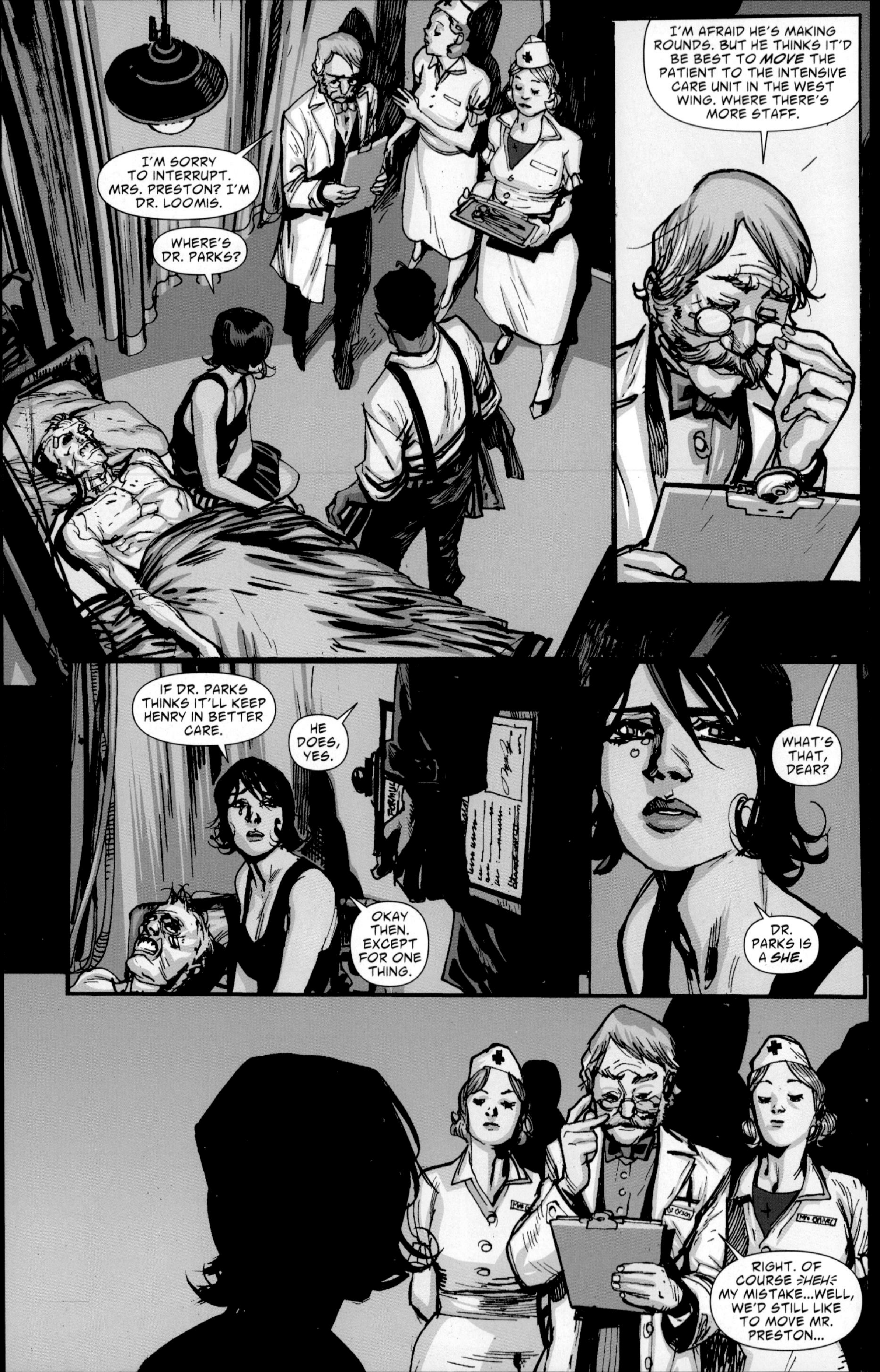
I'M SORRY TO INTERRUPT. MRS. PRESTON? I'M DR. LOOMIS.
WHERE'S DR. PARKS?
I'M AFRAID HE'S MAKING ROUNDS. BUT HE THINKS IT'D BE BEST TO *MOVE* THE PATIENT TO THE INTENSIVE CARE UNIT IN THE WEST WING. WHERE THERE'S MORE STAFF.
IF DR. PARKS THINKS IT'LL KEEP HENRY IN BETTER CARE.
HE DOES, YES.
OKAY THEN. EXCEPT FOR ONE THING.
WHAT'S THAT, DEAR?
DR. PARKS IS A *SHE.*
RIGHT. OF COURSE =HEH= MY MISTAKE...WELL, WE'D STILL LIKE TO MOVE MR. PRESTON...

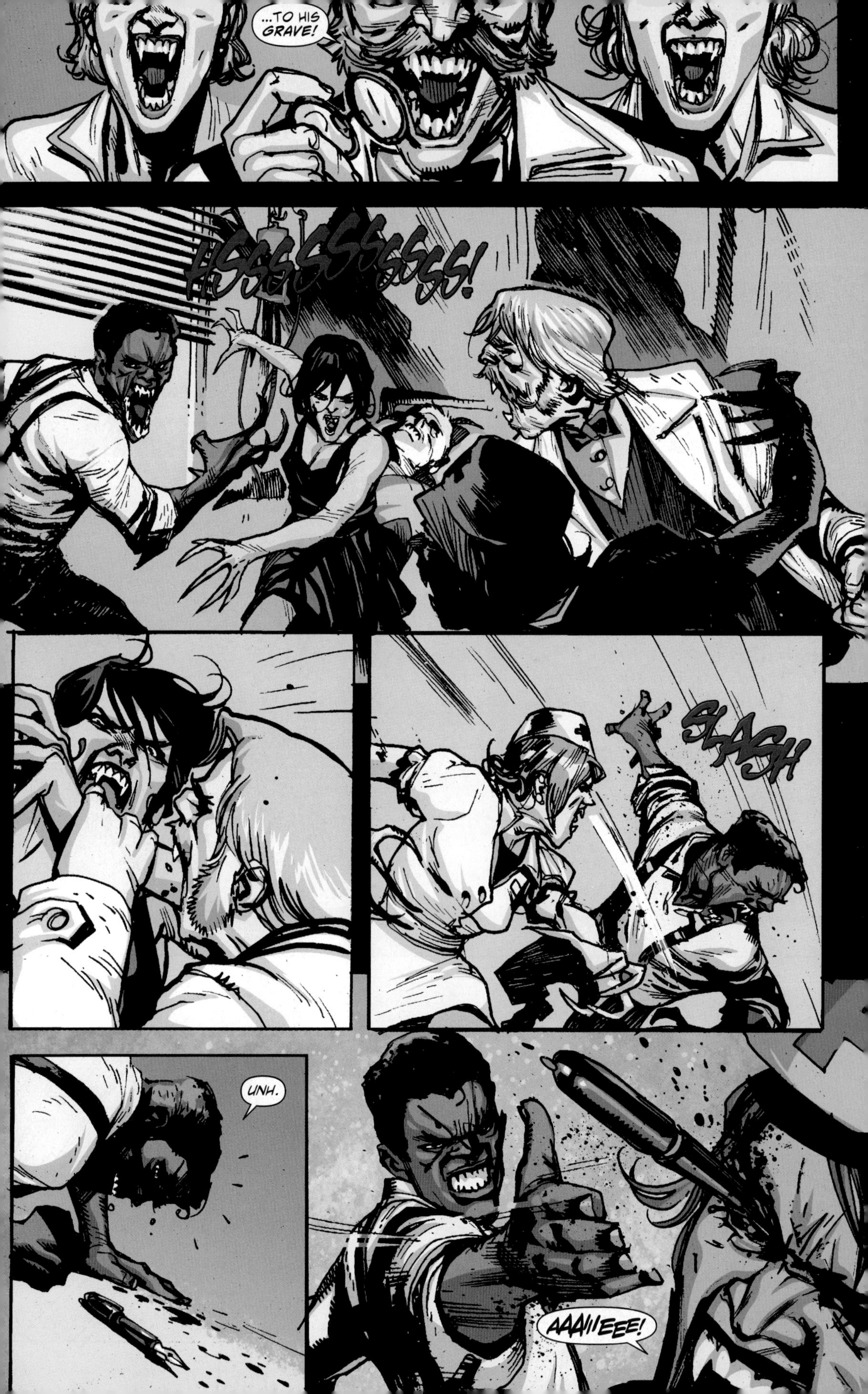
...TO HIS GRAVE!
HSSSSSSSSSS!
SLASH
UNH.
AAAIIIEEE!

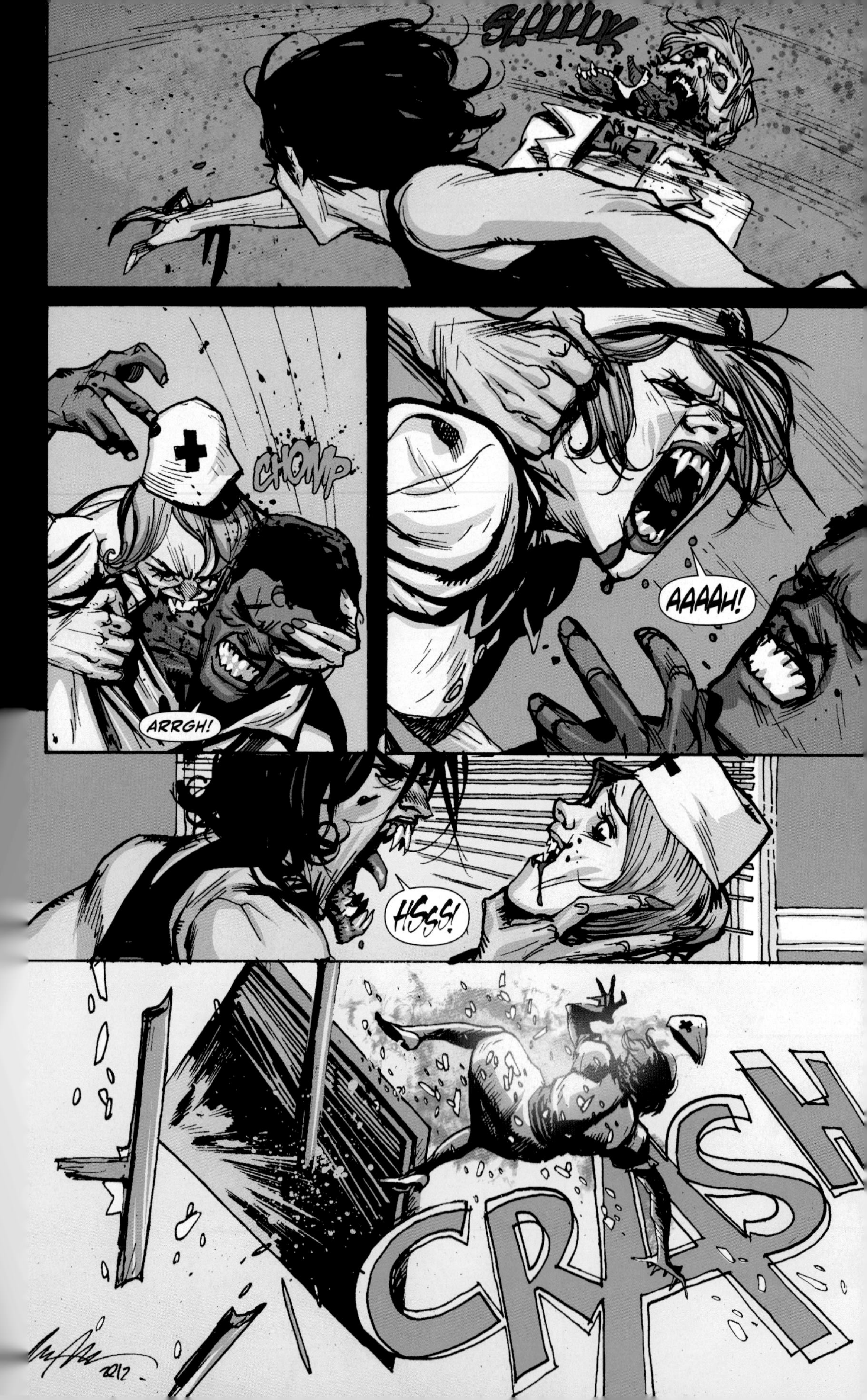
SHLUUUK
CHOMP
ARRGH!
AAAAH!
HSSS!
CRASH

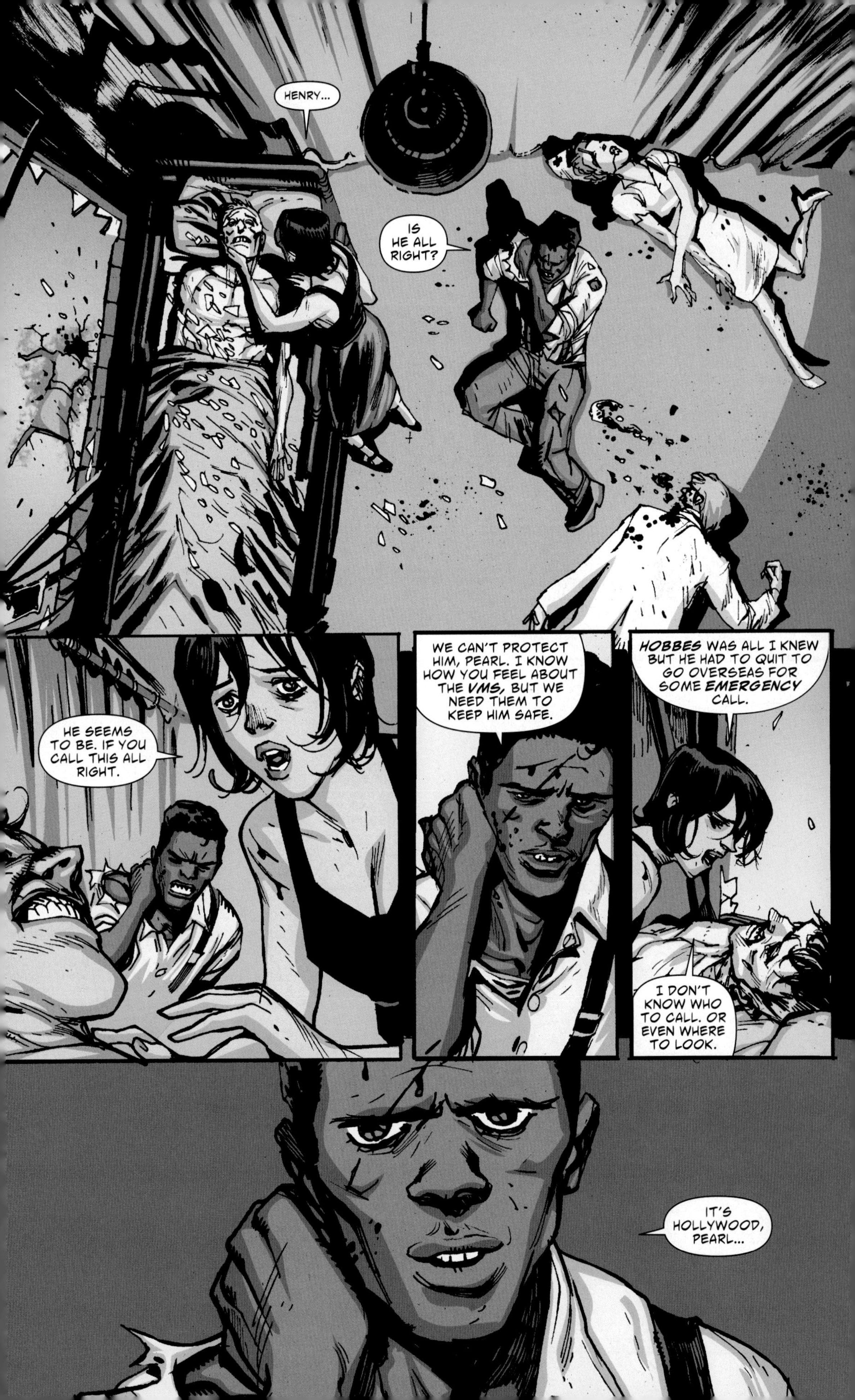
HENRY...
IS HE ALL RIGHT?
HE SEEMS TO BE. IF YOU CALL THIS ALL RIGHT.
WE CAN'T PROTECT HIM, PEARL. I KNOW HOW YOU FEEL ABOUT THE VMS, BUT WE NEED THEM TO KEEP HIM SAFE.
HOBBES WAS ALL I KNEW BUT HE HAD TO QUIT TO GO OVERSEAS FOR SOME EMERGENCY CALL.
I DON'T KNOW WHO TO CALL. OR EVEN WHERE TO LOOK.
IT'S HOLLYWOOD, PEARL...

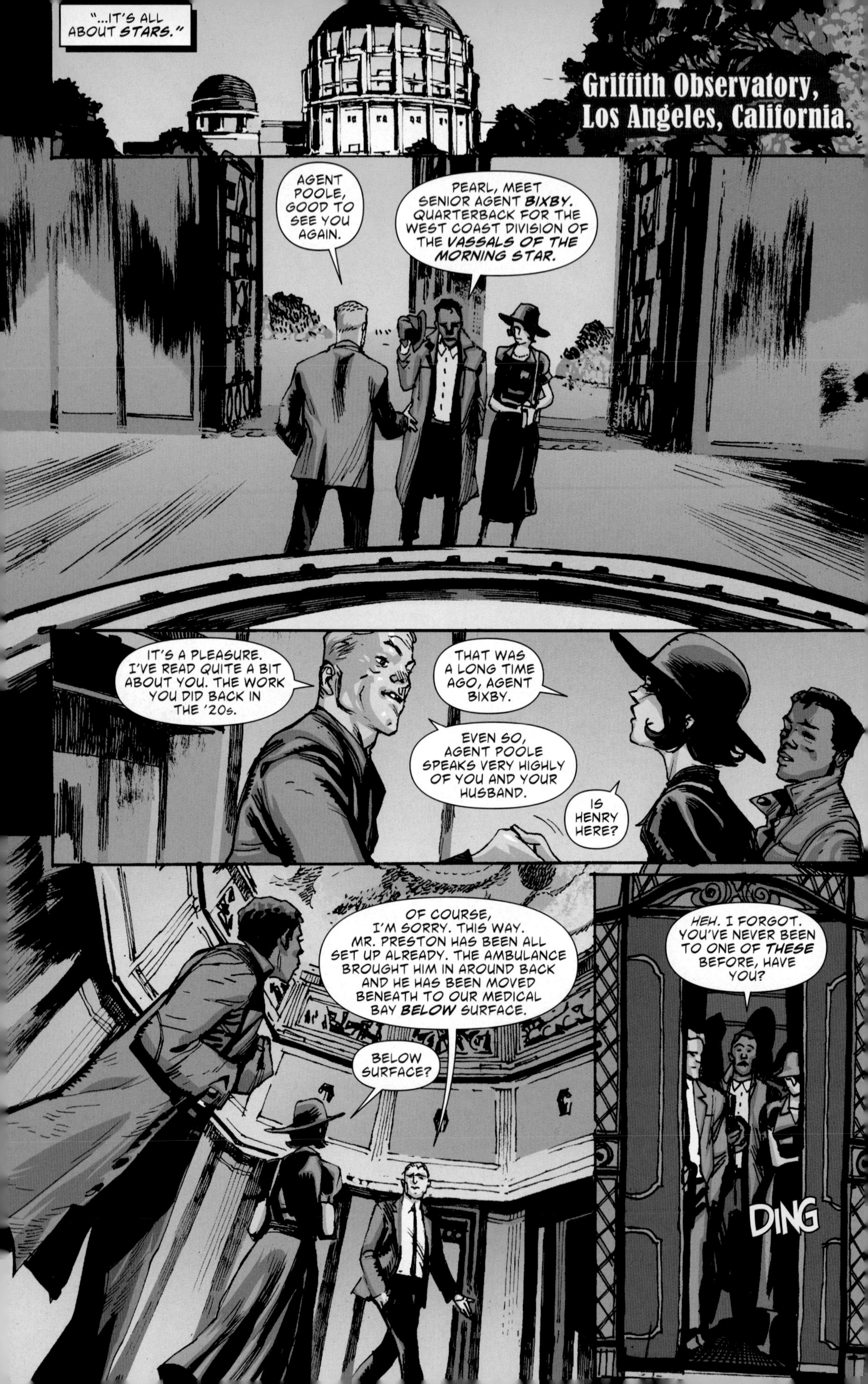
"...IT'S ALL ABOUT STARS."
Griffith Observatory, Los Angeles, California.
AGENT POOLE, GOOD TO SEE YOU AGAIN.
PEARL, MEET SENIOR AGENT BIXBY. QUARTERBACK FOR THE WEST COAST DIVISION OF THE VASSALS OF THE MORNING STAR.
IT'S A PLEASURE. I'VE READ QUITE A BIT ABOUT YOU. THE WORK YOU DID BACK IN THE '20s.
THAT WAS A LONG TIME AGO, AGENT BIXBY.
EVEN SO, AGENT POOLE SPEAKS VERY HIGHLY OF YOU AND YOUR HUSBAND.
IS HENRY HERE?
OF COURSE, I'M SORRY. THIS WAY. MR. PRESTON HAS BEEN ALL SET UP ALREADY. THE AMBULANCE BROUGHT HIM IN AROUND BACK AND HE HAS BEEN MOVED BENEATH TO OUR MEDICAL BAY BELOW SURFACE.
BELOW SURFACE?
HEH. I FORGOT. YOU'VE NEVER BEEN TO ONE OF THESE BEFORE, HAVE YOU?
DING

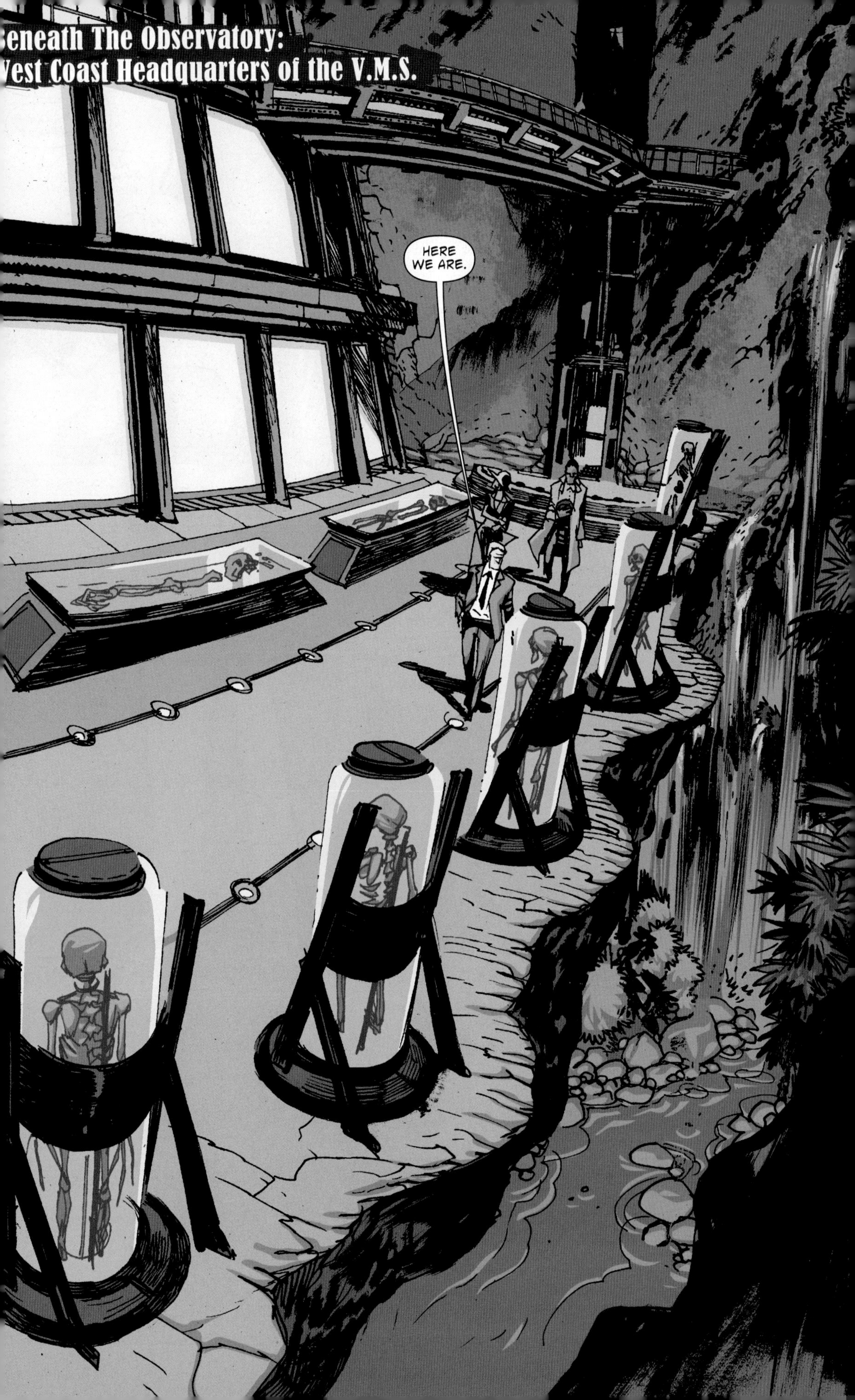
Beneath The Observatory:
West Coast Headquarters of the V.M.S.
HERE WE ARE.

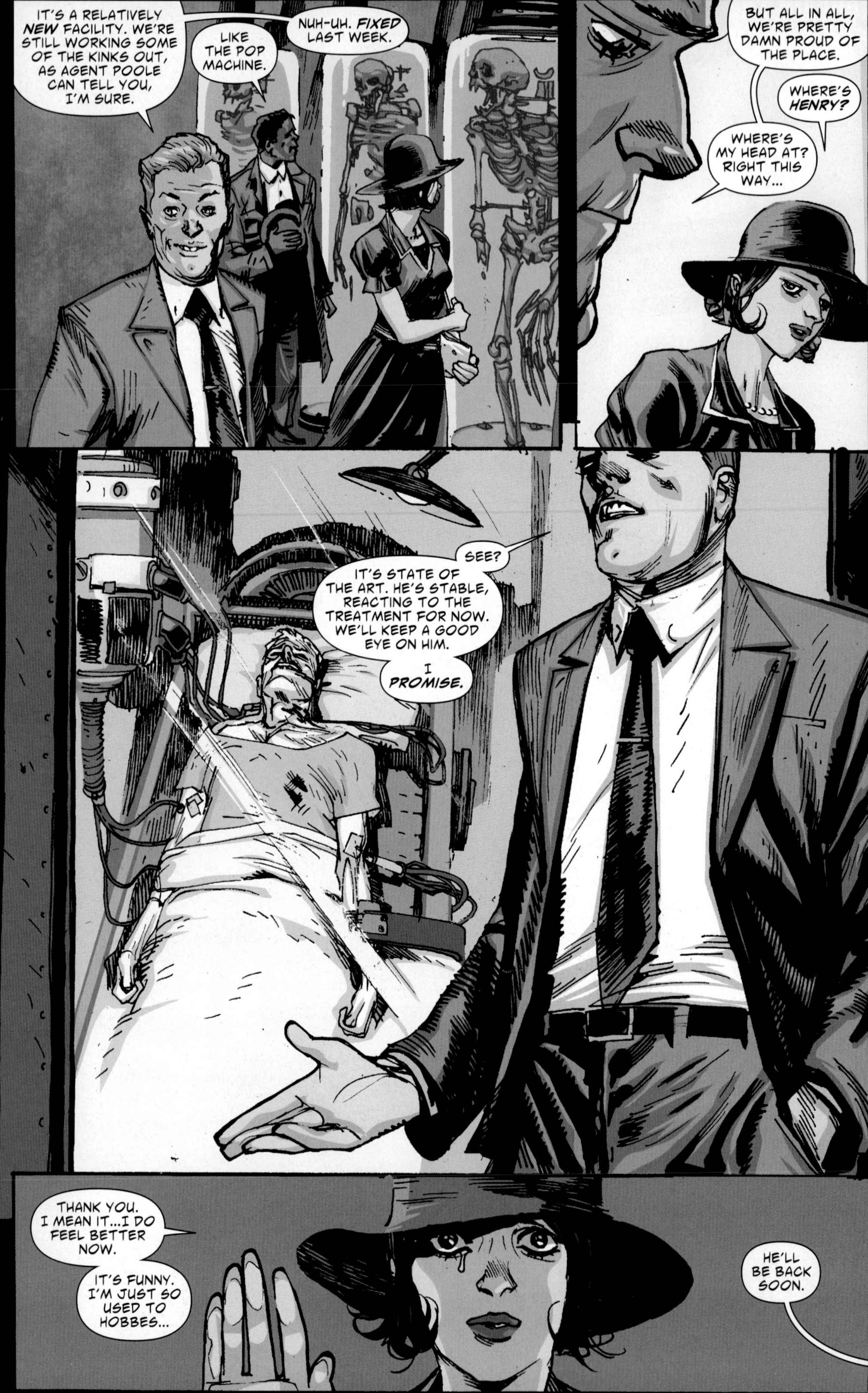
IT'S A RELATIVELY NEW FACILITY. WE'RE STILL WORKING SOME OF THE KINKS OUT, AS AGENT POOLE CAN TELL YOU, I'M SURE.
LIKE THE POP MACHINE.
NUH-UH. FIXED LAST WEEK.
BUT ALL IN ALL, WE'RE PRETTY DAMN PROUD OF THE PLACE.
WHERE'S HENRY?
WHERE'S MY HEAD AT? RIGHT THIS WAY...
SEE?
IT'S STATE OF THE ART. HE'S STABLE, REACTING TO THE TREATMENT FOR NOW. WE'LL KEEP A GOOD EYE ON HIM.
I PROMISE.
THANK YOU. I MEAN IT...I DO FEEL BETTER NOW.
IT'S FUNNY. I'M JUST SO USED TO HOBBES...
HE'LL BE BACK SOON.

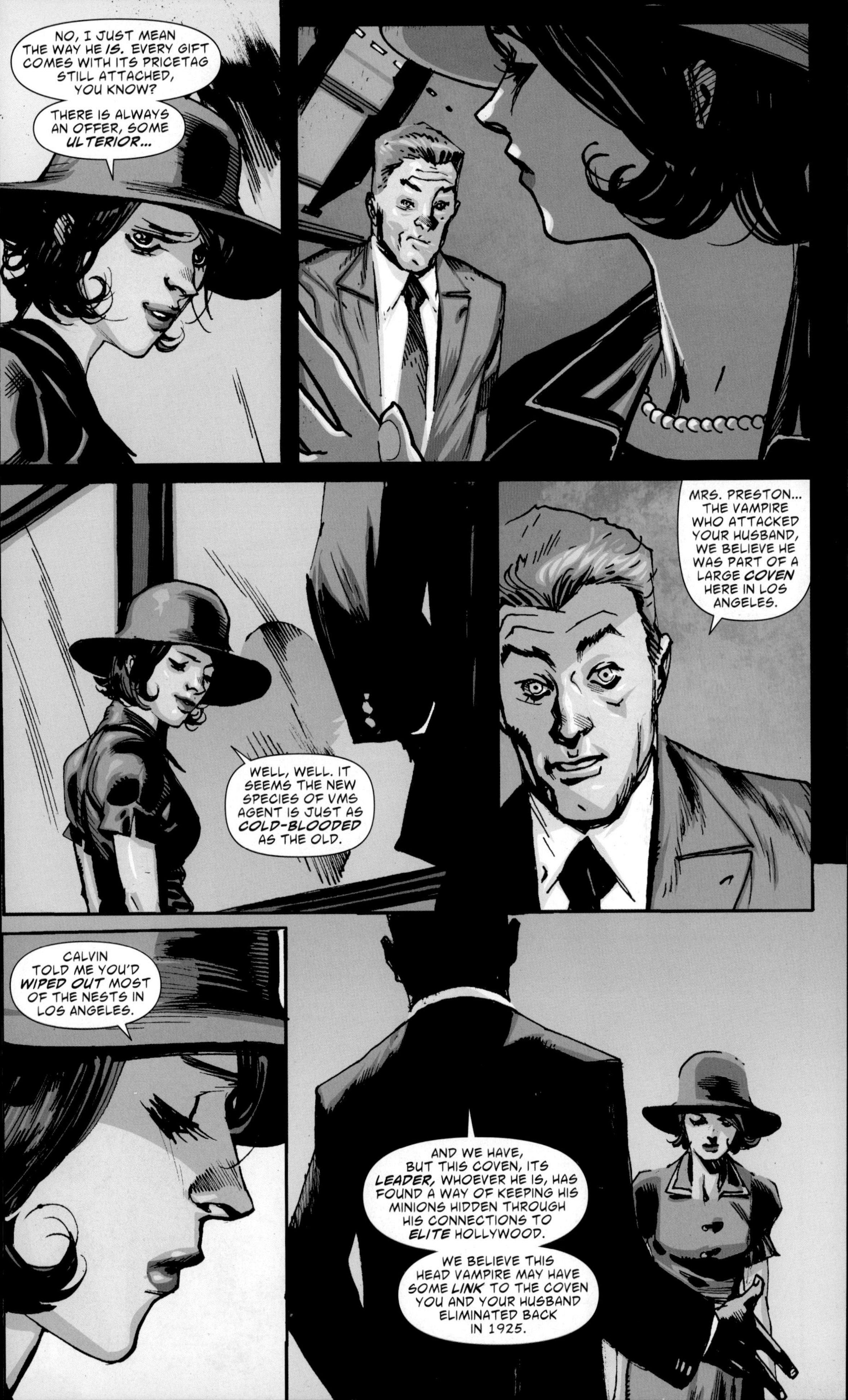
NO, I JUST MEAN THE WAY HE *IS.* EVERY GIFT COMES WITH ITS PRICETAG STILL ATTACHED, YOU KNOW?
THERE IS ALWAYS AN OFFER, SOME *ULTERIOR...*
MRS. PRESTON... THE VAMPIRE WHO ATTACKED YOUR HUSBAND, WE BELIEVE HE WAS PART OF A LARGE *COVEN* HERE IN LOS ANGELES.
WELL, WELL. IT SEEMS THE NEW SPECIES OF VMS AGENT IS JUST AS *COLD-BLOODED* AS THE OLD.
CALVIN TOLD ME YOU'D *WIPED OUT* MOST OF THE NESTS IN LOS ANGELES.
AND WE HAVE, BUT THIS COVEN, ITS *LEADER,* WHOEVER HE IS, HAS FOUND A WAY OF KEEPING HIS MINIONS HIDDEN THROUGH HIS CONNECTIONS TO *ELITE* HOLLYWOOD.
WE BELIEVE THIS HEAD VAMPIRE MAY HAVE SOME *LINK* TO THE COVEN YOU AND YOUR HUSBAND ELIMINATED BACK IN 1925.

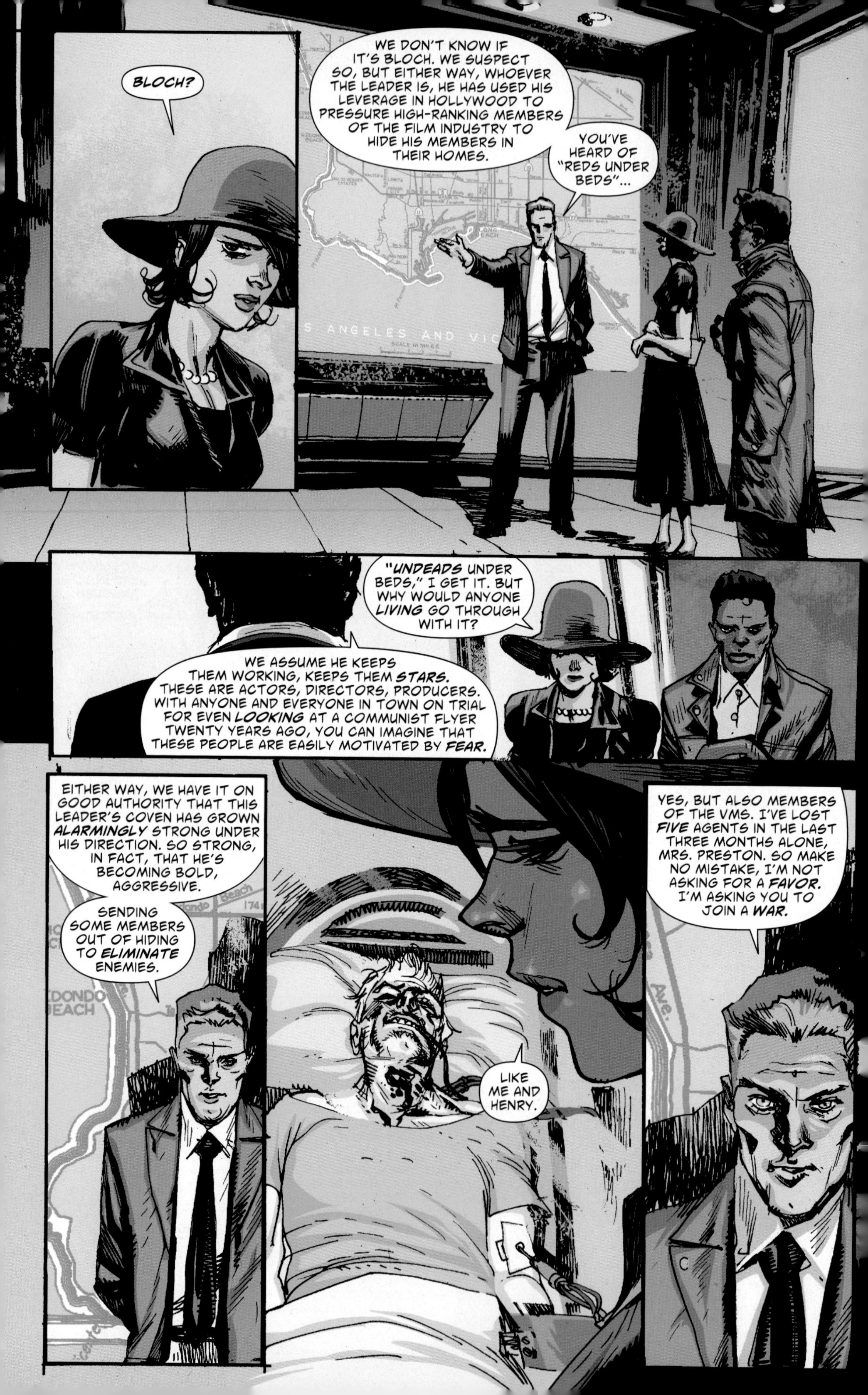
BLOCH?
WE DON'T KNOW IF IT'S BLOCH. WE SUSPECT SO, BUT EITHER WAY, WHOEVER THE LEADER IS, HE HAS USED HIS LEVERAGE IN HOLLYWOOD TO PRESSURE HIGH-RANKING MEMBERS OF THE FILM INDUSTRY TO HIDE HIS MEMBERS IN THEIR HOMES.
YOU'VE HEARD OF "REDS UNDER BEDS"...
LOS ANGELES AND VIC
"*UNDEADS* UNDER BEDS," I GET IT. BUT WHY WOULD ANYONE *LIVING* GO THROUGH WITH IT?
WE ASSUME HE KEEPS THEM WORKING, KEEPS THEM *STARS.* THESE ARE ACTORS, DIRECTORS, PRODUCERS. WITH ANYONE AND EVERYONE IN TOWN ON TRIAL FOR EVEN *LOOKING* AT A COMMUNIST FLYER TWENTY YEARS AGO, YOU CAN IMAGINE THAT THESE PEOPLE ARE EASILY MOTIVATED BY *FEAR.*
EITHER WAY, WE HAVE IT ON GOOD AUTHORITY THAT THIS LEADER'S COVEN HAS GROWN *ALARMINGLY* STRONG UNDER HIS DIRECTION. SO STRONG, IN FACT, THAT HE'S BECOMING BOLD, AGGRESSIVE.
SENDING SOME MEMBERS OUT OF HIDING TO *ELIMINATE* ENEMIES.
LIKE ME AND HENRY.
YES, BUT ALSO MEMBERS OF THE VMS. I'VE LOST *FIVE* AGENTS IN THE LAST THREE MONTHS ALONE, MRS. PRESTON. SO MAKE NO MISTAKE, I'M NOT ASKING FOR A *FAVOR.* I'M ASKING YOU TO JOIN A *WAR.*

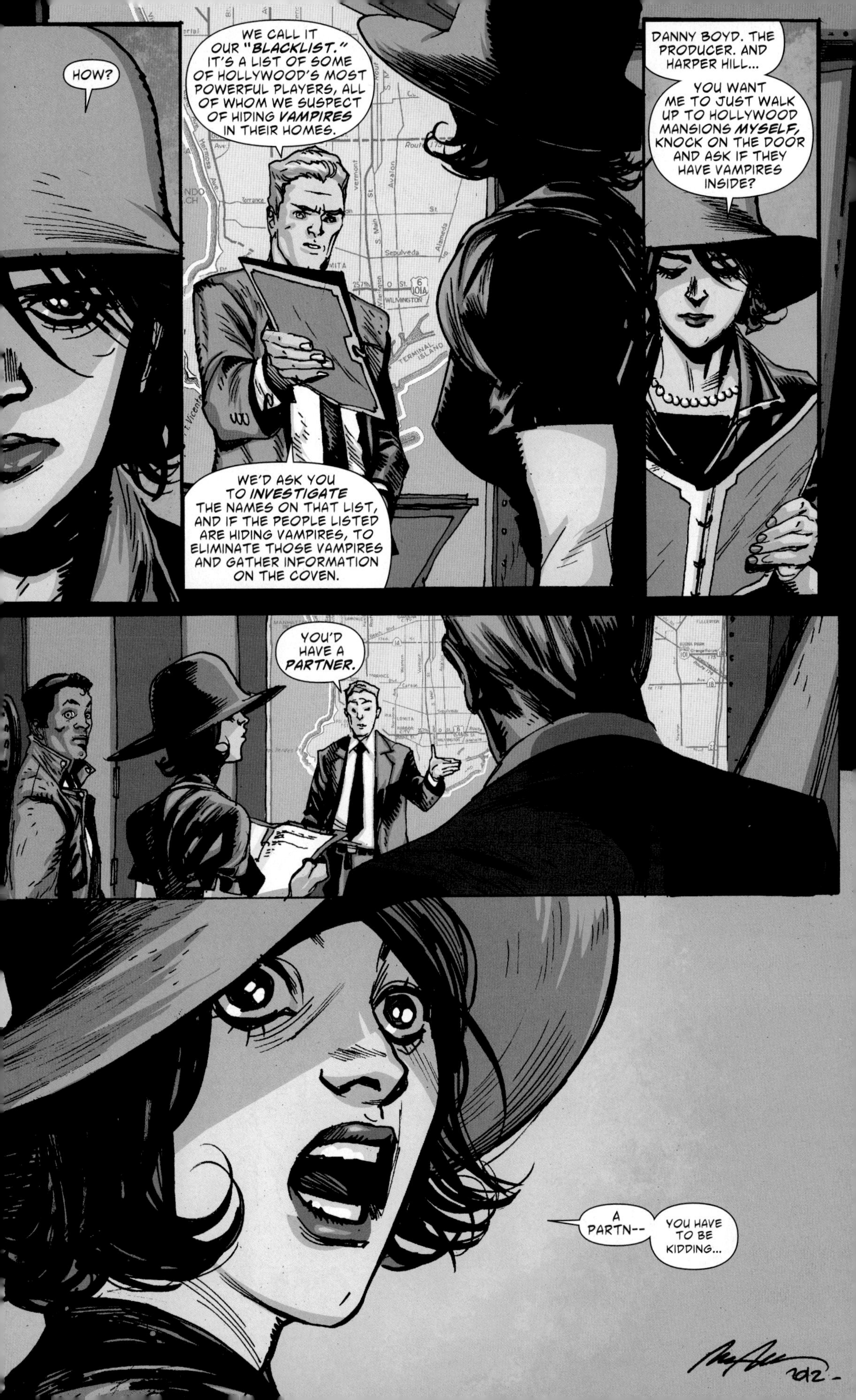
HOW?
WE CALL IT OUR "BLACKLIST." IT'S A LIST OF SOME OF HOLLYWOOD'S MOST POWERFUL PLAYERS, ALL OF WHOM WE SUSPECT OF HIDING VAMPIRES IN THEIR HOMES.
WE'D ASK YOU TO INVESTIGATE THE NAMES ON THAT LIST, AND IF THE PEOPLE LISTED ARE HIDING VAMPIRES, TO ELIMINATE THOSE VAMPIRES AND GATHER INFORMATION ON THE COVEN.
DANNY BOYD. THE PRODUCER. AND HARPER HILL...
YOU WANT ME TO JUST WALK UP TO HOLLYWOOD MANSIONS MYSELF, KNOCK ON THE DOOR AND ASK IF THEY HAVE VAMPIRES INSIDE?
YOU'D HAVE A PARTNER.
A PARTN--
YOU HAVE TO BE KIDDING...

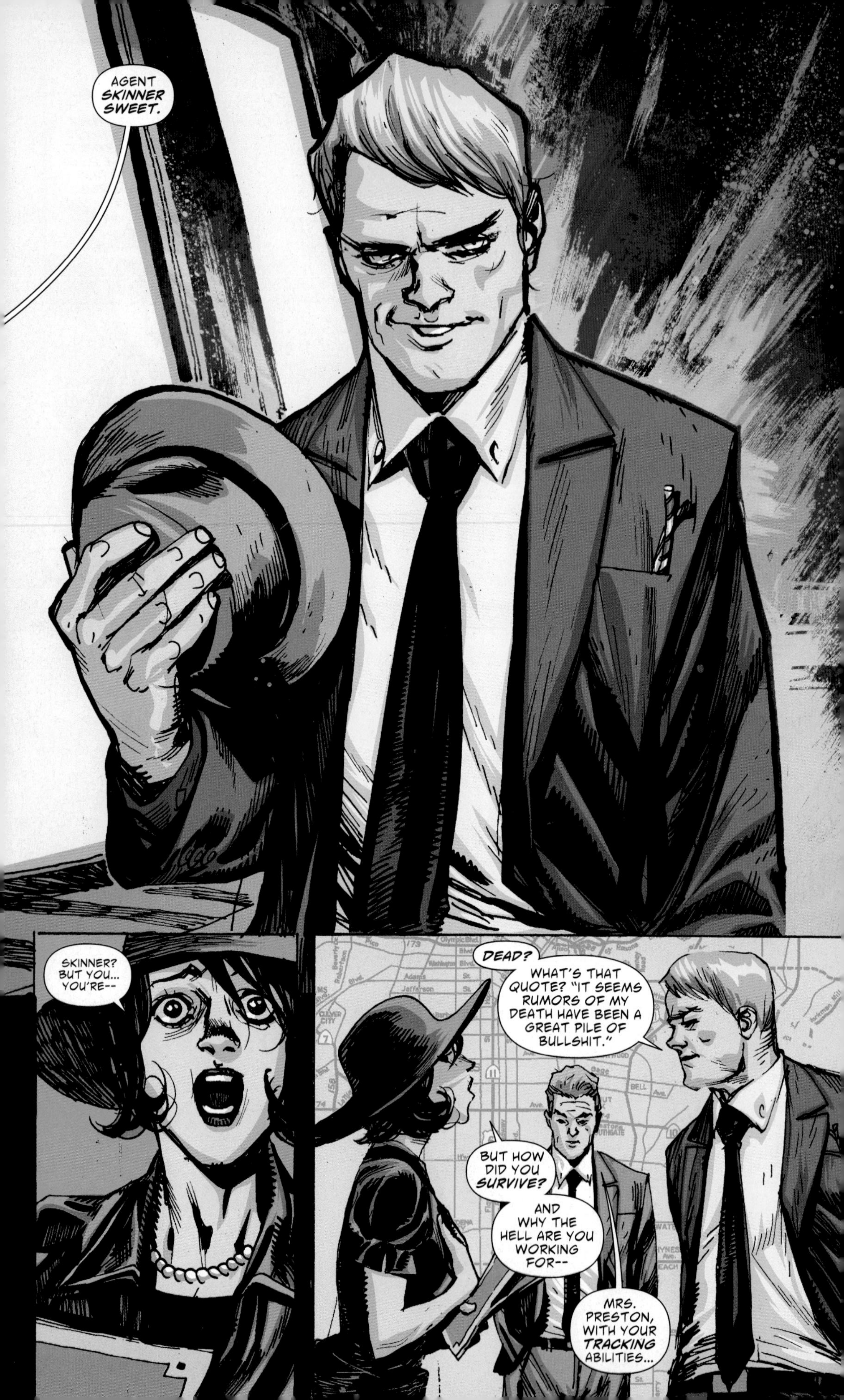
AGENT SKINNER SWEET.
SKINNER? BUT YOU... YOU'RE--
DEAD?
WHAT'S THAT QUOTE? "IT SEEMS RUMORS OF MY DEATH HAVE BEEN A GREAT PILE OF BULLSHIT."
BUT HOW DID YOU SURVIVE?
AND WHY THE HELL ARE YOU WORKING FOR--
MRS. PRESTON, WITH YOUR TRACKING ABILITIES...

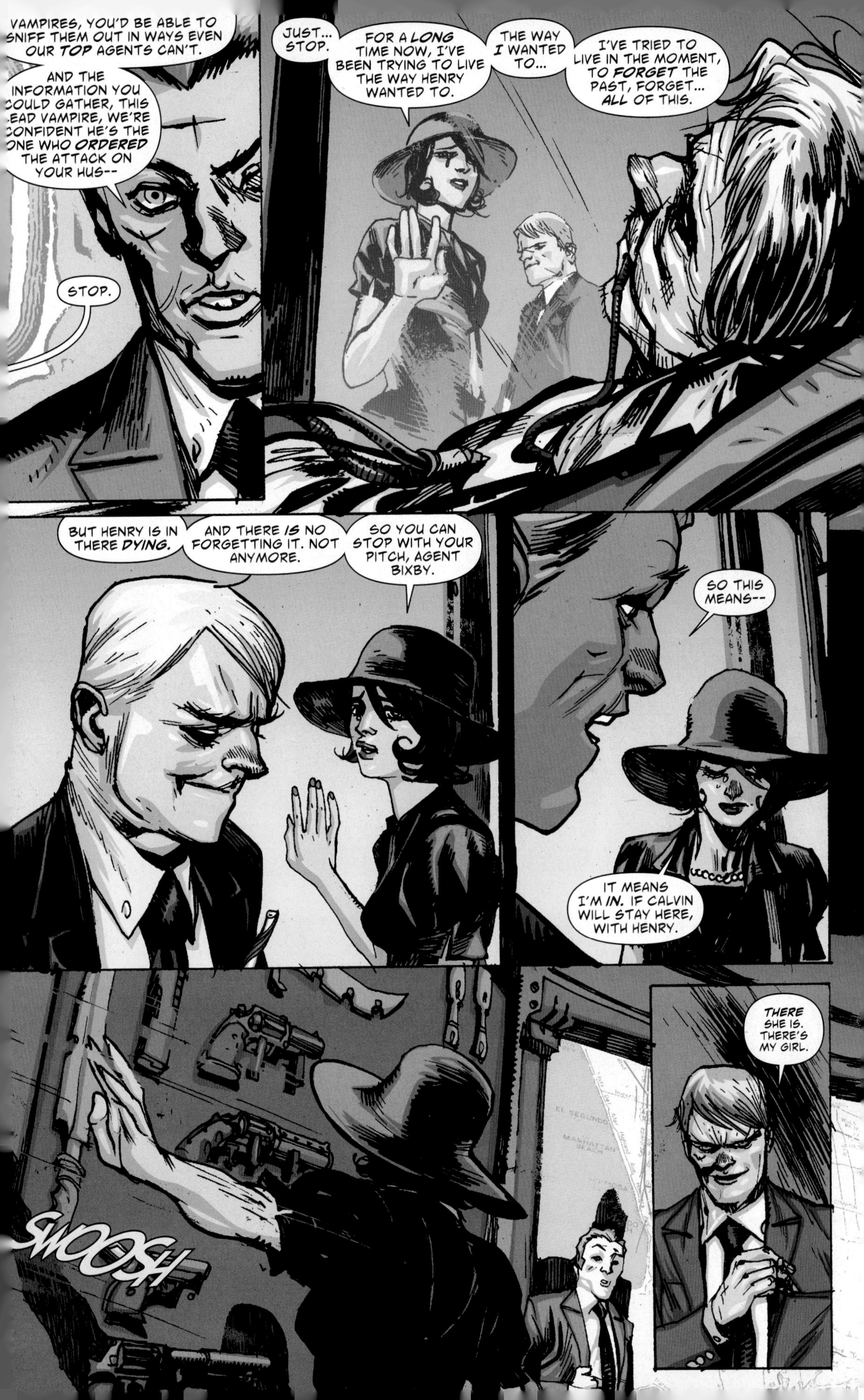
VAMPIRES, YOU'D BE ABLE TO SNIFF THEM OUT IN WAYS EVEN OUR *TOP* AGENTS CAN'T.
AND THE INFORMATION YOU COULD GATHER, THIS LEAD VAMPIRE, WE'RE CONFIDENT HE'S THE ONE WHO *ORDERED* THE ATTACK ON YOUR HUS--
STOP.
JUST... STOP.
FOR A *LONG* TIME NOW, I'VE BEEN TRYING TO LIVE THE WAY HENRY WANTED TO.
THE WAY *I* WANTED TO...
I'VE TRIED TO LIVE IN THE MOMENT, TO *FORGET* THE PAST, FORGET... *ALL* OF THIS.
BUT HENRY IS IN THERE *DYING.*
AND THERE *IS* NO FORGETTING IT. NOT ANYMORE.
SO YOU CAN STOP WITH YOUR PITCH, AGENT BIXBY.
SO THIS MEANS--
IT MEANS I'M *IN.* IF CALVIN WILL STAY HERE, WITH HENRY.
SWOOSH
EL SEGUNDO
MANHATTAN BEACH
THERE SHE IS. THERE'S MY GIRL.

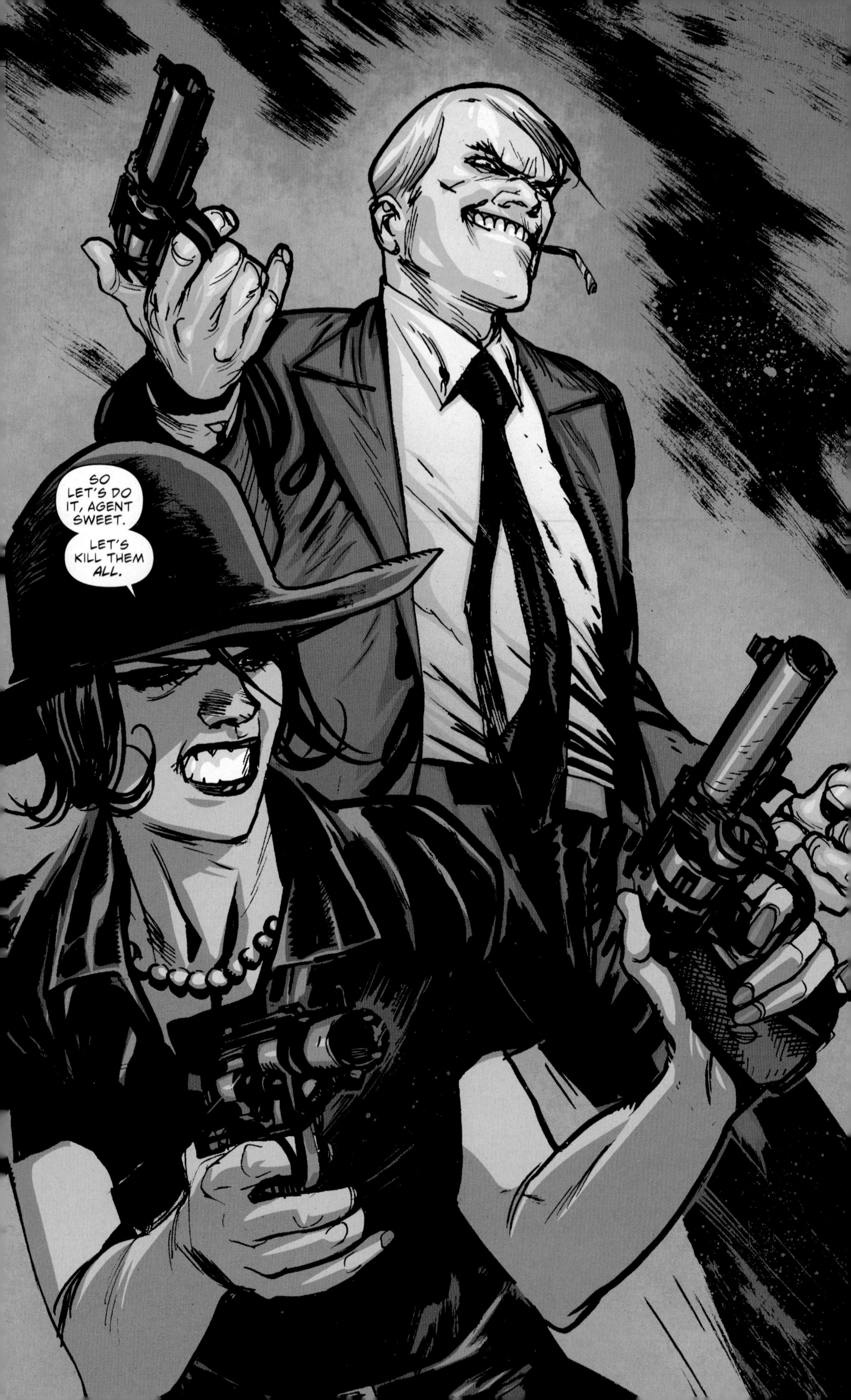
SO LET'S DO IT, AGENT SWEET.
LET'S KILL THEM ALL.

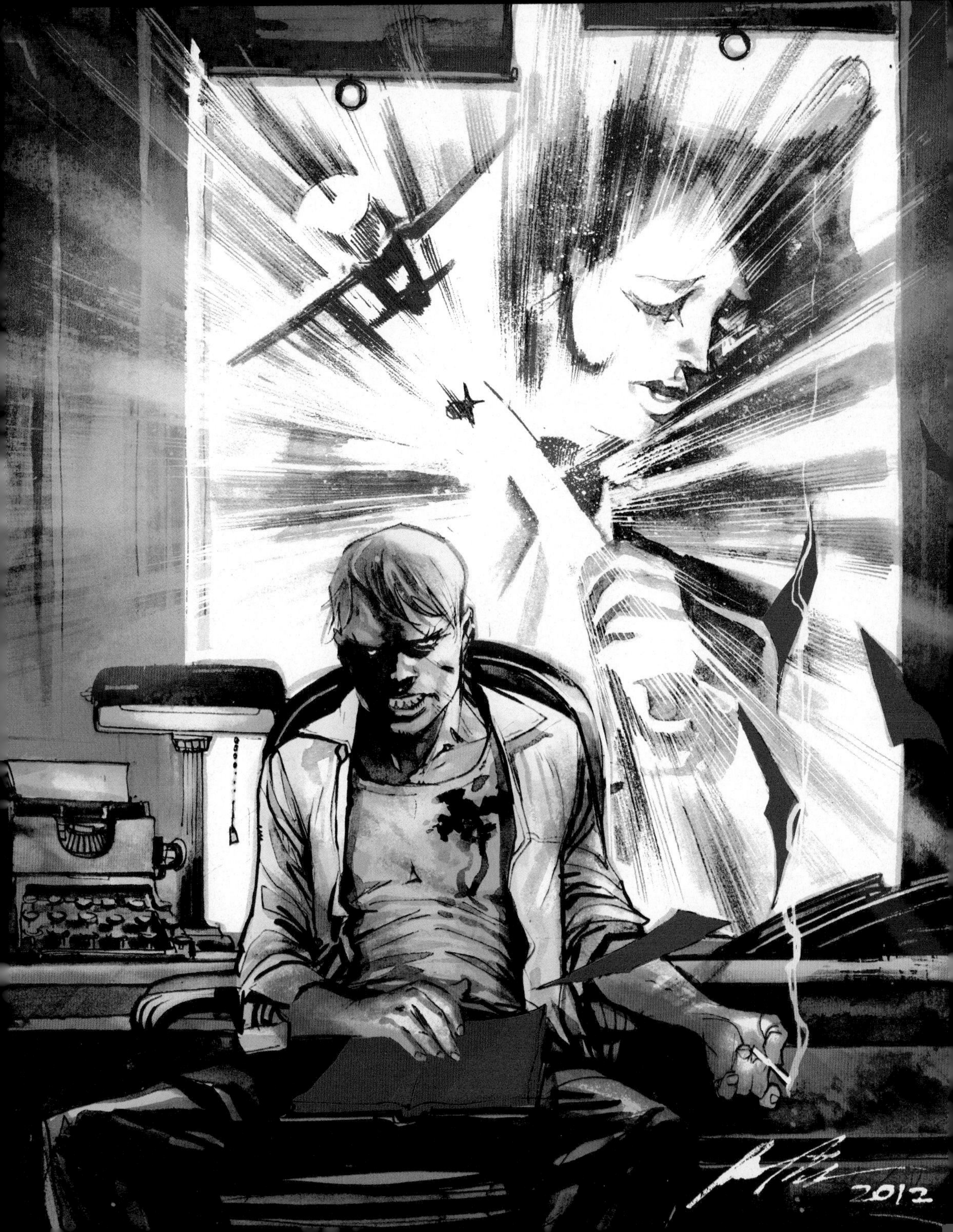
2012

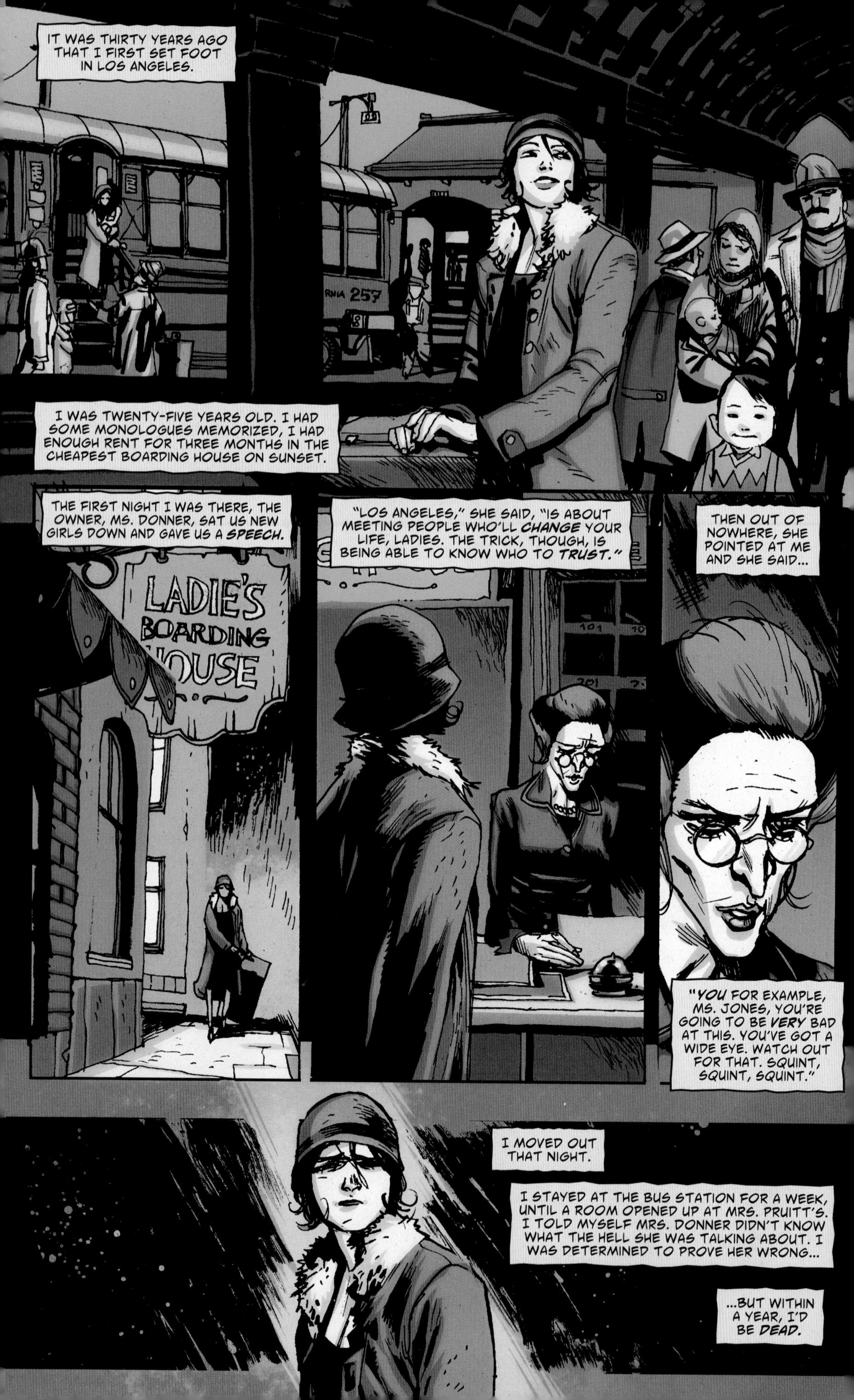
IT WAS THIRTY YEARS AGO THAT I FIRST SET FOOT IN LOS ANGELES.
RNIA 257
I WAS TWENTY-FIVE YEARS OLD. I HAD SOME MONOLOGUES MEMORIZED, I HAD ENOUGH RENT FOR THREE MONTHS IN THE CHEAPEST BOARDING HOUSE ON SUNSET.
THE FIRST NIGHT I WAS THERE, THE OWNER, MS. DONNER, SAT US NEW GIRLS DOWN AND GAVE US A *SPEECH.*
LADIE'S BOARDING HOUSE
"LOS ANGELES," SHE SAID, "IS ABOUT MEETING PEOPLE WHO'LL *CHANGE* YOUR LIFE, LADIES. THE TRICK, THOUGH, IS BEING ABLE TO KNOW WHO TO *TRUST.*"
THEN OUT OF NOWHERE, SHE POINTED AT ME AND SHE SAID...
"*YOU* FOR EXAMPLE, MS. JONES, YOU'RE GOING TO BE *VERY* BAD AT THIS. YOU'VE GOT A WIDE EYE. WATCH OUT FOR THAT. SQUINT, SQUINT, SQUINT."
I MOVED OUT THAT NIGHT.
I STAYED AT THE BUS STATION FOR A WEEK, UNTIL A ROOM OPENED UP AT MRS. PRUITT'S. I TOLD MYSELF MRS. DONNER DIDN'T KNOW WHAT THE HELL SHE WAS TALKING ABOUT. I WAS DETERMINED TO PROVE HER WRONG...
...BUT WITHIN A YEAR, I'D BE *DEAD.*

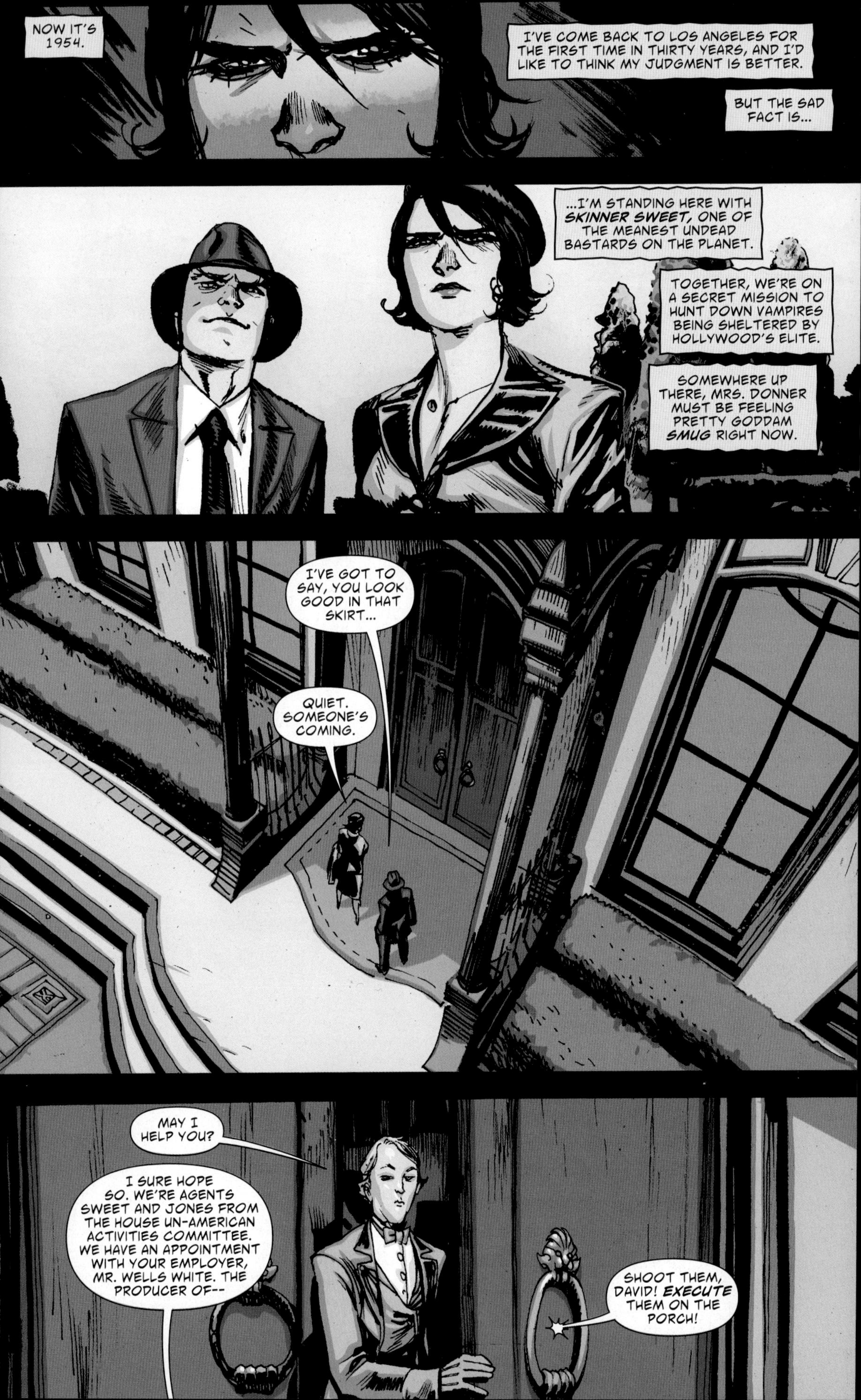
NOW IT'S 1954.
I'VE COME BACK TO LOS ANGELES FOR THE FIRST TIME IN THIRTY YEARS, AND I'D LIKE TO THINK MY JUDGMENT IS BETTER.
BUT THE SAD FACT IS...
...I'M STANDING HERE WITH SKINNER SWEET, ONE OF THE MEANEST UNDEAD BASTARDS ON THE PLANET.
TOGETHER, WE'RE ON A SECRET MISSION TO HUNT DOWN VAMPIRES BEING SHELTERED BY HOLLYWOOD'S ELITE.
SOMEWHERE UP THERE, MRS. DONNER MUST BE FEELING PRETTY GODDAM SMUG RIGHT NOW.
I'VE GOT TO SAY, YOU LOOK GOOD IN THAT SKIRT...
QUIET. SOMEONE'S COMING.
MAY I HELP YOU?
I SURE HOPE SO. WE'RE AGENTS SWEET AND JONES FROM THE HOUSE UN-AMERICAN ACTIVITIES COMMITTEE. WE HAVE AN APPOINTMENT WITH YOUR EMPLOYER, MR. WELLS WHITE. THE PRODUCER OF--
SHOOT THEM, DAVID! EXECUTE THEM ON THE PORCH!

HA, HA! I AM ONLY JOKING, OF COURSE! YOU ENTER MY HOME AS **WELCOME** GUESTS, AGENTS SWEET, YOU SAID? AND JONES? COME IN!

PRESTON, ACTUALLY.

PRESTON, THEN!

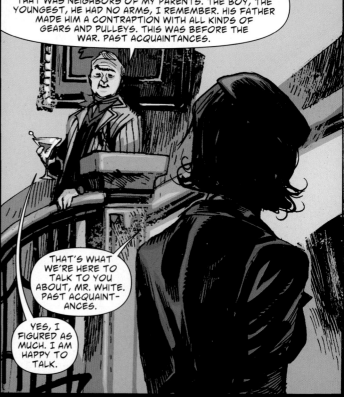

YOU KNOW, THERE WAS A PRESTON FAMILY, BACK IN AUSTRIA, THAT WAS NEIGHBORS OF MY PARENTS. THE BOY, THE YOUNGEST, HE HAD NO ARMS, I REMEMBER. HIS FATHER MADE HIM A CONTRAPTION WITH ALL KINDS OF GEARS AND PULLEYS. THIS WAS BEFORE THE WAR. PAST ACQUAINTANCES.

THAT'S WHAT WE'RE HERE TO TALK TO YOU ABOUT, MR. WHITE. PAST ACQUAINTANCES.

YES, I FIGURED AS MUCH. I AM HAPPY TO TALK.

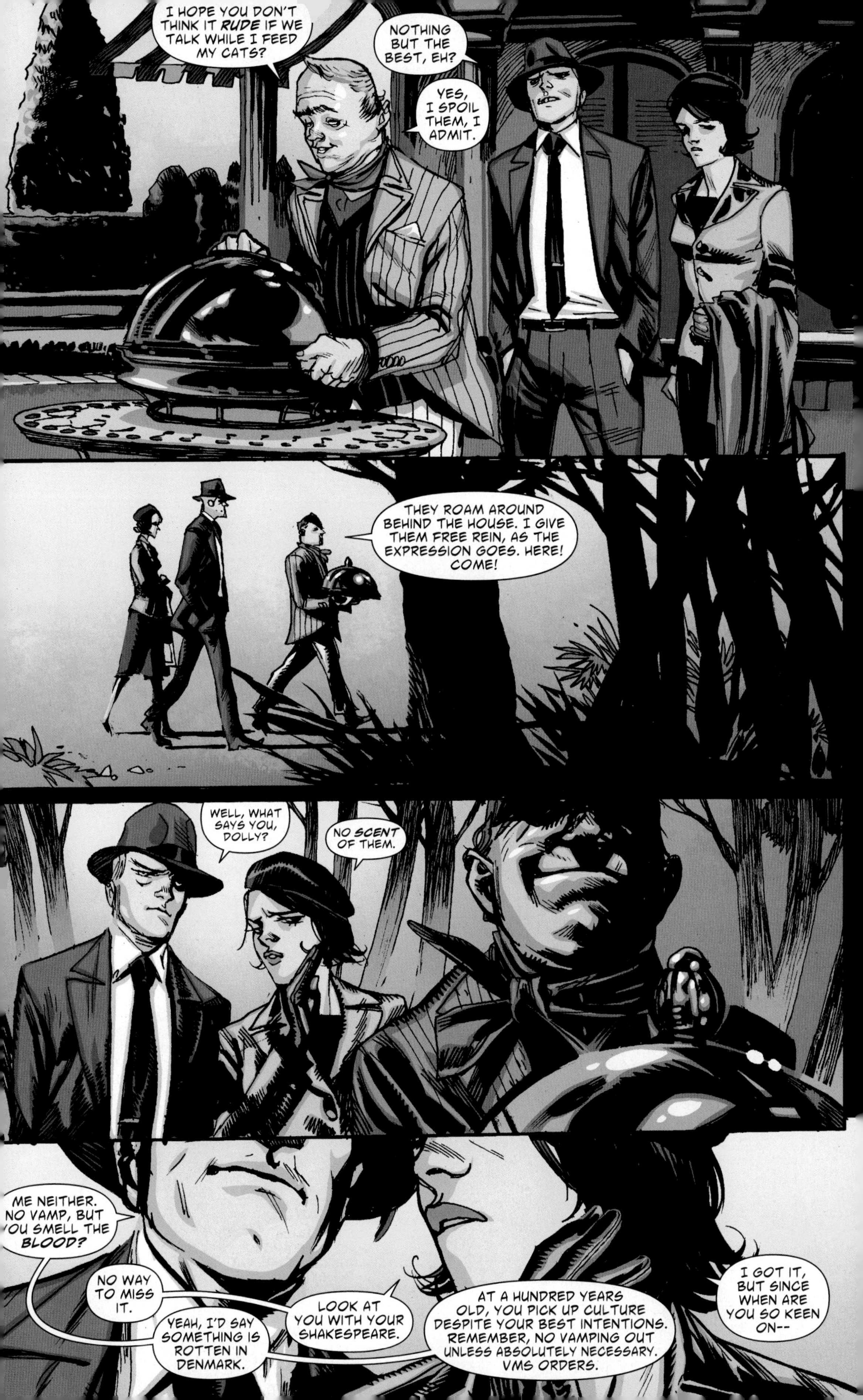
I HOPE YOU DON'T THINK IT RUDE IF WE TALK WHILE I FEED MY CATS?
NOTHING BUT THE BEST, EH?
YES, I SPOIL THEM, I ADMIT.
THEY ROAM AROUND BEHIND THE HOUSE. I GIVE THEM FREE REIN, AS THE EXPRESSION GOES. HERE! COME!
WELL, WHAT SAYS YOU, DOLLY?
NO SCENT OF THEM.
ME NEITHER. NO VAMP, BUT YOU SMELL THE BLOOD?
NO WAY TO MISS IT.
YEAH, I'D SAY SOMETHING IS ROTTEN IN DENMARK.
LOOK AT YOU WITH YOUR SHAKESPEARE.
AT A HUNDRED YEARS OLD, YOU PICK UP CULTURE DESPITE YOUR BEST INTENTIONS. REMEMBER, NO VAMPING OUT UNLESS ABSOLUTELY NECESSARY. VMS ORDERS.
I GOT IT, BUT SINCE WHEN ARE YOU SO KEEN ON--

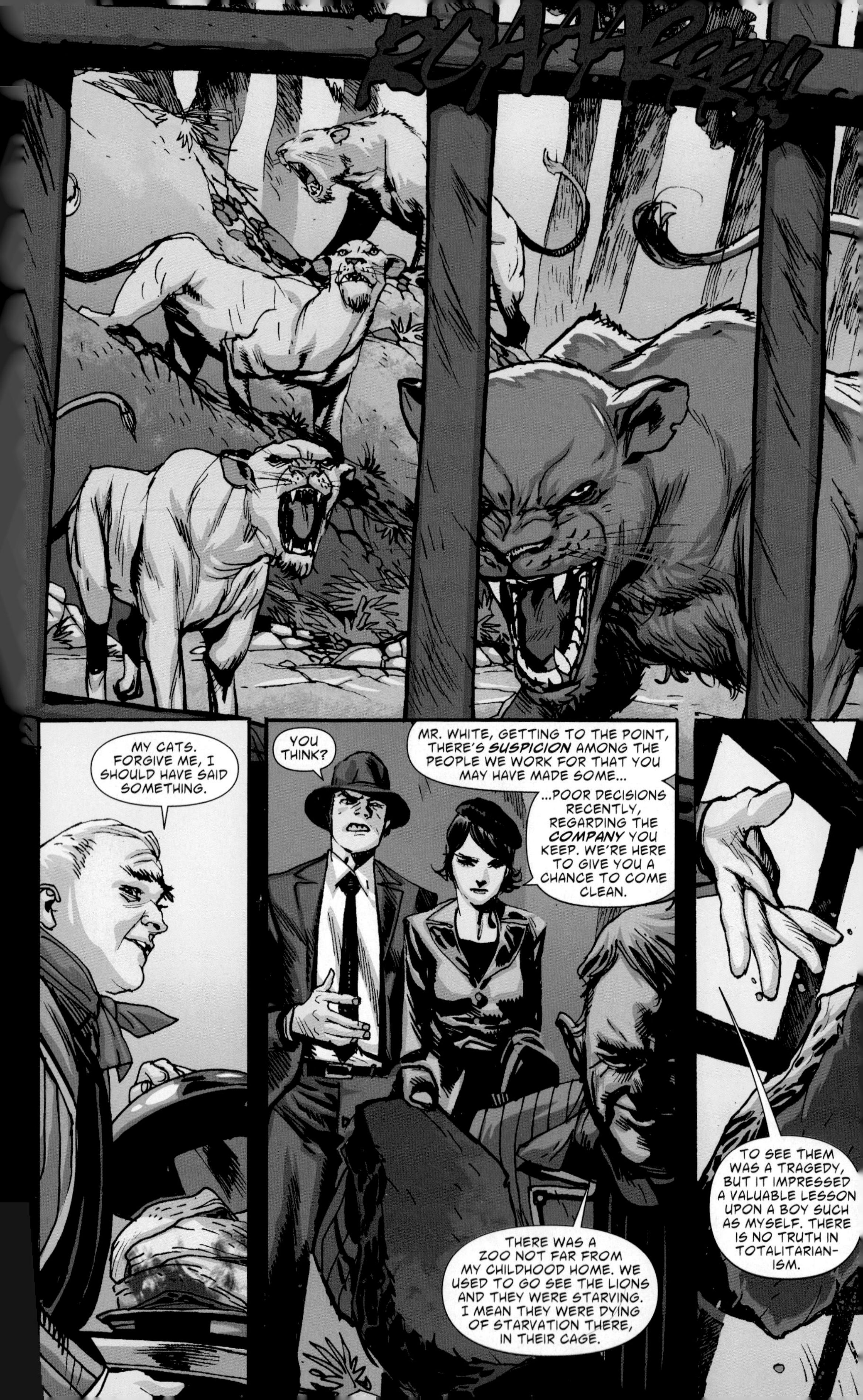
ROAAARRR!!
MY CATS. FORGIVE ME, I SHOULD HAVE SAID SOMETHING.
YOU THINK?
MR. WHITE, GETTING TO THE POINT, THERE'S *SUSPICION* AMONG THE PEOPLE WE WORK FOR THAT YOU MAY HAVE MADE SOME...
...POOR DECISIONS RECENTLY, REGARDING THE **COMPANY** YOU KEEP. WE'RE HERE TO GIVE YOU A CHANCE TO COME CLEAN.
THERE WAS A ZOO NOT FAR FROM MY CHILDHOOD HOME. WE USED TO GO SEE THE LIONS AND THEY WERE STARVING. I MEAN THEY WERE DYING OF STARVATION THERE, IN THEIR CAGE.
TO SEE THEM WAS A TRAGEDY, BUT IT IMPRESSED A VALUABLE LESSON UPON A BOY SUCH AS MYSELF. THERE IS NO TRUTH IN TOTALITARIAN-ISM.

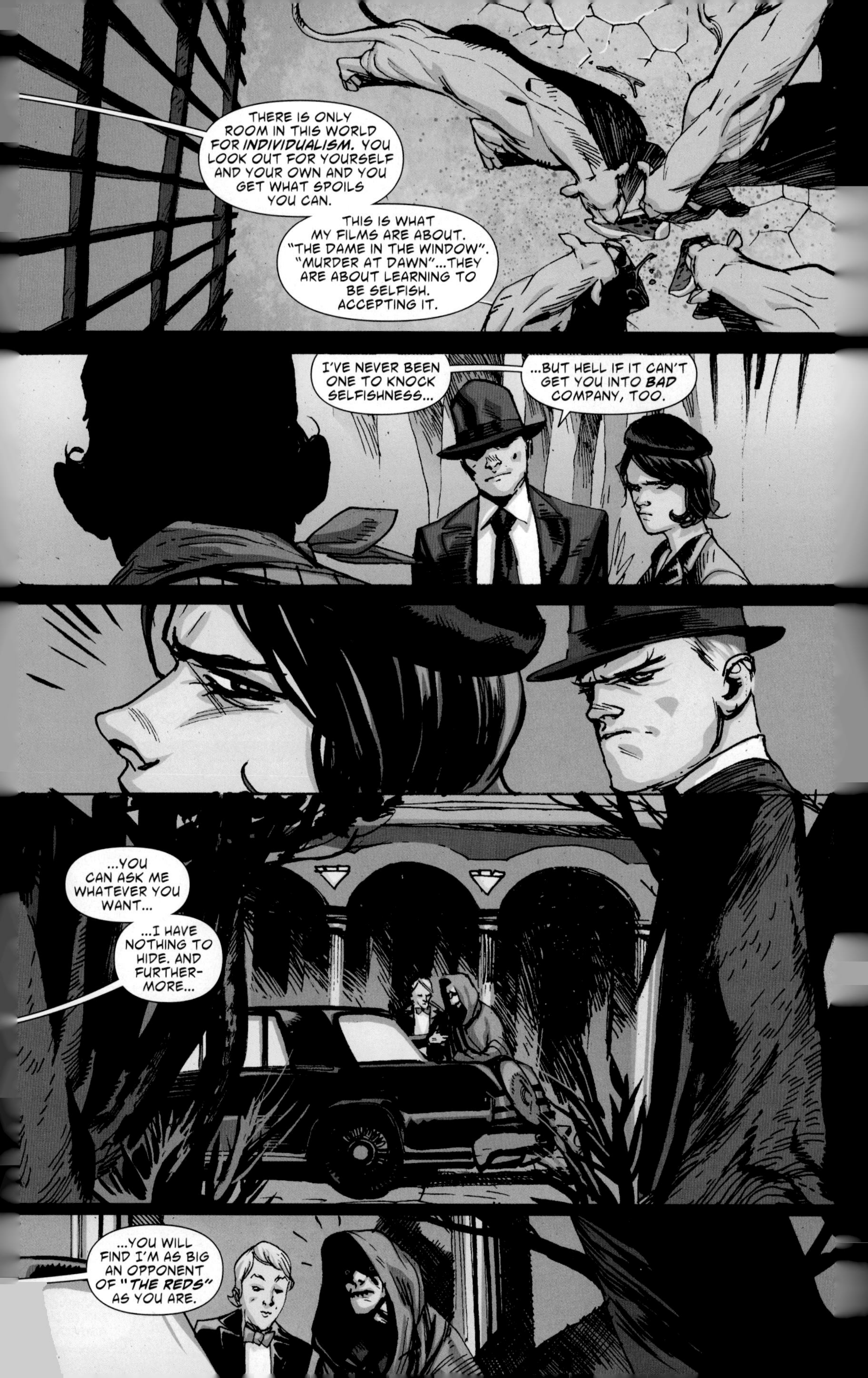

THERE IS ONLY ROOM IN THIS WORLD FOR *INDIVIDUALISM.* YOU LOOK OUT FOR YOURSELF AND YOUR OWN AND YOU GET WHAT SPOILS YOU CAN.
THIS IS WHAT MY FILMS ARE ABOUT. "THE DAME IN THE WINDOW". "MURDER AT DAWN"...THEY ARE ABOUT LEARNING TO BE SELFISH. ACCEPTING IT.
I'VE NEVER BEEN ONE TO KNOCK SELFISHNESS...
...BUT HELL IF IT CAN'T GET YOU INTO *BAD* COMPANY, TOO.
...YOU CAN ASK ME WHATEVER YOU WANT...
...I HAVE NOTHING TO HIDE. AND FURTHER-MORE...
...YOU WILL FIND I'M AS BIG AN OPPONENT OF *"THE REDS"* AS YOU ARE.

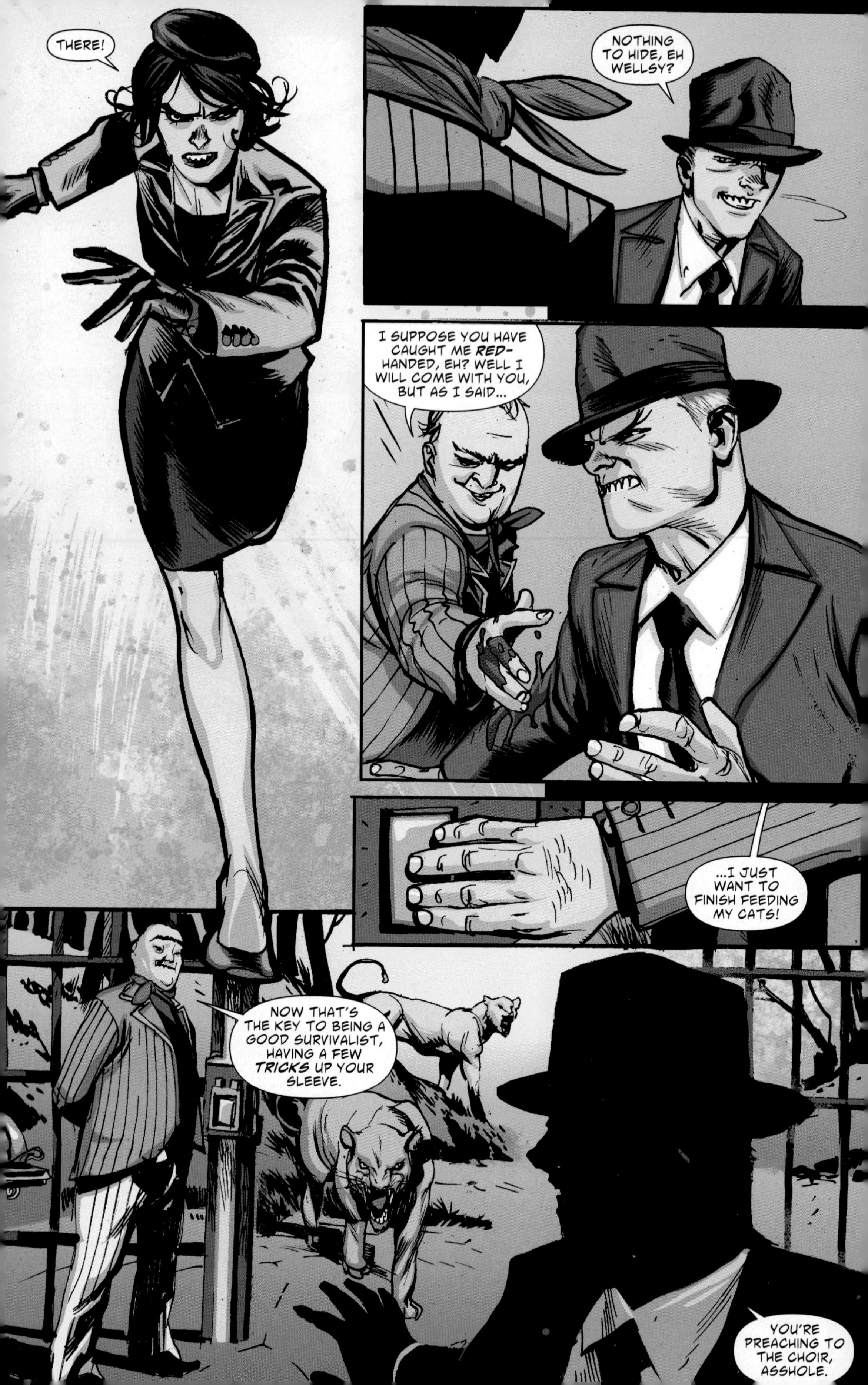
THERE!
NOTHING TO HIDE, EH WELLSY?
I SUPPOSE YOU HAVE CAUGHT ME RED-HANDED, EH? WELL I WILL COME WITH YOU, BUT AS I SAID...
...I JUST WANT TO FINISH FEEDING MY CATS!
NOW THAT'S THE KEY TO BEING A GOOD SURVIVALIST, HAVING A FEW TRICKS UP YOUR SLEEVE.
YOU'RE PREACHING TO THE CHOIR, ASSHOLE.

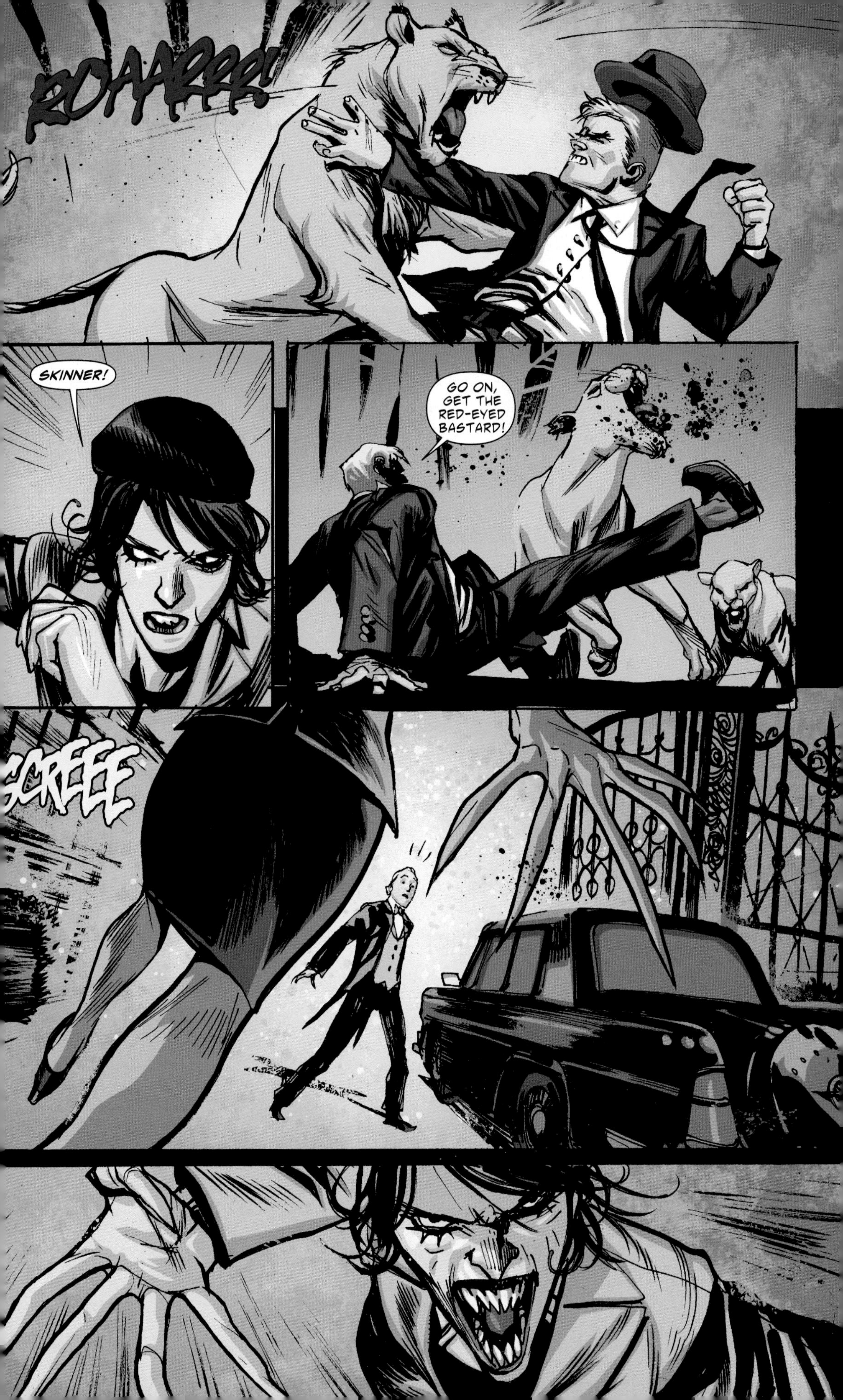
ROAARRR!
SKINNER!
GO ON, GET THE RED-EYED BASTARD!
SCREEE

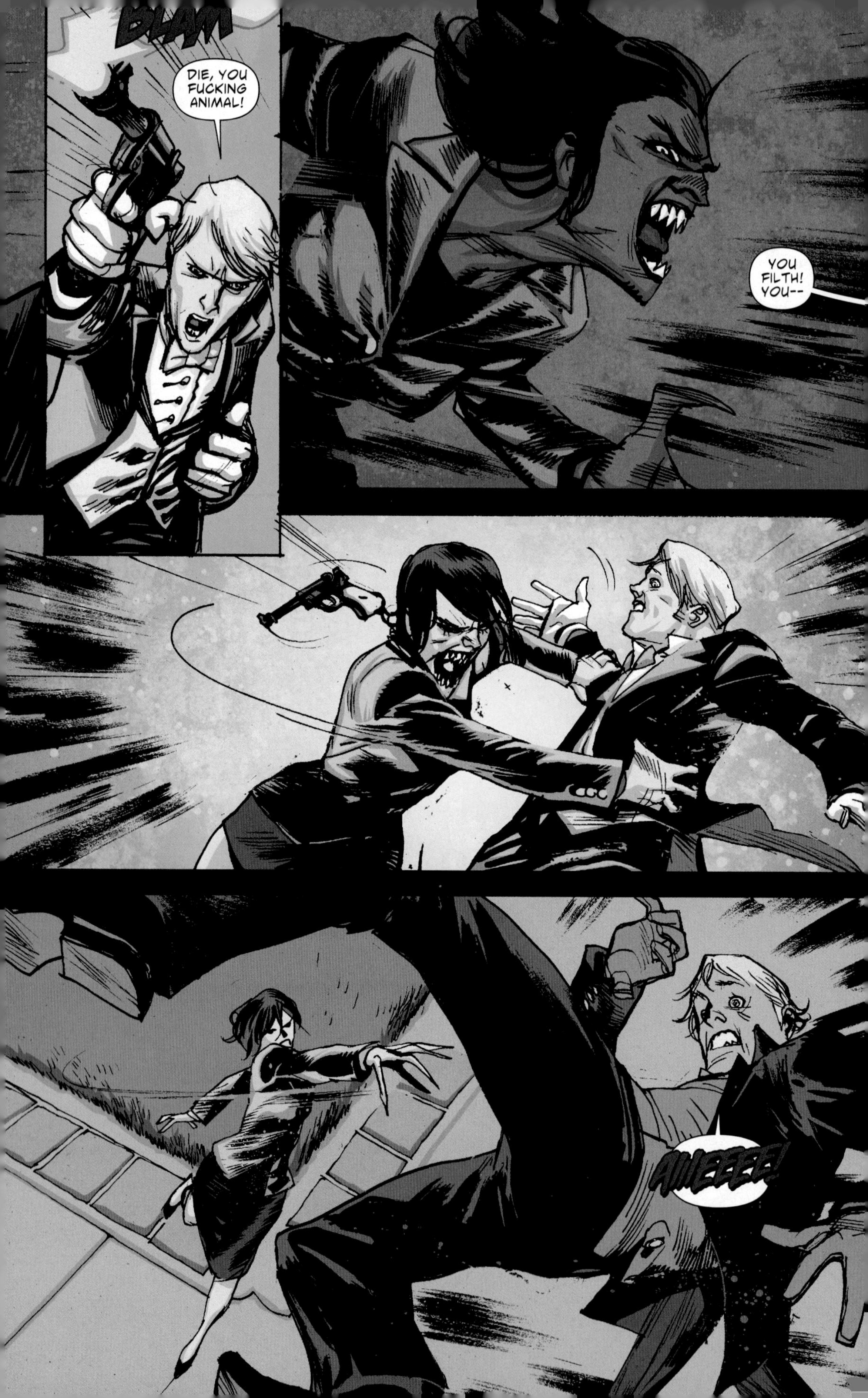
BLAM
DIE, YOU FUCKING ANIMAL!
YOU FILTH! YOU--
AIIEEEEE!

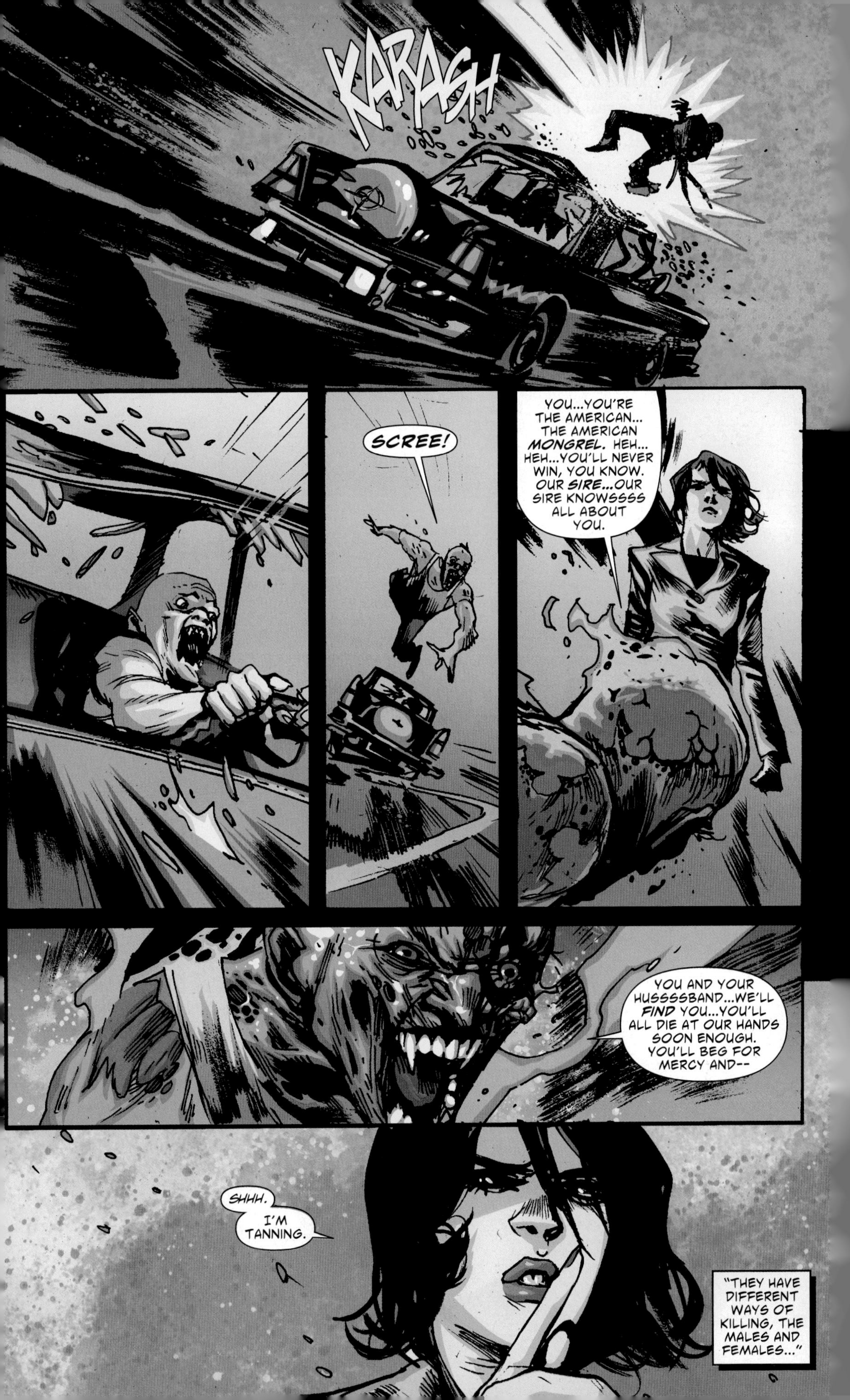
KARASH
SCREE!
YOU...YOU'RE THE AMERICAN... THE AMERICAN MONGREL. HEH... HEH...YOU'LL NEVER WIN, YOU KNOW. OUR SIRE...OUR SIRE KNOWSSSS ALL ABOUT YOU.
YOU AND YOUR HUSSSSBAND...WE'LL FIND YOU...YOU'LL ALL DIE AT OUR HANDS SOON ENOUGH. YOU'LL BEG FOR MERCY AND--
SHHH.
I'M TANNING.
"THEY HAVE DIFFERENT WAYS OF KILLING, THE MALES AND FEMALES..."

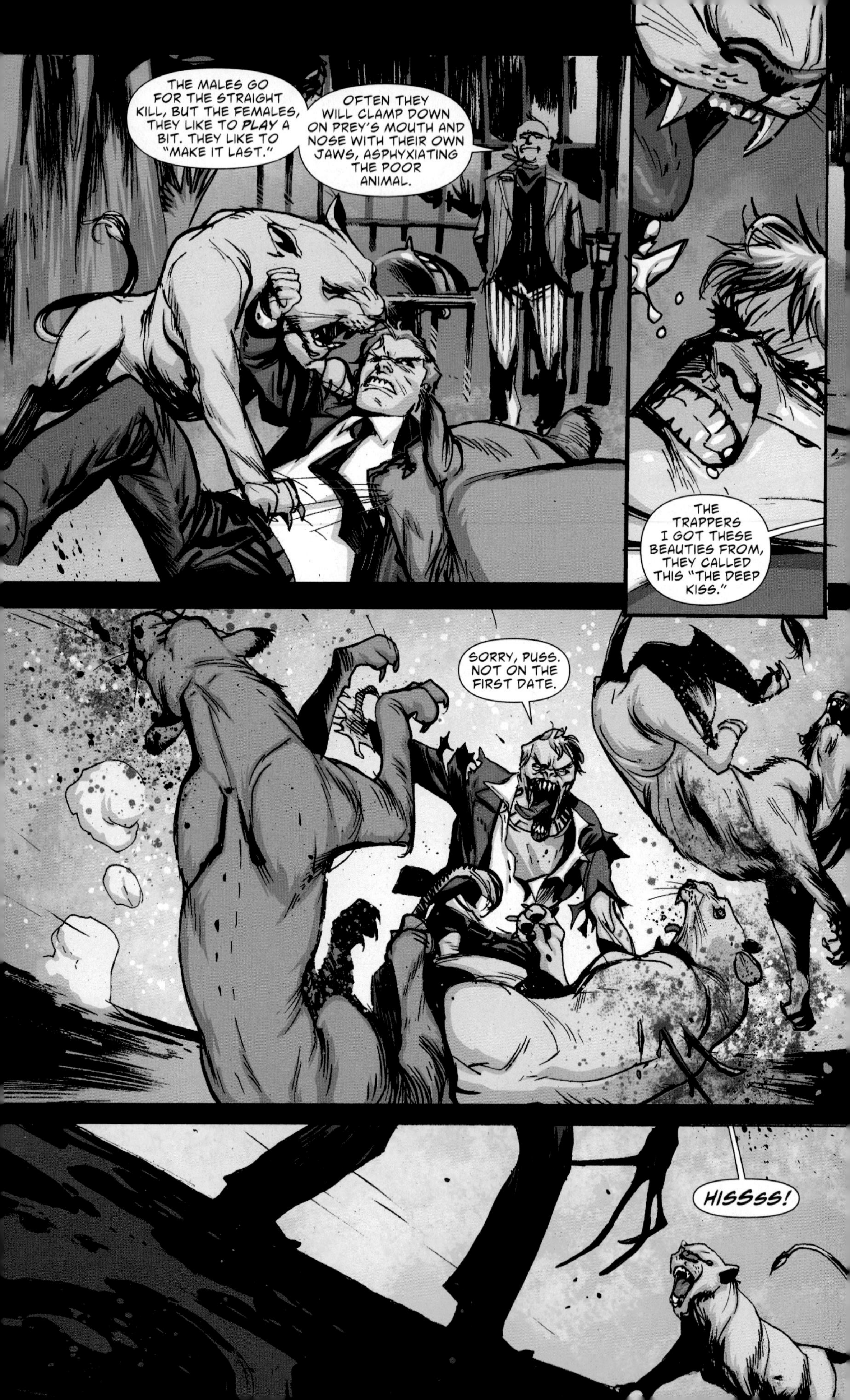
THE MALES GO FOR THE STRAIGHT KILL, BUT THE FEMALES, THEY LIKE TO *PLAY* A BIT. THEY LIKE TO "MAKE IT LAST."
OFTEN THEY WILL CLAMP DOWN ON PREY'S MOUTH AND NOSE WITH THEIR OWN JAWS, ASPHYXIATING THE POOR ANIMAL.
THE TRAPPERS I GOT THESE BEAUTIES FROM, THEY CALLED THIS "THE DEEP KISS."
SORRY, PUSS. NOT ON THE FIRST DATE.
HISSSS!

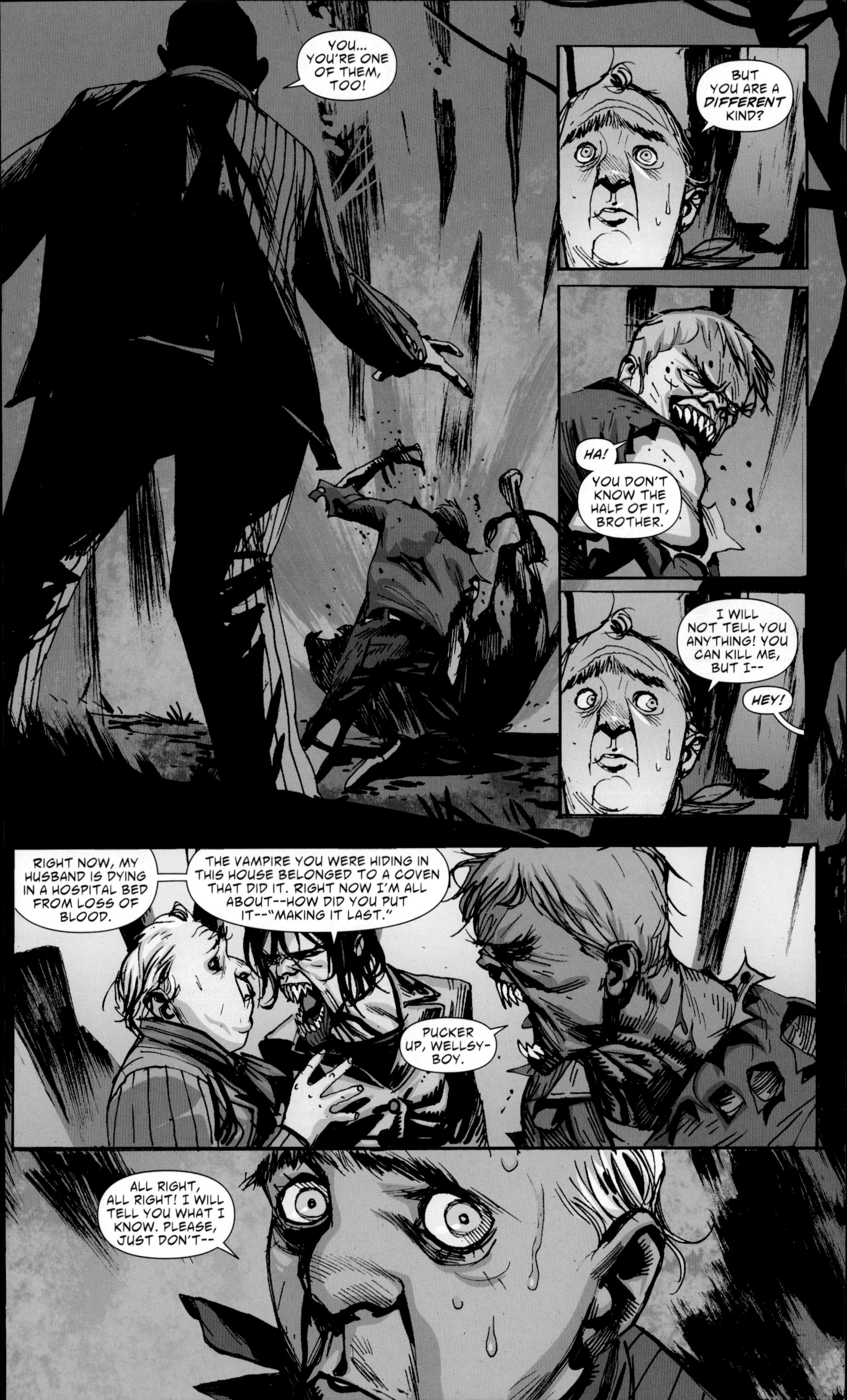
YOU... YOU'RE ONE OF THEM, TOO!
BUT YOU ARE A *DIFFERENT* KIND?
HA!
YOU DON'T KNOW THE HALF OF IT, BROTHER.
I WILL NOT TELL YOU ANYTHING! YOU CAN KILL ME, BUT I--
HEY!
RIGHT NOW, MY HUSBAND IS DYING IN A HOSPITAL BED FROM LOSS OF BLOOD.
THE VAMPIRE YOU WERE HIDING IN THIS HOUSE BELONGED TO A COVEN THAT DID IT. RIGHT NOW I'M ALL ABOUT--HOW DID YOU PUT IT--"MAKING IT LAST."
PUCKER UP, WELLSY-BOY.
ALL RIGHT, ALL RIGHT! I WILL TELL YOU WHAT I KNOW. PLEASE, JUST DON'T--

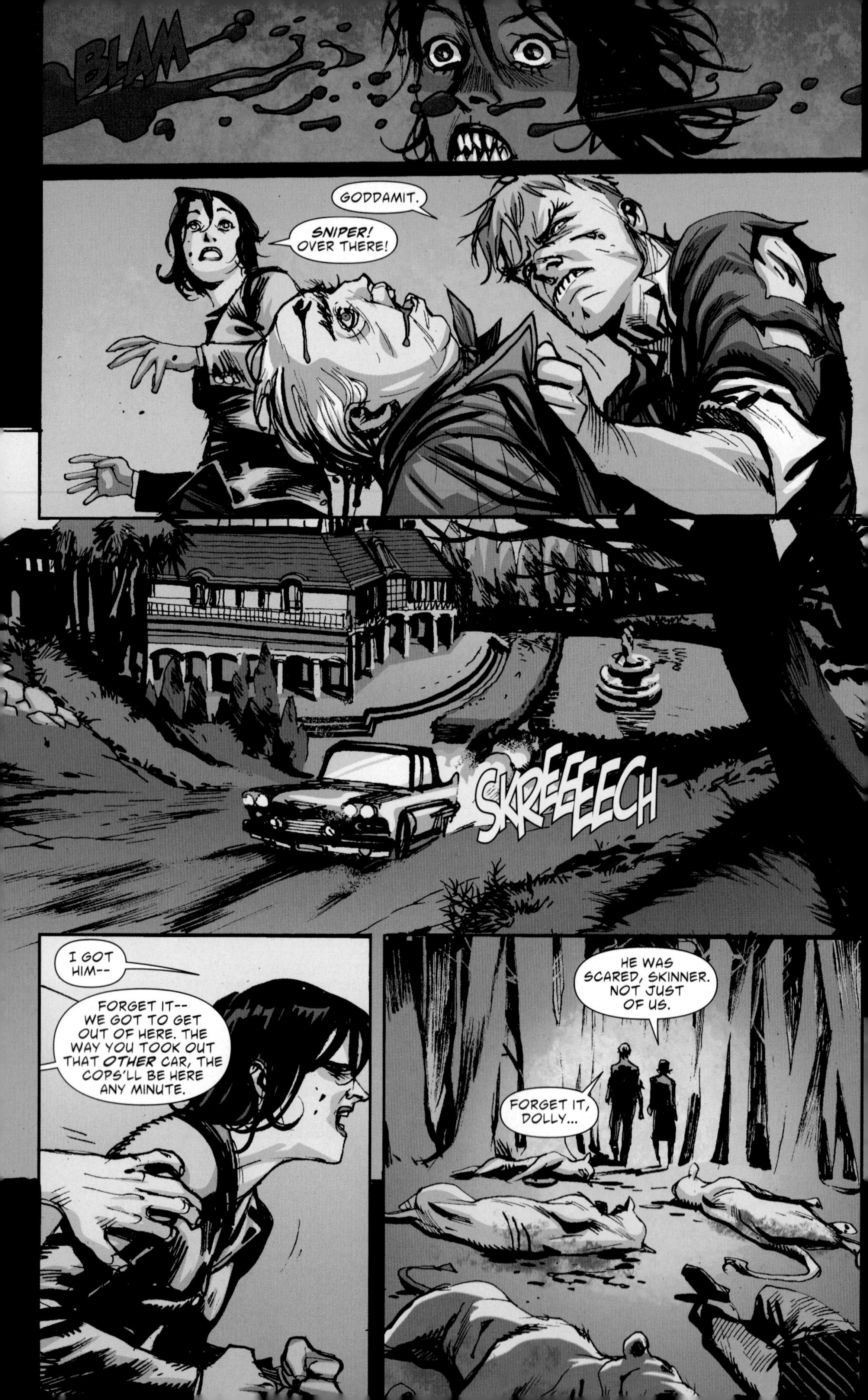
BLAM
GODDAMIT.
SNIPER! OVER THERE!
SKREEEEECH
I GOT HIM--
FORGET IT-- WE GOT TO GET OUT OF HERE. THE WAY YOU TOOK OUT THAT OTHER CAR, THE COPS'LL BE HERE ANY MINUTE.
HE WAS SCARED, SKINNER. NOT JUST OF US.
FORGET IT, DOLLY...

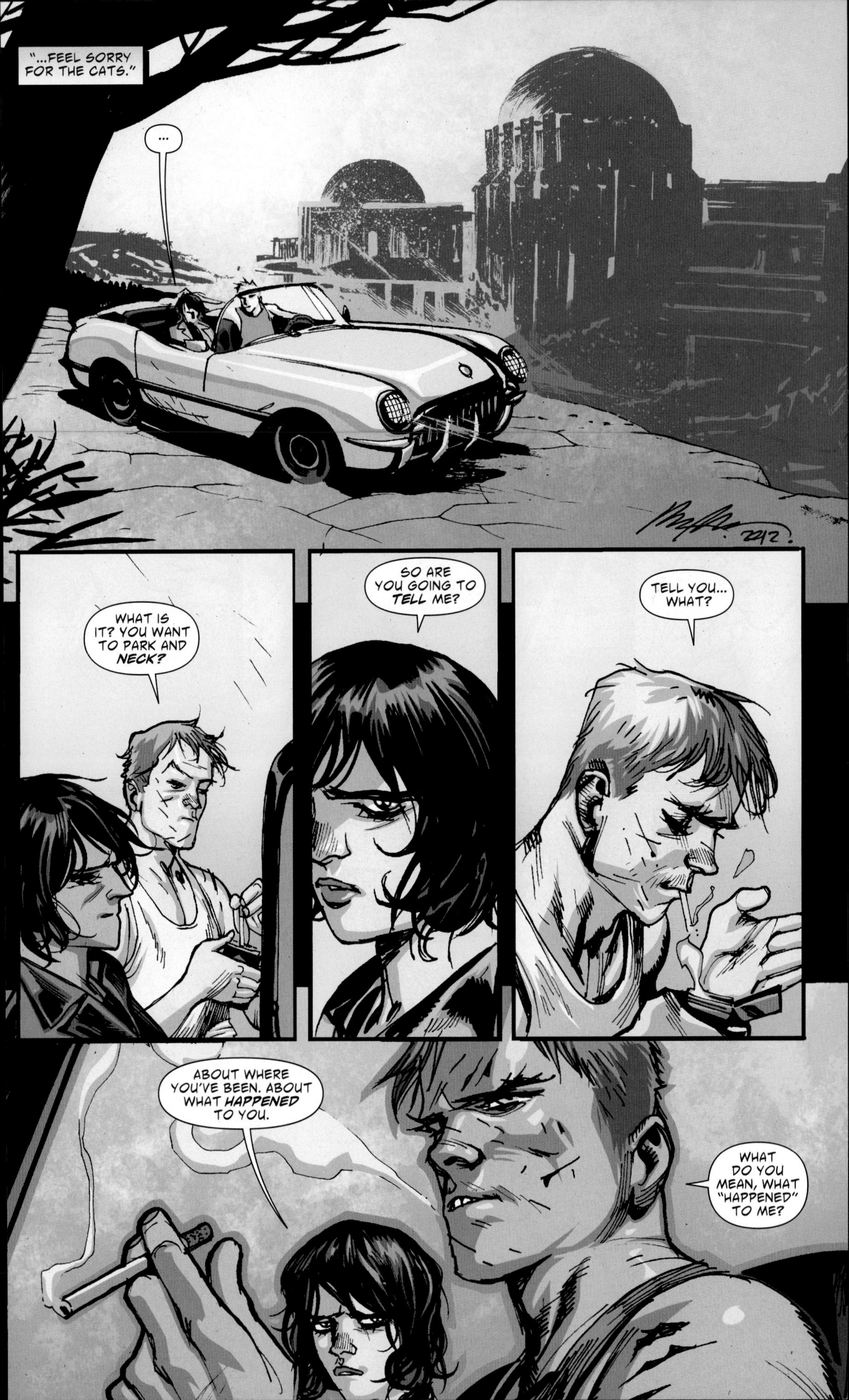

"...FEEL SORRY FOR THE CATS."
...
WHAT IS IT? YOU WANT TO PARK AND NECK?
SO ARE YOU GOING TO TELL ME?
TELL YOU... WHAT?
ABOUT WHERE YOU'VE BEEN. ABOUT WHAT HAPPENED TO YOU.
WHAT DO YOU MEAN, WHAT "HAPPENED" TO ME?

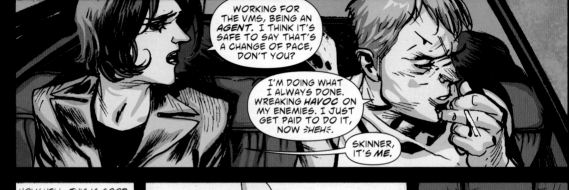

WORKING FOR THE VMS, BEING AN *AGENT.* I THINK IT'S SAFE TO SAY THAT'S A CHANGE OF PACE, DON'T YOU?

I'M DOING WHAT I ALWAYS DONE. WREAKING *HAVOC* ON MY ENEMIES. I JUST GET PAID TO DO IT, NOW ≥HEH≤.

SKINNER, IT'S *ME.*

HOLY HELL, THIS IS GOOD. LAST I REMEMBER, YOU *STABBED* ME IN THE CHEST, LEFT ME FOR DEAD ON A HUNK OF ROCK IN THE JAPLANDS. AND NOW YOU SHOULD *CARE* ABOUT ME, ABOUT WHERE I BEEN, WHAT I DONE.

WE SHOULD GO INSI--

YOU KNOW, DOLLY...

THE WAY YOU TOOK OUT JEEVES BACK THERE, AND THE WAY YOU HANDLED WHITE...

...YOU MIGHT SEE SOMETHING DIFFERENT IN *ME,* BUT I SEE SOMETHING DIFFERENT IN *YOU,* TOO.

CAN'T SAY I DON'T *LIKE* IT.

COME ON, WE'VE GOT TO MAKE THE REPORT.

≥HEH≤ YEAH, I'LL BE RIGHT IN. SAVE ME A SEAT.

"I'M AFRAID THE CHANGES IN HIS CONDITION HAVE BEEN *MINOR* AT BEST."

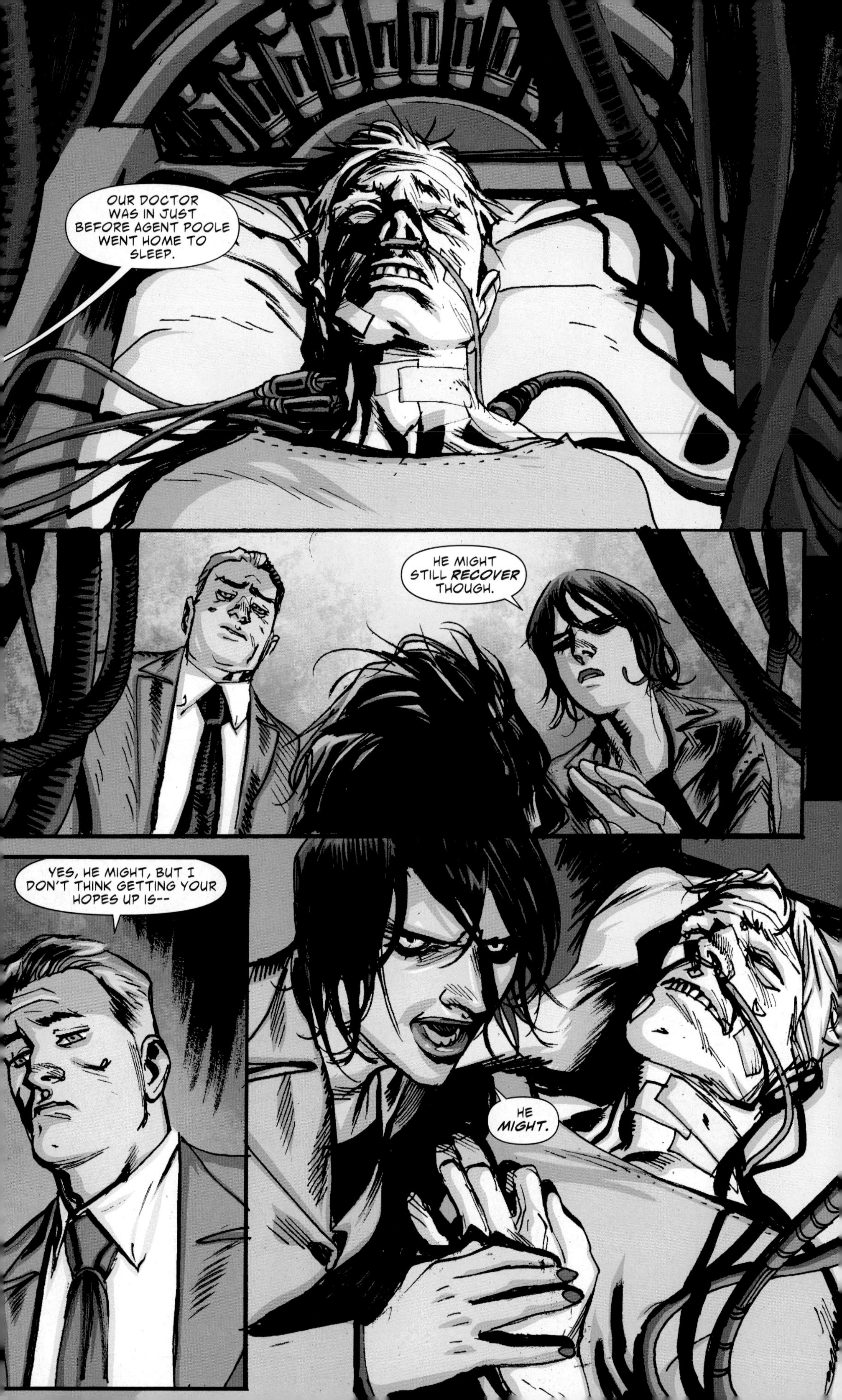
OUR DOCTOR WAS IN JUST BEFORE AGENT POOLE WENT HOME TO SLEEP.
HE MIGHT STILL *RECOVER* THOUGH.
YES, HE MIGHT, BUT I DON'T THINK GETTING YOUR HOPES UP IS--
HE *MIGHT*.

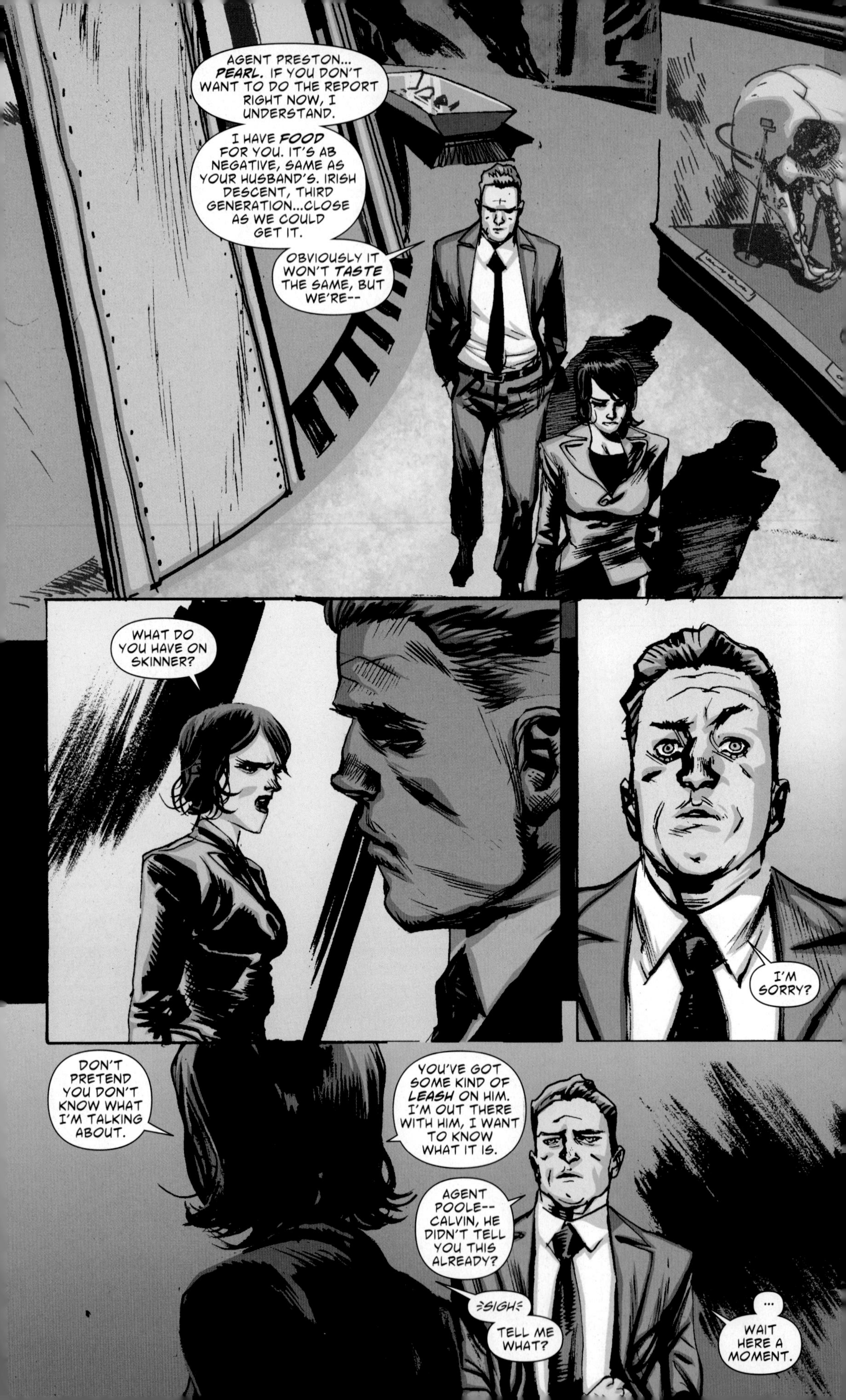
AGENT PRESTON... PEARL. IF YOU DON'T WANT TO DO THE REPORT RIGHT NOW, I UNDERSTAND.
I HAVE FOOD FOR YOU. IT'S AB NEGATIVE, SAME AS YOUR HUSBAND'S. IRISH DESCENT, THIRD GENERATION...CLOSE AS WE COULD GET IT.
OBVIOUSLY IT WON'T TASTE THE SAME, BUT WE'RE--
WHAT DO YOU HAVE ON SKINNER?
I'M SORRY?
DON'T PRETEND YOU DON'T KNOW WHAT I'M TALKING ABOUT.
YOU'VE GOT SOME KIND OF LEASH ON HIM. I'M OUT THERE WITH HIM, I WANT TO KNOW WHAT IT IS.
AGENT POOLE-- CALVIN, HE DIDN'T TELL YOU THIS ALREADY?
SIGH
TELL ME WHAT?
...
WAIT HERE A MOMENT.

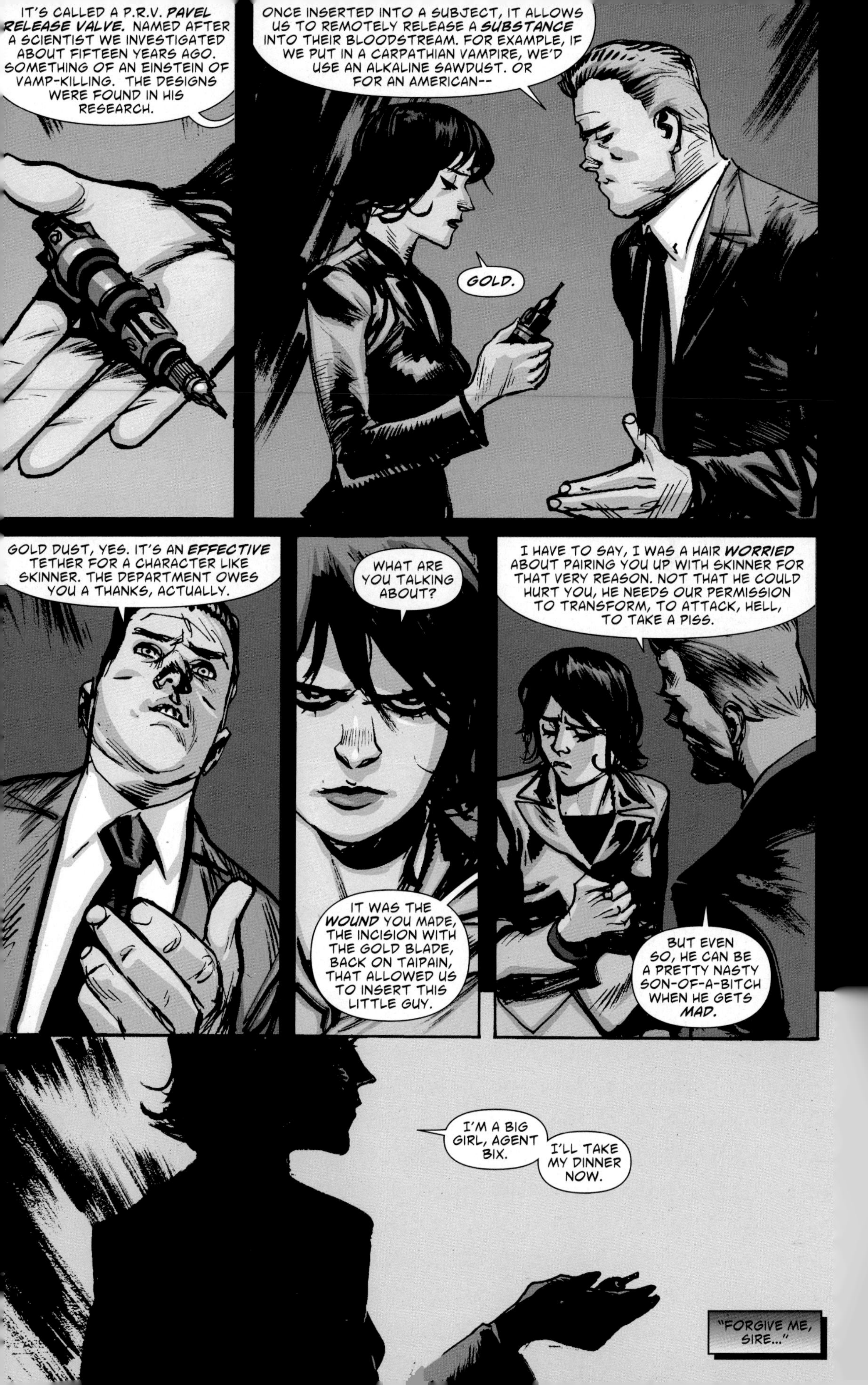
IT'S CALLED A P.R.V. PAVEL RELEASE VALVE. NAMED AFTER A SCIENTIST WE INVESTIGATED ABOUT FIFTEEN YEARS AGO. SOMETHING OF AN EINSTEIN OF VAMP-KILLING. THE DESIGNS WERE FOUND IN HIS RESEARCH.
ONCE INSERTED INTO A SUBJECT, IT ALLOWS US TO REMOTELY RELEASE A SUBSTANCE INTO THEIR BLOODSTREAM. FOR EXAMPLE, IF WE PUT IN A CARPATHIAN VAMPIRE, WE'D USE AN ALKALINE SAWDUST. OR FOR AN AMERICAN--
GOLD.
GOLD DUST, YES. IT'S AN EFFECTIVE TETHER FOR A CHARACTER LIKE SKINNER. THE DEPARTMENT OWES YOU A THANKS, ACTUALLY.
WHAT ARE YOU TALKING ABOUT?
IT WAS THE WOUND YOU MADE, THE INCISION WITH THE GOLD BLADE, BACK ON TAIPAIN, THAT ALLOWED US TO INSERT THIS LITTLE GUY.
I HAVE TO SAY, I WAS A HAIR WORRIED ABOUT PAIRING YOU UP WITH SKINNER FOR THAT VERY REASON. NOT THAT HE COULD HURT YOU, HE NEEDS OUR PERMISSION TO TRANSFORM, TO ATTACK, HELL, TO TAKE A PISS.
BUT EVEN SO, HE CAN BE A PRETTY NASTY SON-OF-A-BITCH WHEN HE GETS MAD.
I'M A BIG GIRL, AGENT BIX.
I'LL TAKE MY DINNER NOW.
"FORGIVE ME, SIRE..."

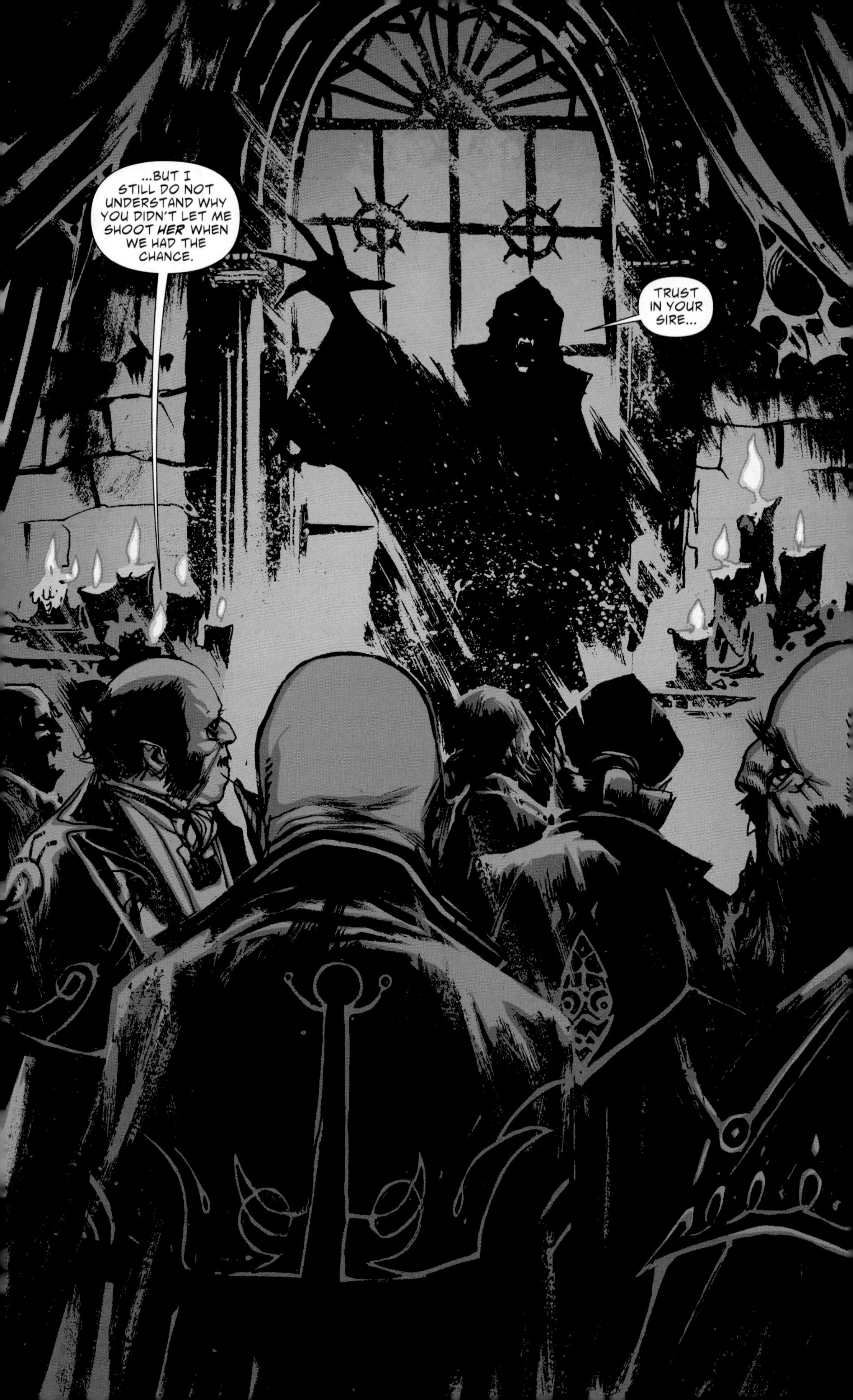
...BUT I STILL DO NOT UNDERSTAND WHY YOU DIDN'T LET ME SHOOT HER WHEN WE HAD THE CHANCE.
TRUST IN YOUR SIRE...

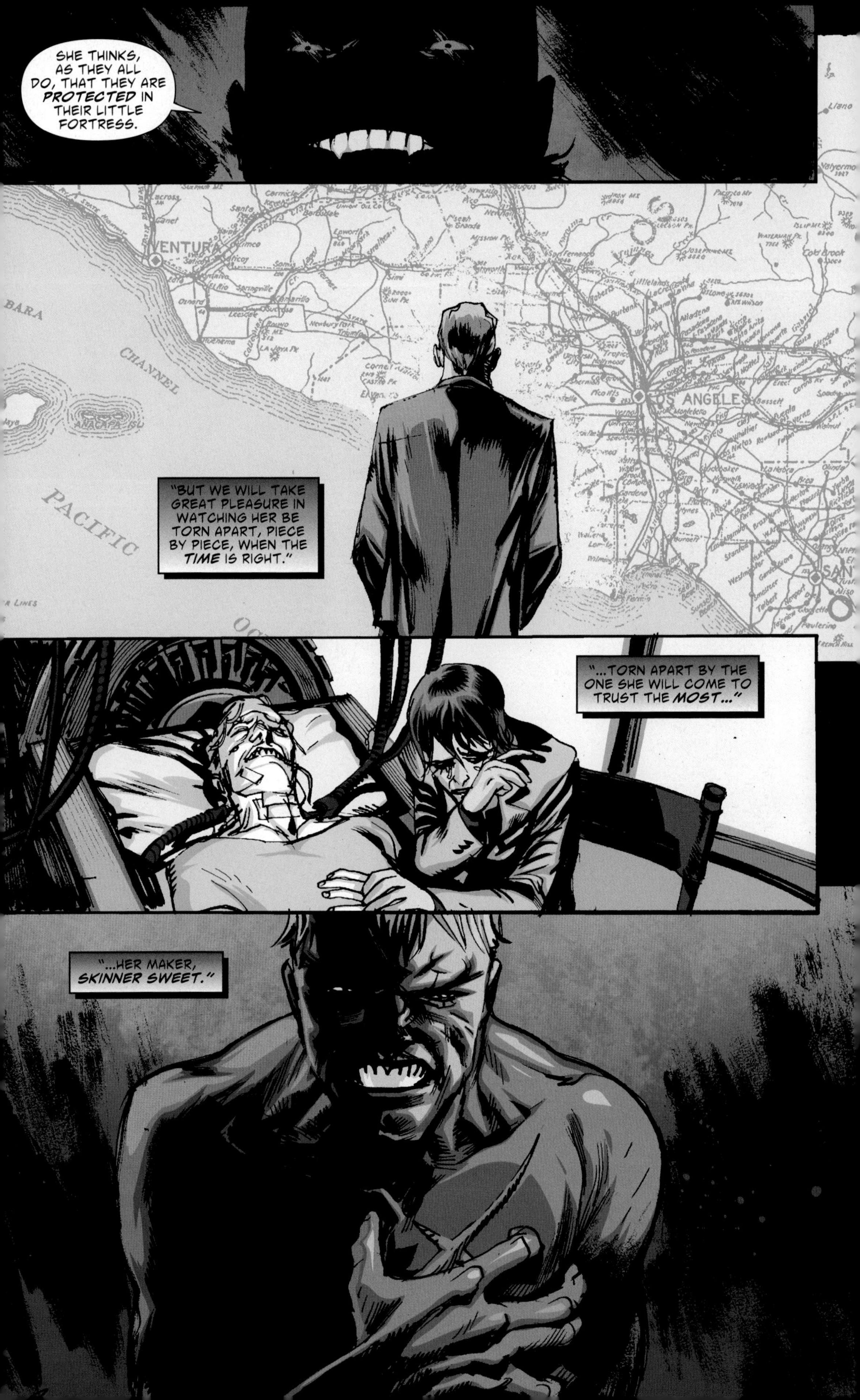

SHE THINKS, AS THEY ALL DO, THAT THEY ARE PROTECTED IN THEIR LITTLE FORTRESS.
"BUT WE WILL TAKE GREAT PLEASURE IN WATCHING HER BE TORN APART, PIECE BY PIECE, WHEN THE TIME IS RIGHT."
"...TORN APART BY THE ONE SHE WILL COME TO TRUST THE MOST..."
"...HER MAKER, SKINNER SWEET."

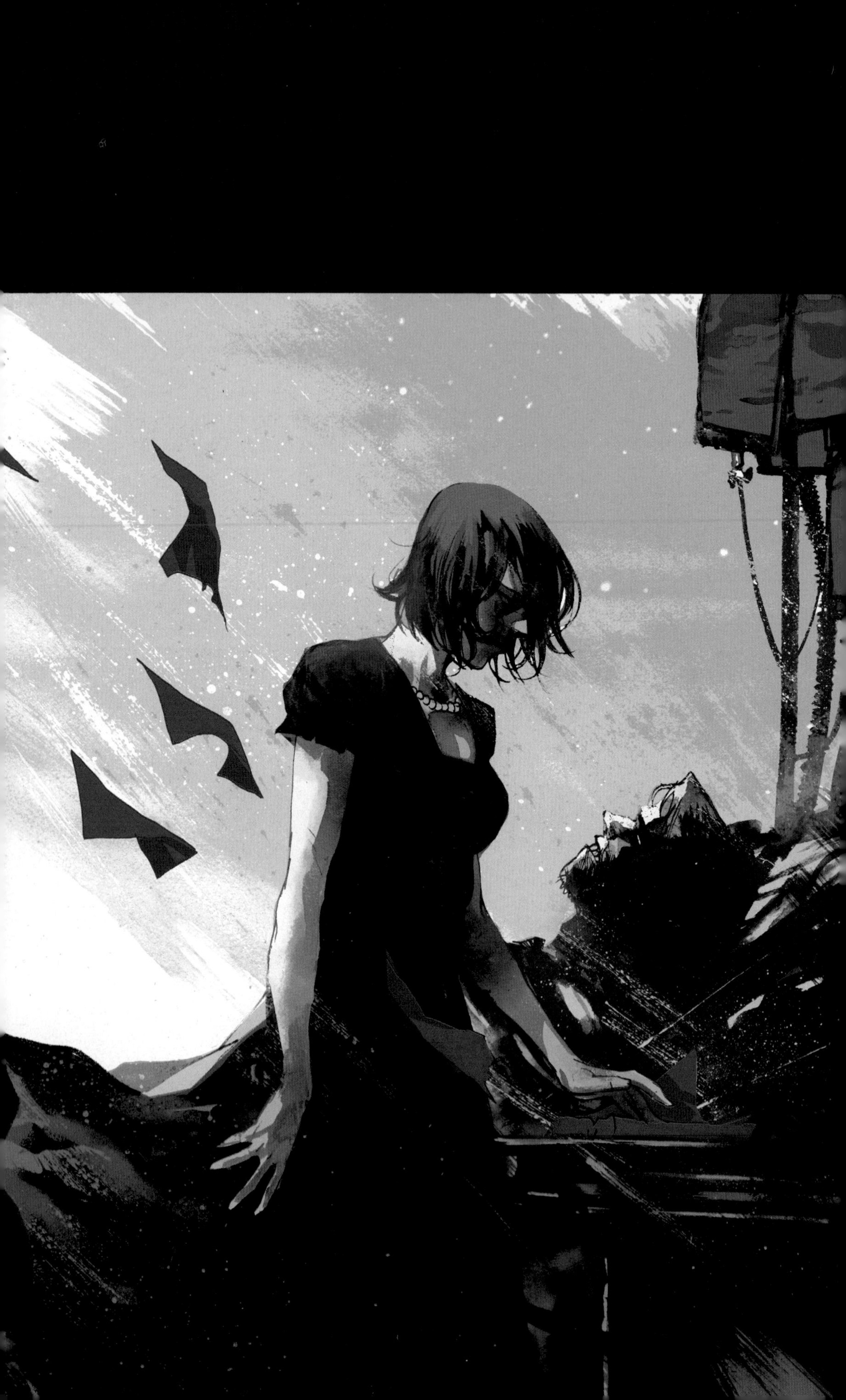

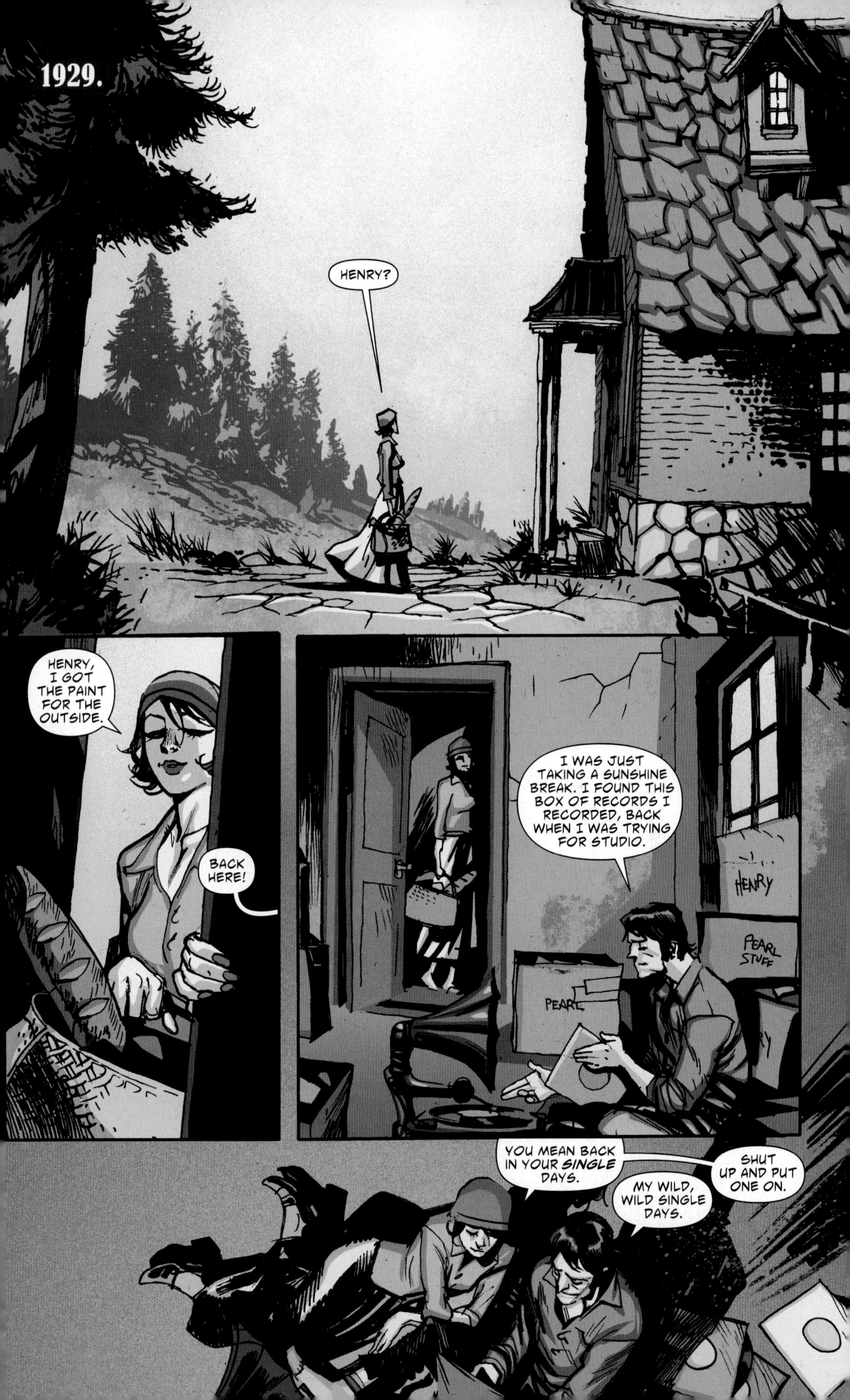
1929.
HENRY?
HENRY, I GOT THE PAINT FOR THE OUTSIDE.
BACK HERE!
I WAS JUST TAKING A SUNSHINE BREAK. I FOUND THIS BOX OF RECORDS I RECORDED, BACK WHEN I WAS TRYING FOR STUDIO.
HENRY
PEARL STUFF
PEARL
YOU MEAN BACK IN YOUR SINGLE DAYS.
MY WILD, WILD SINGLE DAYS.
SHUT UP AND PUT ONE ON.

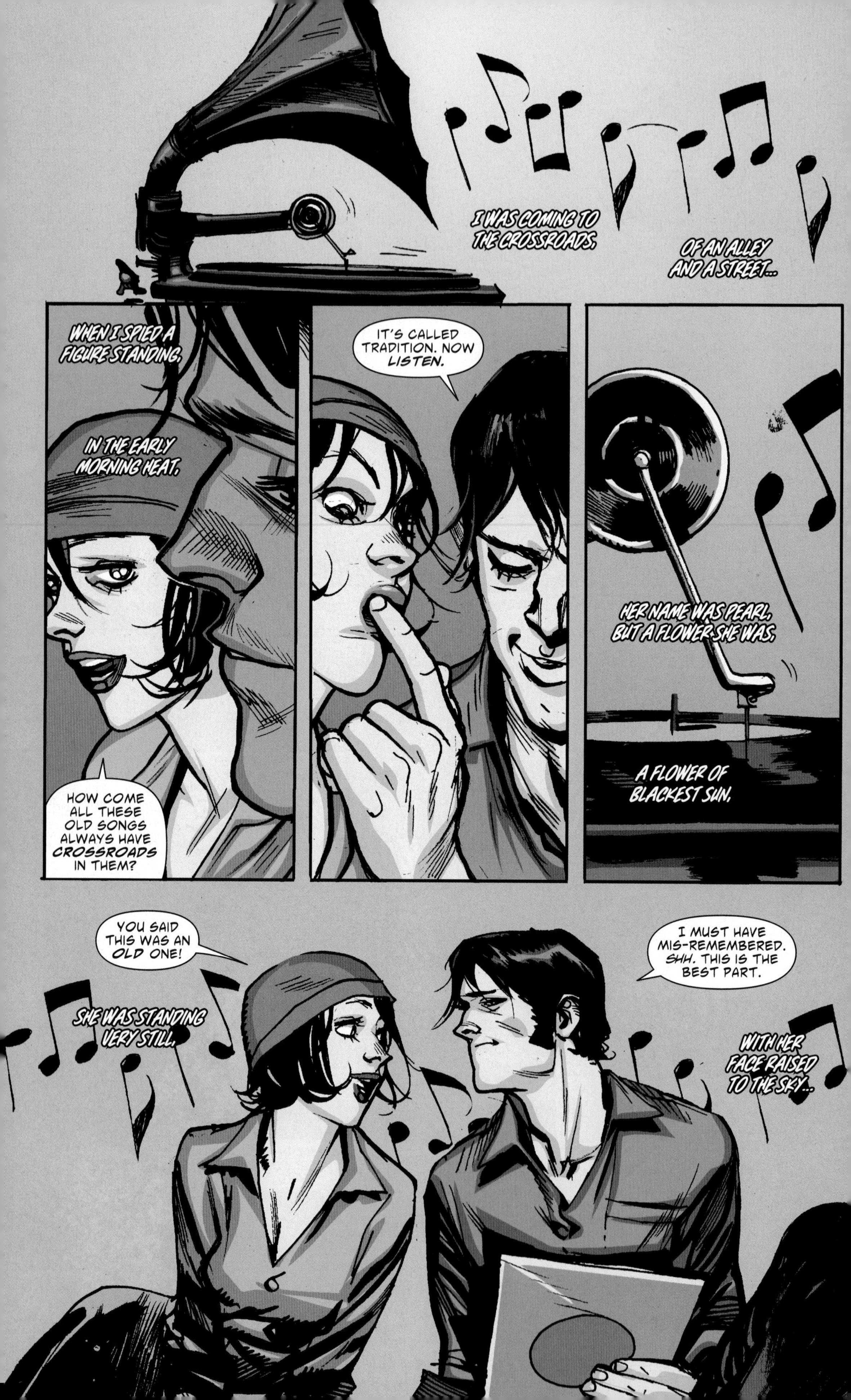

I WAS COMING TO THE CROSSROADS,
OF AN ALLEY AND A STREET...
WHEN I SPIED A FIGURE STANDING,
IN THE EARLY MORNING HEAT.
HOW COME ALL THESE OLD SONGS ALWAYS HAVE CROSSROADS IN THEM?
IT'S CALLED TRADITION. NOW LISTEN.
HER NAME WAS PEARL, BUT A FLOWER SHE WAS,
A FLOWER OF BLACKEST SUN,
YOU SAID THIS WAS AN OLD ONE!
I MUST HAVE MIS-REMEMBERED. SHH. THIS IS THE BEST PART.
SHE WAS STANDING VERY STILL,
WITH HER FACE RAISED TO THE SKY...

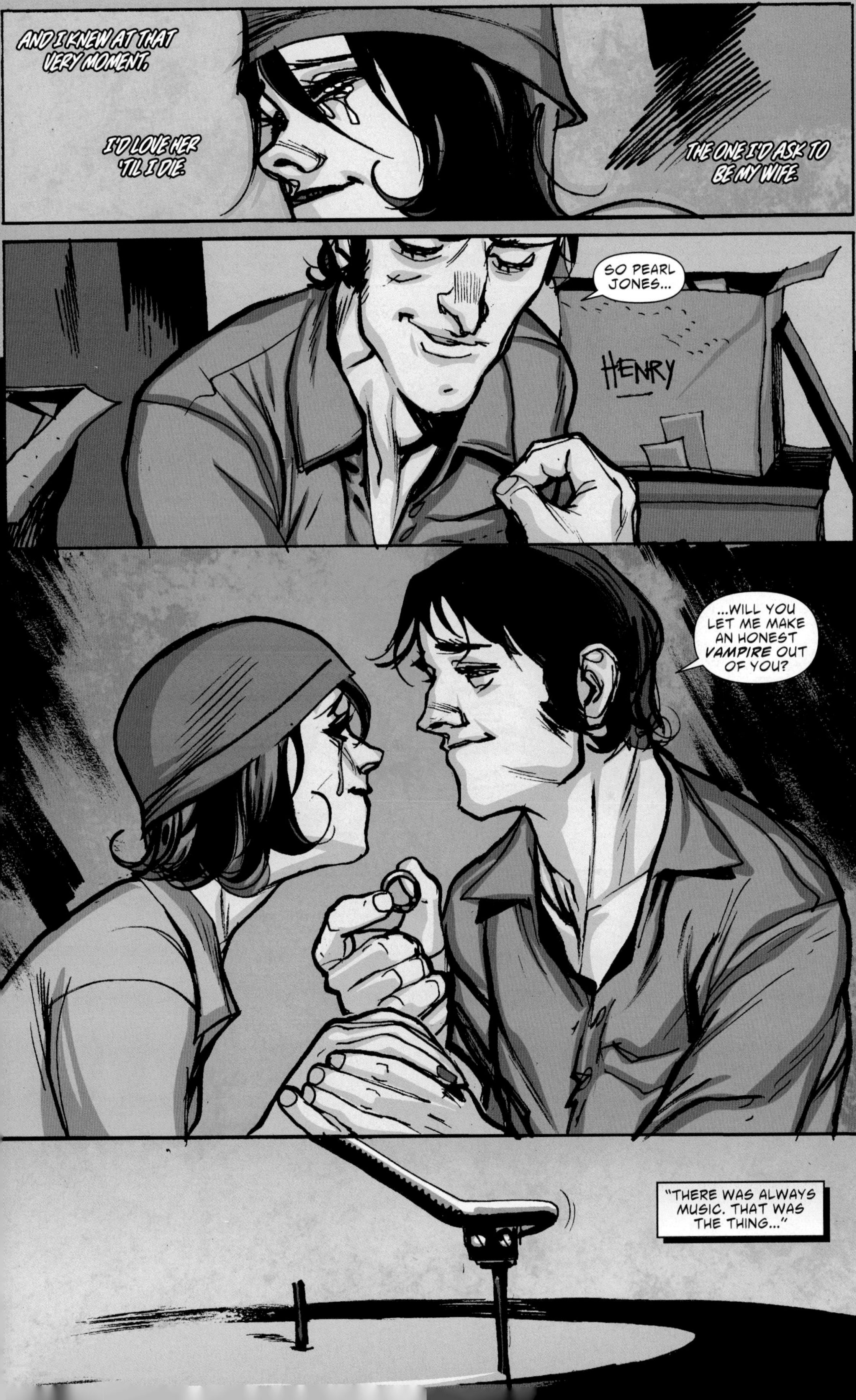
AND I KNEW AT THAT VERY MOMENT,
I'D LOVE HER 'TIL I DIE.
THE ONE I'D ASK TO BE MY WIFE.
SO PEARL JONES...
HENRY
...WILL YOU LET ME MAKE AN HONEST VAMPIRE OUT OF YOU?
"THERE WAS ALWAYS MUSIC. THAT WAS THE THING..."

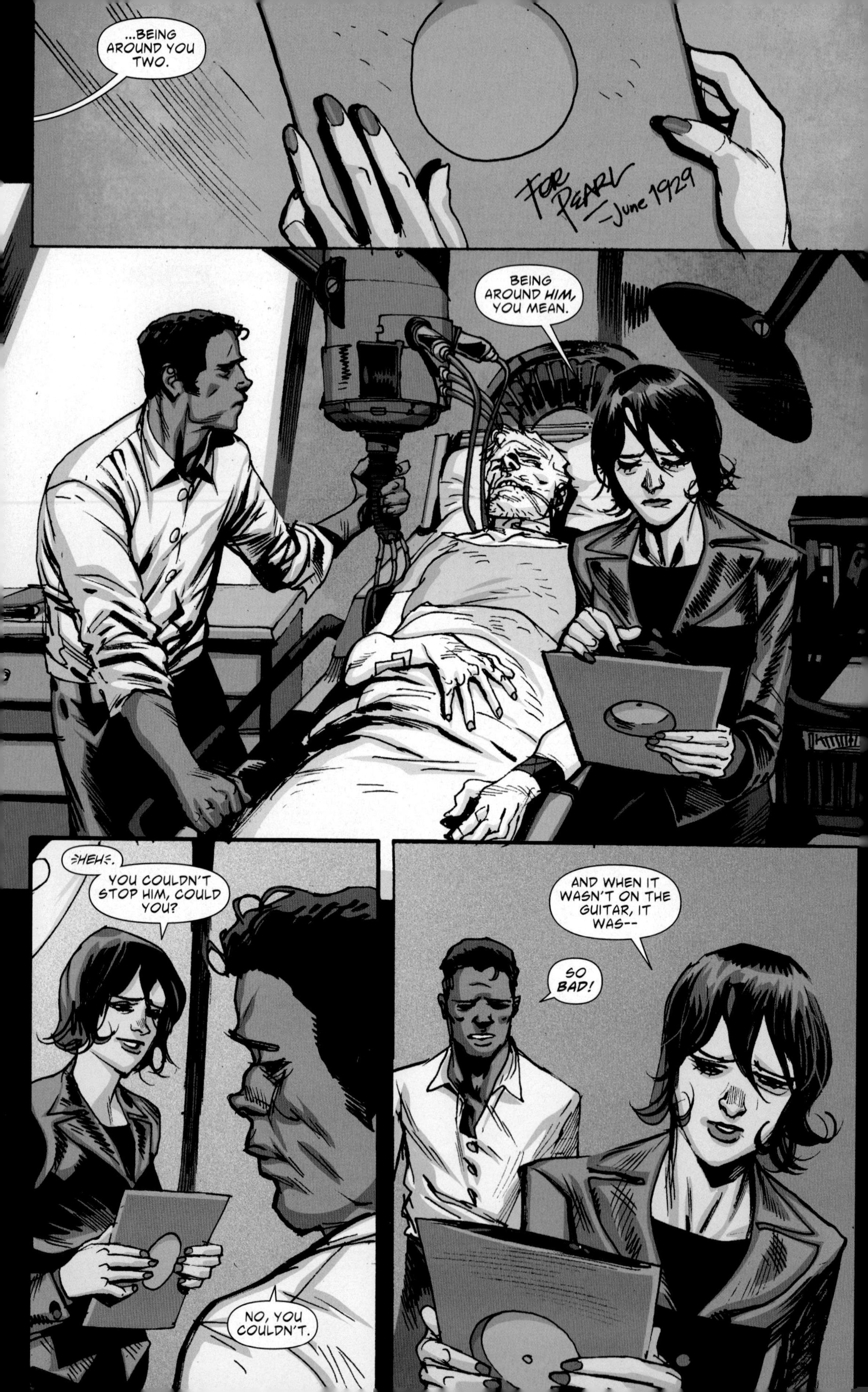
...BEING AROUND YOU TWO.
FOR PEARL —June 1929
BEING AROUND HIM, YOU MEAN.
HEH.
YOU COULDN'T STOP HIM, COULD YOU?
NO, YOU COULDN'T.
AND WHEN IT WASN'T ON THE GUITAR, IT WAS--
SO BAD!

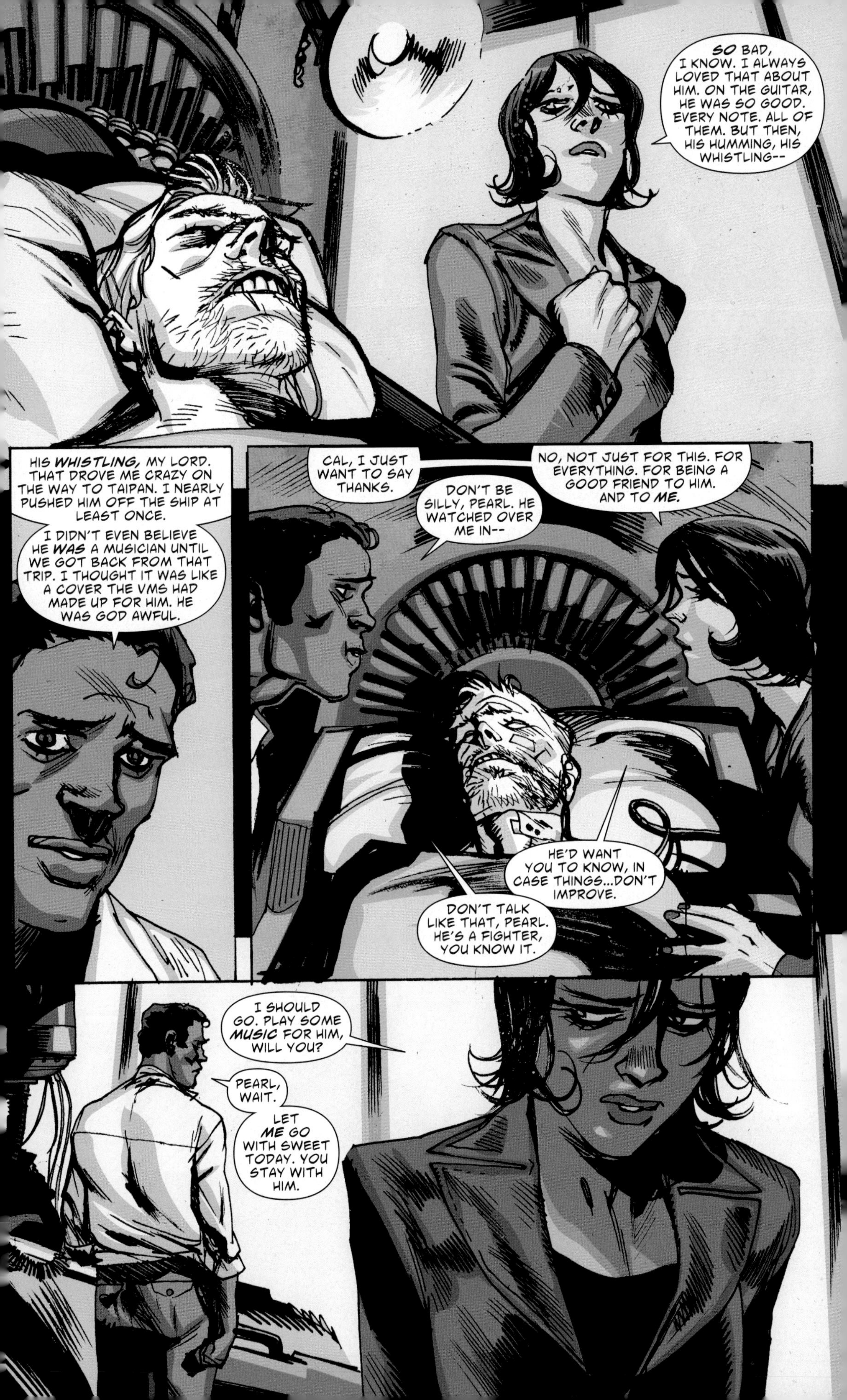
SO BAD, I KNOW. I ALWAYS LOVED THAT ABOUT HIM. ON THE GUITAR, HE WAS SO GOOD. EVERY NOTE. ALL OF THEM. BUT THEN, HIS HUMMING, HIS WHISTLING--
HIS WHISTLING, MY LORD. THAT DROVE ME CRAZY ON THE WAY TO TAIPAN. I NEARLY PUSHED HIM OFF THE SHIP AT LEAST ONCE.
I DIDN'T EVEN BELIEVE HE WAS A MUSICIAN UNTIL WE GOT BACK FROM THAT TRIP. I THOUGHT IT WAS LIKE A COVER THE VMS HAD MADE UP FOR HIM. HE WAS GOD AWFUL.
CAL, I JUST WANT TO SAY THANKS.
DON'T BE SILLY, PEARL. HE WATCHED OVER ME IN--
NO, NOT JUST FOR THIS. FOR EVERYTHING. FOR BEING A GOOD FRIEND TO HIM. AND TO ME.
HE'D WANT YOU TO KNOW, IN CASE THINGS...DON'T IMPROVE.
DON'T TALK LIKE THAT, PEARL. HE'S A FIGHTER, YOU KNOW IT.
I SHOULD GO. PLAY SOME MUSIC FOR HIM, WILL YOU?
PEARL, WAIT.
LET ME GO WITH SWEET TODAY. YOU STAY WITH HIM.

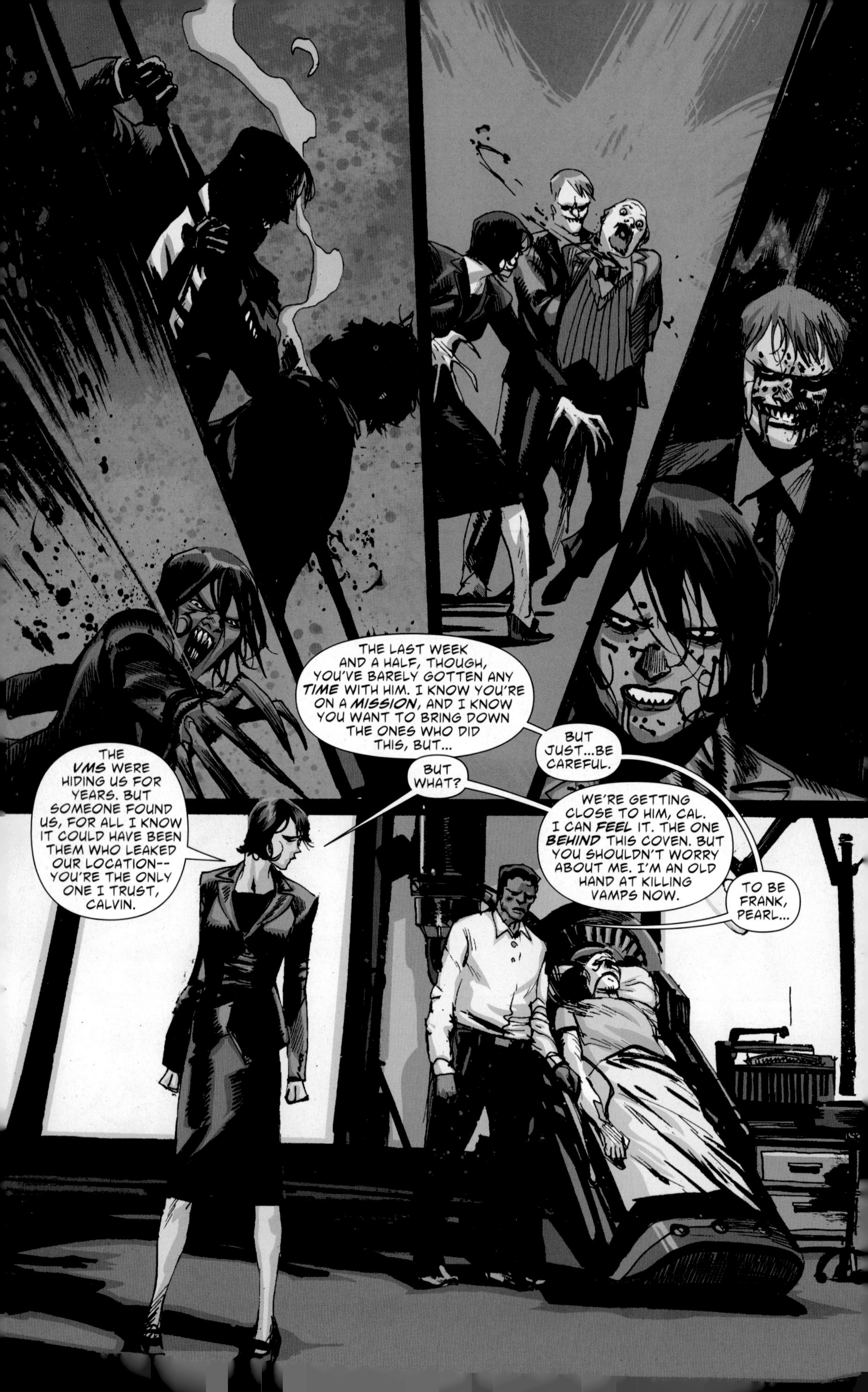
THE LAST WEEK AND A HALF, THOUGH, YOU'VE BARELY GOTTEN ANY TIME WITH HIM. I KNOW YOU'RE ON A MISSION, AND I KNOW YOU WANT TO BRING DOWN THE ONES WHO DID THIS, BUT...
BUT WHAT?
BUT JUST...BE CAREFUL.
THE VMS WERE HIDING US FOR YEARS. BUT SOMEONE FOUND US, FOR ALL I KNOW IT COULD HAVE BEEN THEM WHO LEAKED OUR LOCATION--YOU'RE THE ONLY ONE I TRUST, CALVIN.
WE'RE GETTING CLOSE TO HIM, CAL. I CAN FEEL IT. THE ONE BEHIND THIS COVEN. BUT YOU SHOULDN'T WORRY ABOUT ME. I'M AN OLD HAND AT KILLING VAMPS NOW.
TO BE FRANK, PEARL...

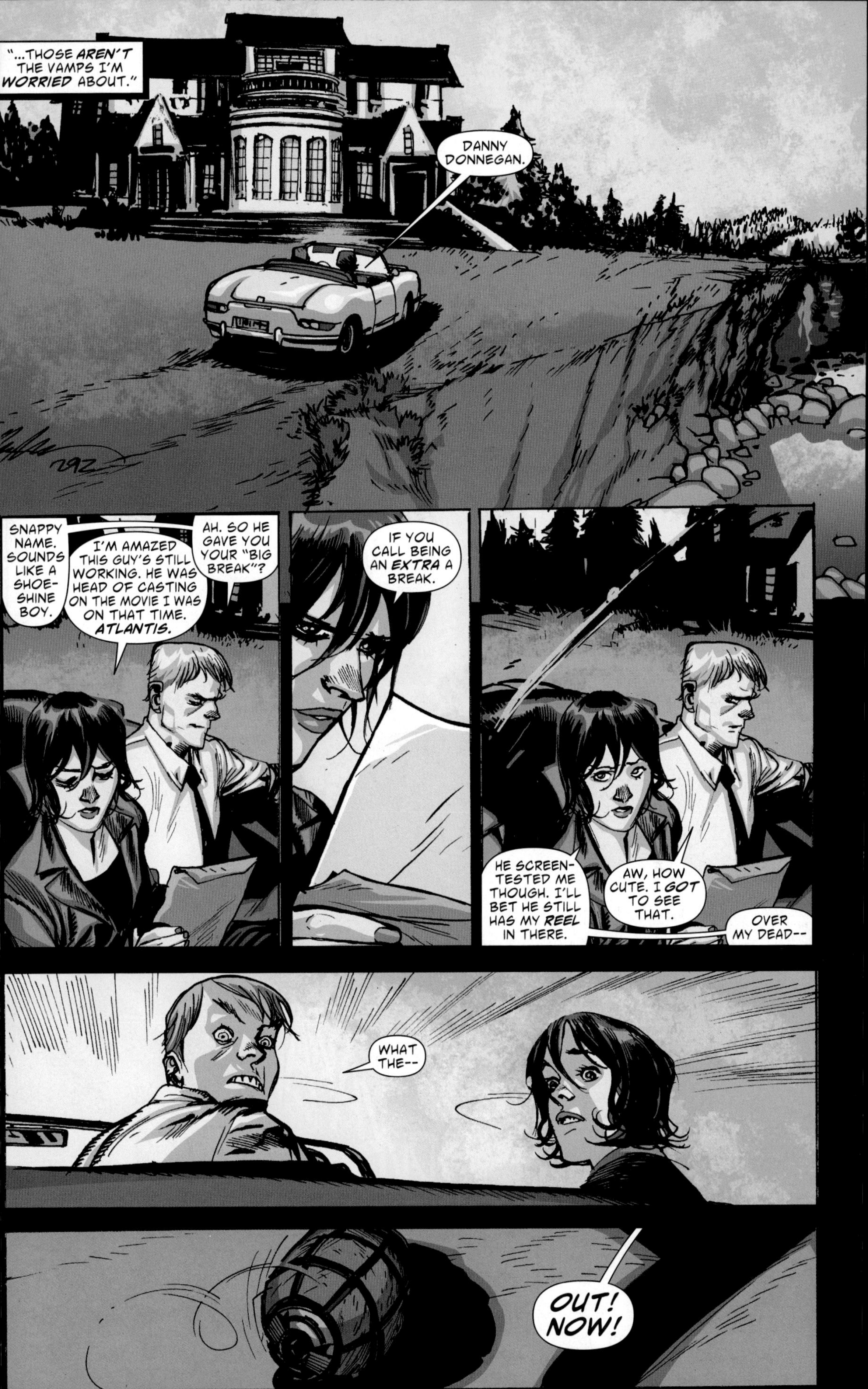
"...THOSE AREN'T THE VAMPS I'M WORRIED ABOUT."
DANNY DONNEGAN.
SNAPPY NAME. SOUNDS LIKE A SHOE-SHINE BOY.
I'M AMAZED THIS GUY'S STILL WORKING. HE WAS HEAD OF CASTING ON THE MOVIE I WAS ON THAT TIME. ATLANTIS.
AH. SO HE GAVE YOU YOUR "BIG BREAK"?
IF YOU CALL BEING AN EXTRA A BREAK.
HE SCREEN-TESTED ME THOUGH. I'LL BET HE STILL HAS MY REEL IN THERE.
AW, HOW CUTE. I GOT TO SEE THAT.
OVER MY DEAD--
WHAT THE--
OUT! NOW!

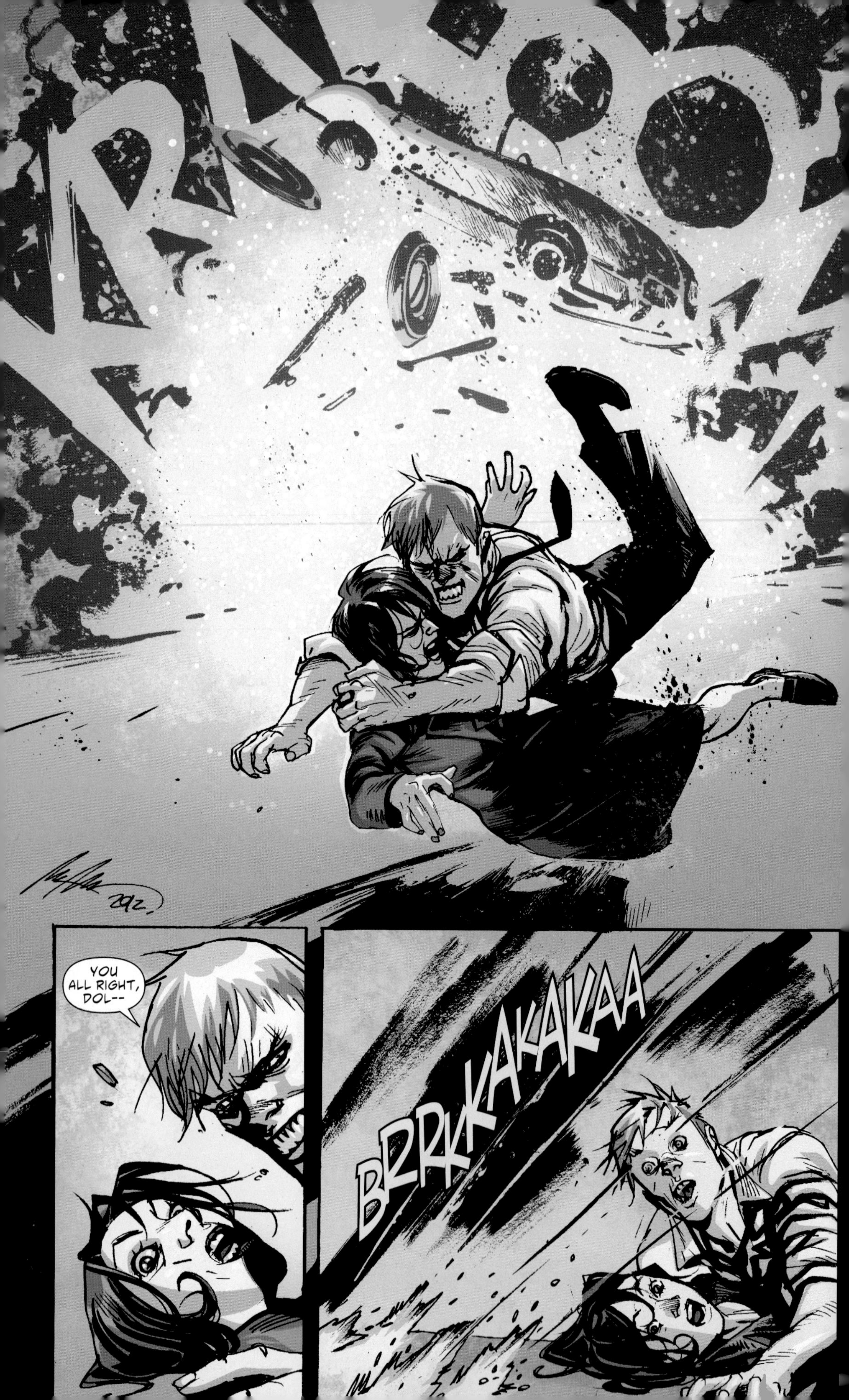
YOU ALL RIGHT, DOL--
BRRKKAKAKAA

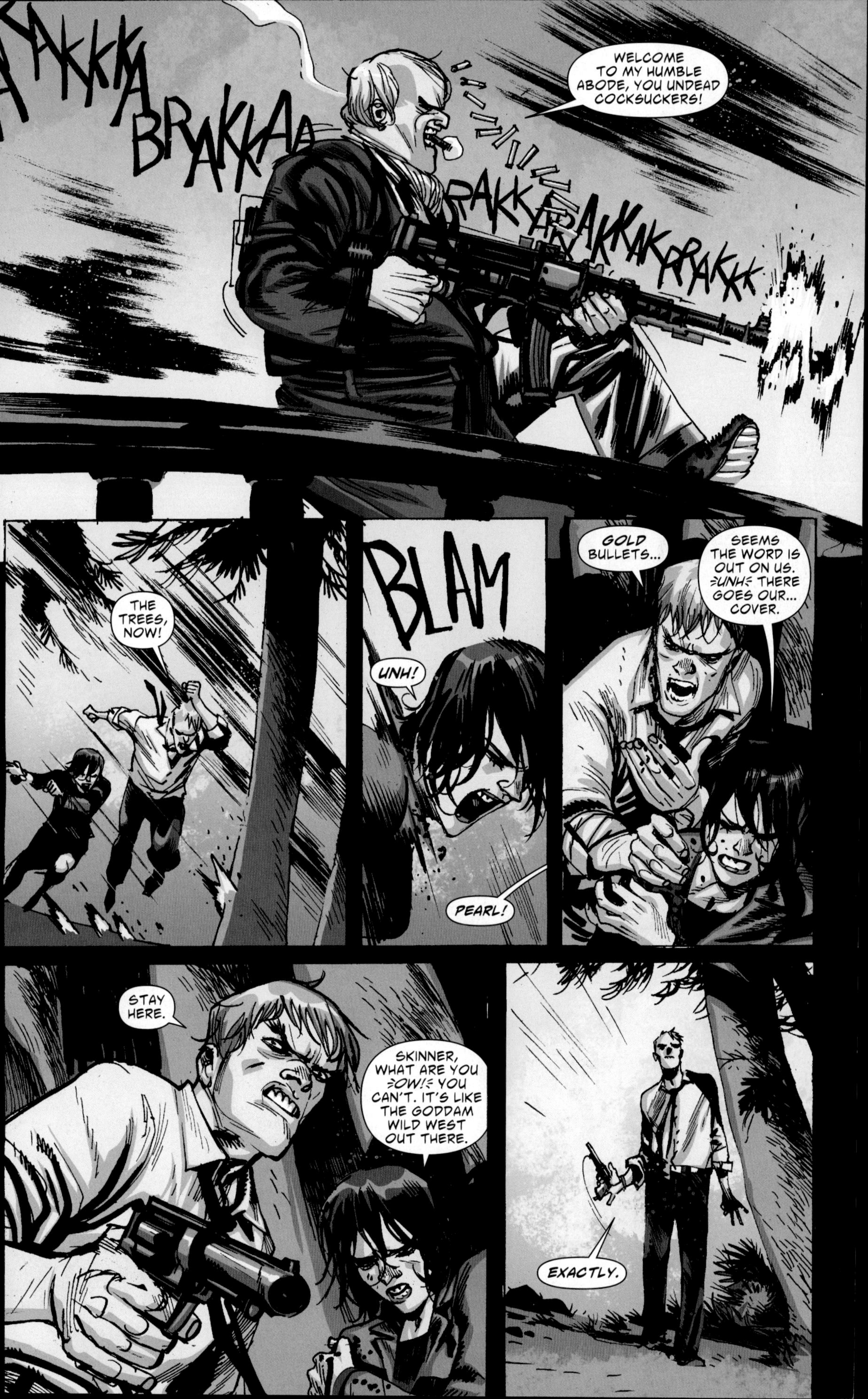

KAKKKA BRAKKAA
WELCOME TO MY HUMBLE ABODE, YOU UNDEAD COCKSUCKERS!
RAKKARAKKAKRAKKK
THE TREES, NOW!
BLAM
UNH!
PEARL!
GOLD BULLETS...
SEEMS THE WORD IS OUT ON US. UNH THERE GOES OUR... COVER.
STAY HERE.
SKINNER, WHAT ARE YOU OW! YOU CAN'T. IT'S LIKE THE GODDAM WILD WEST OUT THERE.
EXACTLY.

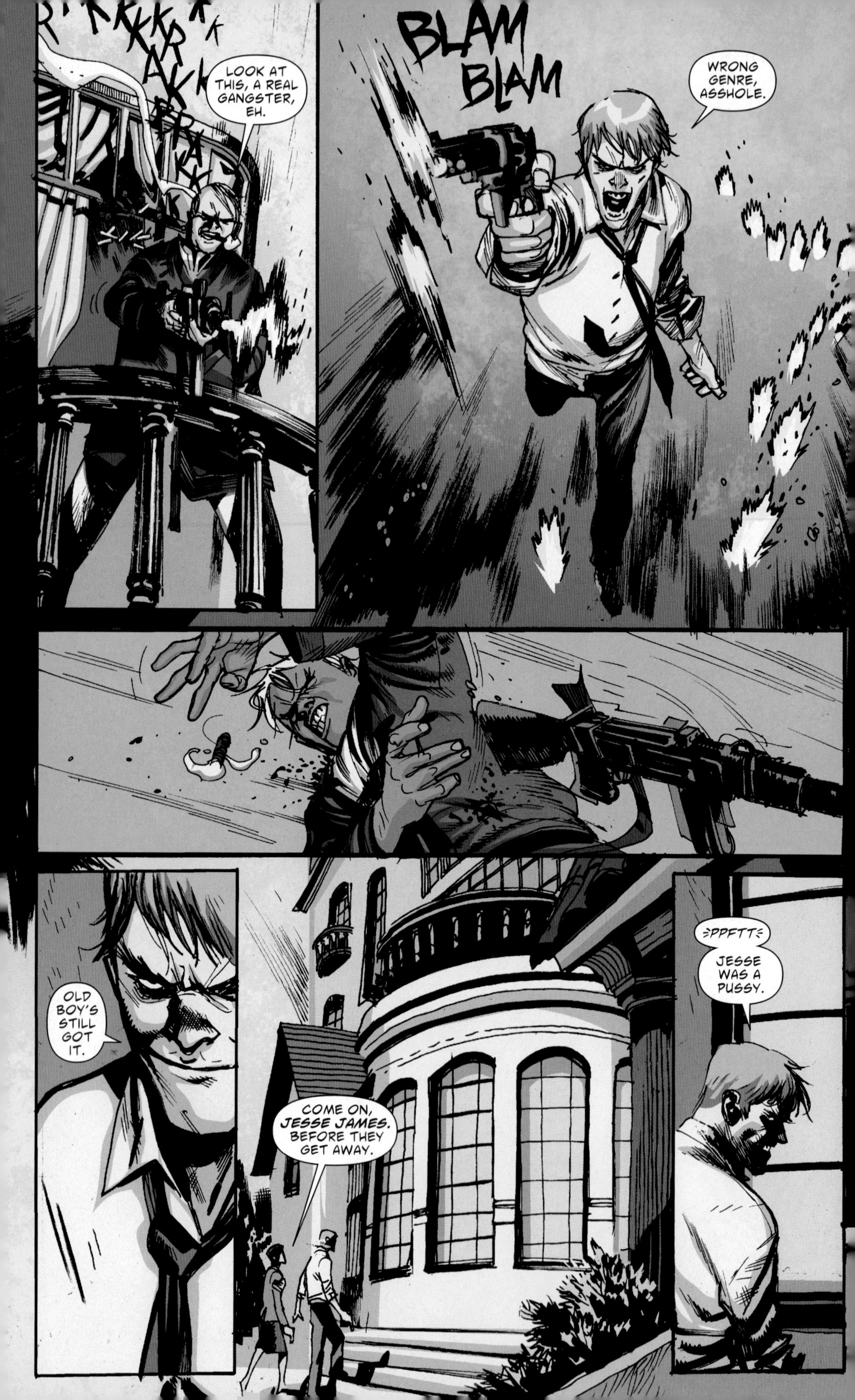

RAKKKRAKK
LOOK AT THIS, A REAL GANGSTER, EH.
BLAM BLAM
WRONG GENRE, ASSHOLE.
OLD BOY'S STILL GOT IT.
COME ON, JESSE JAMES. BEFORE THEY GET AWAY.
PPFTT
JESSE WAS A PUSSY.

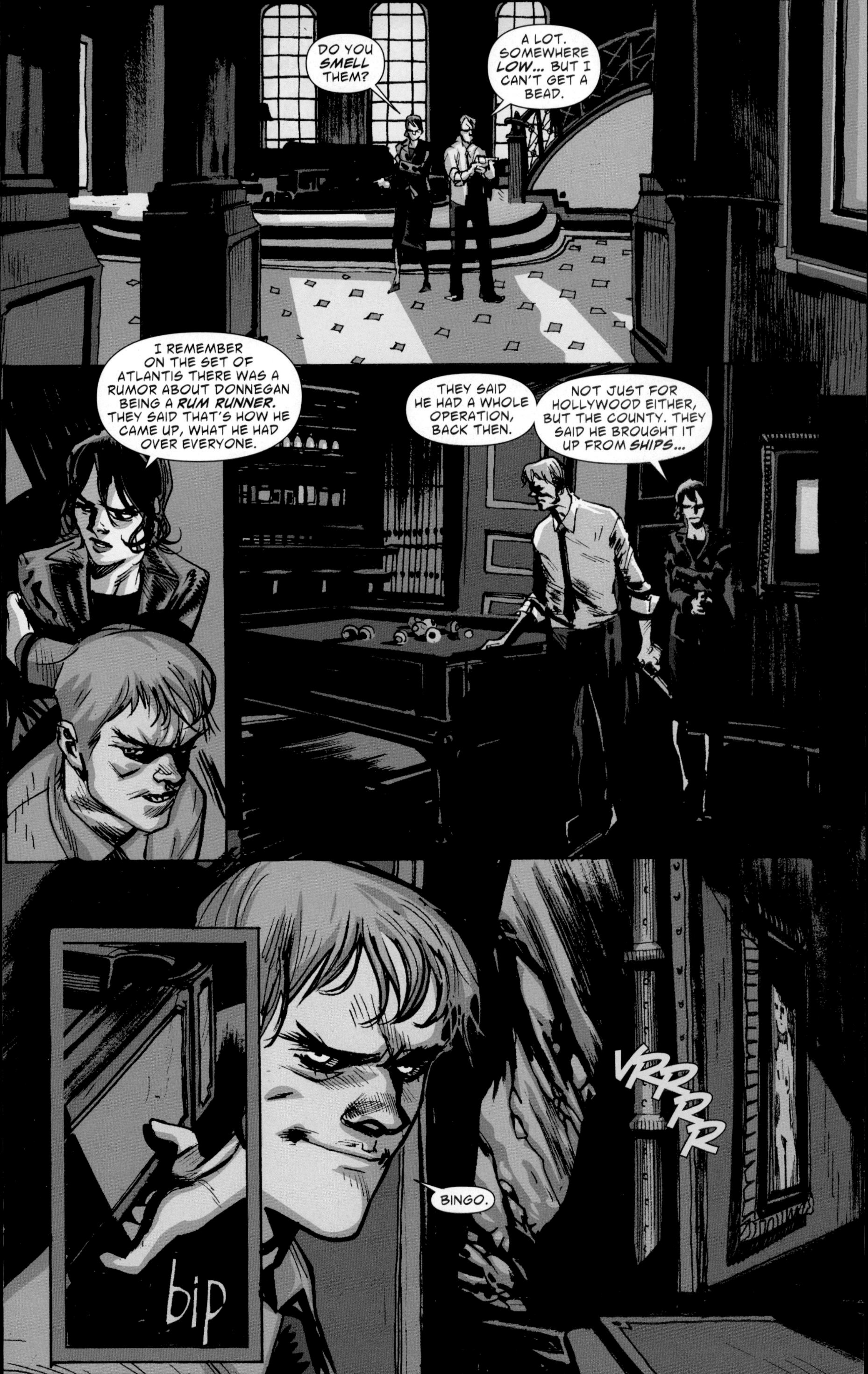
DO YOU SMELL THEM?
A LOT. SOMEWHERE LOW... BUT I CAN'T GET A BEAD.
I REMEMBER ON THE SET OF ATLANTIS THERE WAS A RUMOR ABOUT DONNEGAN BEING A RUM RUNNER. THEY SAID THAT'S HOW HE CAME UP, WHAT HE HAD OVER EVERYONE.
THEY SAID HE HAD A WHOLE OPERATION, BACK THEN.
NOT JUST FOR HOLLYWOOD EITHER, BUT THE COUNTY. THEY SAID HE BROUGHT IT UP FROM SHIPS...
VRRRRR
BINGO.
bip

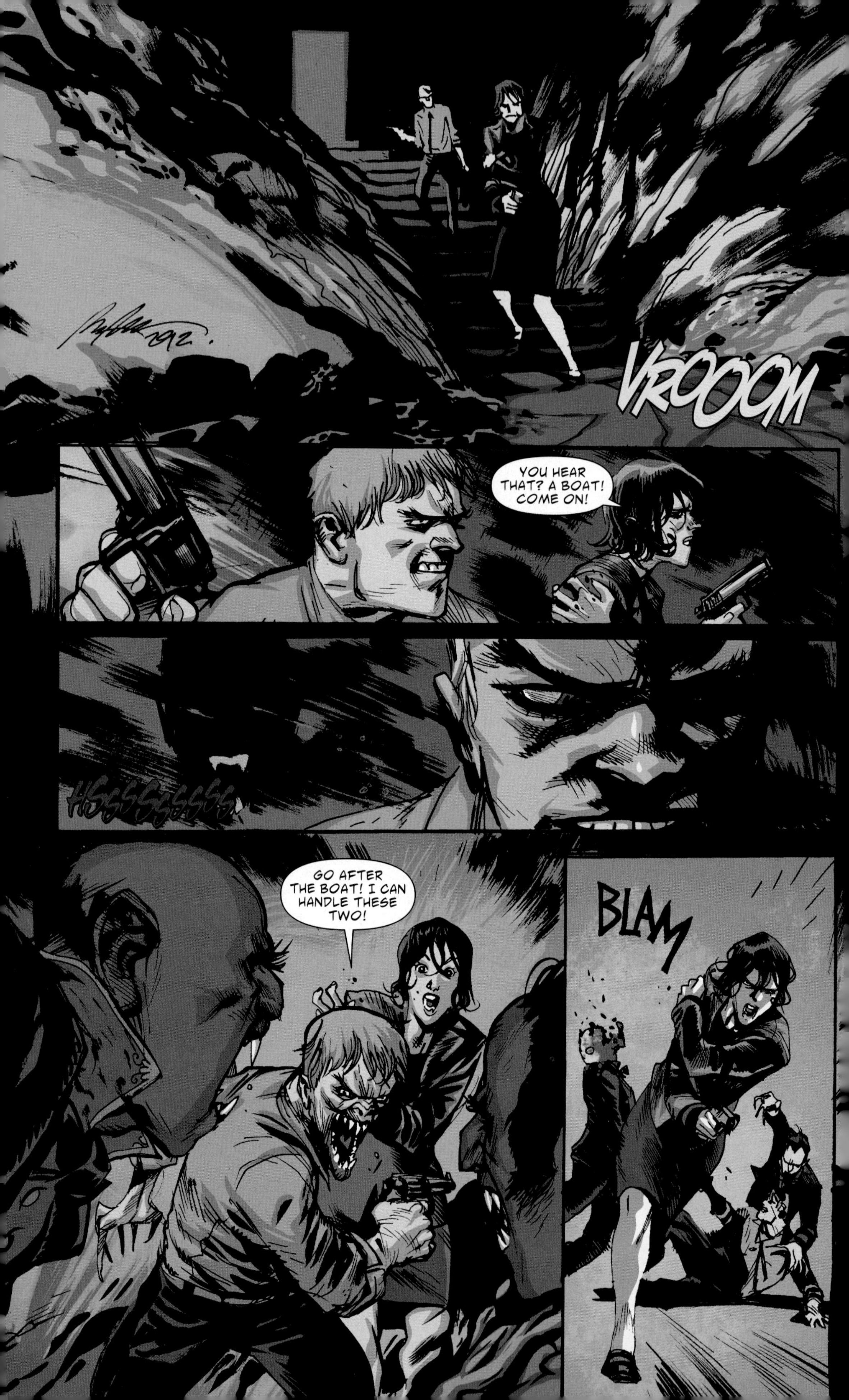
VROOOM
YOU HEAR THAT? A BOAT! COME ON!
HSSSSSSSSS
GO AFTER THE BOAT! I CAN HANDLE THESE TWO!
BLAM

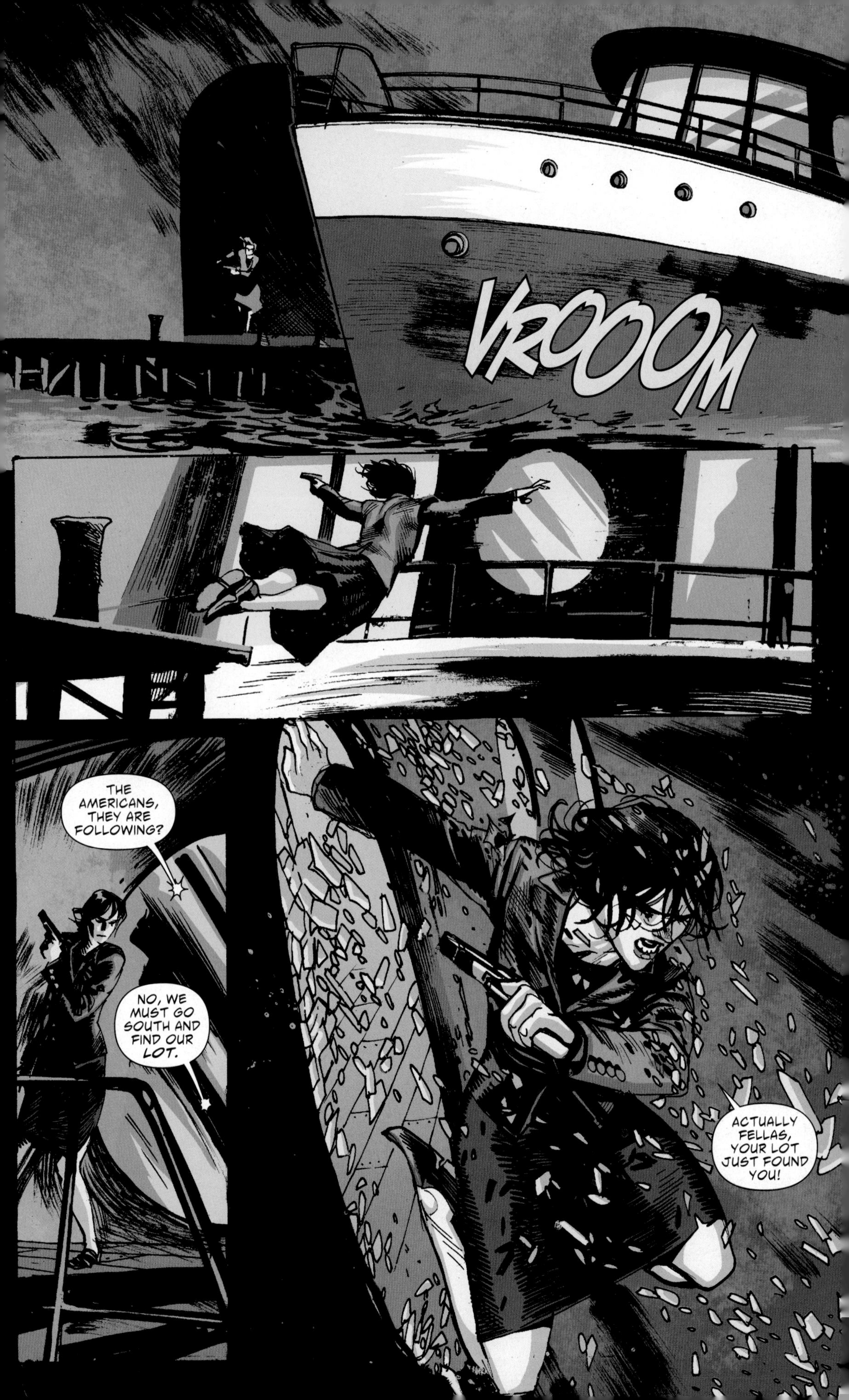
VROOOM
THE AMERICANS, THEY ARE FOLLOWING?
NO, WE MUST GO SOUTH AND FIND OUR LOT.
ACTUALLY FELLAS, YOUR LOT JUST FOUND YOU!

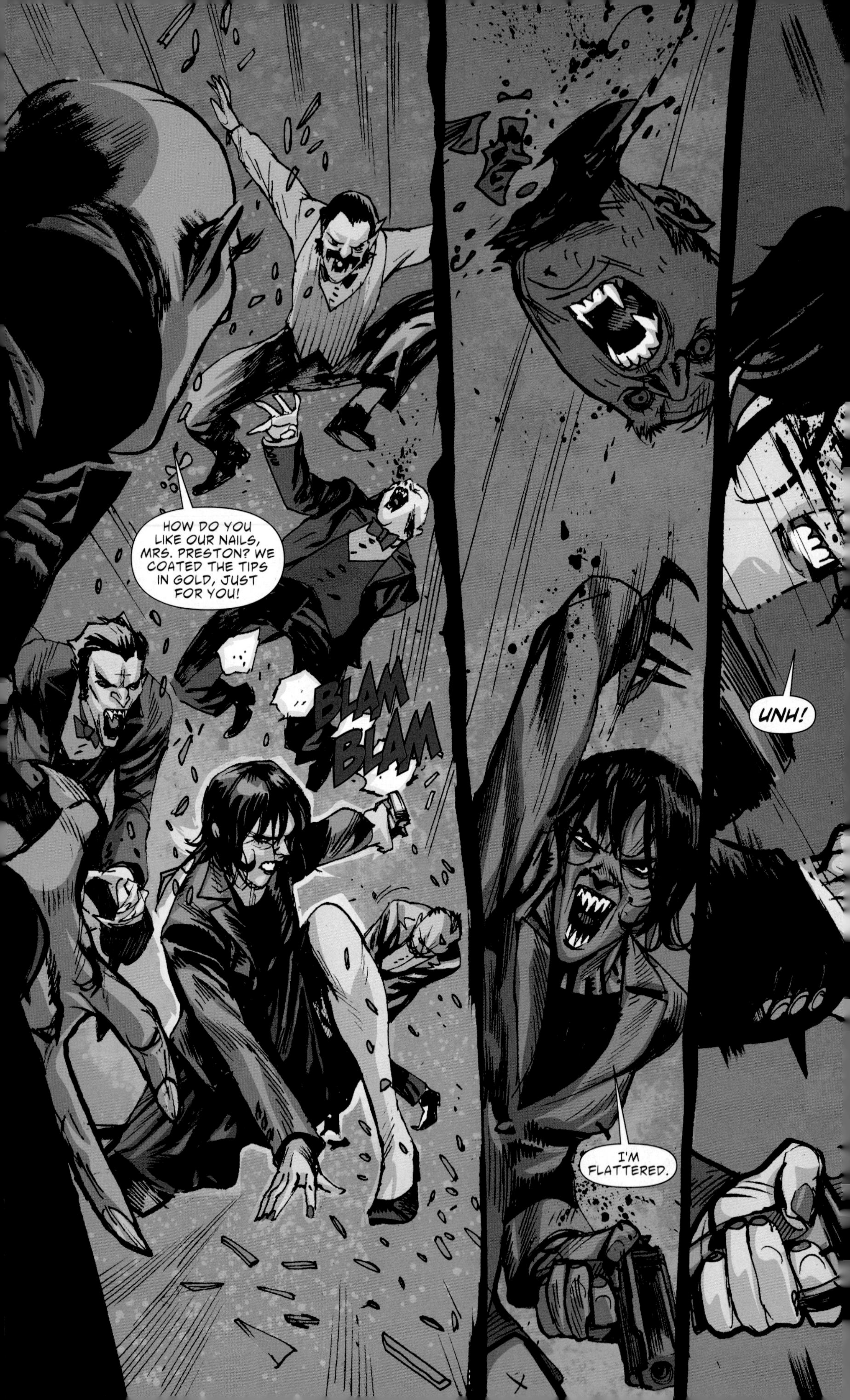
HOW DO YOU LIKE OUR NAILS, MRS. PRESTON? WE COATED THE TIPS IN GOLD, JUST FOR YOU!
BLAM BLAM
UNH!
I'M FLATTERED.

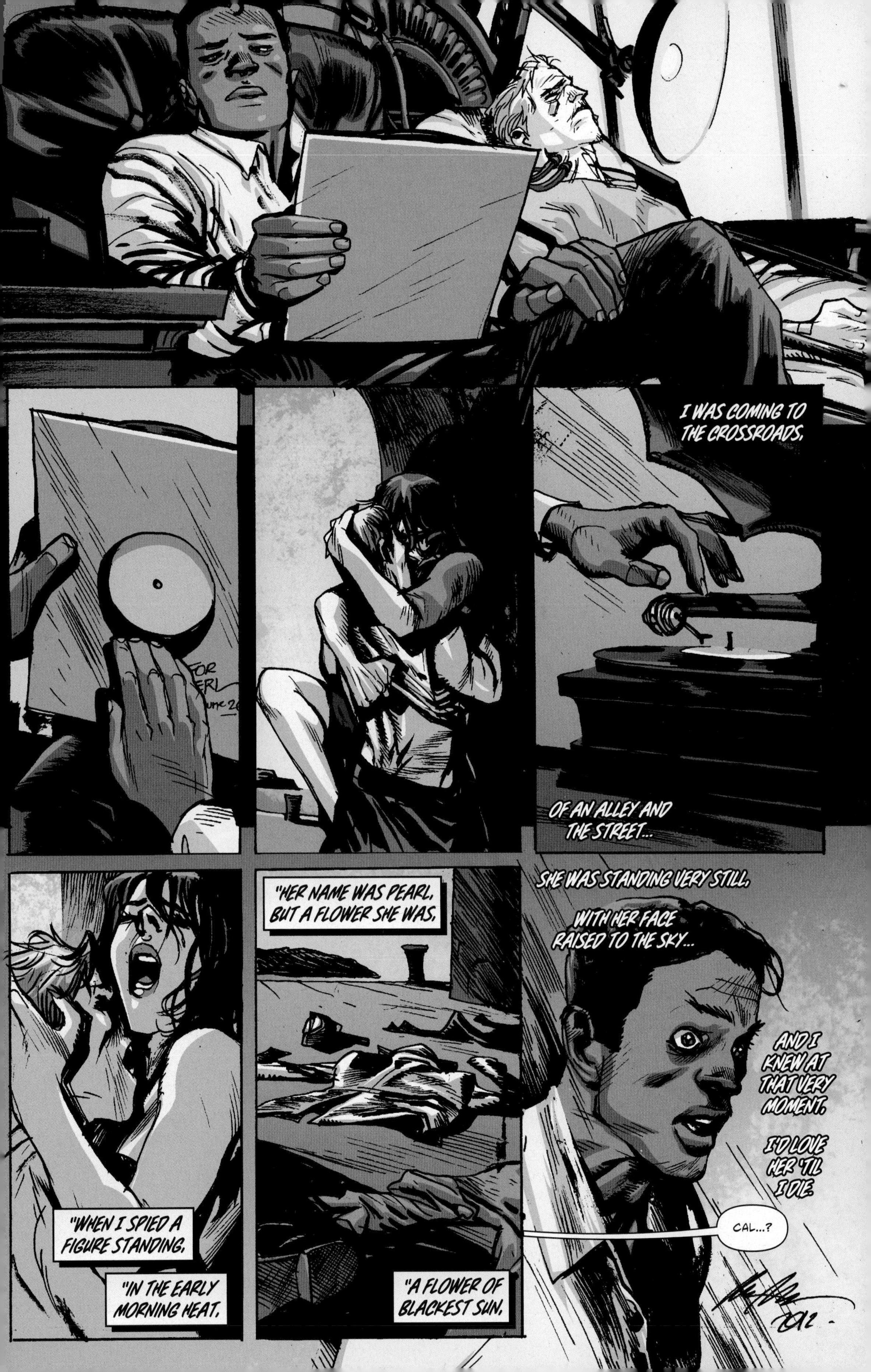
I WAS COMING TO THE CROSSROADS,
OF AN ALLEY AND THE STREET...
"WHEN I SPIED A FIGURE STANDING,
"IN THE EARLY MORNING HEAT,
"HER NAME WAS PEARL, BUT A FLOWER SHE WAS,
"A FLOWER OF BLACKEST SUN,
SHE WAS STANDING VERY STILL,
WITH HER FACE RAISED TO THE SKY...
AND I KNEW AT THAT VERY MOMENT,
I'D LOVE HER 'TIL I DIE.
CAL...?

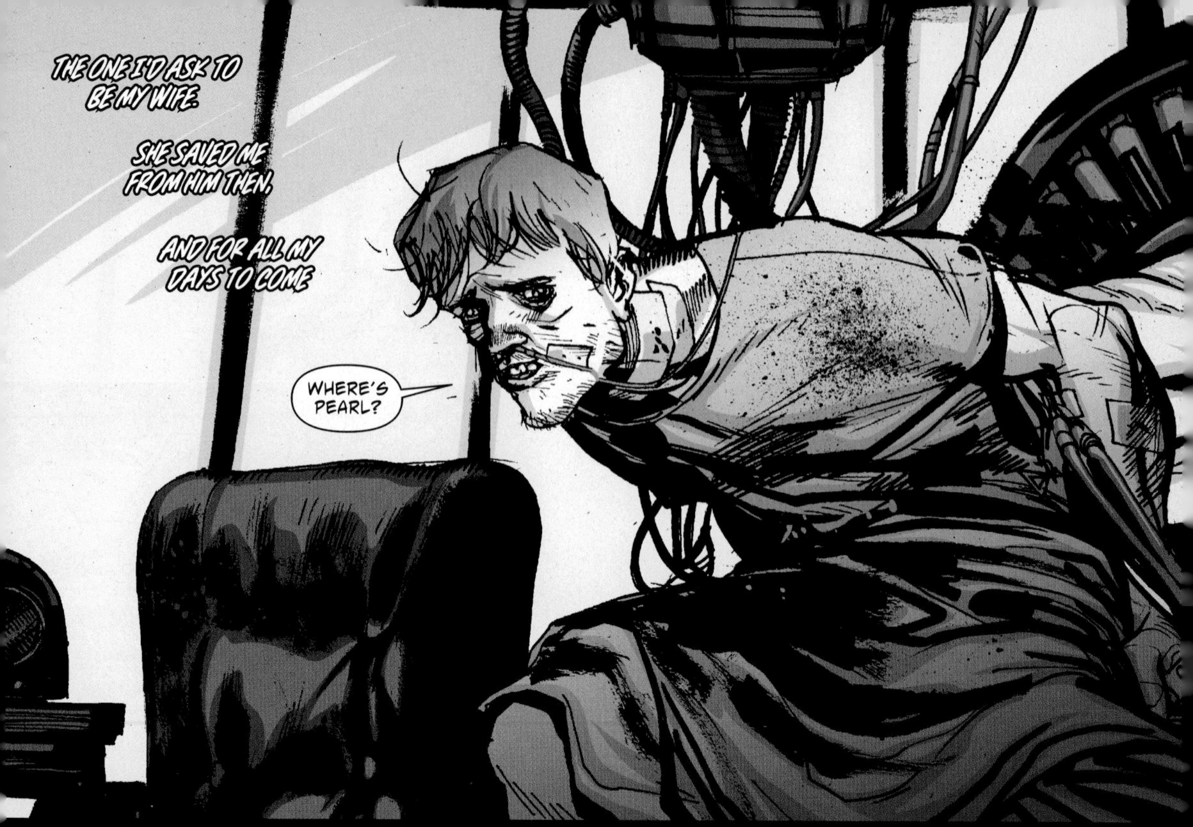
THE ONE I'D ASK TO BE MY WIFE.
SHE SAVED ME FROM HIM THEN,
AND FOR ALL MY DAYS TO COME
WHERE'S PEARL?

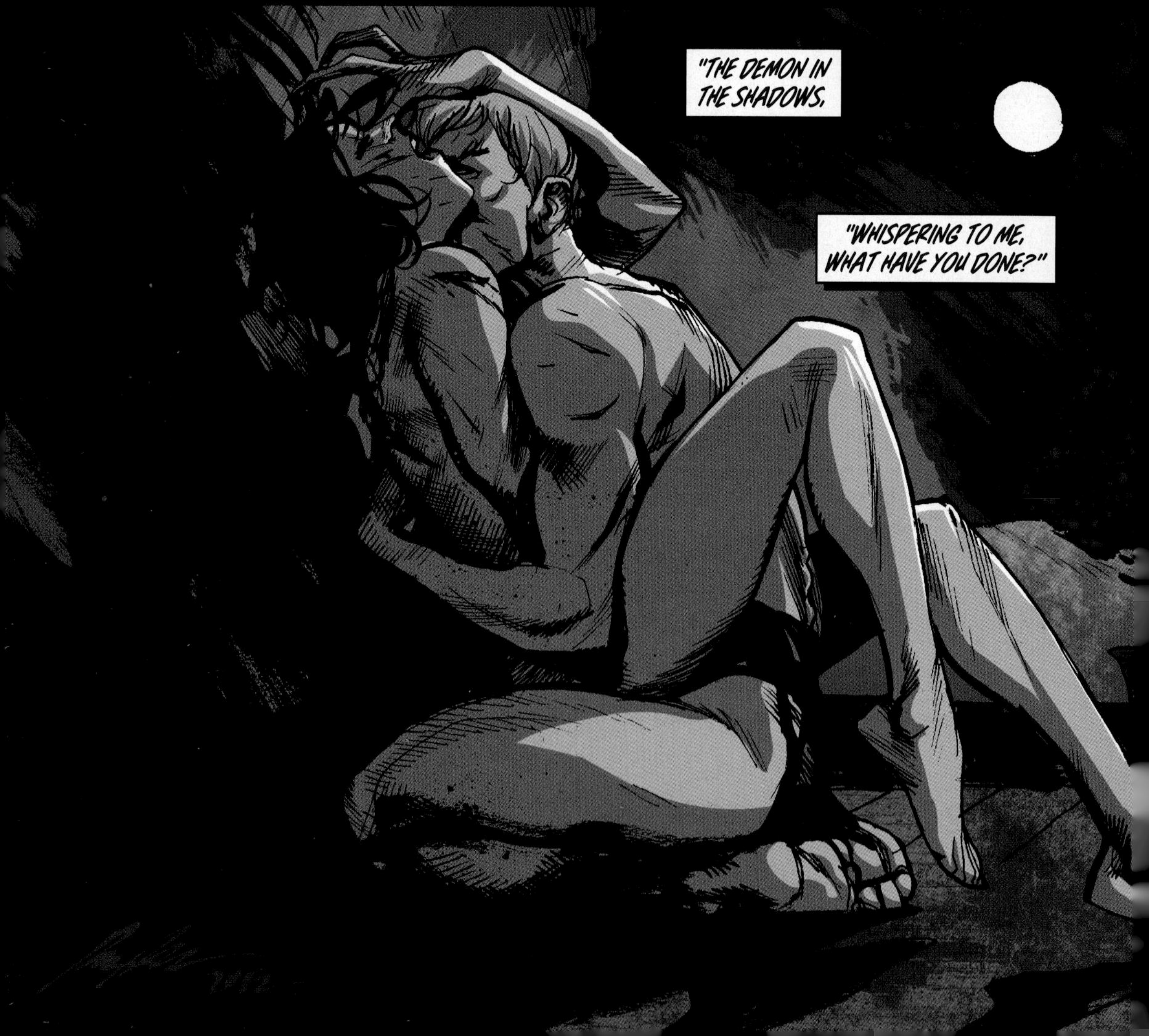
"THE DEMON IN THE SHADOWS,
"WHISPERING TO ME, WHAT HAVE YOU DONE?"

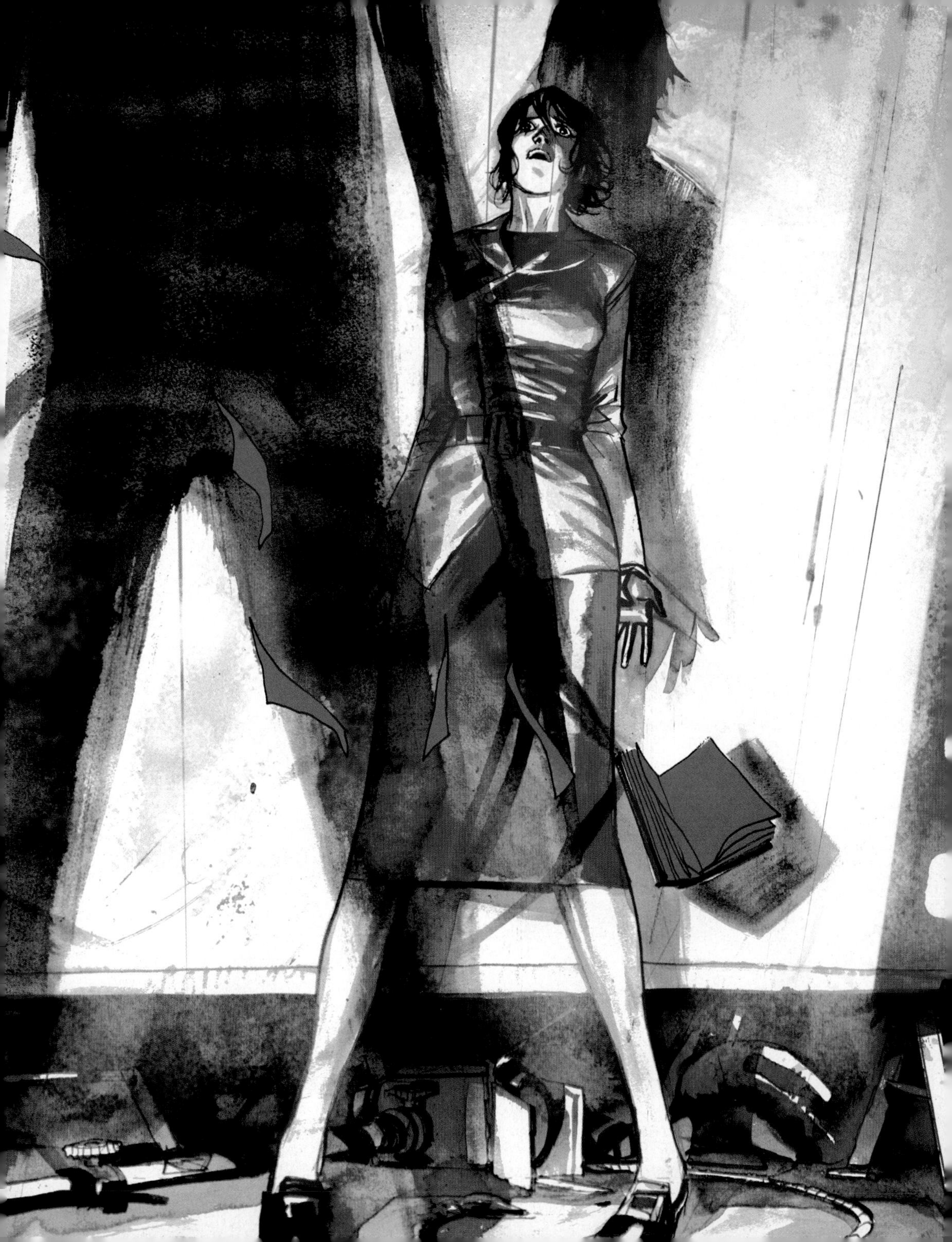

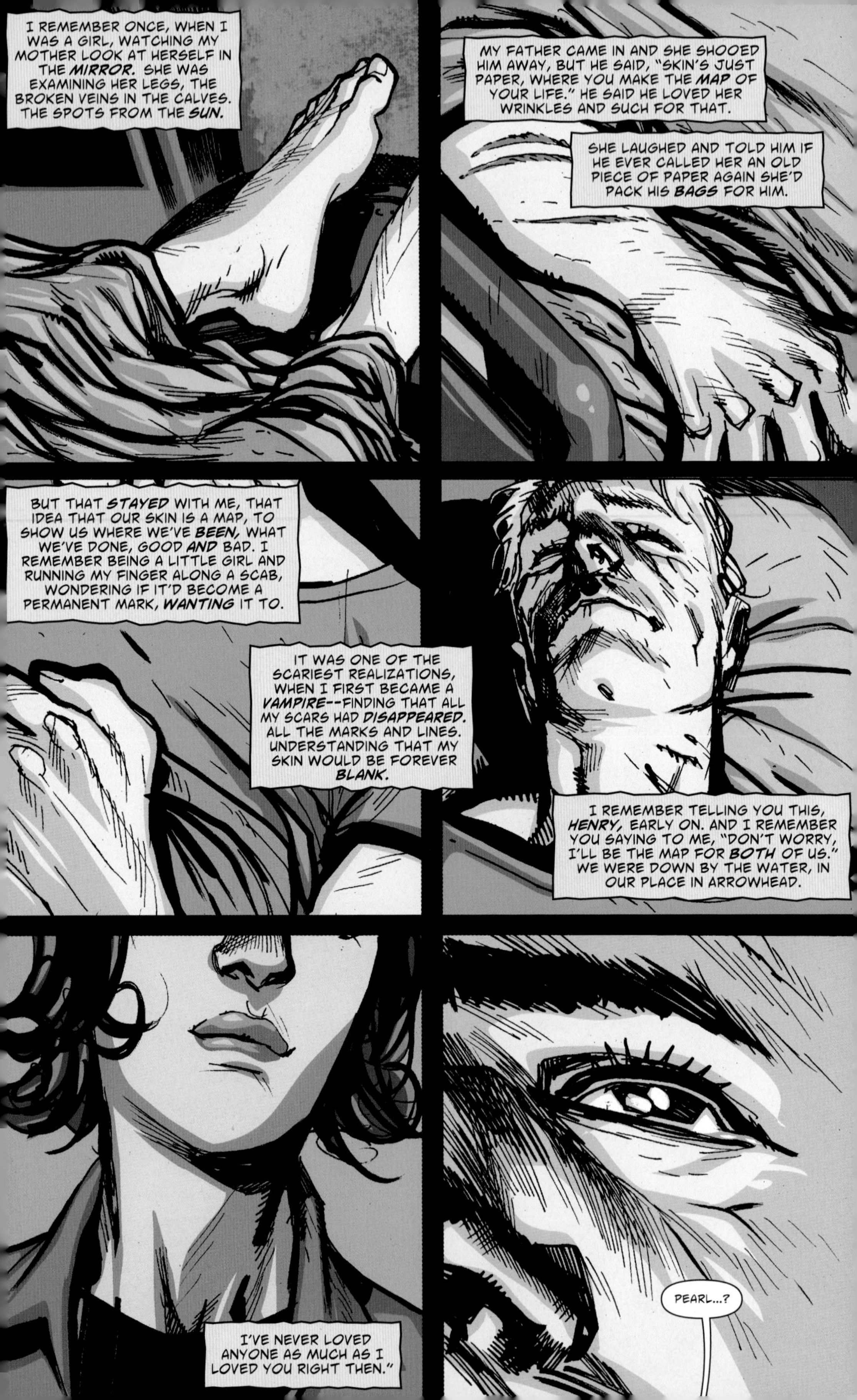
I REMEMBER ONCE, WHEN I WAS A GIRL, WATCHING MY MOTHER LOOK AT HERSELF IN THE MIRROR. SHE WAS EXAMINING HER LEGS, THE BROKEN VEINS IN THE CALVES. THE SPOTS FROM THE SUN.
MY FATHER CAME IN AND SHE SHOOED HIM AWAY, BUT HE SAID, "SKIN'S JUST PAPER, WHERE YOU MAKE THE MAP OF YOUR LIFE." HE SAID HE LOVED HER WRINKLES AND SUCH FOR THAT.
SHE LAUGHED AND TOLD HIM IF HE EVER CALLED HER AN OLD PIECE OF PAPER AGAIN SHE'D PACK HIS BAGS FOR HIM.
BUT THAT STAYED WITH ME, THAT IDEA THAT OUR SKIN IS A MAP, TO SHOW US WHERE WE'VE BEEN, WHAT WE'VE DONE, GOOD AND BAD. I REMEMBER BEING A LITTLE GIRL AND RUNNING MY FINGER ALONG A SCAB, WONDERING IF IT'D BECOME A PERMANENT MARK, WANTING IT TO.
IT WAS ONE OF THE SCARIEST REALIZATIONS, WHEN I FIRST BECAME A VAMPIRE--FINDING THAT ALL MY SCARS HAD DISAPPEARED. ALL THE MARKS AND LINES. UNDERSTANDING THAT MY SKIN WOULD BE FOREVER BLANK.
I REMEMBER TELLING YOU THIS, HENRY, EARLY ON. AND I REMEMBER YOU SAYING TO ME, "DON'T WORRY, I'LL BE THE MAP FOR BOTH OF US." WE WERE DOWN BY THE WATER, IN OUR PLACE IN ARROWHEAD.
I'VE NEVER LOVED ANYONE AS MUCH AS I LOVED YOU RIGHT THEN."
PEARL...?

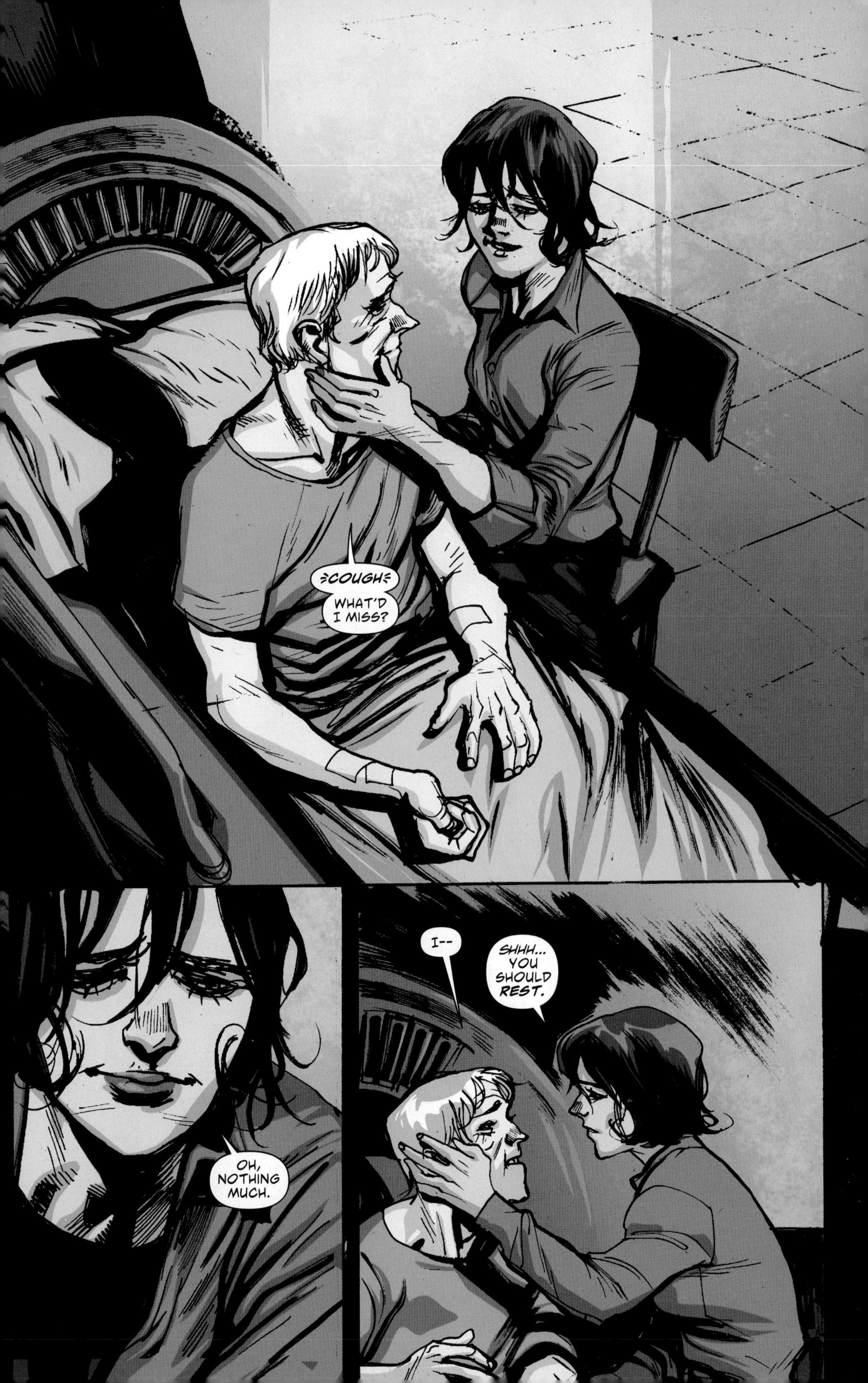
COUGH
WHAT'D I MISS?
OH, NOTHING MUCH.
I--
SHHH... YOU SHOULD REST.

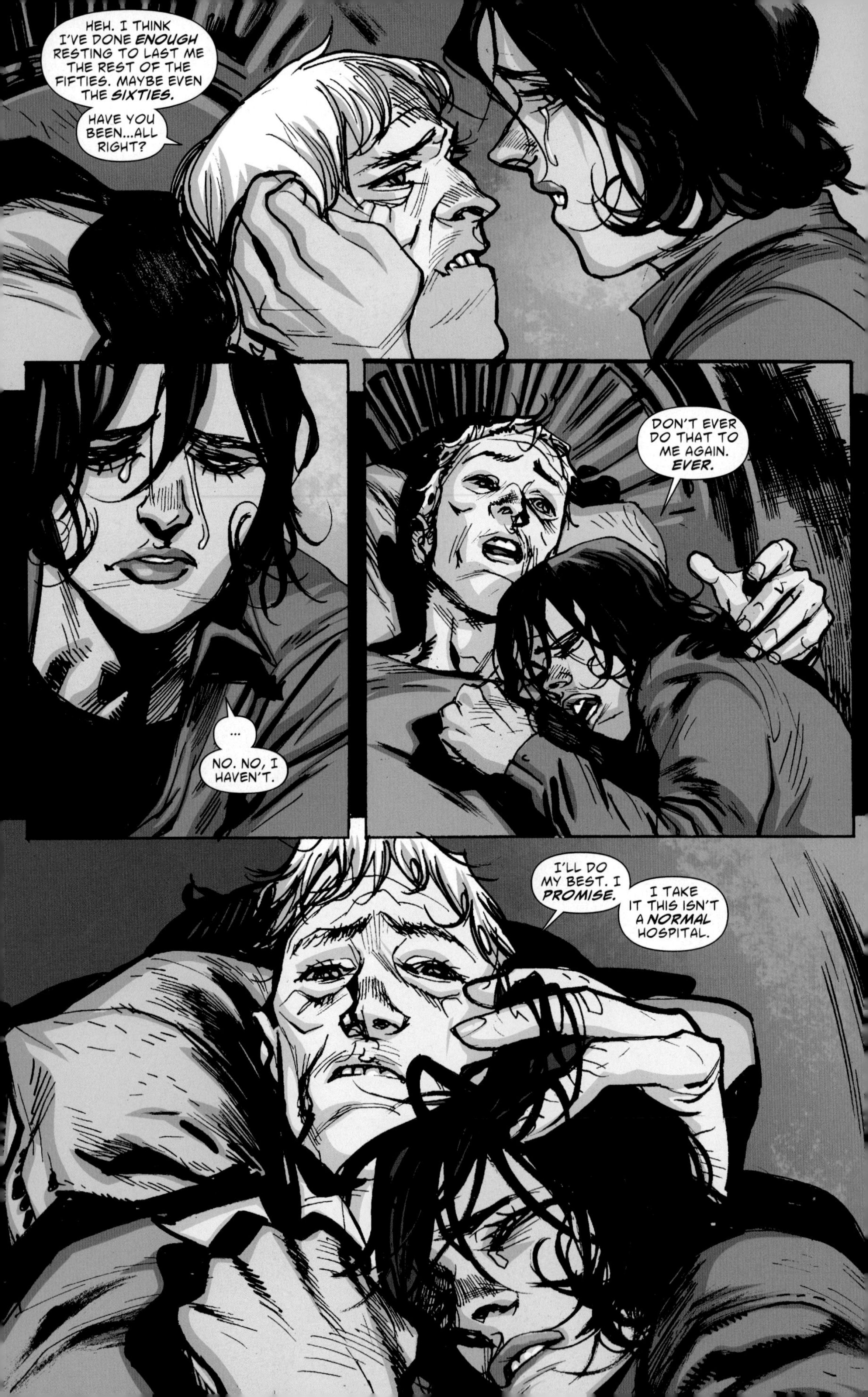
HEH. I THINK I'VE DONE ENOUGH RESTING TO LAST ME THE REST OF THE FIFTIES. MAYBE EVEN THE SIXTIES.
HAVE YOU BEEN...ALL RIGHT?
...
NO. NO, I HAVEN'T.
DON'T EVER DO THAT TO ME AGAIN. EVER.
I'LL DO MY BEST. I PROMISE.
I TAKE IT THIS ISN'T A NORMAL HOSPITAL.

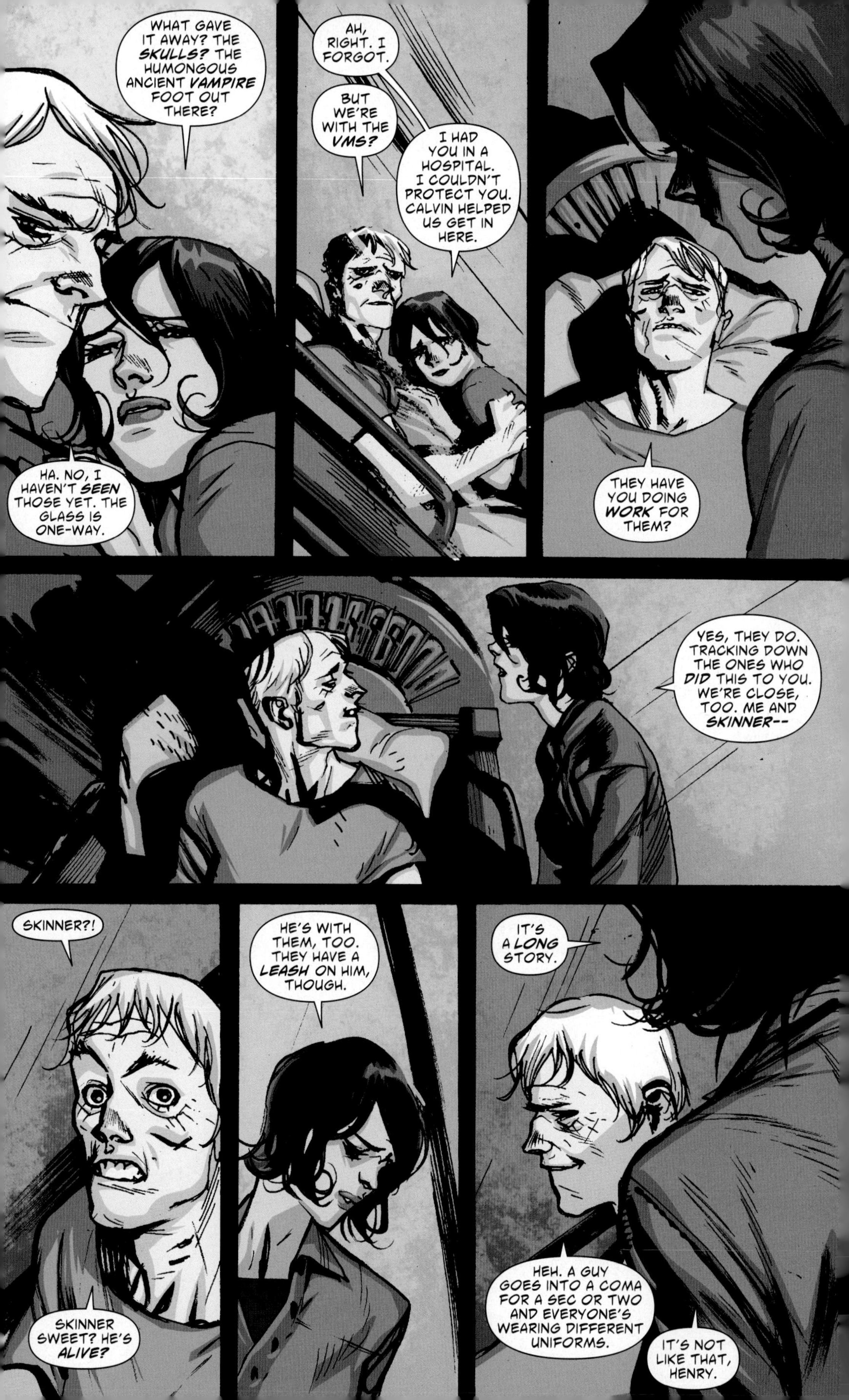
WHAT GAVE IT AWAY? THE SKULLS? THE HUMONGOUS ANCIENT VAMPIRE FOOT OUT THERE?
HA. NO, I HAVEN'T SEEN THOSE YET. THE GLASS IS ONE-WAY.
AH, RIGHT. I FORGOT.
BUT WE'RE WITH THE VMS?
I HAD YOU IN A HOSPITAL. I COULDN'T PROTECT YOU. CALVIN HELPED US GET IN HERE.
THEY HAVE YOU DOING WORK FOR THEM?
YES, THEY DO. TRACKING DOWN THE ONES WHO DID THIS TO YOU. WE'RE CLOSE, TOO. ME AND SKINNER--
SKINNER?!
SKINNER SWEET? HE'S ALIVE?
HE'S WITH THEM, TOO. THEY HAVE A LEASH ON HIM, THOUGH.
IT'S A LONG STORY.
HEH. A GUY GOES INTO A COMA FOR A SEC OR TWO AND EVERYONE'S WEARING DIFFERENT UNIFORMS.
IT'S NOT LIKE THAT, HENRY.

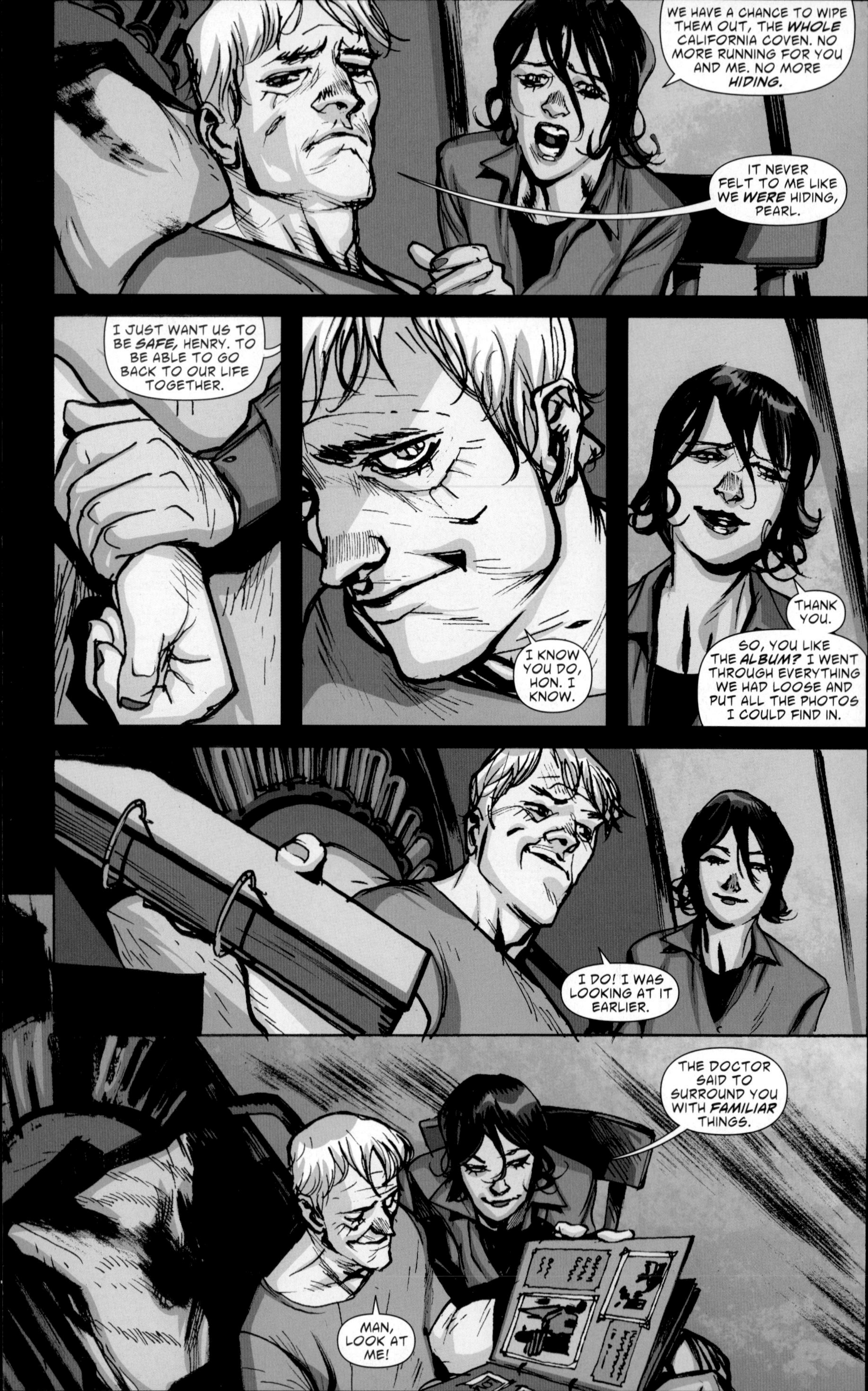
WE HAVE A CHANCE TO WIPE THEM OUT, THE WHOLE CALIFORNIA COVEN. NO MORE RUNNING FOR YOU AND ME. NO MORE HIDING.
IT NEVER FELT TO ME LIKE WE WERE HIDING, PEARL.
I JUST WANT US TO BE SAFE, HENRY. TO BE ABLE TO GO BACK TO OUR LIFE TOGETHER.
I KNOW YOU DO, HON. I KNOW.
THANK YOU.
SO, YOU LIKE THE ALBUM? I WENT THROUGH EVERYTHING WE HAD LOOSE AND PUT ALL THE PHOTOS I COULD FIND IN.
I DO! I WAS LOOKING AT IT EARLIER.
THE DOCTOR SAID TO SURROUND YOU WITH FAMILIAR THINGS.
MAN, LOOK AT ME!

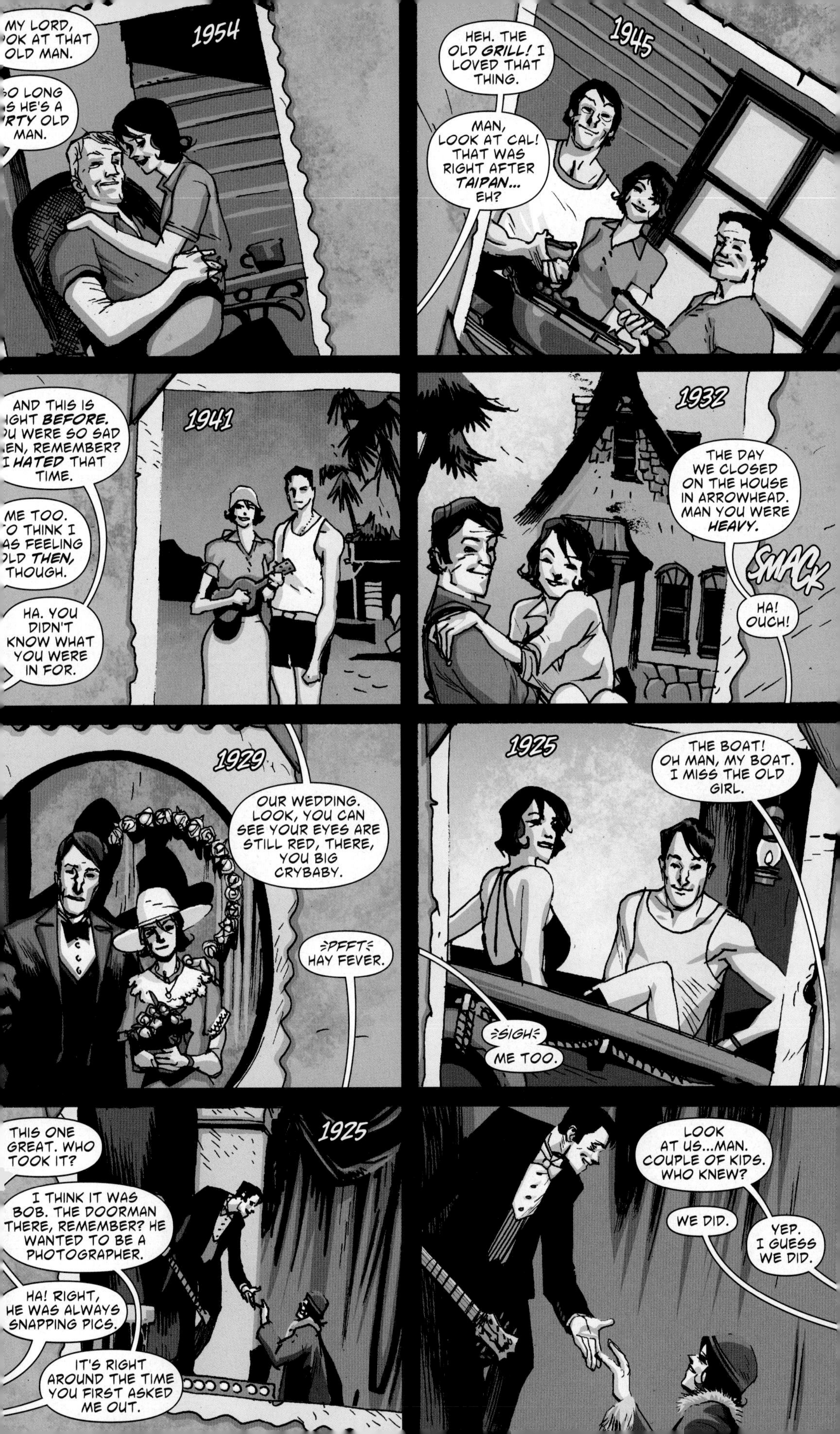
1954
MY LORD, OOK AT THAT OLD MAN.
SO LONG AS HE'S A DIRTY OLD MAN.
1945
HEH. THE OLD GRILL! I LOVED THAT THING.
MAN, LOOK AT CAL! THAT WAS RIGHT AFTER TAIPAN... EH?
1941
AND THIS IS RIGHT BEFORE. YOU WERE SO SAD THEN, REMEMBER? I HATED THAT TIME.
ME TOO. TO THINK I WAS FEELING OLD THEN, THOUGH.
HA. YOU DIDN'T KNOW WHAT YOU WERE IN FOR.
1932
THE DAY WE CLOSED ON THE HOUSE IN ARROWHEAD. MAN YOU WERE HEAVY.
SMACK
HA! OUCH!
1929
OUR WEDDING. LOOK, YOU CAN SEE YOUR EYES ARE STILL RED, THERE, YOU BIG CRYBABY.
PFFT HAY FEVER.
1925
THE BOAT! OH MAN, MY BOAT. I MISS THE OLD GIRL.
SIGH
ME TOO.
THIS ONE GREAT. WHO TOOK IT?
1925
I THINK IT WAS BOB. THE DOORMAN THERE, REMEMBER? HE WANTED TO BE A PHOTOGRAPHER.
HA! RIGHT, HE WAS ALWAYS SNAPPING PICS.
IT'S RIGHT AROUND THE TIME YOU FIRST ASKED ME OUT.
LOOK AT US...MAN. COUPLE OF KIDS. WHO KNEW?
WE DID.
YEP. I GUESS WE DID.

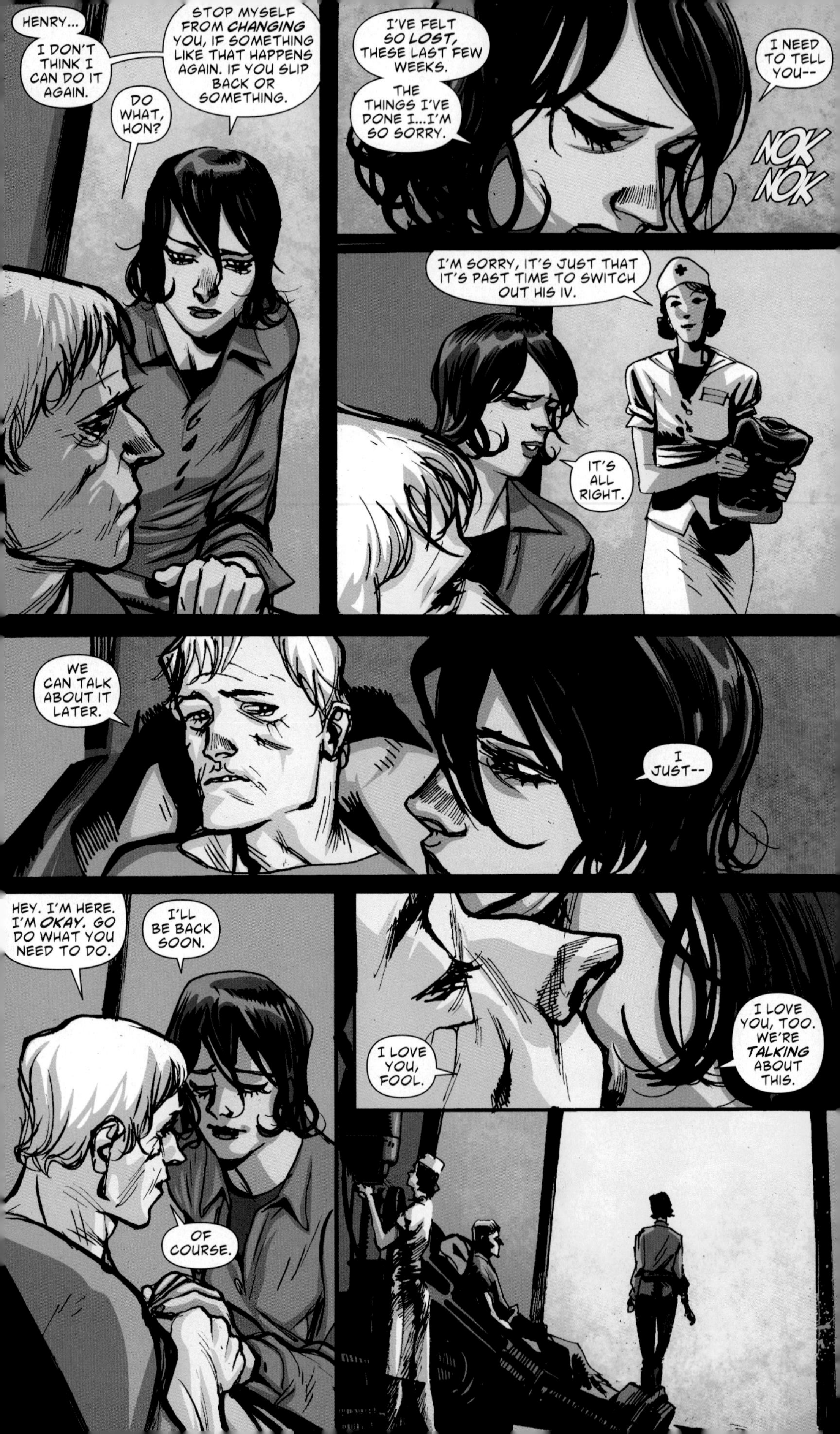
HENRY...
I DON'T THINK I CAN DO IT AGAIN.
DO WHAT, HON?
STOP MYSELF FROM CHANGING YOU, IF SOMETHING LIKE THAT HAPPENS AGAIN. IF YOU SLIP BACK OR SOMETHING.
I'VE FELT SO LOST, THESE LAST FEW WEEKS.
THE THINGS I'VE DONE I...I'M SO SORRY.
I NEED TO TELL YOU--
NOK NOK
I'M SORRY, IT'S JUST THAT IT'S PAST TIME TO SWITCH OUT HIS IV.
IT'S ALL RIGHT.
WE CAN TALK ABOUT IT LATER.
I JUST--
HEY. I'M HERE. I'M OKAY. GO DO WHAT YOU NEED TO DO.
I'LL BE BACK SOON.
OF COURSE.
I LOVE YOU, FOOL.
I LOVE YOU, TOO. WE'RE TALKING ABOUT THIS.

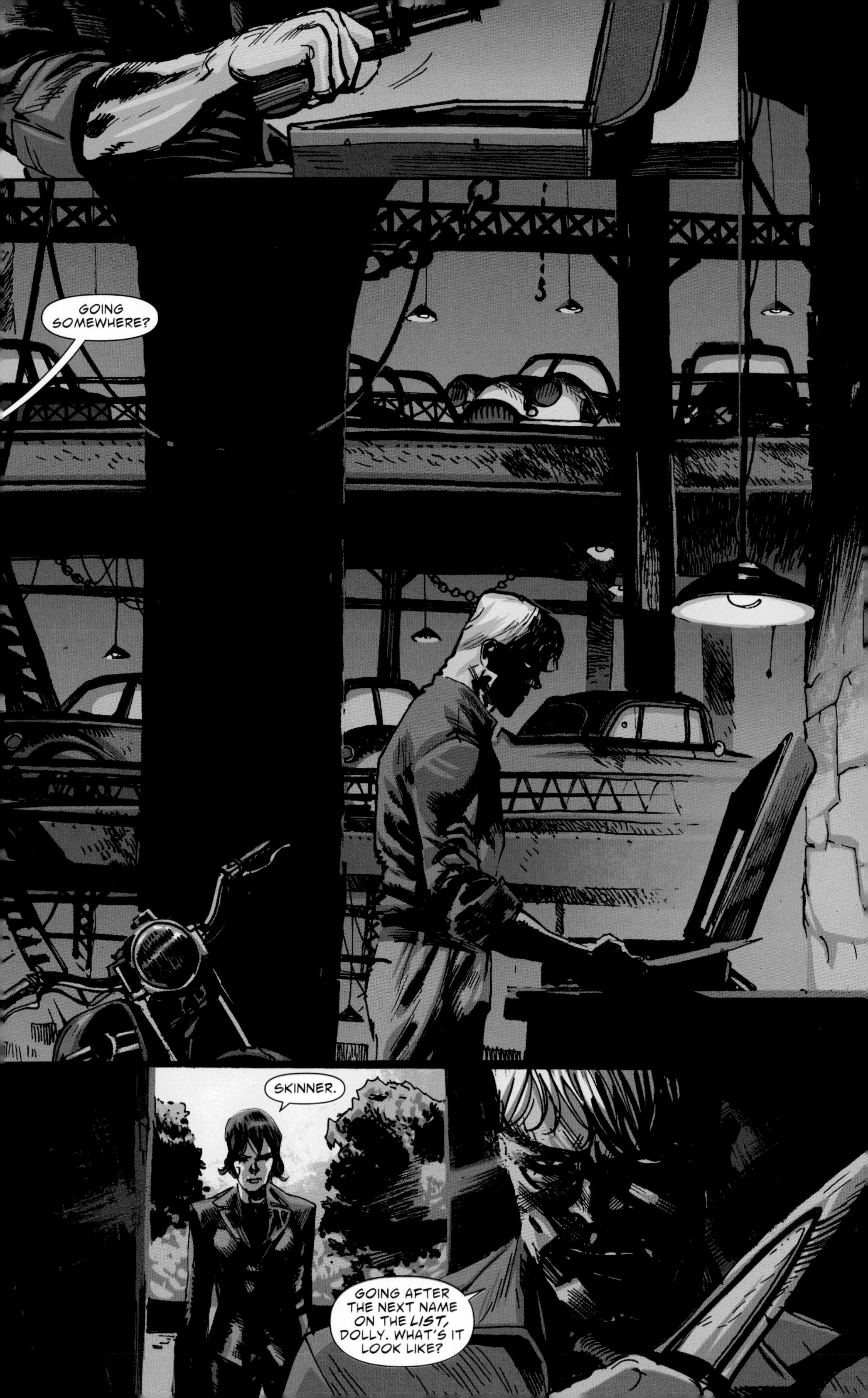
GOING SOMEWHERE?
SKINNER.
GOING AFTER THE NEXT NAME ON THE LIST, DOLLY. WHAT'S IT LOOK LIKE?

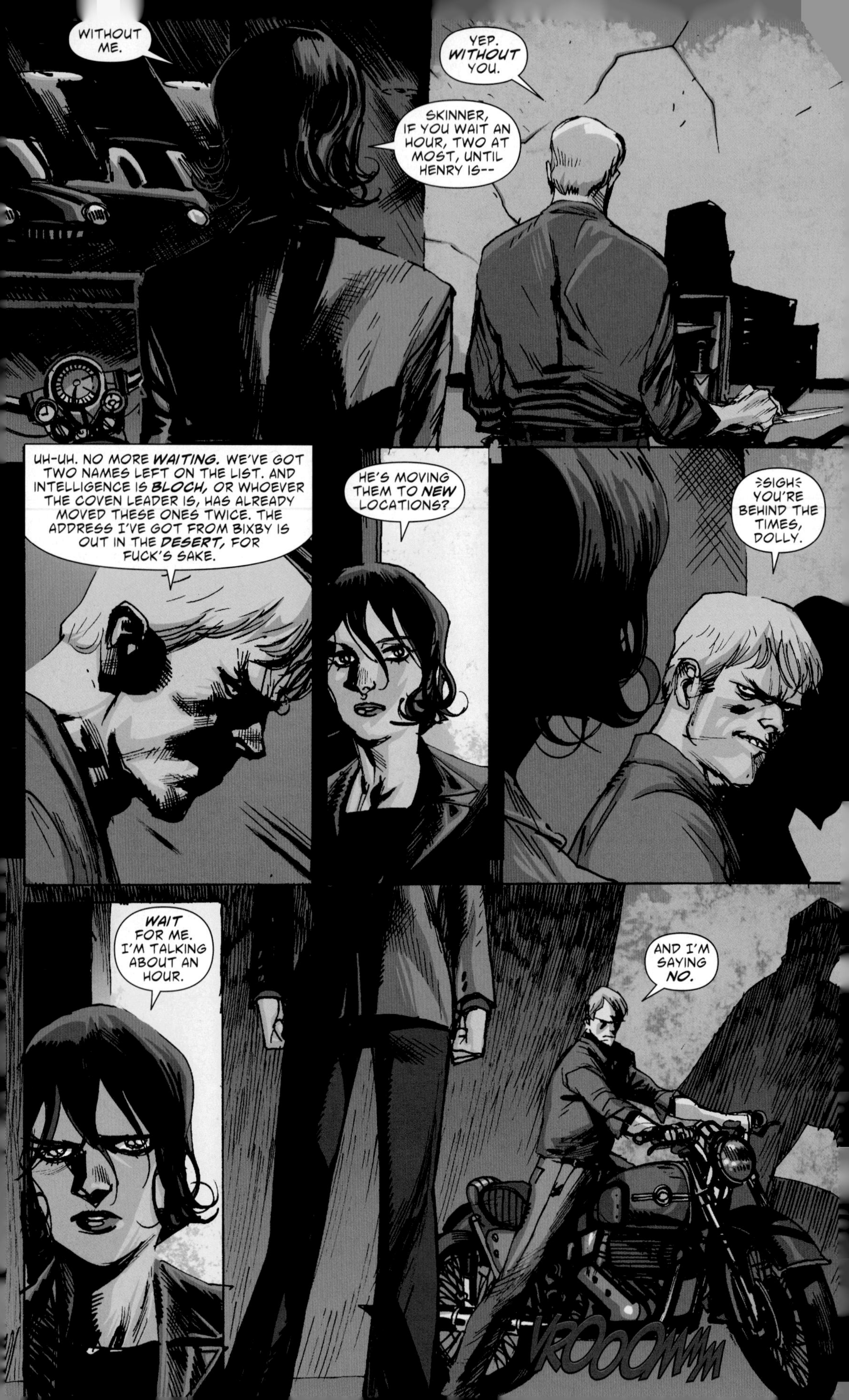
WITHOUT ME.
YEP. WITHOUT YOU.
SKINNER, IF YOU WAIT AN HOUR, TWO AT MOST, UNTIL HENRY IS--
UH-UH. NO MORE WAITING. WE'VE GOT TWO NAMES LEFT ON THE LIST. AND INTELLIGENCE IS BLOCH, OR WHOEVER THE COVEN LEADER IS, HAS ALREADY MOVED THESE ONES TWICE. THE ADDRESS I'VE GOT FROM BIXBY IS OUT IN THE DESERT, FOR FUCK'S SAKE.
HE'S MOVING THEM TO NEW LOCATIONS?
SIGH YOU'RE BEHIND THE TIMES, DOLLY.
WAIT FOR ME. I'M TALKING ABOUT AN HOUR.
AND I'M SAYING NO.
VROOOMMM

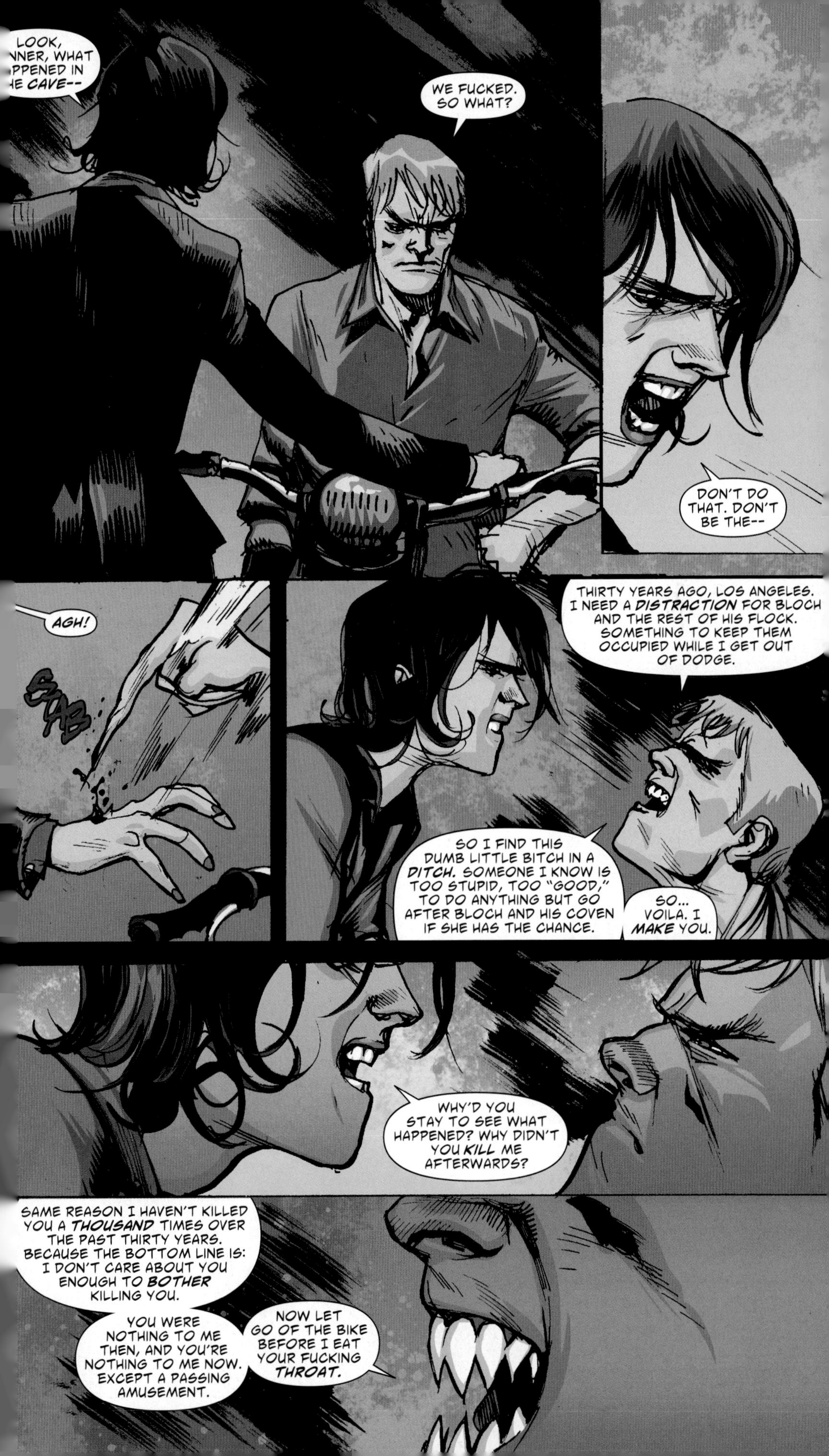
LOOK, ...NNER, WHAT ...PPENED IN ...HE CAVE--
WE FUCKED. SO WHAT?
DON'T DO THAT. DON'T BE THE--
AGH!
STAB
THIRTY YEARS AGO, LOS ANGELES. I NEED A DISTRACTION FOR BLOCH AND THE REST OF HIS FLOCK. SOMETHING TO KEEP THEM OCCUPIED WHILE I GET OUT OF DODGE.
SO I FIND THIS DUMB LITTLE BITCH IN A DITCH. SOMEONE I KNOW IS TOO STUPID, TOO "GOOD," TO DO ANYTHING BUT GO AFTER BLOCH AND HIS COVEN IF SHE HAS THE CHANCE.
SO... VOILA. I MAKE YOU.
WHY'D YOU STAY TO SEE WHAT HAPPENED? WHY DIDN'T YOU KILL ME AFTERWARDS?
SAME REASON I HAVEN'T KILLED YOU A THOUSAND TIMES OVER THE PAST THIRTY YEARS. BECAUSE THE BOTTOM LINE IS: I DON'T CARE ABOUT YOU ENOUGH TO BOTHER KILLING YOU.
YOU WERE NOTHING TO ME THEN, AND YOU'RE NOTHING TO ME NOW. EXCEPT A PASSING AMUSEMENT.
NOW LET GO OF THE BIKE BEFORE I EAT YOUR FUCKING THROAT.

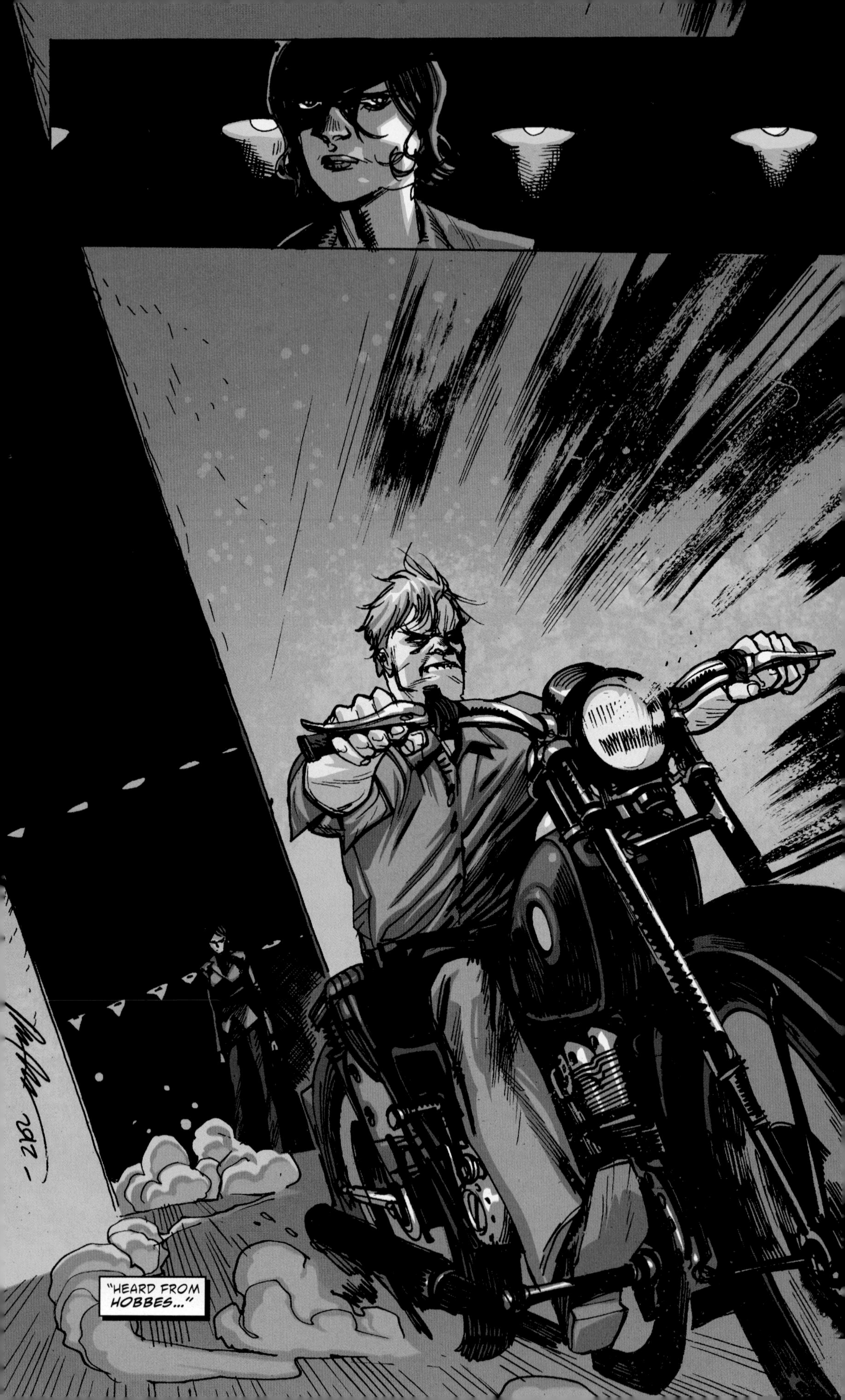
"HEARD FROM HOBBES..."

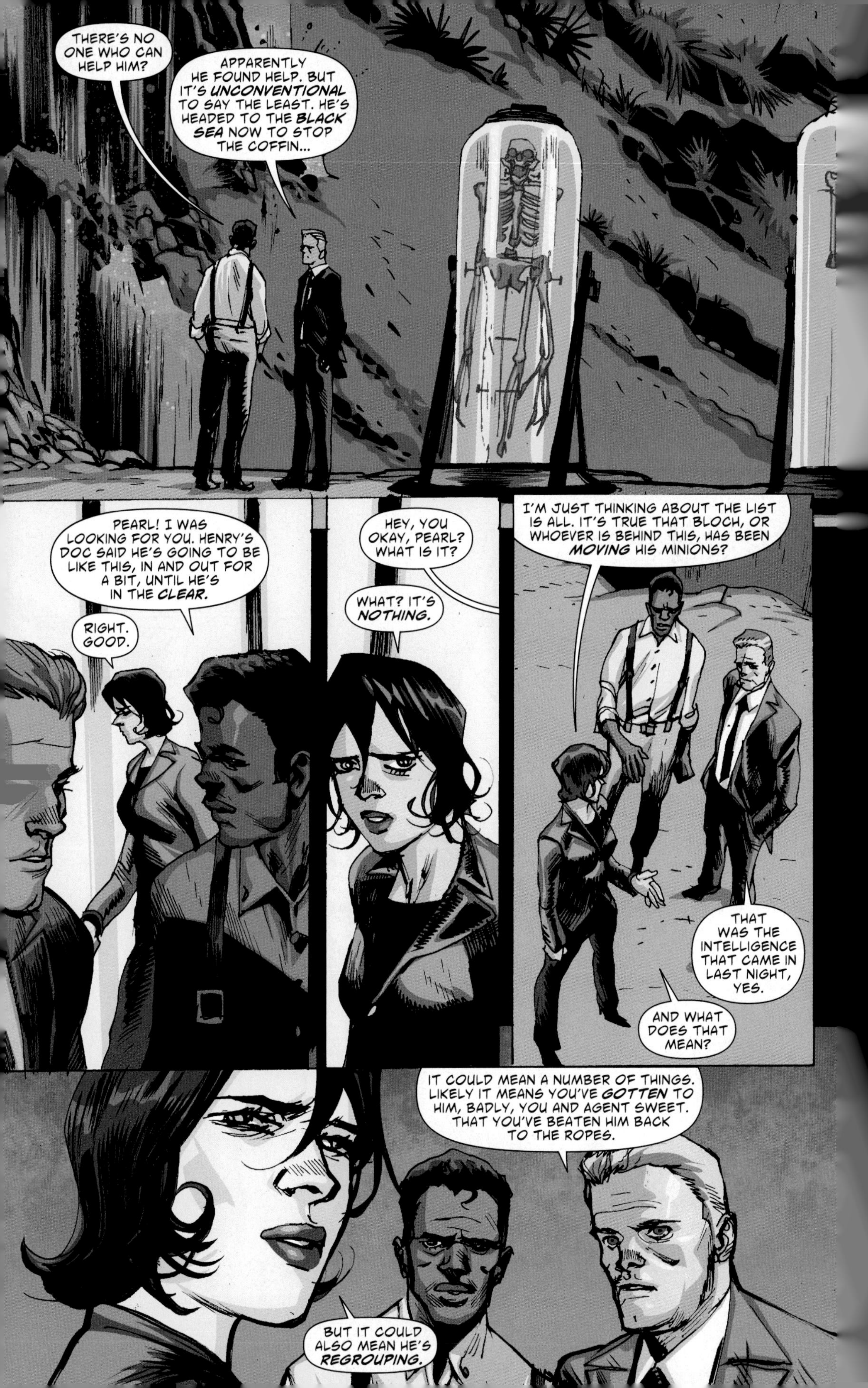
THERE'S NO ONE WHO CAN HELP HIM?
APPARENTLY HE FOUND HELP. BUT IT'S UNCONVENTIONAL TO SAY THE LEAST. HE'S HEADED TO THE BLACK SEA NOW TO STOP THE COFFIN...
PEARL! I WAS LOOKING FOR YOU. HENRY'S DOC SAID HE'S GOING TO BE LIKE THIS, IN AND OUT FOR A BIT, UNTIL HE'S IN THE CLEAR.
RIGHT. GOOD.
HEY, YOU OKAY, PEARL? WHAT IS IT?
WHAT? IT'S NOTHING.
I'M JUST THINKING ABOUT THE LIST IS ALL. IT'S TRUE THAT BLOCH, OR WHOEVER IS BEHIND THIS, HAS BEEN MOVING HIS MINIONS?
THAT WAS THE INTELLIGENCE THAT CAME IN LAST NIGHT, YES.
AND WHAT DOES THAT MEAN?
IT COULD MEAN A NUMBER OF THINGS. LIKELY IT MEANS YOU'VE GOTTEN TO HIM, BADLY, YOU AND AGENT SWEET. THAT YOU'VE BEATEN HIM BACK TO THE ROPES.
BUT IT COULD ALSO MEAN HE'S REGROUPING.

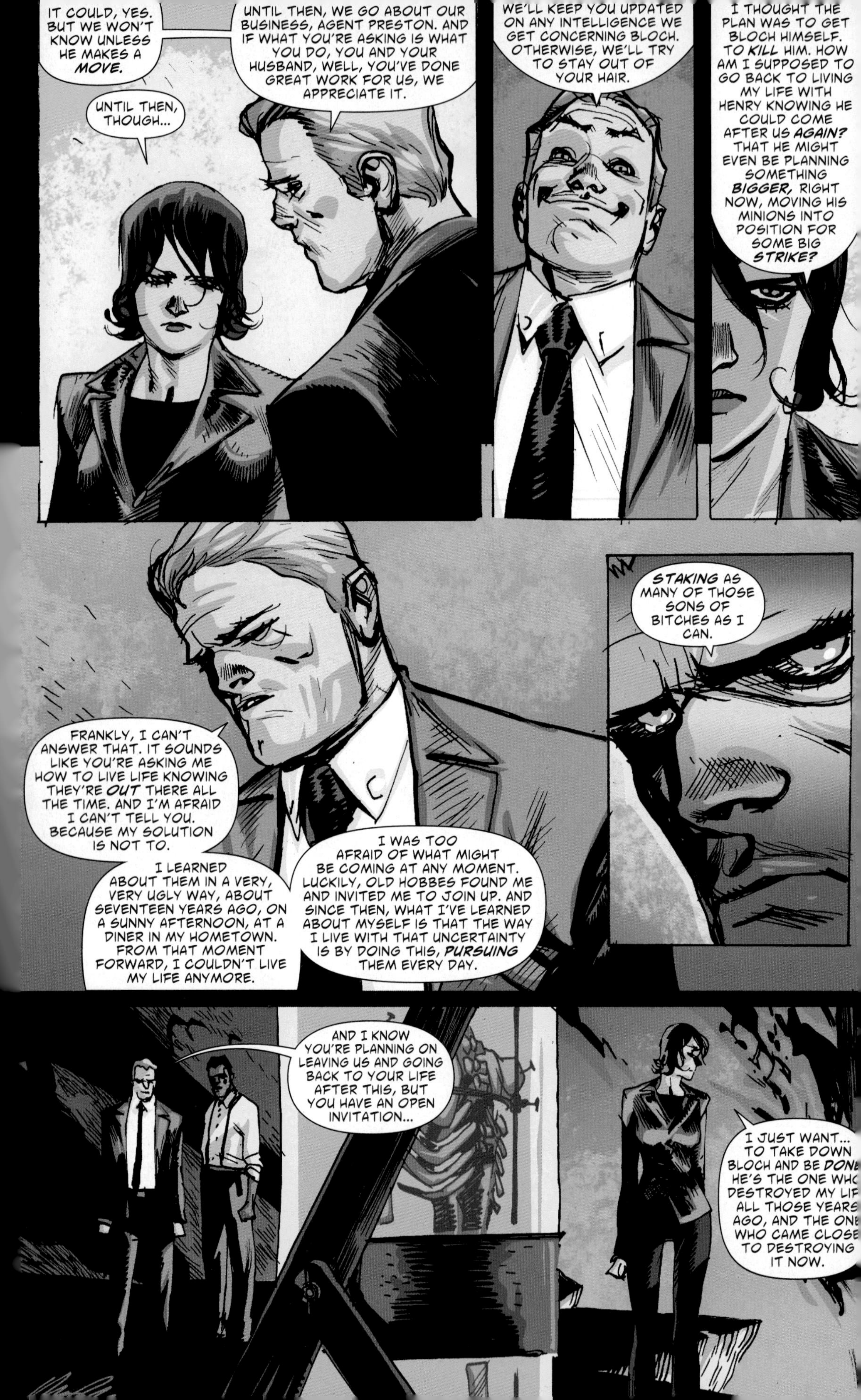
IT COULD, YES. BUT WE WON'T KNOW UNLESS HE MAKES A *MOVE.*
UNTIL THEN, THOUGH...
UNTIL THEN, WE GO ABOUT OUR BUSINESS, AGENT PRESTON. AND IF WHAT YOU'RE ASKING IS WHAT YOU DO, YOU AND YOUR HUSBAND, WELL, YOU'VE DONE GREAT WORK FOR US, WE APPRECIATE IT.
WE'LL KEEP YOU UPDATED ON ANY INTELLIGENCE WE GET CONCERNING BLOCH. OTHERWISE, WE'LL TRY TO STAY OUT OF YOUR HAIR.
I THOUGHT THE PLAN WAS TO GET BLOCH HIMSELF. TO *KILL* HIM. HOW AM I SUPPOSED TO GO BACK TO LIVING MY LIFE WITH HENRY KNOWING HE COULD COME AFTER US *AGAIN?* THAT HE MIGHT EVEN BE PLANNING SOMETHING *BIGGER,* RIGHT NOW, MOVING HIS MINIONS INTO POSITION FOR SOME BIG *STRIKE?*
FRANKLY, I CAN'T ANSWER THAT. IT SOUNDS LIKE YOU'RE ASKING ME HOW TO LIVE LIFE KNOWING THEY'RE *OUT* THERE ALL THE TIME. AND I'M AFRAID I CAN'T TELL YOU. BECAUSE MY SOLUTION IS NOT TO.
I LEARNED ABOUT THEM IN A VERY, VERY UGLY WAY, ABOUT SEVENTEEN YEARS AGO, ON A SUNNY AFTERNOON, AT A DINER IN MY HOMETOWN. FROM THAT MOMENT FORWARD, I COULDN'T LIVE MY LIFE ANYMORE.
I WAS TOO AFRAID OF WHAT MIGHT BE COMING AT ANY MOMENT. LUCKILY, OLD HOBBES FOUND ME AND INVITED ME TO JOIN UP. AND SINCE THEN, WHAT I'VE LEARNED ABOUT MYSELF IS THAT THE WAY I LIVE WITH THAT UNCERTAINTY IS BY DOING THIS, *PURSUING* THEM EVERY DAY.
STAKING AS MANY OF THOSE SONS OF BITCHES AS I CAN.
AND I KNOW YOU'RE PLANNING ON LEAVING US AND GOING BACK TO YOUR LIFE AFTER THIS, BUT YOU HAVE AN OPEN INVITATION...
I JUST WANT... TO TAKE DOWN BLOCH AND BE *DON* HE'S THE ONE WH DESTROYED MY LIF ALL THOSE YEAR AGO, AND THE ON WHO CAME CLOS TO DESTROYING IT NOW.

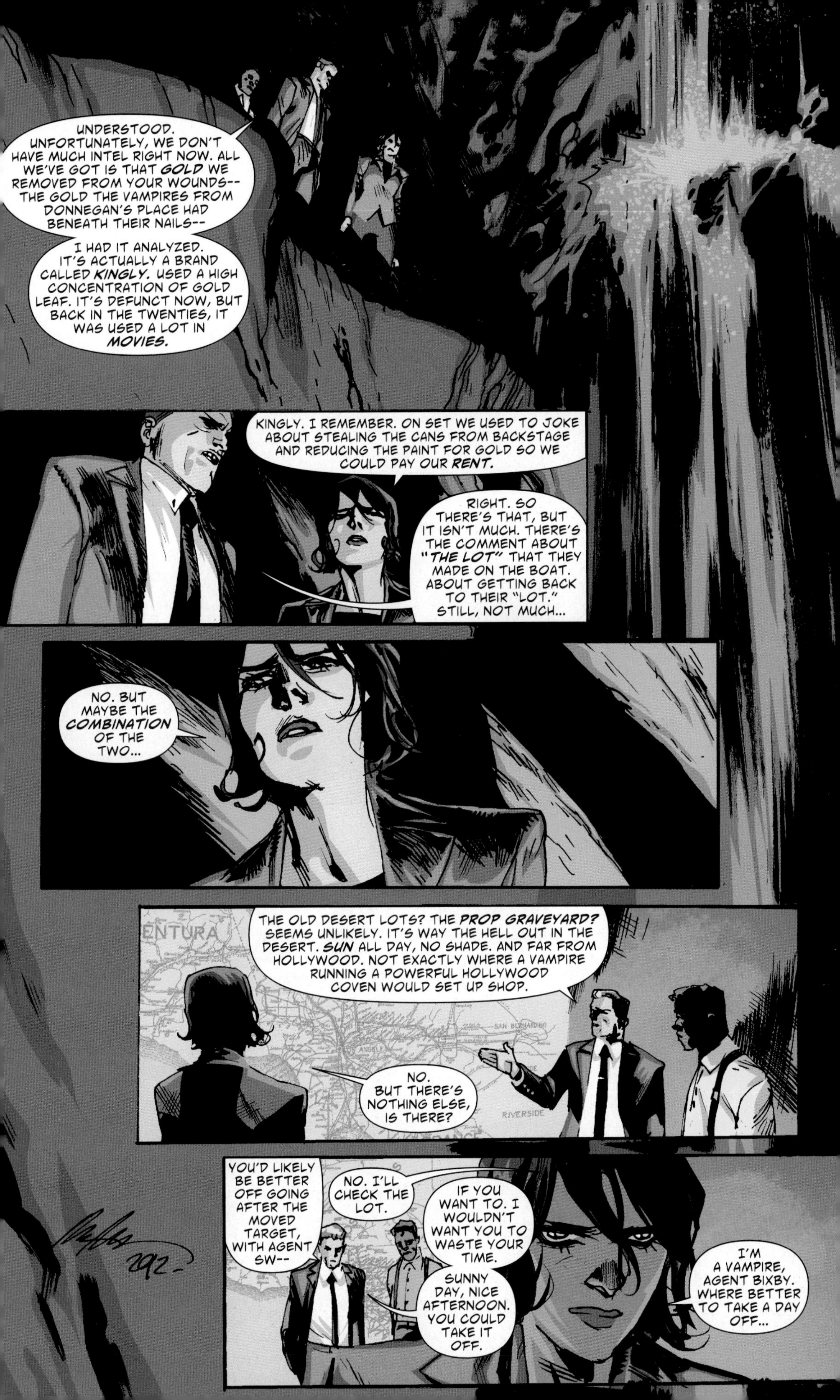
UNDERSTOOD. UNFORTUNATELY, WE DON'T HAVE MUCH INTEL RIGHT NOW. ALL WE'VE GOT IS THAT GOLD WE REMOVED FROM YOUR WOUNDS-- THE GOLD THE VAMPIRES FROM DONNEGAN'S PLACE HAD BENEATH THEIR NAILS--
I HAD IT ANALYZED. IT'S ACTUALLY A BRAND CALLED KINGLY. USED A HIGH CONCENTRATION OF GOLD LEAF. IT'S DEFUNCT NOW, BUT BACK IN THE TWENTIES, IT WAS USED A LOT IN MOVIES.
KINGLY. I REMEMBER. ON SET WE USED TO JOKE ABOUT STEALING THE CANS FROM BACKSTAGE AND REDUCING THE PAINT FOR GOLD SO WE COULD PAY OUR RENT.
RIGHT. SO THERE'S THAT, BUT IT ISN'T MUCH. THERE'S THE COMMENT ABOUT "THE LOT" THAT THEY MADE ON THE BOAT. ABOUT GETTING BACK TO THEIR "LOT." STILL, NOT MUCH...
NO. BUT MAYBE THE COMBINATION OF THE TWO...
THE OLD DESERT LOTS? THE PROP GRAVEYARD? SEEMS UNLIKELY. IT'S WAY THE HELL OUT IN THE DESERT. SUN ALL DAY, NO SHADE. AND FAR FROM HOLLYWOOD. NOT EXACTLY WHERE A VAMPIRE RUNNING A POWERFUL HOLLYWOOD COVEN WOULD SET UP SHOP.
ENTURA
SAN BERNARDINO
RIVERSIDE
NO. BUT THERE'S NOTHING ELSE, IS THERE?
YOU'D LIKELY BE BETTER OFF GOING AFTER THE MOVED TARGET, WITH AGENT SW--
NO. I'LL CHECK THE LOT.
IF YOU WANT TO. I WOULDN'T WANT YOU TO WASTE YOUR TIME.
SUNNY DAY, NICE AFTERNOON. YOU COULD TAKE IT OFF.
I'M A VAMPIRE, AGENT BIXBY. WHERE BETTER TO TAKE A DAY OFF...

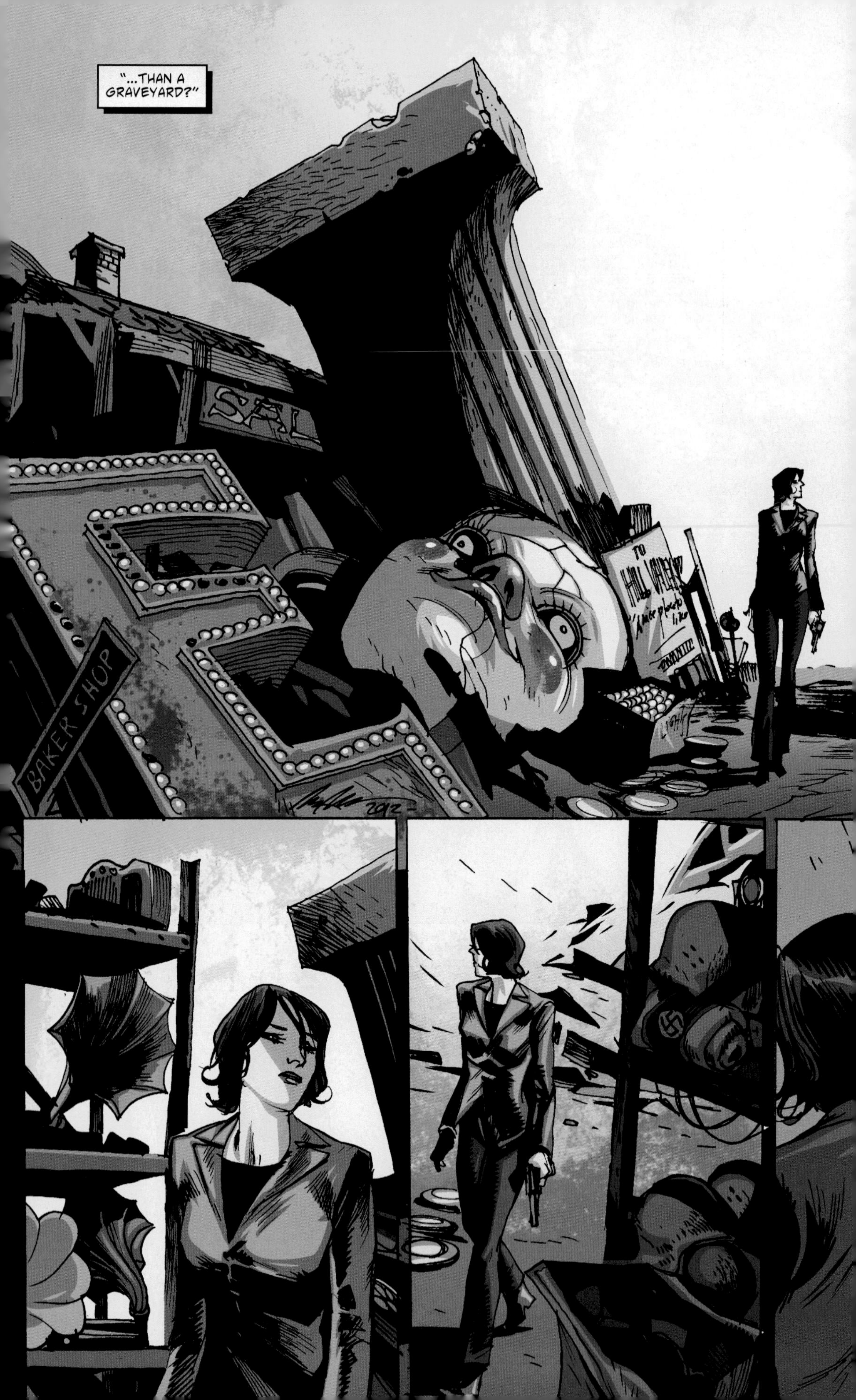
"...THAN A GRAVEYARD?"
SAL
BAKER SHOP
TO HILL VALLEY
LIGHT

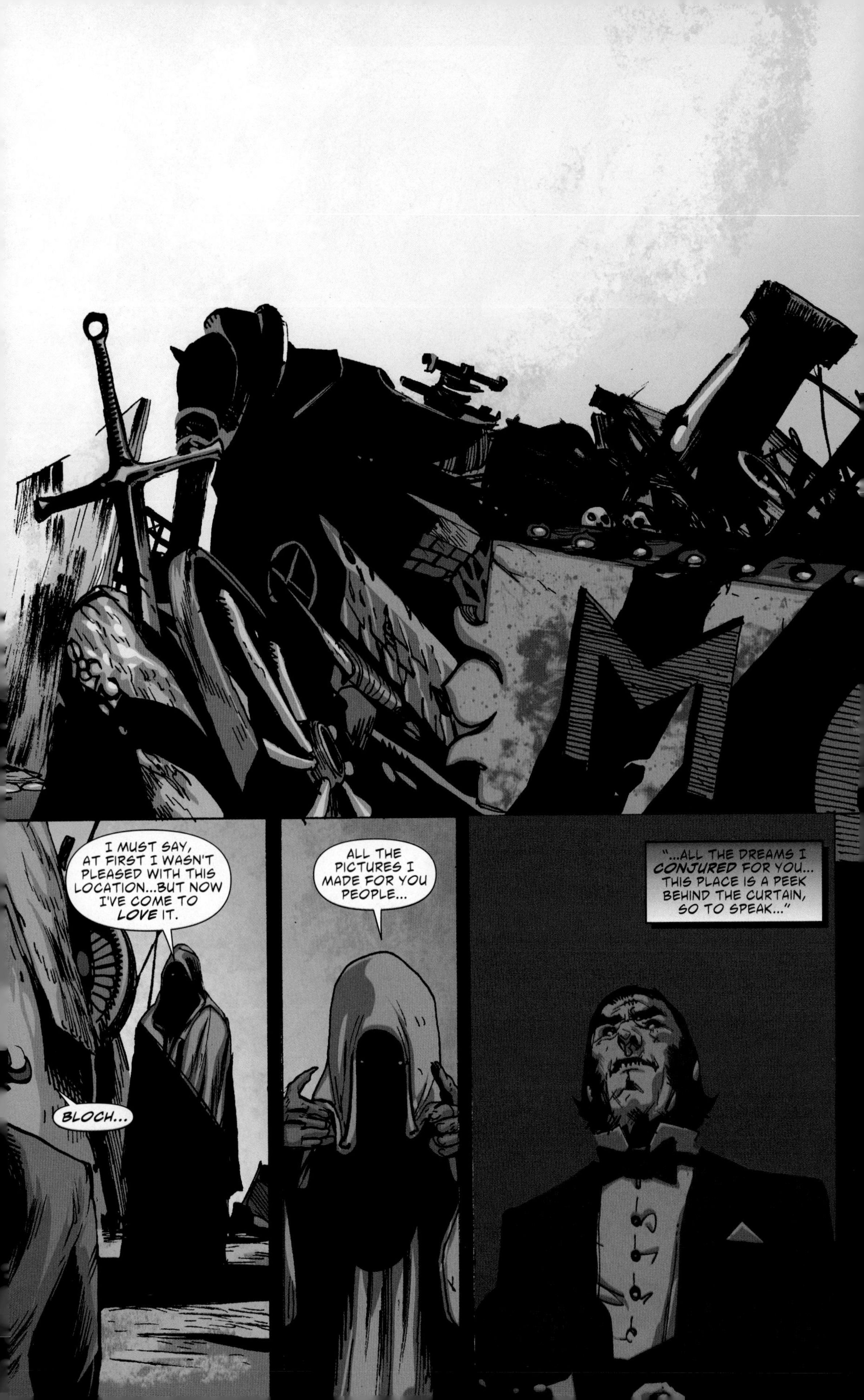
I MUST SAY, AT FIRST I WASN'T PLEASED WITH THIS LOCATION...BUT NOW I'VE COME TO LOVE IT.
BLOCH...
ALL THE PICTURES I MADE FOR YOU PEOPLE...
"...ALL THE DREAMS I CONJURED FOR YOU... THIS PLACE IS A PEEK BEHIND THE CURTAIN, SO TO SPEAK..."

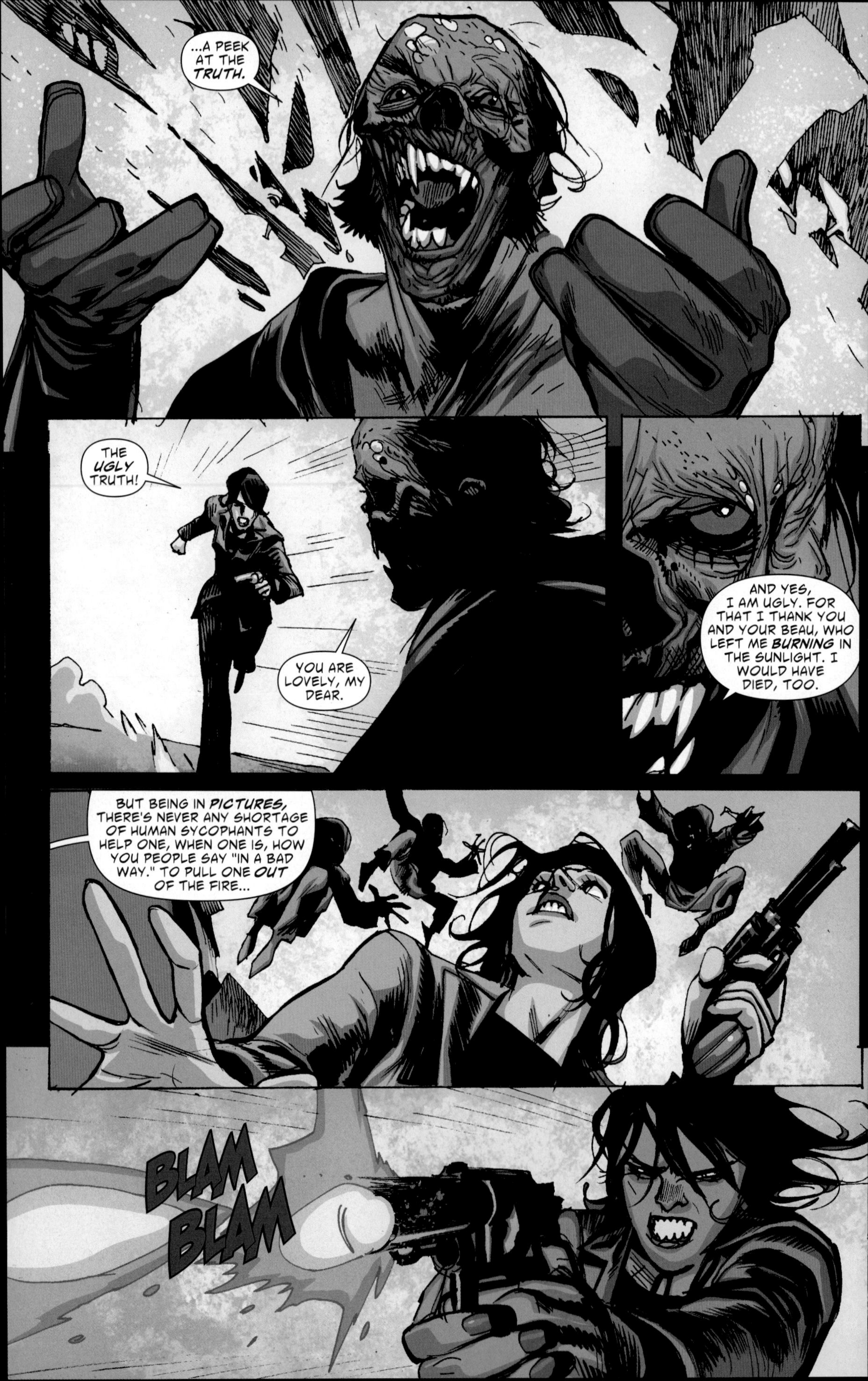
...A PEEK AT THE *TRUTH.*
THE *UGLY* TRUTH!
YOU ARE LOVELY, MY DEAR.
AND YES, I AM UGLY. FOR THAT I THANK YOU AND YOUR BEAU, WHO LEFT ME *BURNING* IN THE SUNLIGHT. I WOULD HAVE DIED, TOO.
BUT BEING IN *PICTURES,* THERE'S NEVER ANY SHORTAGE OF HUMAN SYCOPHANTS TO HELP ONE, WHEN ONE IS, HOW YOU PEOPLE SAY "IN A BAD WAY." TO PULL ONE *OUT* OF THE FIRE...
BLAM
BLAM

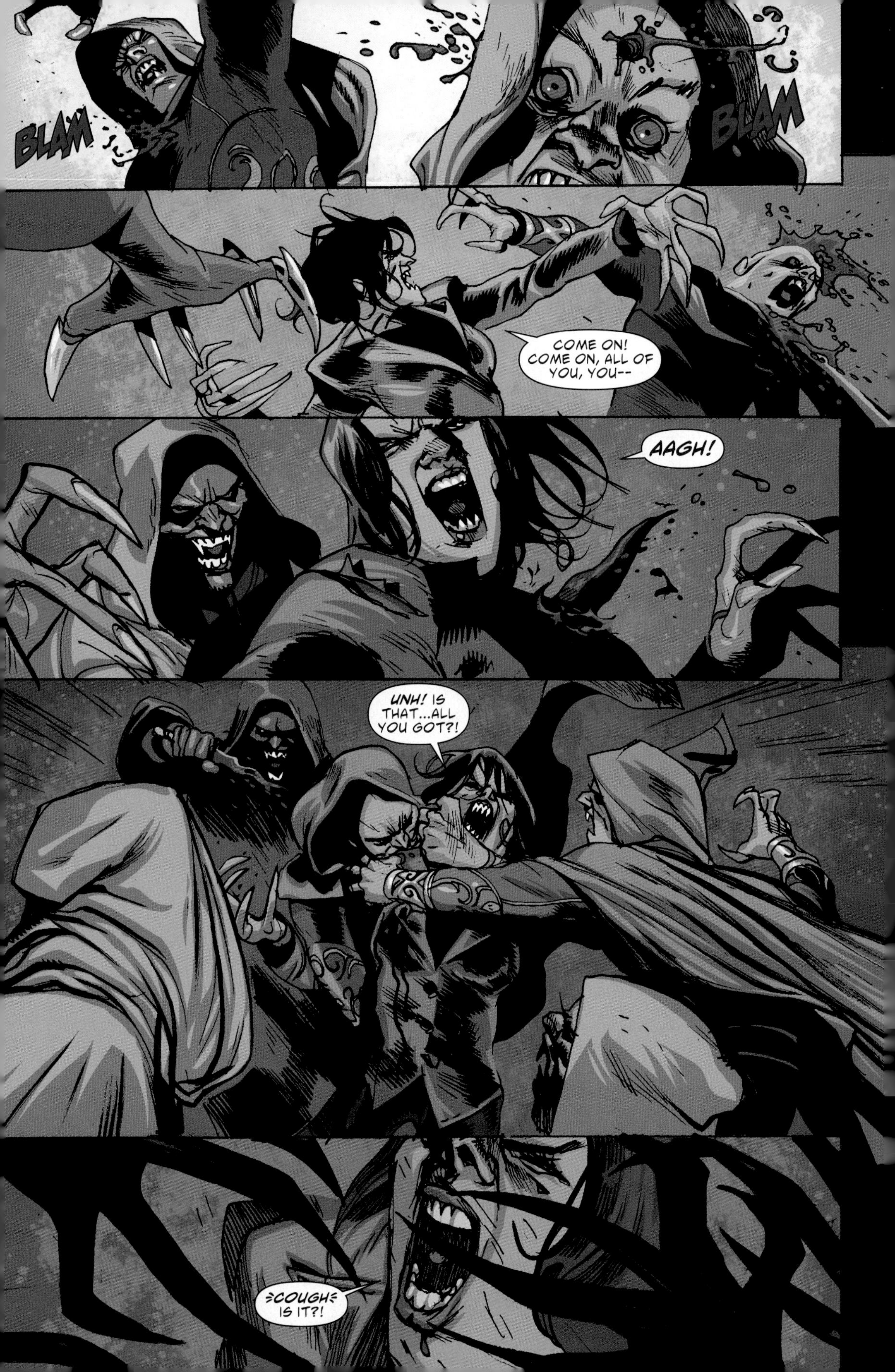
BLAM
BLAM
COME ON! COME ON, ALL OF YOU, YOU--
AAGH!
UNH! IS THAT...ALL YOU GOT?!
COUGH IS IT?!

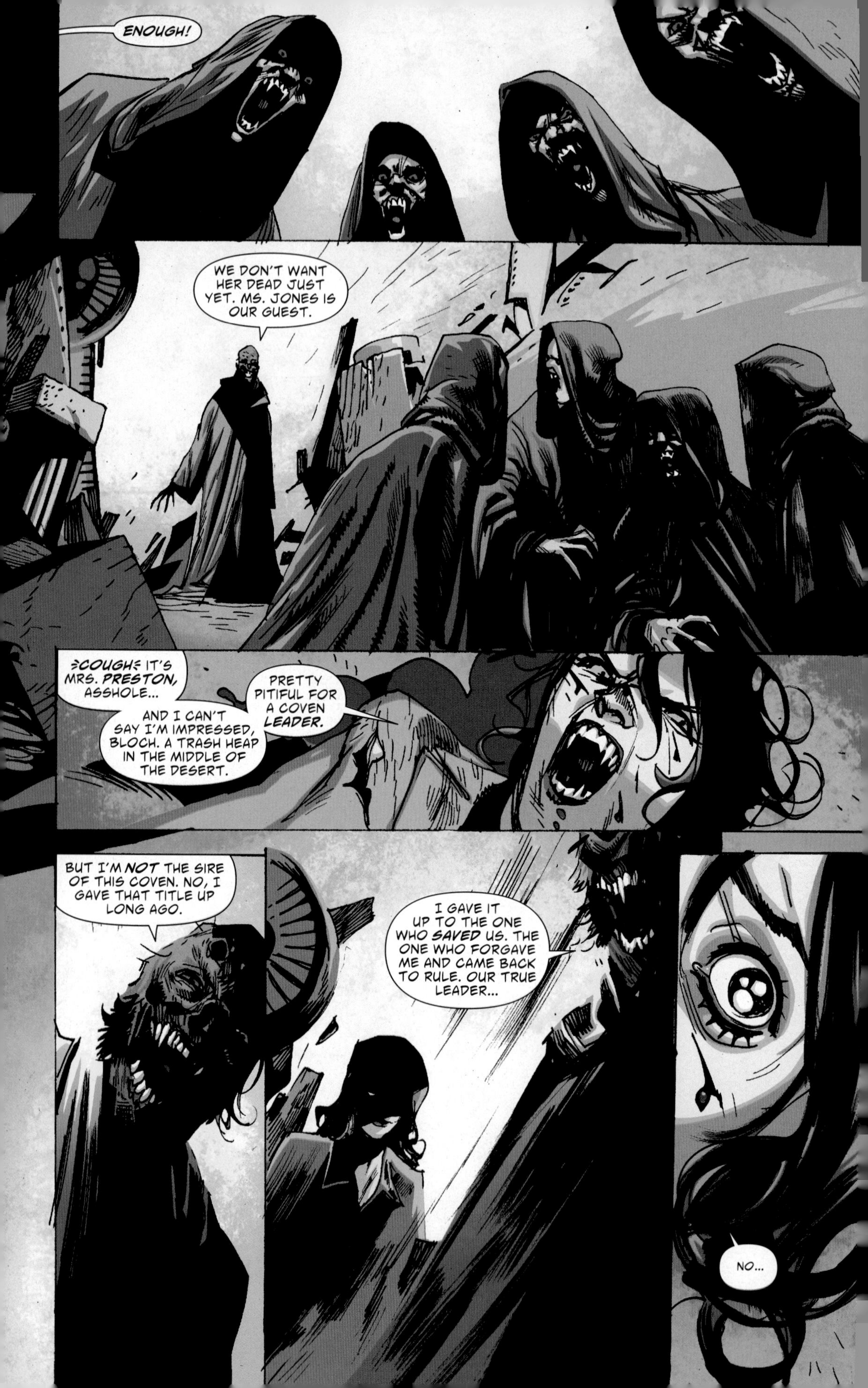
ENOUGH!
WE DON'T WANT HER DEAD JUST YET. MS. JONES IS OUR GUEST.
COUGH IT'S MRS. PRESTON, ASSHOLE...
AND I CAN'T SAY I'M IMPRESSED, BLOCH. A TRASH HEAP IN THE MIDDLE OF THE DESERT.
PRETTY PITIFUL FOR A COVEN LEADER.
BUT I'M NOT THE SIRE OF THIS COVEN. NO, I GAVE THAT TITLE UP LONG AGO.
I GAVE IT UP TO THE ONE WHO SAVED US. THE ONE WHO FORGAVE ME AND CAME BACK TO RULE. OUR TRUE LEADER...
NO...

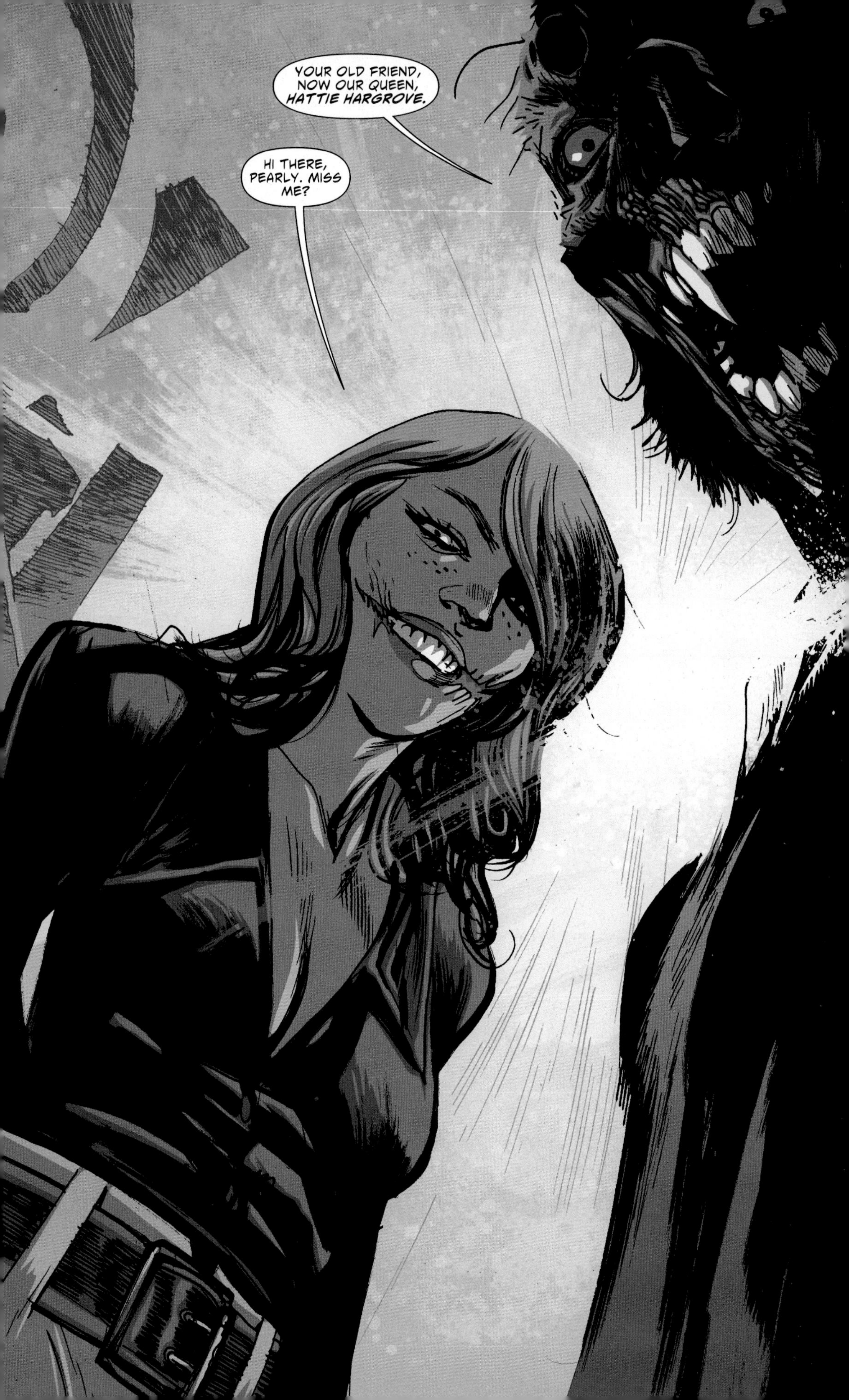
YOUR OLD FRIEND, NOW OUR QUEEN, HATTIE HARGROVE.
HI THERE, PEARLY. MISS ME?

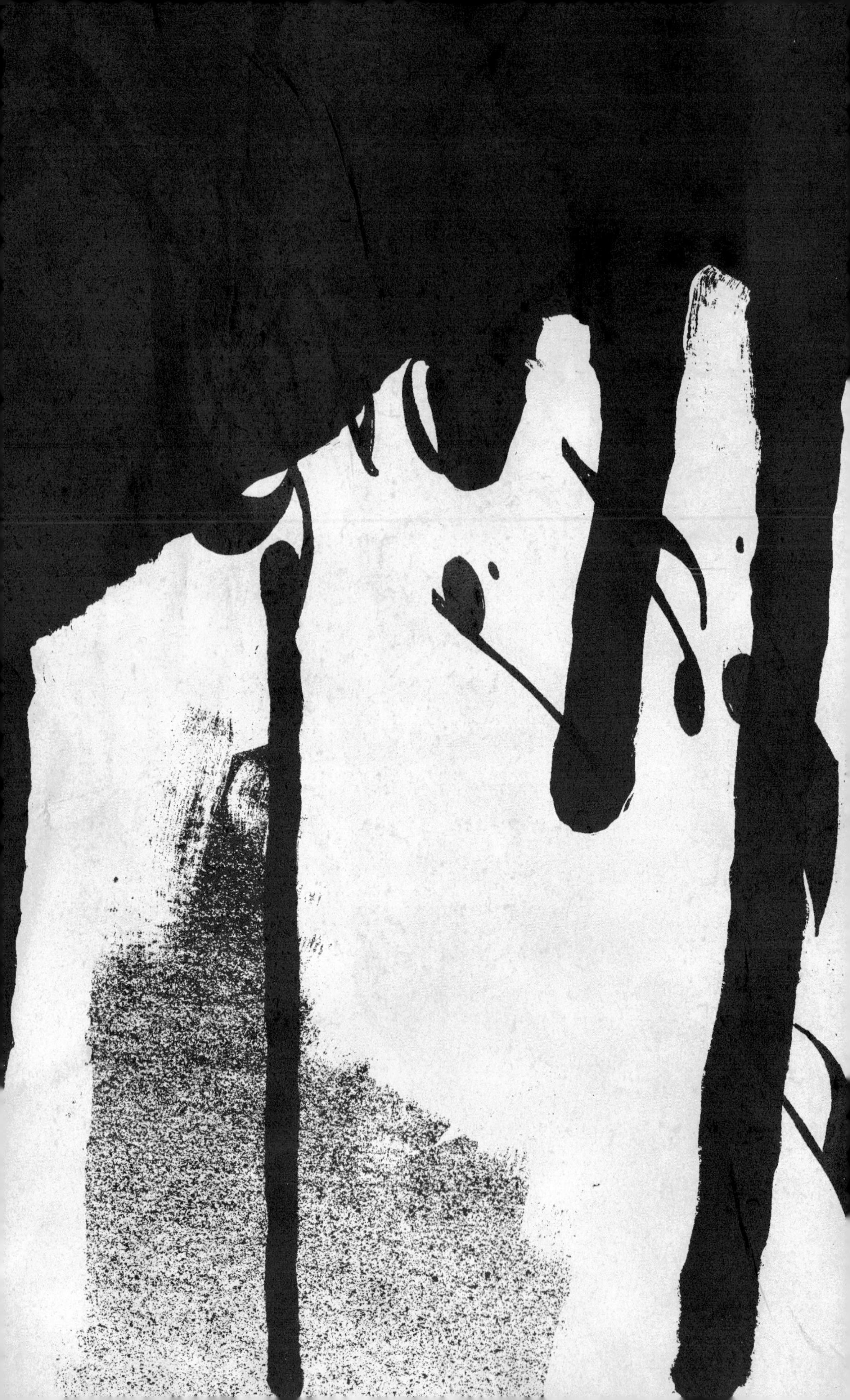

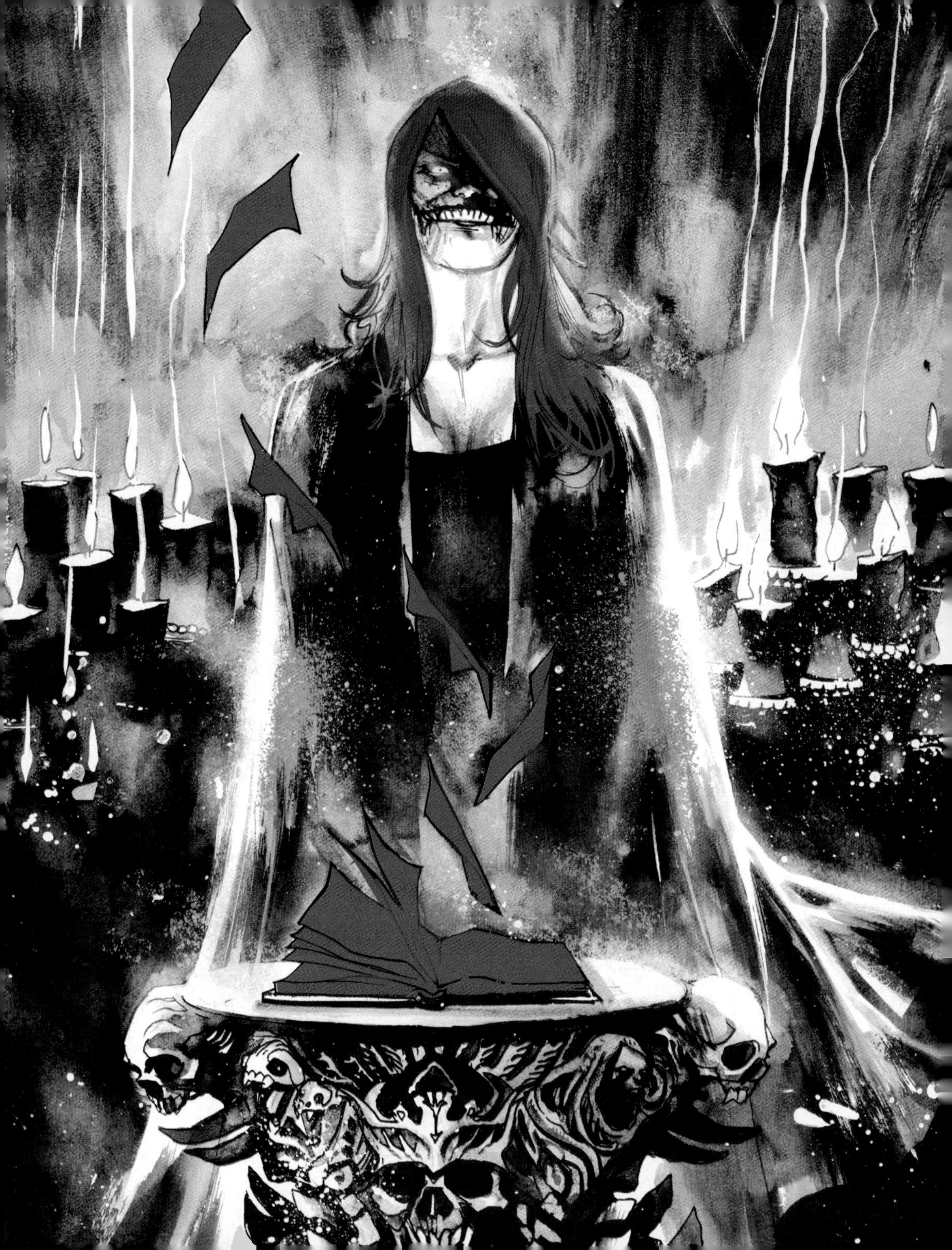

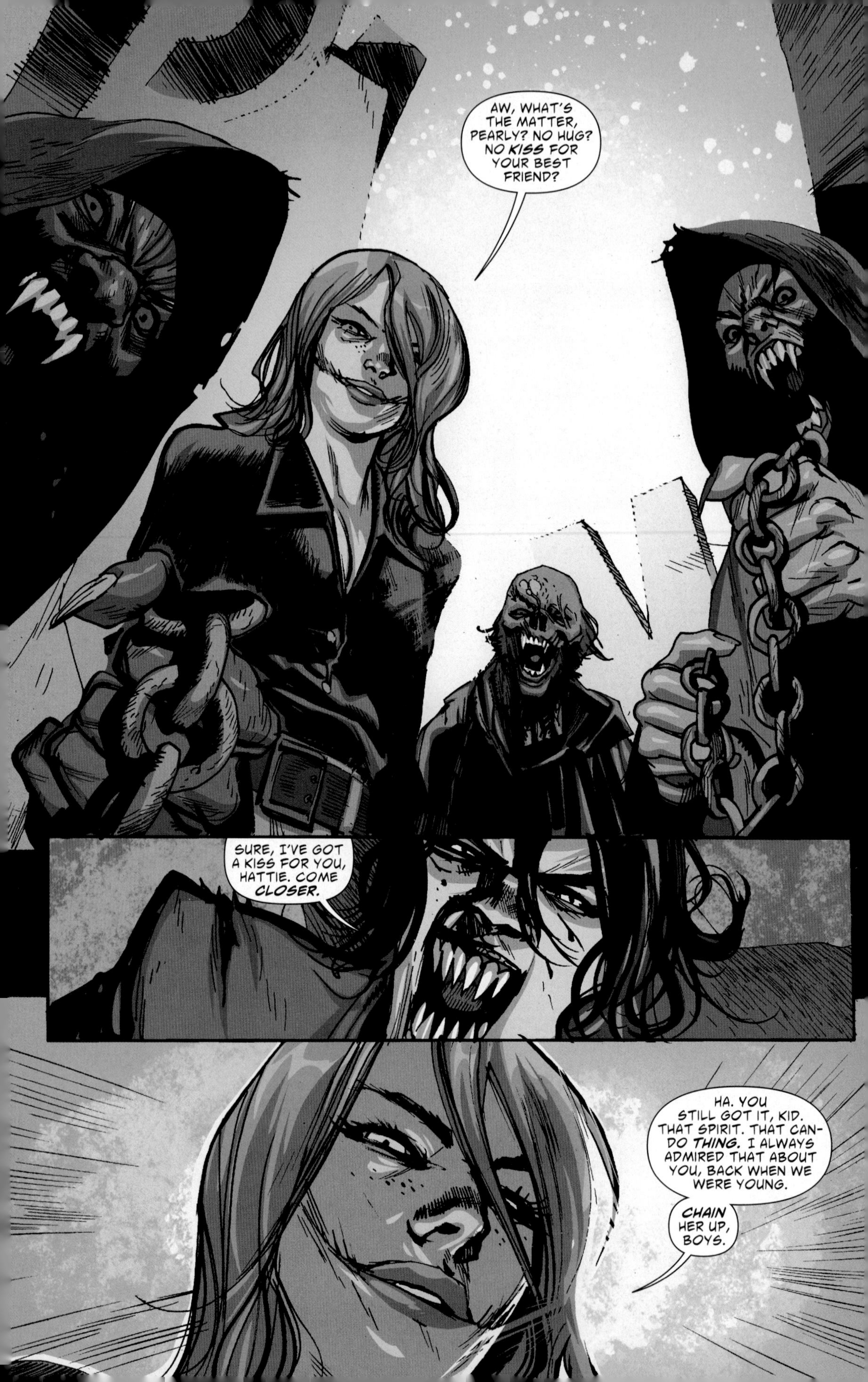
AW, WHAT'S THE MATTER, PEARLY? NO HUG? NO *KISS* FOR YOUR BEST FRIEND?
SURE, I'VE GOT A KISS FOR YOU, HATTIE. COME *CLOSER*.
HA. YOU STILL GOT IT, KID. THAT SPIRIT. THAT CAN-DO *THING*. I ALWAYS ADMIRED THAT ABOUT YOU, BACK WHEN WE WERE YOUNG.
CHAIN HER UP, BOYS.

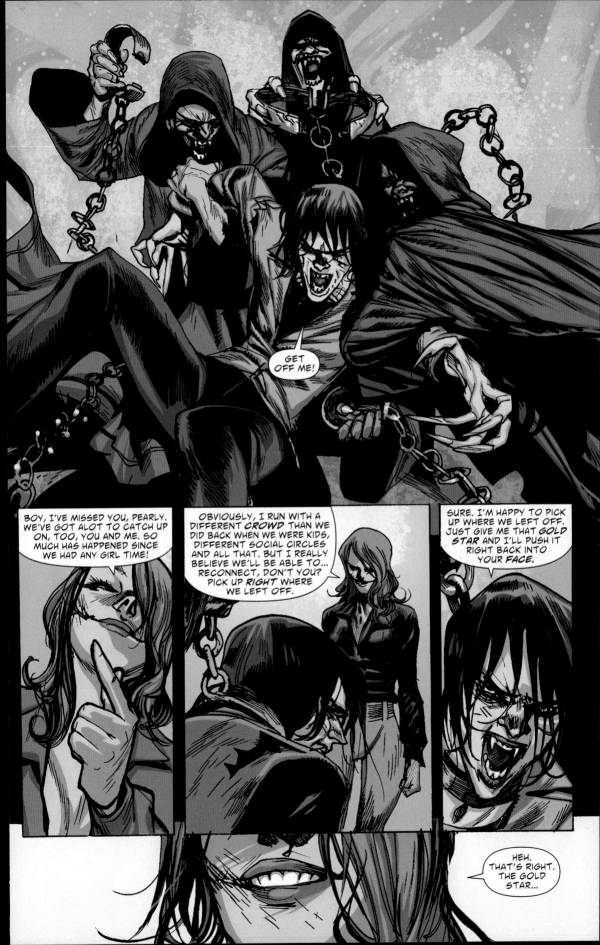

GET OFF ME!

BOY, I'VE MISSED YOU, PEARLY. WE'VE GOT ALOT TO CATCH UP ON, TOO, YOU AND ME. SO MUCH HAS HAPPENED SINCE WE HAD ANY GIRL TIME!

OBVIOUSLY, I RUN WITH A DIFFERENT *CROWD* THAN WE DID BACK WHEN WE WERE KIDS, DIFFERENT SOCIAL CIRCLES AND ALL THAT. BUT I REALLY BELIEVE WE'LL BE ABLE TO... RECONNECT, DON'T YOU? PICK UP *RIGHT* WHERE WE LEFT OFF.

SURE. I'M HAPPY TO PICK UP WHERE WE LEFT OFF. JUST GIVE ME THAT *GOLD STAR* AND I'LL PUSH IT RIGHT BACK INTO YOUR *FACE.*

HEH. THAT'S RIGHT. THE GOLD STAR...

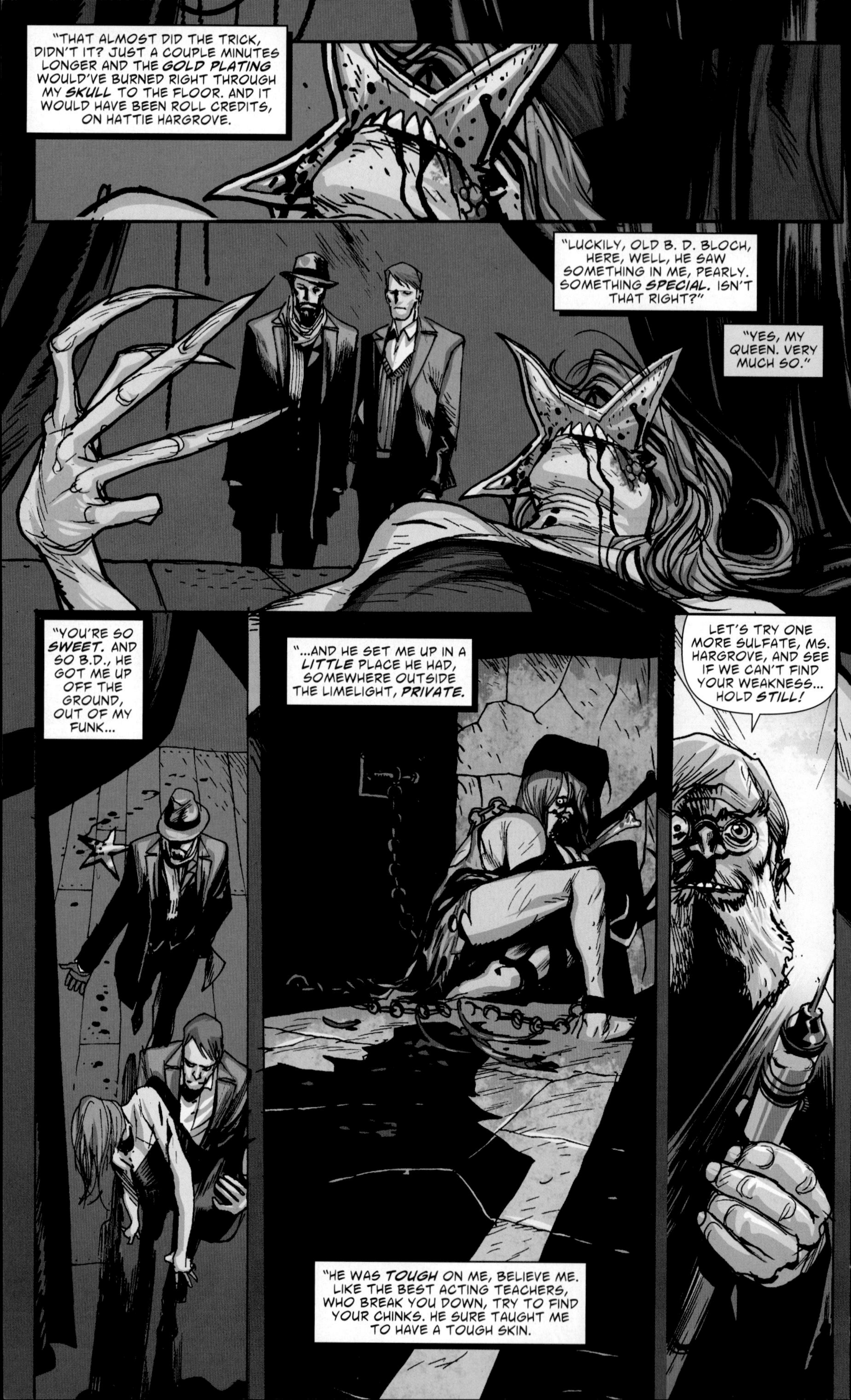
"THAT ALMOST DID THE TRICK, DIDN'T IT? JUST A COUPLE MINUTES LONGER AND THE GOLD PLATING WOULD'VE BURNED RIGHT THROUGH MY SKULL TO THE FLOOR. AND IT WOULD HAVE BEEN ROLL CREDITS, ON HATTIE HARGROVE.
"LUCKILY, OLD B. D. BLOCH, HERE, WELL, HE SAW SOMETHING IN ME, PEARLY. SOMETHING SPECIAL. ISN'T THAT RIGHT?"
"YES, MY QUEEN. VERY MUCH SO."
"YOU'RE SO SWEET. AND SO B.D., HE GOT ME UP OFF THE GROUND, OUT OF MY FUNK...
"...AND HE SET ME UP IN A LITTLE PLACE HE HAD, SOMEWHERE OUTSIDE THE LIMELIGHT, PRIVATE.
LET'S TRY ONE MORE SULFATE, MS. HARGROVE, AND SEE IF WE CAN'T FIND YOUR WEAKNESS... HOLD STILL!
"HE WAS TOUGH ON ME, BELIEVE ME. LIKE THE BEST ACTING TEACHERS, WHO BREAK YOU DOWN, TRY TO FIND YOUR CHINKS. HE SURE TAUGHT ME TO HAVE A TOUGH SKIN.

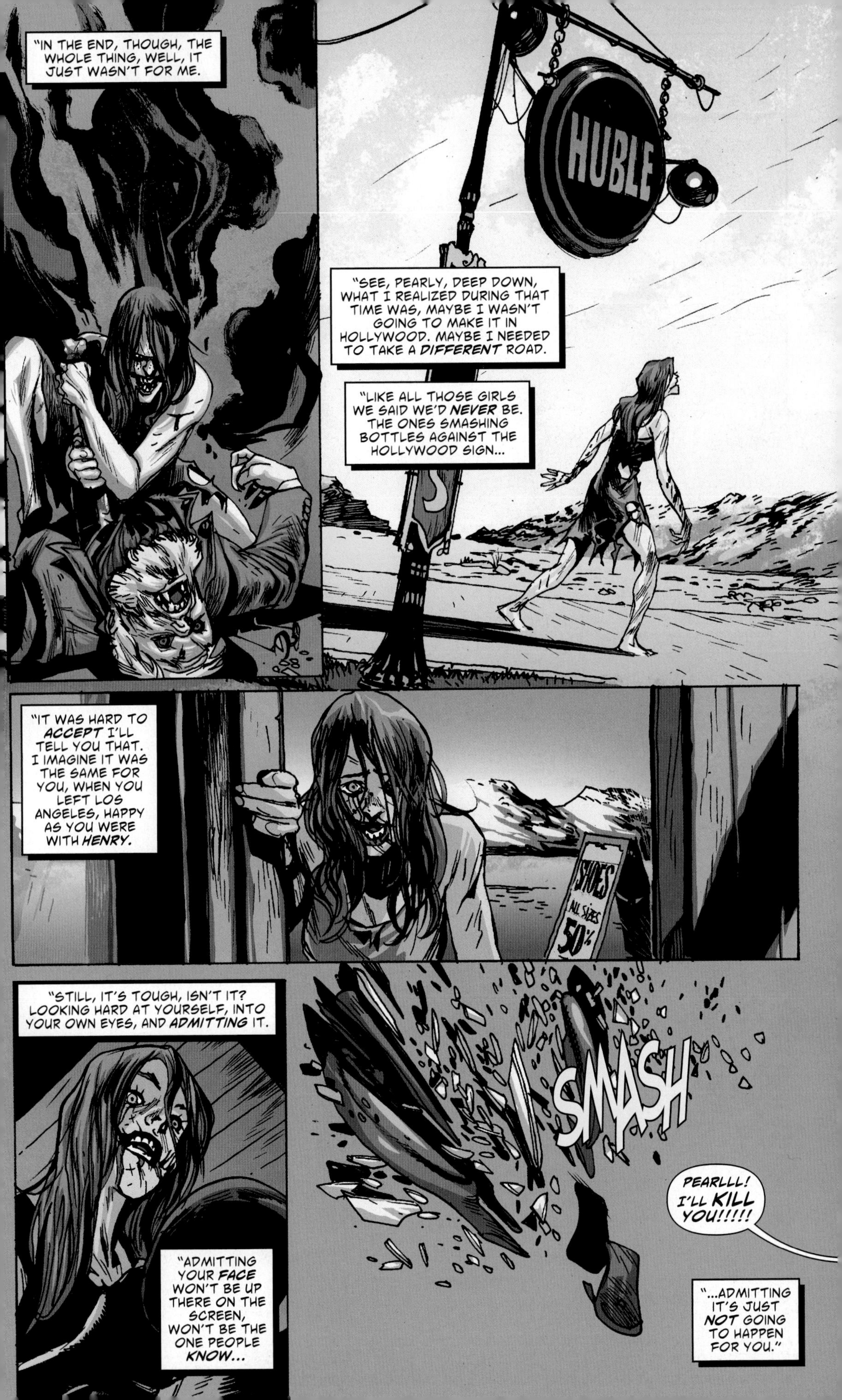
"IN THE END, THOUGH, THE WHOLE THING, WELL, IT JUST WASN'T FOR ME.
HUBLE
"SEE, PEARLY, DEEP DOWN, WHAT I REALIZED DURING THAT TIME WAS, MAYBE I WASN'T GOING TO MAKE IT IN HOLLYWOOD. MAYBE I NEEDED TO TAKE A DIFFERENT ROAD.
"LIKE ALL THOSE GIRLS WE SAID WE'D NEVER BE. THE ONES SMASHING BOTTLES AGAINST THE HOLLYWOOD SIGN...
"IT WAS HARD TO ACCEPT I'LL TELL YOU THAT. I IMAGINE IT WAS THE SAME FOR YOU, WHEN YOU LEFT LOS ANGELES, HAPPY AS YOU WERE WITH HENRY.
SHOES ALL SIZES 50%
"STILL, IT'S TOUGH, ISN'T IT? LOOKING HARD AT YOURSELF, INTO YOUR OWN EYES, AND ADMITTING IT.
"ADMITTING YOUR FACE WON'T BE UP THERE ON THE SCREEN, WON'T BE THE ONE PEOPLE KNOW...
SMASH
PEARLLL! I'LL KILL YOU!!!!!
"...ADMITTING IT'S JUST NOT GOING TO HAPPEN FOR YOU."

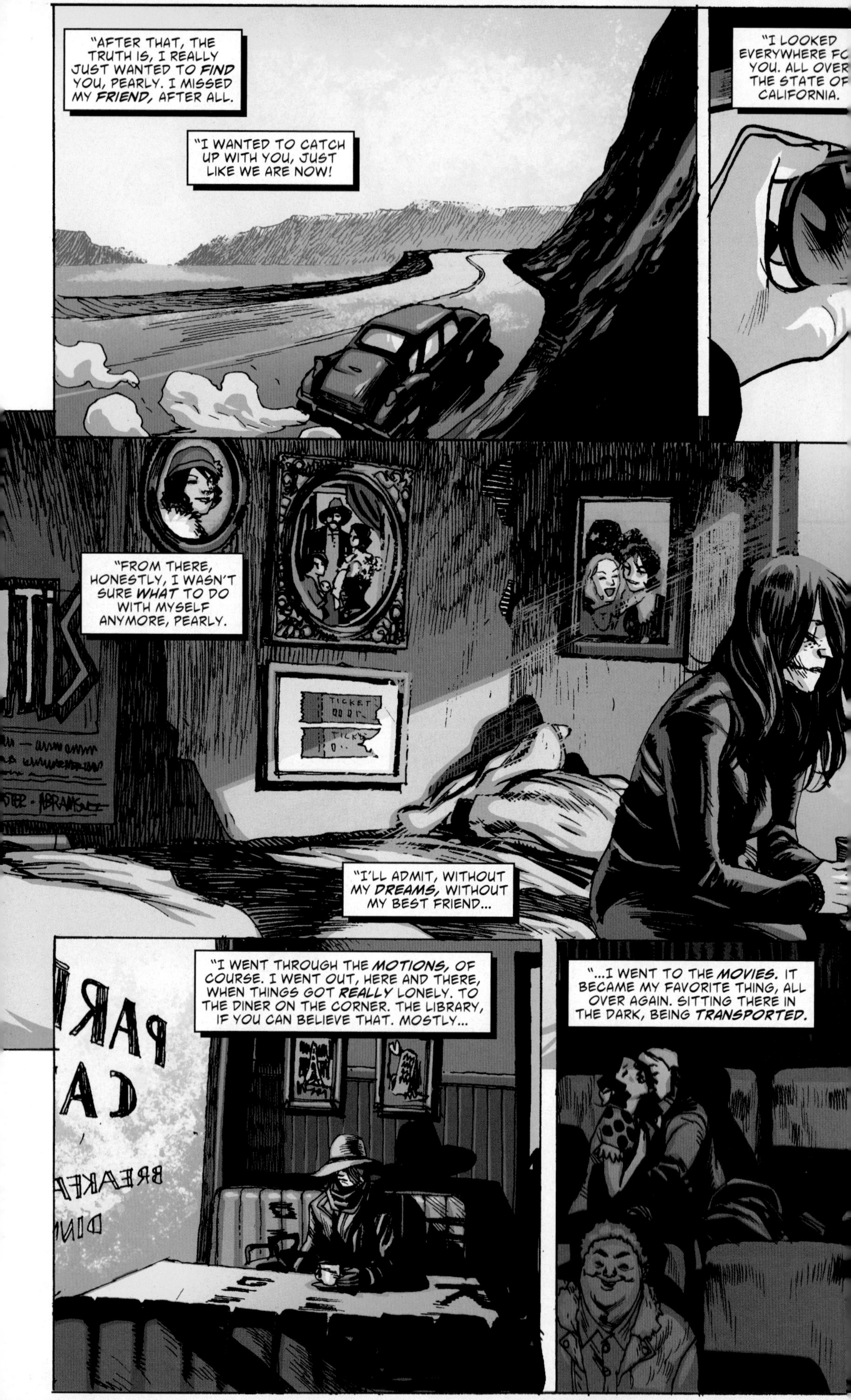
"AFTER THAT, THE TRUTH IS, I REALLY JUST WANTED TO *FIND* YOU, PEARLY. I MISSED MY *FRIEND,* AFTER ALL.
"I WANTED TO CATCH UP WITH YOU, JUST LIKE WE ARE NOW!
"I LOOKED EVERYWHERE FO YOU. ALL OVER THE STATE OF CALIFORNIA.
"FROM THERE, HONESTLY, I WASN'T SURE *WHAT* TO DO WITH MYSELF ANYMORE, PEARLY.
"I'LL ADMIT, WITHOUT MY *DREAMS,* WITHOUT MY BEST FRIEND...
"I WENT THROUGH THE *MOTIONS,* OF COURSE. I WENT OUT, HERE AND THERE, WHEN THINGS GOT *REALLY* LONELY. TO THE DINER ON THE CORNER. THE LIBRARY, IF YOU CAN BELIEVE THAT. MOSTLY...
"...I WENT TO THE *MOVIES.* IT BECAME MY FAVORITE THING, ALL OVER AGAIN. SITTING THERE IN THE DARK, BEING *TRANSPORTED.*

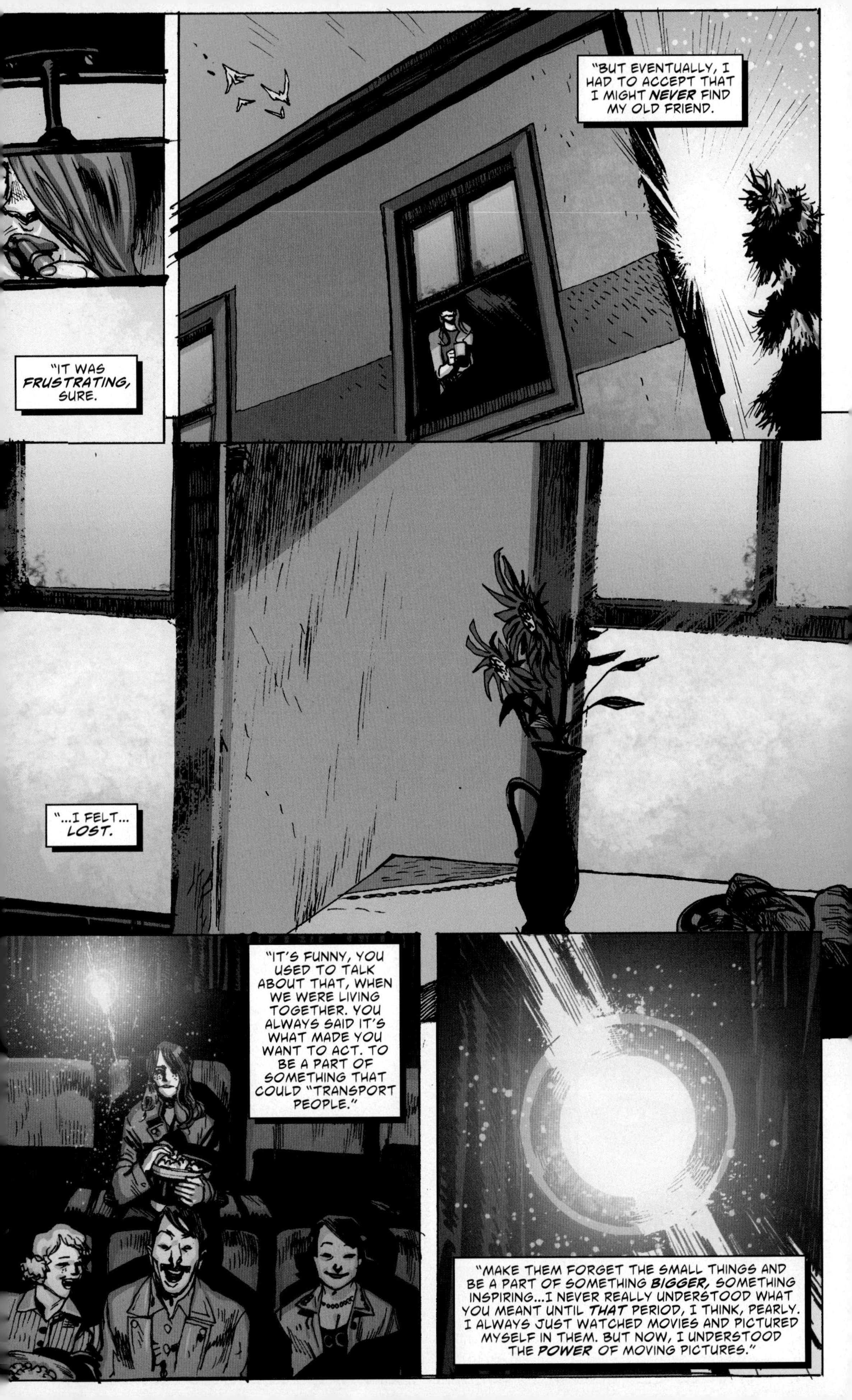
"IT WAS FRUSTRATING, SURE.
"BUT EVENTUALLY, I HAD TO ACCEPT THAT I MIGHT NEVER FIND MY OLD FRIEND.
"...I FELT... LOST.
"IT'S FUNNY, YOU USED TO TALK ABOUT THAT, WHEN WE WERE LIVING TOGETHER. YOU ALWAYS SAID IT'S WHAT MADE YOU WANT TO ACT. TO BE A PART OF SOMETHING THAT COULD "TRANSPORT PEOPLE."
"MAKE THEM FORGET THE SMALL THINGS AND BE A PART OF SOMETHING BIGGER, SOMETHING INSPIRING...I NEVER REALLY UNDERSTOOD WHAT YOU MEANT UNTIL THAT PERIOD, I THINK, PEARLY. I ALWAYS JUST WATCHED MOVIES AND PICTURED MYSELF IN THEM. BUT NOW, I UNDERSTOOD THE POWER OF MOVING PICTURES."

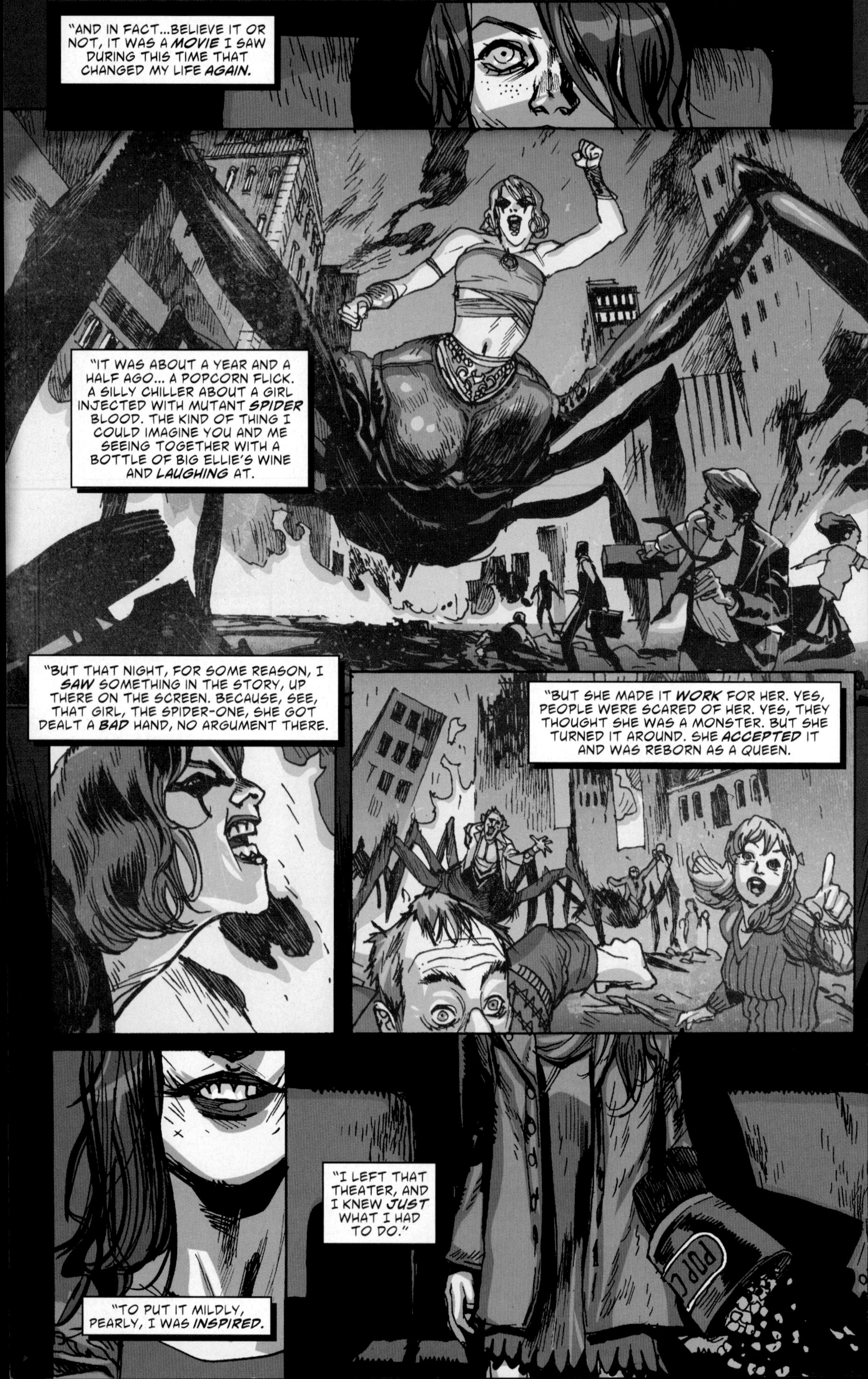
"AND IN FACT...BELIEVE IT OR NOT, IT WAS A MOVIE I SAW DURING THIS TIME THAT CHANGED MY LIFE AGAIN.
"IT WAS ABOUT A YEAR AND A HALF AGO... A POPCORN FLICK. A SILLY CHILLER ABOUT A GIRL INJECTED WITH MUTANT SPIDER BLOOD. THE KIND OF THING I COULD IMAGINE YOU AND ME SEEING TOGETHER WITH A BOTTLE OF BIG ELLIE'S WINE AND LAUGHING AT.
"BUT THAT NIGHT, FOR SOME REASON, I SAW SOMETHING IN THE STORY, UP THERE ON THE SCREEN. BECAUSE, SEE, THAT GIRL, THE SPIDER-ONE, SHE GOT DEALT A BAD HAND, NO ARGUMENT THERE.
"BUT SHE MADE IT WORK FOR HER. YES, PEOPLE WERE SCARED OF HER. YES, THEY THOUGHT SHE WAS A MONSTER. BUT SHE TURNED IT AROUND. SHE ACCEPTED IT AND WAS REBORN AS A QUEEN.
"I LEFT THAT THEATER, AND I KNEW JUST WHAT I HAD TO DO."
"TO PUT IT MILDLY, PEARLY, I WAS INSPIRED.

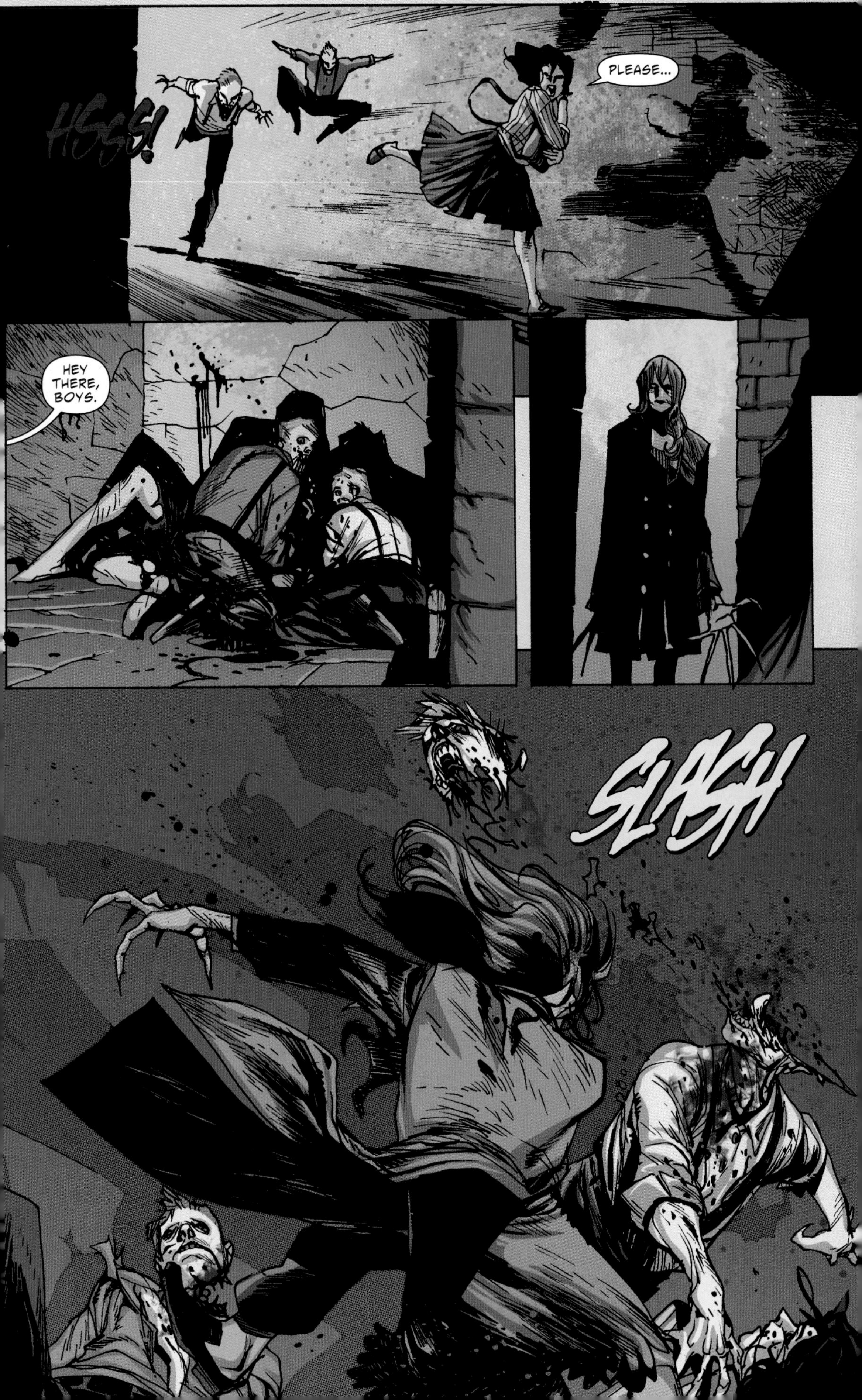
HSSS!
PLEASE...
HEY THERE, BOYS.
SLASH

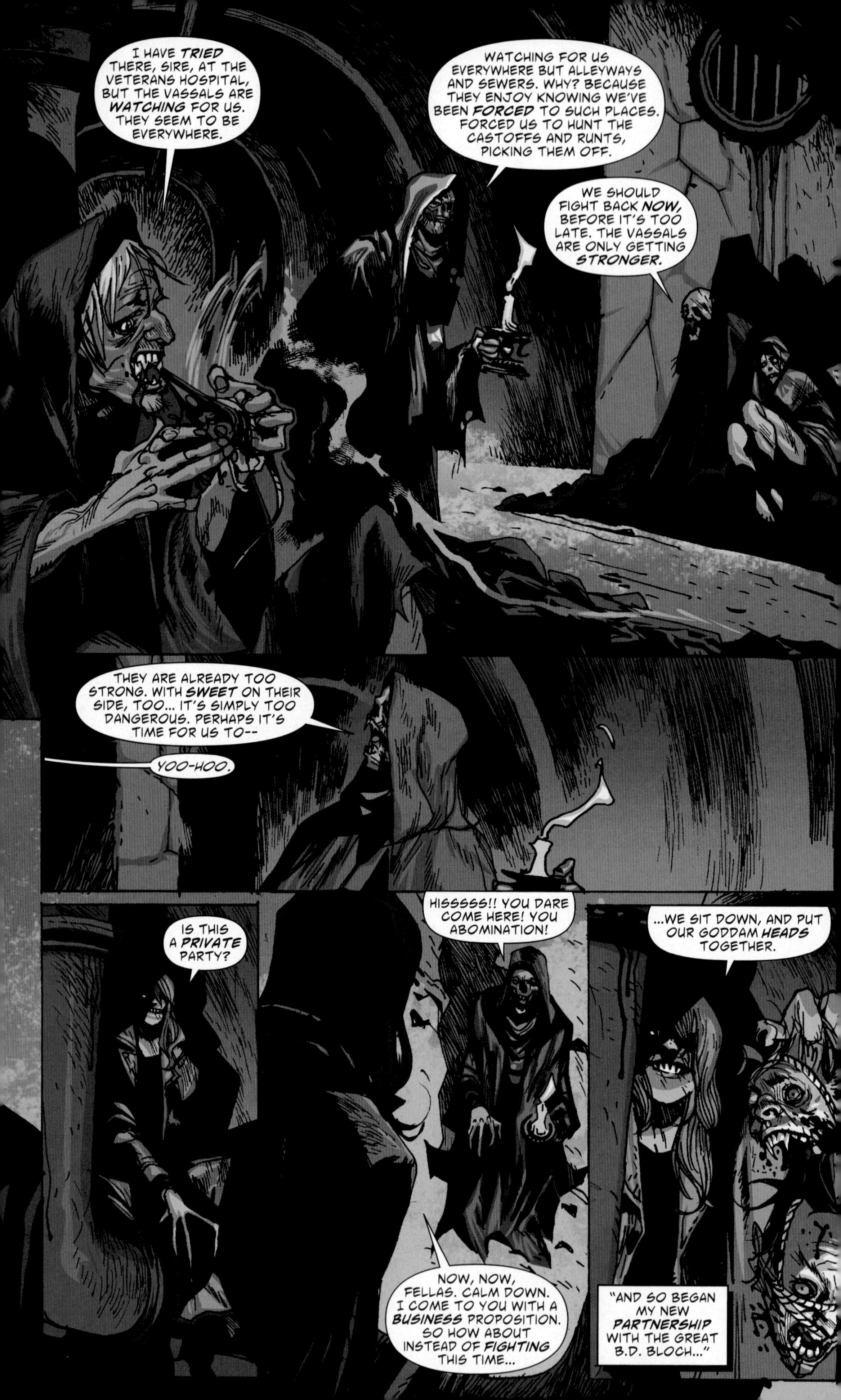

I HAVE TRIED THERE, SIRE, AT THE VETERANS HOSPITAL, BUT THE VASSALS ARE WATCHING FOR US. THEY SEEM TO BE EVERYWHERE.
WATCHING FOR US EVERYWHERE BUT ALLEYWAYS AND SEWERS. WHY? BECAUSE THEY ENJOY KNOWING WE'VE BEEN FORCED TO SUCH PLACES. FORCED US TO HUNT THE CASTOFFS AND RUNTS, PICKING THEM OFF.
WE SHOULD FIGHT BACK NOW, BEFORE IT'S TOO LATE. THE VASSALS ARE ONLY GETTING STRONGER.
THEY ARE ALREADY TOO STRONG. WITH SWEET ON THEIR SIDE, TOO... IT'S SIMPLY TOO DANGEROUS. PERHAPS IT'S TIME FOR US TO--
YOO-HOO.
IS THIS A PRIVATE PARTY?
HISSSSS!! YOU DARE COME HERE! YOU ABOMINATION!
NOW, NOW, FELLAS. CALM DOWN. I COME TO YOU WITH A BUSINESS PROPOSITION. SO HOW ABOUT INSTEAD OF FIGHTING THIS TIME...
...WE SIT DOWN, AND PUT OUR GODDAM HEADS TOGETHER.
"AND SO BEGAN MY NEW PARTNERSHIP WITH THE GREAT B.D. BLOCH..."

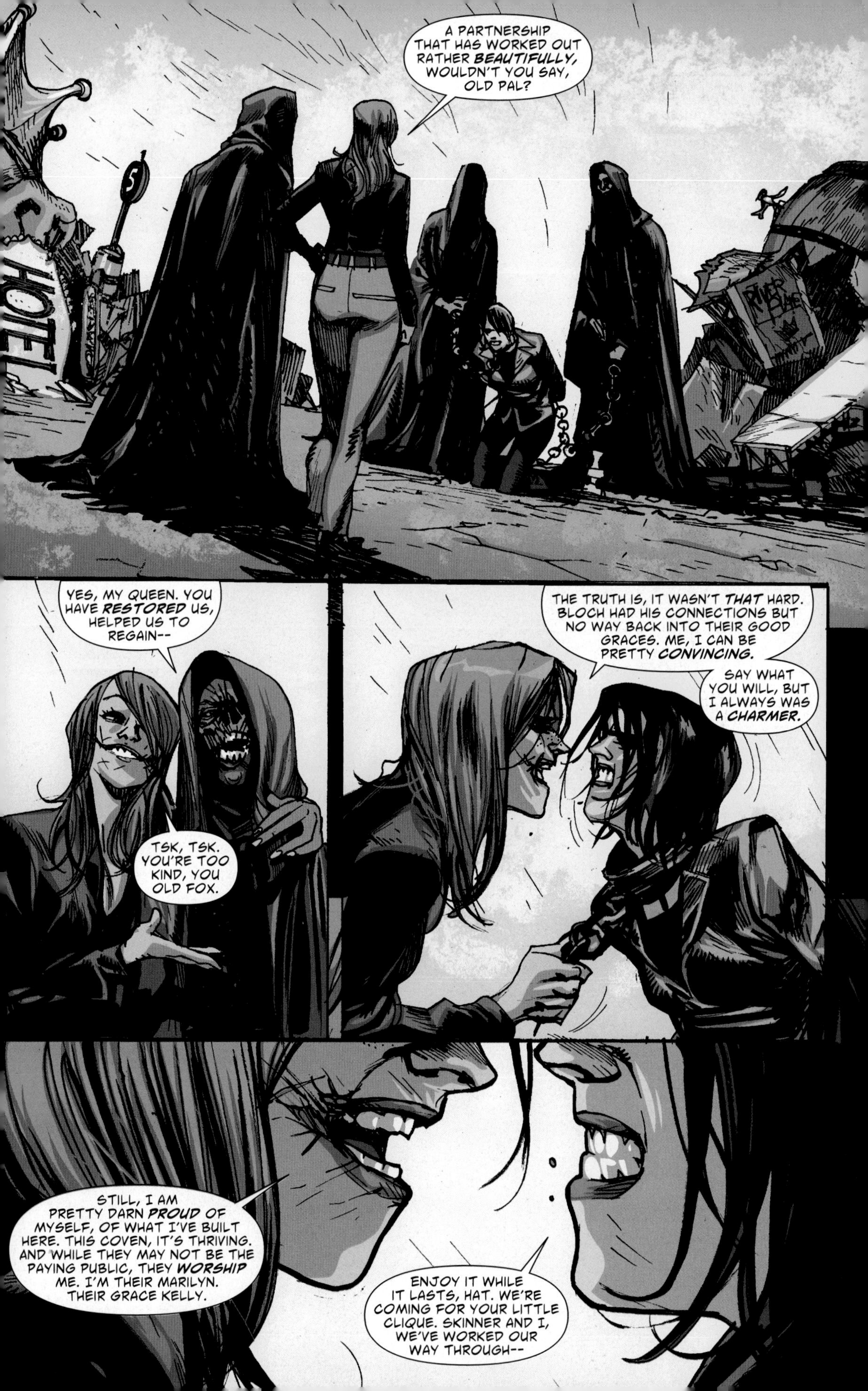
A PARTNERSHIP THAT HAS WORKED OUT RATHER BEAUTIFULLY, WOULDN'T YOU SAY, OLD PAL?
HOTEL
YES, MY QUEEN. YOU HAVE RESTORED US, HELPED US TO REGAIN--
TSK, TSK. YOU'RE TOO KIND, YOU OLD FOX.
THE TRUTH IS, IT WASN'T THAT HARD. BLOCH HAD HIS CONNECTIONS BUT NO WAY BACK INTO THEIR GOOD GRACES. ME, I CAN BE PRETTY CONVINCING.
SAY WHAT YOU WILL, BUT I ALWAYS WAS A CHARMER.
STILL, I AM PRETTY DARN PROUD OF MYSELF, OF WHAT I'VE BUILT HERE. THIS COVEN, IT'S THRIVING. AND WHILE THEY MAY NOT BE THE PAYING PUBLIC, THEY WORSHIP ME. I'M THEIR MARILYN. THEIR GRACE KELLY.
ENJOY IT WHILE IT LASTS, HAT. WE'RE COMING FOR YOUR LITTLE CLIQUE. SKINNER AND I, WE'VE WORKED OUR WAY THROUGH--

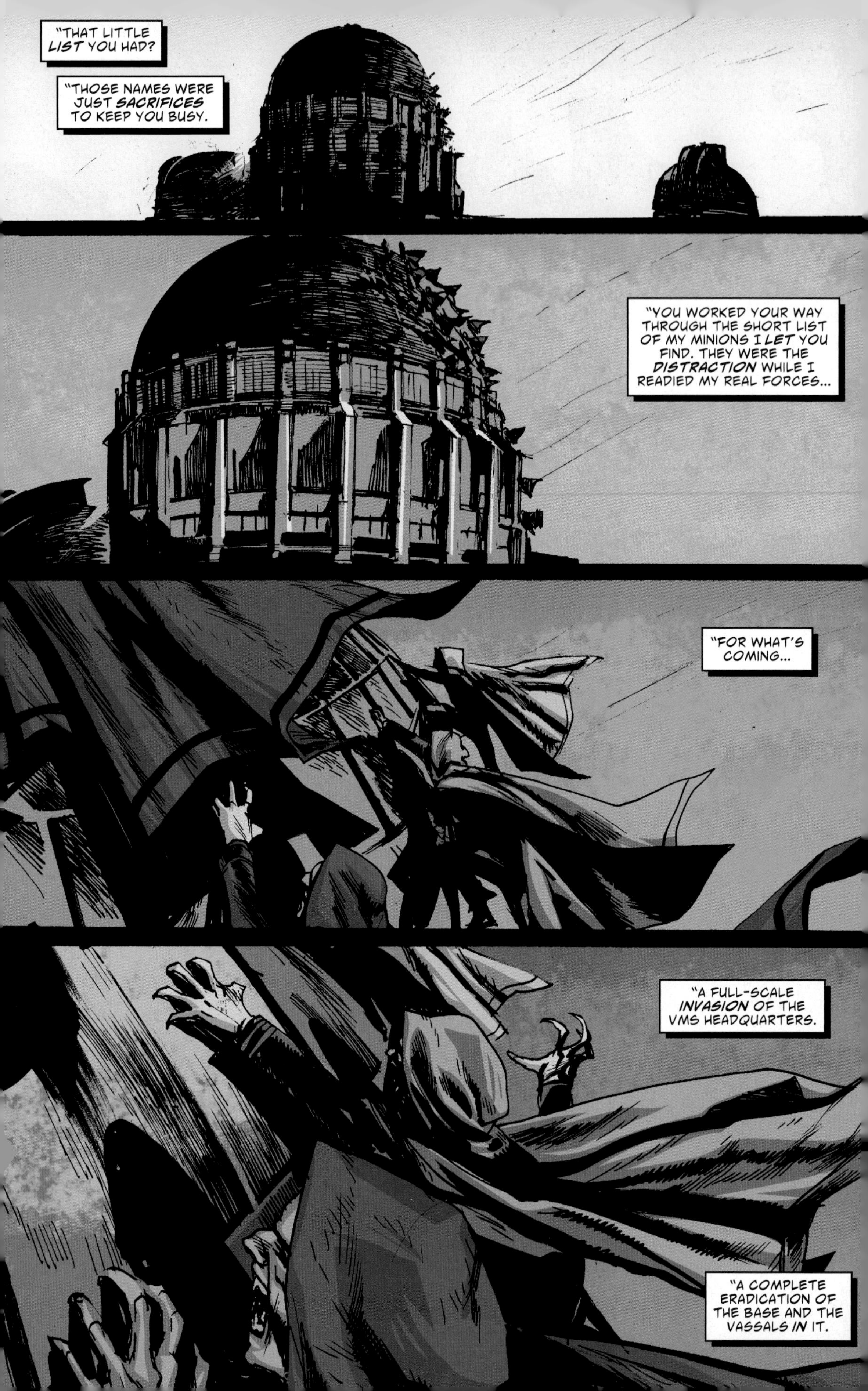
"THAT LITTLE LIST YOU HAD?
"THOSE NAMES WERE JUST SACRIFICES TO KEEP YOU BUSY.
"YOU WORKED YOUR WAY THROUGH THE SHORT LIST OF MY MINIONS I LET YOU FIND. THEY WERE THE DISTRACTION WHILE I READIED MY REAL FORCES...
"FOR WHAT'S COMING...
"A FULL-SCALE INVASION OF THE VMS HEADQUARTERS.
"A COMPLETE ERADICATION OF THE BASE AND THE VASSALS IN IT.

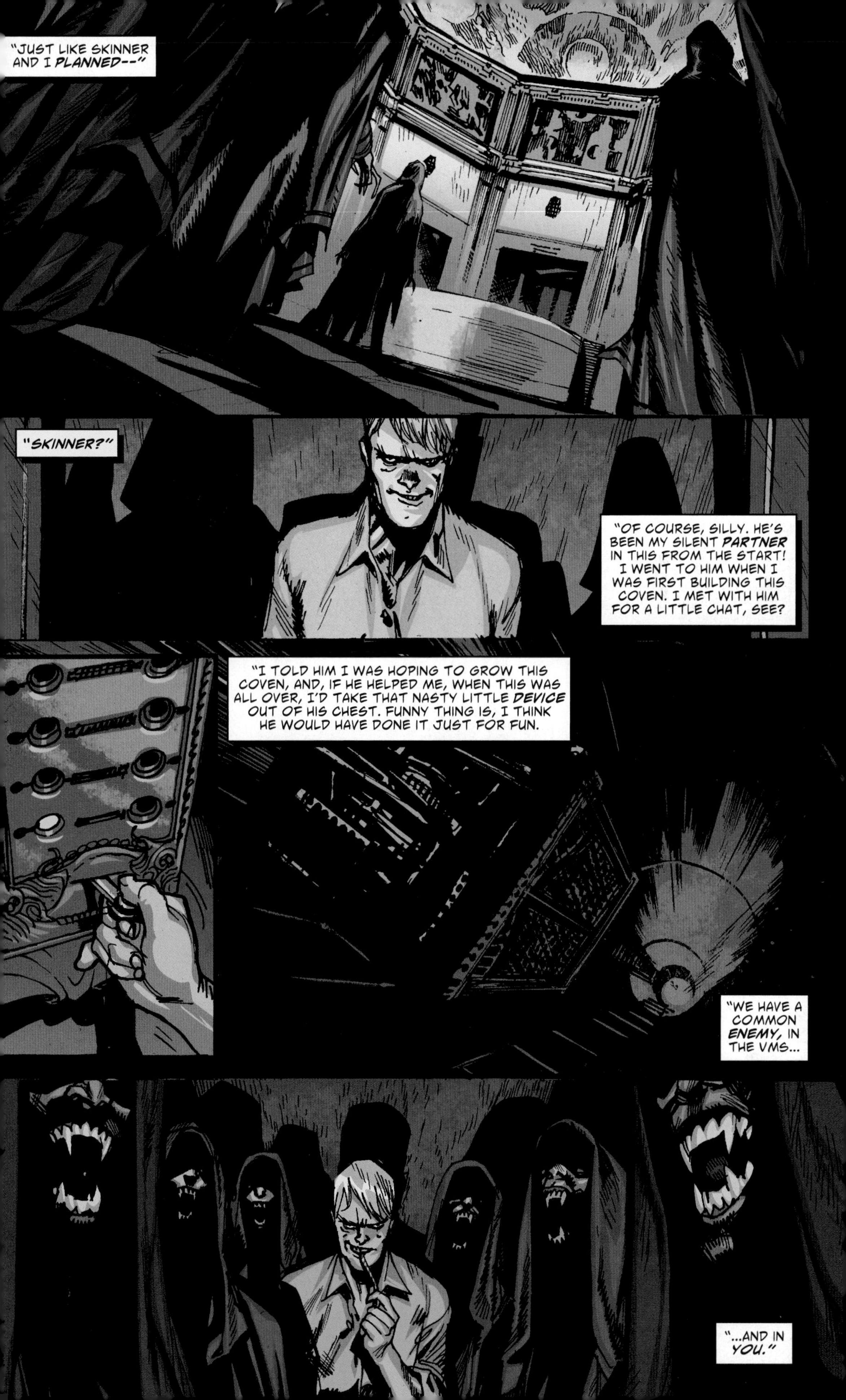
"JUST LIKE SKINNER AND I *PLANNED*--"
"*SKINNER?*"
"OF COURSE, SILLY. HE'S BEEN MY SILENT *PARTNER* IN THIS FROM THE START! I WENT TO HIM WHEN I WAS FIRST BUILDING THIS COVEN. I MET WITH HIM FOR A LITTLE CHAT, SEE?
"I TOLD HIM I WAS HOPING TO GROW THIS COVEN, AND, IF HE HELPED ME, WHEN THIS WAS ALL OVER, I'D TAKE THAT NASTY LITTLE *DEVICE* OUT OF HIS CHEST. FUNNY THING IS, I THINK HE WOULD HAVE DONE IT JUST FOR FUN.
"WE HAVE A COMMON *ENEMY,* IN THE VMS...
"...AND IN *YOU.*"

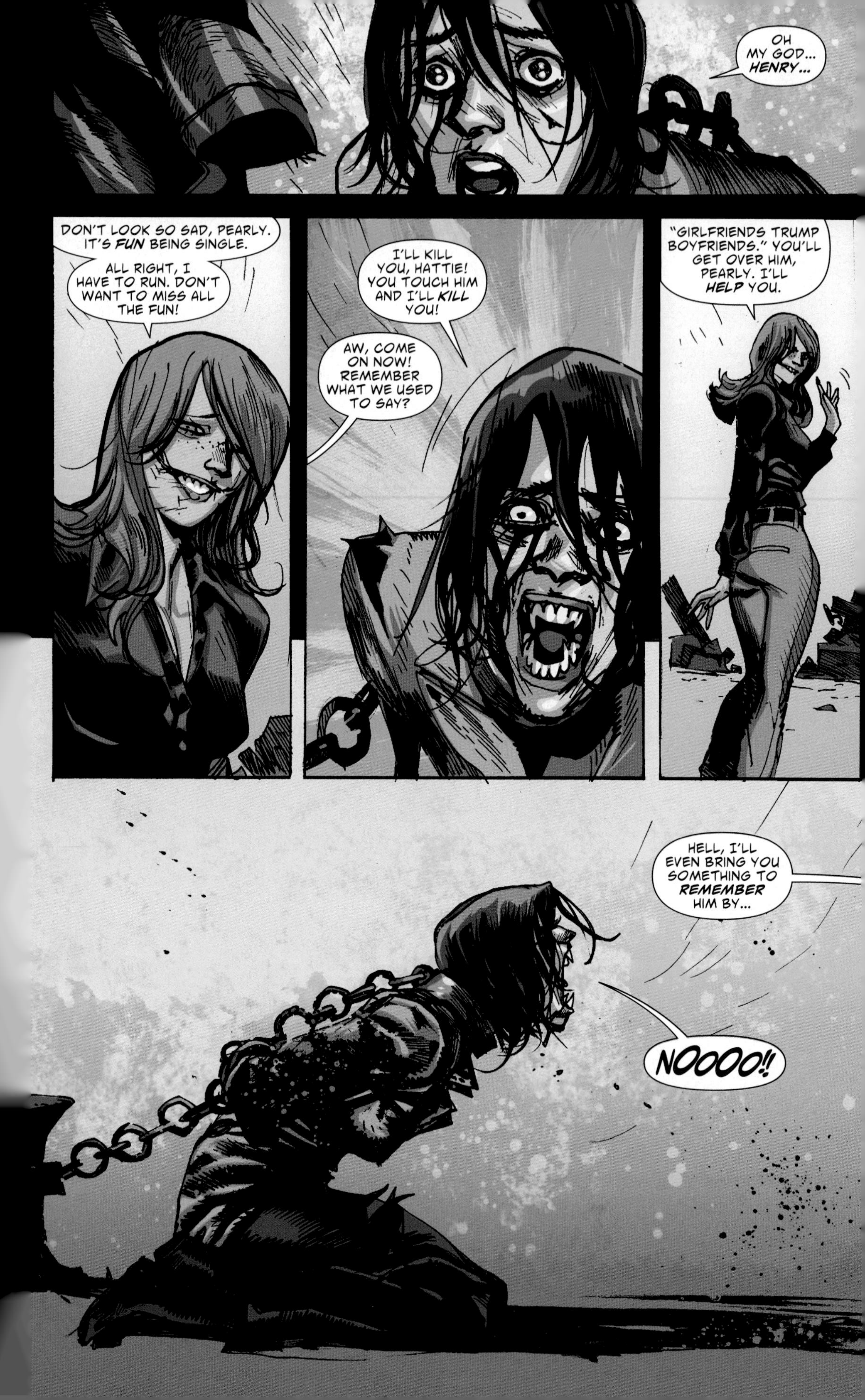
OH MY GOD... HENRY...
DON'T LOOK SO SAD, PEARLY. IT'S FUN BEING SINGLE.
ALL RIGHT, I HAVE TO RUN. DON'T WANT TO MISS ALL THE FUN!
I'LL KILL YOU, HATTIE! YOU TOUCH HIM AND I'LL KILL YOU!
AW, COME ON NOW! REMEMBER WHAT WE USED TO SAY?
"GIRLFRIENDS TRUMP BOYFRIENDS." YOU'LL GET OVER HIM, PEARLY. I'LL HELP YOU.
HELL, I'LL EVEN BRING YOU SOMETHING TO REMEMBER HIM BY...
NOOOO!!

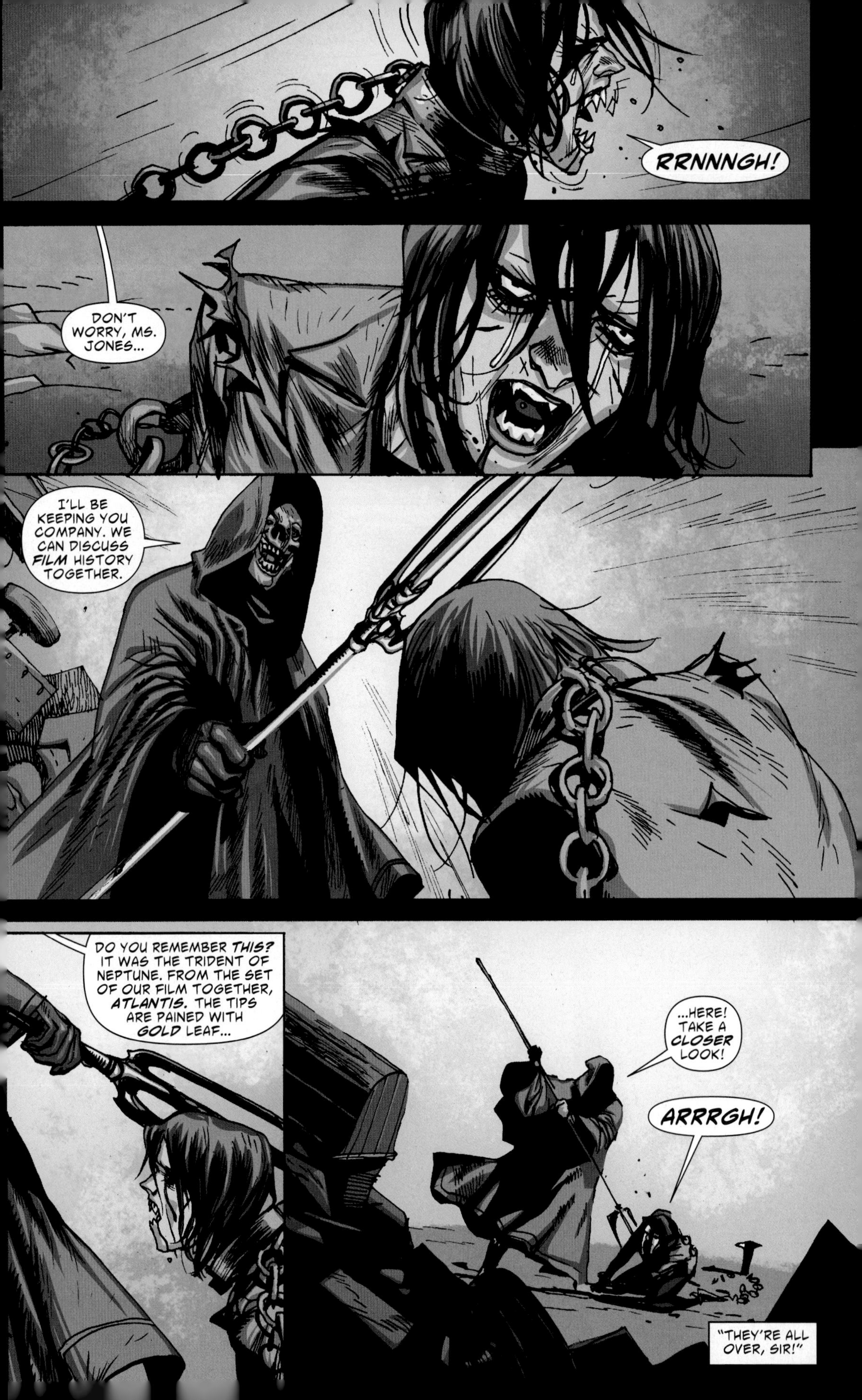
RRNNNGH!
DON'T WORRY, MS. JONES...
I'LL BE KEEPING YOU COMPANY. WE CAN DISCUSS FILM HISTORY TOGETHER.
DO YOU REMEMBER THIS? IT WAS THE TRIDENT OF NEPTUNE. FROM THE SET OF OUR FILM TOGETHER, ATLANTIS. THE TIPS ARE PAINED WITH GOLD LEAF...
...HERE! TAKE A CLOSER LOOK!
ARRRGH!
"THEY'RE ALL OVER, SIR!"

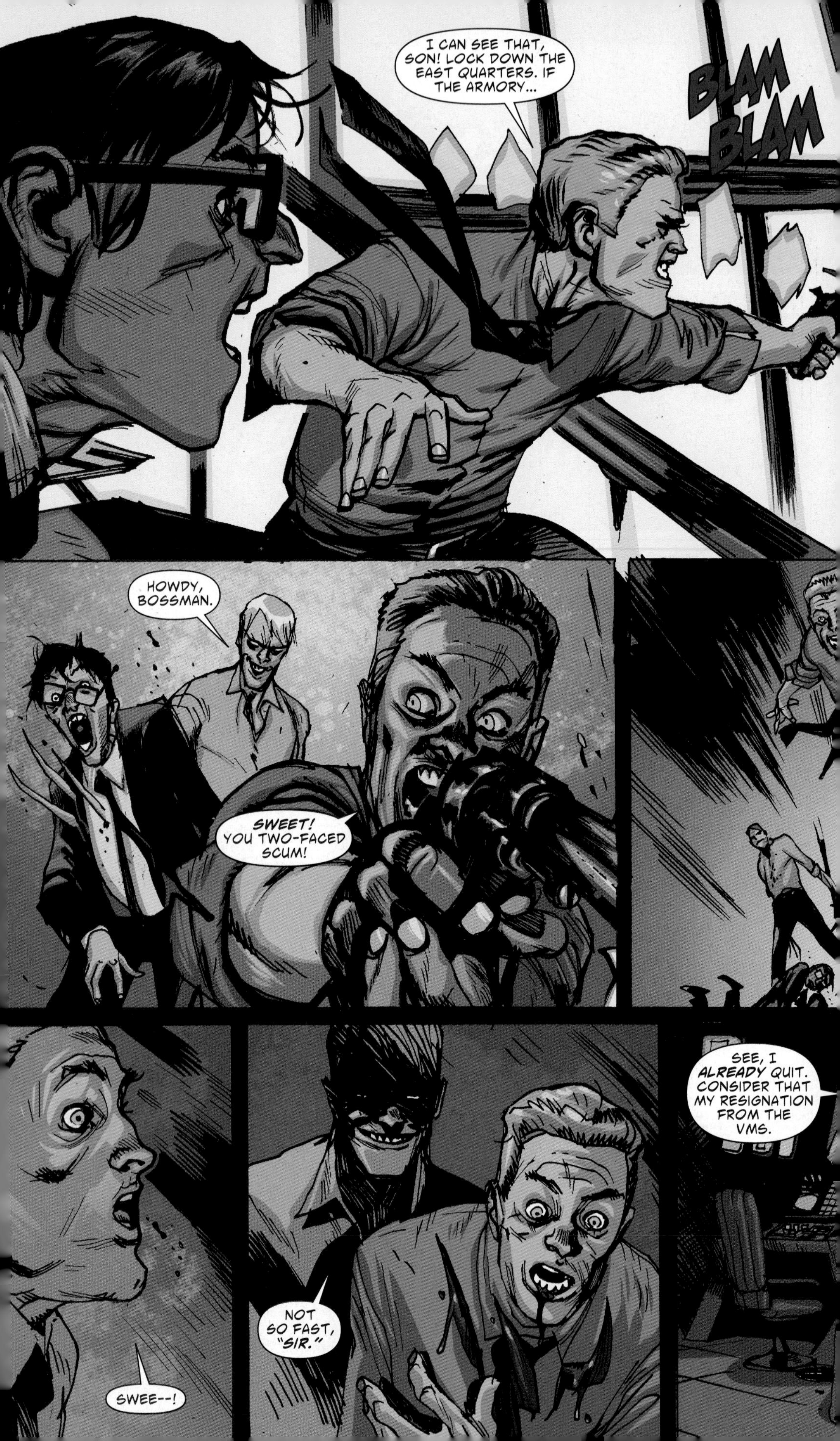
I CAN SEE THAT, SON! LOCK DOWN THE EAST QUARTERS. IF THE ARMORY...
BLAM BLAM
HOWDY, BOSSMAN.
SWEET! YOU TWO-FACED SCUM!
SWEE--!
NOT SO FAST, "SIR."
SEE, I ALREADY QUIT. CONSIDER THAT MY RESIGNATION FROM THE VMS.

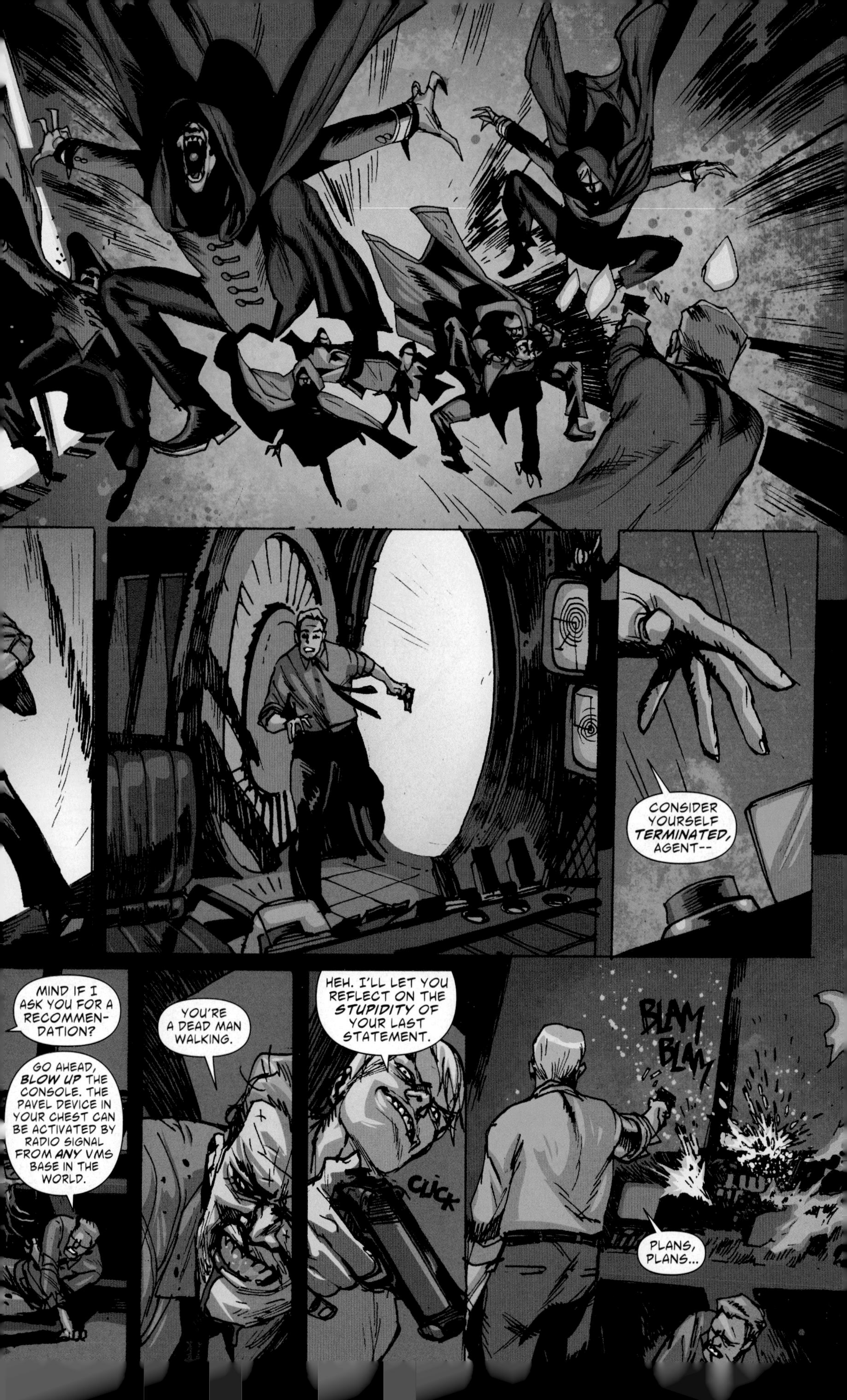
CONSIDER YOURSELF TERMINATED, AGENT--
MIND IF I ASK YOU FOR A RECOMMEN-DATION?
GO AHEAD, BLOW UP THE CONSOLE. THE PAVEL DEVICE IN YOUR CHEST CAN BE ACTIVATED BY RADIO SIGNAL FROM ANY VMS BASE IN THE WORLD.
YOU'RE A DEAD MAN WALKING.
HEH. I'LL LET YOU REFLECT ON THE STUPIDITY OF YOUR LAST STATEMENT.
CLICK
BLAM
BLAM
PLANS, PLANS...

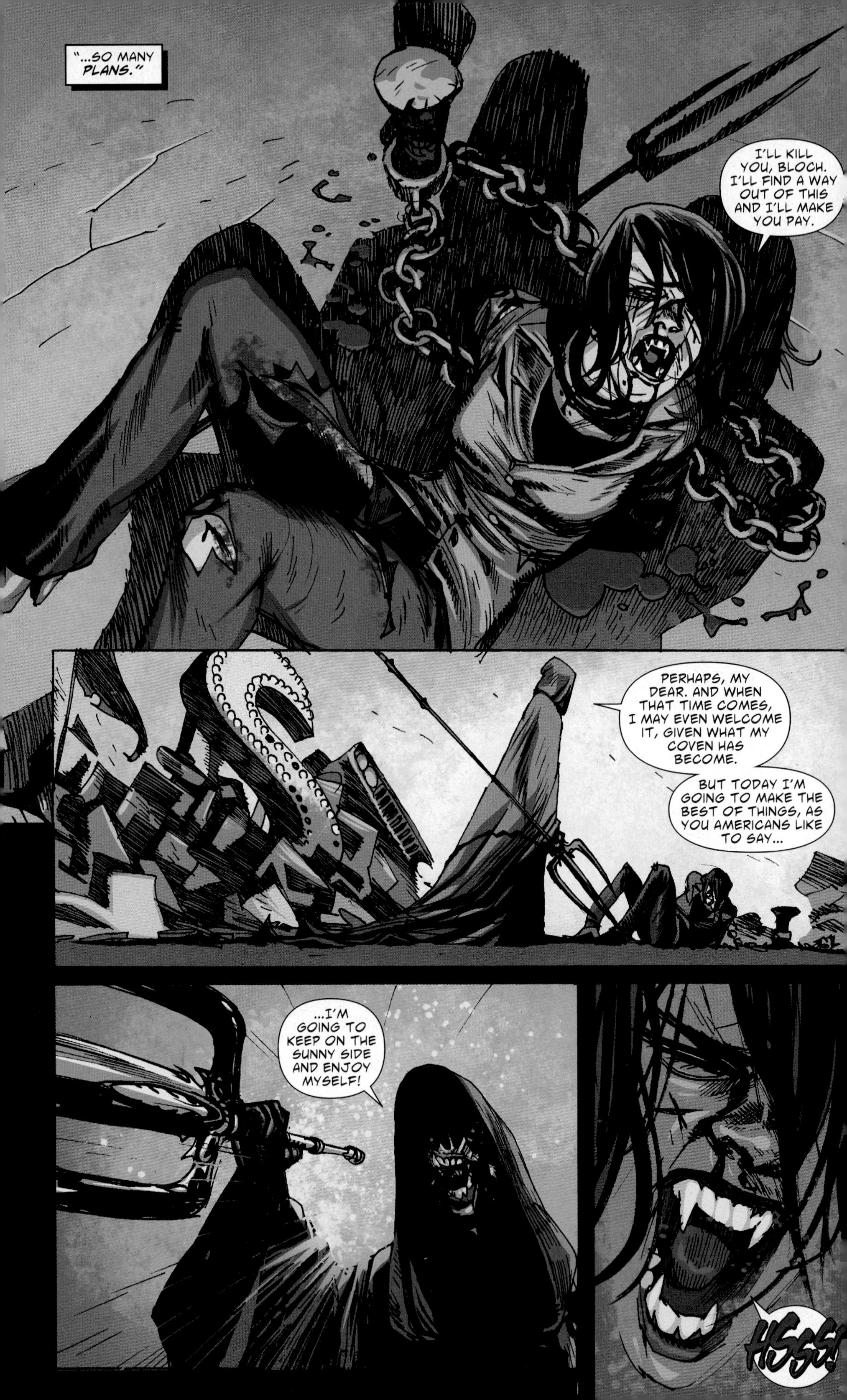
"...SO MANY PLANS."
I'LL KILL YOU, BLOCH. I'LL FIND A WAY OUT OF THIS AND I'LL MAKE YOU PAY.
PERHAPS, MY DEAR. AND WHEN THAT TIME COMES, I MAY EVEN WELCOME IT, GIVEN WHAT MY COVEN HAS BECOME.
BUT TODAY I'M GOING TO MAKE THE BEST OF THINGS, AS YOU AMERICANS LIKE TO SAY...
...I'M GOING TO KEEP ON THE SUNNY SIDE AND ENJOY MYSELF!
HSSS!

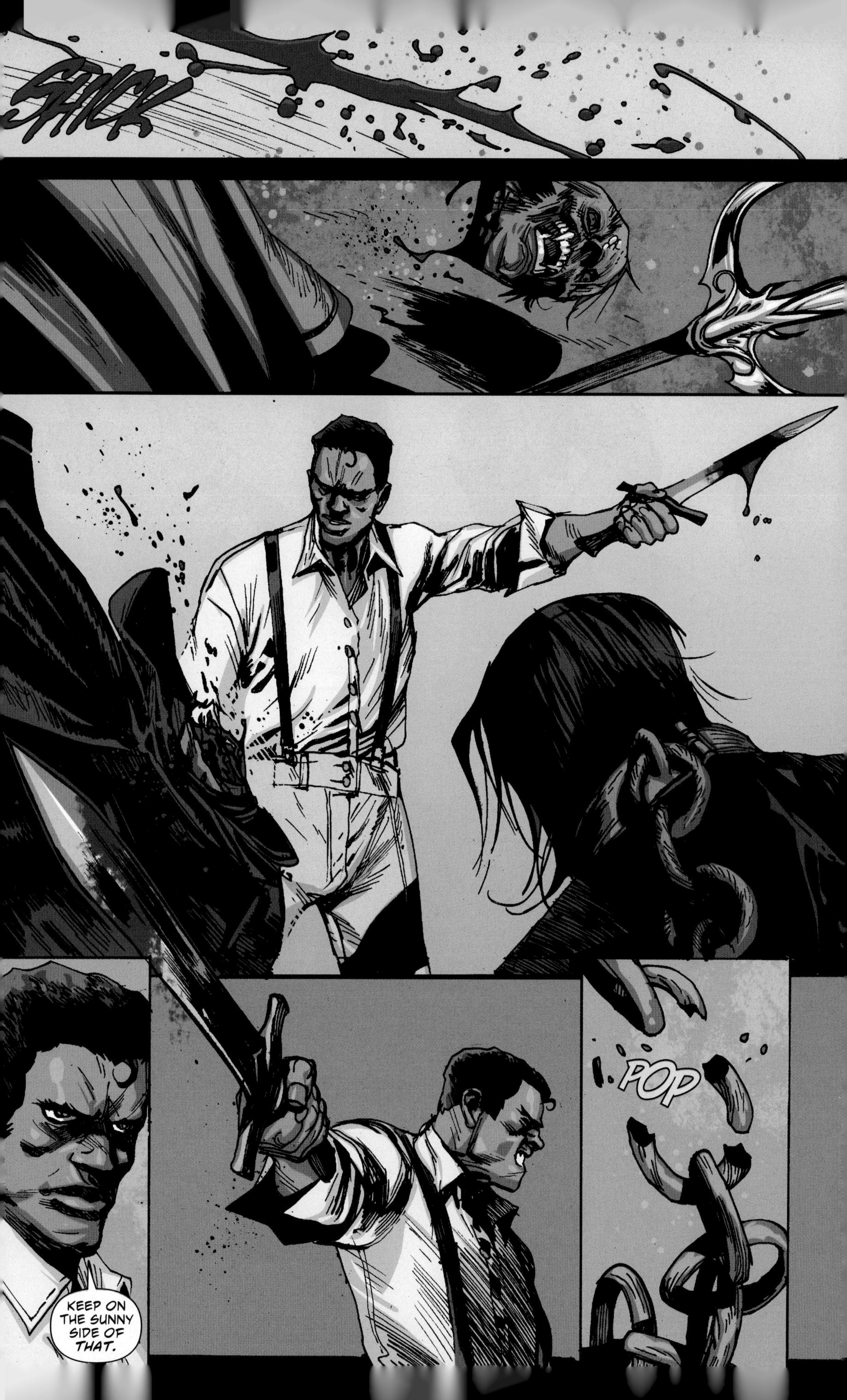
SHICK
POP
KEEP ON THE SUNNY SIDE OF THAT.

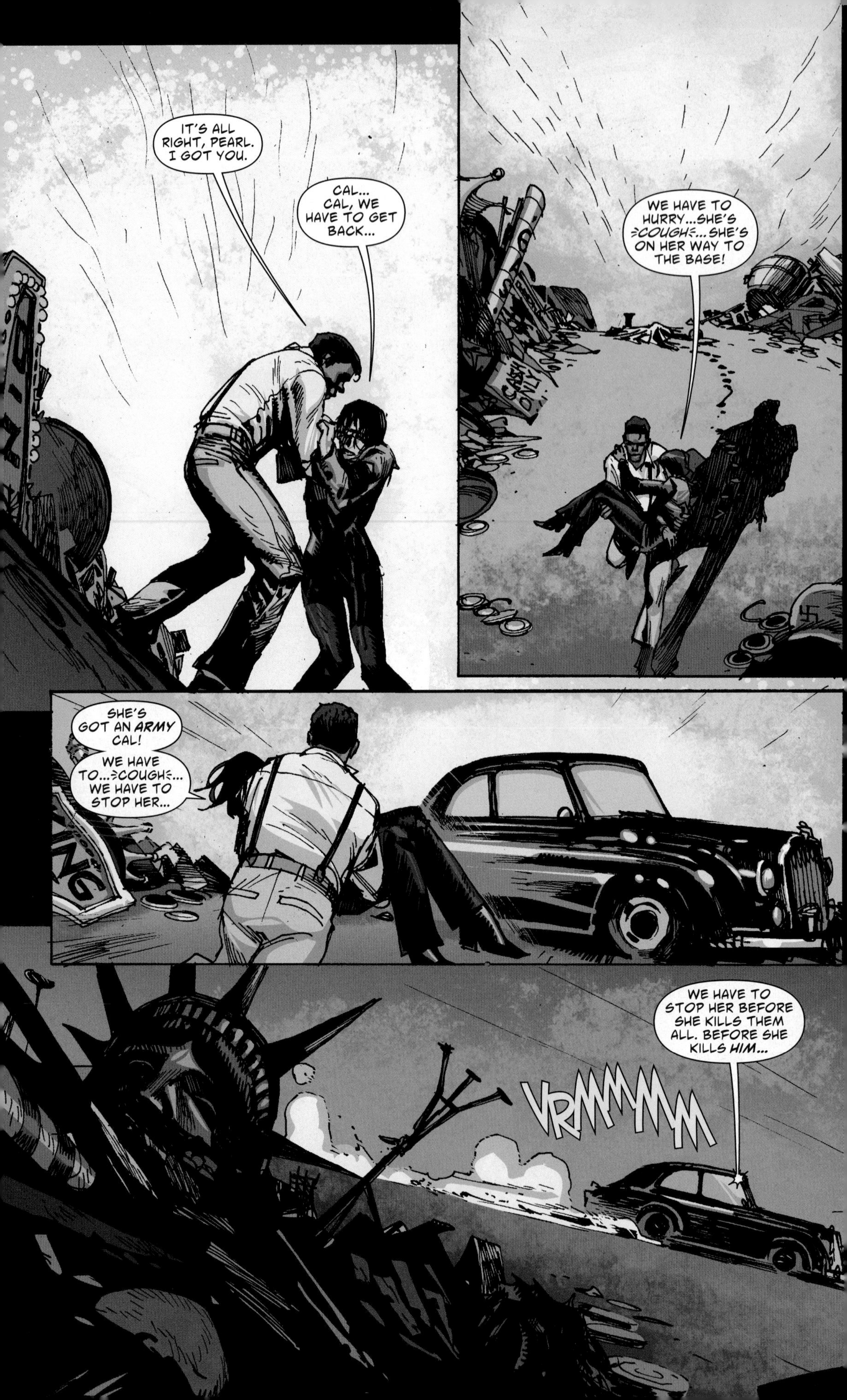
IT'S ALL RIGHT, PEARL. I GOT YOU.
CAL... CAL, WE HAVE TO GET BACK...
WE HAVE TO HURRY...SHE'S ≈COUGH≈...SHE'S ON HER WAY TO THE BASE!
SHE'S GOT AN ARMY CAL!
WE HAVE TO...≈COUGH≈... WE HAVE TO STOP HER...
WE HAVE TO STOP HER BEFORE SHE KILLS THEM ALL. BEFORE SHE KILLS HIM...
VRMMMM

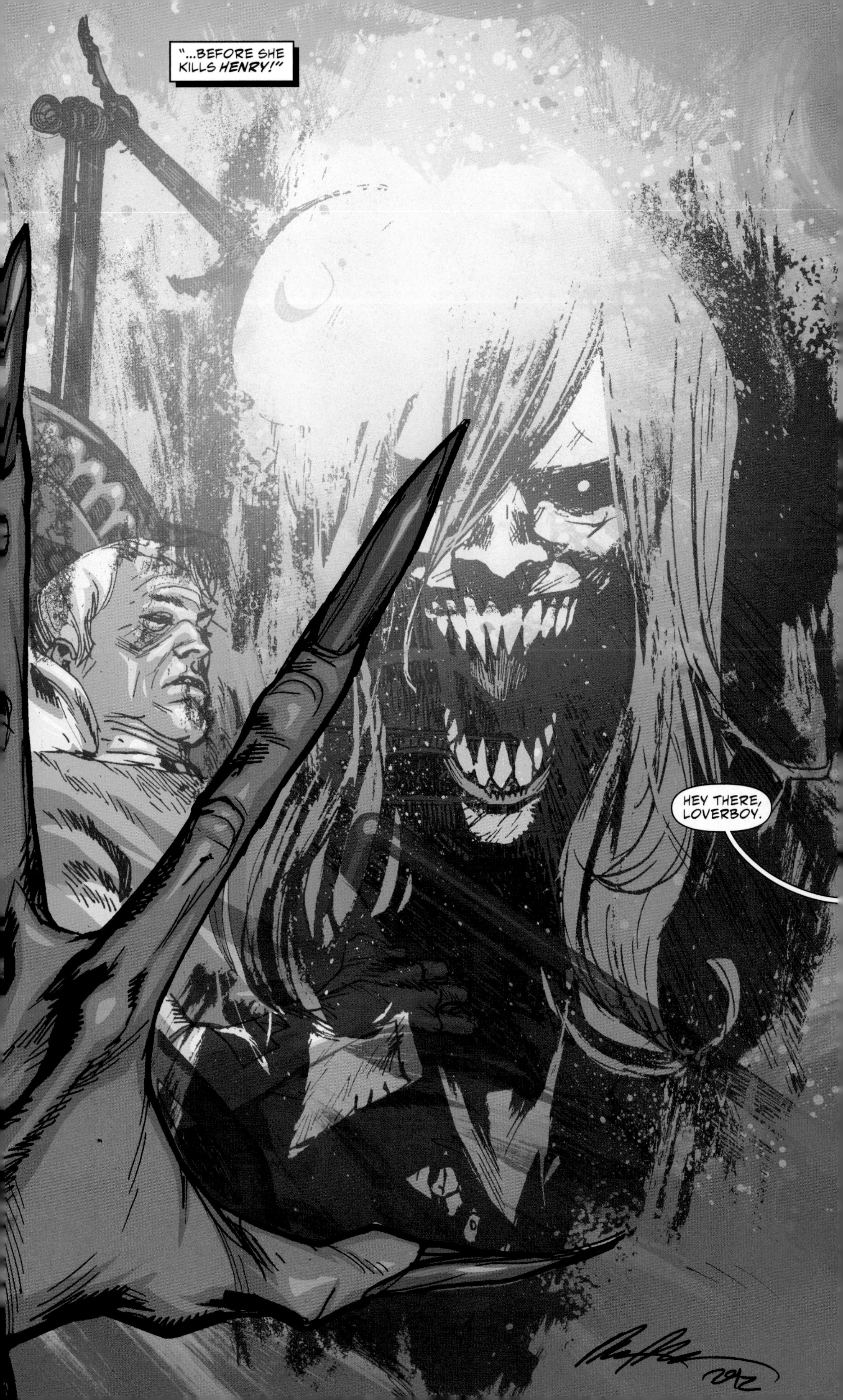
"...BEFORE SHE KILLS HENRY!"
HEY THERE, LOVERBOY.

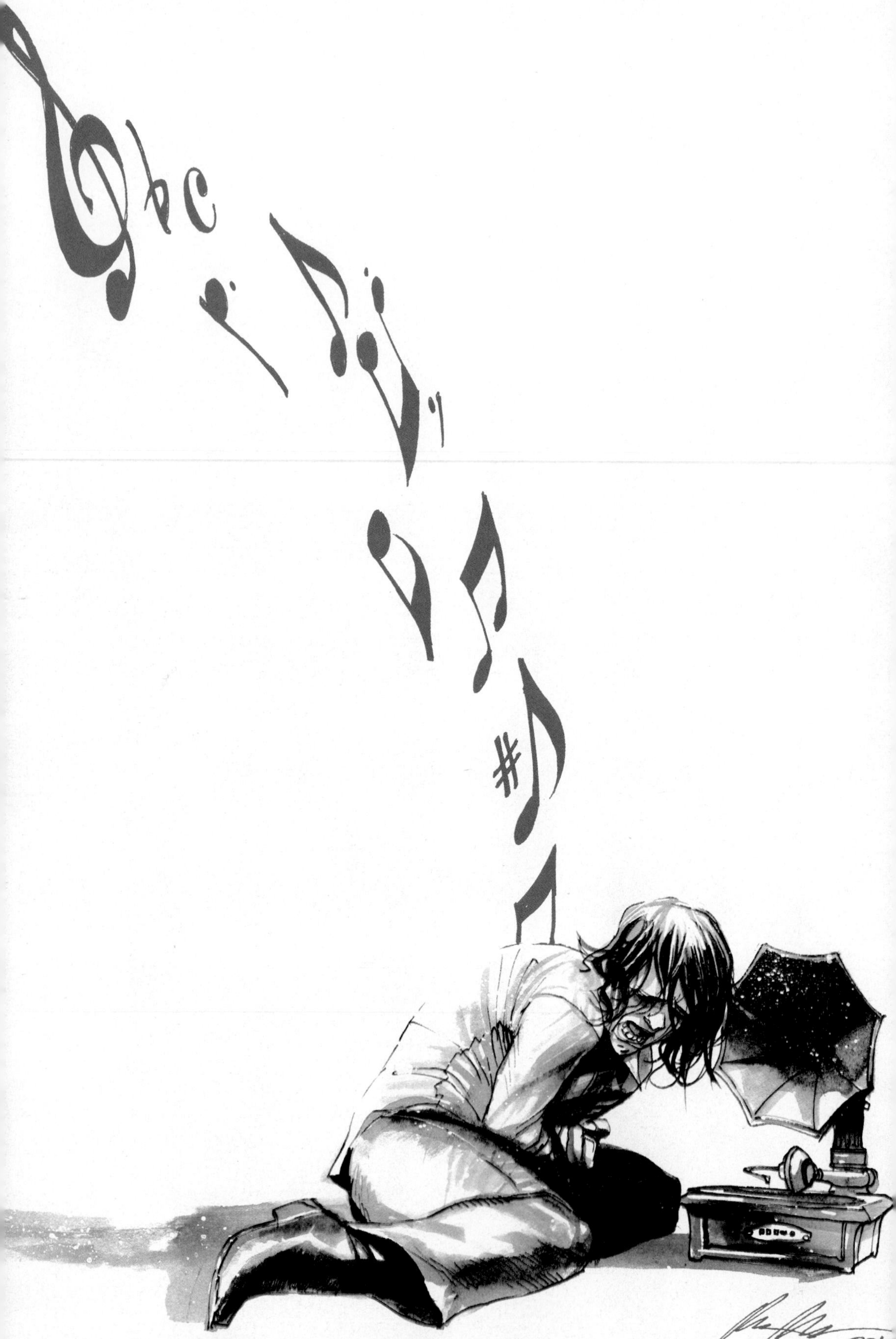

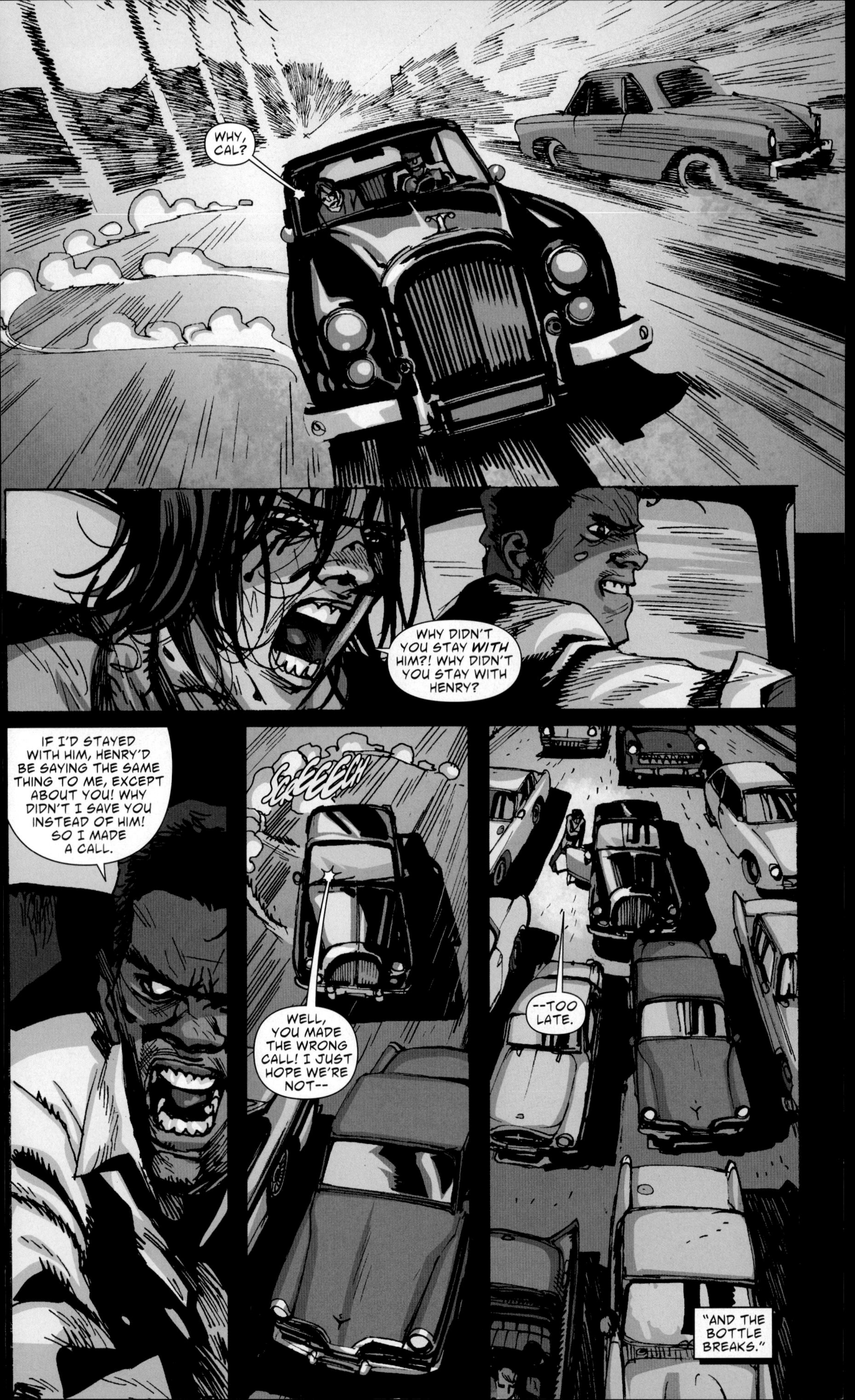
WHY, CAL?
WHY DIDN'T YOU STAY *WITH* HIM?! WHY DIDN'T YOU STAY WITH HENRY?
IF I'D STAYED WITH HIM, HENRY'D BE SAYING THE SAME THING TO ME, EXCEPT ABOUT YOU! WHY DIDN'T I SAVE YOU INSTEAD OF HIM! SO I MADE A CALL.
WELL, YOU MADE THE WRONG CALL! I JUST HOPE WE'RE NOT--
--TOO LATE.
"AND THE BOTTLE BREAKS."

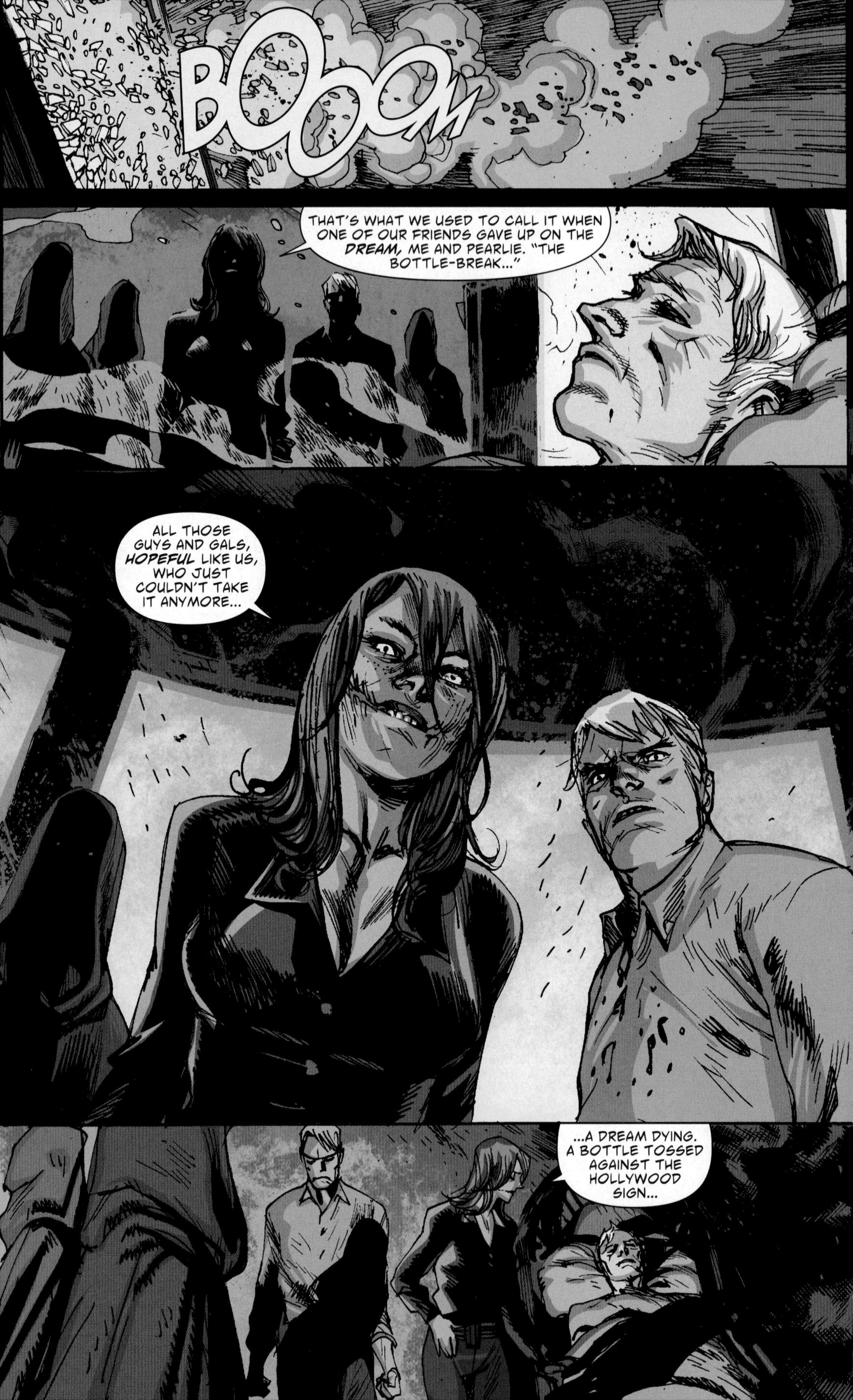
BOOOM
THAT'S WHAT WE USED TO CALL IT WHEN ONE OF OUR FRIENDS GAVE UP ON THE DREAM, ME AND PEARLIE. "THE BOTTLE-BREAK..."
ALL THOSE GUYS AND GALS, HOPEFUL LIKE US, WHO JUST COULDN'T TAKE IT ANYMORE...
...A DREAM DYING. A BOTTLE TOSSED AGAINST THE HOLLYWOOD SIGN...

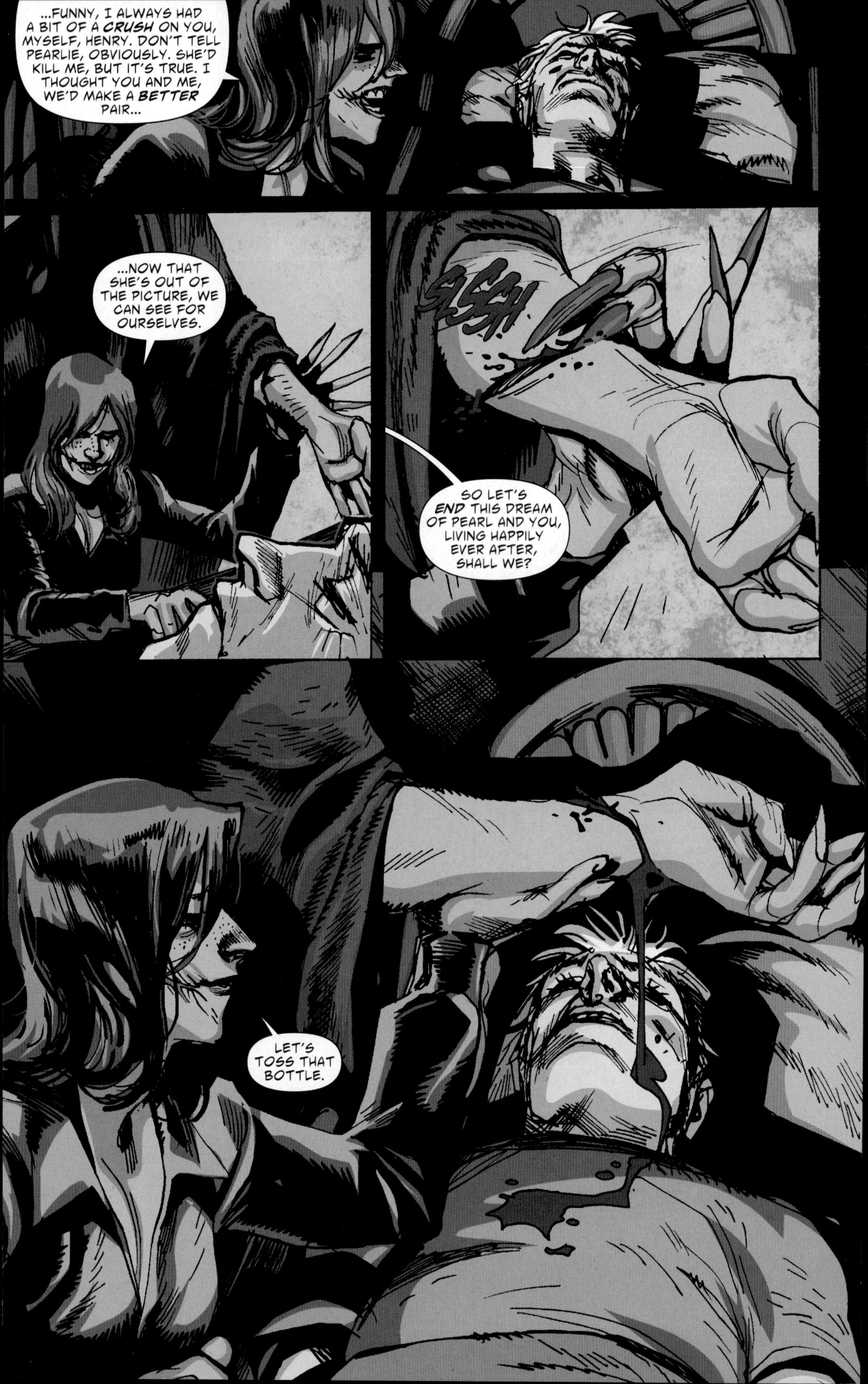
...FUNNY, I ALWAYS HAD A BIT OF A CRUSH ON YOU, MYSELF, HENRY. DON'T TELL PEARLIE, OBVIOUSLY. SHE'D KILL ME, BUT IT'S TRUE. I THOUGHT YOU AND ME, WE'D MAKE A BETTER PAIR...
...NOW THAT SHE'S OUT OF THE PICTURE, WE CAN SEE FOR OURSELVES.
SLSSCH!
SO LET'S END THIS DREAM OF PEARL AND YOU, LIVING HAPPILY EVER AFTER, SHALL WE?
LET'S TOSS THAT BOTTLE.

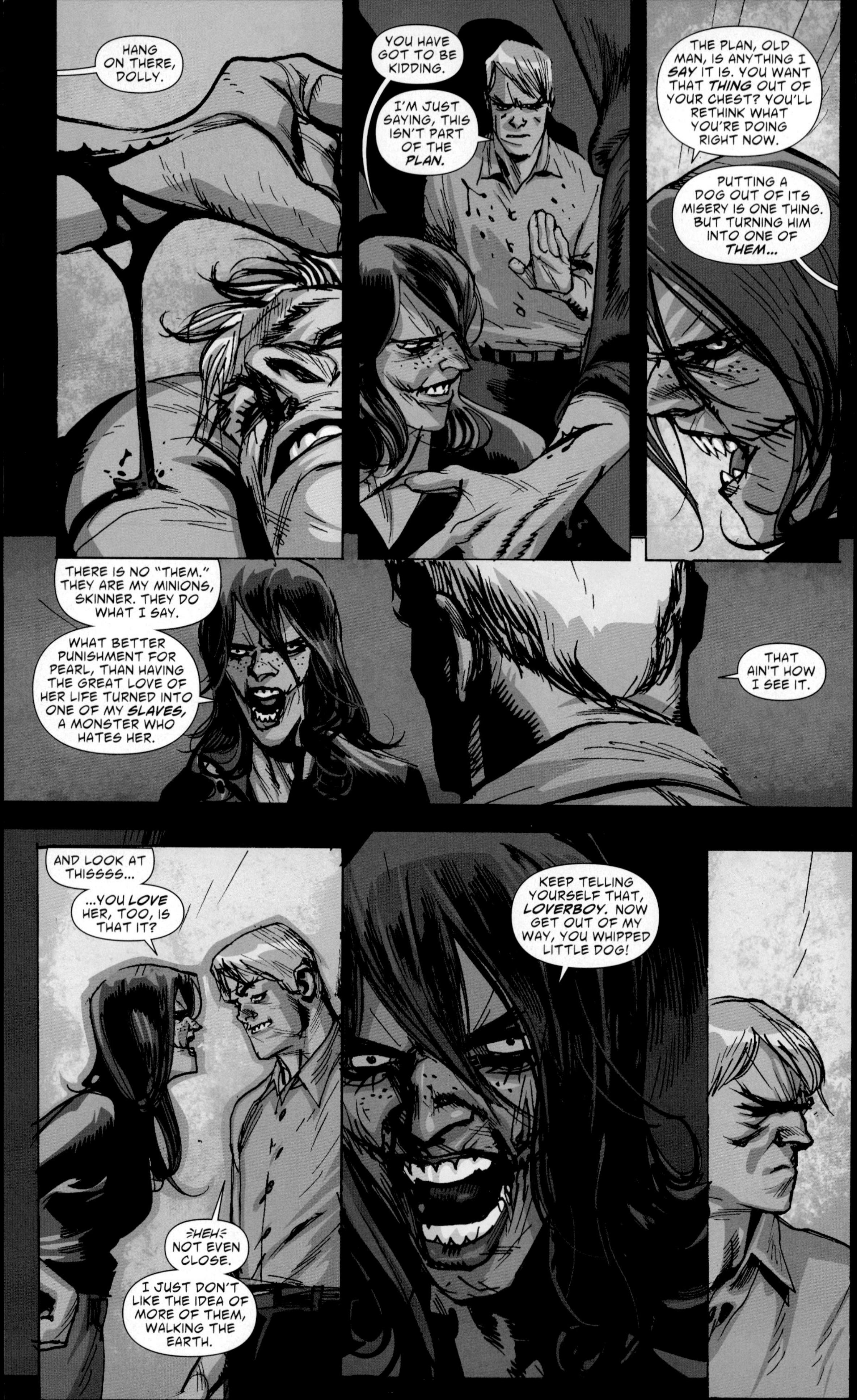
HANG ON THERE, DOLLY.
YOU HAVE GOT TO BE KIDDING.
I'M JUST SAYING, THIS ISN'T PART OF THE PLAN.
THE PLAN, OLD MAN, IS ANYTHING I SAY IT IS. YOU WANT THAT THING OUT OF YOUR CHEST? YOU'LL RETHINK WHAT YOU'RE DOING RIGHT NOW.
PUTTING A DOG OUT OF ITS MISERY IS ONE THING. BUT TURNING HIM INTO ONE OF THEM...
THERE IS NO "THEM." THEY ARE MY MINIONS, SKINNER. THEY DO WHAT I SAY.
WHAT BETTER PUNISHMENT FOR PEARL, THAN HAVING THE GREAT LOVE OF HER LIFE TURNED INTO ONE OF MY SLAVES, A MONSTER WHO HATES HER.
THAT AIN'T HOW I SEE IT.
AND LOOK AT THISSSS...
...YOU LOVE HER, TOO, IS THAT IT?
HEH
NOT EVEN CLOSE.
I JUST DON'T LIKE THE IDEA OF MORE OF THEM, WALKING THE EARTH.
KEEP TELLING YOURSELF THAT, LOVERBOY. NOW GET OUT OF MY WAY, YOU WHIPPED LITTLE DOG!

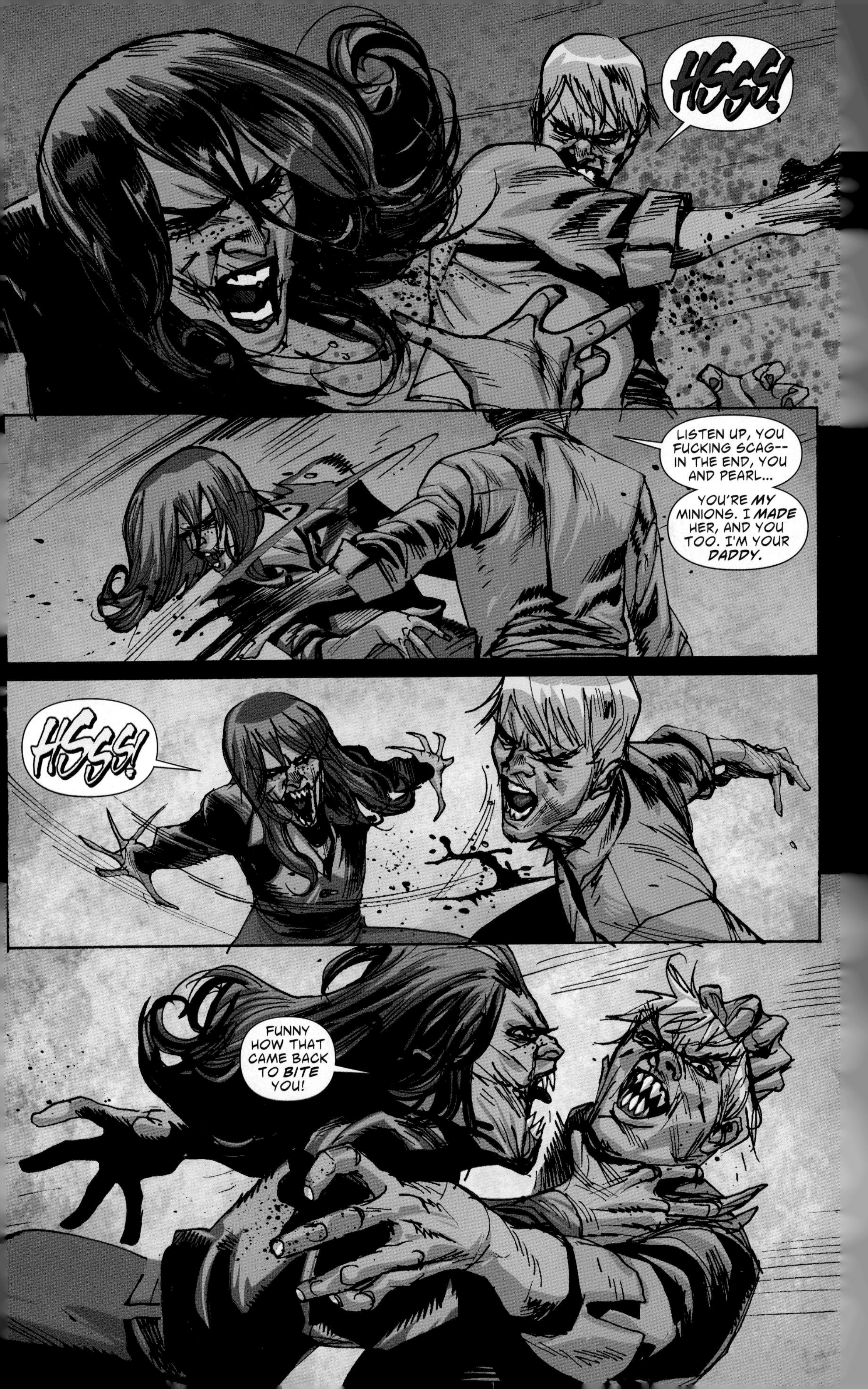
HISSS!
LISTEN UP, YOU FUCKING SCAG-- IN THE END, YOU AND PEARL...
YOU'RE MY MINIONS. I MADE HER, AND YOU TOO. I'M YOUR DADDY.
HISSS!
FUNNY HOW THAT CAME BACK TO BITE YOU!

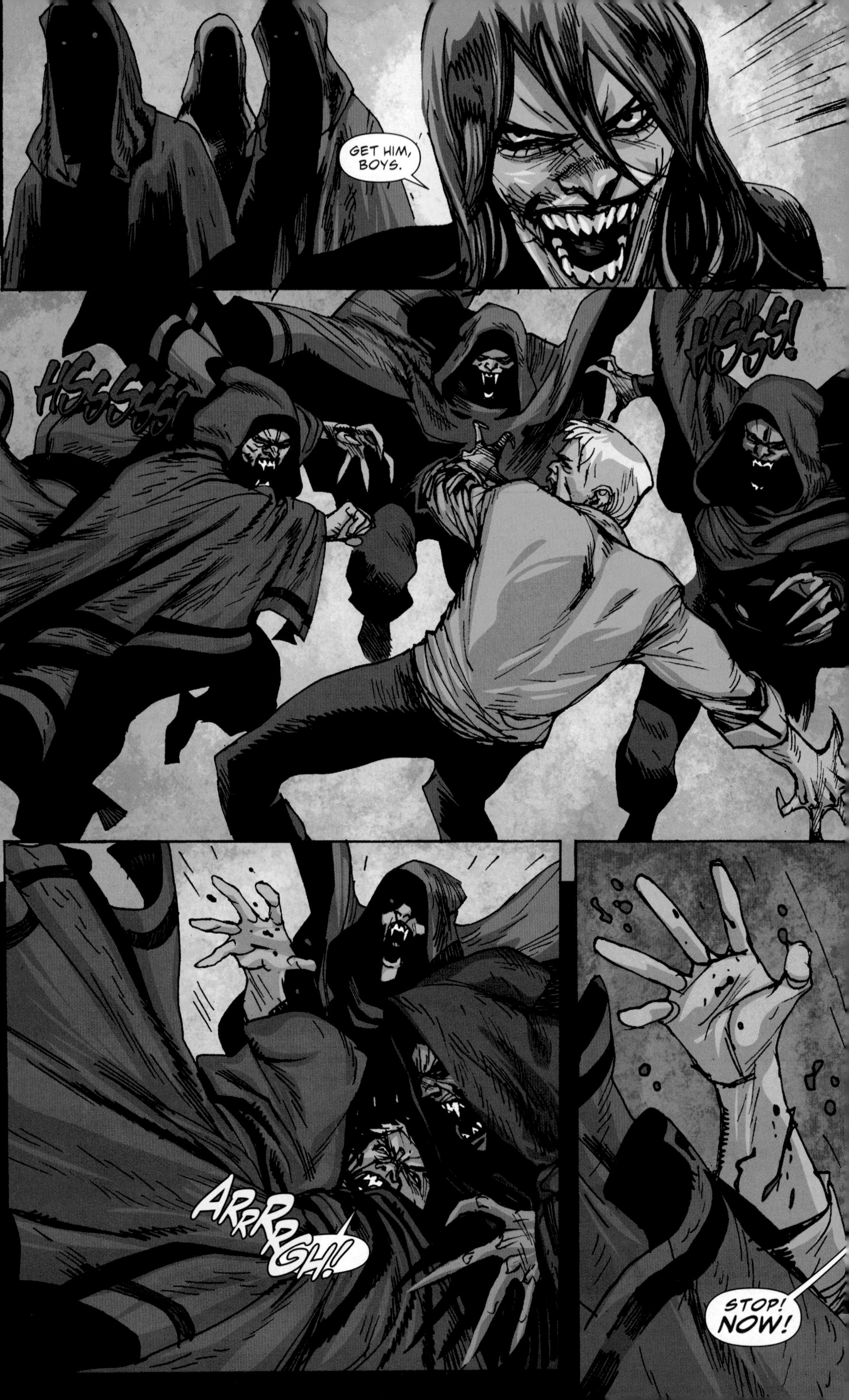
GET HIM, BOYS.
HSSSSS!
HSSS!
ARRRRGH!
STOP! NOW!

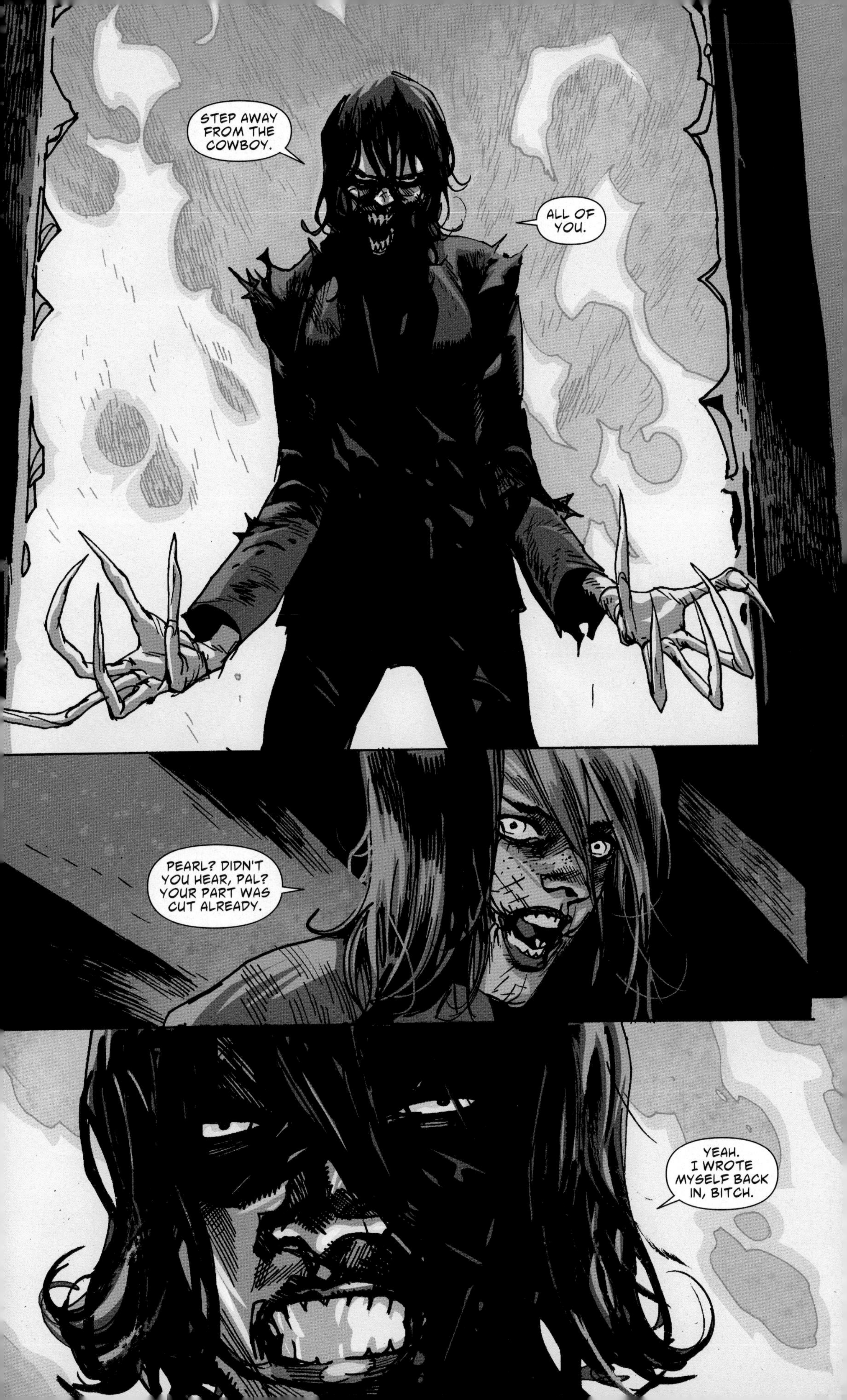
STEP AWAY FROM THE COWBOY.
ALL OF YOU.
PEARL? DIDN'T YOU HEAR, PAL? YOUR PART WAS CUT ALREADY.
YEAH. I WROTE MYSELF BACK IN, BITCH.

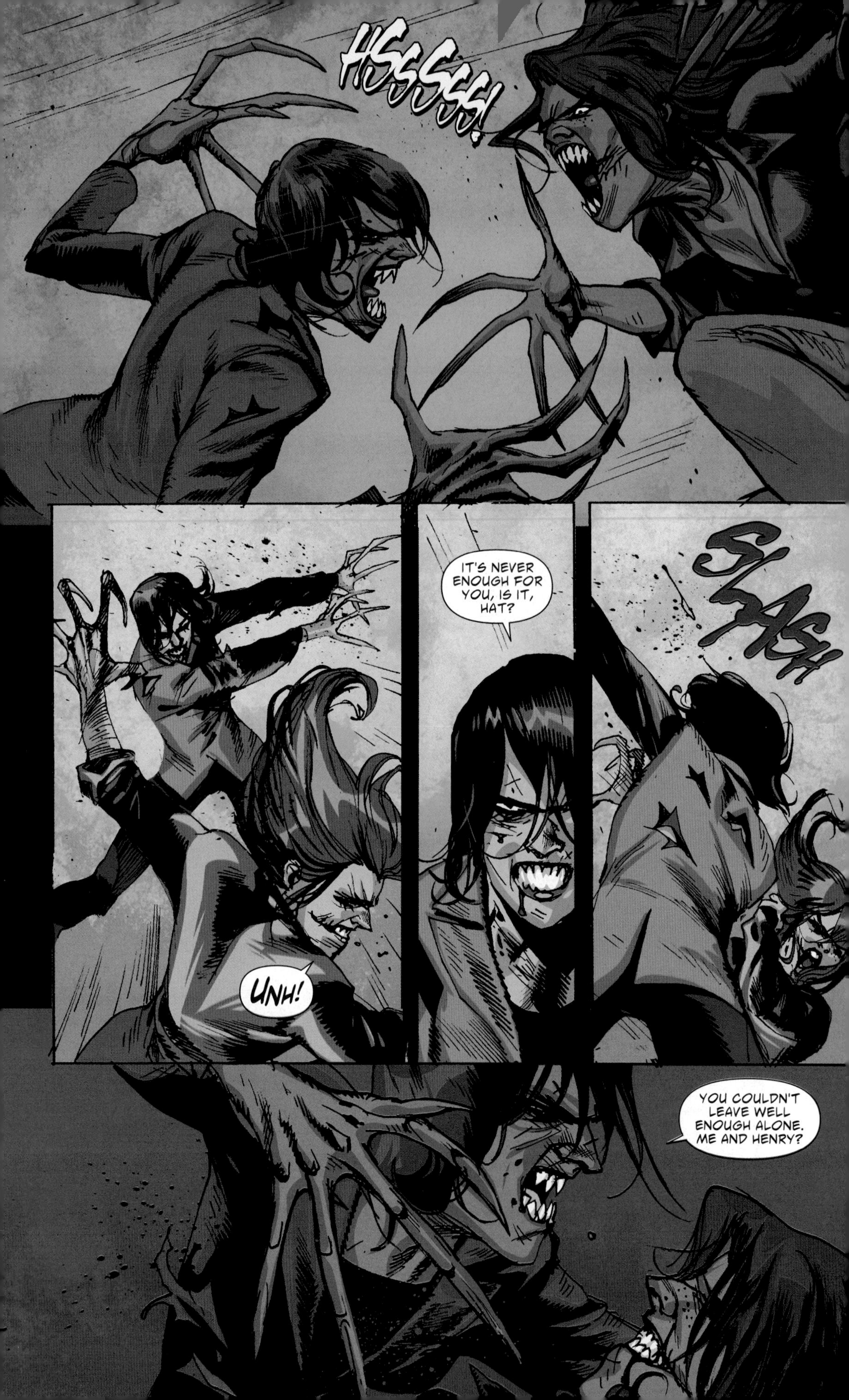
HSSSSSS!
UNH!
IT'S NEVER ENOUGH FOR YOU, IS IT, HAT?
SLASH!
YOU COULDN'T LEAVE WELL ENOUGH ALONE. ME AND HENRY?

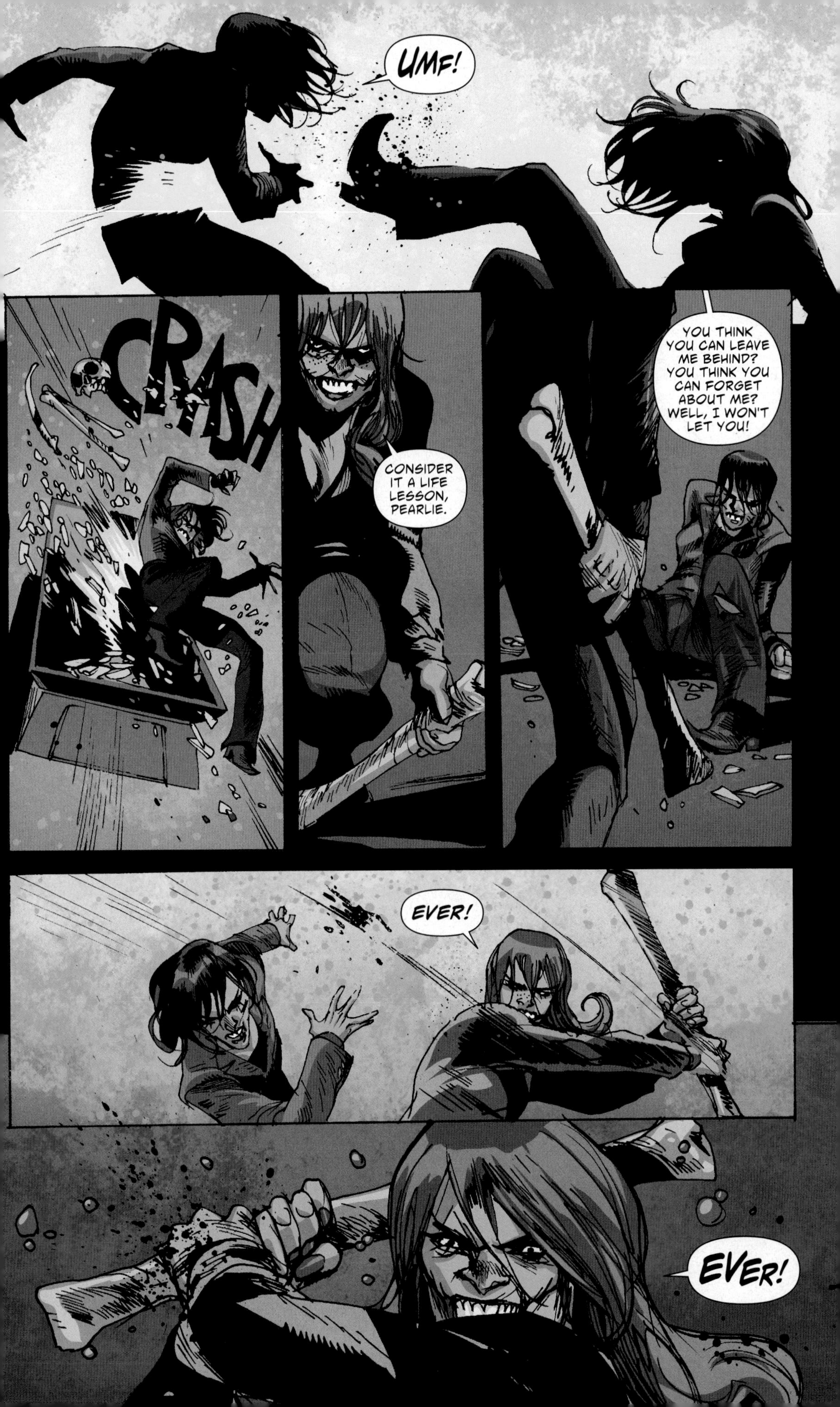
UMF!
CRASH
CONSIDER IT A LIFE LESSON, PEARLIE.
YOU THINK YOU CAN LEAVE ME BEHIND? YOU THINK YOU CAN FORGET ABOUT ME? WELL, I WON'T LET YOU!
EVER!
EVER!

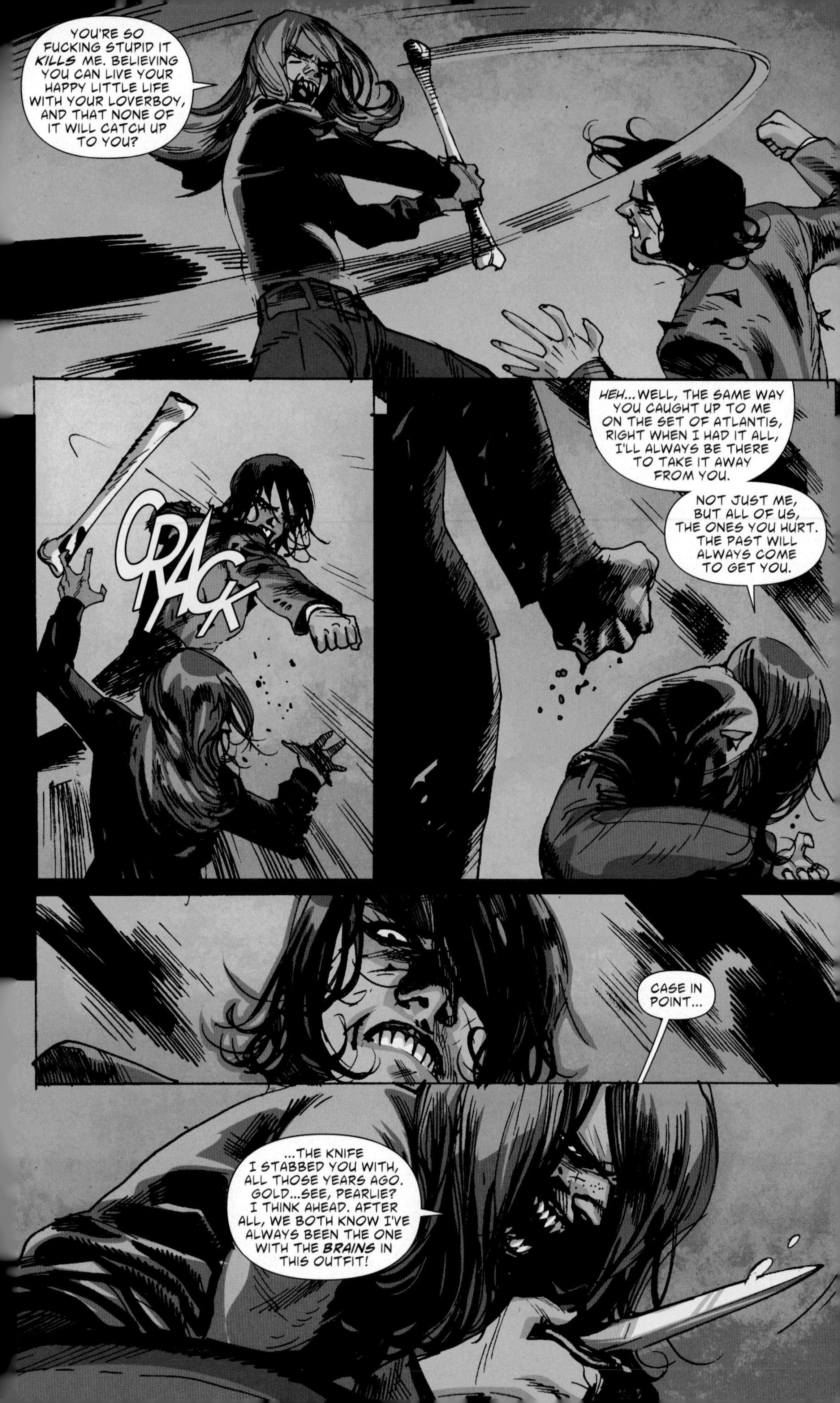
YOU'RE SO FUCKING STUPID IT KILLS ME. BELIEVING YOU CAN LIVE YOUR HAPPY LITTLE LIFE WITH YOUR LOVERBOY, AND THAT NONE OF IT WILL CATCH UP TO YOU?
CRACK
HEH...WELL, THE SAME WAY YOU CAUGHT UP TO ME ON THE SET OF ATLANTIS, RIGHT WHEN I HAD IT ALL, I'LL ALWAYS BE THERE TO TAKE IT AWAY FROM YOU.
NOT JUST ME, BUT ALL OF US, THE ONES YOU HURT. THE PAST WILL ALWAYS COME TO GET YOU.
CASE IN POINT...
...THE KNIFE I STABBED YOU WITH, ALL THOSE YEARS AGO. GOLD...SEE, PEARLIE? I THINK AHEAD. AFTER ALL, WE BOTH KNOW I'VE ALWAYS BEEN THE ONE WITH THE BRAINS IN THIS OUTFIT!

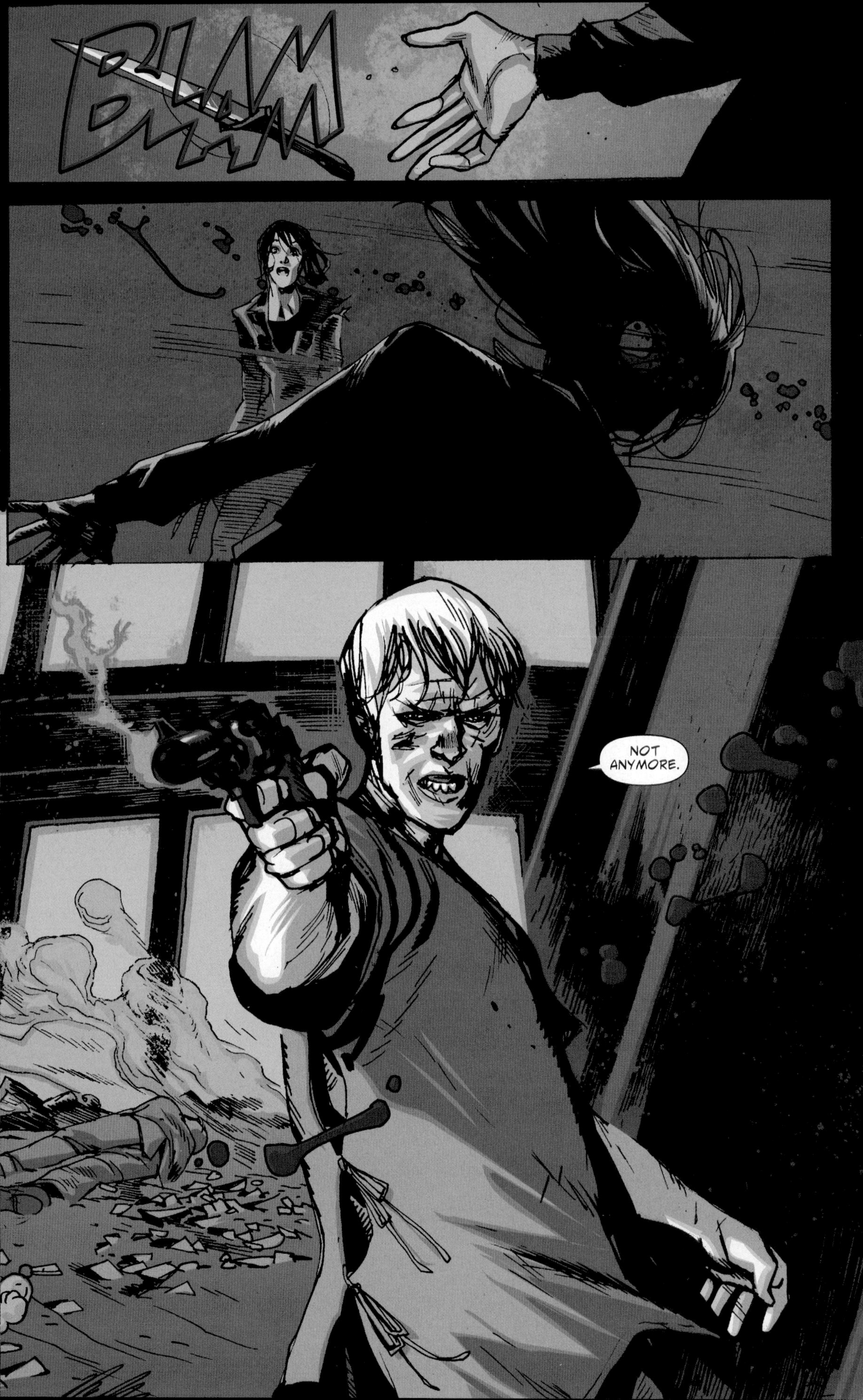
BLAM
BLAM
NOT ANYMORE.

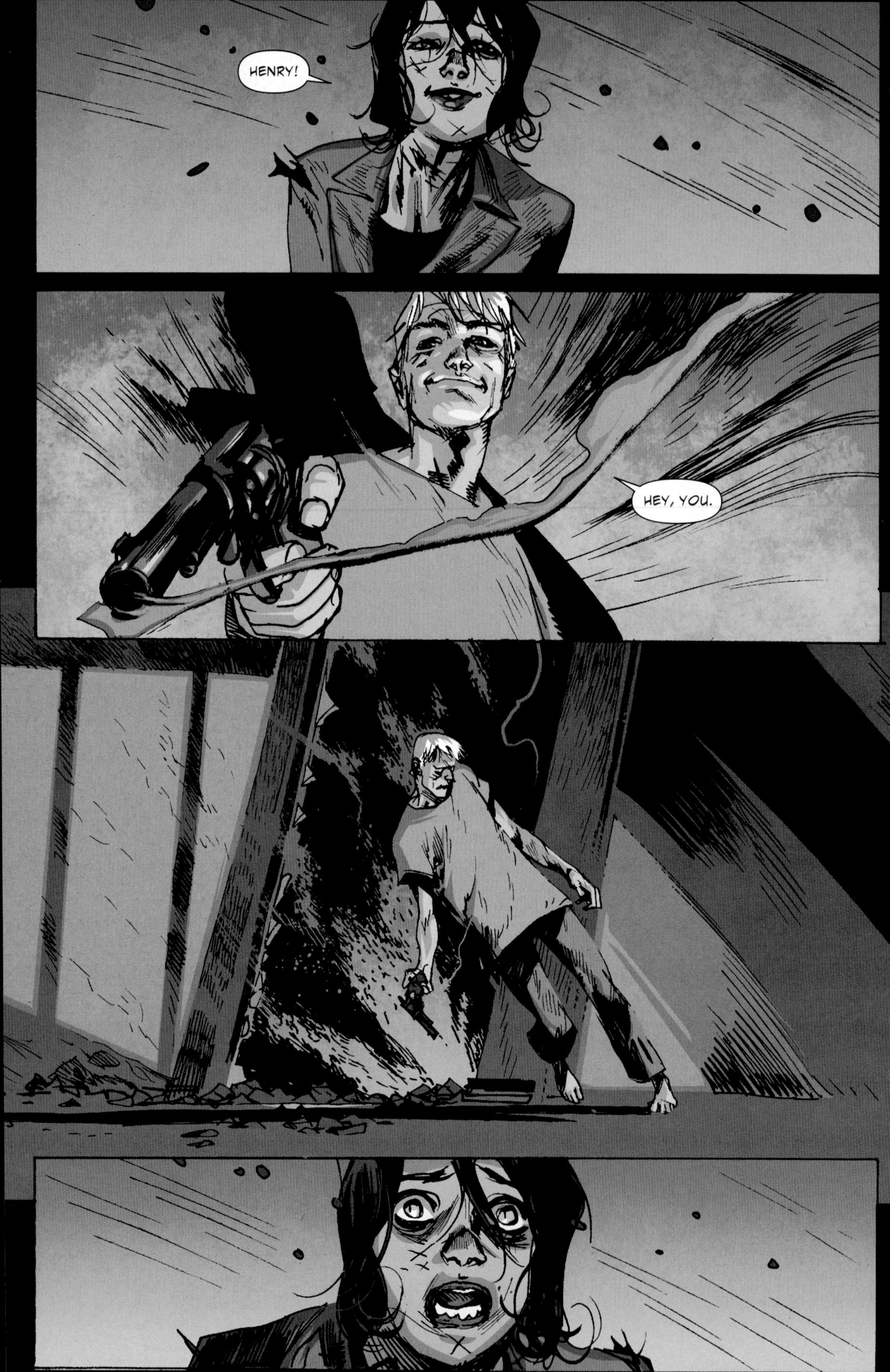
HENRY!
HEY, YOU.

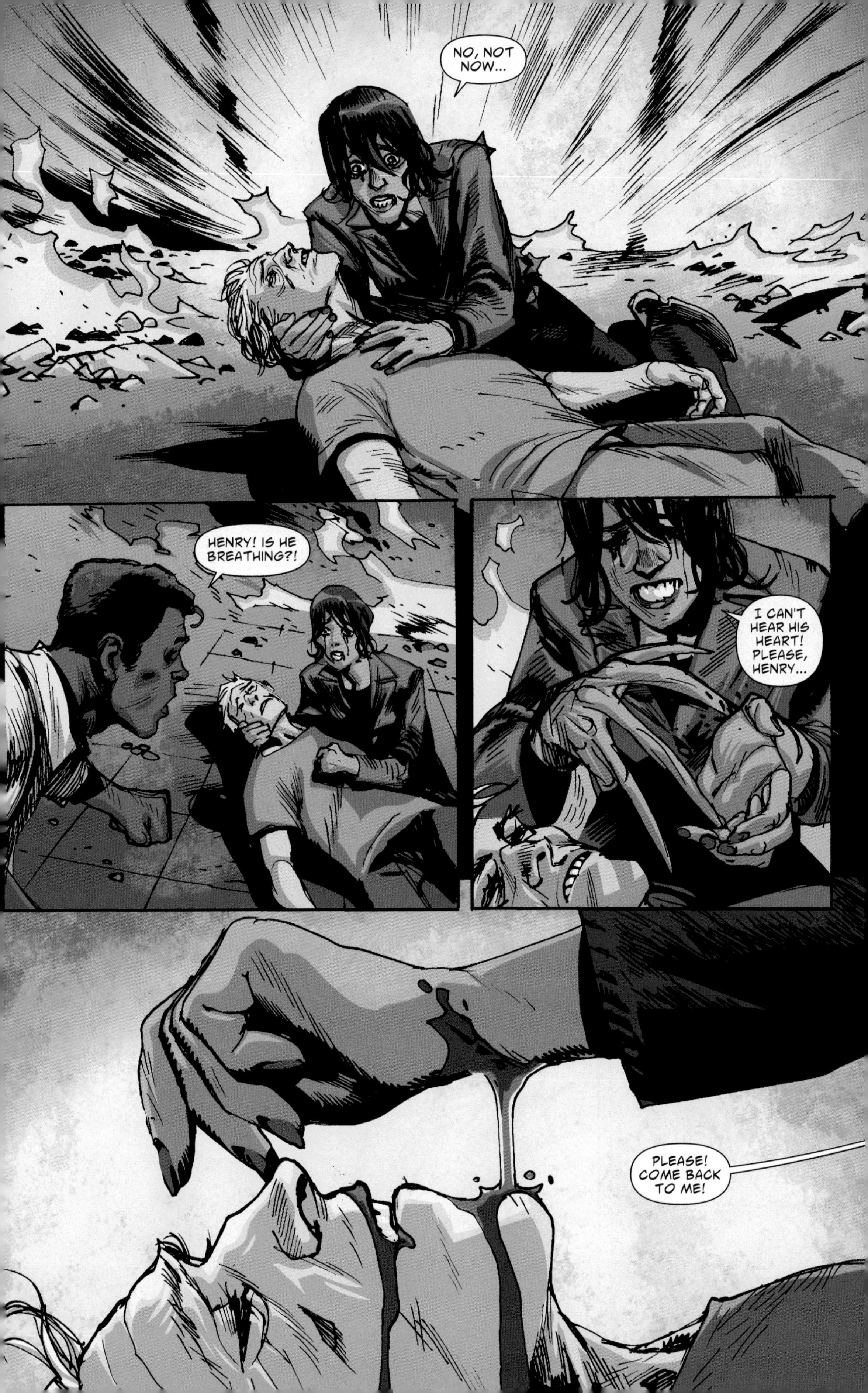
NO, NOT NOW...
HENRY! IS HE BREATHING?!
I CAN'T HEAR HIS HEART! PLEASE, HENRY...
PLEASE! COME BACK TO ME!

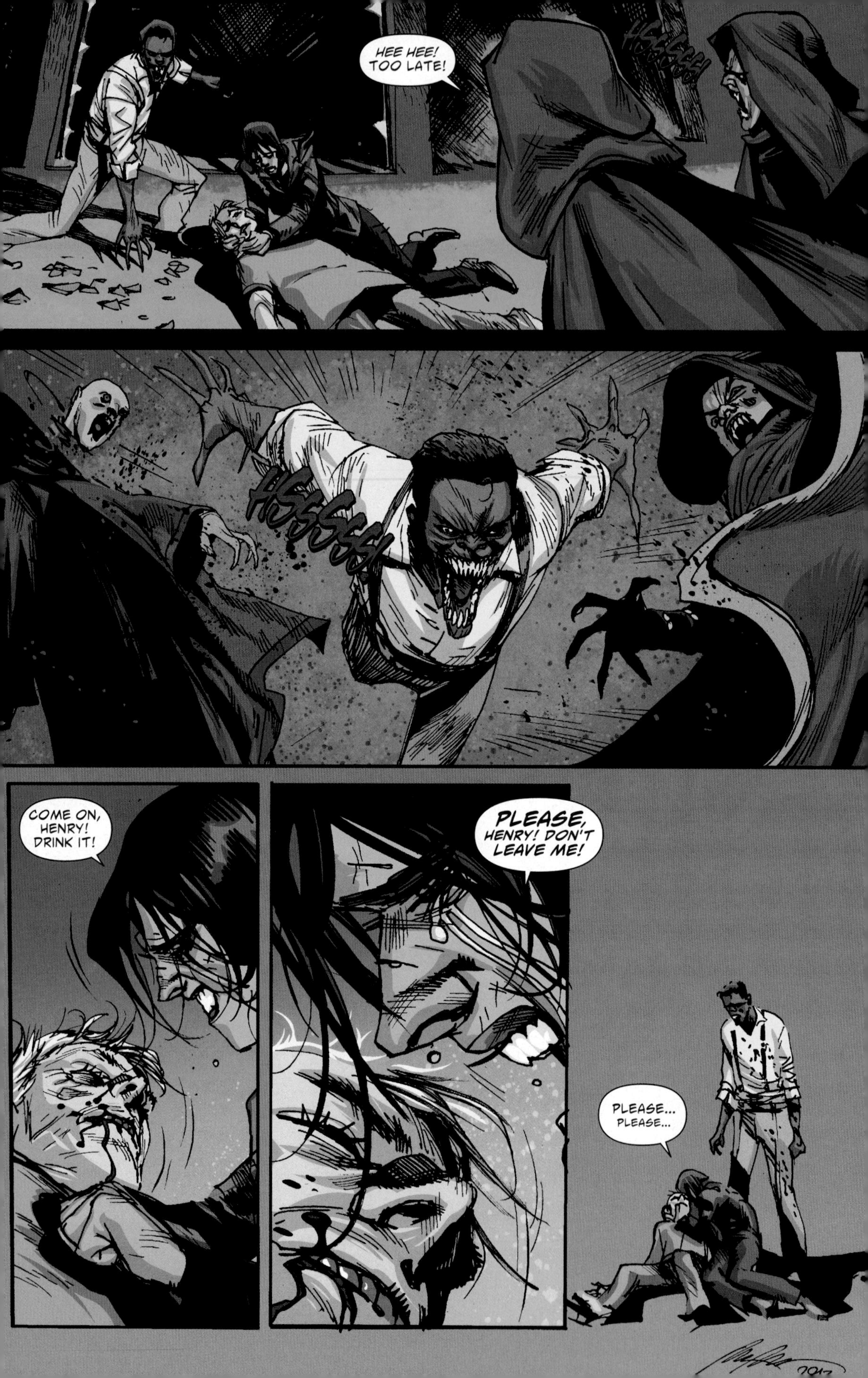
HEE HEE! TOO LATE!
HSSSSS!
HSSSSS!
COME ON, HENRY! DRINK IT!
PLEASE, HENRY! DON'T LEAVE ME!
PLEASE... PLEASE...

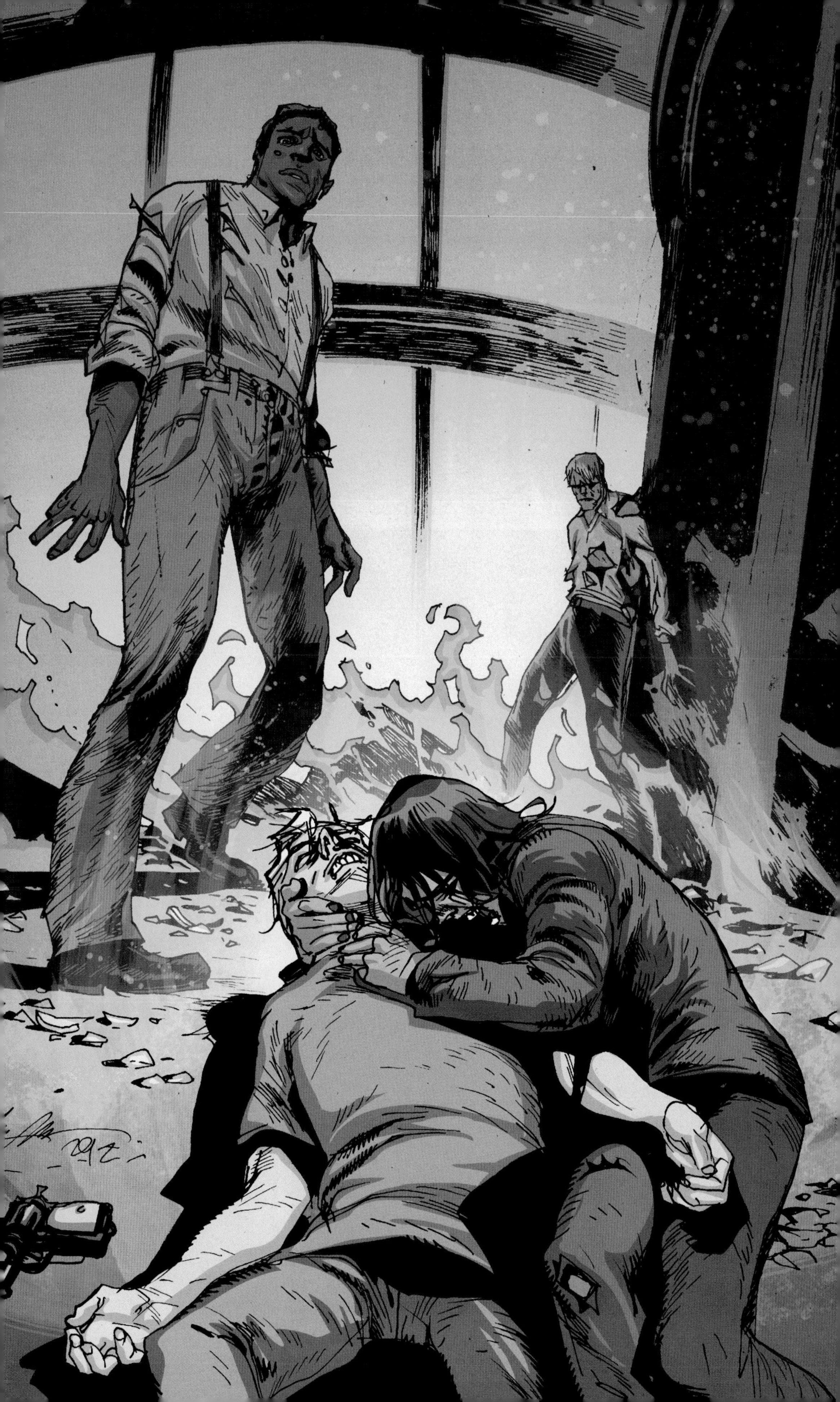

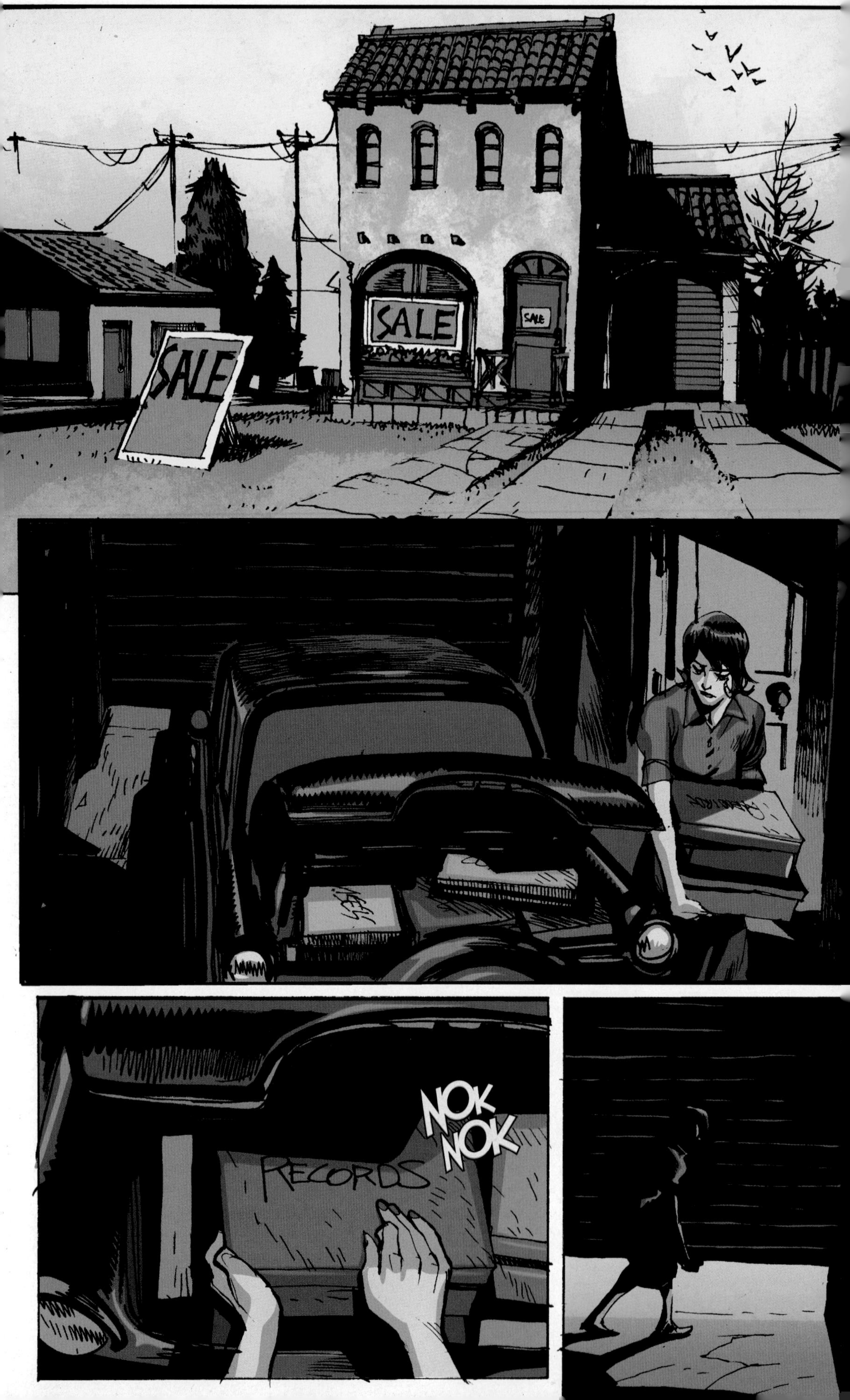

SALE
SALE
SALE
NOK
NOK
RECORDS

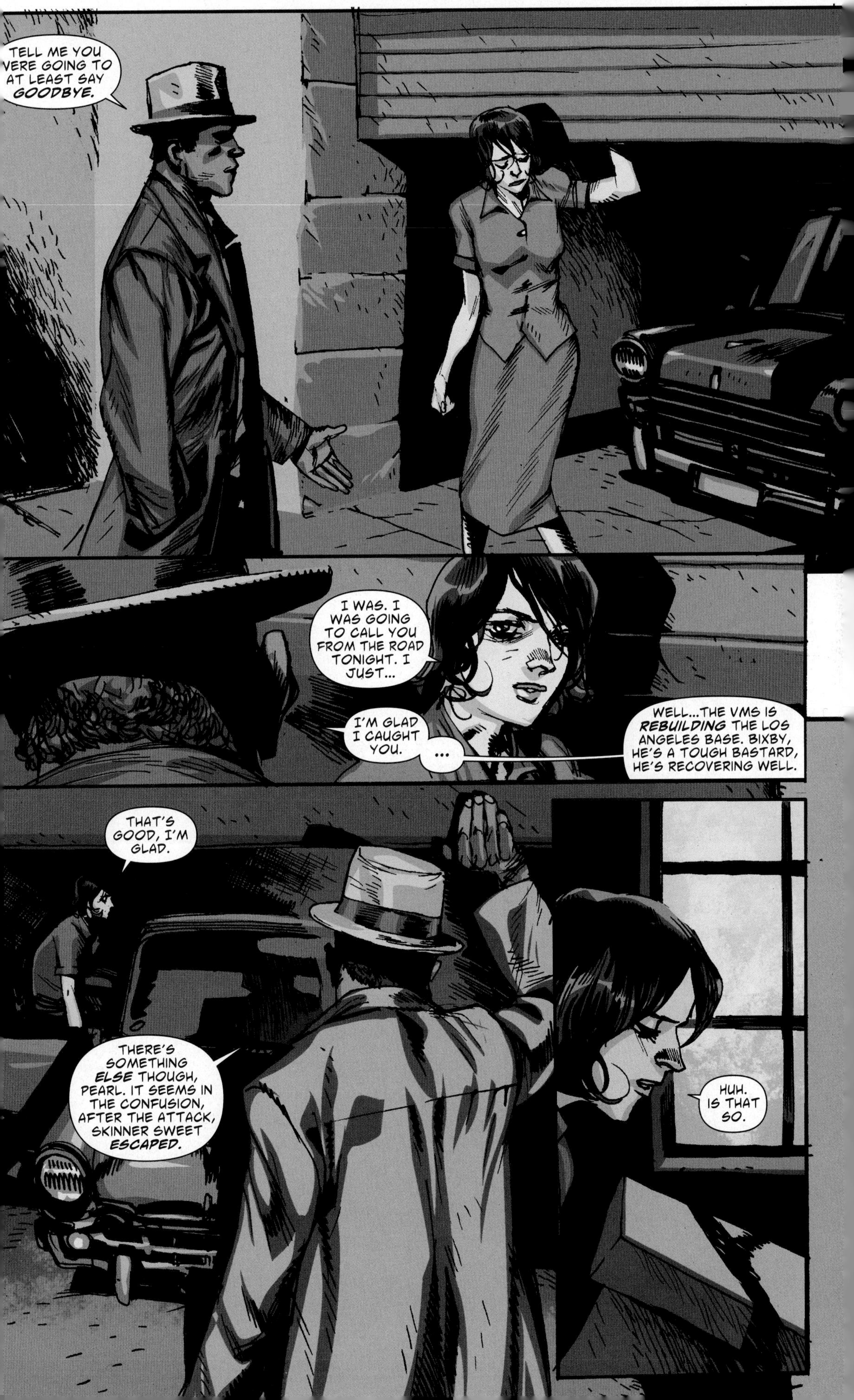
TELL ME YOU WERE GOING TO AT LEAST SAY GOODBYE.
I WAS. I WAS GOING TO CALL YOU FROM THE ROAD TONIGHT. I JUST...
I'M GLAD I CAUGHT YOU.
...
WELL...THE VMS IS REBUILDING THE LOS ANGELES BASE. BIXBY, HE'S A TOUGH BASTARD, HE'S RECOVERING WELL.
THAT'S GOOD, I'M GLAD.
THERE'S SOMETHING ELSE THOUGH, PEARL. IT SEEMS IN THE CONFUSION, AFTER THE ATTACK, SKINNER SWEET ESCAPED.
HUH. IS THAT SO.

IT IS. VMS NURSE CAME BY TO CHECK ON HIM, AND HE WAS *GONE*. NO SIGN OF HIM...

...EXCEPT FOR *THIS*.

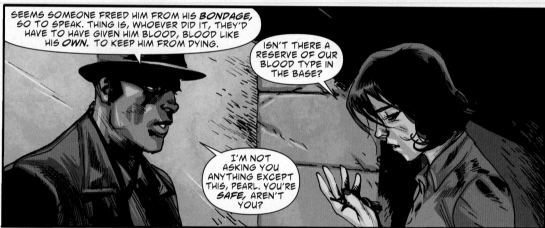

SEEMS SOMEONE FREED HIM FROM HIS *BONDAGE*, SO TO SPEAK. THING IS, WHOEVER DID IT, THEY'D HAVE TO HAVE GIVEN HIM BLOOD, BLOOD LIKE HIS *OWN*. TO KEEP HIM FROM DYING.

ISN'T THERE A RESERVE OF OUR BLOOD TYPE IN THE BASE?

I'M NOT ASKING YOU ANYTHING EXCEPT THIS, PEARL. YOU'RE *SAFE*, AREN'T YOU?

FROM SKINNER?

HEH

HE AND I WILL *NEVER* MEET AGAIN.

YOU KNOW, PEARL, I'D BE A FOOL NOT TO ASK YOU TO *STAY* WITH US, WITH THE VMS. YOU COULD HELP CONTINUE THE FIGHT. AT LEAST FOR A BIT. IT'D GIVE YOU SOMETHING TO TAKE YOUR *MIND* OFF THINGS.

THANKS, CAL, BUT I THINK MY MIND'S BEEN OFF THINGS FOR TOO LONG.

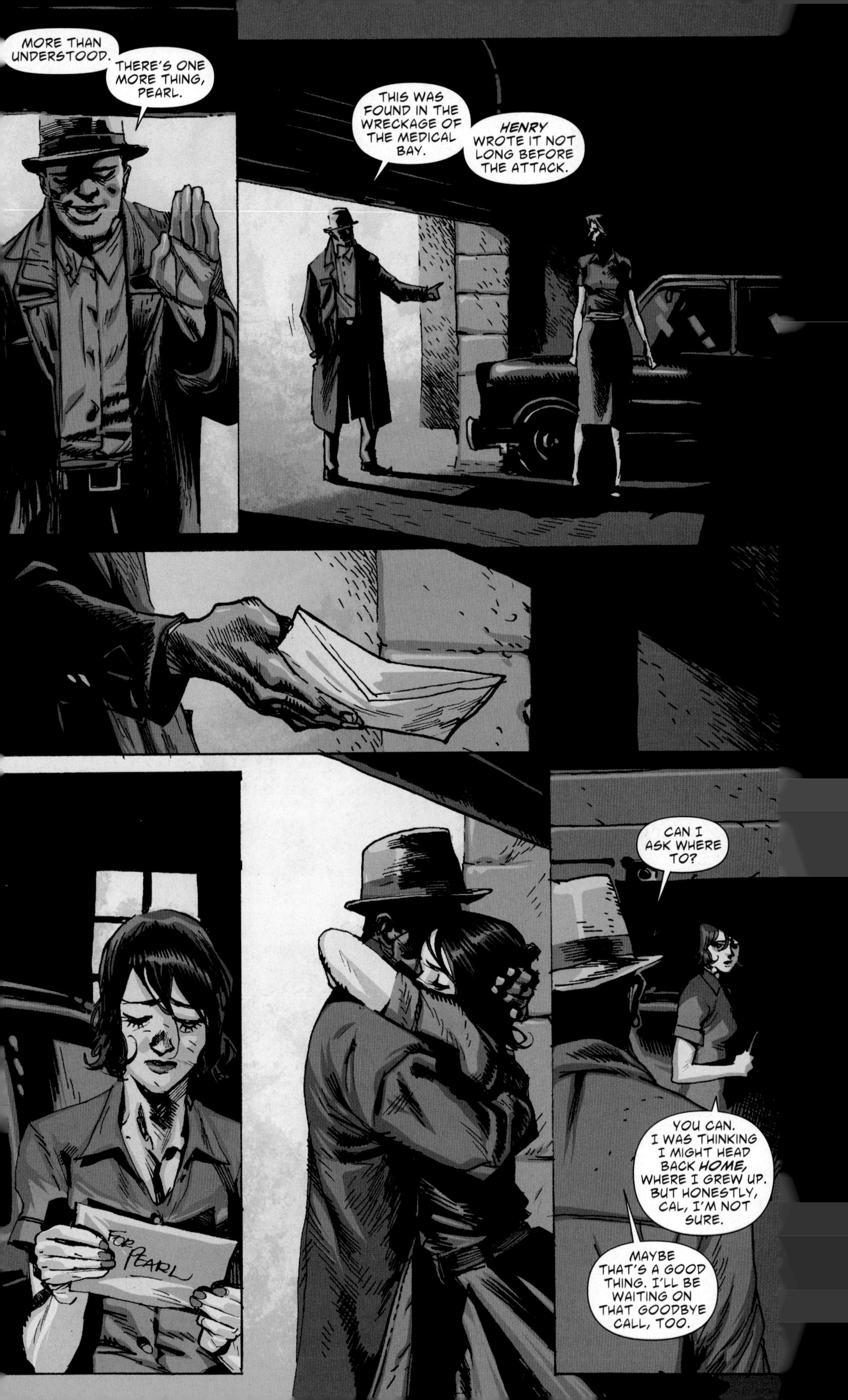
MORE THAN UNDERSTOOD.
THERE'S ONE MORE THING, PEARL.
THIS WAS FOUND IN THE WRECKAGE OF THE MEDICAL BAY.
HENRY WROTE IT NOT LONG BEFORE THE ATTACK.
FOR PEARL
CAN I ASK WHERE TO?
YOU CAN. I WAS THINKING I MIGHT HEAD BACK HOME, WHERE I GREW UP. BUT HONESTLY, CAL, I'M NOT SURE.
MAYBE THAT'S A GOOD THING. I'LL BE WAITING ON THAT GOODBYE CALL, TOO.

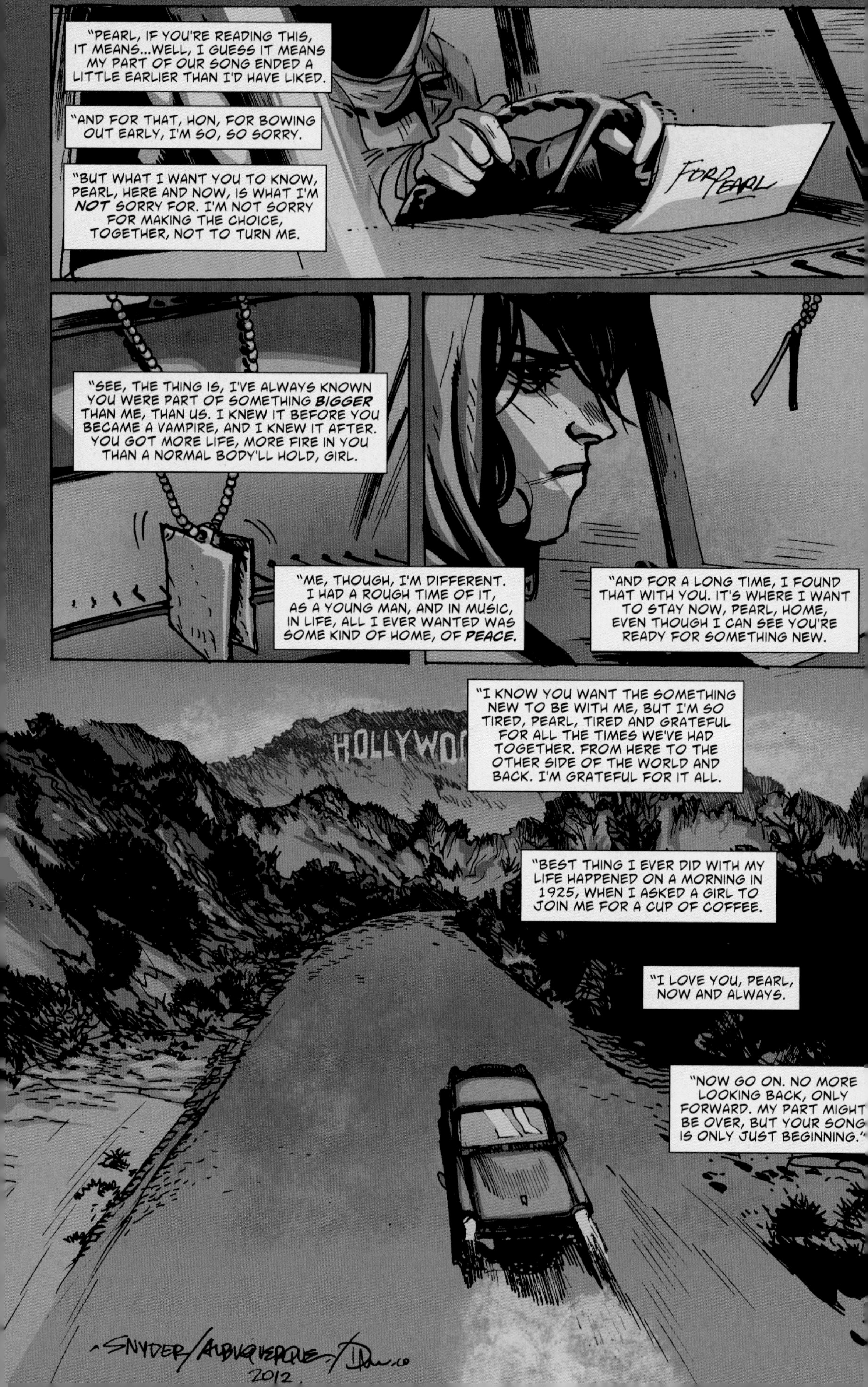
"PEARL, IF YOU'RE READING THIS, IT MEANS...WELL, I GUESS IT MEANS MY PART OF OUR SONG ENDED A LITTLE EARLIER THAN I'D HAVE LIKED.
"AND FOR THAT, HON, FOR BOWING OUT EARLY, I'M SO, SO SORRY.
"BUT WHAT I WANT YOU TO KNOW, PEARL, HERE AND NOW, IS WHAT I'M NOT SORRY FOR. I'M NOT SORRY FOR MAKING THE CHOICE, TOGETHER, NOT TO TURN ME.
FOR PEARL
"SEE, THE THING IS, I'VE ALWAYS KNOWN YOU WERE PART OF SOMETHING BIGGER THAN ME, THAN US. I KNEW IT BEFORE YOU BECAME A VAMPIRE, AND I KNEW IT AFTER. YOU GOT MORE LIFE, MORE FIRE IN YOU THAN A NORMAL BODY'LL HOLD, GIRL.
"ME, THOUGH, I'M DIFFERENT. I HAD A ROUGH TIME OF IT, AS A YOUNG MAN, AND IN MUSIC, IN LIFE, ALL I EVER WANTED WAS SOME KIND OF HOME, OF PEACE.
"AND FOR A LONG TIME, I FOUND THAT WITH YOU. IT'S WHERE I WANT TO STAY NOW, PEARL, HOME, EVEN THOUGH I CAN SEE YOU'RE READY FOR SOMETHING NEW.
"I KNOW YOU WANT THE SOMETHING NEW TO BE WITH ME, BUT I'M SO TIRED, PEARL, TIRED AND GRATEFUL FOR ALL THE TIMES WE'VE HAD TOGETHER. FROM HERE TO THE OTHER SIDE OF THE WORLD AND BACK. I'M GRATEFUL FOR IT ALL.
HOLLYWO
"BEST THING I EVER DID WITH MY LIFE HAPPENED ON A MORNING IN 1925, WHEN I ASKED A GIRL TO JOIN ME FOR A CUP OF COFFEE.
"I LOVE YOU, PEARL, NOW AND ALWAYS.
"NOW GO ON. NO MORE LOOKING BACK, ONLY FORWARD. MY PART MIGHT BE OVER, BUT YOUR SONG IS ONLY JUST BEGINNING."
SNYDER/ALBUQUERQUE 2012

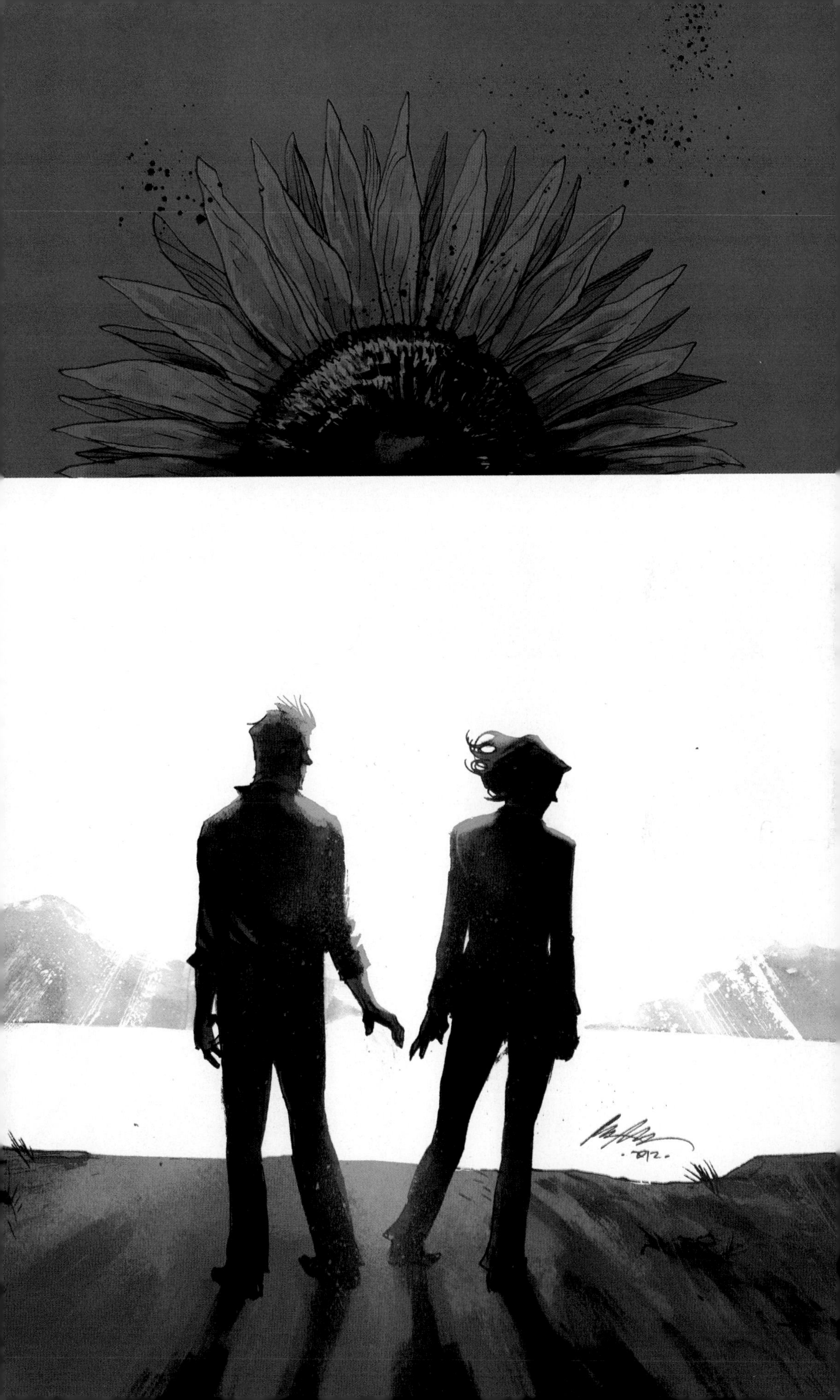

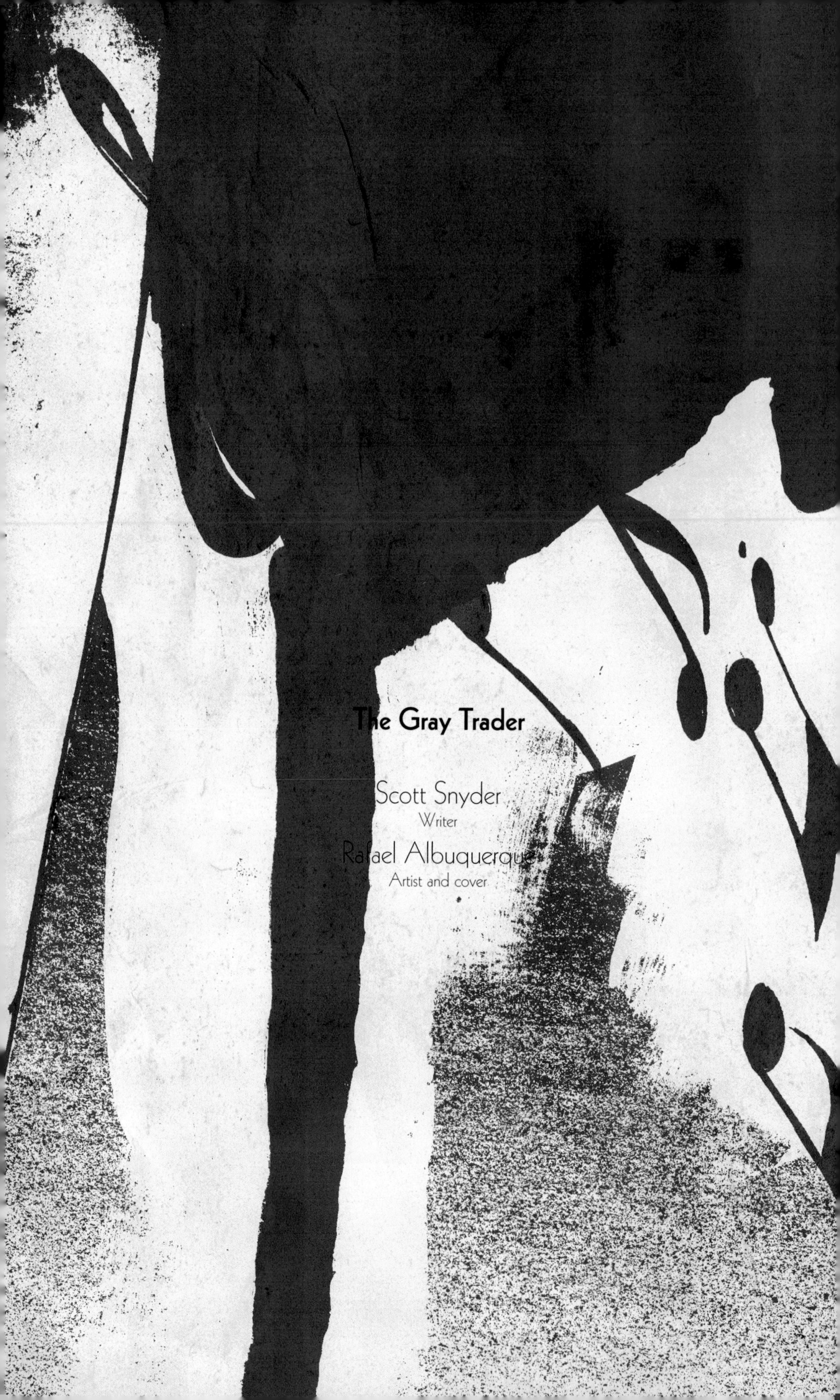

The Gray Trader

Scott Snyder
Writer

Rafael Albuquerque
Artist and cover

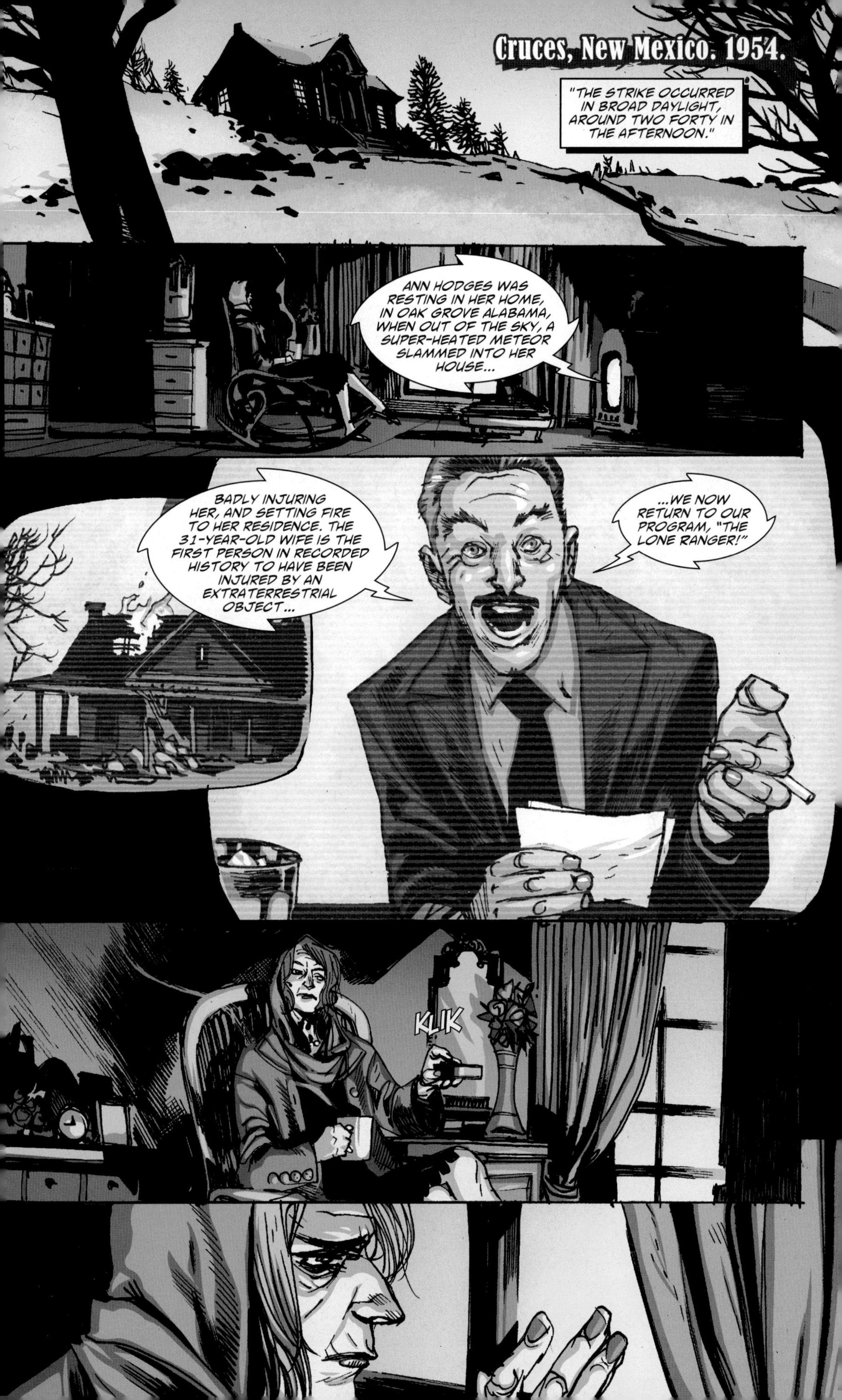

Cruces, New Mexico. 1954.
"THE STRIKE OCCURRED IN BROAD DAYLIGHT, AROUND TWO FORTY IN THE AFTERNOON."
ANN HODGES WAS RESTING IN HER HOME, IN OAK GROVE ALABAMA, WHEN OUT OF THE SKY, A SUPER-HEATED METEOR SLAMMED INTO HER HOUSE...
BADLY INJURING HER, AND SETTING FIRE TO HER RESIDENCE. THE 31-YEAR-OLD WIFE IS THE FIRST PERSON IN RECORDED HISTORY TO HAVE BEEN INJURED BY AN EXTRATERRESTRIAL OBJECT...
...WE NOW RETURN TO OUR PROGRAM, "THE LONE RANGER!"
KLIK

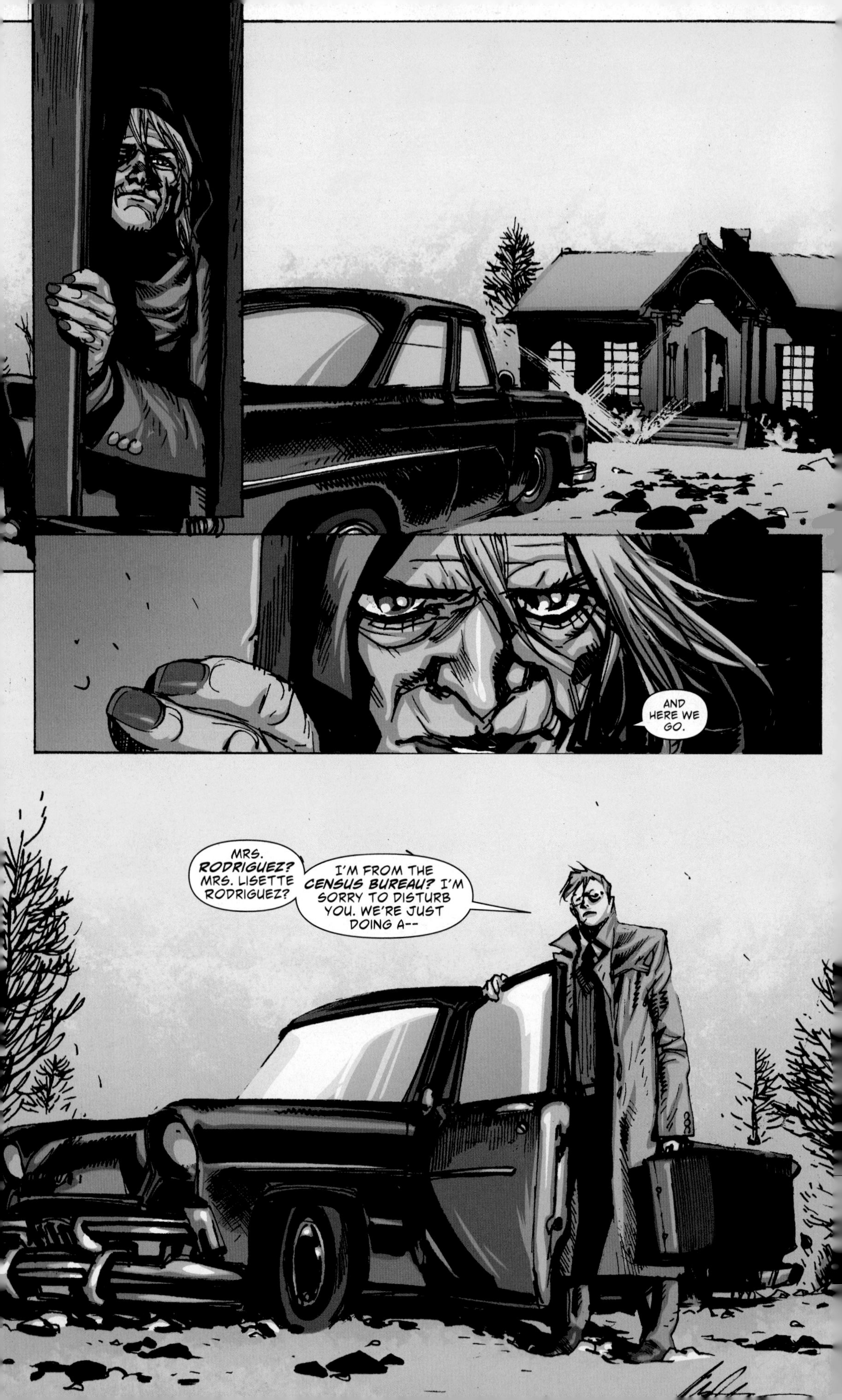

AND HERE WE GO.
MRS. RODRIGUEZ? MRS. LISETTE RODRIGUEZ?
I'M FROM THE CENSUS BUREAU? I'M SORRY TO DISTURB YOU. WE'RE JUST DOING A--

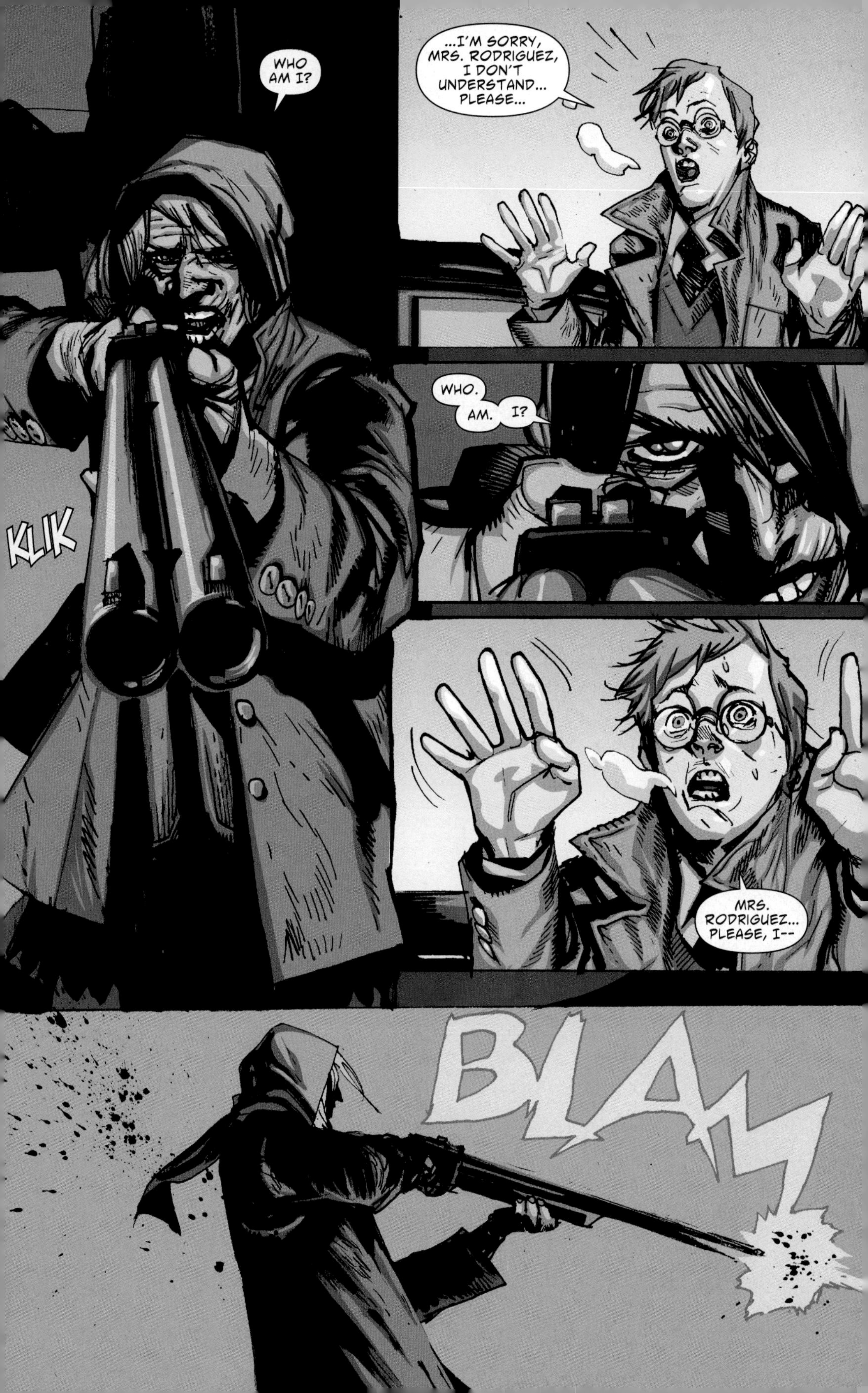
WHO AM I?
KLIK
...I'M SORRY, MRS. RODRIGUEZ, I DON'T UNDERSTAND... PLEASE...
WHO. AM. I?
MRS. RODRIGUEZ... PLEASE, I--
BLAM

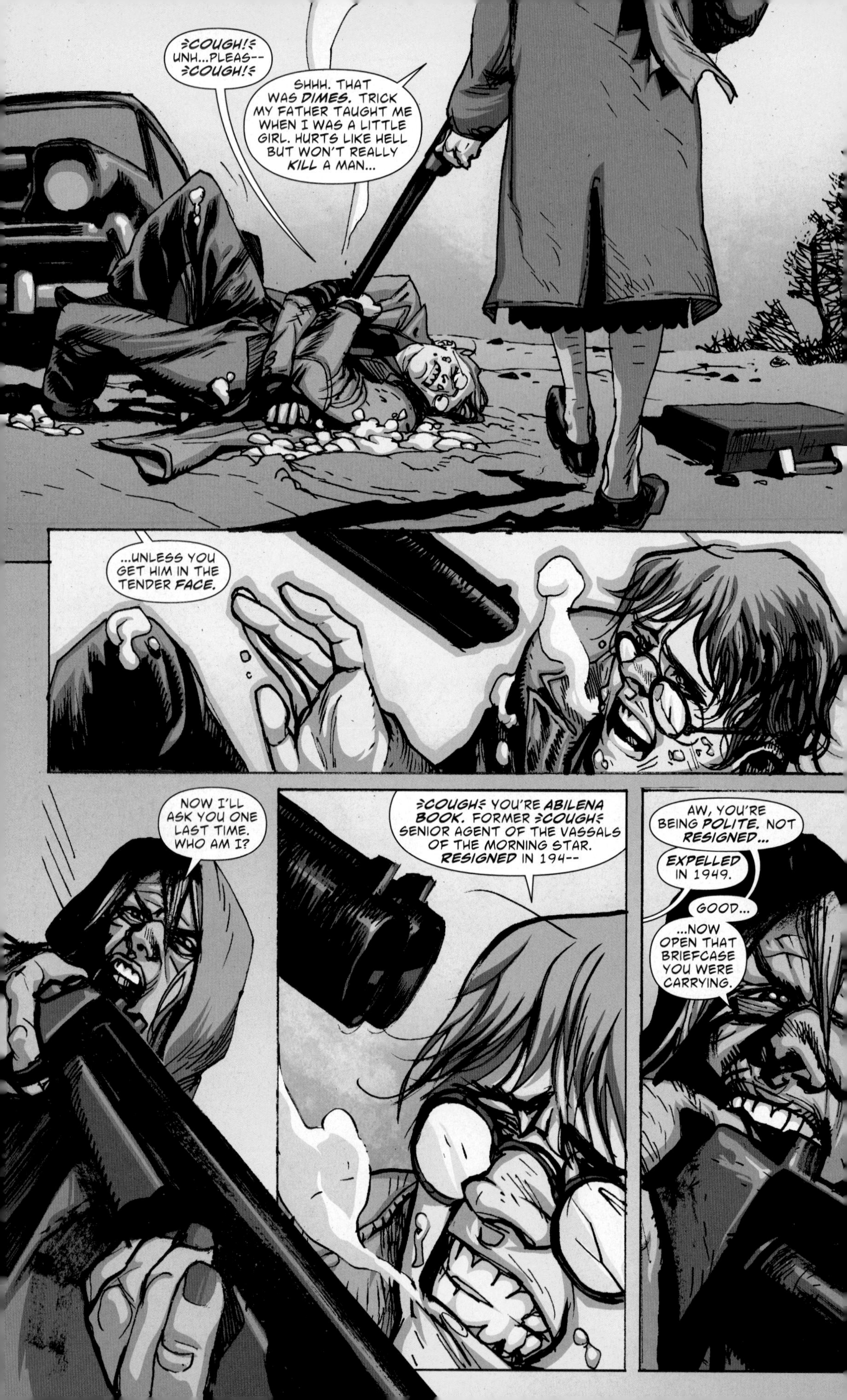

COUGH! UNH...PLEAS-- *COUGH!*
SHHH. THAT WAS DIMES. TRICK MY FATHER TAUGHT ME WHEN I WAS A LITTLE GIRL. HURTS LIKE HELL BUT WON'T REALLY KILL A MAN...
...UNLESS YOU GET HIM IN THE TENDER FACE.
NOW I'LL ASK YOU ONE LAST TIME. WHO AM I?
COUGH YOU'RE ABILENA BOOK. FORMER *COUGH* SENIOR AGENT OF THE VASSALS OF THE MORNING STAR. RESIGNED IN 194--
AW, YOU'RE BEING POLITE. NOT RESIGNED...
EXPELLED IN 1949.
GOOD...
...NOW OPEN THAT BRIEFCASE YOU WERE CARRYING.

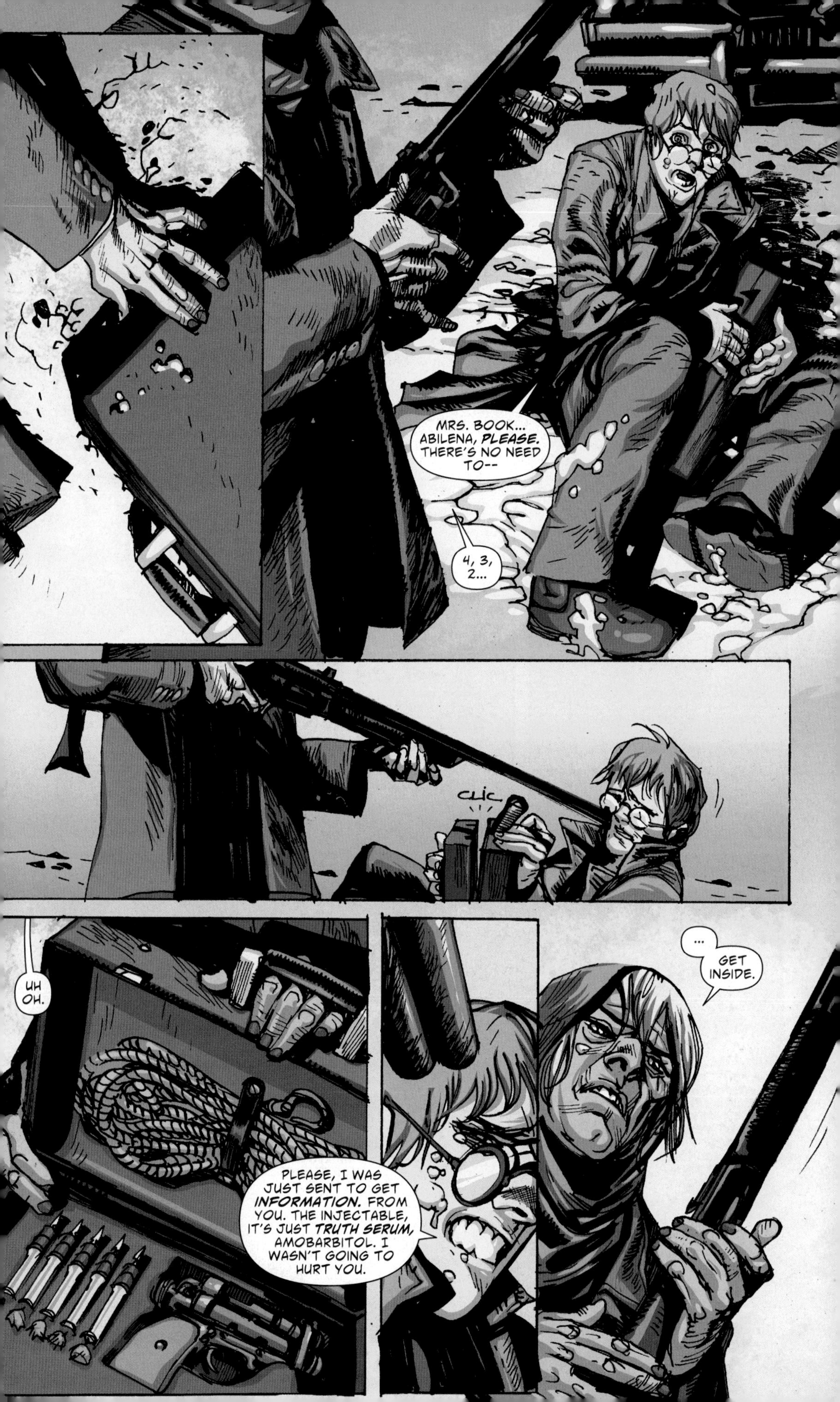
MRS. BOOK... ABILENA, PLEASE. THERE'S NO NEED TO--
4, 3, 2...
CLIC
UH OH.
... GET INSIDE.
PLEASE, I WAS JUST SENT TO GET INFORMATION. FROM YOU. THE INJECTABLE, IT'S JUST TRUTH SERUM, AMOBARBITOL. I WASN'T GOING TO HURT YOU.

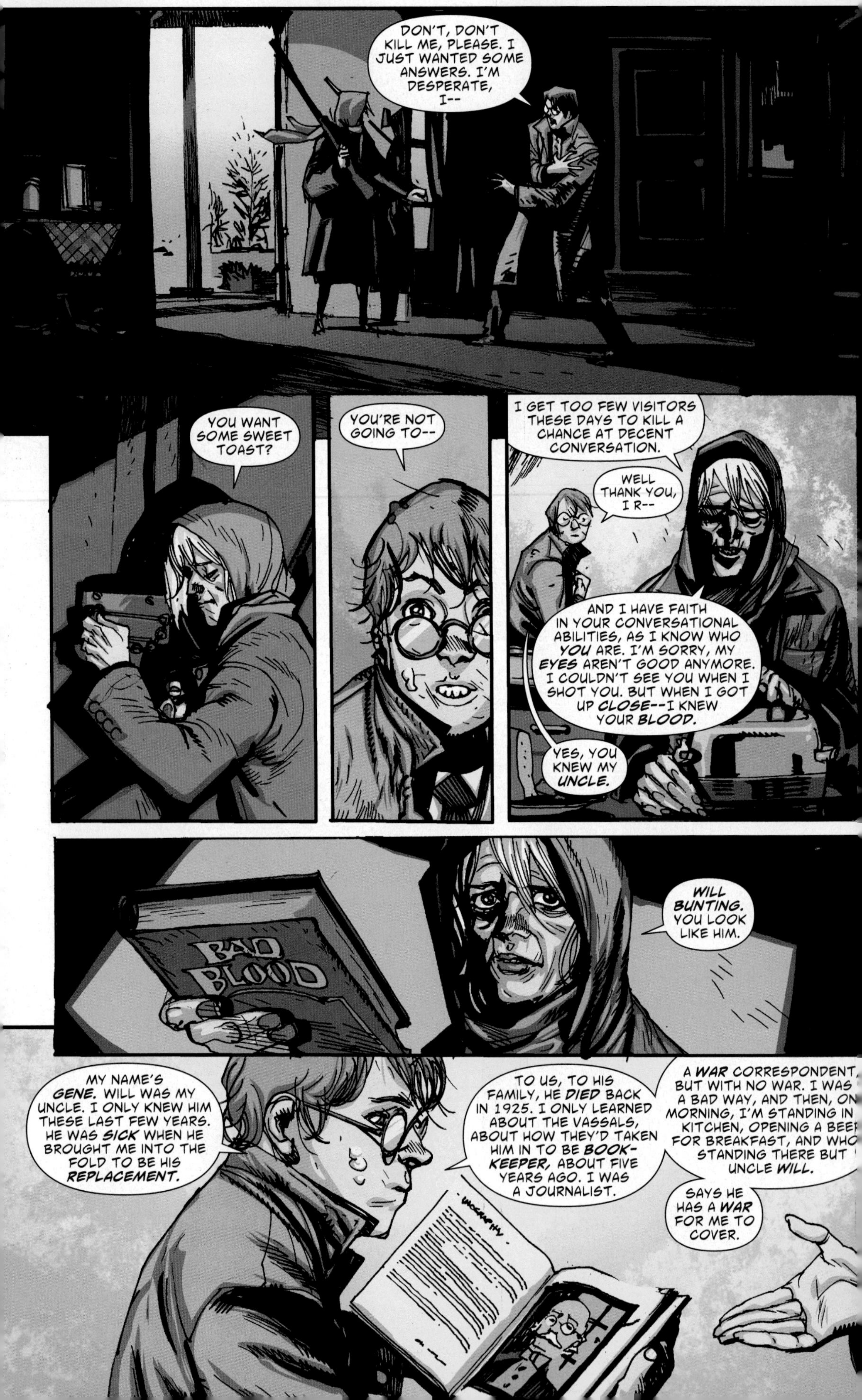

DON'T, DON'T KILL ME, PLEASE. I JUST WANTED SOME ANSWERS. I'M DESPERATE, I--
YOU WANT SOME SWEET TOAST?
YOU'RE NOT GOING TO--
I GET TOO FEW VISITORS THESE DAYS TO KILL A CHANCE AT DECENT CONVERSATION.
WELL THANK YOU, I R--
AND I HAVE FAITH IN YOUR CONVERSATIONAL ABILITIES, AS I KNOW WHO YOU ARE. I'M SORRY, MY EYES AREN'T GOOD ANYMORE. I COULDN'T SEE YOU WHEN I SHOT YOU. BUT WHEN I GOT UP CLOSE--I KNEW YOUR BLOOD.
YES, YOU KNEW MY UNCLE.
BAD BLOOD
WILL BUNTING. YOU LOOK LIKE HIM.
MY NAME'S GENE. WILL WAS MY UNCLE. I ONLY KNEW HIM THESE LAST FEW YEARS. HE WAS SICK WHEN HE BROUGHT ME INTO THE FOLD TO BE HIS REPLACEMENT.
TO US, TO HIS FAMILY, HE DIED BACK IN 1925. I ONLY LEARNED ABOUT THE VASSALS, ABOUT HOW THEY'D TAKEN HIM IN TO BE BOOK-KEEPER, ABOUT FIVE YEARS AGO. I WAS A JOURNALIST.
A WAR CORRESPONDENT BUT WITH NO WAR. I WAS A BAD WAY, AND THEN, ON MORNING, I'M STANDING IN KITCHEN, OPENING A BEE FOR BREAKFAST, AND WHO STANDING THERE BUT UNCLE WILL.
SAYS HE HAS A WAR FOR ME TO COVER.

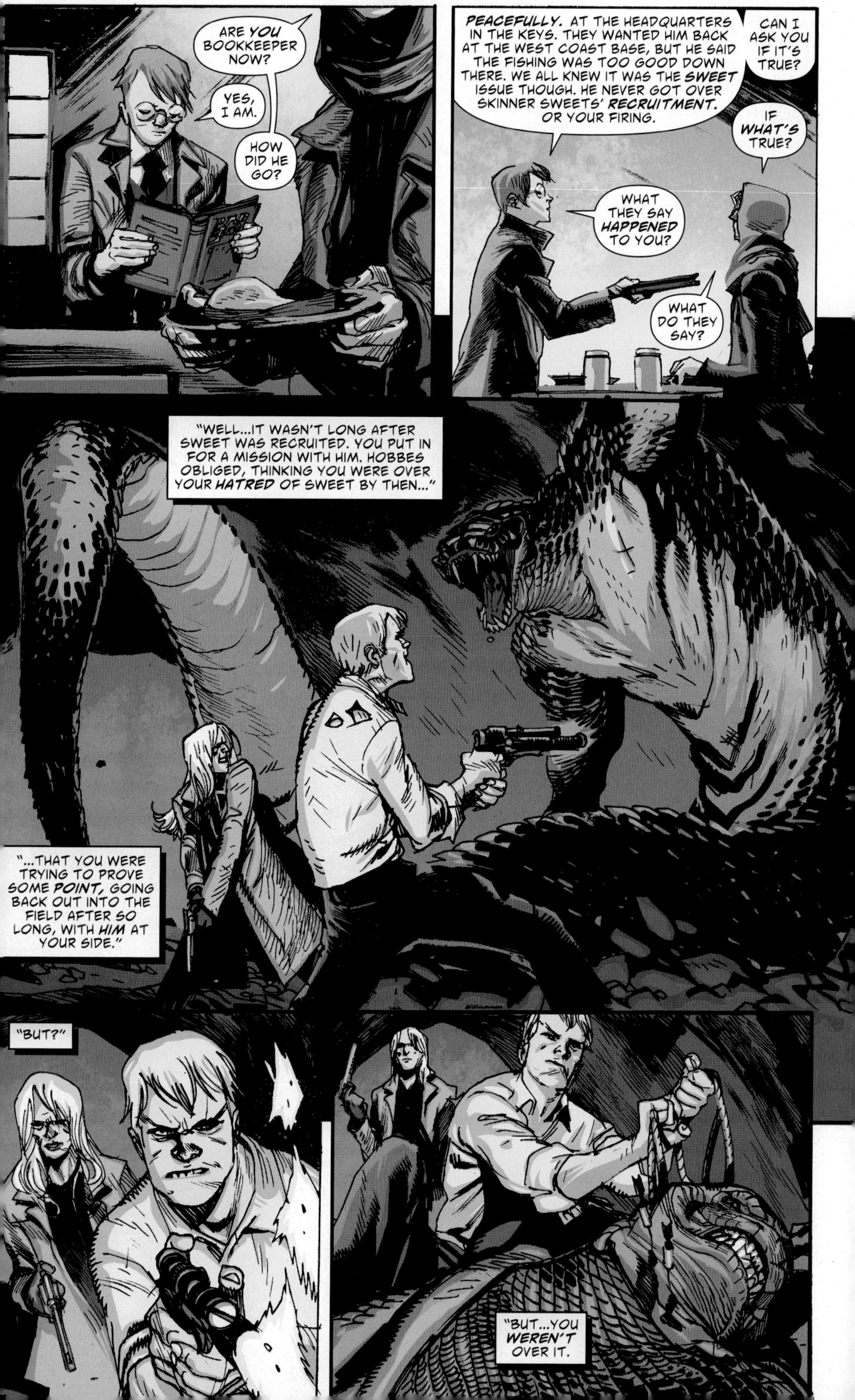
ARE YOU BOOKKEEPER NOW?
YES, I AM.
HOW DID HE GO?
PEACEFULLY. AT THE HEADQUARTERS IN THE KEYS. THEY WANTED HIM BACK AT THE WEST COAST BASE, BUT HE SAID THE FISHING WAS TOO GOOD DOWN THERE. WE ALL KNEW IT WAS THE SWEET ISSUE THOUGH. HE NEVER GOT OVER SKINNER SWEETS' RECRUITMENT. OR YOUR FIRING.
CAN I ASK YOU IF IT'S TRUE?
IF WHAT'S TRUE?
WHAT THEY SAY HAPPENED TO YOU?
WHAT DO THEY SAY?
"WELL...IT WASN'T LONG AFTER SWEET WAS RECRUITED. YOU PUT IN FOR A MISSION WITH HIM. HOBBES OBLIGED, THINKING YOU WERE OVER YOUR HATRED OF SWEET BY THEN..."
"...THAT YOU WERE TRYING TO PROVE SOME POINT, GOING BACK OUT INTO THE FIELD AFTER SO LONG, WITH HIM AT YOUR SIDE."
"BUT?"
"BUT...YOU WEREN'T OVER IT.

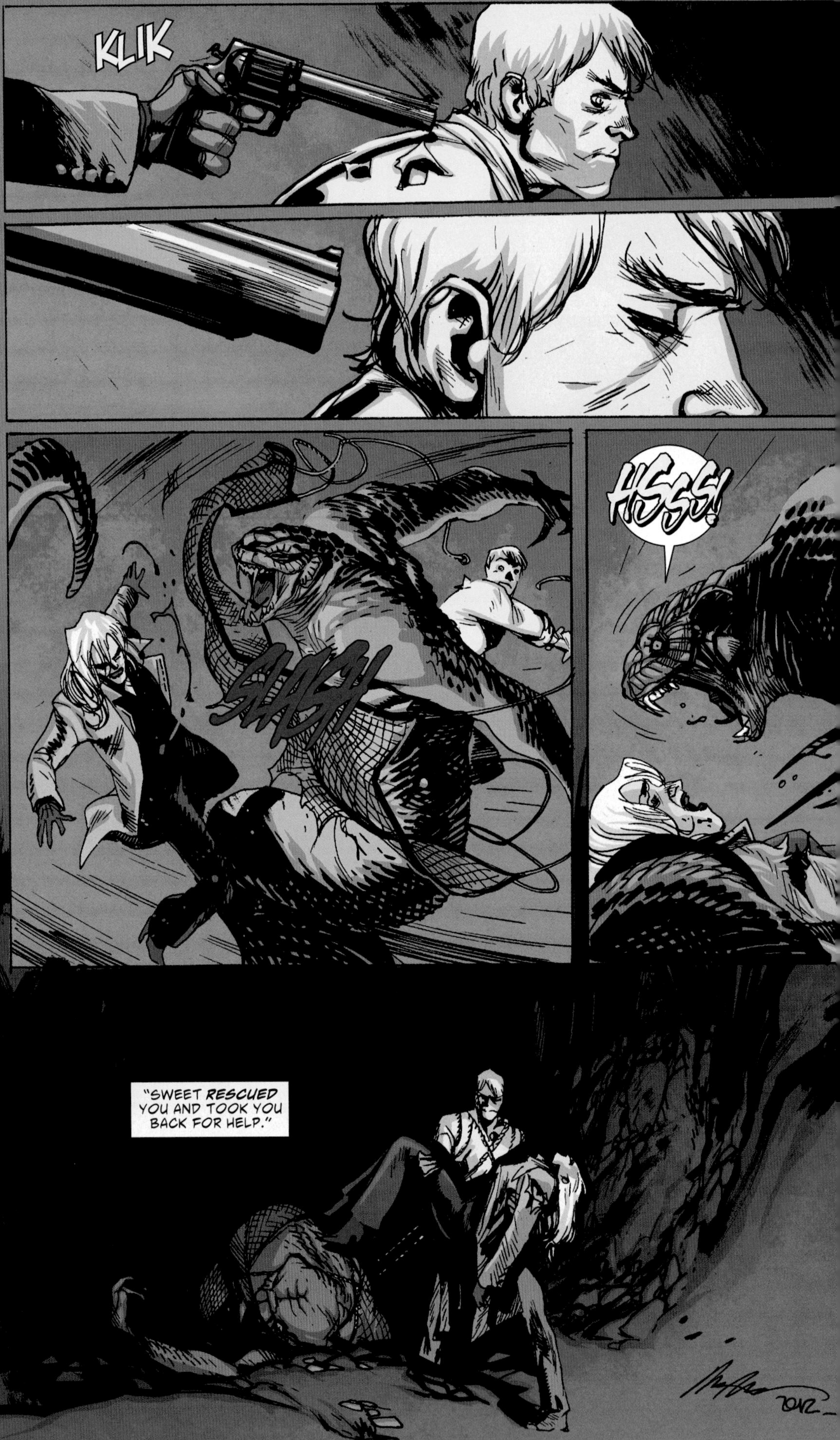
KLIK
HISSS!
SLASH
"SWEET RESCUED YOU AND TOOK YOU BACK FOR HELP."

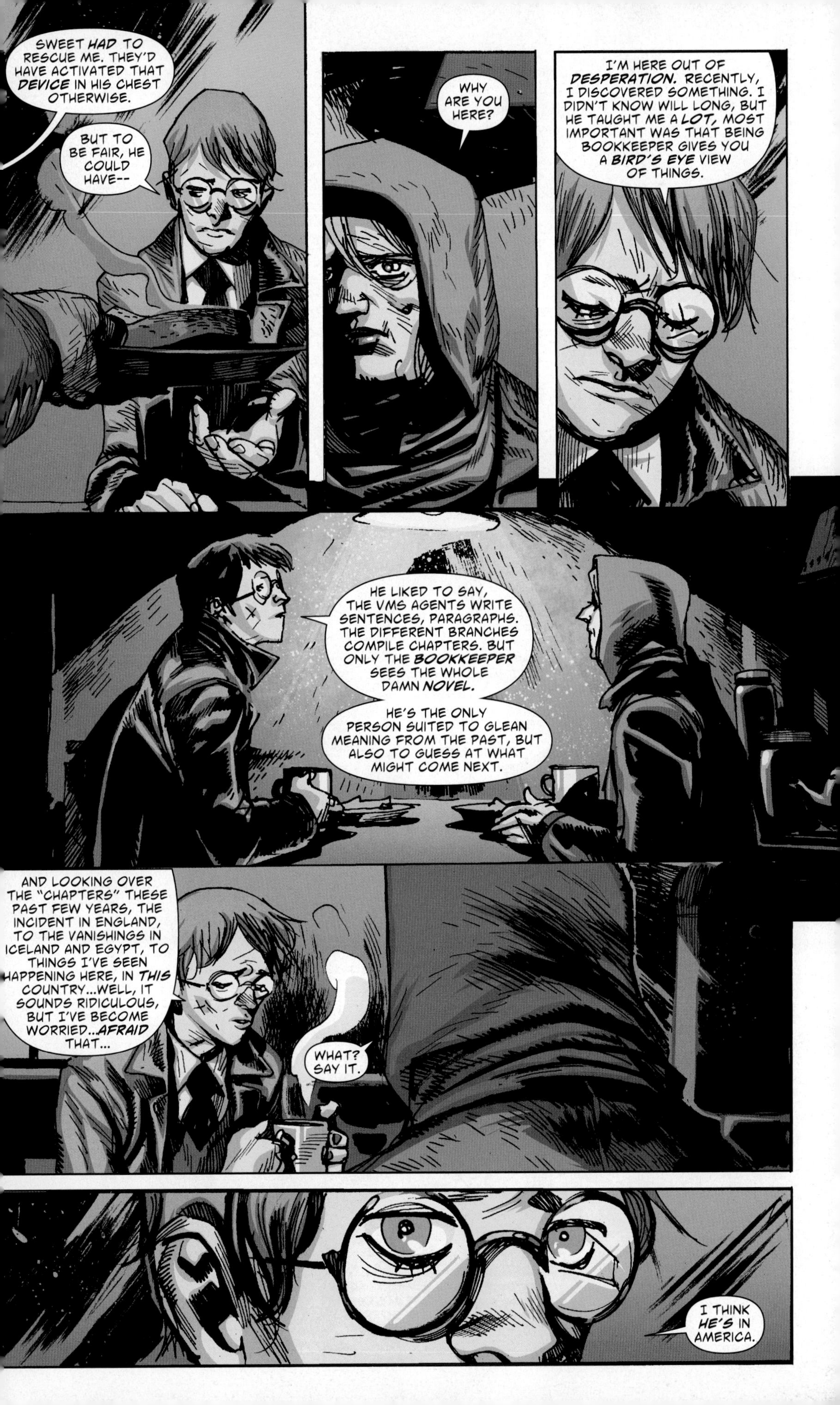
SWEET HAD TO RESCUE ME. THEY'D HAVE ACTIVATED THAT DEVICE IN HIS CHEST OTHERWISE.
BUT TO BE FAIR, HE COULD HAVE--
WHY ARE YOU HERE?
I'M HERE OUT OF DESPERATION. RECENTLY, I DISCOVERED SOMETHING. I DIDN'T KNOW WILL LONG, BUT HE TAUGHT ME A LOT, MOST IMPORTANT WAS THAT BEING BOOKKEEPER GIVES YOU A BIRD'S EYE VIEW OF THINGS.
HE LIKED TO SAY, THE VMS AGENTS WRITE SENTENCES, PARAGRAPHS. THE DIFFERENT BRANCHES COMPILE CHAPTERS. BUT ONLY THE BOOKKEEPER SEES THE WHOLE DAMN NOVEL.
HE'S THE ONLY PERSON SUITED TO GLEAN MEANING FROM THE PAST, BUT ALSO TO GUESS AT WHAT MIGHT COME NEXT.
AND LOOKING OVER THE "CHAPTERS" THESE PAST FEW YEARS, THE INCIDENT IN ENGLAND, TO THE VANISHINGS IN ICELAND AND EGYPT, TO THINGS I'VE SEEN HAPPENING HERE, IN THIS COUNTRY...WELL, IT SOUNDS RIDICULOUS, BUT I'VE BECOME WORRIED...AFRAID THAT...
WHAT? SAY IT.
I THINK HE'S IN AMERICA.

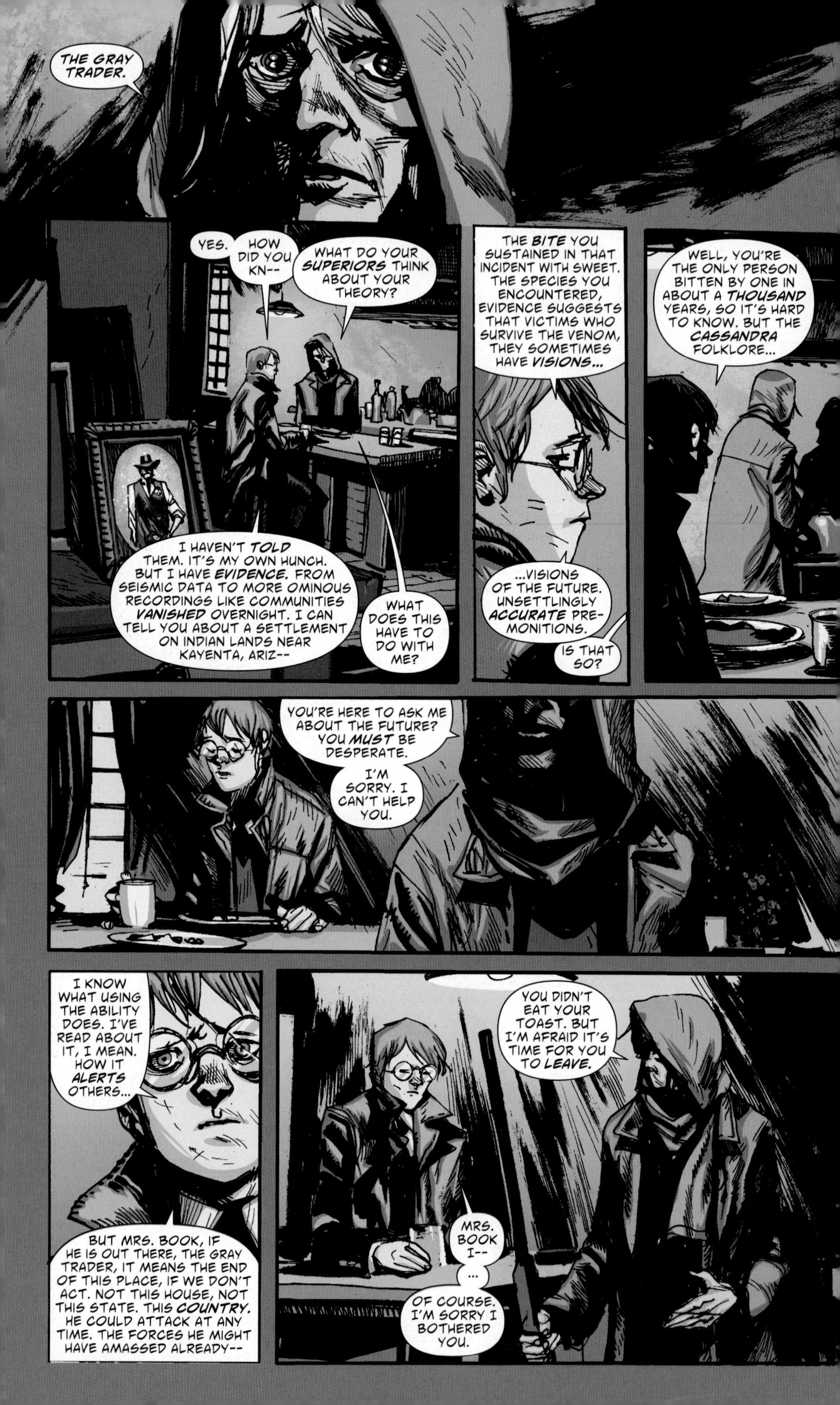

THE GRAY TRADER.
YES.
HOW DID YOU KN--
WHAT DO YOUR SUPERIORS THINK ABOUT YOUR THEORY?
I HAVEN'T TOLD THEM. IT'S MY OWN HUNCH. BUT I HAVE EVIDENCE. FROM SEISMIC DATA TO MORE OMINOUS RECORDINGS LIKE COMMUNITIES VANISHED OVERNIGHT. I CAN TELL YOU ABOUT A SETTLEMENT ON INDIAN LANDS NEAR KAYENTA, ARIZ--
WHAT DOES THIS HAVE TO DO WITH ME?
THE BITE YOU SUSTAINED IN THAT INCIDENT WITH SWEET. THE SPECIES YOU ENCOUNTERED, EVIDENCE SUGGESTS THAT VICTIMS WHO SURVIVE THE VENOM, THEY SOMETIMES HAVE VISIONS...
...VISIONS OF THE FUTURE. UNSETTLINGLY ACCURATE PREMONITIONS.
IS THAT SO?
WELL, YOU'RE THE ONLY PERSON BITTEN BY ONE IN ABOUT A THOUSAND YEARS, SO IT'S HARD TO KNOW. BUT THE CASSANDRA FOLKLORE...
YOU'RE HERE TO ASK ME ABOUT THE FUTURE? YOU MUST BE DESPERATE.
I'M SORRY. I CAN'T HELP YOU.
I KNOW WHAT USING THE ABILITY DOES. I'VE READ ABOUT IT, I MEAN. HOW IT ALERTS OTHERS...
BUT MRS. BOOK, IF HE IS OUT THERE, THE GRAY TRADER, IT MEANS THE END OF THIS PLACE, IF WE DON'T ACT. NOT THIS HOUSE, NOT THIS STATE. THIS COUNTRY. HE COULD ATTACK AT ANY TIME. THE FORCES HE MIGHT HAVE AMASSED ALREADY--
YOU DIDN'T EAT YOUR TOAST. BUT I'M AFRAID IT'S TIME FOR YOU TO LEAVE.
MRS. BOOK I--
...
OF COURSE. I'M SORRY I BOTHERED YOU.

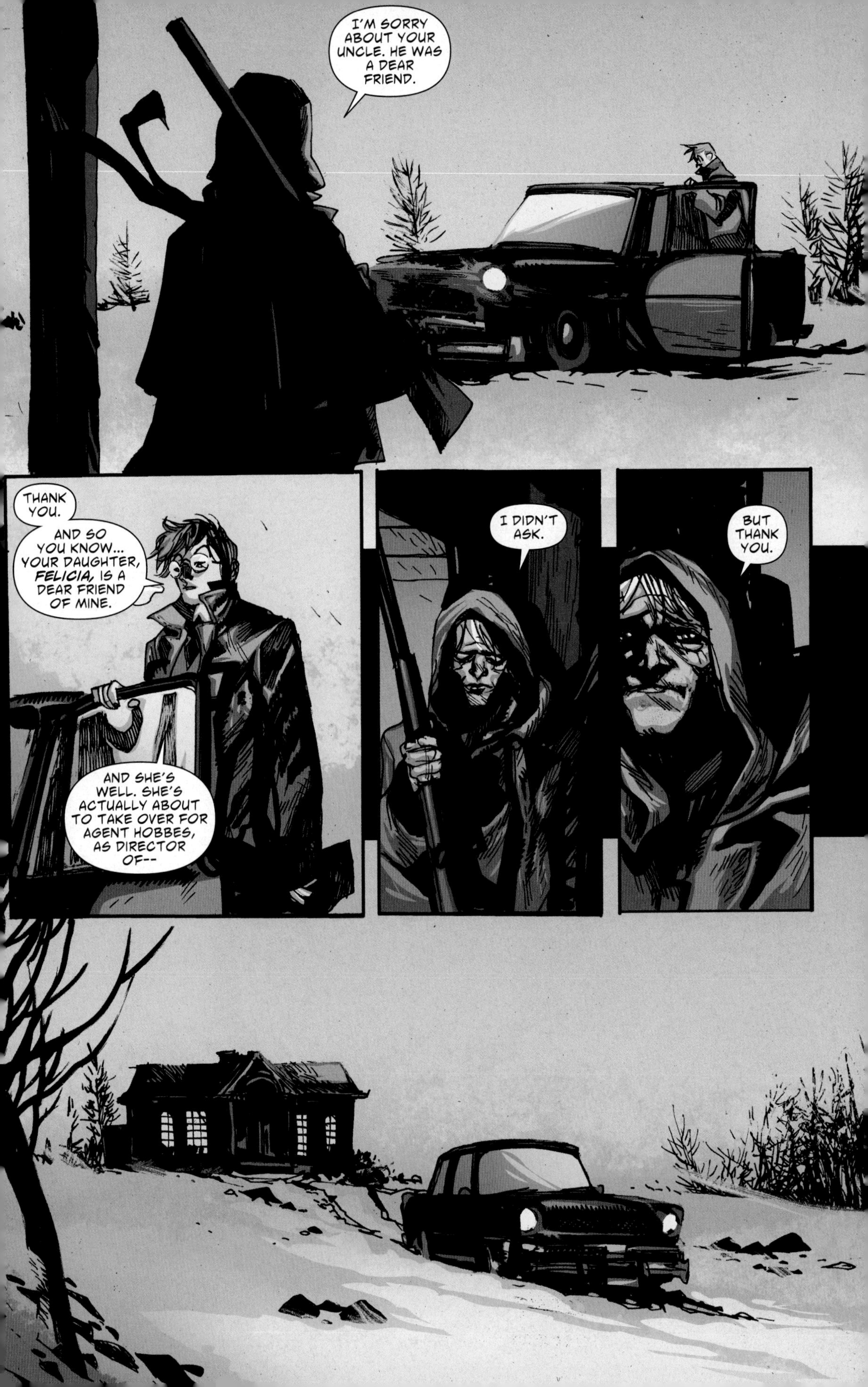
I'M SORRY ABOUT YOUR UNCLE. HE WAS A DEAR FRIEND.
THANK YOU.
AND SO YOU KNOW... YOUR DAUGHTER, *FELICIA,* IS A DEAR FRIEND OF MINE.
AND SHE'S WELL. SHE'S ACTUALLY ABOUT TO TAKE OVER FOR AGENT HOBBES, AS DIRECTOR OF--
I DIDN'T ASK.
BUT THANK YOU.

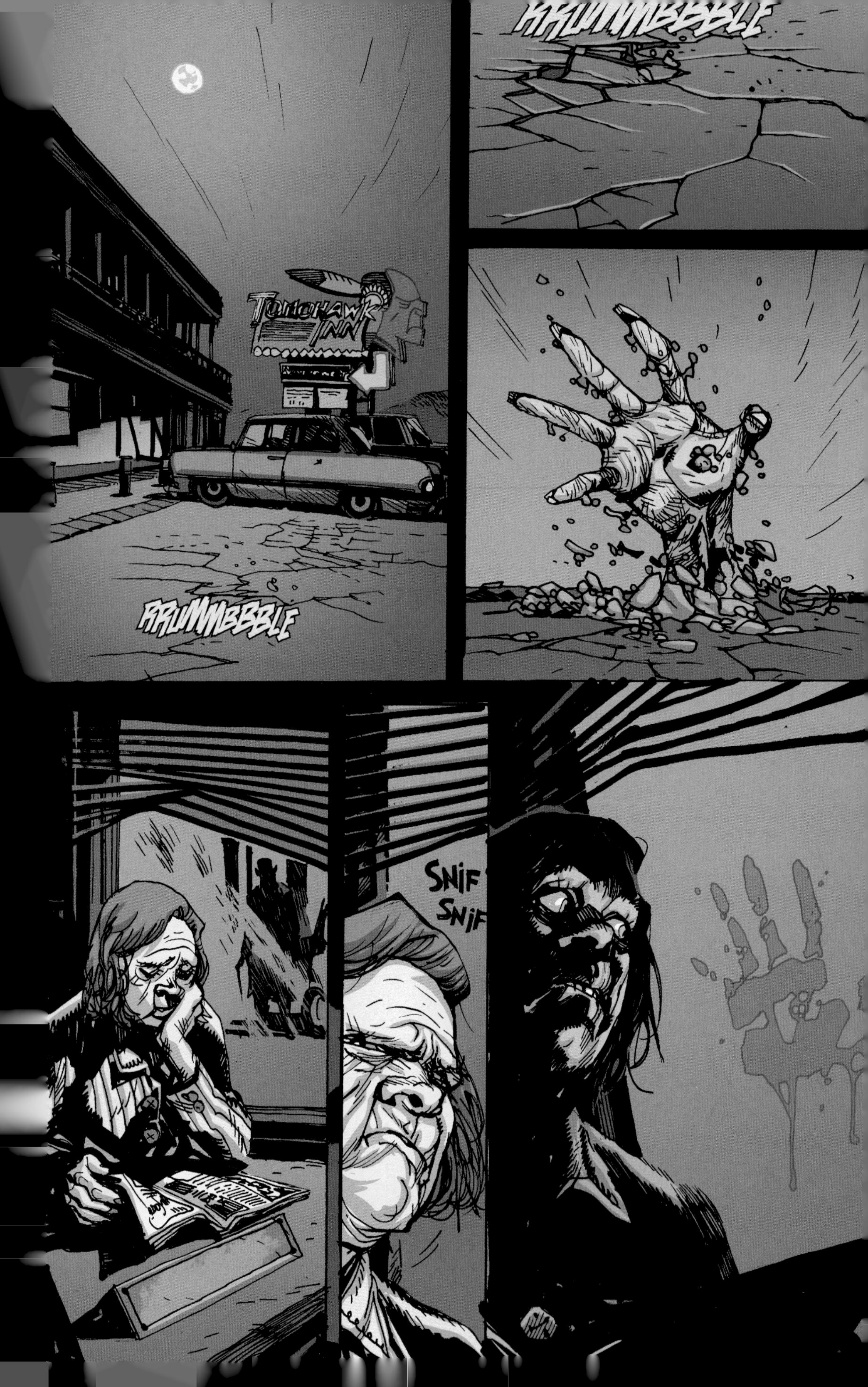
TOMAHAWK INN
RRUMMBBBLE
SNIF
SNIF

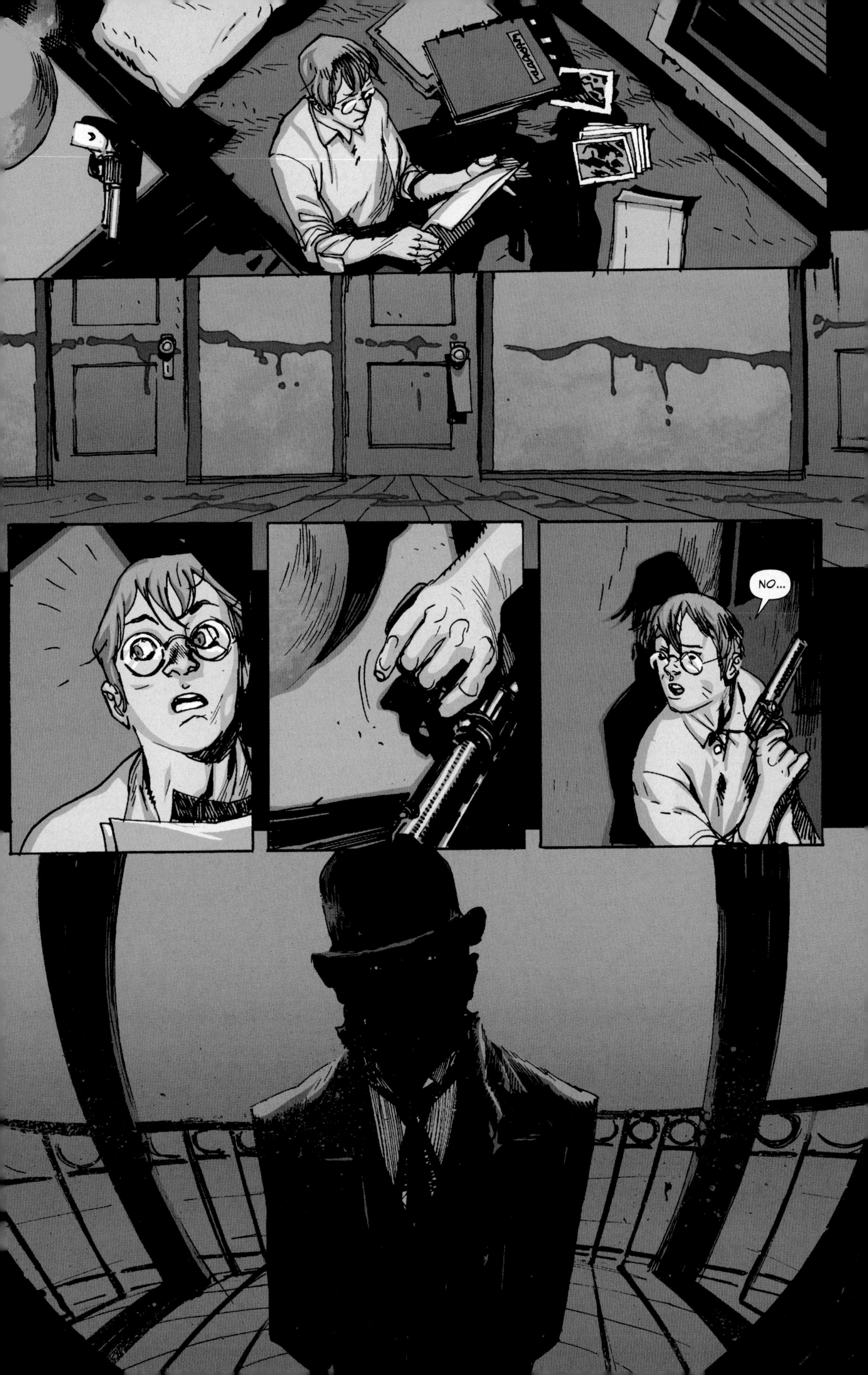
NO...

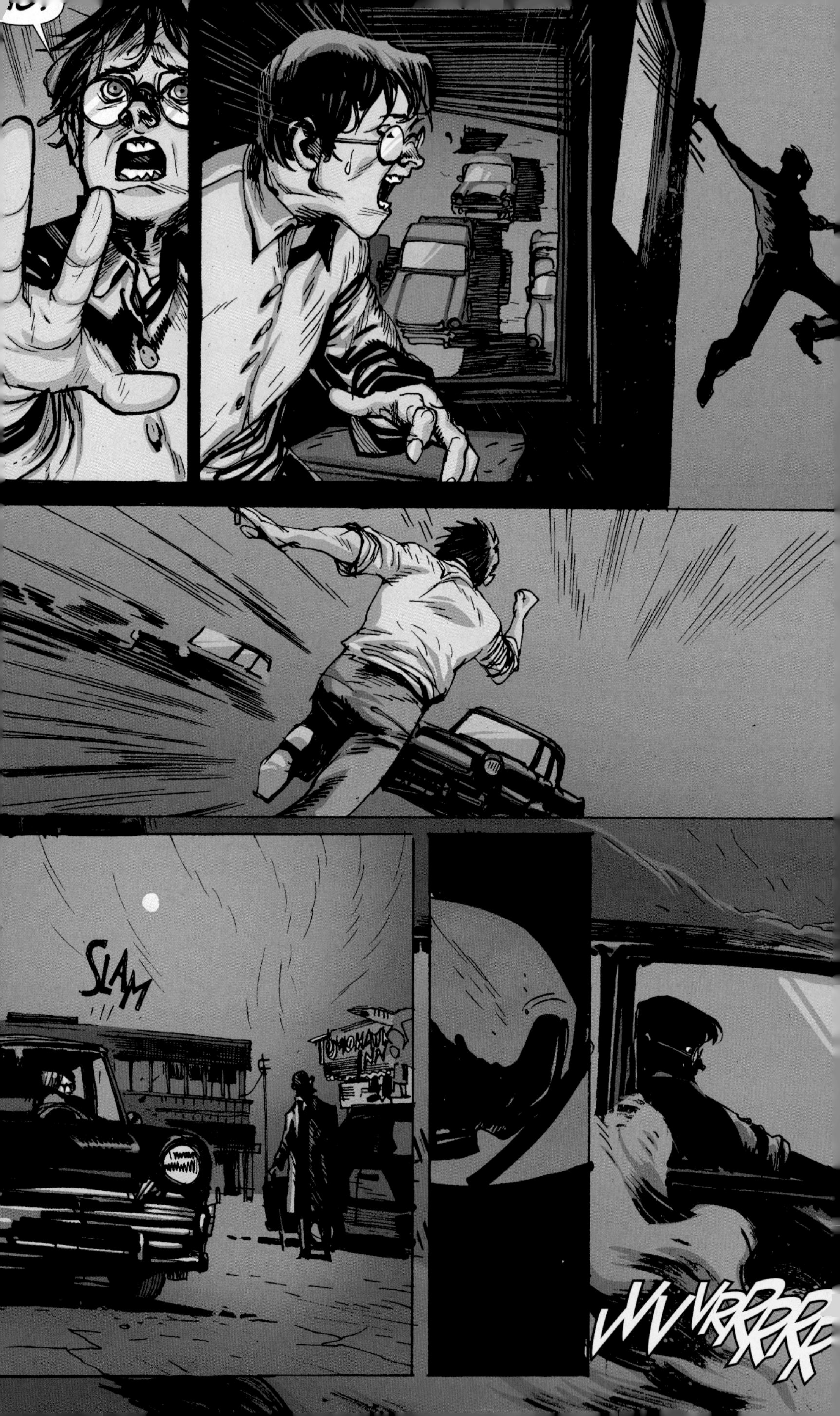
SLAM
TOMOHAWK INN

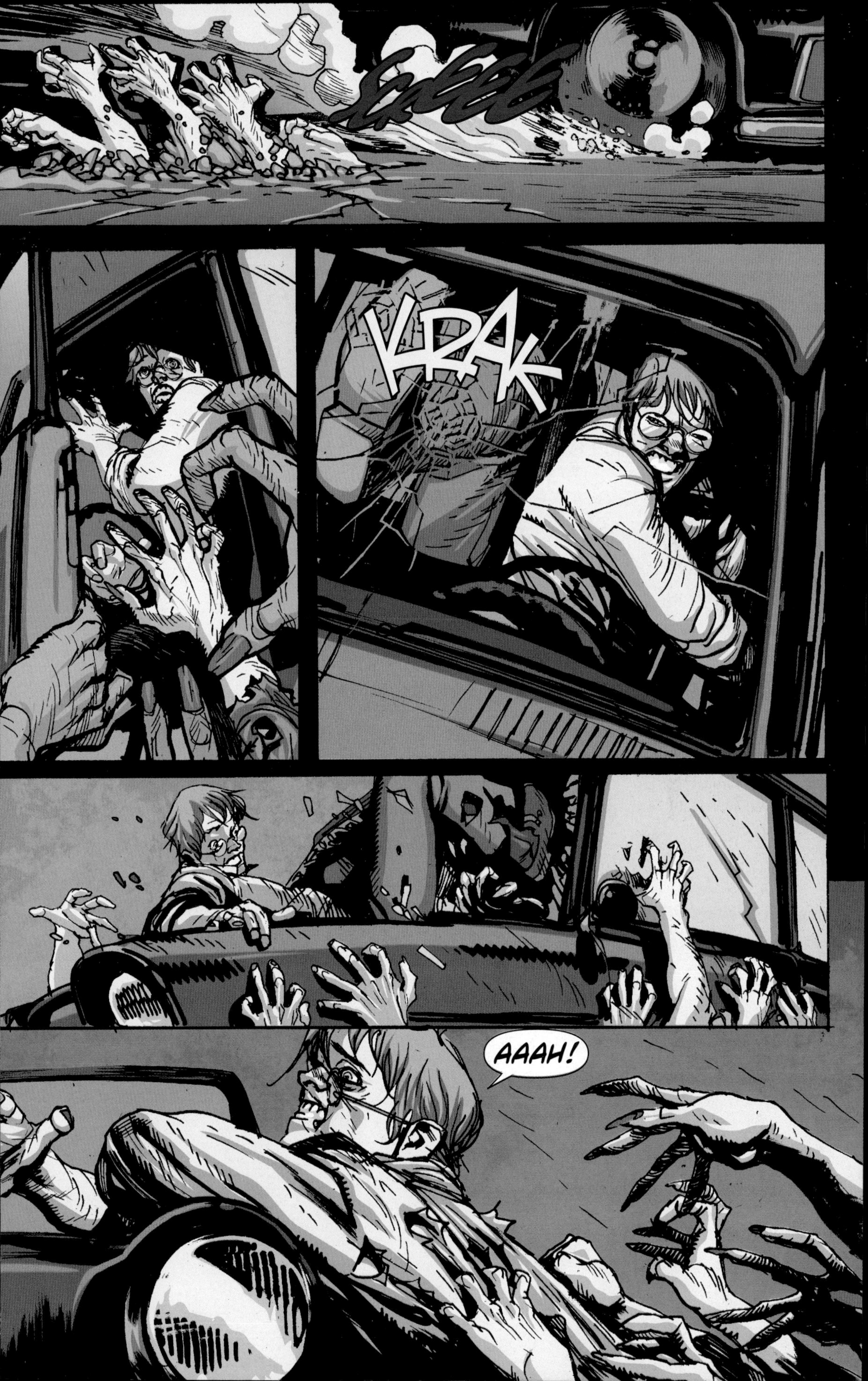

KRAK
AAAH!

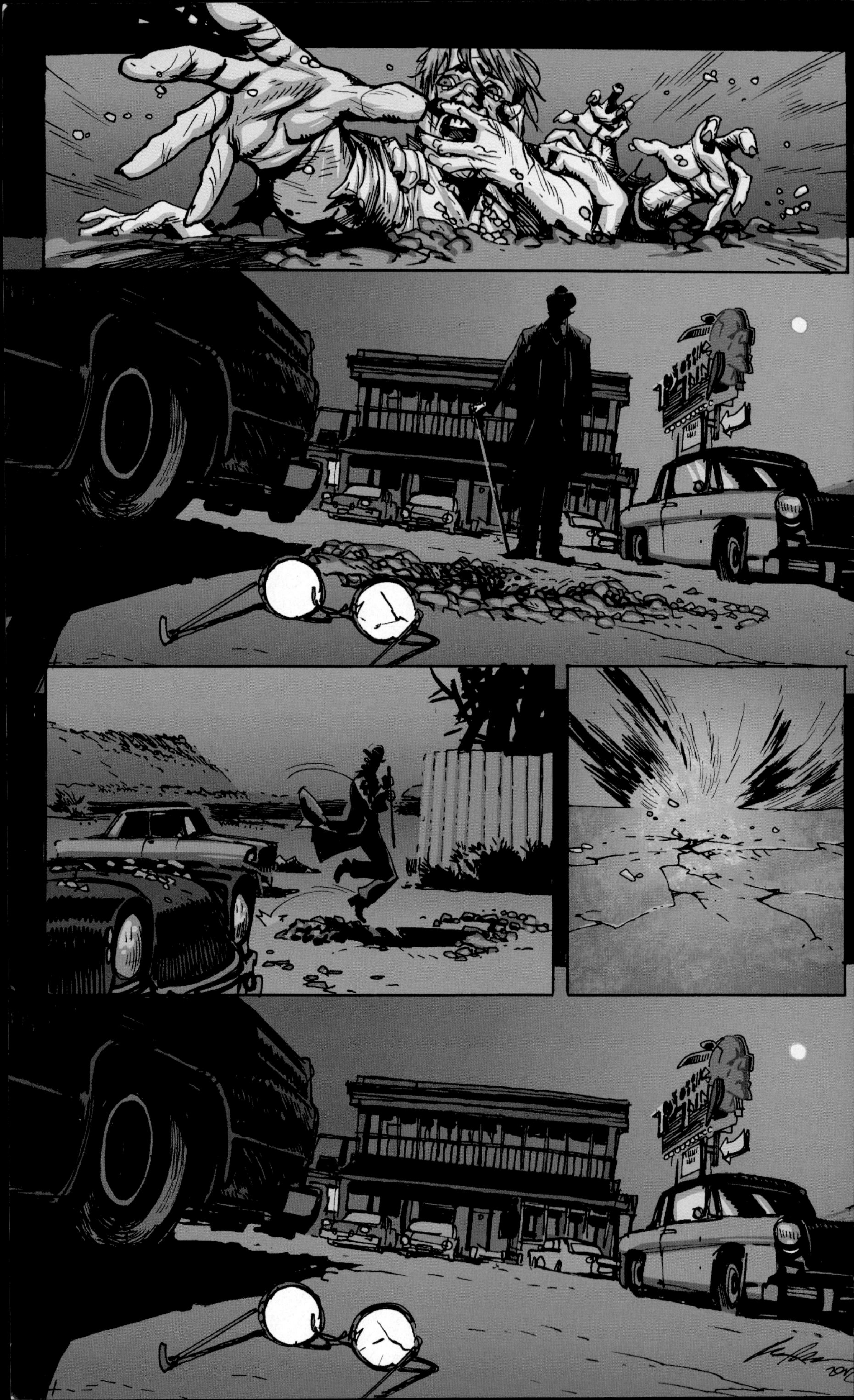

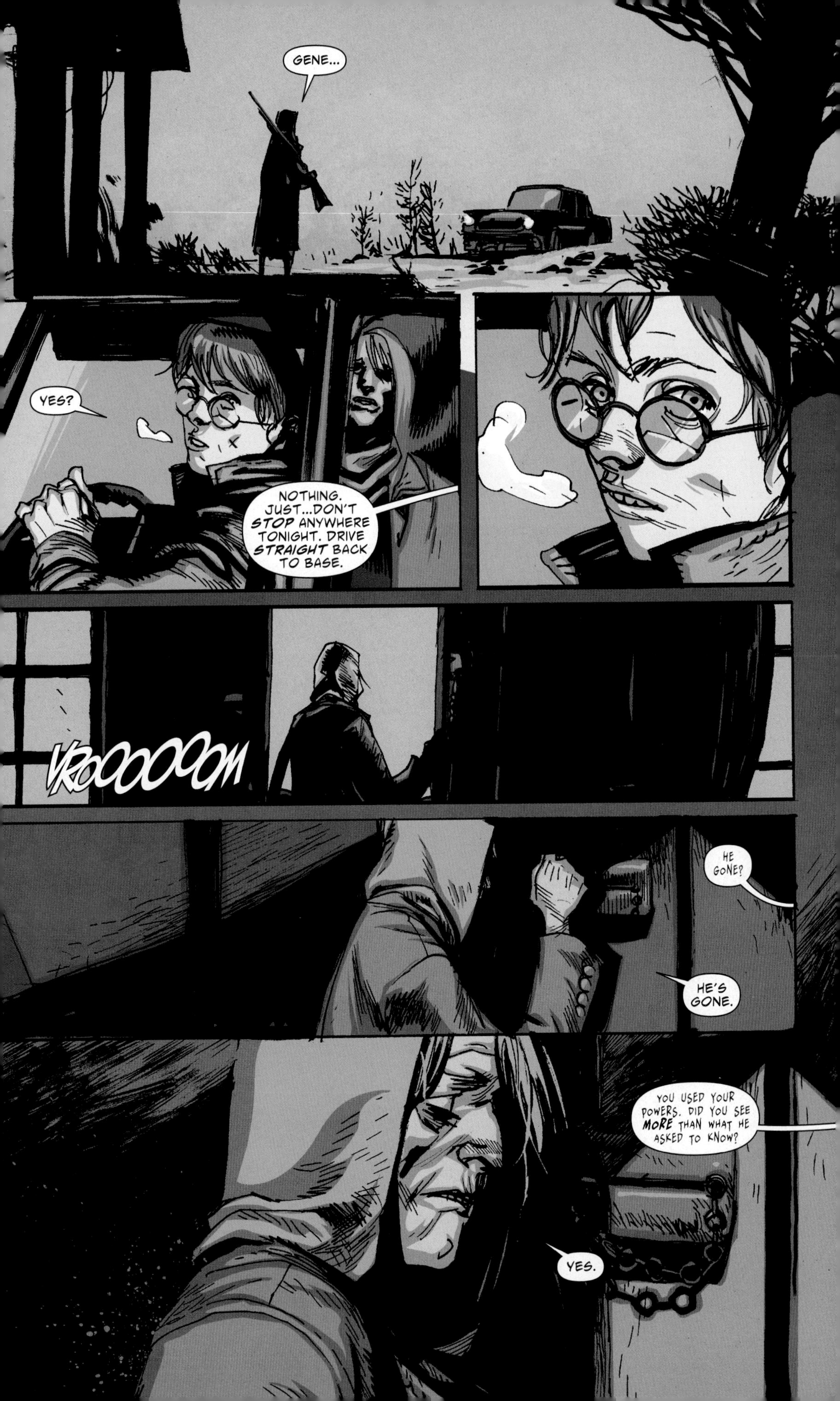
GENE...
YES?
NOTHING. JUST...DON'T STOP ANYWHERE TONIGHT. DRIVE STRAIGHT BACK TO BASE.
VROOOOOOM
HE GONE?
HE'S GONE.
YOU USED YOUR POWERS. DID YOU SEE MORE THAN WHAT HE ASKED TO KNOW?
YES.

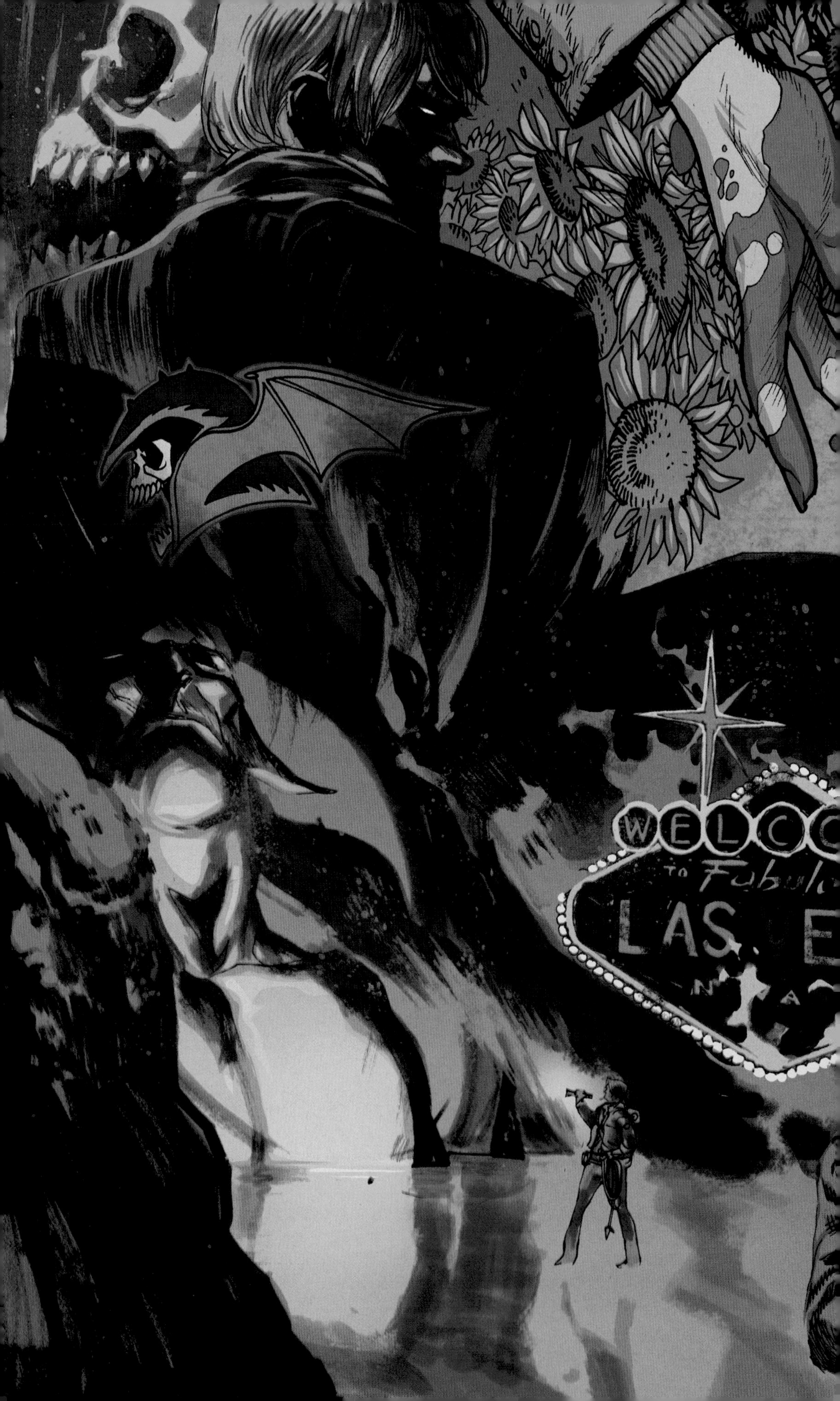
WELC
to Fabul
LAS

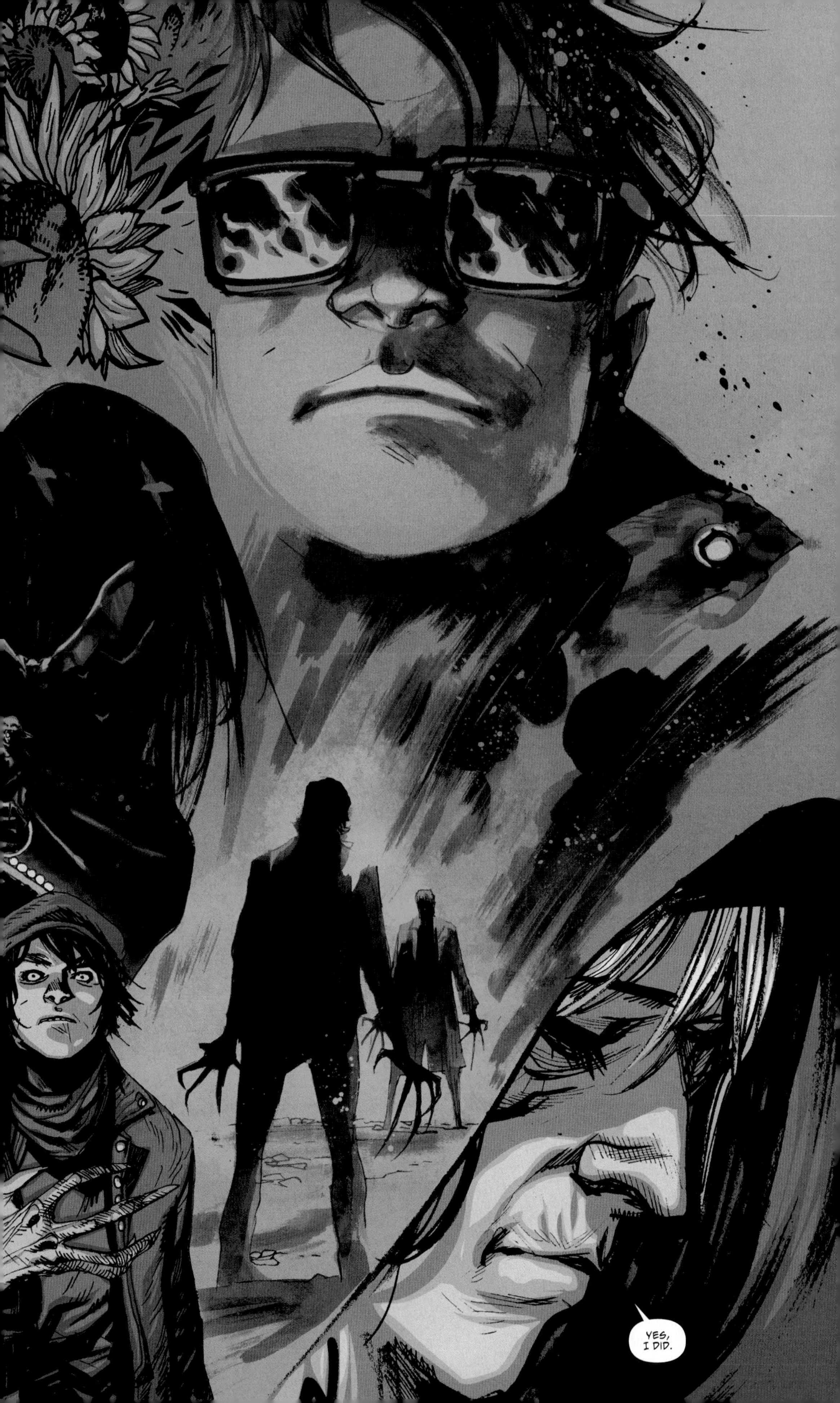
YES, I DID.

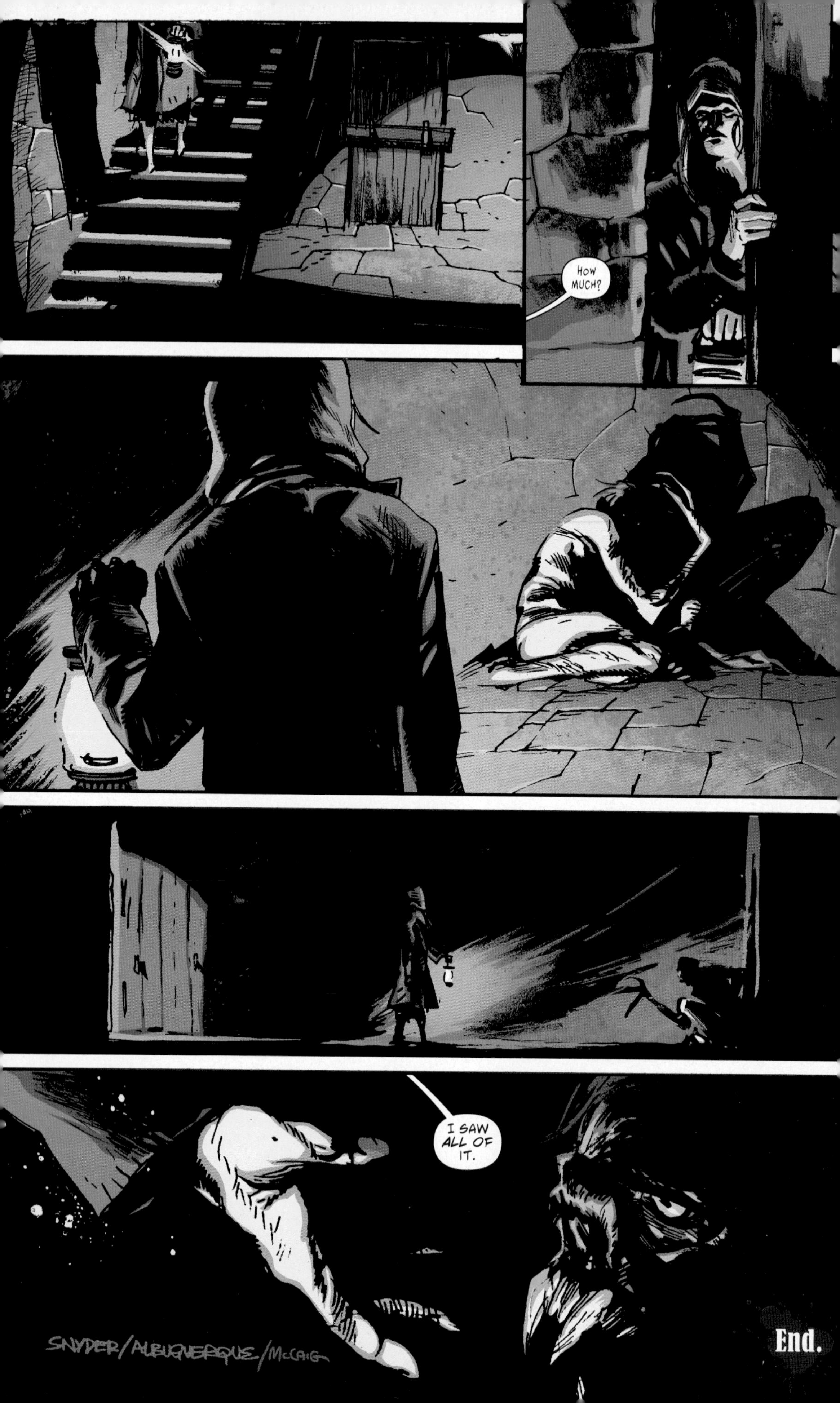
HOW MUCH?
I SAW ALL OF IT.
SNYDER/ALBUQUERQUE/McCAIG
End.

American Vampire #28 variant cover Art by Greg Capullo

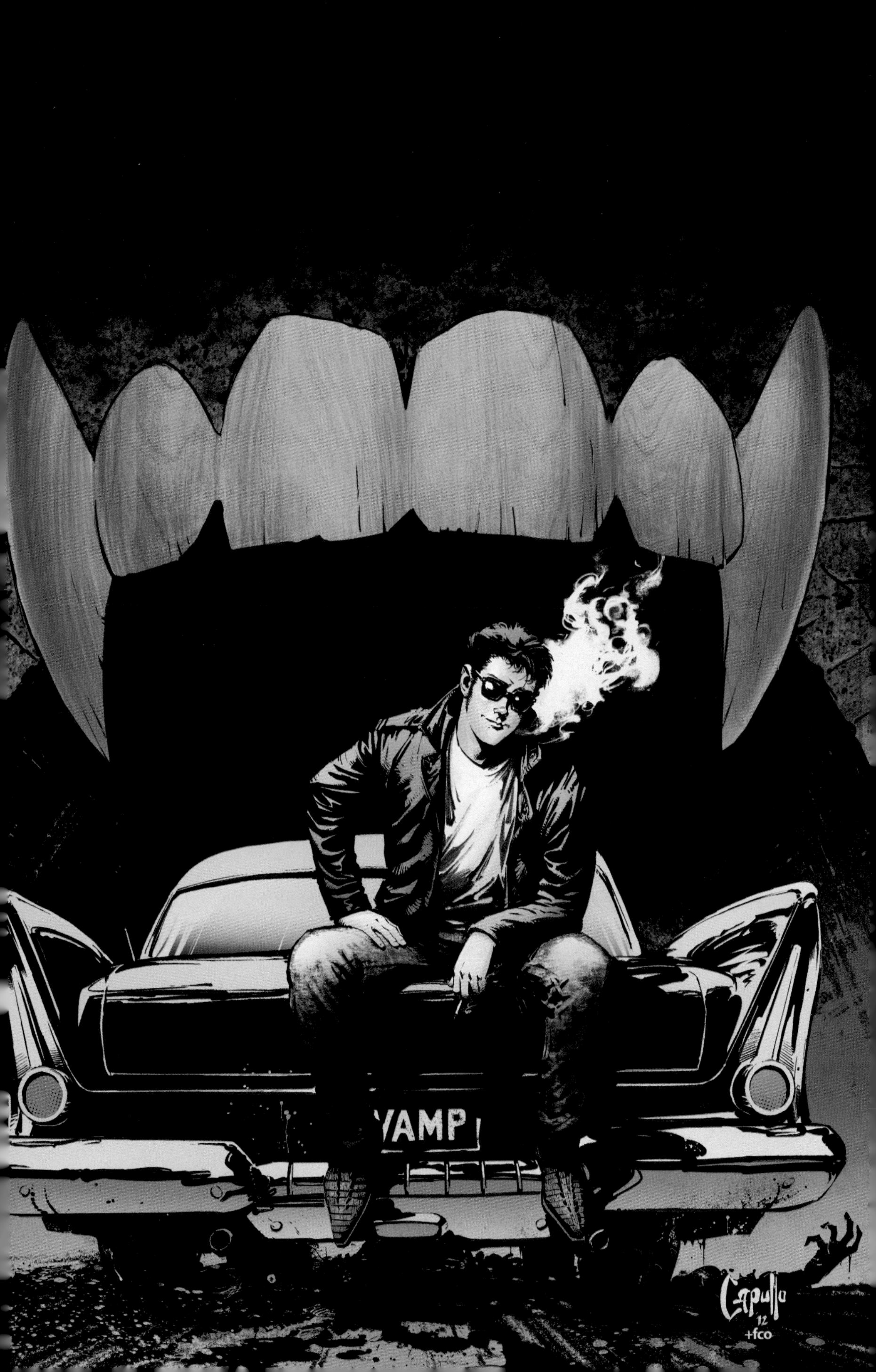
VAMP
Capullo
'12
+fco

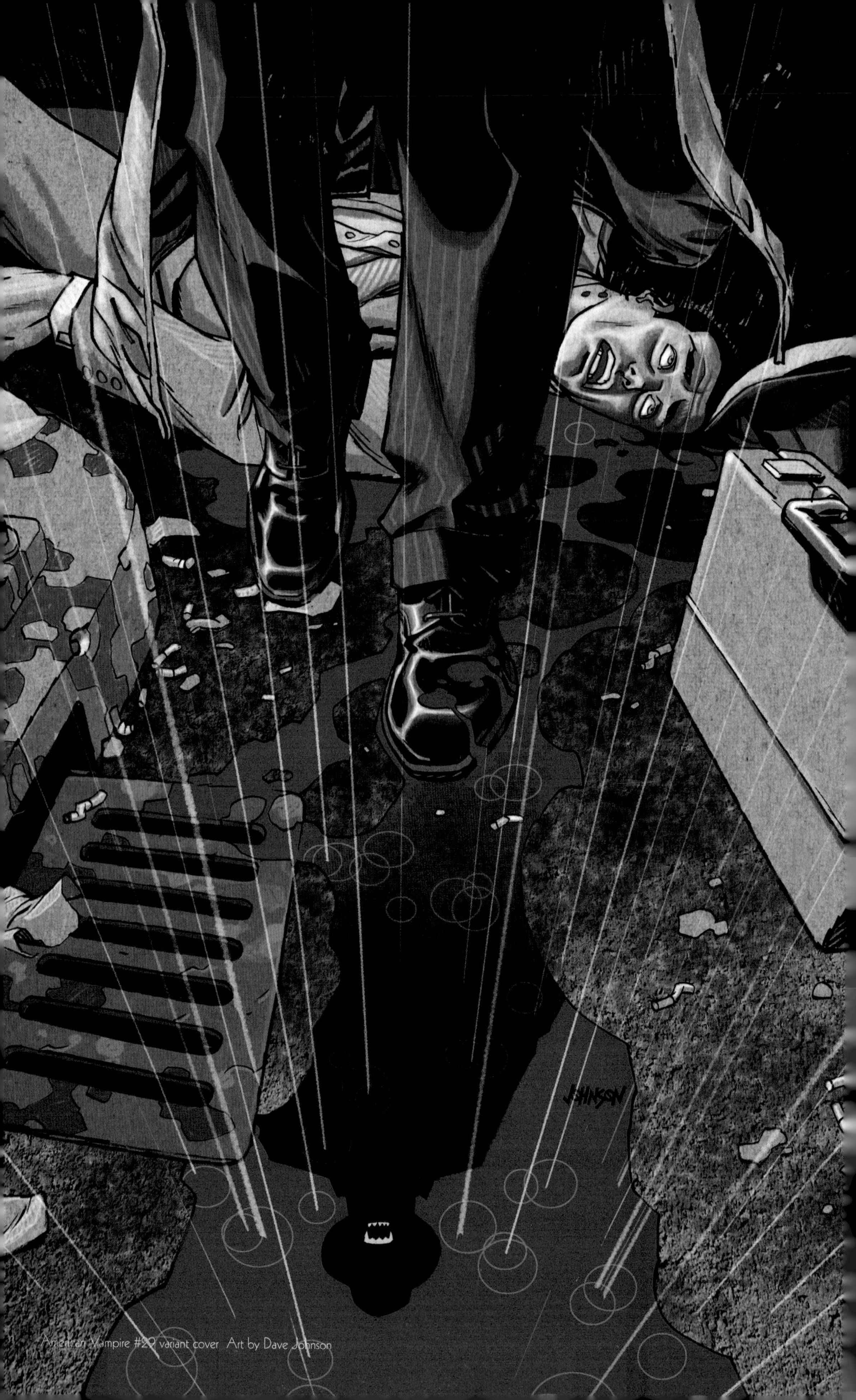
JOHNSON

American Vampire #29 variant cover Art by Dave Johnson

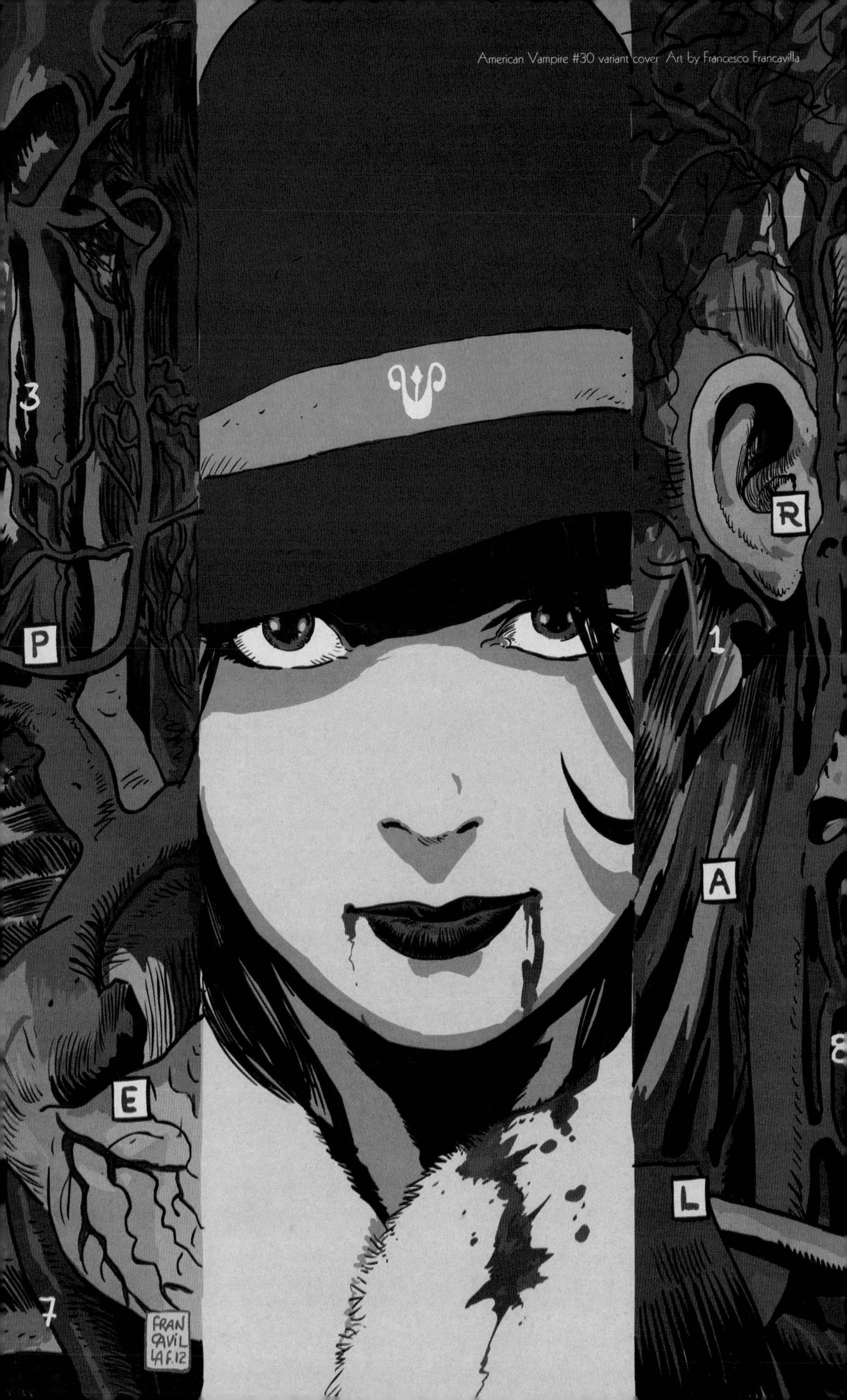
3
P
E
7
FRAN
CAVIL
LA F.12
R
1
A
8
L
American Vampire #30 variant cover Art by Francesco Francavilla

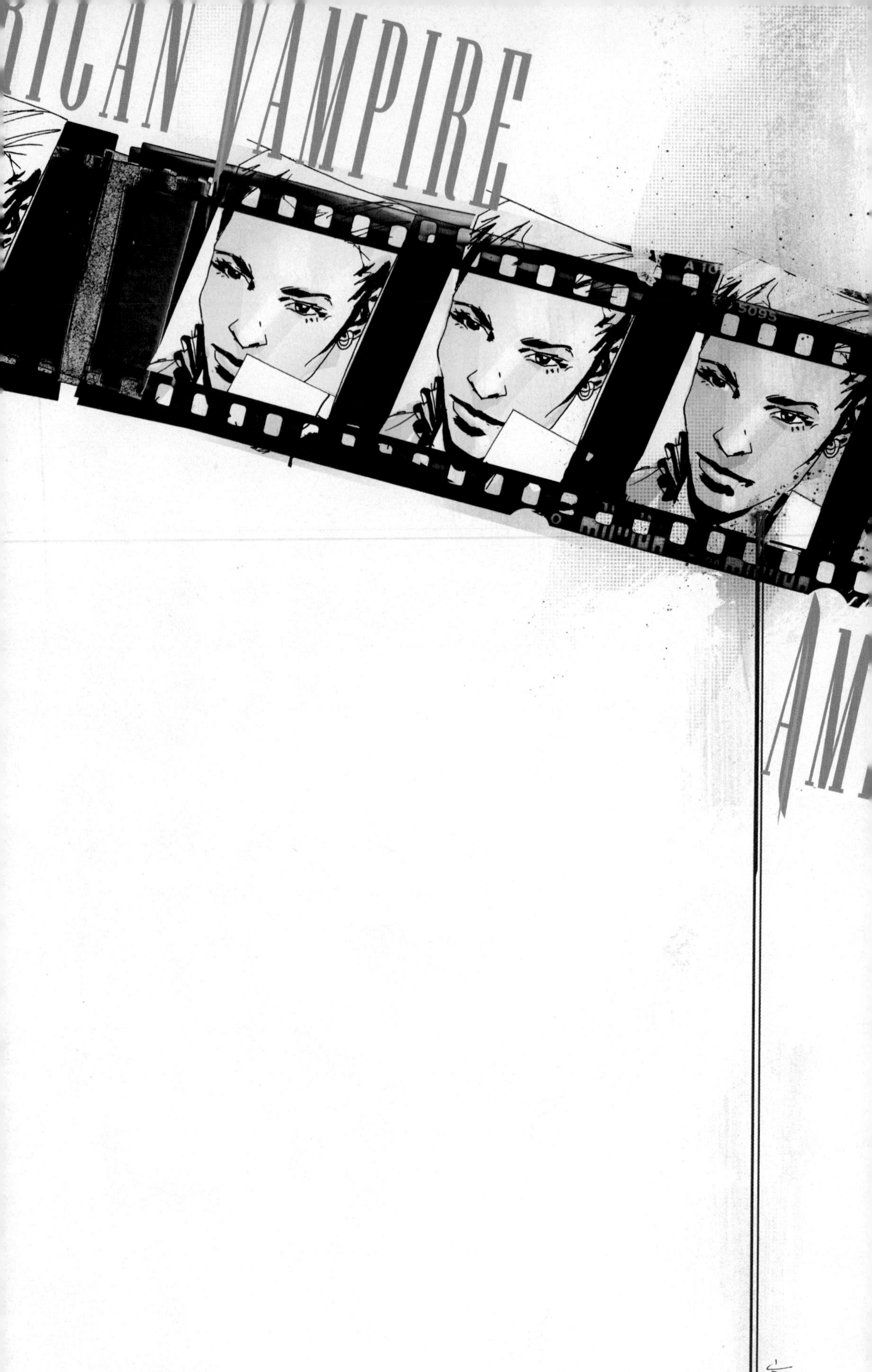
RICAN VAMPIRE
5095

American Vampire #31 variant cover Art by Jock

American Vampire #32 variant cover Art by Dustin Nguyen

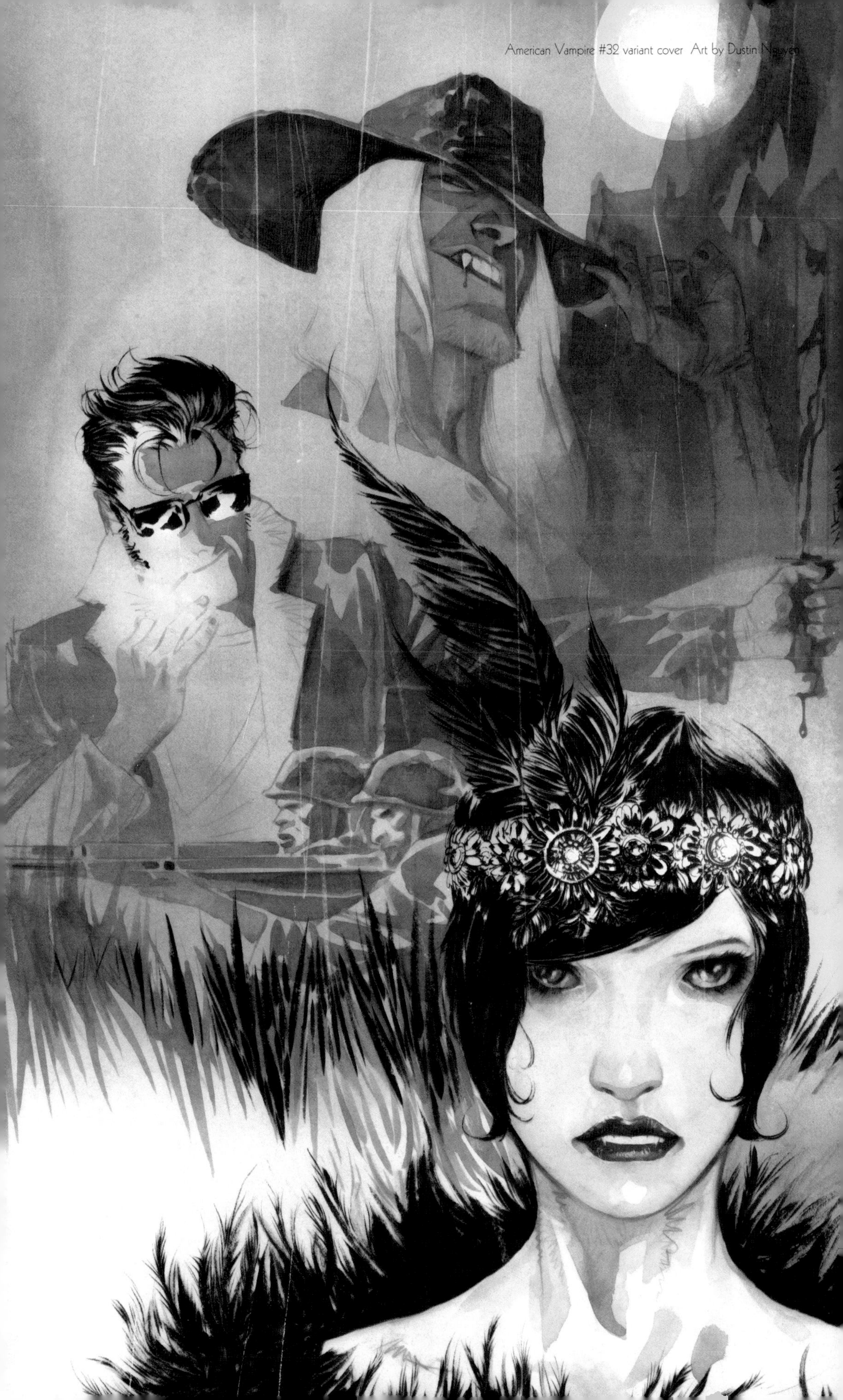

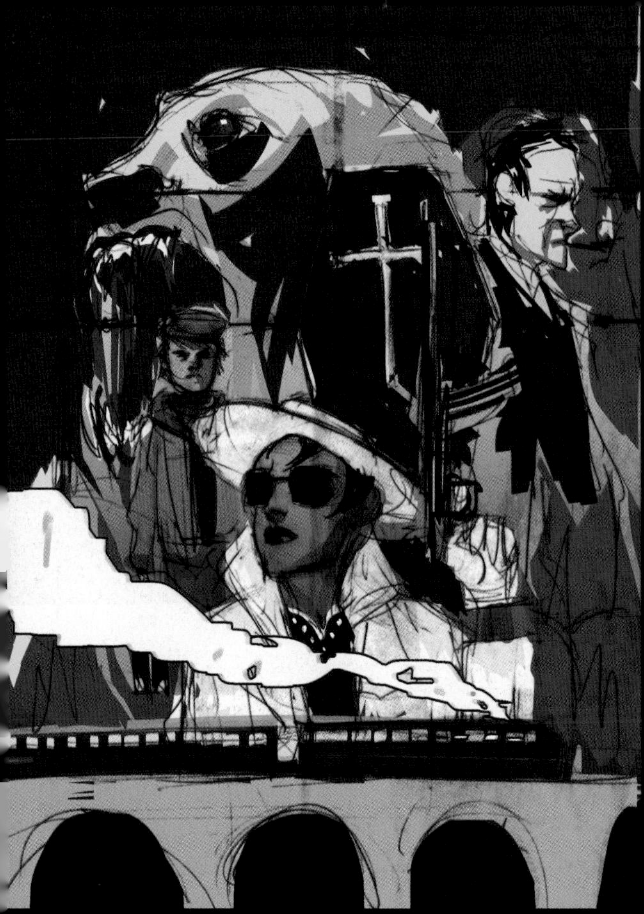

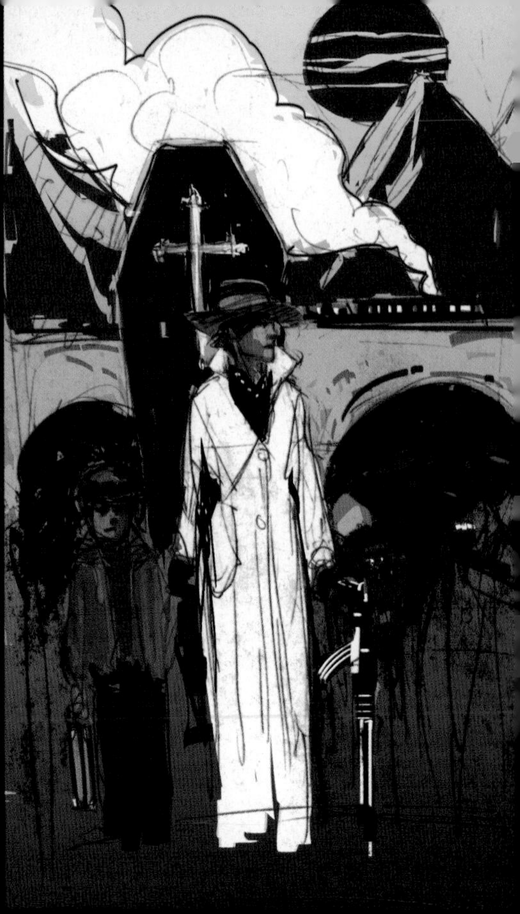

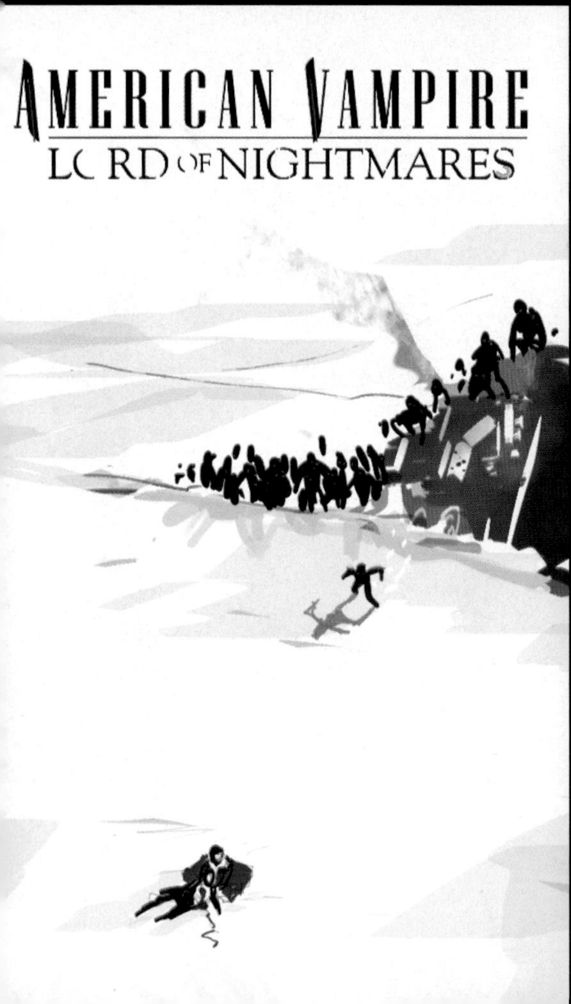
AMERICAN VAMPIRE
LORD OF NIGHTMARES

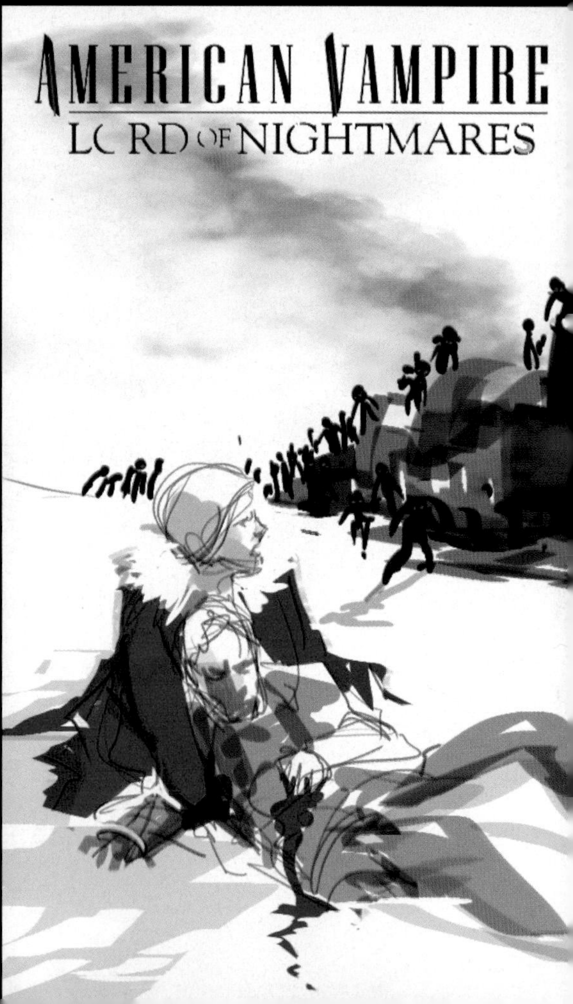
AMERICAN VAMPIRE
LORD OF NIGHTMARES

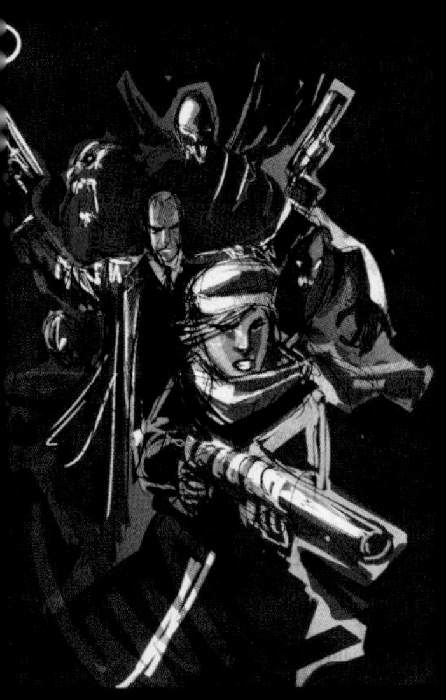

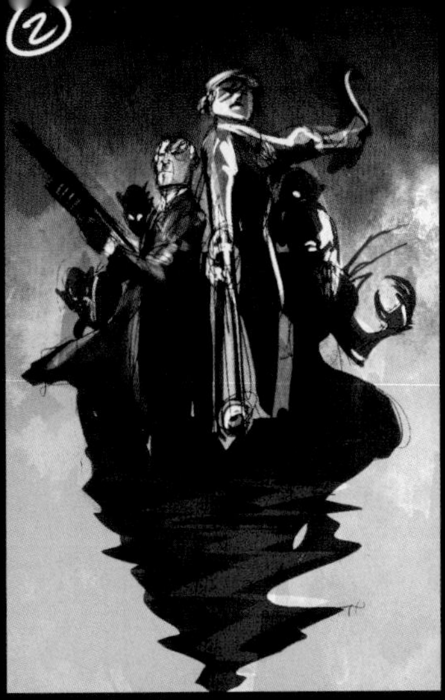
2

Felicia pointing gun at us-
monsters shadow turn into blood at thier feet

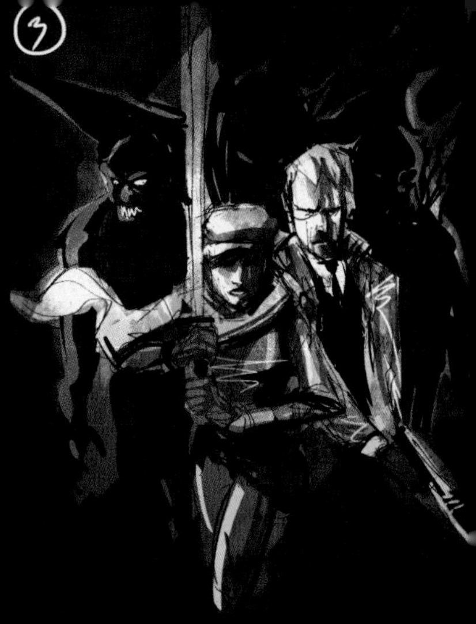
3

felicia with sword, or some old school vampire killing weapon

COVER SKETCHES AND CHARACTER DESIGNS BY DUSTIN NGUYEN FOR " LORD OF NIGHTMARES."

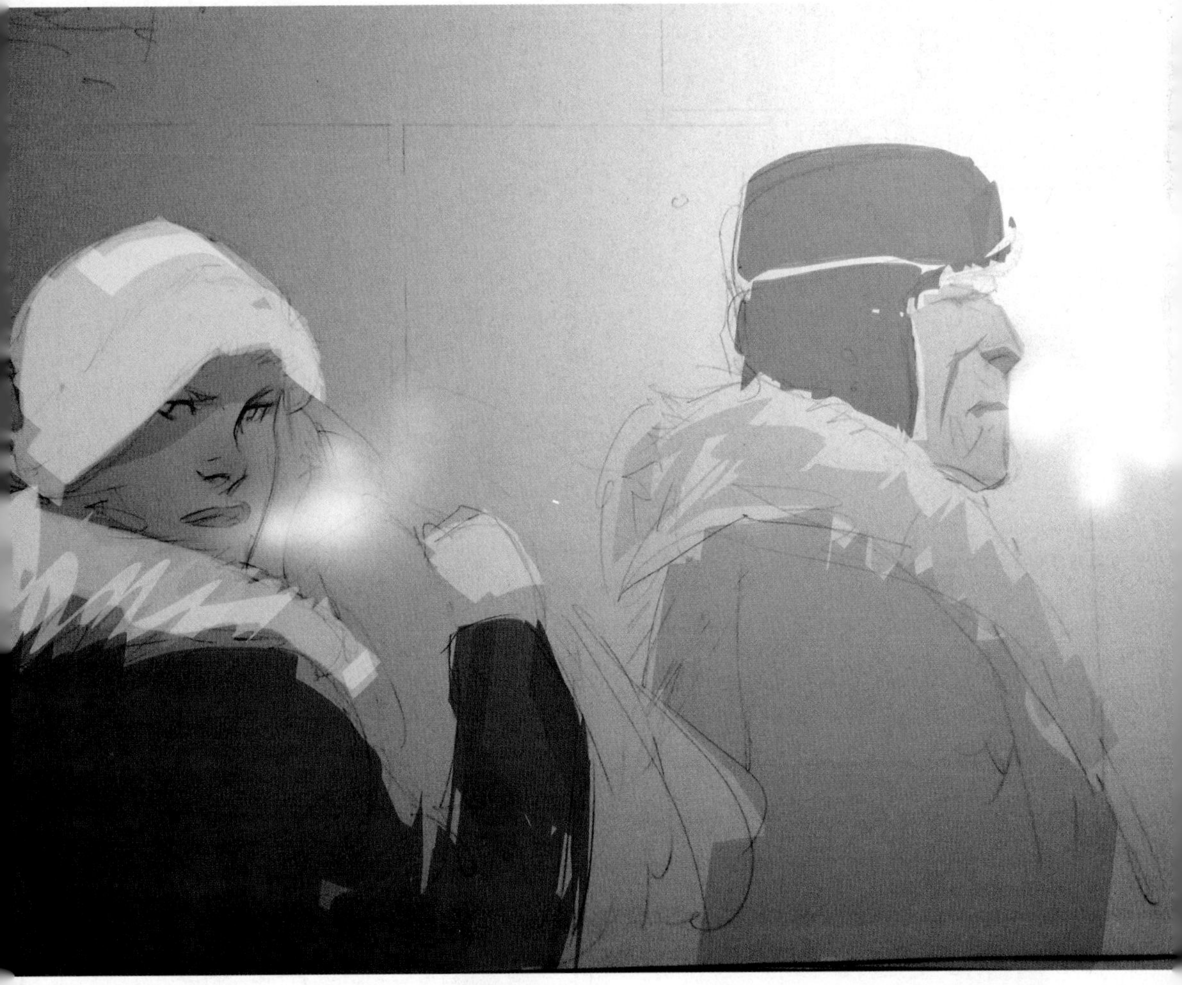

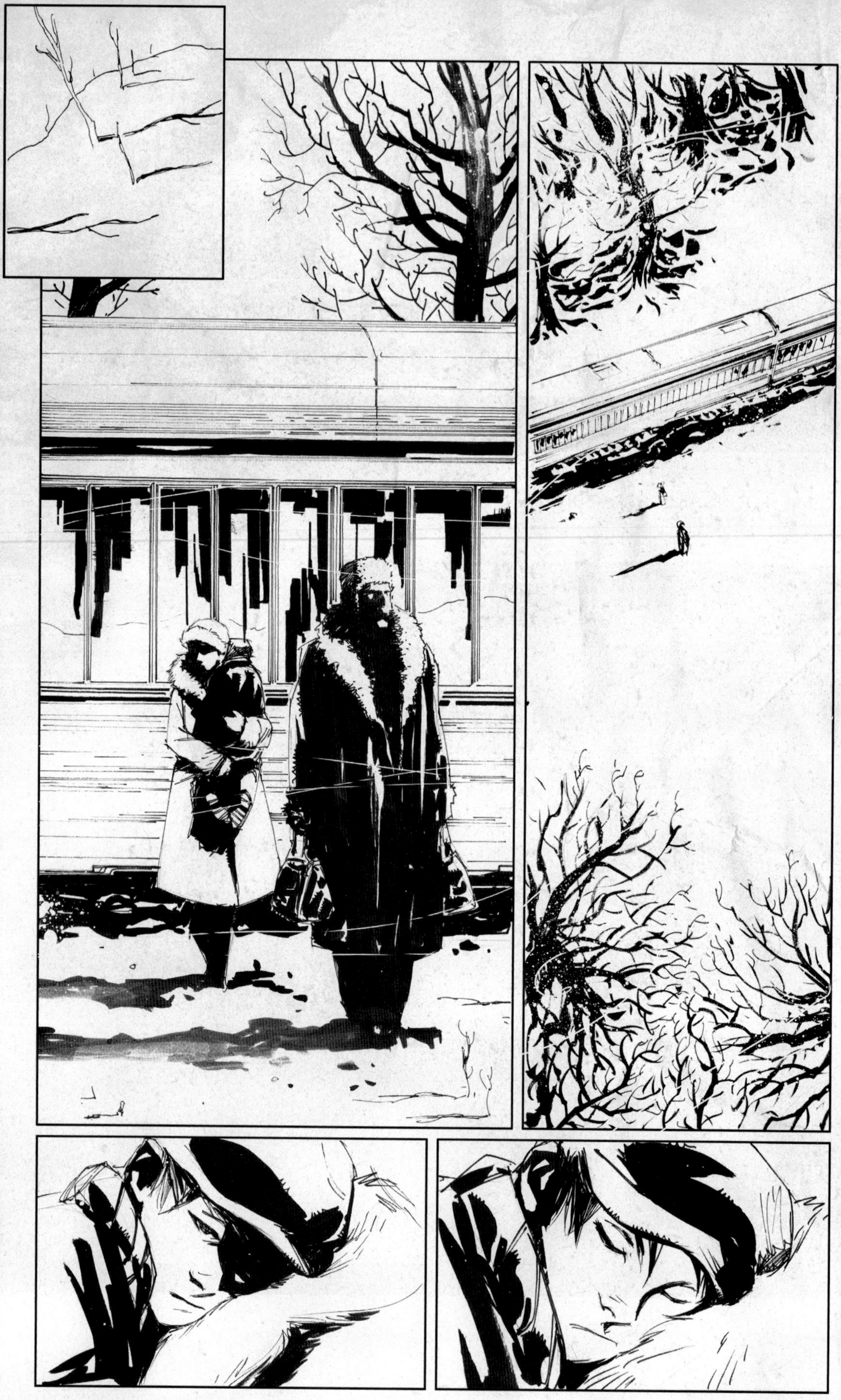

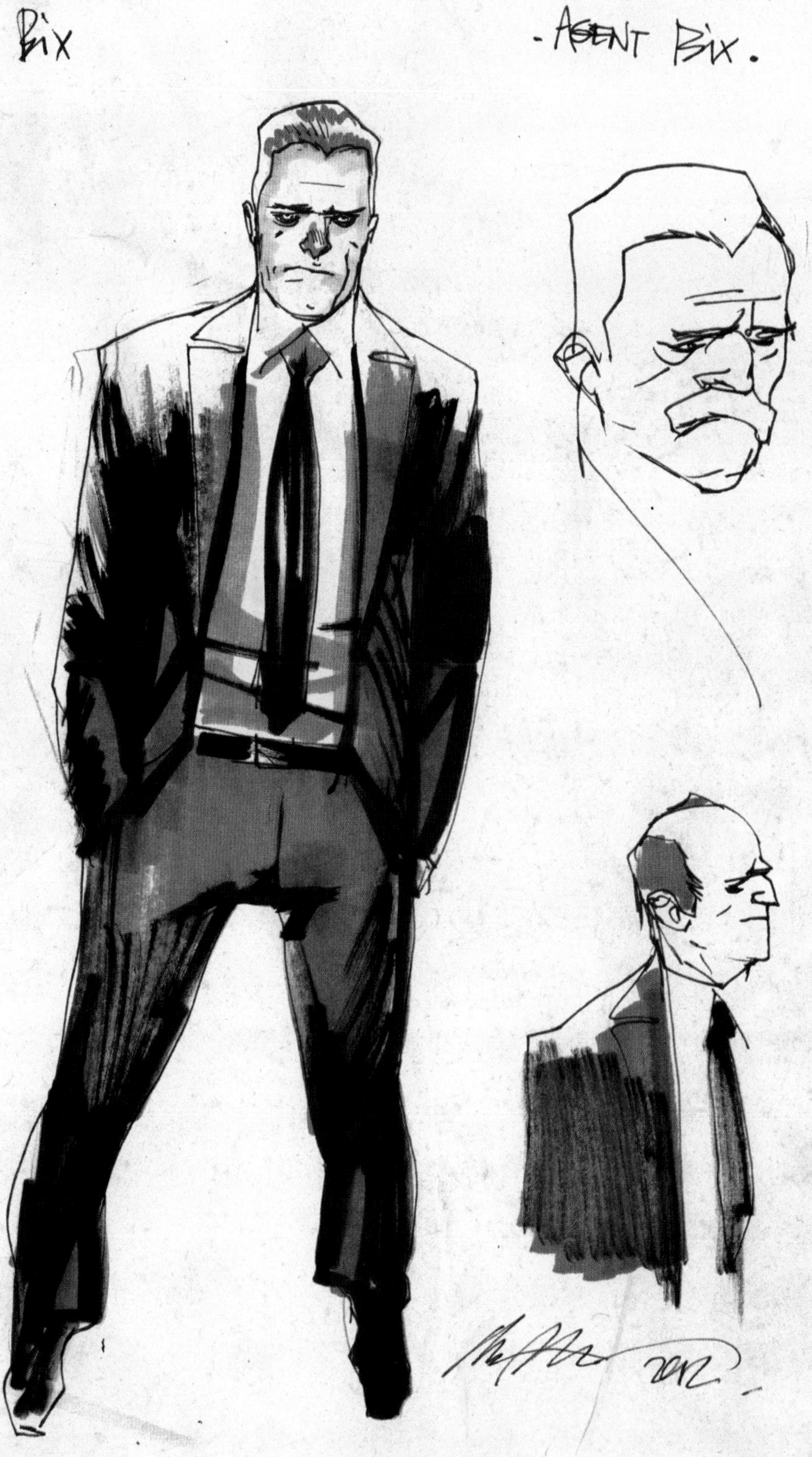
Bix
- Agent Bix -
2012

Character designs by Rafael Albuequerque "The Black List."

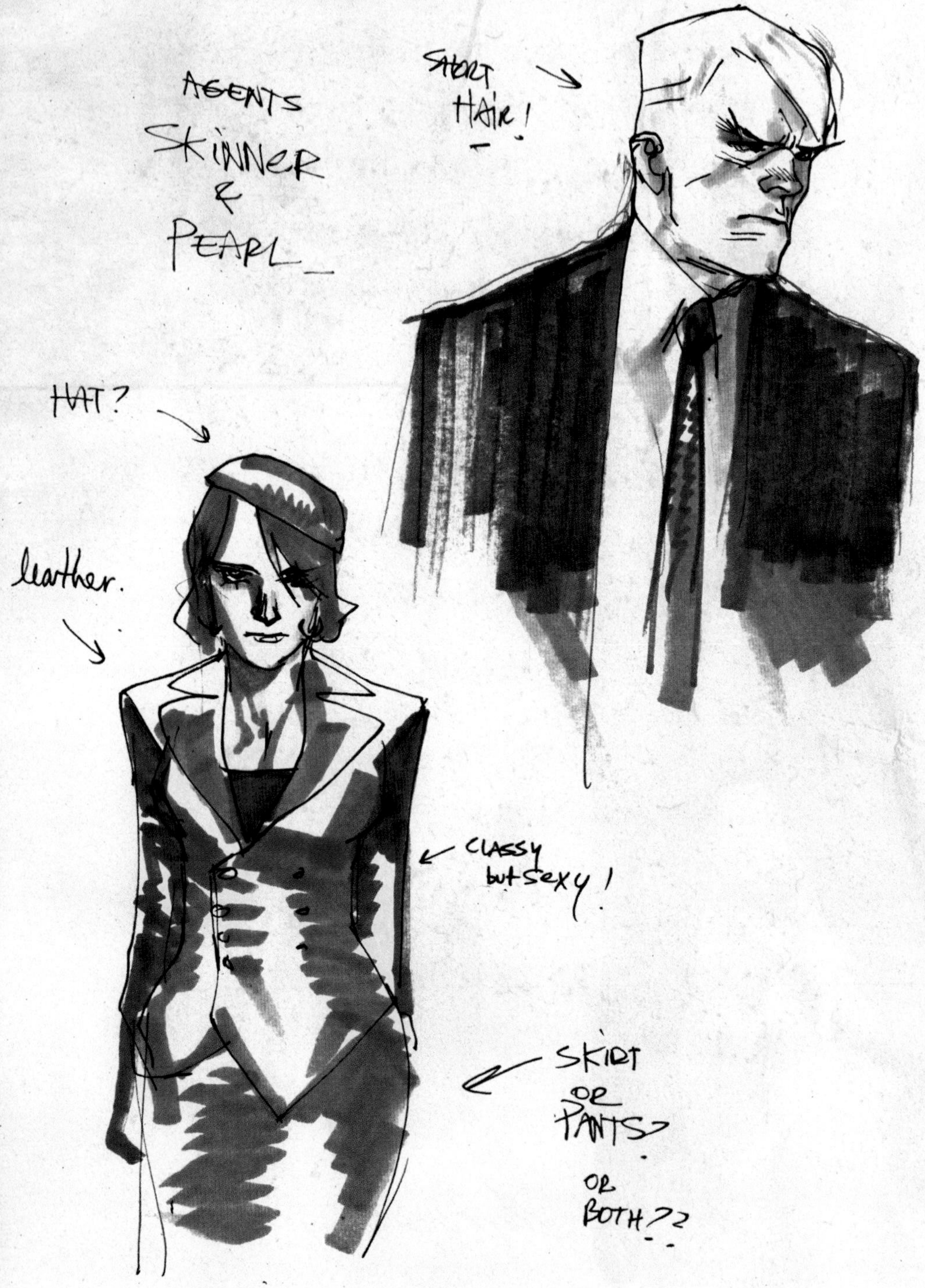

AGENTS
SKINNER
&
PEARL_
SHORT
HAIR!
HAT?
leather.
CLASSY
but sexy!
SKIRT
OR
PANTS?
OR
BOTH??

- CAL -

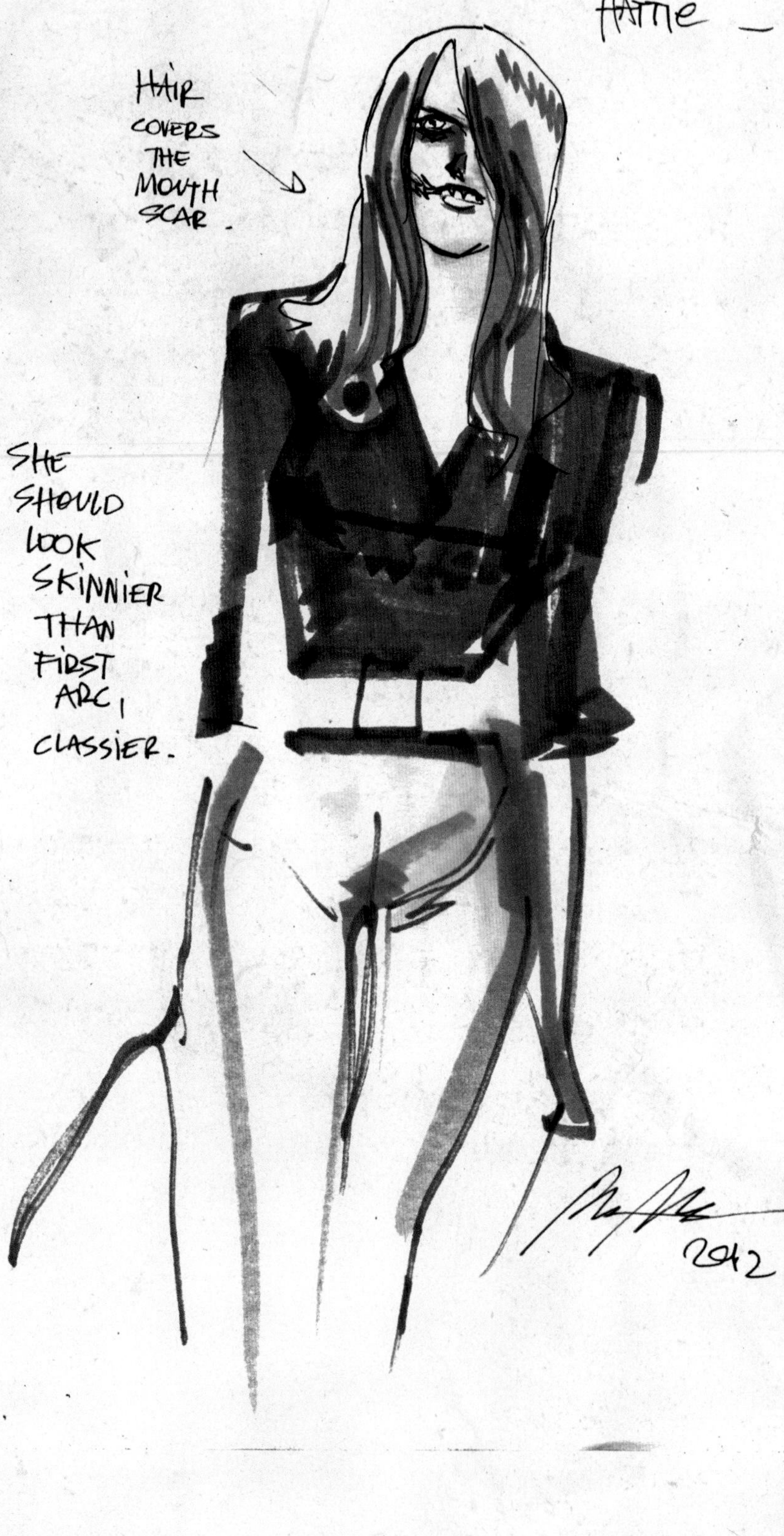
HATTIE –
HAIR COVERS THE MOUTH SCAR.
SHE SHOULD LOOK SKINNIER THAN FIRST ARC, CLASSIER.
2012

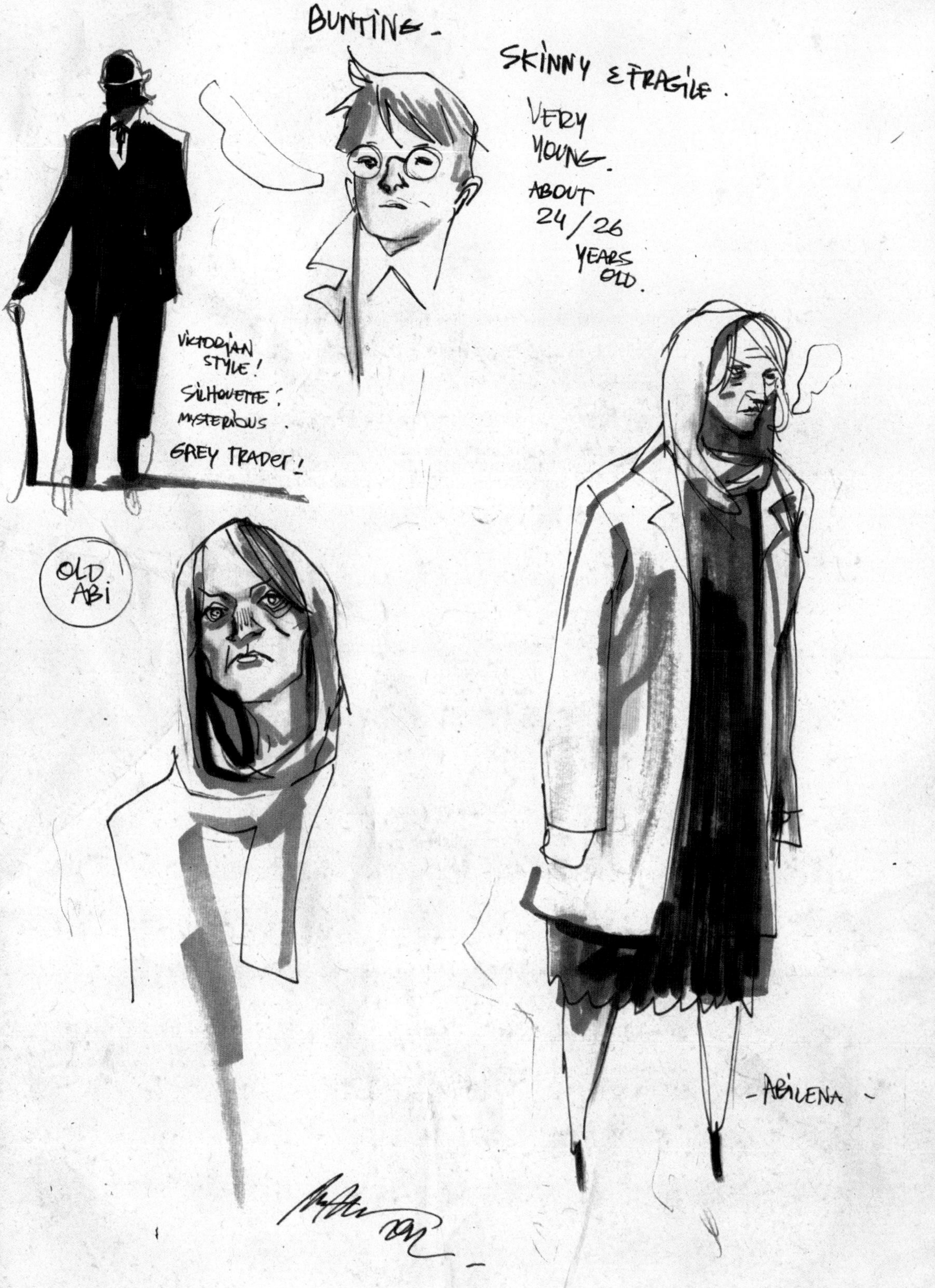
BUNTING -
SKINNY & FRAGILE.
VERY YOUNG.
ABOUT 24/26 YEARS OLD.
VIKTORIAN STYLE!
SILHOUETTE!
MYSTERIOUS.
GREY TRADER!
OLD ABI
- ABILENA -

Scott Snyder is the best-selling and award-winning writer of BATMAN and SWAMP THING as well as the short story collection Voodoo Heart (The Dial Press). He teaches writing at Sarah Lawrence College, New York University and Columbia University. He lives on Long Island with his wife, Jeanie, and his sons Jack and Emmett. He is a dedicated and un-ironic fan of Elvis Presley.

Rafael Albuquerque was born in Porto Alegre, Brazil, and has been working in the American comic book industry since 2005. Best known from his work on the *Savage Brothers*, BLUE BEETLE and SUPERMAN/BATMAN, he has also published the creator-owned graphic novels *Crimeland* (2007) and *Mondo Urbano*, published in 2010.

Dustin Nguyen is an American comic artist whose body of work includes mainly titles throughout the DC Comics universe. His past projects include WILDCATS V3.0, BATMAN, BATGIRL, SUPERMAN/BATMAN, DETECTIVE COMICS, MANIFEST ETERNITY, BATGIRL, BATMAN: STREETS OF GOTHAM, and many others. Currently, he co-writes and illustrates DC's BATMAN: LI'L GOTHAM. He stays up late at night and resides somewhere in California with his lovely wife Nicole and their kids Bradley and Kaeli.

"Looking for a vampire story with some real bite? Then, boys and girls, Scott Snyder has a comic book for you."
—USA WEEKEND

FROM THE NEW YORK TIMES #1 BESTSELLING AUTHOR OF *BATMAN: THE BLACK MIRROR*

SCOTT SNYDER
with RAFAEL ALBUQUERQUE and STEPHEN KING

AMERICAN VAMPIRE
VOL. 2

with RAFAEL ALBUQUERQUE and MATEUS SANTOLOUCO

AMERICAN VAMPIRE
VOL. 3

with RAFAEL ALBUQUERQUE and SEAN MURPHY

"At a time when vampire stories engulf pop culture, this one's actually fresh and original."
— ENTERTAINMENT WEEKLY

AMERICAN VAMPIRE
SCOTT SNYDER   RAFAEL ALBUQUERQUE
and
STEPHEN KING

VERTIGO

VERTIGO

"A science fiction tragedy about the treatment of animals and its ultimate cost to our sense of humanity."
—PUBLISHERS WEEKLY, Best Comic Books of 2005

"[A] startling, disturbing and perhaps enlightening series... a provocative tale." —ATLANTA JOURNAL CONSTITUTION

"Writer Morrison and illustrator Quitely meld incisive dialogue with action visualized from a four legged point of view."
—WASHINGTON POST

ANIMAL MAN VOLS. 1-3

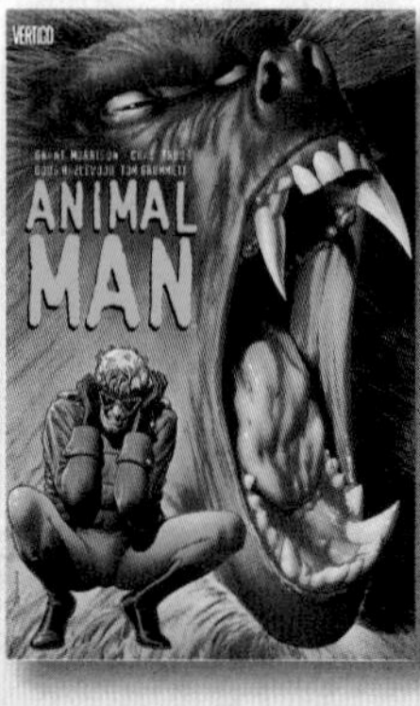
VERTIGO
ANIMAL
MAN

with CHAS TRUOG
& TOM GRUMMETT

FLEX MENTALLO: MAN OF MUSCLE MYSTERY THE DELUXE EDITION

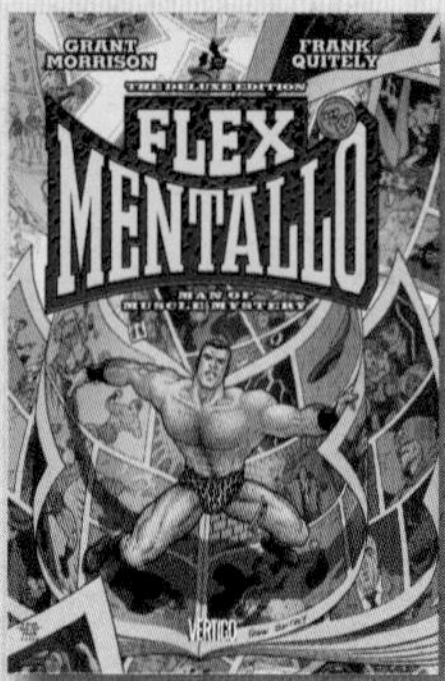
GRANT MORRISON
FRANK QUITELY
THE DELUXE EDITION
FLEX
MENTALLO
MAN OF MUSCLE MYSTERY
VERTIGO

with FRANK QUITELY

JOE THE BARBARIAN

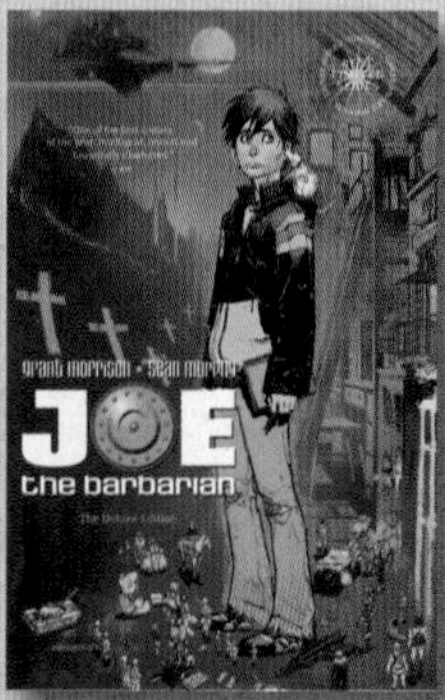
grant morrison • sean murphy
JOE
the barbarian

with SEAN MURPHY

FROM THE WRITER OF *THE INVISIBLES*

GRANT MORRISON

with FRANK QUITELY

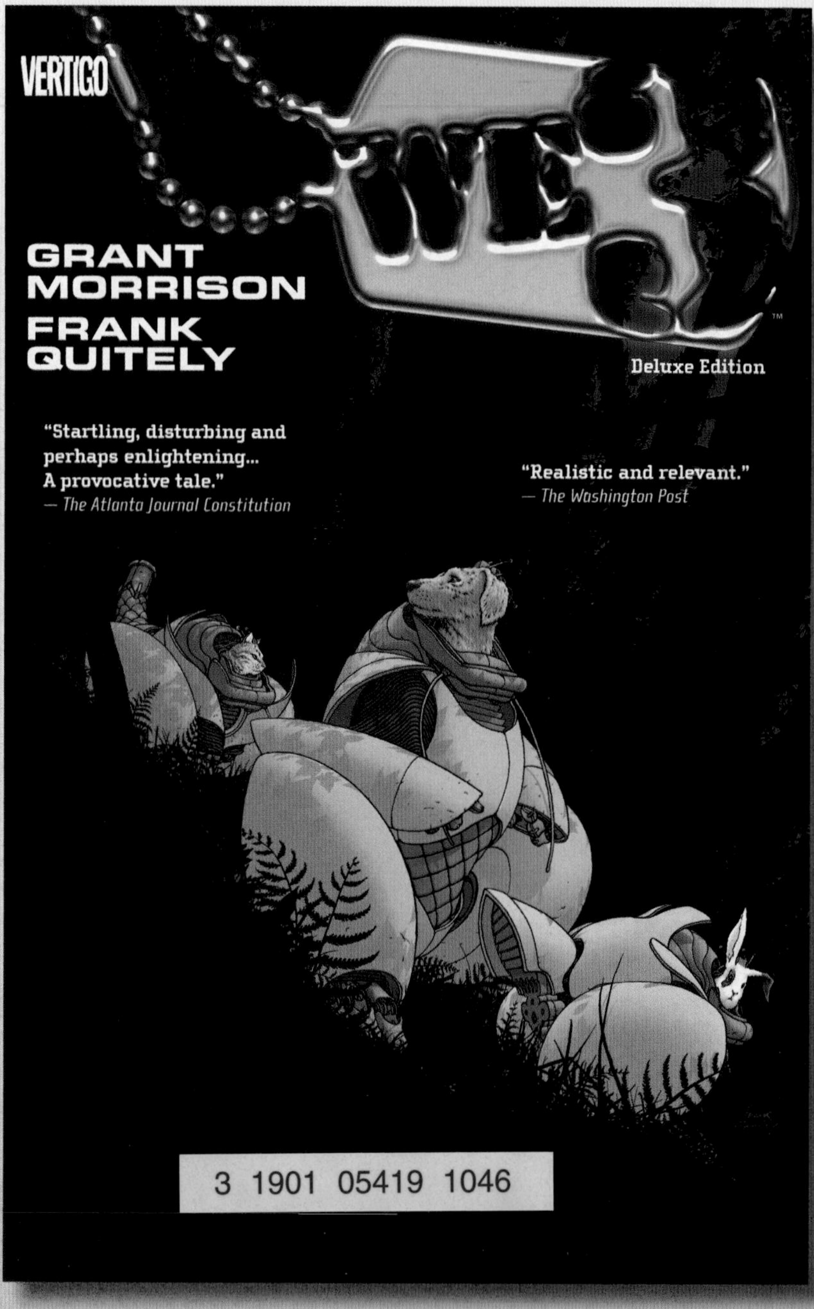
VERTIGO
WE3
GRANT
MORRISON
FRANK
QUITELY
Deluxe Edition
"Startling, disturbing and perhaps enlightening... A provocative tale."
— The Atlanta Journal Constitution
"Realistic and relevant."
— The Washington Post

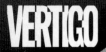